Studies in Fiscal Federalism

ECONOMISTS OF THE TWENTIETH CENTURY

General Editors

Mark Perlman,
University Professor of Economics, University of Pittsburgh

Mark Blaug,
Professor Emeritus, University of London,
Consultant Professor, University of Buckingham
and Visiting Professor, University of Exeter

This innovative series comprises specially invited collections of articles and papers by economists whose work has made an important contribution to economics in the late twentieth century.

The proliferation of new journals and the ever-increasing number of new articles make it difficult for even the most assiduous economist to keep track of all the important recent advances. By focusing on those economists whose work is generally recognized to be at the forefront of the discipline, the series will be an essential reference point for the different specialisms included.

Published titles:

Monetarism and Macroeconomic Policy
Thomas Mayer

The World Economy in Perspective
Essays on International Trade and European Integration
Herbert Giersch

Studies in Fiscal Federalism

Wallace E. Oates
Professor of Economics
University of Maryland

Edward Elgar

23384164
DLC

6-3-92

© Wallace E. Oates 1991

Published by
Edward Elgar Publishing Limited
Gower House
Croft Road
Aldershot
Hants GU11 3HR
England

Edward Elgar Publishing Company
Old Post Road
Brookfield
Vermont 05036
USA

British Library Cataloguing in Publication Data
Oates, Wallace E. (Wallace Eugene) *1937–*
   Studies in fiscal federalism. – (Economists of the
   twentieth century).
   1. Public finance
   I. Title   II. Series
   336.012

Library of Congress Cataloguing in Publication Data
Oates, Wallace E.
   Studies in fiscal federalism / Wallace E. Oates.
      p.   cm. – (Economists of the twentieth century)
   Essays originally published between Feb. 1968 and June 1989.
   Includes bibliographical references.
   1. Intergovernmental fiscal relations. 2. Intergovernmental
fiscal relations–United States. I. Title. II. Series.
HJ192.O19   1991
351.72'5–dc20   91–12597
                                                                         CIP

ISBN 1 85278 520 9

Printed in Great Britain by
Billing & Sons Ltd, Worcester

To My Mother,
Irene G. Oates,
And to the Memory of My Father,
Eugene A. Oates

Contents

PART IV   THE PROVISION OF LOCAL PUBLIC GOODS

PART V   CAPITALIZATION AND LOCAL FINANCE

PART VI   PUBLIC CHOICE AND FISCAL FEDERALISM

Introduction

This collection of essays addresses issues in public finance with several levels of government or, in the jargon of the trade, fiscal federalism. The public sector is not a monolithic, unified agent. It has a complex structure both horizontally in terms of numerous agencies and vertically in terms of different levels of government. It is the latter–the vertical design and functioning of the public sector–that is the subject of this volume.

We live in a time of dramatic fiscal 'reconstruction' in the socialist countries and of a continuing and fascinating evolution of government structure elsewhere. 'Devolution' or 'decentralization' is the current battle cry, as nations try to enhance the effectiveness with which their government sectors respond to social needs by moving decision-making responsibilities away from the centre and closer to the people they serve. And yet, at the same time, we observe some significant enterprises involving fiscal centralization: the emerging top layer of government in the European Community brings the centralization of a number of economic functions that have previously rested with member countries.

The growing complexity of the vertical structure of the public sector casts serious doubt on any simplistic forecasts of tendencies toward either centralization or decentralization. Late in the nineteenth century, Alexis de Tocqueville opined that '...in the democratic ages which are opening upon us...centralization will be the natural government'.[1] This 'forecast' was echoed a few decades later in the form of 'Bryce's Law'–the contention that 'Federalism is simply a transitory step on the way to governmental unity'.[2]

Subsequent events, however, have proven these predictions premature. Instead, fiscal federalism appears on a course of increasing complexity or specialization. New levels of government and new forms of public agencies are coming into being in a process of fiscal evolution that attempts to make the public sector more responsive to the often bewildering variety of demands placed upon it. The task before us here is to gain a better understanding of the vertical structure and workings of the public sector. It is clear that the effectiveness of government will depend in important ways on just how we assign functions to different levels of government and on the mix of policy instruments at their disposal.

My own interest in this set of issues reaches back almost three decades to my years as a graduate student at Stanford University. Studying public finance in the early 1960s, my classmates and I leaned heavily on Richard Musgrave's recently published treatise, *The Theory of Public Finance* (1959). In fact, this was our 'bible'. Musgrave's monumental volume pulled the field together in a modern and analytical way. In this comprehensive work, running in excess of 600 pages, I came across a scant, but most tantalizing, five pages (pp.179–83) that sketched out a conceptual framework for the analysis of fiscal federalism. Drawing on his tripartite division of the public sector, Musgrave concluded his brief treatment with the contention that

> The heart of fiscal federalism thus lies in the proposition that the policies of the Allocation Branch should be permitted to differ between states, depending on the preferences of their citizens. The objectives of the Distribution and Stabilization Branches, however, require primary responsibility at the central level.[3]

These five pages became the point of departure for my dissertation and much of my subsequent research. The dissertation (*The Economics of Federalism: The Stabilization and Tax Harmonization Problems*, 1965) explored two central issues in fiscal federalism. Following its completion, I arrived as a new Assistant Professor at Princeton University and there embarked on an effort to provide a more comprehensive treatment of fiscal federalism. The first fruit of this effort was a paper published in 1968 in the *Canadian Journal of Economics*, 'The Theory of Public Finance in a Federal System'. This paper appears as the first entry in this volume–it provided the impetus to a yet more comprehensive undertaking that resulted in my first book, *Fiscal Federalism* (1972).

In the first two parts of this volume, I have drawn together those of my papers that attempt to provide a general view of the economics of fiscal federalism and, in particular, of the roles of different levels of government. This begins with my early *Canadian Journal of Economics* paper (Chapter 1) that essentially develops in some detail Musgrave's view of the assignment of functions to different levels of government. It presents a formal model of macroeconomic policy and draws out the arguments supporting the primary role of the central government in macroeconomic management and in the redistribution of income. The basic role of 'local' government, I argue, is in the provision of local services with outputs tailored to the particular tastes and circumstances of individual jurisdictions. Part I concludes with a more recent survey of fiscal federalism.

My sense now is that although Musgrave's vertical alignment of fiscal functions retains much of its validity, the lines were probably drawn a bit too sharply. It is impossible to assign the separate fiscal functions in wholly exclusive ways to different levels of government. We might wish on grounds of intellectual 'neatness' to envision a clear and tidy division of economic responsibility among levels of government–such as that described by Lord Bryce who argued that a federal system was 'like a great factory wherein two sets of machinery are at work, their revolving wheels apparently intermixed, their bands crossing one another, yet each doing its own work without touching or hampering the other.'[4] But, in truth, federalism, as the political scientists stress, is much more of a cooperative enterprise with the actions of various levels of government interacting with one another.

At the same time, all is not 'chaos'. Musgrave's basic prescription contains some fundamental and important insights. Charles Brown and I, in a more recent paper that opens Part II of this volume (Chapter 5), show that a wholly decentralized system of support for the poor is likely to prove inadequate, even in terms of the desire of the well-to-do to provide poor relief. Generous local programmes to help the indigent have the potential to attract new recipients from elsewhere–and such potential mobility can induce (and, some evidence suggests, has induced) local officials to choose inefficiently low levels of assistance to the poor. These insights have at times been forgotten–as I argue in the second paper in Part II (Chapter 6) that provides an assessment of the New Federalism proposals under the Reagan Administration. The original Reagan proposals contained a provision that would have shifted the responsibility for welfare programmes back to the states and localities–the proposal did not survive the intense debate that it produced. It is the case that different levels of government have some 'comparative advantage' in carrying out certain fiscal functions and, although this may not lead to a neat and clearly defined menu of responsibilities for each level of government, it can provide some useful guidelines for federal fiscal structure.

Part III of this volume contains a set of papers on intergovernmental grants. It begins with a pair of papers that David Bradford and I published almost twenty years ago (Chapters 8 and 9). These papers stemmed from our dissatisfaction with the existing literature at that time which treated intergovernmental grants as if they were grants to an individual decision maker–and not to a community. It seemed to us that a real theory of inter-governmental grants had to account for the fact that these are not simply grants to individuals, but grants to a collectivity. Such a theory had to reach beyond the standard analysis of individual choice. In these papers, Bradford and I developed such a framework in which the outcomes were explicitly treated as the result of a collective decision on the part of the recipients. In the course of this work, we proved a set of equivalence theorems that demonstrated that under certain fairly general conditions, such grants to a community were fully equivalent, both in terms of their allocative and distributive outcomes, to a set of grants directly to the individuals in the community. For example, these theorems imply that a lump-sum grant to a community will have precisely the same impact on local spending and tax policies as if these grant monies were allocated in a particular way directly to the individuals comprising the community.

The theory and intuition underlying these results is clear and compelling, in principle at least. However, subsequent empirical work has tended to show that such an equivalence does not, in fact, hold. A number of econometric studies have found that a much larger fraction of unconditional grant monies to state and local governments (on the order of 40 to 50 cents on the dollar) will be spent for local budgetary purposes than will increments to private disposable income (resulting in, perhaps, 10 to 15 cents of additional state-local spending on the dollar).[5] This phenomenon has become known in the literature as the 'flypaper effect'–that is, 'money sticks where it hits'.

The flypaper effect is a disturbing and challenging finding. Taken at face value, it suggests a breakdown in democratic fiscal institutions, for it suggests that state and local officials do not follow the will of their constituencies–they spend grant monies on local projects that their citizens would prefer to have returned in the form of local tax reductions. Public finance economists have responded to this finding in a variety of ways: some claim it to be primarily an econometric 'illusion' that will go away if things are modelled and measured properly; others have developed bureaucratic models of behaviour in which local officials do indeed spend more than their constituencies would wish. The third paper in Part III (Chapter 10) represents a contribution in the latter spirit. It presents a model in which imperfect information on the part of the citizenry is used by local public officials to push public spending above the efficient level. While such a model can provide a plausible explanation of observed grant behaviour, there remains a variety of other possible explanations as well. We are in great need of some careful empirical studies that can discriminate among these alternatives and shed some light on the nature of budgetary decision making in the presence of intergovernmental grants.

The final paper in Part III (Chapter 11) provides a review of the intergovernmental grant system in the USA. It finds, among other things, that the normative theory of intergovernmental grants does not provide a very good description of the existing system. Important anomalies abound, attesting to the pervasive influence of political forces in determining the structure of the intergovernmental fiscal system. One implication of this finding is that careful analysis and reform of the grant system can yield large returns in terms of a more effective realization of society's allocative and distributive goals.

Part IV contains a variety of papers on the provision of 'local' public goods. It begins with a paper that David Bradford, Shlomo Maital (then Rick Malt) and I undertook (Chapter 12) to test William Baumol's hypothesis of the 'cost disease' for public services–his contention that the *relative* cost of public services tends to rise over time because of their resistance to cost-saving, technical change. While we produced some evidence in support of Baumol's hypothesis, the more enduring contribution of the paper, it seems to me, has been the conceptual structure it provides for the treatment of local public goods.

In particular, we formulated a general view of local services in which the characteristics of the local populace enter themselves as arguments in the production function. We distinguished between 'D-output', consisting of a vector of directly produced services (e.g. the frequency of police patrols, or the number of teachers and books in the school system) that was the result of locally purchased inputs, and 'C-output', the actual level of the final service (e.g. the level of public safety, or the level of achievement in the school system). Our contention was that it is the latter definition of output, C-output, that matters to citizens and that enters into their utility functions. D-outputs we took to be arguments in the production function for C-outputs (or final outputs). But final outputs, we argued, depend in important ways on the characteristics of the people who live in the community. The level of safety, for example, or the quality of local schools, will depend in fundamental ways on the people who live in the jurisdiction. Communities with law-abiding residents and highly able and motivated pupils will tend, other things equal, to have higher levels of public safety and superior schools. Thus, community composition, as well as budgetary inputs, determine the level of output of local services.

I have developed the implications of this view of local production functions in a number of subsequent papers. In particular, it suggests that communities, in order to improve the quality of local amenities, will desire to have some form of control over entry into the community–some influence over the *kinds* of people that choose to reside there. This, I am convinced, explains to a substantial extent the jealousy with which local governments guard their zoning prerogatives. Local zoning measures provide a way, be it an admittedly crude one, through which local jurisdictions can exercise some control over community composition. Edwin Mills and I have referred to this phenomenon as 'public-goods zoning', the use of zoning ordinances to influence the make-up of the local jurisdiction.[6] My 1977 paper in the Ashenfelter–Oates volume (Chapter 15) presents some suggestive evidence in support of this view and also explores informally some of its efficiency implications. Of particular note are the complications it raises for the efficiency properties of a Tiebout world with unfettered mobility of individual households. If there are important interactions between residents through the production function for local services, then a Tiebout outcome need no longer be an efficient one. My colleague, Robert Schwab, and I have recently developed all this in a more formal and rigorous way–and show in a paper currently in the publication process that in such a setting there can be an efficiency case for equalizing lump-sum grants to local government.[7]

The decentralized provision of local services can, in principle, promise significant welfare gains through the tailoring of outputs to local tastes and circumstances. An interesting and important issue is the *extent* of the potential gains from local finance. Such gains can, in principle, be measured–although there have not been many attempts to do so. In one paper in this collection

('Suburban Exploitation of Central Cities and Governmental Structure' (Chapter 14)), David Bradford and I undertook (in an illustrative way at least) to measure the gains from decentralized finance in a metropolitan setting. Using a sample of local jurisdictions in New Jersey, we estimated demand functions for local public education and then estimated the welfare gains from the decentralized provision of education relative to those from a unified system. The estimated gains are quite sizeable. This result, incidentally, stems largely from our relatively low estimate of the price elasticity of demand – for the gains from decentralized finance become larger as the demand for local public goods becomes more price-inelastic. This is an issue that deserves further study.

Finally, I want to call attention here to a body of ongoing work on the implications of fiscal competition among local jurisdictions. Some economists have suggested that such competition is likely to have unfortunate results. They contend that in their eagerness to attract new business investment and jobs, local public officials are likely to hold down local tax rates and levels of local services excessively, resulting in suboptimal levels of local public services. This is a disturbing charge for, if true, it seriously undermines the case for decentralized fiscal choice.

Until quite recently, there was little systematic theory or evidence that addressed this issue–only some anecdotal reports. The last paper in Part IV (Chapter 18) provides a theoretical analysis of interjurisdictional competition. In this paper, Schwab and I find that for our basic model, competition among jurisdictions for new business enterprise produces efficient results–local fiscal competition is, we find, efficiency-enhancing, not a source of distortions in the local public sector.

At the same time, these results are not highly robust. They are hedged by a number of important qualifications. If, for example, local officials behave in a Niskanen fashion and seek to maximize the size of the local budget, they will, in our models, not only set tax rates too high, but will also establish excessively lax environmental standards to attract more business investment and expand the local tax base. Alternatively, if local government is constrained in its choice of tax instruments to a tax on local capital, then as Zodrow and Mieszkowski and others have shown, inefficiently low levels of local public goods are the predicted result.[8] Or, in a setting of 'imperfect competition' with jurisdictional interactions, Mintz and Tulkens find that Nash equilibria exhibit some tendency toward underprovision of local services.[9] Some insightful empirical work on the extent of such competition and its effects would be a most welcome complement to the ongoing theoretical work on this issue.

Part V presents three empirical papers on the capitalization of local fiscal differentials. These papers purported to provide tests of tax capitalization and of the Tiebout hypothesis. Using a sample of New Jersey municipalities, I found in the two *Journal of Political Economy* papers (Chapters 19 and 20) that not only were property tax differentials between communities largely capitalized into house values, but so were differences in outputs of local services such as local education. The interpretation of these findings has turned out to be a good deal more complex than I appreciated at the time. As Edel and Sclar showed later, a perfect Tiebout equilibrium should exhibit *no* capitalization.[10] Nevertheless, it is clear that capitalization is strong evidence that households (some at least) 'shop' among communities for local amenities.

Perhaps, more important, the subsequent capitalization literature has made use of the estimated coefficients on local output and amenity variables to develop estimates of consumer willingness-to-pay for local services. Through the use of the hedonic approach, there are now many dozens of capitalization studies which can serve as a basis for generating demand functions for local public goods.

Part VI turns to a series of papers on topics in public choice and fiscal federalism. The first paper (Chapter 22) examines the effect of tax structure on the public budget. It presents the results of an econometric study of the influence of the income elasticity of the revenue system on the growth in public spending. The paper was prompted by the debate over revenue sharing in which proponents of the revenue-sharing proposal claimed that state and local governments were unable to meet their growing expenditure responsibilities because their tax bases did not grow commensurately with the rest of the economy. As I show, this line of argument suggests a basic form of 'fiscal illusion' on the part of the citizenry. My findings indicate that there is some positive effect of 'automatic' revenue increases on spending–but only a quite small one. The effect does not seem to me of sufficient magnitude to provide any real support for revenue sharing. I might add that some careful, subsequent work on this question by Feenberg and Rosen, making use of much improved measures of the income elasticity of the tax system, has confirmed my finding that the income elasticity of the revenue system has little impact on the growth in public spending.[11] This is an encouraging finding in one respect: it suggests that growth in public spending is not driven so much by the form of the tax system as, we might hope, by the demand for public services.

A second public-choice hypothesis, this one advanced jointly by Geoffrey Brennan and James Buchanan, stems from their view of the public sector as Leviathan–a monolithic agent that systematically seeks to maximize its budgetary size, irrespective of the wishes of the populace.[12] Their contention is that decentralization of the public sector is a potentially effective mechanism to control Leviathan's expansive tendencies. The basic argument is that, just as competition in the private sector exercises its disciplinary force, so competition among different units of government at a decentralized level can break the monopolistic hold of a large central government. As Brennan and Buchanan put it, 'interjurisdictional mobility of persons in pursuit of "fiscal gains" can offer partial or possibly complete substitutes for explicit fiscal constraints on the taxing power' (p. 184).

This is not only a very provocative policy recommendation for containing growth of the public sector–it also suggests a hypothesis by which the Leviathan view of government can be put to an empirical test. The logic of the Brennan and Buchanan argument implies that, other things equal, we should expect to find that the size of the government sector varies inversely with the extent of fiscal decentralization.

Part VI in this volume contains a pair of papers using this approach to test for the 'existence' of Leviathan. The 1985 *American Economic Review* paper (Chapter 24) presents an econometric study of the relationship between government size and the extent of fiscal decentralization, using two quite different samples: a cross-sectional sample of 43 countries and a second cross-sectional sample consisting of the state-local sectors in the USA. In neither case was I able to find any evidence of a significant negative relationship between the extent of fiscal decentralization and the size of government (as measured by tax receipts as a fraction of GNP).

Some subsequent work has muddied the waters a bit. In particular, two studies making use of county data for the USA have produced some evidence that the presence of more general-purpose local governments is associated with a smaller overall size of the county public sector. It may be that in this smaller geographical setting, the potential mobility of households is higher and acts to constrain local government budgetary behaviour. However, even here the results are not uniformly supportive of Leviathan. In the second *American Economic Review* paper on Leviathan (Chapter 25), I describe this later literature and offer some reflections on this whole line of research. While the evidence may be somewhat conflicting, it seems to me that there is not enough clear support available to make a convincing case that decentralization in itself constrains government growth. *If* we want smaller government, then other measures are probably in order.

Chapter 26 is a survey paper on the fascinating, but elusive, topic of fiscal illusion. The growing literature on fiscal illusion points to a number of channels through which there can take place a 'misperception' of fiscal parameters by the electorate. In a setting of budget-maximizing public agencies, such misperceptions can be manipulated by public officials to the end of budgetary expansion. This literature purports to provide evidence in support of a variety of such outcomes. My contention in the survey, however, is that little of this work is well founded, as yet, either theoretically or empirically. We do not have a systematic theory of fiscal illusion. Although certain of the hypotheses that have been put forward are plausible, they often have some troubling implications. Some imply, for example, that citizens never learn–they continue to misperceive such things as the tax price that they face even though actual outcomes must reveal to them *ex post* that their decisions were based on mistaken fiscal information. Likewise, the empirical literature on fiscal illusion is, on the whole, not very compelling. Most of the findings in the literature, it seems to me, are at least as well explained by alternative hypotheses as by the presumed fiscal illusion for which, it is claimed, they provide support. We badly need a basic theory of fiscal illusion and an empirical effort based on this theory to ascertain the importance of such illusion in determining fiscal outcomes.

While I welcome the opportunity to bring together this body of research in fiscal federalism, I hope that it (along with this introduction) suggests the rich agenda of research that remains. There is much that we do not understand at all well about the design and functioning of an intergovernmental fiscal system. And I hope that this volume points the way to some of the work that needs to be done to enhance this understanding.

As is evident from a perusal of the papers in this volume, I have been the great beneficiary in my research of a number of splendid and talented co-authors. I have always enjoyed joint research efforts. Not only is joint work often stimulating and a great pleasure, but it offers an opportunity to do *better* work than can be done on one's own. Good joint work can simply bring more imagination and skill to bear on a research problem. At any rate, I want to express my gratitude to those that I have worked with on the papers appearing in this volume: David Bradford, Charles Brown, John Heinberg, James Litvack, Shlomo Maital, Robert Schwab and John Wallis. Finally, I want to thank Edward and Sandy Elgar for their encouragement and support of this undertaking.

Notes

1. *Democracy in America, Volume II* (New York: Alfred A. Knoph, 1980), p. 296.
2. Edward McWhinney, *Comparative Federalism*, Second Edition (Toronto: University of Toronto Press, 1965), p. 105.
3. Richard A. Musgrave, *The Theory of Public Finance* (New York: McGraw-Hill, 1959), pp. 181–2.
4. Lord Bryce, *The American Commonwealth* (New York: Macmillan, 1986), p. 325.
5. For a useful survey of this econometric work, see Edward M. Gramlich, 'Intergovernmental Grants: A Review of the Empirical Literature', in W. Oates (ed.), *The Political Economy of Fiscal Federalism* (Lexington, Mass: Heath-Lexington, 1975), pp. 219–40.
6. Edwin S. Mills and Wallace E. Oates (eds), *Fiscal Zoning and Land Use Controls* (Lexington, Mass: Heath-Lexington, 1975), pp. 7–8.
7. Robert M. Schwab and Wallace E. Oates, 'Community Composition and the Provision of Local Public Goods: A Normative Analysis', *Journal of Public Economics* (forthcoming).
8. George R. Zodrow and Peter Mieszkowski, 'Pigou, Tiebout, Property Taxation, and the Underprovision of Local Public Goods', *Journal of Urban Economics* (1986), **19**, pp. 296–315.
9. Jack Mintz and Henry Tulkens, 'Commodity Tax Competition between Member States of a Federation', *Journal of Public Economics* (1986), **29**, pp. 133–72.
10. Mathew Edel and Elliott Sclar, 'Taxes, Spending, and Property Values: Supply Adjustment in a Tiebout-Oates Model', *Journal of Political Economy* (September–October 1974), **84**, pp. 941–54.

11. Daniel R. Feenberg and Harvey S. Rosen, 'Tax Structure and Public Sector Growth', *Journal of Public Economics* (March 1987), **32**, pp. 185–201.
12. Geoffrey Brennan and James Buchanan, *The Power to Tax: Analytical Foundations of a Fiscal Constitution* (Cambridge: Cambridge University Press, 1980).

PART I

FISCAL FEDERALISM: AN OVERVIEW

[1]

THE THEORY OF PUBLIC FINANCE IN A FEDERAL SYSTEM°

WALLACE E. OATES   *Princeton University*

La théorie des finances publiques dans un état fédéral. Comme l'a soutenu Richard Musgrave, l'activité économique du secteur public est nécessaire pour maintenir le plein emploi avec des prix stables, pour atteindre une distribution optimale du revenu et de la richesse et pour en arriver à un allocation efficace des ressources. Le but du présent article est d'étudier comment la responsabilité doit être partagée, dans un état fédéral, entre le pouvoir central et les autres niveaux de gouvernement pour atteindre les objectifs qu'on vient d'énumérer.

L'analyse révèle que les objectifs de stabilité et de distribution du secteur public doivent être la responsabilité du pouvoir central. Le manque de contrôle sur la masse monétaire, les limites aux émissions d'obligations ainsi que « l'ouverture » (au commerce des marchandises et aux mouvements de capitaux) de petites unités économiques réduisent considérablement la possibilité d'une politique efficace de stabilisation par les gouvernements provinciaux et municipaux. Un modèle simple pour une économie locale, incorporant les mouvements de marchandises et de titres financiers, donne un multiplicateur de budget équilibré de zéro et un multiplicateur très faible pour les dépenses publiques financées par des emprunts. De plus, la mobilité des individus et des entreprises rend les niveaux inférieurs de gouvernement incapables d'une politique de redistribution efficace. Par exemple, les efforts d'un pouvoir local pour redistribuer le revenu en faveur de résidents plus pauvres se solderaient par l'exode des riches.

Les arguments économiques à la défense du fédéralisme sont fondés sur le problème de l'allocation efficace des ressources. Dans un modèle fédéral « idéal », un individu choisit l'endroit qui offre la combinaison de services publics et de taxes qui lui convient le mieux. Dans un système fédéral visant l'efficacité, l'action du pouvoir central sera toutefois nécessaire pour obvier aux avantages et désavantages externes entre les différentes unités économiques et pour coordonner les structures fiscales locales.

In his monumental volume on public finance, Richard Musgrave[1] suggests that public economic policy has three basic objectives: (1) to establish an efficient allocation of resources; (2) to attain the desired distribution of income and wealth; and (3) to maintain high and stable levels of employment and output. Thus, for analytic purposes, Musgrave divides the public fiscal department into three branches: an Allocation, a Distribution, and a Stabilization Branch. In terms of this conceptual scheme, Musgrave then explores the economic role of the public sector.

The bulk of his analysis is in terms of a system consisting of a private sector and a *single* level of government. This leaves open the important question of how, in a federal system (like that of Canada or the United States), the responsibility for economic policy is best divided among the various levels of government. The purpose of this paper is to expand Musgrave's brief but most

°The author is grateful to Mancur Olson and Rudolph Penner for a number of helpful comments on an earlier draft of this paper. More basically, however, he is deeply indebted to John Gurley, Ronald McKinnon, and Edward Shaw for their assistance with his dissertation on which this paper is largely founded.
[1]*The Theory of Public Finance* (New York, 1959), 5.

Canadian Journal of Economics/Revue canadienne d'Economique, I, no. 1
February/février 1968

suggestive treatment of the problem.[2] The procedure will be to examine in turn each of the three branches in an effort to determine the respective roles of different levels of government in the implementation of economic policy. This task consists, to a significant degree, of taking ideas formulated in the treatment of other theoretical questions and applying them to tax and spending problems in a federal environment. This application produces, I believe, some valuable insights into the economic theory of federalism.

I / The Stabilization Branch

The purpose of this section is to examine the nature of the stabilization problem in a federal system in order to discern the roles of different levels of government in maintaining full employment with stable prices. For this purpose, it is useful to adopt a simplified federal model in which there are only two levels of government: a central government, entrusted with public matters of national scope, and "local" government bodies, which function to meet "local" needs. All government units are assumed to possess independent tax and expenditure authority. Since the nature and effectiveness of stabilization policy by central governments are now relatively well understood, the bulk of this section consists of an investigation into the efficacy of stabilization policies at the local level of government.

At the outset, it is to be stressed that local government cannot have access to one of the two basic sets of stabilization tools, namely monetary authority. The power to create and destroy money must be limited to the central government; to allow a local government the capacity to make new money would be equivalent to giving that government an unlimited claim on the real resources of other localities. Thus, as regards conventional stabilization measures, local governments must rely solely on tax and expenditure programs.

A LOCAL INCOME AND PAYMENTS MODEL

In order to investigate the potential of fiscal policy at the local-government level, we first set forth a simple income and payments model to describe a local economy. The model embodies two important simplifications. First, it is assumed that the localities are small and highly open in the sense that they have a high average and marginal propensity to import out of income. Further, we assume that the demand for any community's exports depends primarily on national economic conditions and thus can be taken as exogenously determined.

Second, we specify that, within the nation as a whole, financial capital is highly mobile. In fact, it is useful here to adopt the polar case of "perfect" capital mobility: all securities, irrespective of locality of issue, are assumed to be perfect substitutes for one another and to move without cost among the localities. This assumption implies that interest-rate differentials between communities cannot persist. In addition, we specify that a locality is also small in the sense that it can be treated as a price taker in the national securities

[2]*Ibid.*, 132–3, 179–83.

market; thus, the rate of interest is, for the community, an exogenously determined variable.

The model also includes a simple portfolio-balance argument in terms of financial assets. It must be emphasized that for small, highly open communities, it is dangerous to ignore movements of financial assets in response to trade flows. An increase in local income, for example, gives rise to a relatively large increase in imports, the counterpart to which is an outflow from the community of financial assets. This drain of financial assets must itself come to have a depressive effect on spending and income levels in the community.

The model itself is summarized in equations (1) to (3)[3]:

(1) $C(Y_d, i_0, A) + G_0 + X_0 - I(Y_d, i_0, A, G_0) - Y = 0,$ commodities market

(2) $L(Y_d, i_0, A) - A = 0,$ financial-asset market

(3) $X_0 - I(Y_d, i_0, A, G_0) = 0,$ trade balance

where

Y = real income,
Y_d = disposable income,
i_0 = rate of interest (exogenously determined),
X_0 = flow of exports (exogenously determined),
I = flow of imports,
G_0 = local-government expenditure (exogenously determined),
A = real value of the *net* financial-asset holdings of the private sector.

The level of income and output, Y, is assumed to be perfectly elastic at the given price level and to adjust in Keynesian fashion to the level of aggregate demand. The demand in both the commodity and financial-asset markets depends on disposable income, the rate of interest, and the real value of private, *net* financial-asset holdings. In this regard, since local governments have no monetary powers and since the price of bonds in terms of money is fixed by the externally determined rate of interest, it is convenient to aggregate the money and bond markets into a single financial-asset market. Private economic units still attempt to establish a portfolio balance as between money and bonds, but since this can be done by trading with "foreigners" at a fixed price, there is no need to take explicit account in the model of this phenomenon.

The trade-balance constraint expressed in equation (3) is a necessary condition for complete stock and flow equilibrium in the model. If (3) is not satisfied, this would imply that there is either an inflow or outflow of financial assets, which would change A and thereby disturb any existing equilibrium in the commodity and financial-assets markets. The system consists of three equations, but only two of them are independent, and they serve to determine the two dependent variables: Y and A. If, for example, (1) and (3) are satisfied, it follows from Walras' Law that the financial-asset market must be in equilibrium.

[3]For a more extensive treatment of the derivation of a similar model, see R. McKinnon and W. Oates, *The Implications of International Economic Integration for Monetary, Fiscal, and Exchange-Rate Policy*, Princeton Studies in International Finance 16 (Princeton, NJ, 1966).

To get a feeling for the way in which the model works, consider an exogenous increase in the stock of financial assets, A. Such an injection of assets into the system has a positive wealth effect in the demand functions. As a result, the local economy will have an excess demand for commodities and an excess supply of financial assets, in response to which the level of income will tend to rise. But as Y increases, imports also rise, which leads to a deficit in the balance of trade. This deficit will drain the excess supply of financial assets from the economy. Note that this drain will continue until the entire increment of financial assets is absorbed, for only then will income and thus imports return to their original, equilibrium values and thereby restore balance-of-payments equilibrium. Thus, an injection of financial assets into the system results only in a temporary rise in income, for the additional assets flow out of the economy in response to a deficit in the balance of trade. This result is not surprising, for A and Y are the dependent variables in the system; assuming the model to be stable, a change in either of these variables sets to work forces to restore the initial equilibrium solution.

LOCAL-GOVERNMENT FISCAL POLICY

Through the use of its fiscal tools in this system, what effect can a local government expect to have on the community's level of output and income? Because of certain important constraints to be discussed later, local government is compelled to place much greater reliance on balanced-budget spending than is the central government, which has much greater latitude in the use of deficit financing. Thus, we consider first the impact of balanced-budget spending in the local income model.

It is convenient, as a point of departure, to adopt one final set of assumptions, a set of symmetry conditions concerning the spending patterns of the public and private sectors. Specifically, we assume, at the margin, that government expenditures are divided between imports and commodities produced within the community in the same proportion as private expenditures. Further, we specify that the wealth effect results in a similar division of expenditures on commodities. Symbolically, we have that:

(4) $\partial I / \partial Y_d = \alpha [\partial C / \partial Y_d]$,

(5) $\partial I / \partial G = \alpha$,

(6) $\partial I / \partial A = \alpha [\partial C / \partial A]$,

where $0 < \alpha < 1$.

Consider now a balanced-budget increase (i.e., $dG = dT$) in local-government spending. The immediate impact is to raise the level of spending in the locality, since the government's marginal propensity to spend is unity while that of the private sector is assumed to be less than one. However, given our symmetry assumptions concerning the pattern of expenditures, a rise in total spending implies an increase in imports. Thus, the increase in public expenditures will give rise to a deficit in the balance of trade, and an outflow of financial assets will result. This drain of financial assets from the local economy will tend to depress spending and income until the balance of trade again returns to zero. Given that X_0 remains unchanged, the final equilibrium solution must involve an unchanged level of imports, for only then will the outflow of financial assets cease. Thus, we have:

(7) $\quad dI = \left(\dfrac{\partial I}{\partial Y_d}\right) dY_d + \left(\dfrac{\partial I}{\partial A}\right) dA + \left(\dfrac{\partial I}{\partial G}\right) dG = 0.$

Substituting (4)–(6) into (7) gives:

(8) $\quad dI = \alpha\left(\dfrac{\partial C}{\partial Y_d}\right) dY_d + \alpha\left(\dfrac{\partial C}{\partial A}\right) dA + \alpha dG$

$\qquad\quad = \alpha\left[\left(\dfrac{\partial C}{\partial Y_d}\right) dY_d + \left(\dfrac{\partial C}{\partial A}\right) dA\right] + \alpha dG$

$\qquad\quad = \alpha dC + \alpha dG = \alpha(dC + dG) = 0.$

Therefore,

(9) $\ dC = - dG.$

Thus, private expenditure contracts by the *full* amount of the positive increment in government spending, and the balanced-budget multiplier is zero. If, then, the pattern of local-government spending as between locally produced commodities and imports is the same as that of the private sector, balanced-budget government spending simply supplants an equivalent amount of private expenditure with no net effect on the equilibrium level of income and output.[4]

The only way the local government can influence the community's equilibrium level of income through balanced-budget spending is through biasing its expenditures in favor of locally produced commodities, that is, by violating symmetry condition (5). In the limiting case, where all government expenditures are directed to commodities produced at "home," the G_0 argument drops out of the import-demand function altogether. It is thus clear that G_0 can be at any level without directly influencing the balance of trade; Y_d need no longer decline when G rises in order to keep imports equal to exports. Thus, the levels of Y_d and A are determined independently of G_0. This means that, in this limiting case, the balanced-budget multiplier is unity; the equilibrium level of income rises by the amount of the increase in public expenditure so as to maintain Y_d at its previous equilibrium level.[5]

---

[4] In a simple Keynesian system with no balance-of-trade constraint, the standard proof that the balanced-budget multiplier is unity depends critically on the assumption that the entire increment of government spending is directed to domestically produced goods. In general, the balanced-budget multiplier in an open system is less than one and may even be negative. On this point, see, for example, W. J. Baumol and M. H. Peston, "More on the Multiplier Effects of a Balanced Budget," *American Economic Review*, 45 (March 1955), 140–8. It should also be noted that the above analysis abstracts from possible repercussion effects on the community's level of exports.

[5] Proof that the balanced-budget multiplier is unity where $(\partial I/\partial G) = 0$.

We have that: $dT = dG$ and $dI = 0$.

$dI = (\partial I/\partial Y_d)\, dY_d + (\partial I/\partial A)\, dA = 0.$

Using symmetry assumptions (4) and (6):

$dI = \alpha dC = 0.$ Therefore, $dC = 0.$

$dY = dC + dG = 0 + dG = dG$

Thus, $dY/dG = 1.$

In the less extreme case, where public expenditures involve some imports, but relatively less than in the private sector, the multiplier is positive, but less than unity. The rationale for this result is that, in such cases, government spending assumes something of an "import-substitution" character. By reducing the community's overall (i.e., public plus private) propensity to import, a higher level of income and financial-asset holdings becomes consistent with any given level of exports and imports. Conversely, should the government's pattern of expenditures entail more imports than that of the private sector, the equilibrium level of income would decline, and the balanced-budget multiplier would thus become negative. In conclusion, given an unchanged level of exports, local government, in the balanced-budget case, can raise the equilibrium level of income and employment only to the extent that it can reduce the community's propensity to import, and even then the balanced-budget multiplier will (except in the limiting case) be less than unity.

Consider next the case where the increase in local-government spending is debt-financed. The initial impact of such a program on the demand for commodities is equal to the full increment of public spending, dG, for there is no reduction in disposable income from increased taxes. Income rises, a deficit in the balance of trade results and financial assets flow out of the local economy. However, at the same time, financial assets are being pumped into the system at a rate equal to dG. Thus, a deficit in the trade balance of amount dG can exist without disturbing the state of private financial-asset holdings. This means that, in the case of public deficit-finance, equation (3), the balance-of-trade constraint, must be altered to:

(10) $(X - I) + D = 0,$

where $D = $ the deficit in the public budget. This is clear because, if private financial-asset holdings, A, are to remain unchanged (which is a necessary condition for equilibrium in the system), the new public securities entering the economy must flow out of the community.[6] Thus, the increment in government spending and the inflow of financial assets into the local economy will bid up spending until the deficit in the trade balance becomes equal to the deficit in the public budget, at which point private, net financial-asset holdings will cease to change further.

Income and financial-asset holdings thus rise to a level consistent with the increased level of imports. If we again adopt the symmetry conditions (1)–(3), we have, following the argument in (7)–(9),

(11) $dI = \alpha \, (dC + dG);$

but now $dI = dG$. Therefore,

(12) $\alpha(dC + dG) = dG,$ or

(13) $dC = [(1 - \alpha)/\alpha] \, dG.$

From (1), we obtain

[6]This assumes that a resident of the community does not associate a public issue of bonds with an increase in his own liabilities. For a justification of this assumption, see my "Budget Balance and Equilibrium Income: A Comment on the Efficacy of Fiscal and Monetary Policy in an Open Economy," *Journal of Finance*, 21 (Sept. 1966), 491–2.

(14) $dY = dC + dG + dX - dI = dC + dG - dG = [(1 - \alpha)/\alpha]\, dG.$

Therefore,

(15) $dY/dG = (1 - \alpha)/\alpha.$

The deficit-spending multiplier thus depends solely on the relative openness of the system; it bears no relationship to the marginal propensity to save. The more open the local economy, the less expansionary is the impact of deficit spending on the equilibrium level of income. If the local economy is a highly open one with α in excess of ½, then the multiplier is less than unity.[7] Thus, even in the case of deficit-financed expenditures, the multiplier for a highly open local economy is not likely to be very large.[8]

The model also makes clear a most important characteristic of local-government debt, namely that it tends to flow out of the community. The deficit-spending multiplier depends on an unlimited willingness of the local government to alter its net asset position by creating an *external* debt for the community as a whole. Where deficit spending by the central government is in the main held by domestic residents, locally issued securities will in contrast flow largely into the hands of "foreigners."[9] Thus, local governments must treat this debt with considerably greater concern than need the central government, for the eventual repayment of local debt and interest charges will represent a transfer of income to "outsiders." This suggests that local governments have a real incentive for avoiding aggressive deficit-finance programs for stabilization purposes. Not only are the multiplier effects associated with the spending likely to be small, but there is the further disadvantage of saddling the community with a significant external debt.

Thus, in our federal model, a local government is severely constrained in its ability to influence the community's level of output and income. Local government can employ only fiscal stabilization tools, and problems of openness and external indebtedness seriously impair the freedom and effectiveness with which these tools may be used.[10]

A further difficulty regarding local-government stabilization policy arises when the compensatory problem is placed in the context of the nation as a

[7]As in the case of balanced-budget spending, the multiplier is larger if the government biases its expenditures in favour of locally produced goods. In the limiting case where $(\partial I/\partial G) = 0$, the deficit-spending multiplier is equal to $1/\alpha$.
[8]Even in the case of a simple Keynesian system where no consideration is given to balance-of-payments forces, the deficit-spending multiplier is not very large for a highly open economy. Specifically, the multiplier is equal to the reciprocal of the sum of the marginal propensity to save and the marginal propensity to import. If the latter is in excess of $1/2$, then the deficit-spending multiplier must be less than 2.
[9]This has been pointed out by Jesse Burkhead in *State and Local Taxes for Public Education* (Syracuse, NY, 1963), 11.
[10]It is interesting to note that, even if a local government did have access to tools of monetary policy, it could not, by these means, alter the community's equilibrium level of income. As was discussed earlier, an injection of any kind of financial assets into the system results in a balance-of-trade deficit, which drains the entire increment of assets from the economy. Thus, an injection of money into a local economy will not affect the equilibrium level of income. Money is neutral in this model, not because changes in the stock of money induce proportional changes in the price level, but rather because nominal money holdings are restored to their initial equilibrium level through transactions with "outsiders."

whole. The impotence of conventional fiscal measures at the local level implies that local government, if it is to influence significantly the local level of employment, must find other stabilization tools. One method with some promise is to attempt to attract new spending from external sources into the community. In fact, in the United States, the bulk of the attack by state and local government on unemployment has taken the form of inducements to new industry to locate in one's own state or community. To this end, these governments have adopted a wide variety of programs, including such measures as low-interest loans and tax exemptions to incoming business. However, when viewed from the national level, these policies are largely of a "beggar-thy-neighbour" character; they represent an attempt to attract industry and spending away from other states and localities. Thus, such programs clearly are not suitable to remedying unemployment on a national scale.

The importance of this point is clear when one recognizes that the high degree of interdependence between communities means that movements in real income among the various localities tend to parallel one another. Recessions and booms tend to a great extent to be national in scope. Under these conditions, one could hardly anticipate that independent local programs, relying largely on beggar-thy-neighbour policies, would produce an effective national stabilization program.[11]

Thus, the case for the central government to assume primary responsibility for the stabilization function appears to rest on a firm economic foundation. Our local income and payments model suggests that local government cannot use conventional stabilization tools to much effect and must instead rely mainly on beggar-thy-neighbour policies, policies which from a national standpoint are likely to produce far from the desired results.[12] The central government, on the other hand, is free to adopt monetary policies and fiscal programs involving deficit finance where it is necessary to fulfill the compensatory function. Thus, the Stabilization Branch must do its job primarily at the central-government level.[13]

---

[11]Stanley Engerman reaches a somewhat similar conclusion: "Thus, as long as stabilization measures are left to particular states, there can be no expectation of an optimal national policy, for there may be either smaller or larger changes in demand than would be considered desirable. In the contemporary situation, given both financial constraints and interstate strategy, the presumption that stabilization measures will be insufficient if they are left to lower-level governments appears most reasonable." "Regional Aspects of Stabilization Policy," in R. Musgrave, ed., *Essays in Fiscal Federalism* (Washington DC, 1965), 53, 56.

[12]The conclusions reached here admittedly apply with less force to a federal system in which the "communities" are relatively closed, self-sufficient economies.

[13]For an application of some of these ideas to stabilization and exchange-rate policies on an international scale, both under systems of floating and fixed exchange rates, see: J. M. Fleming, "Domestic Financial Policies under Fixed and under Floating Exchange Rates," *IMF Staff Papers*, Nov. 1962, 369–80; A. Krueger, "The Impact of Alternative Government Policies under Varying Exchange Systems," *Quarterly Journal of Economics*, 79 (May 1965), 195–208; R. Mundell, "Capital Mobility and Stabilization Policy under Fixed and Flexible Exchange Rates," *Canadian Journal of Economics and Political Science*, 29 (Nov. 1963), 475–85; McKinnon and Oates, *The Implications of International Economic Integration*; and W. Oates, "Budget Balance and Equilibrium Income: A Comment on the Efficacy of Fiscal and Monetary Policy in an Open Economy," *Journal of Finance*, 21 (Sept. 1966), 489–98.

II / The Distribution Branch

Like the Stabilization Branch, the Distribution Branch is in general seriously constrained in its operations at sub-central levels of government. The scope for an active redistributive policy depends critically upon the existing degree of mobility of both individuals and other economic resources. At the local level of government, for example, the obstacles to movement among a group of adjacent communities, especially in the long run when commitments must be renewed, are usually not very great. Thus, an attempt by a local government to undertake an aggressive redistributive program is likely to have disastrous results.[14] If a community were to institute a highly progressive income tax to redistribute income in favour of the poor, many wealthy residents would simply move to nearby communities where they could receive more favourable fiscal treatment. Thus, in the end, mobility would largely defeat the purpose of the program.

As we move to geographically larger jurisdictions (e.g., states or provinces), the impediments to movement increase; thus, the capacity for successful redistributive programs is enlarged. But, in the United States, for example, mobility even at the state level is considerable, and the scope for redistributive programs is hence modest.[15] The degree of immobility necessary to allow an effective and substantial program of income redistribution is usually present only at the national level. Thus, the primary responsibility for implementing redistributive policies must in most cases rest with the central government.

More generally, it should be stressed that a high degree of mobility of resources restricts the choice of tax programs at state and local levels. Not only people, but to an even greater degree, such things as business capital are highly responsive to differences in local fiscal treatment. A community, for example, simply cannot impose a heavy tax on productive activity in the locality without incurring the risk of inducing existing business enterprise to move to other communities or, perhaps even more serious, of discouraging the entry of potential new investment.[16] The importance of this consideration is

[14]On this point, see G. Stigler, "Tenable Range of Functions of Local Government," in Joint Economic Committee, Subcommittee on Fiscal Policy, *Federal Expenditure Policy for Economic Growth and Stability* (Washington, DC, 1957), 213–19.

[15]In this connection, see W. L. Gillespie, "Effect of Public Expenditures on the Distribution of Income," in Musgrave, ed., *Essays in Fiscal Federalism*, 122–86. This study of the redistributive impact of public expenditures and revenues in the United States suggests that, at the state-local levels, the over-all budgetary impact on family incomes in excess of $5000 is roughly neutral. Gillespie found that for this group the largely regressive character of state-local taxes is approximately offset by an equalizing pattern of public expenditures. There does, however, appear to be some redistribution of income at these levels in favour of those with family incomes less than $5000.

[16]To the extent that local-government expenditures provide improved public services resulting in lower costs to business, the damaging effect of local taxes on business may be avoided. However, the bulk of local government spending goes toward functions like education, recreation, and public welfare, which do not necessarily provide a direct benefit to local business. Thus, substantial local taxes on business are likely on net to result in an increase in costs for local firms. Another point of interest is that it is by no means clear just how responsive business firms in fact are to differences in local fiscal treatment. However, local public officials seem to believe that businessmen are very sensitive to such differentials. And this is what is important, for it means that local fiscal policy will be structured so as to avoid perverse incentives to business location.

clear from the great number of fiscal programs which sub-central level governments in fact adopt to attract business capital into their areas. It means that these governments must resort in the main to taxes which do not fall so heavily (or at least so obviously) on mobile resources. This explains to some extent the primary reliance of state and local government in the United States on property and sales taxes instead of on personal and corporate income taxation.[17] Canadian municipalities likewise have adopted property taxes as their primary source of revenue.

HORIZONTAL EQUITY IN A FEDERAL SYSTEM

"Perhaps the most widely accepted principle of equity in taxation is that people in equal positions should be treated equally."[18] However, as Buchanan has shown,[19] compliance with this principle requires, in a federal system, special equalizing measures. The source of the problem arises from the fact that, even if the central government treats equals equally, while at the same time each local government provides a uniform fiscal-package for equals within its boundaries, the *over-all* impact of central and local-government budgets is likely to violate the horizontal-equity criterion. The difficulty is that. if we consider two communities with an identical output of public goods and services, the wealthier of the two communities will, *ceteris paribus*, be able to meet its revenue requirements with a lower level of tax *rates*. To raise a given amount of revenue per resident, lower tax rates are required in a community the higher is the level of per-capita income. Thus, for a specified amount of local public services, an individual in a wealthier community will have a smaller tax bill than his equal in a poorer locality.[20] Therefore, from the standpoint of the system as a whole, equals tend not to be treated equally.[21]

[17]S. Mushkin, "Federal Grants and Federal Expenditures," *National Tax Journal*, 10 (Sept. 1957), 193–213; and J. Maxwell, *Financing State and Local Government* (Washington. DC, 1965), 128.

[18]Musgrave, *The Theory of Public Finance*, 160.

[19]James M. Buchanan, "Federalism and Fiscal Equity," *American Economic Review*, 40 (Sept. 1950), 583–90, reprinted in American Economic Association, *Readings in the Economics of Taxation* (Homewood, Ill., 1959), 93–109.

[20]There is, as Buchanan has shown in "Federalism and Fiscal Equity," also an efficiency aspect to this problem. An individual, other things equal. will tend to be attracted to a wealthier community, since he can there obtain a given level of output of public goods for a smaller tax payment. Thus, varying levels of income between communities create "artificial" incentives for location, incentives which do not reflect differences in productivity or other relevant economic considerations. This means that there will be a tendency towards a distortion in the allocation of resources in the form of over-migration into relatively wealthy communities. For a further examination of this "efficiency-in-location" problem, see the Buchanan-Scott exchange in the *Journal of Political Economy*, 60 (Buchanan, "Federal Grants and Resource Allocation," 208–17; A. D. Scott, "Federal Grants and Resource Allocation," 534–6; Buchanan's reply, 536–8); A. D. Scott, "A Note on Grants in Federal Countries," *Economica*, NS 17 (Nov. 1950), 416–22; C. Tiebout, "An Economic Theory of Fiscal Decentralization." in NBER *Public Finances: Needs, Sources, and Utilization* (Princeton, NJ, 1961), 93–4; R. Musgrave, "Approaches to a Fiscal Theory of Political Federalism," in *ibid.*, 120–2. and comments by Buchanan, 122–9, and reply by Musgrave, 132–3; A. D. Scott, "The Economic Goals of Federal Finance," *Public Finance*, 3 (1964), 241–88.

[21]This problem does not arise if local taxation is on a benefit basis. "If state taxes. imposed to finance public services, are allocated on a benefit basis, all citizens of the federation will be taxed on a benefit basis by their respective states. In this case, no central equalization is needed since the requirement of horizontal equity is met by the very condition of universal taxation according to benefits received." Musgrave, "Approaches to a Fiscal Theory," 119.

One can respond to this problem in either of two ways. First, it can be argued that, in a federal system, equal treatment of equals by the central government and independently by each local government is sufficient. "Complete over-all horizontal equality is not achieved, chiefly because its achievement is not a prime goal in a federation."[22] Thus, one can simply ignore the question of over-all horizontal equity. Alternatively, following Buchanan,[23] one can contend that central-government measures are needed to satisfy the horizontal-equity criterion. To this end, the central government can adopt either of two programs: (1) geographically discriminating tax rates at the central-government level to equalize the *total* tax bill of all individuals of equal income who reside in communities with the same level of public services[24]; or (2) redistributive payments among communities to equalize the fiscal capacity of all communities. Either of these measures would result in the like treatment of equals. Buchanan, while favouring the first, suggests that the second is probably more feasible.

In this context, it is interesting to note that the central governments in both Canada and Australia have for many years provided unconditional, equalizing grants to provinces and states. In contrast, in the United States conditional grants have been the primary vehicle for returning funds to states and municipalities. However, the tendency of late in the United States has been to include equalizing provisions in grant formulae so that the federal-government share in matching grants is larger for relatively poor states.[25] In fact, most federal public-assistance funds are now distributed among the states on such a variable-matching basis. The inclusion of terms in grant formulae to account both for need and fiscal capacity implies that the differential in tax rates between wealthy and poor states or communities to realize similar levels of public services has been reduced. Furthermore, the United States is now considering seriously the adoption of unconditional grants to the states along the lines of the Heller-Pechman Plan, a proposal which allows for modest equalization.

However, the primary motivation for equalizing grants has not been the problem of horizontal equity; it has rather been a concern for achieving a greater equality in the distribution of income and, perhaps more important, for improving the quality of public services in poorer areas. But to the degree that greater equality in the distribution of income is achieved, either by direct interpersonal transfers or by payments to poorer state and municipal governments, the objective of horizontal equity is better satisfied. Thus, to a large extent, the means to these two objectives of a more equal distribution of income and of "treating equals equally" are the same.

For our purposes, it is important to stress that the responsibility for attaining these goals must rest primarily with the central government. The mobility of economic units severely constrains the scope for local redistribution of income,

---

[22]Scott, "The Economic Goals of Federal Finance," 251.
[23]In "Federalism and Fiscal Equity."
[24]Buchanan generalizes his treatment in "Federalism and Fiscal Equity" by dealing with the "fiscal residuum" (i.e., tax bill minus expenditure benefits). In these terms, over-all horizontal equity requires that the fiscal residua for equals be equal irrespective of community of residence.
[25]See Mushkin, "Federal Grants and Federal Expenditures."

and the achievement of horizontal equity, as Buchanan has shown, implies central-government intervention. Thus, the Distribution Branch, like the Stabilization Branch, must perform its function primarily at the national level.

III / The Allocation Branch

The economic case for federalism is found in the Allocation Branch.[26] Where the Stabilization and Distribution branches of the public fiscal department must work primarily at the central-government level, there are compelling reasons for believing that, in the Allocation Branch, the provision of certain goods and services is best placed in the hands of local governing bodies. In the first place, one might expect that local government would be more responsive to the particular preferences of the community as regards expenditure and revenue policies. A greater reliance on the central government would probably result in a substantially higher degree of uniformity in public services among communities.

However, there is a second economic rationale for federalism, which may be of even greater importance. Public goods, by their very nature, involve compromise among the residents of a nation or community. Some individuals, for example, may prefer a high level of national defence, while others would desire a lower level of expenditures (and taxes) for this function. However, everyone in a particular nation or community must consume the same set of public goods. Thus, compromise is inevitable. There is no way out of this problem at the national level; we all, for example, by necessity receive essentially the same amount of national defence. However, at the local level, there is at least a partial solution, namely consumer mobility.[27] If, for example, an individual is unhappy with the pattern of expenditures and the structure of taxes in his community, he can, in a federal system, always move to another community which provides a "fiscal package" better suited to his tastes. Thus, in a federal economy, the efficiency of resource allocation as regards local public goods tends to be enhanced by so-called "voting-on-foot." In much the same way as consumers purchase private goods, they can to some degree select a community which provides a pattern of public goods and taxes which is in accord with their tastes.[28] Thus, we can envision a federal system in which communities provide varying levels and combinations of public goods and in

[26]A strong case for decentralized finance can also be made on political grounds. It can be argued, for example, that a federal system, in contrast to a wholly centralized form of government, provides safeguards against the excessive concentration of public power, fosters diversity and innovation, and promotes the development of a responsible and experienced citizenry by providing wider opportunities for participation in public decision-making; see, for example, John Stuart Mill's essay, *Considerations on Representative Government*, R. B. McCallum, ed. (Oxford, 1948), chap. 15. In this paper, however, we limit the argument to the economics of federalism.

[27]See Stigler, "Tenable Range of Functions of Local Government," and C. Tiebout, "A Pure Theory of Local Expenditures," *Journal of Political Economy*, 64 (Oct., 1956), 416–24.

[28]This conception of a federal system has, I believe, increasing relevance with the growing urbanization in most countries. An individual working in a central city often has a wide choice of suburban communities in which to live, and the quality of the local school system, for example, may be of considerable importance in his selection of a place of residence.

which individuals locate themselves, to some extent at least, according to their fiscal preferences.[29]

AN IDEAL FEDERAL MODEL

It is useful at this point to develop in a little more detail an "ideal" federal system and then to consider later certain important complications to this ideal model. To this end, consider, as earlier, an economic system consisting of a collection of communities, each with its own government possessed of tax and expenditure authority. The communities are tied together in a federation which provides for a central government with the power to tax economic units in all the communities to meet the cost of providing needed national public services. We assume that there are two public goods, produced in the system. The first is a national collective-consumption good, a good which all individuals in the economy "enjoy in common in the sense that each individual's consumption of such a good leads to no subtraction from any other individual's consumption of the good. . . ."[30] In formal terms, this implies that the total quantity of the good produced enters into each individual's utility function.

In this system, a primary responsibility of the Allocation Branch at the central-government level is to provide the optimal level of output of the national public good. This implies, as Samuelson and others have shown, that production of the public good should be extended to the point where the sum of all individuals' marginal rates of substitution for a unit of the public good is equal to its marginal cost.

Second, we assume that local governments provide a public good. However, this good is of a slightly different character from that produced by the central government. Specifically, the local public good is such that, although each individual in the community consumes the same quantity of the good, the utility he derives from its consumption depends not only on the quantity of the good produced, but also on the number of other people who consume the good (i.e., on the population of the community).[31] For example, the satisfaction an individual derives from the use of a local park depends not only on the size and facilities of the park, but also on the number of other visitors to the park. The more crowded the park is, the less an individual may enjoy his trip there. Thus, the local public good in this model is not a pure, collective-consumption good, for it is subject to costs of congestion.[32]

---

[29]On non-economic grounds, one can raise certain objections to this solution. Scott, for example, points out that "In itself, this migration will be regarded as a good thing by those who value an exchange optimum. But it will be regarded as a bad thing by those who value the continuation of grouping of peoples in a federation according to other characteristics, such as tradition, culture, law, language, or religion." "The Economic Goals of Federal Finance," 269.

[30]P. Samuelson, "The Pure Theory of Public Expenditures," *Review of Economics and Statistics*, 36 (Nov. 1954), 387.

[31]See James M. Buchanan, "An Economic Theory of Clubs," *Economica*, 32 (Feb. 1965), 1–14. Breton would prefer to call this a "non-private good"; see A. Breton, "The Theory of Government Grants," *Canadian Journal of Economics and Political Science*, 31 (May 1965), 175–87.

[32]This characterization of the local public good is not unrealistic, since most of the services provided by state and local government are in fact subject to costs of congestion (e.g., school systems, roads, recreation facilities, etc.). However, there is a fundamental theoretical

Adopting an approach suggested by James Buchanan,[33] the costs of congestion can be played off against the benefits from expanding the population of the community so as to define the optimal size of a community. Consider a locality which provides a given output of a particular good (e.g., a centrally located park). The admission of additional residents to the community benefits existing residents by allowing the costs of the construction and operation of the park to be divided among more persons. Thus, the cost (or tax bill) per resident varies inversely with the population of the community. On the other hand, as the community grows and more people use the park, a point will be reached at which additional residents impose costs of congestion on existing park users. Furthermore, the larger the population of the community, the less are the savings per resident of yet another newcomer to the locality. Thus, we can define the optimal-size population of the community as that for which the marginal gain from an additional resident is equal to the marginal cost of congestion (assuming that marginal congestion costs rise or at least do not decline more rapidly than marginal gain). After this point, the sum of the marginal rates of substitution of the existing residents for a further entrant is negative (i.e., marginal congestion cost to current residents exceeds the marginal benefits from reduced taxes per resident). Finally, we assume that, at this point, residents take action, perhaps in the form of zoning laws or building restrictions, to stem the flow of entrants and to maintain the community at its optimal size.

The introduction of the congestion factor does complicate matters a bit, for an individual in his selection of a place of residence now must take into consideration both the level of output of the local public good and the degree of congestion. Thus, our efficiency conditions are considerably more complicated than in the case of the national public good.[34] Nevertheless, one might expect that where there are a large number of communities with diverse levels of output of the local public good and with varying crowding conditions, an individual will in most cases be able to find a community which provides a reasonable satisfaction of his preferences.

Thus, we have an economy in which the Allocation Branch at the central-government level provides the efficient output of the national public good, and in which this Branch at the local level produces a wide variety of levels of output of the local public good. Individuals, with assumed full knowledge

---

justification for making the local public good subject to crowding. If there were no crowding constraint, it would make little sense to have different communities produce the good. In this case, one community could provide the good for everyone, and the optimal solution would involve the existence of only a single community. Thus, the congestion condition is necessary to prevent the degeneration of the model into a single-community system.

[33]In "An Economic Theory of Clubs."

[34]The establishment of a new community, especially if its level of output of public goods closely approximates that of several other communities, represents a loss of resources in the sense that residents of this community could have consumed the output of public goods in other communities. The gain resulting from a new community stems primarily from the reduction in congestion costs it affords (and also to some degree from the greater diversity its existence may offer). Thus, as an approximation, it can be argued that the *number* of communities is optimal when the reduction in congestion costs resulting from an additional community has been reduced to equality with the costs of producing another community's output of local public goods.

of the offerings of the various communities, select a community of residence which provides a fiscal package well suited to their preferences. It remains to move somewhat closer to reality by introducing some complications into the model in order to determine what sorts of adjustments in public policies these conditions require.

SOME OBSTACLES TO ACHIEVING AN EFFICIENT UTILIZATION OF RESOURCES IN A FEDERAL SYSTEM

The "ideal" federal model just described provides a powerful case for a federal system as a means for realizing an efficient allocation of resources. If instead, a single level of output of each public good were provided by a central government, the potential increase in welfare from better satisfying diverse individual preferences for many of these goods would be lost. Nevertheless, the adoption of a federal system does in general entail certain inefficiencies which may require further public action.

The production of local public goods may, for example, result in spill-over benefits (or costs) to residents of other communities. In the case of spill-over benefits, the output of these goods is likely to be suboptimal, for a local government, seeking to maximize the welfare of its own residents, will disregard the impact of its activities on outsiders.[35] Thus, the central government should, in this instance, subsidize the production of local public goods with a unit subsidy equal to the spill-over benefits per unit of output, thereby "internalizing" the spill-over.

Somewhat less appreciated, however, is the fact that taxes levied by a local government may not fall wholly on its own residents. Through a variety of means, the taxes paid in one community may be shifted onto residents of other localities. A tax on local production, for example, may result in part in higher prices of output, which are paid largely by outsiders who purchase these goods. These spill-over costs from taxes appear to be of considerable magnitude; Charles McLure, in a recent study of the United States,[36] estimates that, on the average, roughly 20 to 25 per cent of the taxes levied at the state level are shifted onto residents of other states. The implication of such spill-over costs (assuming for the moment an absence of spill-over benefits) is that local public goods will tend to be overproduced. A community, by equating marginal benefits with marginal costs to its *own* residents, will extend production past the point where marginal benefits equal the sum of marginal costs to *all* residents of the country. Thus, where spill-overs consist both of benefits from the production of local public goods and the shifting of local taxes onto residents of other communities, the central government must, on efficiency criteria, determine the *net* spill-over benefit and employ a unit subsidy where this figure is positive or an appropriate unit tax where it is negative.[37]

Furthermore, the whole problem of efficiency in taxation acquires additional

[35]Breton, "The Theory of Government Grants."
[36]"The Interstate Exporting of State and Local Taxes: Estimates for 1962," *National Tax Journal*, March 1967.
[37]For a provocative treatment of the problems resulting from spill-overs among communities, see Alan Williams, "The Optimal Provision of Public Goods in a System of Local Government," *Journal of Political Economy*, 74 (Feb. 1966), 18–33.

dimensions in a federal system. Economists are familiar with the sorts of inefficiencies which arise when a tax is levied on a particular product or on the earnings of a factor of production. But in a federal system, further complications arise. In a simple two-factor model (e.g., labour and capital), if community A chooses to tax the use of labour and community B capital, substantial losses in total output can result. In a competitive system with mobile factors of production, such a situation will give rise to intercommunity differences in relative factor prices. Thus, the relative price and hence the marginal product of capital would tend to be higher in community B than in A. This is clearly inefficient, for it means that the aggregate level of real output could be increased by simply relocating units of the factors of production; the movement of a unit of capital from A into B would result, *ceteris paribus*, in greater output.[38] There is therefore something to be said for sub-central governments adopting similar tax structures so as to minimize the loss of output resulting from an inefficient pattern of location of productive activity.[39]

Finally, it should be stressed that taxes, which are efficient when imposed at the national level, may be highly inefficient when employed at the local level. A tax, for example, on people with brown eyes is a neutral (and efficient) tax for a closed system as a whole, as there is no way in which it can be shifted. Such a tax does not *directly* affect the terms on which individuals make choices (i.e., it has only income, no direct substitution, effects). However, the same tax is not neutral if employed by a single community, for it may, in this case influence an individual's choice of community of residence. The point here is that a tax on a factor or commodity whose supply is fixed is a neutral and an efficient tax. However, those inputs or goods which are fixed in supply at the national level may, as a result of intercommunity mobility, be in quite elastic supply to any particular community. Thus, in a federal system, there may be good reason for different levels of government to adopt quite different types of taxes.

[38]This inefficiency will tend to create artificial, inefficient patterns of comparative advantage among the various communities. A community, for example, with a natural comparative advantage in producing relatively capital-intensive goods, may, after levying a tax on capital, find itself specializing in the production of labour-intensive commodities. For an excellent study of the tax-harmonization problem in the European Common Market, see the *EEC Reports on Tax Harmonization* (the Tinbergen Report) (Amsterdam, 1963). In addition, Musgrave (*The Theory of Public Finance*, 180) and G. Break (*Intergovernmental Fiscal Relations in the United States* (Washington, DC, 1967)) treat some specific problems regarding the integration of state and local tax structures.

[39]Even if all communities employ the same tax, some inefficiencies will yet remain, since the tax rate among communities will vary, other things equal, according to the levels of output of local public goods. Thus, if all communities taxed the use of capital, the relative price of capital will tend to be higher in those communities whose residents prefer more in the way of local public goods. But this is to be expected. "The very purpose of fiscal federalism . . . is to permit different groups living in various states to express different preferences for public services; and this inevitably leads to differences in the levels of taxation and public services. The resulting differentiation in tax levels may interfere with the most efficient allocation of resources and location of industries for the region as a whole; but such is the cost of political subdivision, be it on an intranational or international level." Musgrave, *The Theory of Public Finance*, 179–80.

THE OPTIMAL-SIZE PUBLIC UNIT

In the ideal model, we considered a simplified federal model with only two levels of government and two "nicely behaved" public goods. In this system, we were able to define the optimal-size community by balancing marginal tax savings against marginal congestion costs. However, a federal system is more usually characterized by a number of different levels of government which provide a complex array of public goods and services. In addition to the central government, one generally encounters state or provincial governments, local government units, plus perhaps county or regional public bodies. Furthermore, residents frequently construct *ad hoc* public units, cutting through various levels of government, to deal with specific problems.

In this more complex sort of a federal world, a new and important question arises, namely "What is the optimal-size government unit to perform a specific function?" This problem obviously has important political dimensions, but we will limit the discussion here to the economic aspects of this decision. The first and most obvious factor to be considered is the spatial distribution of the benefits provided by the good or service. If, for example, production of the good has little impact on persons outside the community, this suggests that local government is the appropriate decision-making unit. However, if benefits are more widespread, a higher level of government is indicated. Normally, one would not expect the spatial distribution of the benefits (and possibly costs) from a particular public good to coincide precisely with the existing jurisdictions of governing units.[40] In this case, as discussed earlier, certain adjustments need to be made to account for the resulting spill-over costs and benefits.

However, the spatial nature of benefits is only one relevant consideration. Public goods frequently exhibit significant economies of scale. In such cases, the cost savings resulting from production on a larger scale at a higher level of government may warrant the transfer of a specific function to a level of government higher than would be indicated solely by the spatial distribution of benefits. It is thus clear that the determination of the optimal level of government to provide a specific good or service is likely to involve compromise. On the basis of the spatial character of benefits, a level of government may be appropriate which is quite different from that suggested by the nature of the cost function for the good.

Even this, however, is a somewhat oversimplified view of the problem. There are many facets to the provision of most public goods and services. And, for one reason or another, the interests of practically all levels of government are involved in providing something like educational services. Thus, at the policy level, Mushkin and Adams[41] have recently stressed that the relevant question is not so much which level of government should provide the service but

---

[40]Another approach to this problem is not to hold rigidly fixed the existing structure of government, but to allow some flexibility as regards the size of existing jurisdictions and more important some adaptability in the formation of public units based on a cooperative effort between different levels of government. On this, see S. Mushkin and R. Adams, "Emerging Patterns of Federalism," *National Tax Journal*, 19 (Sept. 1966), 225–47.
[41]"Emerging Patterns of Federalism."

rather what mix of government participation is optimal. The spatial distribution of benefits, possible economies of scale, and, in practice, a number of political variables must jointly serve to provide the answer to this question.

Summary and conclusions

The central thesis of this paper is that, in a federal system, the Distribution and Stabilization branches of the public fiscal department must perform their functions primarily at the central-government level. In contrast, in the Allocation Branch, local government, as well as the central government, has important responsibilities in the provision of needed public goods and services.[42]

1. In the Stabilization Branch, the effective use of an independent fiscal policy by local governments is seriously constrained by the openness of the community, which implies a small conventional multiplier, by restrictive balance-of-payment forces, and by the growth of external indebtedness in response to deficit-financed expenditures. Furthermore, since in a federation cyclical fluctuations are generally of a nationwide character, it is essential that there be a centrally planned and directed compensatory policy.

2. In the Distribution Branch, the mobility of economic units generally places stringent restrictions on the capabilities of local governments to alter the existing distribution of income. Attempts, for example, by a local government to institute a more equal distribution of income tend to result in a movement of the wealthy out of the community. Furthermore, the achievement of horizontal equity in a federal system implies either intercommunity transfers or a discriminating central-government income tax. Thus, the central government must in the main assume responsibility for maintaining the "optimal" distribution of income.

3. In the Allocation Branch, the responsiveness of local government to community needs and the desirability of providing consumers with a wide choice of "fiscal packages" suggest an important role for government at the local level. In our "ideal" model, the central government provides the efficient output of the national public good, while numerous local governments offer individuals a wide variety of output of the local public good.

(a) The existence of spill-over benefits and costs between communities indicate a need for central-government policies to correct for the resulting inefficiencies in resource allocation.

(b) The problem of efficiency in taxation has added dimensions in a federal system. As a consequence, community co-ordination to "harmonize" local tax structures is needed to keep inefficiencies from becoming excessive.

(c) In a more complicated system with many levels of government and a detailed menu of public goods and services, compromises as between the spatial character of spill-over effects and possible economies of scale are inevitable in determining the optimal *mix* of government participation in providing a particular good or service.

---

[42]Musgrave reaches a similar conclusion in his treatment of the problem in *The Theory of Public Finance*, 181–2.

[2]

An Economist's Perspective on Fiscal Federalism

Wallace E. Oates

The federal system was created with the intention of combining the different advantages which result from the magnitude and the littleness of nations.

Alexis de Tocqueville
Democracy in America

De Tocqueville's observation on the origin of federal government takes on new dimensions from the perspective of recent economic events and research. In the realm of macroeconomic policy, for example, the importance of size has become increasingly apparent: the monetary and fiscal authorities of a small, highly "open" country in today's international economy have only a limited scope for independent action; in various limiting cases, they may lose entirely their control over the size of the domestic money supply and the availability of credit.[1] On the other hand, the "littleness" of fiscal jurisdictions continues to offer compelling advantages for the provision of a number of important public services. In fact, fiscal data covering recent decades for a large number of countries indicate a growth in the budgets of decentralized levels of government relative to that of the national authority.

Recent fiscal history has been, to a significant extent, the response to a continuing tension between the economic and political forces inducing greater centralization and the opposing centrifugal attractions of local fiscal control. In the United States, this has given birth to federal revenue sharing with state and local governments. On a larger scale, the ongoing drama in the European community reflects the pushes and pulls of the gains from economic unification versus the desirability of fiscal autonomy. The effort continues to forge new fiscal institutions to combine ". . . the different advantages which result from the magnitude and the littleness of nations."

These events have stimulated a renewal of interest in the study of multilevel finance that has resulted in the emergence of fiscal federalism as a subject of study in its own right. In this paper, I want to explore at a relatively general

21

level what the basic principles of economics have to say about the organization and functioning of the public sector in a federal system. I stress that the perspective will be on the *economics* of federalism in the more narrow and conventional sense; the subject is the implications of economic analysis for the traditional concerns of the economist—the allocation of resources and the distribution of income.

This will raise some controversial issues. We find, for example, that the objective of efficient resource allocation suggests that individuals should segregate themselves by communities according to their demands for public services. However, it is precisely this sort of segregation that, for political or even ethical reasons, we may be quite reluctant to tolerate. In some instances, then, economic analysis points in directions that may leave us uneasy because of their implied social and political consequences. Nevertheless, it is my purpose here simply to follow the economic logic to its own conclusions. Even where this leads to propositions that are "normatively" unsettling, the analysis is still likely to reveal some fundamental forces at work in the economic system with which we must contend, regardless of our objectives for social policy.

I should also emphasize that the term *federalism* for the economist is not to be understood in a narrow constitutional sense. In economic terms, all governmental systems are more or less federal; even in a formally unitary system, for example, there is typically a considerable extent of de facto fiscal discretion at decentralized levels. Instead of being dichotomously federal or nonfederal, governments vary along some multidimensional spectrum in the degree to which fiscal decision-making is decentralized. As Livingston (1952, p. 86) has argued, "The essence of federalism lies not in the institutional or constitutional structure but in the society itself" [see also Oates (1972, chap.1)]. For purposes of economic analysis, I find it more useful to envision a "centralized solution" to the problem of resource allocation in the public sector as one that emphasizes standardized levels of services across all jurisdictions, while the "federal" approach stresses greater scope for decentralized choice in the provision of these services.

Finally, I should point out that certain portions of this chapter have a strongly U.S. flavor. In particular, the local-finance literature has explored in great detail the mobility model, whose applicability seems largely confined to modern metropolitan areas in which individuals often work in one place and reside in another. These models predict a process of segregation by socioeconomic class, which seems to characterize urban areas in the United States rather better than in some other countries. The applicability of this line of analysis to certain other nations (or supranational bodies like the European community) is open to real question. However, other parts of the chapter deal with issues relevant to the intergovernmental structure of nearly all countries.

AN ECONOMIST'S PERSPECTIVE ON FISCAL FEDERALISM   5

I. The Division of Fiscal Functions Among Levels of Government

There seems to be a consensus on the proposition that the primary responsibility for macroeconomic stabilization policies and for the redistribution of income and wealth must rest with the central government. The basic point is not that local governments in the aggregate have no impact on total demand or the distribution of income, but rather that the constraints on an individual local government leave it very little scope for an effective stabilization or redistributive policy within its jurisdiction.

On the macroeconomic side, local governments do not possess the power to create or destroy money. Moreover, any attempts to influence the level of local economic activity by deliberate fiscal measures will be dissipated by the deflection of most of the new demand to goods and services produced elsewhere; typically, the local economy is highly open, i.e., it has a large average and marginal propensity to import, so the local authority is unable to contain the new spending within its borders.

Similarly, the mobility of individual economic units among different localities places fairly narrow limits on the capacity for local income redistribution. For example, an aggressive policy to redistribute income from the rich to the poor in a particular locality, may, in the end, simply chase the relatively wealthy to other jurisdictions and attract those with low incomes. The likely outcome is a community homogeneous in poor residents (an unappealing prospect for most local jurisdiction).[2] The ability to redistribute income to a significant extent depends largely on impediments to mobility of the sort provided by national borders (and, in some instances, even these may not be fully adequate).

The Decentralization Theorem

Decentralized choice in the public sector comes into its own in Musgrave's allocation branch. Consider an economy composed of two communities in which a single public service is provided. For the moment, let us ignore the problem of mobility by assuming that each individual's location is permanently fixed in one or the other of these two localities. Finally, let us postulate that there are no spillover effects in the provision of the public service; the benefits from these outputs are confined solely to the residents of the community in which they are provided, so that, in Breton's (1965, p. 180) terminology, a "perfect mapping" exists.

The spirit of the *unitary solution* to the provision of the public service would be to ensure a uniform level of the service over both communities. However, it is easy to see that in economic terms this will generally be inefficient. If the demands in the two communities for the public service differ (and if there are no economies of scale from centralized provision of the service), then we can increase welfare by diversifying outputs in the two communities in accordance with local demands. I have elsewhere (1972, pp. 33–38, 54–63) described this rather straightforward proposition as the decentralization theorem. Its importance in the context of public-sector outputs is that, subject to certain conditions, it establishes a presumption in favor of the *federal solution* to resource allocation in the government sector: the decentralized provision of public services in response to local demands.

The conditions necessary for the validity of the proposition are also important: the absence of both spillover effects and any economies of scale. If, for example, the central government can achieve cost savings by providing a uniform service level across both localities, then this must be weighed against the potential welfare gains from diversified local outputs to ascertain the appropriate level of government to provide the service. These kinds of tradeoffs constitute the problem of determining the optimal size jurisdiction for providing a particular public service. This determination is further complicated by the presence of several public services. In order to reduce the decision-making costs implicit in a myriad of different levels of government, it will normally make sense to consolidate the provision of several services under the roof of one governmental unit, although this may mean that the optimal jurisdiction size for each service in isolation no longer corresponds precisely to the actual jurisdiction of the responsible government.

In practice, however, possibly the most difficult dimension of this optimal-jurisdiction problem has proved to be the geographical delineation of the benefits and costs. It is not clear, for example, just what the geographical range of *significant* benefits is for functions like education and police services. For instance, it can be argued that I have an "option value" for levels of public outputs in other communities because I may at some point move to one of them.

Consumer Mobility and the Tiebout Model

A large portion of the local-finance literature has addressed the issues that arise when consumers move among communities, at least in part in response to fiscal differentials. The immediate appeal of the mobility model is the enhanced potential that it offers for realizing the welfare gains from diversified local outputs. We can envision a world in which different communities offer varying levels of public services and in which each individual selects as a community of residence a locality with a service level corresponding to his level of demand. By "voting with their feet," individuals at the same time reveal their preferences and promote an efficient allocation of resources with the public sector.

AN ECONOMIST'S PERSPECTIVE ON FISCAL FEDERALISM 7

The origin of this line of analysis in the economics literature is the classic article by Tiebout (1956). Tiebout sketched out a model which, in contrast to Samuelson's allegations concerning the inefficiencies resulting from decentralized choice for public goods, showed that, for a particular class of public goods (those whose consumption is restricted to a specific geographical area), individual choice can, at least in principle, generate an efficient outcome. In Tiebout's world, perfectly mobile consumers, living solely on dividend income, choose to reside in communities that provide their desired levels of public outputs. The resulting solution closely parallels the market solution for private goods:

Just as the consumer may be visualized as walking to a private market place to buy his goods, the prices of which are set, we place him in the position of walking to a community where the prices (taxes) of community services are set. Both trips take the consumer to market. There is no way in which the consumer can avoid revealing his preferences in a spatial economy. Spatial mobility provides the local public-goods counterpart to the private market's shopping trip [Tiebout (1956, p. 422)].

The Tiebout model, however, involves a number of heroic assumptions *and* omissions, the investigation of which spurred later research. It is quite striking, for example, that a paper which purports to describe individual location decisions in response to local services uses a nonspatial model and makes no mention of local taxation! In addition, a number of the assumptions verge on the outrageous: Tiebout's consumers, for example, are completely footloose in the sense that the location of their jobs or friends has no influence on their choice of a community of residence—the selection is made solely on fiscal criteria.

The large literature that has followed on Tiebout's paper has tried to relax some of these assumptions and to enrich the analysis. Buchanan and Goetz (1972) have shown that certain inefficiencies are likely where the individual must commute to a place of work. On another front, Schuler (1974) has begun the integration of the model into an explicitly spatial framework. However, rather than attempt a comprehensive survey of the work on the mobility model, I shall explore a couple of issues that I find of particular interest and relevance to the political economy of fiscal federalism.

The first concerns the tendencies in the mobility model to the formation of communities that are stratified by income class.[3] The Tiebout solution involves a sorting-out process in which individuals with similar demands for local services locate together; since we might generally expect the demand for local services to exhibit a positive income elasticity, this in itself should encourage a tendency toward segregation by income. However, there is a second inducement to income homogeneity implicit in the use of income-related taxes to finance local services. High-income residents in a particular community have a fiscal incentive to exclude those with lower incomes, since the latter will make only a relatively small contribution to the local treasury. We thus have both a taste element and a pecuniary incentive operating in the local public sector to produce a system of communities which are relatively homogeneous in income.

This segregation solution has some interesting implications. First, note how it removes the potential for any income redistribution through local budgets. Even though communities employ income-related taxes (such as property or personal income taxes), no redistribution whatsoever occurs in the limiting case of perfect income segregation, since everyone in a particular community has the same income.

A second intriguing aspect of this outcome is its apparent instability. It will generally be in the interest of a relatively poor individual to locate in a high-income community, where at the existing tax rate he will get a partial free ride from the larger tax payments of his neighbors. We can thus envision a process in which wealthy households establish a community with high levels of public outputs only to find themselves invaded by lower-income families seeking the pecuniary advantages of the large tax base—a continuing game of hide-and-seek with no stable solution.

How do we bring stability into this world? In the United States, at least, the answer to this is fairly clear: higher-income communities have adopted exclusionary zoning regulations specifically to keep out poorer families. Such ordinances typically require a minimum lot size and, perhaps, certain housing characteristics to ensure that only a wealthy family can afford to purchase or build a house. Zoning regulations have thus been the policy instrument to achieve a stable composition of the local community.

Until quite recently, there has been little formal economic analysis of zoning activities. In general, there seemed to be some presumption that the use of local property taxation introduced certain inefficiencies or distortions in the local housing market (as well as into local decisions concerning public services) and the introduction of zoning impediments to mobility among local jurisdictions probably made things even worse. However, Hamilton (1975) has demonstrated that this need not be the case; in fact, the Hamilton model shows that a system of many communities, each using property taxation and zoning ordinances that specify a minimum value for local houses, effectively converts the property tax into a pure benefit tax and restores all the efficiency properties of the Tiebout solution. Moreover, the equilibrium in the Hamilton model is a stable one: no household will have any incentive to relocate.

This is an intriguing result from the perspective of public policy. Our amended mobility model is one in which households segregate themselves, largely by income class, to consume desired levels of public outputs and effectively wall themselves in from potential lower-income entrants by means of exclusionary zoning ordinances. And the outcome is efficient resource allocation in the local public sector! What can hardly escape notice is that this is precisely the system that is presently under severe attack in the popular literature and in the courts in the United States. The tide of opinion contends that this system both fails to accommodate regional housing needs for lower-income households and gives rise to intolerable differences in the quality of public services (particularly schools) across different localities. We thus seem to have another of the (frequent) conflicts between economic efficiency and norms of social justice.

In concluding this section, let me comment briefly on the applicability of the mobility model. The model itself appears to make strong demands on consumer responses to local-sector differentials; households must undertake the expensive act of moving to satisfy their demands for local services. How realistic is this? As stated, it seems an unlikely description of the behavior of a typical household. Census data do indicate that the average family does, in fact, move surprisingly frequently; in the United States, for example, the 1970 census indicated that only about half the families sampled were living in the same house as in 1965. However, the vast majority of these moves are surely not motivated primarily by fiscal considerations; they are the result of a change in the location of employment or, perhaps, in family status. Whatever the motivation for the move, once the individual begins to survey the available alternatives, he can take into account the levels of local public services, particularly the quality of local schools and the degree of public safety. For an individual working in a central city, there typically exists a wide range of potential residential communities within the suburbs, and when choosing among these communities, he can be expected to devote significant attention to such things as the reputation of the local public school system.

The mobility model may thus provide a reasonable approximation to behavior *within metropolitan areas.* There is, moreover, a growing empirical literature whose findings are consistent with this view. However, the case for the mobility model is much weaker in a regional context; the constraint imposed by place of employment is probably sufficient in most cases to restrict the scope of choice among residential communities to a single metropolitan area (or even part of that area).

The Measurement of the Welfare Gains from Decentralized Public Choice

The economic rationale for a federal system is to be found in the capacity of decentralized government units to improve resource allocation in the public sector through the diversification of public outputs in accordance with local tastes. This, of course, has long been recognized. A more difficult and intriguing question is the order of magnitude of the economic gains to be realized from such diversification. How much is the decentralized provision of public outputs worth?

There is, in principle at least, a straightforward way to answer this question:

the measurement of the increase in consumers' surplus associated with varying levels of local public services. Let us suppose, for purposes of illustration, that we can divide the population in two groups, within each of which the demand for a particular public output is the same for all persons. In terms of Figure 1-1, each of the people in group 1 possesses a demand of D_1, while the demand curve for those in group 2 is D_2. Assuming that the public service can be provided at constant cost per head,[4] the desired level of consumption of people in group 1 is Q_1, and that of group 2 individuals is Q_2.

The spirit of the centralized solution to the provision of the public service is a standardized level of the service to everyone. In Figure 1-1 suppose that this uniform output is a compromise between the higher and lower demands at, say, Q_c. The welfare loss to each group 1 person is then simply the shaded triangle ABC, which represents the excess of costs to each person over his valuation of the "excessive" units of consumption. Similarly, there is a welfare loss to each group 2 individual equal to the shaded triangle CDE (in this case, the excess of marginal valuation over cost for the "lost" units of consumption.)[5]

Two points regarding Figure 1-1 are worthy of note. First, the extent of the welfare loss from centralized provision is obviously critically dependent on the variation in individual demands; if Q_1 and Q_2 were quite close, then Q_c could provide a close approximation to the most desired outputs for all individuals

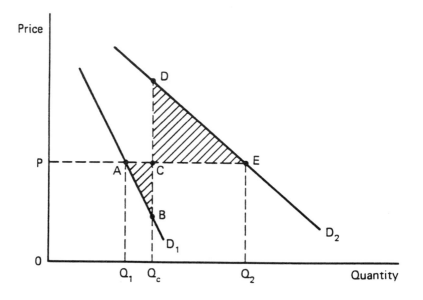

Figure 1-1. Welfare Losses from Centralization

with little resulting loss in consumer surplus. Second, note that the magnitude of the loss in consumer surplus varies inversely with the price elasticity of demand. The steeper the demand curves in Figure 1-1, the larger will be the area of the shaded triangles (which reflects the more rapid decline in the marginal valuation of additional units of consumption for group 1 persons or the increased marginal valuation of lost units for group 2 individuals).[6] The loss in welfare from imposing a uniform level of consumption of a public service over all jurisdictions will, therefore, depend on the extent of the variation in the most desired quantity among the localities and on the price elasticities of individual demands.

While this analysis suggests a direct way to measure the gains from diversified local outputs, it is not an easy matter to implement the technique for a number of reasons (not the least of which are the difficulties in measuring units of public output and in obtaining reliable estimates of individual demand functions). One recent illustrative attempt by Bradford and Oates (1974) generated an estimate of the welfare loss from imposing a standardized level of expenditure per pupil in all school districts in northeastern New Jersey. Assuming that each family was located in a municipality providing the family's most desired school budget, Bradford and Oates estimated a multiplicative demand function for school expenditures and then used this function to calculate the loss in consumer surplus resulting from the introduction of a hypothetical uniform level of spending equal simply to the existing average expenditure per pupil.[7] The computations indicated a substantial welfare loss from the hypothetical centralization of school spending: for a dollar transferred from a high-expenditure school district to a lower-spending district, the loss in consumer surplus was, *on average*, about 50 cents. Moreover, estimates of the price elasticity of demand for other local public services by Bergstrom and Goodman (1973) are typically quite low (on the order of -0.2), which suggests that welfare losses from uniform consumption may well be considerable.

Boss (1974) has recently presented an alternative, and extremely intriguing, approach to the measurement of the value of decentralized choice. Boss studied a fiscal-reform referendum to centralize the financing of local schools in Oregon. In brief, the proposal would have entailed the standardizing of school operating budgets on a statewide basis to replace existing local budget determination. The program also involved a radical shift away from local property taxation to statewide business and individual income taxation. The tax proposal was such that an estimated 85 percent of the taxpayers in Oregon would have enjoyed a net decrease in their tax payments. However; 58 percent of the voters going to the polls rejected the plan. Boss analyzed the referendum results on a county-by-county basis: for each county he calculated the median tax change and then used this to estimate a predicted "yes" vote. Interestingly, the predicted vote exhibited a high correlation with the actual vote, which suggests that the voters in Oregon did respond systematically to net tax gains. However, the predicted "yes" vote consistently exceeded the true vote (on average, by some 42 percent); Oregon voters apparently placed a positive value on local fiscal control. Boss went on to estimate this valuation and found that a voter typically would have required compensation on the order of $150 for the loss of local budget determination for schools.

While all these calculations are hedged by critical assumptions and qualifications, they do at least suggest that people attach some economic value to local fiscal choice and that the measurement of this valuation may not be a wholly intractable problem. This implies, moreover, that attempts to impose centrally determined uniform levels of public outputs can be expected to encounter opposition, not only of a formal political sort but also in terms of individual behavior seeking either private sources of services or alternative ways to obtain desired levels of outputs.[8]

II. Fiscal Equity in a Federal System

In the discussion of the mobility model, we examined some existing conflicts between economic efficiency and equity in the provision of local services. At a policy level, matters of fiscal equity have, in fact, weighed very heavily in the formulation of budgetary programs. Most countries rely, to a greater or lesser extent, on equalizing intergovernmental grants to compensate for perceived geographical inequities. These grants typically incorporate variables to reflect need and fiscal capacity in an attempt to reduce the differences among localities in their ability to provide acceptable levels of public outputs. A district, for example, with an abnormally large fraction of its population in the school-age years and with a relatively small tax base will typically receive more grant assistance per capita than a jurisdiction in a more favorable fiscal position. In this section, I want to examine further some of these issues of fiscal equity.

Horizontal Equity in a Federal System

The principle that people in equal positions should be treated equally is one of the traditional canons of equitable taxation. However, Buchanan (1950) pointed out some years ago that decentralized finance is likely to violate this principle. Since the size of the tax base per capita will vary from one jurisdiction to the next, it follows that different tax rates will be required to raise the same amount of revenue per head. A resident of a locality with a relatively large tax base will thus face a lower tax rate and have a lower tax bill than his counterpart in a district with a smaller tax base. Buchanan concluded that the central government could introduce either a geographically discriminating income tax or, preferably, a set of unconditional grants to local governments to restore the equal treatment of equals.

There is one important assumption implicit in all this: the absence of significant consumer mobility. If we pose this problem in terms of the mobility model, we find that it resolves itself. Suppose, for example, that one jurisdiction possesses a notable fiscal advantage over the others; this could take the form of a relatively large tax base or, alternatively, superior efficiency in the provision of a public output (such as the lower cost of maintaining clean air in a town located on a hill). In an environment of mobile individuals, the value of such differences will be capitalized into local property values. Consumers will bid for places in the fiscally advantaged community until the increased price of property exactly offsets the fiscal gain. Mobility thus ensures that equals will be treated equally, for whatever fiscal advantages are enjoyed will be paid for in the form of a higher actual (or imputed) rent. In the mobility model, horizontal equity is self-policing.

This suggests that significant horizontal inequities should be ironed out by market forces within the metropolitan economy. This may not be true, however, at the regional level, where the mobility model appears less applicable. Here the obstacles to mobility may permit unequal treatment of equals to persist. Such unequal treatment has provided some of the motivation for equalizing intergovernmental grants in many countries. If one examines the constitutions or basic legislation authorizing these grant programs, there typically appears some reference to assistance that allows all jurisdictions to provide an adequate level of services by an effort not appreciably different from the others. *Effort* in this sense is often interpreted to refer to the fraction of income paid in taxes. The basic idea seems to be that, if local services were financed through proportional taxation of income, then all jurisdictions *ought* to be able to provide some specified and adequate level of services with (roughly) the same tax rate.

Minimum Service Levels

The second major objective of many of these grant programs is to ensure the provision of certain minimally acceptable levels of public outputs in all localities. The economic rationalization for this objective is not wholly clear. It seems, however, to draw to some extent on both efficiency and equity arguments. On the efficiency side one can argue that many of these services have substantial spillover effects; it is in my interest, for example, that all residents of the country attain a basic proficiency in reading and writing. Moreover, as mentioned earlier, guaranteed service levels can have an option value in that I may find it desirable at some future date to reside in another community (although the force of this argument is blunted if there exists a wide choice among local jurisdictions).

In terms of equity, the basic notion seems to be that everyone should be assured a certain minimum level of public services; to deprive an individual of adequate schooling opportunities or safety is to do him an injustice. This is typically interpreted to mean that all localities should provide at least certain prescribed minimum levels of services.

While a society may deem such minimum service levels an explicit objective of economic and social policy, the curious part is that, in many countries, this objective has been pursued through the use of essentially lump-sum grants. Such grants may serve to equalize the fiscal capacity to provide such services, but they certainly do not ensure the attainment of the minimum level of public outputs. This requires further measures prescribing standards with which the localities must comply. Here again we find a basic source of tension in a federal system between economic efficiency, on the one hand, and equity considerations, on the other: efficiency points in the direction of a wide scope for decentralized choice in the public sector, while the desire to guarantee adequate service levels in all jurisdictions motivates centrally imposed constraints on local fiscal behavior.

Vertical Equity in a Federal System

We noted in the introduction that the primary responsibility for the redistribution of income must lie with the central government. The point I want to add here is simply that such redistribution is best accomplished by central-government taxation and transfers directly to individuals, not indirectly by intergovernmental grants. The obvious problem is that such grants represent transfers from one group of people to another, whereas a just distribution of income is normally defined over individuals. If, for example, the central government attempts to redistribute income from rich to poor by transferring funds to the governments of poorer jurisdictions, it is bound to find itself engaging in some perverse transfers, because there will no doubt be at least a few low-income individuals in the wealthy locality and some high-income persons in the poorer jurisdiction. Equalizing intergovernmental grants are not an adequate substitute for a nationwide negative income tax.

III. Public Revenues in a Federal System

In the concluding section I want to explore the subjects of taxation and revenue sharing in a federal system. The problems of the efficiency and incidence of a tax are typically a good deal more complicated at the local than at the national level because of the effects of the tax on the interjurisdictional flows of commodities and factors of production. Moreover, these flows impose certain types of constraints on local taxation that may not exist for the central government.

We have already noted the inability of a local government to employ strongly redistributive tax measures because of the resulting outmigration of the heavily taxed individuals. To the extent that we desire significantly progressive taxation, we must look primarily to the central government. Moreover, with a little ingenuity local governments may be able to shift a substantial portion of their tax burdens onto residents of other jurisdictions. The taxation of certain locally produced goods may, for example, be largely borne in the form of higher prices paid by outsiders. One particular favorite is the heavy taxation of tourists with excise taxes on hotel and restaurant bills and on other services to finance a major portion of the local budget. This "exporting" of local taxes appears not to be a trivial phenomenon: McLure (1967) has estimated that in the United States approximately 20 to 25 percent of state taxes are shifted onto the residents of other states.

In addition to these issues of incidence, local taxation has a relatively high potential for the distortion of patterns of resource use. The supply of capital, for example, *may* be quite price inelastic for the country as a whole, so that national taxation of capital will involve only minor deadweight losses. In contrast, the supply of capital to a single local jurisdiction is likely to be highly elastic; the same tax at the local level will divert units of capital elsewhere where they have a lower marginal product. Another interesting example involves heavy reliance on local sales taxes. To the extent that one jurisdiction pushes its tax rate above that of neighboring localities, it creates an incentive for consumers to waste the additional time and resources to travel elsewhere to purchase items available locally. There is, in fact, some evidence for the United States suggesting that even relatively small differentials in local sales-tax rates have had noticeable effects on the geographical purchasing patterns of consumers.[9]

What all this suggests is that the design of an efficient and equitable system of local taxation is an extremely demanding task. In particular, we may expect the usual sorts of income and commodity taxes to generate greater deadweight losses per unit of revenues at the local than the national level and, in addition, to induce certain anomalies in incidence through such things as tax exporting.[10]

The central government, largely free from some of these constraints, has distinct advantages in the field of taxation. Besides the capacity for a more progressive revenue structure and the avoidance of certain deadweight losses because of national uniformity, centralized taxation typically results in some cost savings from economies of scale in tax administration. In the United States, for instance, the administrative costs of the federal individual income tax amount to only about one-half of 1 percent of revenues. In contrast, at the state level these costs for income or sales taxation are roughly 1 to 2 percent of tax receipts [Pechman (1971, p. 53), Maxwell (1969, p. 102)].

Revenue Sharing

One way to realize some of these advantages of centralized taxation without relinquishing local expenditure authority is through revenue sharing: the central government can effectively act as a tax-collection agent for local governments. From this perspective revenue sharing is best seen as a substitution of centrally raised tax receipts for local revenues. The national revenue authority simply collects a prescribed level of taxes, which it then distributes in the form of lump-sum grants to local governments. It is important, however, that local authorities continue to raise some significant portion of their own revenues, for *at the margin*, fiscally responsible local choice requires that each community finance its own expenditures.

The popular case for revenue sharing has, however, taken a rather different tack; it has stressed the so-called fiscal mismatch between central and local governments. This argument focuses on the constraints on local budgets imposed by the relative income inelasticity of their tax systems. Because of growing demands for local services and their rising relative costs, the expansion in local spending necessary to keep pace with the growth in demand for public outputs is more than proportionate to the growth in income. However, most local revenue systems exhibit an income elasticity not much in excess of unity, so that revenue needs expand more rapidly than actual receipts at existing tax rates. The result is the persistent recurrence of a "revenue gap," with the implication that political obstacles to raising tax rates or instituting new taxes result in a systematic underprovision of public services.

Heller (1966, p. 118) made this point quite eloquently in the United States during the 1960s:

At the Federal level, economic growth and a powerful tax system, interacting under modern fiscal management, generate new revenues faster than they generate new demands on the Federal purse. But at the state-local level, the situation is reversed. Under the whiplash of prosperity, responsibilities are outstripping revenues.

From this vantage point, the appeal of revenue sharing is that it puts the highly elastic central revenue system at the disposal of local government: it matches growth in expenditure needs with an automatic growth in revenues and thereby moderates the revenue gaps and associated fiscal crises besetting local governments.

The difficulty with this argument is that its premise implies some rather strange behavior on the part of the taxpayer-voters. We normally assume that an individual's demand for public services (as for other commodities) depends on his tastes, his level of income, and the cost (here, a tax-price) to him of these services. There is no reason, in principle, to think that an individual's demand for public outputs is a function of the income elasticity of the revenue system. But this is what the fiscal-mismatch argument seems to imply: people will support increases in the public budget if they can be funded without increases in tax rates (that is, from increments to revenues resulting solely from growth in income), but they will not support this same budgetary expansion if it requires a rise in tax rates. In brief, the implication is that what people care about is not their tax *bill* but rather their tax *rate*. From this perspective, the argument simply is not consistent with our usual models of rational consumer behavior; instead, it implies the presence of a form of fiscal illusion.

The proposition is, however, an empirical one: Does a higher income elasticity of the tax structure result in a more rapid expansion over time in the public budget? To test this hypothesis, I have examined the growth in state and local budgets in the United States over the decade of the 1960s, a period of extraordinary budgetary increases, to see if those states and cities with relatively income-inelastic tax systems experienced comparatively small rises in expenditure. The approach was to take two samples (one consisting of the 48 coterminous states and the other of 33 large central cities) in which, after controlling for the effect of other explanatory variables by multiple-regression analysis, I examined the partial association between the growth in expenditure per capita over the decade 1960–1970 and a proxy variable for the income elasticity of the state's (or city's) revenue system [For a detailed description of the approach and findings, see Oates (1975)].

The findings showed a statistically significant positive coefficient on the tax variable (at a 0.05 level of significance), providing support for the hypothesis that the income elasticity of the tax structure does have some effect on the growth in the public budget. However, the magnitude of the estimated effect was not very large. Among the states, for example, the estimated coefficient indicates that a state government that generated 35 percent of its revenues through individual income taxes would, other things equal, have experienced an expansion in spending per capita over the period 1960–1970 of roughly $35 more than a state that relied wholly on sales and excise taxes. However, this compares to a mean increase in state expenditure per capita of $228 for the decade. It would be difficult, in my judgment, to regard this as a large effect, hardly of sufficient size to justify major fiscal reform.

If, as I am inclined to believe, the effect of revenue sharing on the size of local public budgets is quite modest, then the appropriate perspective on revenue sharing is to regard it as a substitution of central taxation for locally raised revenues. To evaluate the merits of the program, we must then look to the altered pattern of incidence, possible reductions in deadweight losses, and the cost savings from administering a more centralized system of taxation.

Finally, there is one further aspect of revenue sharing on which a "narrow" economic view may be less than adequate. An implicit assumption in the analysis is that the central government can act as a tax collector for local governments without impairing the local-expenditure prerogative. So long as the transfers of funds to local governments are truly of a lump-sum form, there is no reason in principle why the recipient should feel any constraints as to how he employs these resources. This, however, is no doubt rather naïve; so long as the central government is a major supplier of local funds, political

realities can be expected to induce the central government to use this leverage
to achieve some of its own objectives. In the United Kingdom, for example,
central-government grants (primarily of a lump-sum form) now account for
approximately two-thirds of local authority revenues, and this has given rise to
widespread concern over the erosion of local autonomy and has generated
renewed interest in additional sources of tax revenues at the local level. Important as it may be, this particular dimension of revenue sharing is difficult to
incorporate into a purely economic analysis.

My objective in this chapter has been to provide an overview of the *economics* of fiscal federalism. I have tried to develop the implications of the basic
principles of economics for the functioning of a multilevel public sector. Such
an approach does generate a variety of insights which are useful for the analysis
of public budgetary policy. But, as I have tried to emphasize at several points,
it is difficult to cast the analytic net sufficiently wide to capture all the salient
aspects of fiscal programs like revenue sharing. Moreover, the economic logic
sometimes points in directions that can be quite discomforting in terms of their
social implications. Nevertheless, in so doing, it often reveals certain basic tendencies in the system (toward, for example, segregation by income) with which
public policy must come to terms irrespective of its goals.

Notes

1. For a useful survey of this literature, see Whitman (1970).

2. Pauly (1973) has argued that there may be a modest role for local redistributive policies.

3. This discussion draws on Bradford and Oates (1974).

4. If there are cost savings from joint consumption in larger groups, these
must, of course, be weighed off against the gains in consumer surplus from more
diversified consumption.

5. For an algebraic treatment of the measurement of these consumer surpluses, see Barzel (1969); for a summary of Barzel's analysis, see Oates (1972,
pp. 59–63).

6. It is interesting that this is precisely the reverse of the case of the excess
burden resulting from distorting taxes. In partial-equilibrium terms, the excess
burden generated by an excise tax varies directly with the price elasticity of
demand. The source of this difference is that under tax analysis we are varying
price and are thus moving along the vertical axis in Figure 1–1, while for the
problem here we are altering quantity on the horizontal axis.

7. This calculation ignores any spillover effects associated with education.

8. As one possible illustration, the elimination of the selective grammar
schools in the United Kingdom may encourage residential patterns of the
Tiebout type as a means to control the quality of neighborhood schools.

9. In a study of sales taxation in New York City, Hamovitch (1966) estimated that increases in the city's sales tax rate of 1 percentage point had led on past occasions to declines of about 6 percent in taxable sales. Likewise, a cross-sectional econometric study of 173 U.S. metropolitan areas by Mikesell (1970) revealed that an increase of 1 percentage point in the differential between city and suburban sales taxes is associated on average with approximately a 7 percent reduction in retail sales in the central city.

10. Some qualifications are in order. We noted earlier, for example, that in the mobility model, with the appropriate use of local zoning ordinances, local property taxation *can* be perfectly efficient. In addition, a heavier reliance on local land taxation appears to offer considerable potential for reducing the distorting effects of local taxes.

11. It is possible to try to rationalize this fiscal illusion in a kind of Downsian model of rational political ignorance [see Oates (1975)].

References

Barzel, Y. 1969. Two propositions on the optimum level of producing collective goods. *Public Choice* 6:31-37.

Bergstrom, T., and Goodman, R. 1973, Private demands for public goods. *American Economic Review* 63:280-296.

Boss, M. 1974. Economic theory of democracy: An empirical test. *Public Choice* 19:111-115.

Bradford, D., and Oates, W. 1974. Suburban exploitation of central cities and governmental structure. In *Redistribution through Public Choice*, H. Hochman and G. Peterson, eds. Columbia University Press, pp. 43-90.

Breton, A. 1965. A theory of government grants. *Canadian Journal of Economics and Political Science* 31:175-187.

Buchanan, J. 1950. Federalism and fiscal equity. *American Economic Review* 40:583-599.

Buchanan, J., and Goetz, C. 1972. Efficiency limits of fiscal mobility: An assessment of the Tiebout model. *Journal of Public Economics* 1:25-44.

Hamilton, B. 1975. Zoning and property taxation in a system of local governments. *Urban Studies* 12:205-211.

Hamovitch, W. 1966. Effects of increases in sales tax rates on taxable sales in New York City. In *Research Report of the Graduate School in Public Administration, New York University, Financing Government in New York City*. New York: New York University, pp. 619-633.

Heller, W. 1966. *New Dimensions of Political Economy*. Cambridge, Mass.: Harvard University Press.

Livingston, W. 1952. A note on the nature of federalism. *Political Science Quarterly* 67:81-95.

McLure, C. 1967. The interstate exporting of state and local taxes: Estimates for 1962. *National Tax Journal* 20:49-77.

Maxwell, J. 1969. *Financing State and Local Governments*, rev. ed. Washington, D.C.: The Brookings Institution.

Mikesell, J. 1970. Central cities and sales tax differentials: The border city problem. *National Tax Journal* 23:206-213.

Oates, W. 1972. *Fiscal Federalism.* New York: Harcourt Brace Jovanovich.

Oates, W. 1975. Automatic increases in tax revenues: The effect on the size of the public budget. In *Financing the New Federalism: Revenue Sharing, Conditional Grants, and Taxation*, W. Oates, ed. Baltimore: Johns Hopkins Press. pp. 139-160.

Pauly, M. 1973. Income redistribution as a local public good. *Journal of Public Economics* 2:35-58.

Pechman, J. 1971. *Federal Tax Policy*, rev. ed. Washington, D.C.: The Brookings Institution.

Schuler, R. 1974. The interaction between local government and urban residential location. *American Economic Review* 64:682-696.

Tiebout, C. 1956. A pure theory of local expenditures. *Journal of Political Economy* 64:416-424.

Whitman, M. Von N., 1970. Policies for internal and external balance. *Princeton Studies in International Finance* 9. Princeton, N.J.: Princeton University Press.

[3]

THE CHANGING STRUCTURE
OF INTERGOVERNMENTAL FISCAL RELATIONS*

Wallace E. Oates

> "I am of the opinion that, in the democratic ages which are opening upon us... centralization will be the natural government."
>
> Alexis de Tocqueville,
> *Democracy in America.*

Much recent literature echoes the judgment of de Tocqueville that the evolution of the public sector is likely to be one of an increasing centralization of decision-making. With reference to the federal form of government in particular, Edward McWhinney cites "Bryce's Law", the proposition that "... federalism is simply a transitory step on the way to governmental unity".[1] The thesis, more generally, is that a public sector with substantial scope for decentralized choice is an unstable structure; it will give way over time to a system with a greater role for the central government.

A purpose of this paper is to investigate the economic dimensions of the "centralization thesis" to see what sorts of economic forces appear to support this proposition. Can we make a compelling case for total centralization of the public sector as the equilibrium outcome? Is existing evidence on the secular trends in governmental structure consistent with this view? To anticipate the findings, I will contend that neither *a priori* analysis nor recent trends provide unambiguous support for the proposition of increasing centralization. Rather, the tendencies in intergovernmental structure point to the evolution of a more complex, multi-tiered system with a variety of sizes of jurisdictions to provide different public services. In fact, the centralization thesis is a much too simplistic notion to provide much insight into the development of fiscal systems, but it can provide a point of departure for the discussion.

1. *The Case for the Centralization Thesis*

The economic forces promoting a heavier reliance on central choice have their source in the rising incomes, improved transportation, and more

* I am grateful to Stephen Williams for assistance in assembling the data.
1. *Comparative Federalism*, second edition, Toronto, University of Toronto Press, 1965, p. 105.

effective systems of communication that have characterized economic growth. For these developments have given rise to an increasing mobility of and interdependence among economic units. This has had important implications both for the provision of public services and for programs for the redistribution of income.

Most basically, a growing geographical mobility and interdependence have tended to expand the range of many of the external benefits and costs associated with the local provision of certain important services. As regards public education, for example, Burton Weisbord contends that in the United States:

Whereas public primary and secondary education have been considered traditionally as matters to be dealt with locally according to the preferences of each community, we have found that the effects of these local decisions permeate the entire society. Population mobility and fiscal interdependence make education decisions in one part of the nation important to other, even distant, parts.[2]

The implication is that the extended geographical scope of the benefits and costs from public services has, over time, enlarged the optimal-size jurisdiction for the provision of a number of important public services like education.

Neville Topham and Richard Barnett have recently developed one dimension of this in terms of an "option value".[3] In a nation characterized by a high degree of mobility of individuals, a person may care about levels of public services elsewhere, because he is likely at some future time to visit or reside in other jurisdictions. For this reason alone, service levels in other areas may enter the individual's utility function.[4]

Rising real incomes seem also to give rise to an increased demand for public redistributive programs. We find, for example, that wealthier nations devote a larger fraction of the public budget to transfers than do poorer countries.[5] This in itself can promote an increased centralization of the public sector. The mobility of economic units greatly restricts the capacity for redistributive activities at the local level with the result that the central government must typically assume a primary responsibility for the redistribution of income and wealth. Thus a shift in the composition of the public budget toward transfer payments is likely to bring with it an expansion in the role of the central government within the public sector.

Certain features of economic growth, thus, do seem conducive to an increased centralization of government. In brief, as Michael Reagan has put it, "... many more problems today than in the past are national in the sense of being affected by developments elsewhere in the nation or having their own impact upon other parts of the nation".[6]

2. *External Benefits of Public Education*, Princeton, NJ, Princeton University, Industrial Relations Section, 1964, p. 117.

3. *Federalism and the Social Welfare Function*, unpublished manuscript.

4. However, to the extent that the individual has a wide choice among communities within a general area, the option value he places on outputs in a particular jurisdiction may not amount to much.

5. See my *Fiscal Federalism*, New York, Harcourt Brace Jovanovich, 1972, p. 224.

6. *The New Federalism*, New York, Oxford University Press, 1972, p. 77.

2. *Forces Favoring Decentralized Provision of Public Services*

In other ways, however, rising incomes and greater mobility can also increase the effectiveness of the local public sector. In particular, the local-finance literature has developed in some detail the efficiency-enhancing properties of models of decentralized choice in which a consumer seeks out a community of residence which provides a fiscal package well suited to his tastes.[7] Rather than a central government providing a single level of the service over the entire nation, a multitude of local governments can offer the individual a choice among differing service levels. Much as a consumer satisfies his preferences for private goods by purchasing his desired quantity in the market, he can likewise consume his desired service level in the public sector by an appropriate selection of a community in which to live. From this perspective, increased centralization of the public sector with more homogeneous levels of services is likely to involve losses in welfare, for in the words of George Bernard Shaw, "Do not do unto others as you would have them do unto you. They may have different tastes".

There is reason, moreover, to expect the potential welfare gains from decentralized public choice to increase over time. The basic mechanism of the location model which generates these outcomes is consumer mobility which promotes the formation of groups of individuals with similar demands for public services. The development of metropolitan areas in which an individual works in the center city (or one of the suburban "rings") but has a wide choice among suburban communities in which to reside is precisely the kind of world where the local-finance model is most relevant. The increasing degree of mobility within metropolitan areas should permit a fuller realization of the welfare gains from decentralized public choice.

The solution emerging from this type of model is one which typically involves a high degree of segregation across communities by socio-economic class.[8] And this may in itself be regarded as undesirable in terms of its social implications. However, the point is that the rising incomes, improved transportation, and increased mobility that have characterized development in many of the industrialized nations have, in one sense, made the local provision of certain public services more attractive to individuals by permitting the congregation of individuals with similar tastes. Economic growth has thus generated some pressures for a continuing reliance on local budgetary decisions.

The net effect of rising economic affluence on the degree of centralization in the public sector is, therefore, not altogether clear. Some forces seem to be working in the direction of a greater role for the central government, but there are opposing tendencies. An examination of some actual fiscal trends may suggest which set of forces seems to have been the stronger.

---

7. This literature stems from Charles TIEBOUT, "A Pure Theory of Local Expenditures", *Journal of Political Economy*, 64 (Oct. 1956), pp. 416-424.

8. For an analysis of the forces inducing segregation by income class, see D. BRADFORD and W. OATES, "Suburban Exploitation of Central Cities and Governmental Structure", *in* H. HOCHMAN and G. PETERSON, eds., *Redistribution Through Public Choice*, New York, Columbia University Press, 1974, pp. 43-90.

3. *Some Evidence on Trends in Fiscal Centralization*

Both the definition and measurement of the degree of centralization in the public sector raise some extremely difficult issues, which I want to examine later in the paper. Here, however, I simply want to present some data on one widely-used summary measure of fiscal centralization: the centralization ratio defined as the share of the central government in the total public budget.

It is difficult to get figures for most countries that extend back more than a few decades. Often budgetary data are available for the central government, but the aggregates for all the more decentralized levels in the public sector are typically harder to come by. As a result, the picture I am able to present of actual fiscal trends is quite fragmentary and necessarily impressionistic.

Table 1 presents, for scattered years, the central government's share in total expenditure for four countries, three with federal forms of government (Australia, Canada, and the United States) and one unitary state (the United Kingdom). The data suggest some tendencies toward increasing fiscal centralization, at least over the first half of the twentieth century, but the trends are not without ambiguities. For the United Kingdom, for example, the figures assembled by Alan Peacock and Jack Wiseman (supplemented with data for more recent years) indicate that the central government's percentage share of public expenditure is about the same in 1970 as it was in 1890. A drift towards greater centralization is more apparent in the United States, where the centralization ratio rose from about one-third in 1902 to about two-thirds by 1955. Similarly, the data for Canada and Australia show some signs of growing centralization, at least until 1955.

Not surprisingly, the central government's share of the public budget displays dramatic shifts in response to world political and economic conditions. In particular, the two World Wars and the Great Depression provided a powerful impetus to an increased role for the central government. Peacock and Wiseman have suggested that violent social disruptions of this sort give rise to "displacement effects" which serve both to enlarge the public sector as a whole and to enhance the primacy of the central government.[9] In the return to normalcy following such dislocations, they claim that some of this "temporary" expansion is likely to persist.

Somewhat better data are available for more recent years, and they seem to tell a somewhat different story. In Table 2, I have reproduced the centralization ratios for six countries as assembled by Werner Pommerehne. Once again they include some countries with federal constitutions (Canada, Germany, Switzerland, and the United States) and others with a unitary form of government (France and the United Kingdom). The pattern that emerges from these figures is a remarkably consistent one: in every instance, the central government's share in total expenditure has declined over the period 1950 to 1970. Although it is certainly dangerous to draw inferences from data covering a span of only two decades, the trends since World War II surely do not support the centralization thesis. It is interesting as

9. PEACOCK and WISEMAN, *op. cit.*, pp. 26-30.

regards the Peacock and Wiseman hypothesis that this has not been a time of violent social disruption of the sort they see necessary to provide a stimulus for an increased predominance of the central government.

TABLE 1: Central Government Expenditure as a Percentage of Total Government Expenditure for Selected Years

Year	United Kingdom	United States	Canada	Australia
1890	61.6			
1895	57.0			
1900	64.8			
1902		34.5		
1905	48.9			
1910	52.1			
1913		30.2		
1915	86.3			
1920	80.1			
1922		40.5		
1925	65.4			
1927		31.5		
1929				28.4
1930	63.3			
1932		34.3		29.3
1933			46.7	
1935	61.7			
1936		54.7		28.0
1937			44.4	
1940	86.2	49.3		40.5
1941			76.1	
1945	90.6		89.3	80.6
1946		83.5		
1950	76.6	63.7	64.2	51.9
1955	75.0	66.3	66.5	47.4
1960	68.0	64.3	59.7	
1965	60.6	63.3	43.1	
1970	60.0	62.5	38.1	
1974		61.1		

Sources: Alan PEACOCK and Jack WISEMAN, *The Growth of Public Expenditure in the United Kingdom*, London, Oxford University Press, 1961, Table A-20; *Facts and Figures on Government Finance*, 1975 edition, New York, Tax Foundation, 1975, Table 6; M. C. URQUHART and K. A. H. BUCKLEY eds., *Historical Statistics of Canada*, Great Britain, Cambridge University Press, 1965, Government Finance, Series 95 and 142; B. U. RATCHFORD, *Public Expenditures in Australia*, Durham, North Carolina, Duke University Press, 1959, Appendices E and F; Werner W. POMMEREHNE, "Quantitative Aspects of Federalism: A Study of Six Countries", in W. OATES, ed., *The Political Economy of Fiscal Federalism*, Lexington, Mass., D. C. Heath, 1977, Table 15-10, p. 307.

The available evidence, scant as it admittedly is, does not seem consistent with a simplistic view of increasing governmental centralization. However, a number of qualifications are in order. In particular, the centralization ratio may not provide a very reliable measure of the true extent of the centralization of decision-making power. Central governments, through for example an expanding use of conditional grants to lower levels of government, may have come to exert much greater control over patterns of resource use in the public sector.[10] This suggests that we would do well to inquire a bit further into what we mean by centralization and how we ought to measure it.

TABLE 2: Central Government Expenditure as a Percentage of Total Government Expenditure for Six Countries Since 1950

Year	Canada	France	Germany	Switzerland	United Kingdom	United States
1950	52.2	85.6	48.4	32.9	76.6	58.3
1955	59.2	80.5	44.3	33.4	75.0	62.9
1960	50.5	83.2	39.9	30.7	68.0	57.6
1965	43.1	81.7	40.3	26.9	60.6	54.8
1970	38.1	79.3	37.9	26.2	60.0	50.5

Source: Werner W. POMMEREHNE, *op. cit.*

4. On the Concept of Centralization in the Public Sector

In the earlier sections, I have proceeded blithely along as if the degree of governmental centralization were a well defined and easily measurable quantity. It certainly is not. The notion of centralization is full of ambiguities, both at a conceptual level and in terms of measurement. This is of particular importance for the remainder of the paper, for the evolution of intergovernmental structure (as I see it) really has little to do with simplistic statements about more or less centralization; it is more a matter of the development of new institutions, jurisdictions, and instruments as attempts to improve the performance of the public sector. A brief consideration of the meaning of centralization can serve to introduce this discussion.

The term "centralization" is typically thought to "... describe a condition or a trend in an areal hierarchy of power".[11] A system becomes more centralized when decision-making powers shift to an agency whose authority encompasses a larger jurisdiction. However, this really doesn't take us very far. To develop an operational measure of the degree of centralization, we need somehow to quantify "power" in terms of geographical (or population?) space. There is no obvious way to do this. In one treatment of this issue, Herbert Kaufman suggests six alternative criteria for measuring the degree of organizational centralization ranging from the extent of detail in centralized directives to the sources of funding for agency expenditures.[12]

Even if we had an unambiguous measure of the "quantity" of decision-making power, the attempt to generate a summary measure of the degree

10. It is the case, however, that if grants are treated as central-government expenditure (rather than as spending by the recipient), it doesn't seem to alter the trends in Table 2 very much. See POMMEREHNE, *op. cit.*
11. James W. FESLER, "Centralization and Decentralization", *International Encyclopedia of the Social Sciences*, Vol. 2, United States, Macmillan and the Free Press, 1968, p. 370.
12. *Politics and Policies in State and Local Governments*, Englewood Cliffs, New Jersey, Prentice-Hall, 1963, pp. 12-13.

of centralization abounds in index-number problems. In the preceding section, I simply ignored these difficulties under the guise of a centralization ratio defined in terms of the budgetary share of the central government. This, however, is far from satisfactory. Suppose, for instance, that the powers of local governments were reassigned to large regional agencies. We would surely feel that the public sector had, in some sense, become more centralized, but this would have no effect on the earlier-used centralization ratio. As a second example, consider the case where a reorganization of the public sector involves the transfer of certain powers from the central government and from local governments to new regional bodies. Would this constitute more centralization or decentralization of the public sector? The answer obviously depends on the particular set of weights used for governments at different levels in the public-sector hierarchy.

The point I want to make here is simply that there is no unambiguous, non-arbitrary measure of the extent of centralization. This implies that we must take some care in drawing inferences from trends in such things as centralization ratios. More important as the preceding examples suggest, many of the more important changes in intergovernmental structure may have little to do with any simplified notion of the extent of centralization.

5. *On Trends in Intergovernmental Structure*

While there may be no easily interpretable trends in centralization ratios, the structure of the public sector in most countries has by no means been static. In fact, recent decades have brought a number of very dramatic and intriguing alterations in governmental structure. It is, moreover, difficult and somewhat perilous to try to identify a single set of forces or tendencies underlying these transformations across a number of different countries; the very diversity of the changes is itself quite striking. In consequence, I will try here only to give the flavor of some of the kinds of evolution of the public sector that seem to be taking place and to offer a few tentative observations on them.

One development common to a number of countries has been the consolidation of some of the smallest jurisdictions to form areas over which public services can be provided more efficiently. In the United States, for example, this has taken the form largely of the consolidation of school districts. Table 3 indicates that, over the period 1942 to 1972, the number of school districts in the US fell from 108,579 to 15,781. Likewise, local-government reorganization in the United Kingdom and elsewhere has involved combining certain smaller and, in some instances, rural jurisdictions into new governmental units. While this is clearly a move in the direction of greater centralization of the public sector, it is not one that I would emphasize too strongly. In the case of the United States at least, the new jurisdictions are, for the most part, of relatively modest size. Moreover, what evidence we have suggests that the economies of scale inherent in the provision of a wide range of public services are exhausted fairly rapidly; they may justify some consolidation but not the formation of quite large jurisdictions.

Table 3 reveals another trend which I see to be of somewhat greater significance and interest: the rapid growth in the number of special districts. From 1942 to 1972, special districts almost tripled in number; there are now more such districts in the United States than any other form of local government. The rise of special districts reflects an increasing specialization in the local sector. Most of the districts are single-function entities. However, the range of functions is quite wide and diverse: there are special districts for the provision of highways, sewers, housing, libraries, fire protection, natural resources, hospitals, and even cemeteries.

TABLE 3: Governmental Units by Level of Government for Selected Years in the United States

	1942	*1952*	*1962*	*1972*
us Government	1	1	1	1
State Governments	48	50	50	50
Local Governments	155,067	116,756	91,186	72,218
Counties	3,050	3,052	3,043	3,044
Municipalities	16,220	16,807	18,000	18,517
Townships	18,919	17,202	17,142	16,991
School Districts	108,579	67,355	34,678	15,781
Special Districts	8,299	12,340	18,323	23,885
Total	155,116	116,807	91,237	78,269

Sources: 1957 Census of Governments, Washington, us Government Printing Office, 1957, p. 1; *1972 Census of Governments*, Washington, us Government Printing Office, 1973, p. 1.

All this would seem to have a certain economic rationale. We would expect that the appropriate size jurisdiction (in terms of the spatial distribution of benefits and costs and the particular configuration of economies of scale) would vary for different services; the relevant geographical entity for the control of environmental quality, for example, is likely to be quite different from that for fire protection or housing. From this perspective, the proliferation of special districts can be seen as an attempt to fashion jurisdictions of the proper size for the various local services. This phenomena, incidentally, is surely not independent of the growth in the size of the public sector as a whole. This expansion of public activity, in general, has, no doubt, made it feasible to increase the degree of specialization. We may have here a principle for the public sector that parallels Adam Smith's famous dictum for the private sector that "the division of labour is limited by the extent of the market".

Moreover, the creation of new jurisdictions has not been limited to single-purpose public agencies. In fact, probably the most pervasive tendency across a substantial number of countries has been the establishment of new "levels" of government to cope with new demands on the public sector. This has taken the form in many countries of new metropolitan governments with jurisdictions that encompass not only the center city but some of the surrounding suburban area as well. This has been a response to the recognition that the high degree of mobility and interdependence within the modern metropolitan area, with an individual residing in one locality and working in another, requires that certain decisions be made on a metropolitan-wide basis. From the other end, the difficulty of resolving certain problems from the central level has given rise to pressures for the formation of regional governments units (in, for example, Italy and the United Kingdom). This represents, to some extent at least, a move towards decentralization. In the United Kingdom, Alan Peacock suggests that the "deviation in individual and group preferences from those reflected in the existing amount and pattern of government services has become more marked..." and has resulted in "... the growing demand for devolution...".[13]

Finally, the formation of new governments has not been restricted to the lower-tiers. We are in the process of watching in Europe the emergence of a new level of government whose jurisdiction will be the entire membership of the European Economic Community. It is not as yet clear what will be the precise range of responsibilities and powers of the new government. However, the creation of a European level of government on the one hand, contrasting with moves toward devolution in certain of the member countries on the other, does suggest the diverse nature of the pressures operating on the public sector.

The perspective that emerges on the trends in intergovernmental structure is thus a rather complicated one. It does not point clearly to any simplistic thesis of increasing centralization or decentralization. Rather, it suggests the evolution of a more complex system with a greater variety of both levels and types of governments. This does not imply a greater independence on the part of individual governmental units. On the contrary, the development of the public sector has moved toward a greater degree of shared responsibility in the provision of public services. In the recent political-science literature in particular, the older view of federal institutions in which the functions are clearly divided among different levels of government has given way to an emphasis on the interplay among governments in the provision of services.[14] Instead of the older "co-ordinate federalism", the political scientists tell us that we now live in an age of "co-operative federalism".[15] Although a local government may retain ultimate responsibility for providing a particular service, it is now likely to find itself hedged in by a series of restrictions from federal and state officials and encouraged in certain directions by sets of conditional grants. It is obviously quite difficult to conceptualize or to measure "the" degree of centralization in such a world.

Résumé

Une thèse fréquente de ces cent dernières années est que le fédéralisme est simplement une étape transitoire dans un processus qui conduit au gouvernement unitaire; selon les propos de Tocqueville, le gouvernement

13. "The Political Economy of Devolution: The British Case", *in* W. OATES, ed., *The Political Economy of Fiscal Federalism*, p. 51.

14. See, for example, A. H. BIRCH, *Federalism, Finance, and Social Legislation*, Oxford, England, Clarendon Press, 1955; and Geoffrey F. SAWER, *Modern Federalism*, London, C. A. Watts, 1969.

15. BIRCH, Ch. 11, and SAWER, Ch. 8.

centralisé sera la forme normale de gouvernement. Cet article considère cette thèse de la centralisation à la fois sur le plan de la théorie économique et des tendances actuelles de la structure fiscale. Bien qu'il existe des forces favorisant une centralisation accrue du secteur public, la croissance économique connaît aussi des conditions favorables à un choix décentralisé du public. Les données indiquent que, dans plusieurs pays fédéraux ou unitaires, la part des dépenses publiques du gouvernement central a diminué ces dernières décennies. Bien qu'il y ait de sérieuses ambiguïtés inhérentes à toute mesure de centralisation fiscale, les données ne semblent pas soutenir l'hypothèse de la centralisation. L'évolution de la structure fiscale intergouvernementale, plus qu'un processus simpliste d'accroissement de la centralisation ou de la décentralisation, est un phénomène complexe entraînant la création de nouvelles juridictions et une interdépendance croissante entre les niveaux du gouvernement. L'article cite certaines de ces tendances, à savoir la consolidation continue des petites unités locales, la création d'un grand nombre de nouvelles circonscriptions (district, secteur) spéciales (du moins aux Etats-Unis), et un accroissement de la part de responsabilité entre les différents niveaux du gouvernement pour fournir des services publics.

Comments by Manfred Neumann

In my discussion of Professor Oates' and Hanusch's papers I shall first give some comments on the interpretation of the evidence of recent trends relating to the fiscal centralization ratio and, second, I shall turn to a discussion of the trends themselves.

1. For a given federal state there are always some pure public goods which are essential for the very existence of the particular state, viz. defense, diplomacy, and, to some degree, measures of redistribution.

Hence the discussion of centralization vs. decentralization can only be concerned with those public goods the provision of which has not by necessity to be assigned to the federal government. Therefore it seems to me to be misleading to check the validity of the theses of secular centralization of decision making by means of the simple fiscal centralization ratio. Even if all the conceptional shortcomings of such a measure as discussed by Oates are disregarded it would at least be necessary to devise a modified ratio in the computation of which pure public goods are omitted.

Actually, it is striking that the figures cited by Professor Oates all show increases during the wars which was already pointed out by himself. So it is tempting to infer that the decrease of the centralization ratio in the post war years can simply be accounted for by a declining share of defense expenditure and those redistributive measures by the federal governments which were introduced to alleviate the hardships associated with the war.

In order to check this conjecture I did some tentative computations which were based on the figures of Pommerehne for the USA, Canada, and Switzerland und were based on figures drawn from official statistics for Germany.

If the ratio of defense expenditure to total public expenditure is deducted from the centralization ratio the modified ratio so obtained was practically constant in Switzerland and Canada from 1956-1971, whereas it increased for the USA and also for Germany. If, in an alternative modification, defense expenditure is deducted from the denominator as well as from the numerator a slight decrease of this ratio can be observed for all four countries. These calculations are not quite satisfactory, however, since I was unable to get hold of figures for war induced redistributive measures of the federal governments for all countries. That was only possible for Germany. For this country the modified ratio shows a clear increase from 1950 to 1972.

In spite of the incompleteness of my computations I submit that they nevertheless cast some doubts on the conclusion that centralization has declined. These doubts are strengthened if we look at the assignment of decision making from the institutional point of view.

[4]

Decentralization of the Public Sector:
An Overview
WALLACE E. OATES

THE vertical structure of the public sector has important implications for the way in which government functions. It affects the menu of government services, how they are financed, and the potential for innovation, and perhaps even the overall size of government. These issues of 'fiscal federalism' present specialists in public finance with an intriguing set of problems: the assignment of functions and of fiscal instruments to the appropriate levels of government.

In this chapter I provide a brief survey of this literature. After a short review of some general guide-lines for the allocation of functions among levels of government, the chapter turns to a series of issues in the structure and operation of a public sector with several levels of government. The focus in these later sections is on recent research in fiscal federalism.

Allocation of Functions among Levels of Government: Some General Guide-lines

In the existing public-finance literature, a popular approach to the allocation-of-functions issue makes use of Richard Musgrave's tripartite division of the public sector (for example Oates, 1972 and King, 1984). For purposes of discussion, I will consider briefly each of Musgrave's three functions of the public sector: the stabilization, distribution, and allocation functions.

Macroeconomic stabilization

There is much controversy these days over the proper form and scope of macroeconomic policies to stabilize the economy at high levels of output and employment with reasonable price stability. Without becoming embroiled in this debate, one can still make the claim that the primary responsibility for the exercise of countercyclical policy must rest with the central government.

This claim is developed along two lines. First, the central government in nearly all countries exercises basic control over the supply of money and credit. And with good reason—if each level of government were to create and destroy money, there would exist a powerful incentive for local governments to finance their purchases of goods and services with newly created money rather than burdening their constituencies with local taxation. The result in the aggregate would obviously be a rapid national monetary expansion with consequent inflationary pressures.

Second, regional or local economies tend to be highly 'open' in that they import and export relatively large shares of the goods that they produce and consume. Such openness implies serious constraints on the capacity of decentralized governments to employ countercyclical fiscal measures. If a local government, for example, were to undertake a substantial tax cut to stimulate the local economy, it would find that most of the newly generated spending would flow out of the local economy in payment for goods and services produced elsewhere with little ultimate effect on local levels of employment.

In short, the absence of monetary prerogatives and the openness of regional or local economies suggest that the potential for effective macroeconomic stabilization policy is quite limited at decentralized levels of the public sector. Edward Gramlich (1987) has argued recently that decentralized government can make some contribution to an effective countercyclical policy. By the use of 'rainy day' (or stabilization funds), such governments can accumulate funds during periods of expansion and draw on these funds during recessions so as to stabilize spending and tax rates over the course of the business cycle. However, the central government with its broad monetary and fiscal powers must assume the primary role for an active countercyclical policy.

Income distribution

A second function of the public sector is the redistribution of income to achieve a socially just outcome. This typically implies a transfer of funds to low-income households to bring about a somewhat more equal distribution of income. Once again, there are some serious constraints on purely 'local' measures to achieve this objective. First, to the extent that poor relief is perceived as a national goal (or, put somewhat differently, to the extent that people in each jurisdiction care about the well-being of the poor elsewhere), purely local policies will not incorporate the concern for income transfers throughout the nation. Redistributive measures from this perspective are a 'national public good' that requires a central-government presence.

Second, the potential mobility of households and firms can place real constraints on the capacity of decentralized governments to redistribute income. If a local government, for example, were to undertake an aggressive programme to redistribute income from the wealthy to the poor, it would create compelling incentives for high-income persons to move elsewhere and for low-income households to immigrate into the jurisdiction. Such measures may end up creating more equality through an outflow of the wealthy and an inflow of the poor—a process that is not an attractive one from the perspective of most jurisdictions. There is, in fact, some evidence suggesting that, in the USA at least, some mobility of the poor exists and that it discourages to some extent the adoption of measures to assist the poor (see Brown and Oates, 1987).

Nevertheless, there is certainly some scope for decentralized poor relief. As Pauly has argued (1973), there is typically much greater concern in a locality for the locally indigent than for the poor elsewhere. In fact, the claim that assistance to the poor is a national public good is little more than an assertion; there is not much solid evidence to support this claim. This has led President Reagan, for example, to argue that 'Financial assistance to the poor is a legitimate responsibility of states and localities', and to propose the shifting of the major support progammmes in the USA from the central government to state and local levels. However, it is not hard to show that even if poor relief is not a national public good, the potential mobility of the poor creates a type of externality that is the likely source of underprovision of assistance to low-income households under a wholly decentralized system (see Brown and Oates, 1987).

However, this is surely not to deny a useful role for decentralized finance in this function. An active local participation in the administration of policies to assist the poor may significantly enhance the effectiveness of these programmes. This suggests some degree of co-operation among levels of government. King (1984, p. 36) argues, for example, that there should be 'a basic national redistribution policy, and that subcentral authorities should be allowed to alter the degree of distribution in their areas within specified limits'. But it seems clear that the central government (as with the stabilization function) has an important role to play in achieving an equitable distribution of income.

The provision of public goods and services

Decentralized levels of government have their primary rationale in the provision of public goods and services. There are certain public goods, like national defence and foreign policy, that benefit all members of a nation; the central government is obviously the appropriate agent for providing such truly national public services. In contrast, many other public services are of mainly local concern, including such things as refuse-collection systems, local fire protection, and many others. For such services, there is a compelling argument for decentralized provision. Centralized control tends to result in relatively uniform levels of services across local jurisdictions. As de Tocqueville observed over a century ago, 'In great centralized nations the legislator is obliged to give a character of uniformity to the laws, which does not always suit the diversity of customs and of districts.'

Decentralized provision of services, in contrast, provides the scope for adapting levels of output to the circumstances and tastes of individual jurisdictions. There are, in fact, some studies (for example, Bradford and Oates, 1975) suggesting that the magnitude of the welfare losses from the uniform provision of public services can be quite sizeable. Where possible, the argument suggests the levels of public services should be adjusted to the tastes of local constituencies.

The decentralized provision of local services offers the further attraction of providing a menu of outputs from which to choose. Charles Tiebout (1956) has described a model of local finance in which individuals seek out a community that provides the level of outputs best suited to their tastes. The resulting outcome is similar in spirit to that of a private market.

Just as the consumer may be visualized as walking to a private market to buy his goods, the prices of which are set, we place him in the position of walking to a community where the prices (taxes) of community services are set. Both trips take the consumer to market . . . Spatial mobility provides the local-public goods counterpart to the private market's shopping trip (p. 422).

While, in its formal attire, the Tiebout model may seem a little extreme, it does call to our attention the potential gains from allowing some choice to individuals in the consumption of locally provided public services.

The thrust of the argument is that where the output of particular services is primarily of 'local' interest, there is a strong case for assigning the provision of these services to local government. Such government is in a better position to tailor outputs of these services to local tastes and circumstances. This admittedly does not provide a firm menu of those goods and services that should be centralized and those that should be decentralized, but it provides some guide-lines for determining their assignment to a particular level of government.

Public Revenues: Tax Assignment and Intergovernmental Grants

In addition to the assignment of expenditure functions to the various levels of government, we must determine the vertical structure of revenues. In most countries, decentralized units of government raise some substantial portion of their revenues through their own tax instruments, but typically rely on higher levels of government for intergovernmental transfers to fund much of their spending. Consequently, I will address two issues in this section: the tax-assignment problem and systems of intergovernmental grants.

Are certain revenue sources more appropriate for particular levels of government?[1] A cursory survey of revenue systems across the world reveals a

For an excellent collection of papers addressing the tax-assignment problem in a federal system, see McLure (1983). For an approach that incorporates both economic and political aspects of this issue, see Bennett (1987).

marked diversity in structure. Instances can be found where nearly all major forms of taxation are employed at centralized and/or decentralized levels of government. This does not, of course, imply that 'anything goes'; there may well exist substantial distortions and other economic and social ills associated with the actual use of some of these tax structures. The interesting question here is whether or not there are reasons for believing that certain kinds of taxes are more suitable for use by central governments while others are more appropriately employed at decentralized levels of the public sector.

Richard Musgrave (1983) has provided some general guide-lines on this matter.[2] Among these 'principles', Musgrave contends that:

1. Highly progressive redistributional taxes (like a highly progressive personal income tax) should be centralized. The basic point here is that the use of such taxes at decentralized levels establishes pecuniary incentives for migration for both high- and low-income households that can easily lead to locational distortions and a frustration of the redistributional objectives of the tax.[3]

2. More generally, lower-level governments should avoid (non-benefit) taxes on highly mobile tax bases. Such taxes have the potential to induce movements of the tax base with resulting distortions in economic activity.

3. Tax bases that are distributed highly unequally across subcentral jurisdictions should be centralized. Thus, taxes on deposits of natural resources that are concentrated in certain jurisdictions are best taxed by the central government in order to avoid excessive inequities in subcentral tax bases.

4. User taxes and fees are appropriate revenue souces at all levels, but are particularly attractive at highly decentralized levels of government. Their appeal at the local level stems from the absence of any purely pecuniary incentives for location; such taxes or fees require recipients of local services to pay for them in accordance (roughly at least) with the cost of providing the services. In a world of mobile consumers (like that envisioned in the Tiebout model), such user taxes promote an efficient pattern of resource use in the local public sector.

Reflection on these guide-lines suggests that highly decentralized ('local') levels of government will do best to rely on taxes on relatively immobile bases and on user charges and fees. Actual practice conforms somewhat to these principles. In many countries, for example, local governments rely on property taxation as their primary source of tax revenues. In addition, an extensive reliance on charges for various local services is fairly common.

[2] See also Oates (1972, ch. 4).
[3] Just how extensive such distortions are likely to be is a matter about which little is really known. In one recent study, Timothy Goodspeed (1987), using a theoretical model of the local public sector that he employs in some simulation exercises, finds that a modest amount of local redistribution can be achieved with only quite minor distortions in location behaviour.

The structure of decentralized tax systems has potentially important implications for fiscal decision-making. Certain kinds of taxes (for example, taxes on local productive activity which are translated into higher prices of goods that are sold elsewhere) are in large degree exported to residents of other jurisdictions. Such 'tax-exporting' may easily encourage excessive budgets since they are paid by others. More generally, as Gordon (1983) has shown in an optimal taxation approach to the tax-assignment problem, if decentralized jurisdictions seek independently to maximize the welfare of their own residents, they will create externalities for residents of other states through their tax and expenditure policies. It is thus important to encourage the use of tax structures that limit the more serious sources of such distortions in economic activity. User taxes again are the most direct way to circumvent this problem: if individuals and firms face 'taxprices' that reflect the cost of local services, they will have the proper incentives both for efficient location decisions and to support (for example, through voting behaviour) efficient levels of local public outputs.

The general prescription emerging from this discussion suggests that an optimal tax system is one in which the central government places a heavy reliance on progressive, redistributive taxes like a progressive personal income (or expenditure) tax, while highly decentralized (local) governments rely on relatively immobile tax bases like local real estate and on user charges. Middle-level governments (like states or provinces), because of their larger size, have more scope than do local governments for making use of taxes on income and sales.

Subcentral governments typically receive substantial revenues in the form of intergovernmental grants. In some countries, such intergovernmental transfers account for well in excess of half of the revenues of the decentralized part of the public sector. In other countries, they play a more modest but still a quite significant role. There is now a large literature on intergovernmental grants (for example, Oates, 1972, ch. 3; King, 1984, chs. 3–5) that sets forth their economic rationale. In brief, such grants can serve three major objectives:

1. The subsidization of certain specific programmes where there are benefits accruing to those outside the jurisdiction. This calls for matching grants for the programme to encourage an expansion of output to take into account the 'external benefits'.

2. The substitution of more equitable and efficient central tax sources for decentralized revenues in order to produce a more just and economically efficient revenue system overall. This objective suggests that the central government act as a kind of revenue-collecting agent for subcentral units with the transfer of funds taking an unconditional (or revenue-sharing) form.

3. The equalizing of fiscal capacity across subcentral jurisdictions so that all areas are able to achieve the same basic bundle of public services with

(roughly) the same tax effort. The intent here is to achieve 'horizontal fiscal equity' in the public sector.[4]

The economic analysis of intergovernmental grants thus points to a system of transfers in which there are a set of open-end matching grants for particular programmes with benefits reaching outside of the individual subcentral jurisdictions and a set of unconditional (lump-sum) grants which may be distributed by a formula that provides more revenues per capita to fiscally disadvantaged areas.

A cursory examination of existing grant systems suggests that such elements are frequently present. But a closer study (at least in the case of the USA) reveals some striking anomalies. For example, certain major federal matching-grants have federal shares of the order of 90 per cent—far in excess of any conceivable level of external benefits. And some matching grants are closed-end; matching ceases at some level so that they provide no incentive at the margin for any expansion in output after some modest level of provision. In fact, in one recent study, Robert Inman (1989) concludes that economic principles cannot provide a very satisfactory explanation of the structure of existing US grant programmes; he finds that political considerations appear to be much more important in understanding the US system of federal grants. While this is dismaying, it also suggests that careful analysis and reform of the grant system may yield large dividends in terms of a system that better serves the objectives of equity and an effective use of our scarce resources.

There exists a substantial body of empirical work that has attempted to measure the budgetary impact of intergovernmental grants.[5] This work has turned up an intriguing finding: the results suggest that intergovernmental grants have had a highly stimulative effect on the spending of recipients. Even unconditional grants, which come with no apparent strings attached, seem to have induced sizeable increases in recipients' budgets. This is surprising, for, in principle, an unconditional grant to a group of people should be treated in much the same way as an increment to their private income. But the propensity to spend on public services out of grants appears to exceed greatly the additional spending on these services from equivalent increases in private income. This phenomenon is known in the literature as the 'flypaper effect', that is, 'money sticks where it hits'. Grants are not passed along to the extent one might expect in the form of reduced local taxes. It thus appears that an increased reliance on intergovernmental grants contributes to budgetary growth in the overall public sector. There are, however, some important qualifications attached to these results (involving both measurement problems and issues in

[4] For a comprehensive treatment of the geography of local fiscal inequity, see Bennett (1980).
[5] For a useful survey of this work, see Gramlich (1987).

interpretation), so they should not be regarded as the last word on the subject.

There may be a further puzzle in all this. If grants are so stimulative, considerations of symmetry suggest that their removal should have a marked contractionary effect on public spending. Interestingly, this appears not to have been the case in the USA during the 1980s. In the face of fiscal retrenchment by the Reagan administration involving substantial cuts in both the number and size of federal grant programmes, state and local governments seem to have picked up most of the slack; as Gramlich (1987) points out, they have increased their own taxes and largely replaced the lost grant funds wih revenues of their own.[6] Does the flypaper effect work in only one direction?

As the discussion suggests, we have much to learn about the structure and impact of intergovernmental grants. Nevertheless, careful analysis and evaluation can contribute much to the design of a grant system that improves the performance of the public sector.

Finally, I wish to comment briefly on the issue of the 'balance' in a federal revenue system between locally raised revenues and intergovernmental transfers. While there is certainly an important role for systems of intergovernmental grants, an excessive reliance on such systems can undermine the autonomy and vitality of decentralized decision-making. It is crucial, if decentralized levels of government are to have real and effective fiscal discretion, that they raise a significant portion of their own funds (particularly at the margin). This is important for two reasons. First, in a political setting, central funds nearly always come with certain strings attached. If decentralized governments are too heavily dependent on central revenue sources, it is inevitable that central intrusion into expenditure decisions will be widespread. Decisions concerning the menu and level of local programmes will become the result of negotiations between central and local authorities, undercutting the fiscal independence of the local public sector. Second, heavy reliance on grants destroys the incentives for responsible local fiscal decisions. It is essential that localities in choosing to expand or contract various programmes consider carefully the cost of these decisions. If, however, funding comes from 'above', there may be little real cost to the locality associated with these decisions. Thus, the funding *at the margin* of local programmes from own revenues is critical if decentralized choice is to play its proper role in the fiscal system.

---

[6] As Seymour Sacks has pointed out, there are some subtle issues of measurement and interpretation here that require careful analysis. From 1980 to 1982, federal grants to state and local governments declined in nominal dollars and even more sharply as a percentage of GNP. Over the same period, state and local governments increased their revenues from 'own sources' and raised spending in nominal terms. However, state and local spending in real terms and as a percentage of GNP fell slightly. The state and local share of GNP did decline somewhat in the early 1980s.

Decentralization as a Means to Control Public-Sector Growth

A more recent theme—one that has emerged in the public-choice literature during the last decade—concerns the potential for competition among decentralized jurisdictions as a disciplining force to restrain budgetary growth. The twentieth century has brought with it a dramatic growth in most countries in the share of the economy devoted to public-sector budgets. This continuing growth of government has become a major concern both in the scholarly literature and in the political world. There have taken place many conferences with volumes of papers exploring the causes and consequences of this growth (see, for example, Forte and Peacock, 1985). In the political sphere, presidents and prime ministers have been elected on platforms of budgetary restraint.

Geoffrey Brennan and James Buchanan (1977, 1978, 1980) have taken a particularly striking position on the matter. Drawing by analogy on the conventional theory of monopoly in the private sector, they view the government sector as a monolithic agent that systematically seeks to exploit its citizenry through the maximization of the tax revenues that it extracts from the economy. While this view has been hotly debated (see for example, Musgrave, 1981), what is relevant here is Brennan and Buchanan's claim that an effective means to control Leviathan is through decentralization of the public sector. Just as competition among firms in the private sector fosters efficiency, so decentralization can break the hold of a large monopolistic central government. Competition among decentralized government units in the context of the 'interjurisdictional mobility of persons in pursuit of "fiscal gains" can offer partial or possibly complete substitutes for explicit fiscal constraints on the taxing power' (Brennan and Buchanan, 1980, p. 184).

This is an intriguing claim. Can decentralization resulting in more competition in the public sector reduce the size of government? There have recently been some empirical attempts to test this proposition. If true, the proposition would suggest that, other things being equal, the size of the public sector should vary inversely with the extent of fiscal decentralization. In the earliest of these studies, I tested the hypothesis, using two quite different samples: a cross-sectional sample of 43 countries and another cross-sectional sample consisting of the states in the USA (Oates, 1985). In neither case was I able to find any supporting evidence. The partial associations between the size of the government sector and various measures of fiscal decentralization were weak, and, where they were statistically significant, possessed the wrong sign.

However, some later work has provided supporting evidence for Brennan and Buchanan. Michael Nelson (1987), reworking my data for the states in the USA with some alternative measures of decentralization and further disaggregation, found a significant positive association between fiscal decentralization and the size of the state/local sector. Likewise, a recent study by Jeffrey Zax (1987), using a large data base on US counties, finds that the size of the county/local sector tends to be larger, the more centralized is local government within counties. However, another study of US counties, this one by Kevin Forbes and Ernest Zampelli (1987), finds precisely the opposite: their results indicate that the more counties there are within a metropolitan area, the larger, other things being equal, is the metropolitan 'fisc'!

At this juncture, the contrasting findings of these various studies do not provide a clear answer to our question. The Brennan–Buchanan proposition on decentralization and public-sector size must, I think, be regarded as an intriguing conjecture. But one for which there is not, at this point at least, compelling evidence.

Decentralization and Public-Sector Innovation

There is a further aspect of decentralization that has not received much attention in the economic literature but is potentially of real significance: the role of decentralized government in fostering innovation in public-sector programmes. As Gramlich (1987, p. 309) puts it, 'One argument for the decentralized approach is that states and localities can serve as laboratories for testing national policy changes—systems can be tested on a small scale and perhaps better tailored to local conditions.' In fact, there have been some important instances in which states in the USA have led the way in introducing new policies whose success prepared the way for measures at the national level. Early in this century, the state of Wisconsin, for example, enacted a personal income tax in advance of the nation as a whole, and, more recently, California initiated various environmental programmes that provided an impetus to national legislation.[7]

The existing literature is largely empirical with a focus on the process of diffusion of policies among jurisdictions.[8] This work typically finds that the pattern of enactments can be described in terms of a cumulative distribution function that takes the S-curve shape. Walker (1969) has suggested that competition among jurisdictions is the driving force behind his diffusion indices. In a related vein, Pierre Salmon in two recent papers (1987*a*, *b*) has

---

[7] Susan Rose-Ackerman has explored innovation and risk-taking in the public sector in the context of a theoretical model of politicians who seek to maximize their probability of re-election. Her analysis suggests that incumbents are likely to behave in a 'risk-averse' fashion with a basic reluctance to engage in innovative measures. In a two-level federal system, 'the hope of running for a higher office may give low-level politicians an incentive to search for new ways of doing things and increase the competitiveness of state and local politics'. However, even here Rose-Ackerman argues that there are fundamental obstacles to widespread experimentation in the 'laboratories' of state and local government.

[8] See Breton (1988) for a brief description and assessment of this literature.

shown that if the electorate in one jurisdiction evaluates the performance of its officials in terms of information about the policies in other jurisdictions, the forces for adopting new programmes that enhance local welfare will be strengthened. Such awareness can promote the spread of successful policies.

The role of decentralized government as an innovator in public policy has received increased attention recently in the USA. As Nathan and Derthick point out (1987), with the withdrawal of the federal government under the Reagan administration from a wide range of social programmes, the states have stepped in vigorously and imaginatively on a number of fronts. Of particular interest in the 1980s has been the development by the states of some new forms of welfare policies. Many of the states have introduced their own 'workfare' programme that makes benefits contingent on enrolment in various kinds of public job, training, and wage-subsidy programmes. While a comprehensive evaluation of these programmes remains to be made, the initial results seem encouraging: the programmes appear to be popular both with the state governors and the welfare recipients themselves (Gueron, 1986). Experimentation at the state level may in this instance point the way to much-needed welfare reform.

Regulatory Federalism

In addition to the provision of public goods with purchased inputs, government agencies exercise important controls over the economy through the use of regulatory measures that prescribe various forms of activity for individuals and firms in the private sector. For illustrative purposes here, I shall take the case of environmental standards. In many countries, public environmental agencies set standards for environmental quality and employ some form of regulatory system to achieve these standards.

An important issue that has emerged in the policy arena is the extent to which such regulatory functions should be decentralized. In the USA, environmental standard-setting is an interesting case in point. Under the Clean Air Act in 1970, the US Congress directed the Environmental Protection Agency to set national standards for air quality; the EPA responded by specifying maximum permissible concentrations for a set of important air pollutants. Two years later, however, under the Clean Water Act, Congress instructed the states to set their own standards for water quality. Which is the preferable approach: centrally set national standards or locally determined standards for environmental quality?

On first inspection, simple economic analysis appears to provide a straightforward answer: standards should vary across jurisdictions in accordance with local circumstances. The argument here is basically the same as that discussed in the first section of this chapter. The marginal benefits (as determined by tastes, income, etc.) of environmental quality and the marginal costs of abatement are likely to vary across jurisdictions so that the optimal level of pollution will differ from one jurisdiction to another. If uniform national standards are introduced, there will be a loss in social welfare relative to the first-best outcome in which each jurisdiction achieves its own optimal level of environmental quality. Standards should, therefore, be set locally.

There is obviously a case for national standards in the event that pollution from one jurisdiction is transported across the relevant boundaries into neighbouring areas. This is a standard case of externalities; some intervention by a supra-local authority is required if localities are to take into account the effects of their polluting activities on those outside their borders.

But many pollutants have effects that are quite localized. Is there any case for national standards for such pollutants? Such a case has been made. John Cumberland (1979, 1981) for one has argued that national minimum standards for environmental quality are needed to avert 'destructive interregional competition'. The concern is that, in their eagerness to encourage new business investment and the creation of jobs, state or local authorities are likely to compete with one another in terms of reducing standards for environmental quality so as to reduce the costs for prospective business enterprise. The argument here parallels the oft-cited phenomenon of 'tax competition' among jurisdictions to promote economic development. The argument is that decentralized jurisdictions, if left to their own, will fail to select the optimal standards.

These are not easy arguments to evaluate. The case for national standards is strongest if jurisdictions are roughly similar in terms of their optimal levels of environmental quality and if serious distortions from economic competition are likely. There is some preliminary work that bears on these matters. In an ongoing empirical study of a major air pollutant, Albert McGartland, Paul Portney, and I have found that for two cities (Baltimore and St Louis), the optimal level of air pollution varies quite significantly. Requiring both cities to achieve the same level of air quality would appear in our case-study to entail relatively large welfare losses. Moreover, there are some reasons to believe that economic competition among jurisdictions, rather than distorting outcomes, may well be efficiency-enhancing. In one recent paper, Oates and Schwab (1989) present a model in which local jurisdictions set both a local tax rate on capital and a standard for local environmental quality. In this model, jurisdictions can increase their level of wage income by setting lower environmental standards or induce the entry of more capital. However, for the basic model, local choices under simple-majority rule turn out to be socially optimal. Jurisdictions in the model choose the level of environmental quality for which marginal benefits equal marginal abatement costs.

These results are obviously quite preliminary and specific. But they point in the direction of a relatively wide scope for decentralized standard-setting.

Decentralization has its attractions not only for the provision of public goods with purchased inputs but also for the regulation of certain forms of activity with public effects.

Some Concluding Remarks on the Evolution of Multi-level Government

The structure of the public sector is by no means static in character. A process of continuing evolution has led to marked changes in the vertical structure of government. This raises the intriguing question of whether or not there are any underlying trends in this structure. Some observers have contended that the public sector exhibits a continuing tendency towards increased centralization. Over a century ago, Alexis de Tocqueville predicted that 'in the democratic ages which are opening upon us ... centralization will be the natural government'. Referring to the federal form of government in particular, Edward McWhinney has cited Bryce's Law, the proposition that 'federalism is simply a transitory step on the way to governmental unity'. The claim here is that a public sector that relies heavily on decentralized budgetary choice is unstable—that it will move over time in the direction of continually greater reliance on central government.

There is some evidence to support this claim in the first half of the twentieth century. The public sector in the USA, for example, exhibited centralizing tendencies over this period. However, a closer examination of the trends in fiscal concentration since the middle of the century indicates that in many countries there have been no continuing tendencies toward centralization; in several instances, the trend has been toward an increasing fiscal share for decentralized levels of the public sector.

A simplified version of the centralization thesis thus doesn't appear to square with the evidence. There are, however, a number of other interesting dimensions of this process of evolution. In particular, the government sector in several countries seems to be developing into a more complex and highly specialized set of institutions, taking different forms in different countries. In the USA, for example, there has been a dramatic rise in the number of 'special districts'. These are single-function entities that now provide a diverse group of services including highways, hospitals, libraries, sewers, housing, fire protection, and others.

Moreover, public sectors in the Western industrialized countries have introduced new levels of government to cope with new demands on the public sector. Metropolitan area governments have come into being in Britain, the USA, Canada, and other countries in an effort to co-ordinate fiscal decision-making between central cities and their suburban communities. The formation of new governments has not been restricted to lower tiers. Within the European Community, a whole new top layer of government is emerging.

It is not yet fully clear what the ultimate range of responsibilities and powers of this new unit of government will be, but the contrast between a newly created European level of government and the pressures in many countries for moves toward 'devolution' suggests the diversity of forces operating on the public sector.

The complexity of the evolution of the public sector indicates that any simplified notions like that of the centralization thesis are likely to be misleading. There certainly does not seem to be any indication that local government, for example, is on its way out. Local government has, in fact, shown itself capable of taking on new forms in response to the variety of demands for local services. More generally, the complexity of the demands made on the modern public sector will no doubt require the continuing existence of many levels of decision-making to take advantage of the peculiar strengths of each level in dealing with particular problems. An effective public sector will be one with several levels in which responsibilities and fiscal instruments are assigned to the levels that can address and use them most advantageously.

References

Bennett, R. J. (1980), *The Geography of Public Finance* (Methuen, London).

—— (1987), 'Tax Assignment in Multilevel Systems of Government: A Political-Economic Approach and the Case of Spain', *Environment and Planning C: Government and Policy*, 5, p. 267–85.

Bradford, David, and Oates, Wallace, (1975), 'Suburban Exploitation of Central Cities and Governmental Structure', in H. Hochman and G. Peterson (eds.), *Redistribution Through Public Choice* (Columbia University Press, New York), pp. 43–90.

Brennan, Geoffrey, and Buchanan, James (1977), 'Towards a Tax Constitution for Leviathan', *Journal of Public Economics* 8, (Dec.), pp. 255–73.

—— —— (1978), 'Tax Instruments as Constraints on the Disposition of income', *Journal of Public Economics*, 9, pp. 301–18.

—— —— (1980), *The Power to Tax: Analytical Foundations of a Fiscal Constitution* (Cambridge University Press, Cambridge, England, and New York).

Breton, Albert (1988), 'The Existence and Stability of Intergovernmental Competition', preliminary draft.

Brown, Charles, and Oates, Wallace (1987), 'Assistance to the Poor in a Federal System', *Journal of Public Economics*, 32, (Apr.), pp. 307–30.

Cumberland, John (1979), 'Interregional Pollution Spillovers and Consistency of Environmental Policy', in H. Siebert *et al.* (eds.), *Regional Environmental Policy: The Economic Issues* (New York University Press, New York), pp. 255–81.

—— (1981), 'Efficiency and Equity in Interregional Environmental Management', *Review of Regional Studies*, 48, pp. 1–9.

Forbes, Kevin, and Zampelli, Ernest (1987), 'Is Leviathan a Mythical Beast?', unpublished paper.

Forte, Francesco, and Peacock, Alan (1985), *Public Expenditure and Government Growth* (Blackwell, Oxford).

Goodspeed, Timothy (1987), 'A Re-examination of the Use of Ability-to-Pay Taxes by Local Governments', unpublished paper.

Gordon, Roger (1983), 'An Optimal Taxation Approach to Fiscal Federalism', *Quarterly Journal of Economics*, 97, pp. 567–86.

Gramlich, Edward (1977), 'Intergovernmental Grants: A Review of the Empirical Literature', in W. Oates (ed.), *The Political Economy of Fiscal Federalism* (Heath-Lexington, Lexington), pp. 219–40.

—— (1987), 'Federalism and Federal Deficit Reduction', *National Tax Journal*, 40, (Sept.), pp. 299–313.

—— (1985), 'Reforming US Federal Fiscal Arrangements', in John Quigley and Daniel Rubinfled (eds.), *American Domestic Priorities: An Economic Appraisal* (University of California Press, Berkeley), pp. 34–69.

Gueron, Judith (1986), *Work Initiatives for Welfare Recipients* (Manpower Research Demonstration Corporation, New York).

Inman, Robert (1989), 'Federal Assistance and Local Services in the United Sates: The Evolution of a New Federalist Fiscal Order', in Harvey Rosen (ed.), *Fiscal Federalism* (University of Chicago Press, Chicago), forthcoming.

King, David (1984), *Fiscal Tiers: The Economics of Multi-Level Government* (Allen & Unwin, London).

McLure, jun., Charles (ed.) (1983), *Tax Assignment in Federal Countries* (Australian National University Press, Canberra).

Musgrave, Richard (1981), 'Leviathan Cometh—Or Does He?' in Helen Ladd and T. Nicolaus Tideman (eds.), *Tax and Expenditure Limitations* (The Urban Institute, Washington, DC), pp. 77–120.

—— (1983), 'Who Should Tax, Where, and What?', in Charles McLure (ed.), *Tax Assignment in Federal Countries* (Australian National University Press, Canberra), pp. 2–19.

Nathan, Richard, and Derthick, Martha (1987), 'Reagan's Legacy: A New Liberalism among the States', *New York Times*, 18 Dec.

Nelson, Michael (1987), 'Searching for Leviathan: Comment', *American Economic Review*, 77, (Mar.), pp. 198–204.

Oates, Wallace (1972), *Fiscal Federalism* (Harcourt Brace Jovanovich, New York).

—— (1985), 'Searching for Leviathan: An Empirical Study', *American Economic Review*, 75, (Sept.), pp. 748–57.

—— and Schwab, Robert (1989), 'Economic Competition among Jurisdictions: Efficiency Enhancing or Distortion Inducing?' *Journal of Public Economics*, forthcoming.

Pauly, Mark (1973), 'Income Redistribution as a Local Public Good', *Journal of Public Economics*, 2, pp. 35–58.

Salmon, Pierre (1987), 'The Logic of Pressure Groups and the Structure of the Public Sector', *European Journal of Political Economy*, 3, (1–2), pp. 55–86.

—— (1976), 'Decentralization as an Incentive Scheme', *Oxford Review of Economic Policy* 3, (Summer), pp. 24–43.

Tiebout, Charles (1956), 'A Pure Theory of Local Expenditures', *Journal of Political Economy*, 64, (Oct.), pp. 416–24.

Walker, J. L. (1969), 'The Diffusion of Innovations among the American States', *American Political Science Review*, 63, (Sept.), pp. 880–99.

Zax, Jeffrey (1987), 'Is There a Leviathan in Your Neighbourhood?', unpublished paper.

PART II

THE ROLES OF DIFFERENT LEVELS OF GOVERNMENT

[5]

Journal of Public Economics 32 (1987) 307–330. North-Holland

ASSISTANCE TO THE POOR IN A FEDERAL SYSTEM

Charles C. BROWN

University of Michigan, Ann Arbor, MI 48109, USA

Wallace E. OATES*

Department of Economics, University of Maryland, College Park, MD 20742, USA

Received June 1985, revised version received October 1986

This paper explores the roles of different levels of government in assisting the poor. Using a model incorporating utility interdependence, the paper first presents some theoretical results indicating how levels of poor relief vary with the extent of mobility of the poor under both centralized and decentralized systems of support. It then provides a survey of the empirical work on migration of the poor along with a brief historical discussion of the experience under the English Poor Laws. The concluding section turns to normative issues and contends that mobility of the poor is a basic source of inefficiency in wholly decentralized systems of support; this inefficiency, along with certain other equity considerations, establishes a role for the central government in assistance to the poor.

Measures adopted to produce greater equality are, however, exceedingly unsuitable for local authorities. The smaller the locality the more capricious and ineffectual are likely to be any efforts it may make to carry out such a policy. It seems clearly desirable that all such measures should be applied to the largest possible area, and that subordinate authorities should be left to act, like the individual, from motives of self-interest.

Edwin Cannan (1896)

Redistribution is intrinsically a national policy.

George Stigler (1957)

Financial assistance to the poor is a legitimate responsibility of states and localities.

President Reagan (1982)

*We are grateful to Anne Stevens and to the Computer Science Center at the University of Maryland for their valuable assistance and to the National Bureau of Economic Research and the Sloan Foundation for their support of this research. We also appreciate helpful comments on an earlier draft of this paper from Steven Craig, Edward Gramlich, Russell Mathews, David Wildasin, the participants in the Sloan Workshop in Urban Public Economics at the University of Maryland, and two anonymous referees. Finally, Oates wishes to thank Resources for the Future, where he spent a sabbatical leave as a visiting fellow while completing work on this paper.

1. Introduction

As the epigraphs to this paper suggest, there exists a divergence of views on the appropriate intergovernmental structure of programs to assist the poor. One strand of the literature argues that the central government should assume primary responsibility for this task [e.g. Oates (1972), Ladd and Doolittle (1982)]. This contention is typically developed along two lines:

(1) The well-being of the poor is of national concern: it is a national public good in the sense that income levels of the poor enter as arguments in the utility functions of the nonpoor. As a result, individual behavior or 'local' programs will involve an externality with the consequence of suboptimal levels of support.

(2) Even if preferences were such that concern for the poor were limited to residents of one's own jurisdiction, the potential mobility of the poor toward areas with comparatively high levels of assistance would force individual localities to be excessively parsimonious in their relief programs. The point here is that:

> The mobility of individual economic units among different localities places fairly narrow limits on the capacity for local income redistribution. For example, an aggressive policy to redistribute income from the rich to the poor in a particular locality may, in the end, simply chase the relatively wealthy to other jurisdictions and attract those with low incomes. The likely outcome is a community homogeneous in poor residents (an unappealing prospect for most local jurisdictions) [Oates (1977, p. 5)].

Not all of the economic literature, however, subscribes to this position [e.g. Pauly (1973), Tresch (1981, ch. 30)]. And, in fact, actual programs for assistance to the poor have often relied heavily on decentralized finance and administration. Over several centuries under the Poor Laws, England operated a system of poor relief with basic control at the level of the local parish. More recently, existing programs in the United States exhibit a wide range of roles for the different levels of government with the Federal Government providing certain programs, the states and localities others, and with shared responsibility for some of the major assistance programs (like AFDC). The institutional structure across these programs is strikingly diverse. This is of further interest in view of President Reagan's proposal under the New Federalism to shift the major responsibility for assistance to the poor away from the central government to the state and local levels.

Our purpose in this paper is to explore the issue of poor relief in a federal system with particular attention to the implications of mobility of the poor for the design of these programs. We begin with a positive analysis. Making use of a variant of a simple and useful model of Orr (1976) with demon-

Studies in Fiscal Federalism 69

C.C. Brown and W.E. Oates. Assistance to the poor   309

strated explanatory power, we work through a series of conceptual exercises that describe relative levels of cash transfers to the poor under various conditions. In these exercises, we find that the mobility of poor households across jurisdictions is a critical element in determining the outcome. In particular, we demonstrate that in a partial-equilibrium framework, the level of assistance varies inversely with the 'elasticity of mobility' of low-income individuals. The extension of the analysis to a general-equilibrium setting produces some important qualifications to this finding. But using some numerical simulations, we establish the presumption that with mobile poor the movement from a centralized to a decentralized system of poor relief is likely to result in a reduced *average* level of assistance to the poor. Since the extent of mobility is basically an empirical matter, we next survey recent research on migration behavior in response to differentials in levels of support for the poor and on the response of benefit levels to the potential for such migration. Then, following a brief examination of the experience under the English Poor Laws, we turn in the final section of the paper to the normative implications of the analysis. Here we contend that the potential migration of poor households seriously undermines the case for a decentralized system of poor relief. Economic efficiency in such transfer programs itself requires a basic role for the central government to correct the distortions inherent in a wholly decentralized program of assistance to the poor. In addition, there are other equity and efficiency arguments that, depending on a society's values, may imply a further rationale for central intervention.

2. A positive theory of poor relief: Partial equilibrium analysis

Our variant of Orr's model is based on the following simplifying assumptions:

(1) The nation consists of two kinds of people: the nonpoor (N) and the poor (P). Within each group, all individuals are identical: they have the same preferences and the same pre-tax and pre-transfer incomes.

(2) The concern for the poor is expressed as a dependence of the utility of the nonpoor on post-transfer income levels of the poor: $U_N^i = U_N^i(\bar{Y}_N^i, \bar{Y}_P^i)$.[1] Here, the utility of a nonpoor individual in local jurisdiction i depends on his own post-tax income. $\bar{Y}_N^i$ and on the post-transfer income of the poor, $\bar{Y}_P^i$

---

[1]Following Orr, we adopt here the 'altruistic' rationale for support for the poor. There are alternatives. Varian (1980), for example, suggests income security as a motivation for poor relief: one might support assistance to the poor as an insurance policy in case one's own income falls to low levels at some future time. Yet another approach is Peltzman's (1980) vote-maximizing politician who tries to secure the votes of transfer recipients through redistributive measures.

(where $\bar{Y}$ refers to disposable income). The poor care only about their own disposable income: $U_P^i = U_P^i(\bar{Y}_P^i)$. We shall assume (as indicated by the superscript *i*) that the nonpoor care only about the poor within their own jurisdiction and not elsewhere.[2]

(3) All the poor within a particular jurisdiction receive the same amount of transfer income.

(4) Transfers within each jurisdiction are financed by equal (lump-sum) taxes per capita on the nonpoor.

(5) The median voter determines the level of taxes and transfers. The one restriction here is that $N^i > P^i$: the number of nonpoor (N^i) exceeds the number of poor individuals (P^i). Otherwise, the poor could pass a measure to transfer all the income of the nonpoor to themselves.

Before exploring the implications of mobility of the poor, it is helpful as a benchmark to consider briefly the pattern of assistance to the poor in the absence of any such movement. Suppose that the distribution of individuals – both poor and nonpoor – across jurisdictions is given and fixed by, say, historical circumstance. In the context of our model, we can determine the equilibrium pattern of support in any jurisdiction by simply maximizing the utility of one of the (identical) nonpoor individuals:

$$\max U_N^i = U_N^i(\bar{Y}_N^i, \bar{Y}_P^i) \tag{1}$$

subject to the condition that total receipts by the poor equal aggregate tax payments by the nonpoor (which can be stated in the form):

$$\bar{Y}_P^i = Y_P^i + \frac{N^i}{P^i}(Y_N^i - \bar{Y}_N^i). \tag{2}$$

Eq. (2) indicates that the post-transfer income of a poor individual in *i* equals his pre-transfer income, Y_P^i, plus the total tax payments of the nonpoor $N^i(Y_N^i - \bar{Y}_N^i)$ divided by the number of poor. It is important to note that (P^i/N^i) is effectively the 'price' to a nonpoor individual of raising income per capita of the poor by \$1.

The solution to this maximization problem requires that

$$\frac{\partial U_N^i}{\partial \bar{Y}_N^i} = \frac{1}{(P^i/N^i)} \frac{\partial U_N^i}{\partial \bar{Y}_P^i}. \tag{3}$$

Eq. (3) implies that the nonpoor in *i* will continue to transfer income to the

---

[2]Note that this assumption explicitly eliminates one of the major arguments for a central role in assistance to the poor: the contention that such assistance involves a national public good. We shall return to this matter later.

poor in *i* until the marginal utility *to the nonpoor* of a marginal dollar of disposable income to themselves equals the marginal utility *to the nonpoor* of another dollar transferred to the poor. Note that this latter quantity depends not only on the income of the poor but on the 'effectiveness' of a dollar from a nonpoor person in raising the per capita income of the poor. And this in turn depends on the relative number of poor and nonpoor in the jurisdiction. If, for example, the poor are few in number relative to the nonpoor, then it will be comparatively inexpensive to the nonpoor to raise the per capita income of the poor.

Since we have assumed that the nonpoor have identical pre-tax incomes and tastes across all jurisdictions and, likewise, that the poor have the same pre-transfer incomes irrespective of location, it follows that the pattern of assistance to the poor will depend solely on the price (P^i/N^i) of raising the income level of the poor. Those poor fortunate enough to be in jurisdictions where they constitute a relatively small fraction of the population will receive relatively large transfers as compared to their counterparts in localities where the poor are a larger proportion of the residents.

More generally, however, individuals are not 'chained' to their current places of residence. In particular, the poor may have the opportunity to move away from jurisdictions providing relatively low levels of assistance to others with more generous levels of support.[3] In order to say more about the properties of an equilibrium in the presence of such mobility, we must be more specific about the response of the nonpoor to the prospect of a mobile poor population. Any decisions on levels of assistance to the poor must now take into consideration not only the existing number of poor residents in the jurisdiction, but also the impact of the support level on migration behavior. One thing we can say unequivocally in this instance: an increase in the number of poor in any jurisdiction [implying a rise in (P^i/N^i)] is undesirable from the perspective of the nonpoor residents – it reduces their level of utility. This follows because, in the model, the effect of an increase in (P^i/N^i) is to raise the 'price' to the nonpoor of any given level of assistance per poor person. An increase in the fraction of the population that is poor effectively increases the price of the second argument in the utility function of the nonpoor.

This would suggest that, in general, levels of assistance to the poor will be less in the presence of mobility than if the poor remained in their 'home' jurisdictions. For in the determination of the level of support, the nonpoor

---

[3]We shall continue to assume that the nonpoor do not move in response to differentials in assistance programs. This seems reasonable for, as Gramlich and Laren (1984) observe, '... at today's levels, a 30 percent increase in average AFDC benefit levels would raise the disposable income of AFDC recipients approximately this amount, but reduce the disposable income of average income taxpayers by only one-third of one percent' (pp. 495–496). It would thus seem that existing differentials in taxation of the nonpoor to finance transfers to the poor are probably too small to exert much effect in themselves on the location decisions of the nonpoor.

must now subtract from the utility they derive from a higher level of assistance to the poor not only the cost to themselves of the transfers to existing poor residents, but also the cost of the payments to the newly arrived poor who will migrate in response to the higher support levels [Boadway and Wildasin (1984, pp. 509–511)].

We shall now provide a formal proof of this proposition in our partial-equilibrium framework. We introduce an explicit 'migration function' in which the number of poor in a jurisdiction is a function of the level of transfer payments:

$$P = f(T), \quad \text{where } f'(T) > 0 \text{ and } f' \cdot \frac{T}{P} = \eta. \tag{4}$$

The parameter η is the elasticity of the migration function.[4] Substituting the budget constraint into the utility function, we can write:

$$U_N[\bar{Y}_N, \bar{Y}_P] = U_N\left[Y_N - \frac{PT}{N}, Y_P + T \right]. \tag{5}$$

Differentiating (5) with respect to T and setting the resulting expression equal to zero yields:

$$\begin{aligned} Z(T, \eta) &= \frac{\partial U_N}{\partial \bar{Y}_N}\left\{ -\frac{P}{N} - \left(\frac{T}{N} \cdot \frac{dP}{dT} \right) \right\} + \frac{\partial U_N}{\partial \bar{Y}_P} \\ &= \frac{\partial U_N}{\partial \bar{Y}_N}\left\{ -\frac{P}{N}(1+\eta) \right\} + \frac{\partial U_N}{\partial \bar{Y}_P} = 0. \end{aligned} \tag{6}$$

By the implicit-function rule, we obtain:

$$\frac{dT}{d\eta} = -\frac{\partial Z/\partial \eta}{\partial Z/\partial T}, \tag{7}$$

where $\partial Z/\partial T = \partial^2 U_N/\partial T^2 < 0$ by the second-order condition for utility maximization. Next, we note that

$$\frac{\partial Z}{\partial \eta} = \frac{\partial U_N}{\partial \bar{Y}_N}\left(-\frac{P}{N} \right) < 0. \tag{8}$$

---

[4]We note, in this regard, that it is the total number of poor (not the number of migrants) that appears in the denominator of the elasticity formula. In addition, to simplify notation in this section, we have omitted the subscripts and superscripts identifying the particular jurisdiction. All variables are understood to refer to the same, say the *i*th, jurisdiction.

From (7) and (8) it follows that

$$\frac{dT}{d\eta} < 0. \tag{9}$$

Eq. (9) indicates that the level of transfer payments varies inversely with the elasticity of the migration function; in a loose sense, it tells us (as expected) that the greater the potential flow of migrant poor in response to a change in the level of transfers, the lower will be the jurisdiction's level of support for the poor. This result, however, must be interpreted quite carefully. Note that the sign of this derivative is determined while holding T and P constant; we are effectively rotating the migration function around some initial values for P and T.

This can be seen in fig. 1, which depicts the 'demand curve' for transfer payments (D) by the nonpoor and a migration curve (M). The M-curve indicates that the number of poor residents (and hence P/N) rises with the level of support payments.[5] Note that an equilibrium pattern of payment levels and poor residents can only occur at the intersection of the D and M curves – at point A corresponding to the solid curves. If, for example, $T > T_0$,

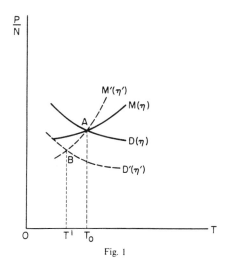

Fig. 1

[5]The M-curve in fig. 1 represents the locus of points satisfying the mobility function described by eq. (4). The D-curve corresponds to eq. (6); it is the locus of points satisfying the conditions for utility-maximization of the nonpoor. As is evident from eq. (6), the D-curve depends on the 'elasticity of migration' (η).

then more poor would enter the jurisdiction pushing down the level of transfer payments until $T = T_0$. In terms of fig. 1, our result in eq. (9) says that if we rotate the M curve about the initial position at point A and increase the elasticity of the function by making the curve steeper (see M'), then the equilibrium level of T will fall. This occurs because the demand function itself depends upon the slope of the migration curve: as M becomes steeper, indicating a greater responsiveness of the poor to payment levels, the D-curve shifts down (to D' in the diagram) reflecting a lower desired level of transfers. The new equilibrium is at B, indicating a fall in support payments from T_0 to T^1. It is important to be quite precise concerning this interpretation of (9). For, as we shall see in the next section, shifts of the M-curve in one direction may not yield a predictable effect on the level of support payments.

3. A two-jurisdiction, general-equilibrium model

A partial-equilibrium analysis is not, however, wholly satisfactory, since there will typically exist some interrelationship among levels of support among jurisdictions. In this section we examine the properties of a simple, two-jurisdiction model where we introduce simultaneous utility-maximization across the two localities. This provides some further insights into the way in which the degree of mobility of the poor influences the equilibrium levels of transfer payments.

Heretofore, we 'defined' mobility in terms of a mobility function. We effectively identified an increase in mobility with an increase in the parameter η, the elasticity of the mobility function. Higher mobility was thus associated with more responsiveness in the location decisions of the poor with respect to the level of support payments. For our two-jurisdiction case, we shall use a related, but somewhat different, measure of mobility: the 'cost' of moving from one jurisdiction to the other. We understand such moving costs to include the net costs of all considerations besides transfers. This would include not only transport costs (e.g. the price of 'bus tickets'), but also the psychic costs of relocation. In addition, moving costs depend upon such conditions as the length of the residency period before a low-income individual becomes eligible for support payments. From this latter perspective, the Supreme Court decision striking down state residency requirements can be seen as reducing the cost of relocation.

For the kth poor individual in jurisdiction i, the decision as to whether to move to jurisdiction j will depend upon the difference in support payments relative to moving costs. More formally, individual k will emigrate from i to j if

$$T^j - T^i > C_k^i + \alpha, \tag{10}$$

where α represents a component of moving costs common to all individuals and C_k^i an individual-specific 'attachment'.[6] A change $d\alpha$ increases moving costs by $d\alpha$ for each individual. It is changes in this parameter α that we will use to generate different equilibria at varying levels of moving costs (or, inversely, at different levels of mobility). If we let $F^i(C)$ and P_0^i represent the cumulative distribution function of C and the initial number of poor in jurisdiction i, then

$$P^i(T^j - T^i, \alpha) = P_0^i - P_0^i F^i(T^j - T^i - \alpha) + P_0^j F^j(T^i - T^j - \alpha). \tag{11}$$

The first term on the RHS of (11) is the initial stock of poor, the second the number of poor who emigrate from i, and the third the number who come to i from the other jurisdiction. Although (11) takes the form of a stock-adjustment process, we note that the model is not itself dynamic in character; we shall make use of (11) in describing the comparative-statics outcomes associated with changes in the parameter α.

If each jurisdiction takes the other's behavior as given, it will choose T^i (or T^j) to maximize

$$U_N^i(\bar{Y}_N^i, \bar{Y}_P^i) = U_N^i\left[Y_N - \frac{T^i P^i(T^j - T^i, \alpha)}{N^i}, \ Y_P^i + T^i \right]. \tag{12}$$

Differentiating with respect to T^i and setting the result equal to zero gives:

$$Z \equiv \frac{\partial U_N^i}{\partial \bar{Y}_N^i} \cdot \frac{\partial \bar{Y}_N^i}{\partial T^i} + \frac{\partial U_N^i}{\partial \bar{Y}_P^i} = 0, \quad \text{for } i = 1, 2. \tag{13}$$

Changes in α will then lead to changes in T^i and T^j. These can be either partial- or general-equilibrium responses. For a partial-equilibrium analysis, we can differentiate (13) for jurisdiction i with respect to T^i and α, and solve

$$\frac{\partial Z^i}{\partial T^i}\,dT^i + \frac{\partial Z^i}{\partial \alpha}\,d\alpha = 0, \quad \text{for } \frac{dT^i}{d\alpha}.$$

---

[6]C_k^i is related to what Grewal and Mathews (1983) have termed the 'locational surplus'. This surplus is the 'algebraical sum of the net benefits which a citizen perceives as accruing to him, in terms of his consumption and production/employment activities as well as his fiscal transactions with governments, by choosing to remain in his present jurisdiction rather than migrating to another jurisdiction' (p. 9). In our notation, $(C_k^i + T^i - T^j)$ is the locational surplus for the kth low-income household in jurisdiction i. We should also note, as a referee pointed out, that moving and attachment costs in eq. (10) must be understood to be annualized costs to make them commensurate with transfer payments. Alternatively, we could take the left-hand side of (10) to represent the present discounted value of the difference between the future streams of transfer payments.

For a general-equilibrium analysis, we differentiate each equation in (13) with respect to T^i, T^j, and α and solve the system of equations,

$$\begin{bmatrix} \partial Z^1/\partial T^1 & \partial Z^1/\partial T^2 \\ \partial Z^2/\partial T^1 & \partial Z^2/\partial T^2 \end{bmatrix} \begin{bmatrix} dT^1 \\ dT^2 \end{bmatrix} = - \begin{bmatrix} \partial Z^1/\partial \alpha \\ \partial Z^2/\partial \alpha \end{bmatrix} d\alpha,$$

for $dT^1/d\alpha$ and $dT^2/d\alpha$. To label the resulting algebra 'tedious' is an understatement. Here, we merely outline the solution; details appear in an appendix available from the authors on request.

Differentiating eq. (13) leaves us with three sorts of derivatives: first-partials of the utility function, second- and cross-partials of the utility function, and derivatives of P^i with respect to its arguments. The first-partials are, of course, positive. Various combinations of the other derivatives of the utility function can be signed either from the second-order conditions for each jurisdiction's maximization of (12) or from strongly-held priors about related comparative-static experiments. In particular, we assume that

$$\frac{\partial T^i}{\partial \bar{Y}^i_N} > 0 \quad \text{and} \quad \frac{\partial T^i}{\partial \bar{Y}^i_P} < 0.$$

The third source of information comes from actually differentiating P^i with respect to its arguments. Most of our conclusions take advantage of the fact that the sum of P^1 and P^2 is constant, and that the assumed response of migration from i to j is based on the *linear* function $(T^j - T^i - \alpha)$. Finally, we assume that $F^{i\prime\prime\prime}$ is non-negative or, equivalently, that the density of C is rising.[7]

In both the partial- and general-equilibrium contexts, our results are qualitatively similar. An increase in α will reduce both of the migration flows in eq. (11), reducing the number of poor in one jurisdiction and increasing it in the other. For the jurisdiction which is on the receiving end of the *net* migration flow, we can say unambiguously that an increase in the mobility of the poor (i.e. a reduction in α) will result in a decline in the level of transfer payments. Increased mobility implies an increased inflow of low-income individuals for any specified level of transfer payments. The response of the nonpoor to this increase in the potential inflow of transfer recipients will be to lower support levels. For the other jurisdiction, however, the effect is ambiguous. Increased mobility implies a greater net outflow of the poor; with

---

[7]For any symmetric density, this holds when less than half the poor are migrating. Allowing $F^{\prime\prime\prime}$ to be negative introduces an ambiguity into our results rather than necessarily reversing them; it turns out that increases in α necessarily correspond to reductions in the elasticity of P with respect to T only when $F^{\prime\prime}$ is positive.

fewer poor, the 'price' (P/N) of raising the disposable income of the poor falls. This effect encourages an increase in the level of transfers and works against the incentive to reduce payments in response to the higher level of mobility. We cannot, in general, determine the sign of $dT/d\alpha$ for such a jurisdiction.

More particularly, if we were to limit migration flows to a one-way movement of the poor from the low-transfer to the high-transfer state, we could show that with increased mobility, the level of transfers would unambiguously decline un the high-support state but could conceivably either rise or fall in the low-transfer state (because of the exodus of some of its poor). Gramlich (1985), using a specific formulation of a model in this spirit with representative values for the parameters, produces some intriguing results. In his simulation exercises, increased mobility of the poor results in a dramatically reduced level of transfers (T) in the high-support state and an *increase* in T in the low-support state. Greater mobility of the poor effectively pushes support levels closer together with a sharp decrease in the average payment across the two jurisdictions. The decrease in the average payment is an interesting, if perhaps an unsurprising, finding. We shall present some evidence shortly that reinforces this finding. While it is our conjecture that a decrease in the *average* payment is probably the 'typical' outcome under increased mobility of the poor, we would note that it is not a proposition that we have been able to derive as a general result.

4. Centralized versus decentralized support for the poor

Having examined the effects of mobility of the poor on levels of support under a system of local poor relief, we turn next to a comparison of support levels under centralized and decentralized systems of assistance.

It is helpful at the outset to examine some of the properties of the centralized outcome using the two-jurisdiction model. Consider the following numerical example:

$$N_1 = 200, \qquad P_1 = 60,$$

$$N_2 = 100, \qquad P_2 = 40,$$

where N_i and P_i refer to the number of nonpoor and poor households, respectively, in jurisdiction i (where $i = 1, 2$). We retain the assumption that the nonpoor care only about the well-being of the poor within their own jurisdiction. Centralization of support has two effects. First, it equalizes the price of support for the poor across the two jurisdictions. Under centralized support, it is *as if* both jurisdictions had ratios of poor to nonpoor of

$$\frac{P}{N} = \frac{P_1 + P_2}{N_1 + N_2} = \frac{60 + 40}{200 + 100} = \tfrac{1}{3}.$$

Note that the distribution of the poor across jurisdictions is irrelevant to the centralized outcome (even though it remains true that the nonpoor are only concerned with the poor within their own locality). Since in our simple model the nonpoor are everywhere identical, they will all desire the same level of transfer payments – that corresponding to the price P/N. Second, by equalizing levels of transfer payments, centralization eliminates any movement of poor households in response to interjurisdictional differentials in support levels. The mobility issue thus vanishes.

Suppose that we take such a centralized outcome as our initial equilibrium and consider a shift to a decentralized system of poor relief. In terms of our numerical example, jurisdiction 1 will now provide for its own poor as will jurisdiction 2. Decentralization will involve two effects: a price effect and a mobility effect. The sign of the mobility effect is unambiguous: as noted earlier, each jurisdiction will incorporate into its choice of a level of transfer payments the prospect that a higher T will, ceteris paribus, result in a larger number of poor households. This will depress the level of transfers. The price effect, however, will differ between the two jurisdictions. In our example, jurisdiction 1 (with a comparatively small fraction of poor residents) will experience a fall in the 'price' of transfer payments to its poor. This will tend to offset the mobility effect so that the impact of decentralization on T_1 is uncertain. For jurisdiction 2, in contrast, the price of transfers rises; this reinforces the mobility effect and leads to an unambiguous fall in T_2. Because of the ambiguous sign for jurisdiction 1, we cannot demonstrate that decentralization will necessarily lower the average level of transfers, although we might expect this often to be the case. That is, we might expect that in most circumstances, the *average* level of transfer payments under a decentralized system of assistance to the poor would be less than the average payment level under a centralized outcome. But even this fairly weak result rests on our assumption of identical tastes of nonpoor individuals in the two jurisdictions.

To obtain some further sense of these relationships, we have undertaken some numerical exercises using specific functional forms for our two-jurisdiction case. For these exercises, we have normalized the pre-transfer income to the nonpoor at 1.0 and set the pre-transfer income of the poor at 0.25. We assumed a utility function of the simplified-CES form:

$$U = [\bar{Y}_N^{(-r)} + b \bar{Y}_P^{(-r)}]^{-(1/r)},$$

where $\sigma = 1/(1 + r)$ is the elasticity of substitution between $\bar{Y}^N$ and $\bar{Y}^P$. We arbitrarily chose five values of σ: 0.33, 0.67, 1.0, 2.0, and 3.0. For each σ, we picked b so that $\bar{Y}_P/\bar{Y}_N$ equalled 0.40 when transfers were provided under a fully centralized system.[8]

We assumed the moving-cost functions $F^i(T^j - T^i - \alpha)$ to be cumulative-normal distributions, with variance one and means of 1.2817 and 1.0365, respectively. Thus, in a benchmark world where moving costs are zero and transfers in the two jurisdictions are equal, $F^1 = \phi(-1.2817) = 0.10$ and $F^2 = \phi(-1.0365) = 0.15$ [where $\phi(z)$ is the standard-normal c.d.f.]. This implies that, in our benchmark case, the number of poor in each jurisdiction is constant, since $F^1 P_1 = 0.10 \times 60 = 6$ move from 1 to 2 and $F^2 P_2 = 0.15 \times 40 = 6$ move from 2 to 1.

The results appear in table 1. The level of transfers under a centralized system is independent of σ by construction; b was chosen for each σ to generate this property. The first major result is that when $\alpha = \infty$ (no mobility), decentralization can either raise or lower average transfers. When $\sigma < 1$, the demand curve in fig. 1 is concave, so that T at $P/N = 0.33$ (the centralized solution) exceeds the weighted average of T at $P/N = 0.3$ and T

Table 1

Transfers under centralized and decentralized systems.

	Elasticity of substitution				
	0.33	0.67	1.0	2.0	3.0
Centralized system	0.13235	0.13235	0.13235	0.13235	0.13235
Decentralized system: $\alpha = \infty$					
T_1	0.14613	0.15868	0.17157	0.21237	0.25648
T_2	0.10987	0.09128	0.07353	0.02500	0.01695
$\bar{T}$	0.13163	0.13172	0.13235	0.13742	0.14711
Decentralized system: $\alpha = 0$					
T_1	0.14085	0.14745	0.15373	0.17084	0.18564
T_2	0.10466	0.08337	0.06475	0.02022	0.01293
$\bar{T}$	0.12637	0.12182	0.11814	0.11059	0.10621

[8]In a centralized system, P/N equals $1/3$ and there are no $\partial P/\partial T$ terms in the first-order conditions. As a result,

$$\frac{\bar{Y}_P}{\bar{Y}_N} = \left(\frac{b}{P/N}\right)^\sigma$$

Since the left-hand side is fixed at 0.40 and P/N is known, it is easy to solve for b as a function of σ. The values of Y_P and T were chosen as representative of actual 1983 data: families receiving 'public assistance and welfare' received an average transfer of \$3,245, bringing their total income to \$8,329. Average family income before taxes was \$24,646. [See U.S. Bureau of the Census (1985, tables 33 and 34).]

80 Studies in Fiscal Federalism

320   *C.C. Brown and W.E. Oates. Assistance to the poor*

at $P/N = 0.4$. When $\sigma > 1$, the reverse is true. Of course, these comparisons hold for 'large' finite α's as well as the polar case in the table. With immobile poor, there is thus no presumption in our model that the average level of transfer payments will be higher or lower under centralized assistance than under localized support for the poor.

The second major result is that increased mobility reduces transfers in each jurisdiction (compare the $\alpha = \infty$ and $\alpha = 0$ results). This happens for a range of intermediate values, too (and for other $\bar{Y}_p$, T pairs), although we cannot show this result need always hold. Interestingly, our finding that transfers fall in the jurisdiction with more poor people contrasts with the implication of the Gramlich–Laren (1984) model [as developed in Gramlich (1985)]. As noted earlier. Gramlich finds that, in his simulations, benefits in the poorer jurisdiction rise. This difference appears to result from the choice of functional form, especially for the migration function.[9] At any rate, it is the case in both the Gramlich and our simulations that in the presence of mobility of the poor, *average* support payments are lower under a system of local poor relief than under a centralized system of assistance. The extent of mobility of transfer recipients seems to be of great importance to the outcome.

5. An examination of the evidence

Our theoretical analysis suggests that migration of the poor in response to differentials in transfers has the potential to depress the levels of these payments. But is there evidence that this has taken place? We shall organize our discussion of the empirical literature around the following two issues:

(1) Is there evidence to indicate that the poor do, in fact, migrate from low-benefit to high-benefit jurisdictions (and in substantial numbers)?

---

[9]Neglecting matching grants, the Gramlich–Laren model can be written

$$\ln T^i = \frac{1}{1+cb}(a_i + cb \ln T^j),$$

where c is the price elasticity of demand for T, b is the elasticity of P^i with respect to T^i/T^j, and the a_i are constant terms reflecting other influences [see Gramlich (1985, p. 63)]. The equilibrium levels of transfers are

$$\ln T^i = \frac{a_i + cb(a_1 + a_2)}{1 + 2cb}.$$

The derivative of $\ln T^i$ with respect to b is

$$\frac{c(a_j - a_i)}{(1+2cb)^2}.$$

Thus, increased mobility (higher b) reduces transfers in the higher-transfer state $(a_i > a_j)$, and increases them in the low-transfer state. Note, however, that the sum of these derivatives must be zero, which is a very strong a priori restriction.

(2) Can we find any response in the level of transfer payments to such migration?

We begin with a brief survey of a large number of econometric studies of migration behavior in the United States that have addressed the first of these issues. These studies typically relate migration over some period between states (or, in some instances, metropolitan areas) to a set of independent variables including measures of per capita income, unemployment rates, etc., in addition to variables indicating welfare benefits in (or differentials in benefits between) the jurisdictions. Some of the early studies were quite crude and aggregative [e.g. Gallaway et al. (1967)]. Using total migration flows, they typically found the welfare-support variables to be statistically insignificant. It is also worth noting that several of these studies used migratory data from the 1950s, when payment levels and differentials were relatively small and various residency requirements were in effect. In contrast, many later studies employed more disaggregated data on migratory flows for more recent periods. These studies typically distinguish between white and nonwhite migration and, in some instances, between different age groups. And many of them use data from the decade of the 1960s. One would have to characterize the findings of these studies as somewhat mixed. But our survey indicates that the large majority of them find some evidence of positive net migration of nonwhite individuals in response to differentials in welfare benefits [see, for example, Kaun (1970), Cebula et al. (1973) and Curran (1977)].

Nonwhite migration, however, is itself an imperfect proxy measure for benefit-induced migration. As Gramlich and Laren (1984) note, only about one-quarter of nonwhite families are recipients of AFDC payments, and only about one-half of AFDC recipients are nonwhite. It would obviously be preferable to target such migration studies on actual (or potential) welfare recipients. Some recent studies have done just this. Southwick (1981) has explored the migratory patterns of AFDC recipients and finds that benefit levels exert a strong influence on AFDC immigration. In his 'Test 5', for example, Southwick estimates a 'migration' elasticity of 2.5: his table 5 indicates that a 10 percent increase in AFDC benefits will lead to an estimated increase of 25 percent in the in-migration of welfare recipients.[10] Likewise, Blank (1983), drawing on micro data for individual AFDC recipients from the Current Population Survey, finds that benefit levels (as well as employment opportunities) exert a significant influence on location decisions. Finally, Gramlich and Laren (1984) have used two quite different

[10]Southwick's elasticity of migration, incidentally, is not the same as the elasticity of our migration function in the preceding section. For Southwick's calculations, the elasticity of migration is defined as the percentage change in the number of *migrant* poor (not total poor) resulting from a 1 percent change in the level of transfer payments (in this case the monthly AFDC benefit).

techniques to estimate the migratory response to benefit levels. The first involves the estimation of a simultaneous-equation model using pooled time-series and cross-sectional data on state AFDC payments for 1974–81; the second employs micro data from a subsample of the 1980 Census and the Panel Study of Income Dynamics (PSID) to estimate a 'transition matrix' describing movements among groups of states with differing benefit levels. Both of these exercises reveal a significant migratory movement of AFDC beneficiaries from lower to higher benefit states. This movement, incidentally, is not large in the short run. Gramlich and Laren describe it as 'sluggish', but over a longer period this mobility 'can alter the interstate distribution of the AFDC population substantially' (p. 506).

The evidence thus provides some support for the view that benefit differentials exert a significant influence on the location decisions of the poor. But is this migratory response to differentials in support levels perceived by state and local policy-makers, and do they react by holding benefits below what they otherwise would be? As we noted earlier, this is a difficult issue to get at empirically. Interestingly, there has been a recognition in the empirical literature that *actual* migration flows may influence benefit levels. Cloward and Piven (1968), for example, have argued that the movement of blacks from the South to northern cities led to an increase in the political power of blacks in the cities with a consequent expansion of welfare rolls and benefit levels. The claim here is that actual migration is associated with *increases* (not decreases) in welfare benefits, in response to the expanded, and hence politically more influential, group of transfer recipients. The first empirical test of this hypothesis is embodied in the estimation of a two-equation model by Cebula (1974); the model contains one equation explaining migration flows and a second describing the response of benefit levels to these flows. In the second equation, Cebula found a direct and significant relationship between the level of benefits and the inflow of nonwhite migrants. However, later work casts doubt on these initial findings. Criticizing Cebula's work, Kumar (1977) has estimated a somewhat different model using Cebula's (and other) data: he finds no significant impact of migration flows on the level of assistance payments. Likewise, Curran (1977), in the estimation of a three-equation model of net immigration of nonwhites to SMSAs between 1965 and 1970, can find no evidence that greater immigration of nonwhites leads to higher welfare payments. And, finally, Southwick (1981), estimating a two-equation model, finds that migration flows of welfare recipients do not have a significant effect on benefit levels. The evidence, on the whole, does not seem to support this version of the 'bi-directional' hypothesis.

However, the hypothesis of interest to us is that *potential* migration depresses benefit levels; the proposition is that public officials, responding to the potential movements of low-income households, select benefit levels below those they would choose in the absence of such mobility. The one attempt to conceptualize and measure this relationship is the simultaneous-equation model, noted earlier, by Gramlich and Laren. Their model incorporates explicitly the differential between own-state and surrounding-state benefit levels and its effect on the size of the welfare population. This, in turn, enters into the determination of the level of welfare benefits (which results from utility-maximization of the decisive voter). Their estimated benefit equation indicates that the 'migration effect [on benefit levels] is strong and significant no matter how the model is estimated' (p. 499). In short, the greater the potential migration of benefit recipients, the lower are the support-payment levels predicted by the Gramlich and Laren equation.

Our reading of the evidence, at this juncture, is that it provides some support both for the view that there is a migratory response to differentials in benefit levels and that the recognition of this migration potential depresses levels of assistance payments. As Gramlich and Laren (1984) put it:

> Our tentative conclusion is that migration of AFDC beneficiaries does appear to be an important phenomenon, though only in the very long run. It does appear to be perceived that way by state legislators, who appear to be very much conditioned by what other states are doing when they set AFDC benefits (p. 510).

6. Local assistance to the poor: The case of the English Poor Laws

Our analysis and some supporting evidence suggest that mobility of the poor in response to differentials in support is a potentially serious obstacle to the successful functioning of a system of local finance. This raises the intriguing question of how England, a relatively small country with short distances between local parishes, managed to operate a system of local relief over several centuries. Although the Elizabethan or Old Poor Law was officially enacted in 1601, it effectively codified practices that had existed for some time [Marshall (1968, p. 11)]. Under these practices, the basic responsibility for both the finance and administration of poor relief rested with the parish. The Old Poor Law required each parish to designate an 'Overseer of the Poor' whose task it was to know all the poor, to administer assistance to them, and to find work for the unemployed.

The English dealt with the problem of migration by prohibiting it. The Law of Settlement and Removal of 1662 (which again formalized earlier practices reaching back at least to the Labour Ordinance of 1349) made it the responsibility of each parish to provide relief for its own, but only its own, poor. Under the Law, church wardens and overseers were directed to remove to his 'home' parish any newcomer likely to become a burden to his adopted parish unless the new arrival could give surety that he would not become indigent or rented property of the value of ten pounds per year or more [Fraser (1976, pp. 26–27)]. In fact, the history of the Poor Laws is largely an account of efforts to deny support to, and to deport, the itinerant poor. Cruel instances abound of whippings, the splitting of families, and the expulsion of widows and unwed mothers. In a further Act in 1795, the settlement law was amended such that only those who applied for local relief were subject to removal. Now only the poor who actually applied for support put themselves in jeopardy of being removed. The threat of removal proved a powerful force in persuading strange paupers to conceal their neediness. The settlement and removal provisions were a cornerstone of the Poor Laws. Even with the enactment of the New Poor Law in 1834 with its attempt to centralize and standardize somewhat the treatment of the poor, settlement and removal was left intact; it survived well into the twentieth century.

In addition to the hardship that it worked on the poor, the settlement law proved quite complex and costly to administer. The removal of a poor person could involve a long and expensive search to determine the person's most recently acquired 'settlement', sometimes involving extensive litigation with other parishes. Such litigation could drag on encompassing one parish after another, until the bill became quite sizeable.

> It took seven years for a case brought by the township of Carlton in Yorkshire against Marsden in Lancashire to be settled, and when the Court of the Queen's Bench finally decided the issue in 1849, the 142 ratepayers of Carlton were left with a legal bill of over 300 pounds [Fraser (1976, pp. 34–35)].

Added to this was the cost of actual removal and transport; Tate (1969, p. 200) notes that constables on the main roads sometimes spent the whole of their time transporting paupers.

During the nineteenth century, an alternative to settlement and removal procedures became popular. Instead of having a relief applicant and his family returned to them under a removal order with little prospect of gainful employment, the parish of settlement sometimes elected to reimburse the parish where the relief recipient was currently located. As Fraser (1976, pp. 35–36) points out: 'A complex system of inter-parochial and inter-union accountancy sprang up... Between 1846 and 1859 the Chorlton-on-Medlock Union was reimbursing 36 unions and parishes, and was at the same time in receipt of payments from about 100 unions or parishes on behalf of their non-resident paupers.'

In view of the cumbersome and expensive character of the English system, one wonders at its longevity. The laws of settlement and removal, in particular, were the subject of fierce criticism from various social reformers and from economists of the stature of Smith and Malthus. The economists opposed these provisions because they restricted the mobility of labor.[11] However, the support for maintaining the local system of poor relief was strong. There was deep distrust of proposals that would replace local with national financing of relief. The source of this distrust was largely the concern that effective control be maintained over recipients and levels of support [Fraser (1976, pp. 42–43)]. Local experience and direct contact with poor persons were seen as necessary to restrict assistance to the truly deserving poor. Moreover, local funding provided a check on levels of assistance that, some feared, would be lost under a system of national finance. In short, a national system of poor relief, it was argued, would lead to a 'profusion' of assistance to the poor that would encompass fraudulent recipients and discourage work effort.

Of central interest for our treatment, however, are the provisions for settlement and removal. Without such provisions to thwart the movement of the poor from one parish to another in search of more generous support, it seems doubtful that much in the way of local poor relief could have been sustained. Meager as such support may have been over much of the period under consideration, poor relief would probably have been even less without some control over the mobility of potential recipients.

7. The normative issue

In the preceding sections we have developed a descriptive theory of poor relief in a federal system and have explored the empirical literature that bears on the issues raised by the theory. We now turn to the normative matter posed at the outset of the paper concerning the roles of different levels of government in providing assistance to the poor. In particular, we are interested in what sorts of insights we can gain from the positive analysis into the design of an effective intergovernmental system of income maintenance.

The simple two-jurisdiction model of section 3 can be used to highlight some of the important issues which arise in a federal system. As others [e.g. Boadway and Wildasin (1984, pp. 505–511)] have noted, migration imposes a garden-variety externality that renders a completely decentralized system inefficient. Pareto efficiency (thinking only of the nonpoor in the two jurisdictions) requires that we maximize $U_N^1(\bar{Y}_N^1, Y_P^1 + T^1)$ subject to $U_N^2(\bar{Y}_N^2, Y_P^2 + T^2)$ being equal to some $\bar{U}_N^2$. The social budget constraint is

$$\bar{Y}_N^1 = Y_N^1 - \frac{P^1 T^1 + N^2(\bar{Y}_N^2 - Y_N^2) + P^2 T^2}{N^1}.$$

[11]Blaug (1963) and others contend that settlement and removal were not, in practice, so serious an impediment to labor mobility as was believed by reformers of the time.

The choice variables are T^1, $\bar{Y}^2_N$, and T^2. The first-order conditions, after some manipulation, yield as a rule for efficiency:

$$\frac{\partial U^i_N / \partial \bar{Y}^i_P}{\partial U^i_N / \partial \bar{Y}^i_N} = \frac{P^i + T^i(\partial P^i / \partial T^i) + T^j(\partial P^j / \partial T^i)}{N^i}, \quad i = 1, 2. \tag{14}$$

Comparing (14) to eq. (6) or (13) makes it clear that the inefficiency is *not* the result of jurisdiction i allowing its choice of T to be affected by costs to it from transfer-induced in-migration; the source of the distortion is rather that jurisdiction i gets no credit for the savings an increase in its transfers would bring to the other jurisdiction.

We can imagine trying to satisfy this efficiency condition by allowing each jurisdiction to subsidize the transfers of its neighbor. Let s^i be the subsidy per dollar of transfer which j offers to i. To obtain an expression for s^i, we can use the fact that $\partial P^j / \partial T^i$ is equal to minus $\partial P^i / \partial T^i$, and rewrite the right-hand side of eq. (14) as

$$\frac{P^i[1 + \eta^i - (T^j / T^i)\eta^i]}{N^i},$$

where $\eta^i = (\partial P^i / \partial T^i)(T^i / P^i)$. The Pigouvian subsidy rate needed to internalize the externality is therefore

$$s^i = \frac{T^j}{T^i} \frac{\eta^i}{(\eta^i + 1)}.$$

Jurisdiction i's transfer costs are then $(1 - s^i)T^i P^i$, and maximizing the utility of its nonpoor satisfies the efficiency condition.[12] The subsidy rate increases with η^i and is proportional to T^j / T^i; the rate is thus higher for a 'poor' low-transfer jurisdiction than for a high-transfer 'rich' one.[13] The subsidy is, in a sense, symmetric: if jurisdiction i is the 'rich' high-transfer jurisdiction, it still receives a subsidy from j, though $s^i < s^j$ if $T^j < T^i$ and $\eta^i = \eta^j$.

Finally, notice that $\partial P^i / \partial T^i$ refers to those migrants whose location changes with a small change in T, not to all migrants. Hence, a system of reimbursement like that of nineteenth-century England (where jurisdiction i reimburses jurisdiction j for *all* of i's poor who migrate to j) does not achieve efficient levels of transfers.

---

[12]Of course, if jurisdiction i were offered a subsidy rate s^i which depended *explicitly* on T^i, each nonpoor resident of jurisdiction i would see $-T^i P^i (\mathrm{d}s^i / \mathrm{d}T^i)$ as part of the price it faces, and a more complicated subsidy rule would be needed.

[13]It is *possible* that $s^i > 1$. This would mean simply that if T^j / T^i is large enough, it would pay jurisdiction j to subsidize jurisdiction i to push T^i beyond the point where $\partial U^i_N / \partial \bar{Y}^i_P = 0$.

In a two-jurisdiction model, the appropriate subsidies could, in principle, be offered by each jurisdiction to the other without central government involvement. But with many jurisdictions, each has an incentive to be a free-rider on the others' payments to jurisdiction i. We thus have a standard kind of public-goods problem with central government intervention needed to achieve an efficient outcome.

As we noted in the Introduction, there is a second line of argument for vesting a primary responsibility for poor relief with the central government: the claim that income levels of the poor are a national public good. In its strongest form, this argument would assert that individuals care equally about the well-being of the poor irrespective of their location. It is difficult, however, to find compelling empirical support for such a claim. Individuals contribute to national (and global) charities to assist the poor, but much (and perhaps most) of such giving has a largely local orientation. Our conjecture is that the appropriate way to characterize the utility functions of the nonpoor would involve, as arguments in these functions, weighted levels of income of the poor with heavier weights attached to the poor in one's own jurisdiction. However, in the absence of more compelling evidence in support of the national public-good argument, we are hesitant to put much reliance on it as a justification for a heavily centralized system of assistance to the poor.

There is, however, another normative argument for central involvement in poor relief that we find more persuasive. Returning to our earlier case of complete immobility of the poor, we recall that the equilibrium support level in our model represents the level of transfers for which we make no *nonpoor* individual better off without making another person worse off; it is the Pareto-efficient level of transfers for the group of nonpoor residents in the jurisdiction. Were we to take the well-being of the poor into consideration by, for example, the maximization of some social-welfare function that included the welfare of all the residents in the jurisdiction, we would presumably determine an optimal level of transfers that is greater than that based solely on the tastes of the nonpoor. From this perspective, we can argue that the equilibrium level of support in the immobility case is less than the socially optimal level; we might take it as a kind of lower bound for the optimal level of transfers. If we now introduce some degree of mobility of the poor, we are likely to get (as we found in the analysis) payment levels that are, on average, less than in the immobility case. This suggests a presumption that levels of assistance to the poor under a wholly decentralized system (at least in the absence of quite stringent residency requirements) will be suboptimal and points to the need for some form of central participation in poor relief. As the analysis indicated earlier, however, there is no guarantee that the movement from a decentralized to a wholly centralized system of support will result in increased levels of transfer payments – although there may be some reason (as our simulations suggest) to expect this as a likely outcome. As an alternative, one can argue for a system of matching grants by which means the central government would effectively reduce the 'price' of transfers in each local jurisdiction.

Finally, we would note another argument for a central role in assisting the poor based on a quite different kind of social value judgment. As we found in the first section of the paper, a decentralized equilibrium would involve varying levels of support for the poor with higher payment levels in jurisdictions where the poor are a relatively small fraction of the population. If we were to allow for varying incomes and tastes across jurisdictions, we would have a further source of variation in local levels of poor relief. While we might justify such variation in support levels on grounds of economic efficiency, there are other criteria for social justice that render such differentials in the treatment of the poor objectionable. Stigler (1957), for example, has voiced such an objection quite strongly; he argues that the redistribution '... decision must be in some sense a national decision, for the proper amount of redistribution, *even if rich and poor were chained to their communities* [our emphasis], could not depend upon the accidents of income composition of a particular community' (p. 217). Some will take issue with Stigler on this matter, but as the argument suggests, the preferred intergovernmental structure for assisting the poor is not solely an economic matter. It will depend to some extent on various social values concerning, for example, the acceptability of substantial geographical variation in levels of support payments.[14]

Whatever one concludes concerning these supplementary arguments for a central role in poor relief, the analysis in this paper points to a basic source of inefficiency in decentralized systems stemming from the mobility of the poor. One mechanism to circumvent these distortions is to prohibit such migration, as was the case under the English Poor Laws. However, this really is not an option any longer in most countries. In the United States, for example, the U.S. Supreme Court has struck down residency requirements for assistance payments. But, more generally, there are compelling social and economic arguments for eliminating impediments to mobility. Migration of transfer recipients exists and must be taken into account in the design and implementation of assistance programs. And this suggests the need, strictly on grounds of economic efficiency, for central intervention to internalize the

[14]Gramlich (1985), for instance, has used his estimates of the U.S. welfare system to predict the response of support levels for the poor to sets of matching rates to internalize spillovers. His estimates suggest that preferences for support levels vary dramatically among the states such that even in the presence of a sensible matching system, payment levels would vary quite widely across the states. He finds these results sufficiently troubling on grounds of social justice to abandon such a scheme; he recommends instead a system with centrally mandated minimum levels of support. States would be free to supplement these national minima.

externalities inherent in decentralized choice. As discussed earlier in this section, the pure economics of the matter suggests a system of matching grants to local jurisdictions to remedy the distortion.

References

Blank, Rebecca M., 1983, Welfare, wages and migration: An analysis of locational choice by female-headed households, unpublished paper.

Blaug, Mark, 1963, The myth of the old poor law and the making of the new, Journal of Economic History 23, 151–184.

Boadway, Robin W. and David E. Wildasin, 1984, Public sector economics, Second edition (Little, Brown and Co., Boston, MA).

Bradford, David F. and Wallace E. Oates, 1974, Suburban exploitation of central cities and governmental structure, in: Harold Hochman and George Peterson, eds., Redistribution through public choice (Columbia University Press, New York), 43–92.

Buchanan, James M., 1974, Who should distribute what in a Federal System? in: Harold Hochman and George Peterson, eds., Redistribution through public choice (Columbia University Press, New York), 22–42.

Cebula, Richard J., 1974, Interstate migration and the Tiebout hypothesis: An analysis according to race, sex, and age, Journal of the American Statistical Association, 876–879.

Cebula, Richard J., Robert M. Kohn and Richard K. Vedder, 1973, Some determinants of interstate migration of blacks, 1965–1970, Western Economic Journal 11, 500–505.

Cloward, R.A. and F.F. Piven, 1968, Migration, politics and welfare, Saturday Review, 31–35.

Curran, C., 1977, Migration and welfare: An analysis of their relationship, Industrial Journal of Economics, 1–16.

Fraser, Derek, ed., 1976, The new poor law in the nineteenth century (St. Martin's Press, New York).

Gallaway, Lowell E., R.F. Gilbert and P.E. Smith, 1967, The economics of labor mobility: An empirical analysis, Western Economic Journal 5, 211–223.

Gramlich, Edward M., 1982, An econometric examination of the New Federalism, Brookings Papers on Economic Activity, 327–370.

Gramlich, Edward M., 1985, Reforming U.S. Fiscal Federalism arrangements, in: John Quigley and Daniel Rubinfeld, eds., American domestic priorities: An economic appraisal (University of California Press, Berkeley, CA), 34–69.

Gramlich, Edward M. and Deborah S. Laren, 1984, Migration and income redistribution responsibilities, Journal of Human Resources 19, 489–511.

Grewal, Bhajan and Russell Mathews, 1983, Federalism, locational surplus, and the redistributive role of subnational governments, unpublished paper.

Kaun, David E., 1970, Negro migration and unemployment, Journal of Human Resources 5, 191–207.

Kumar, Rishi, 1977, More on non-white migration, welfare levels, and the political process, Public choice 32, 151–154.

Ladd, Helen F. and Fred C. Doolittle, 1982, Which level of government should assist the poor?, National Tax Journal 35, 323–336.

Marshall, J.D., 1968, The old poor law, 1795–1834 (Macmillan, London).

Oates, Wallace E., 1972, Fiscal Federalism (Harcourt, Brace, Jovanovich, New York).

Oates, Wallace E., 1977, An economist's perspective on Fiscal Federalism, in: W. Oates, ed., The political economy of Fiscal Federalism (Heath-Lexington, MA), 3–20.

Orr, Larry L., 1976, Income transfers as a public good: An application to AFDC, American Economic Review 66, 359—371.

Pauly, Mark V., 1973, Income redistribution as a local public good, Journal of Public Economics 2, 35–58.

Peltzman, Sam, 1980, The growth of government, Journal of Law and Economics 23, 209–287.

Southwick, Lawrence, 1981, Public welfare programs and recipient migration, Growth and Change 12, 22–32.

Stigler, George, 1957. The tenable range of functions of local government, in: Joint economic committee, U.S. Congress, Federal expenditure policy for economic growth and stability (U.S. Government Printing Office, Washington, DC), 213–219.

Tate, William E., 1969. The parish chest (Cambridge University Press, London).

Tiebout, Charles, 1956. A pure theory of local expenditures, Journal of Political Economy 64, 416–424.

Tresch, Richard W., 1981, Public finance: A normative theory (Business Publications, Plano, Texas).

U.S. Bureau of the Census, 1985, Money income of households, families, and persons in the United States: 1983, Current population reports, Series P-60, No. 146.

Varian, Hal R., 1980, Redistributive taxation as social insurance, Journal of Public Economics 14, 49–68.

[6]

THE NEW FEDERALISM: AN ECONOMIST'S VIEW

Wallace E. Oates

Measures adopted to produce greater equality are, however, exceedingly unsuitable for local authorities. The smaller the locality the more capricious and ineffectual are likely to be any efforts it may make to carry out such a policy. It seems clearly desirable that all such measures should be applied to the largest possible area, and that subordinate authorities should be left to act, like the individual, from motives of self-interest.

Edwin Cannan (1896)

Financial assistance to the poor is a legitimate responsibility of States and localities.

President Reagan (1982)

In his State of the Union address, President Reagan identified the basic premise of the New Federalism: "During the past 20 years, what had been a classic division of functions between the Federal Government and the States and localities has become a confused mess. Traditional understandings about the roles of each level of government have been violated." The source of the problem has been the intrusion of the federal government into many state and local matters with a consequent blurring of the responsibilities for providing various public services. Such sharing of functions "results in neither the Federal or other levels of government being respon-

---

Cato Journal, Vol. 2, No. 2 (Fall 1982). Copyright © Cato Institute. All rights reserved.

The author is Professor of Economics at the University of Maryland, where he is associated with the Bureau of Business and Economic Research, and the Department of Economics, College Park 20742.

sible." In response, the President proposed "to clean up this mess" and to initiate "a major effort to restore American Federalism."

A determination of the proper structure of the federal system requires a coherent view of the appropriate roles of different levels of government. I shall turn first in this paper to the general issue of the assignment of functions in a federal system and subsequently to a description of the administration's proposals and an analysis of their likely effects on the functioning of state and local (and particularly urban) governments. I should emphasize at the outset that the analysis involves both positive and normative elements: At certain points, I seek *solely* to describe or predict the consequences of various components of the New Federalism proposals, while at other junctures I attempt to pass judgment on these prospects based on a prescriptive model of fiscal federalism.

The Division of Functions Among Levels of Government

Like the President, I have never been very comfortable with the popular "marble-cake" perspective on federal forms of government, which sees the functions of the public sector cutting across the layers of government in largely unpredictable and unsystematic ways. This view is neither very helpful in setting forth prescriptions for the vertical structuring of the government sector nor, I believe, fully satisfactory in describing its operation. Admittedly, the division of functions among levels of government is not subject to a precise and unchanging definition. But we can, from an economic perspective at least, propose some general guidelines that possess both normative and positive significance.

The standard textbook in public finance posits three economic functions for the public sector as a whole:

(1) The macroeconomic stabilization function, consisting of the use of various policies to stabilize the economy at high levels of employment with reasonable price stability;

(2) The distribution function of amending the market-determined distribution of income and wealth to one which better satisfies our objectives of social equity (particularly of providing adequate assistance to the poor);

(3) The allocation function, which entails the provision of certain goods and services (like national defense and a system of courts) that for various reasons would not be forthcoming at appropriate levels from the private sector of the economy.

THE NEW FEDERALISM

The peculiarly federal problem in this framework is the proper assignment of these functions to different levels of government.[1] Although there exists considerable controversy over the proper conduct of macroeconomic stabilization policy, there is general recognition that the responsibility for this first function must rest with the central government. Monetary control must be exercised at the central level; likewise, there is little potential for decentralized levels of government to use their fiscal instruments of spending and taxation to smooth explicitly cyclical fluctuations in levels of output and employment. Cyclical swings in economic activity are generally national in scope, and only the federal government has the policy tools to deal with them.

Likewise, there are serious constraints on decentralized levels of government in the pursuit of income redistribution. The high degree of mobility within national borders implies that one jurisdiction cannot tax a certain group significantly more heavily than elsewhere without creating incentives to move. A city, for example, that undertakes an aggressive program of taxation to provide generous support for the poor exposes itself to an influx of low-income households to take advantage of this support and an exodus of the well-to-do to escape relatively high tax bills. In short, mobility within a federal system imposes real constraints on the scope for decentralized redistributive policies. A community may wish collectively to establish what it sees as adequate support for its low-income residents, but be unable to do so because of the prospective movement of economic units that such a program would encourage. In this way, mobility may effectively prevent a community from doing what its members want to do.

At the same time, I don't wish to overstate the case. There is obviously some potential for modest redistributive programs. Moreover, as the size of the jurisdiction increases, the scope for assistance to the poor tends to expand; states obviously have greater possibilities for such policies than do individual municipalities. Edwin Cannan's position (noted at the outset of the paper and based on British experience with the locally administered Poor Laws) may, perhaps, be too strong. Yet the point remains that the scope for decentralized programs for support of the poor is circumscribed. Even where the costs of mobility are, in fact, sufficiently high to allow significant income transfers, the *perceptions* of state and local policymakers as to possible detrimental results can be sufficient to rule out their

[1]For a more detailed treatment of the assignment issue, see Wallace Oates, *Fiscal Federalism* (New York: Harcourt Brace Jovanovich, 1972), chap. 1.

adoption. Simply the threat of business and higher-income residents relocating (or not entering the jurisdiction in the first place) in response to relatively high levels of taxation exercises a sobering restraint on tax policy. State and local governments are acutely aware of the problem of tax competition.

In addition to this constraint on decentralized income redistribution, there is a second kind of economic argument for a basic central role in the funding of income-maintenance programs. This argument is based on the presumed concern of individuals with the alleviation of poverty in all parts of the nation. In the economist's jargon, assistance to the poor possesses some of the properties of a "public good" in that such assistance in one state confers not only benefits directly to the recipients themselves, but also contributes to the well-being of the non-poor across all states.[2] From this perspective, support from the central government becomes the instrument through which the national concern with poverty expresses itself in the income-maintenance programs in the individual states.

Finally, on purely equity grounds, one can contend that a "fair" resolution of the poverty problem requires central-government participation. Poverty is, in a fundamental sense, a national problem; its level and geographical pattern are inextricably interwoven with a diverse set of national economic and social policies. Moreover, the poor are unevenly distributed across the nation; in 1975, for example, the incidence of poverty in several southern states was more than twice that in states like Massachusetts and Minnesota. And it is precisely those states with the highest incidence of poverty that have the least fiscal capacity or ability to provide for the needs of the poor. To place the responsibility for support of the poor with the states and localities implies widely divergent levels of assistance for low-income households across jurisdictions or substantially different tax burdens on the non-poor. In this way, it seems unfair to allow certain higher-income individuals to avoid their share of the burden of financing income-maintenance programs by locating in states or localities with a relatively low incidence of poverty. A fair system, in this view, requires central funding of assistance to the poor that spreads the burden evenly over the non-poor residents of the nation.

[2]For a rigorous formulation of this argument, see H. Hochman and J. Rodgers, "Pareto Optimal Redistribution," *American Economic Review* 59 (September 1969):542–57. In this formulation, the income levels of the poor enter directly into the utility functions of the non-poor; contributions to the poor by one individual (or one state) thus produce external benefits in that they increase the utility of the other non-poor. This creates the usual sorts of free-rider problems associated with the provision of a public good.

THE NEW FEDERALISM

The raison d'être for decentralized government is found in the allocation function. For various services of primarily local interest, there is a compelling case for local provision in accordance with the tastes or preferences of local residents. As de Tocqueville observed over a century ago, "In great centralized nations the legislator is obliged to give a character of uniformity to the laws, which does not always suit the diversity of customs and of districts."[3] Decentralized provision of such services tailored to local preferences can significantly enhance well-being as compared with a "unitary" solution requiring uniform levels of services across all jurisdictions.[4] State and local governments are in a better position to respond to the specific needs of their constituencies for a wide range of services, including localized transport systems, refuse collection, police and fire protection, etc. At the same time, there are, of course, certain "public goods" that are national in character (national defense and foreign policy being the classic cases); for this class of goods and services, the central government must determine levels of provision.

The perspective that emerges from this economic approach to the structure of the federal system is one in which the central government assumes the primary responsibility for the stabilization and distribution functions and in which the allocation function is shared in such a way that different levels of government provide those services whose range of benefits and costs are confined to the residents of their respective jurisdictions. In this way, a federal system can succeed, in de Tocqueville's words, in "combining the different advantages which result from the magnitude and the littleness of nations."[5]

The New Federalism: The Reagan Proposals

With this economic perspective on fiscal federalism as background, I turn next to the specifics of the administration's program for the restructuring of the U.S. federal system. The Reagan effort to redefine and clarify the respective roles of the different levels of government is embodied in four proposals:

1. A "swap" of the federal role in the support of the Aid to Families with Dependent Children (AFDC) and Food Stamp Programs in

[3]Alexis de Tocqueville, *Democracy in America* (New York: Vintage Books, 1945), vol. I, p. 169.

[4]For an exercise in the measurement of these welfare gains, see D. Bradford and Oates, "Suburban Exploitation of Central Cities and Governmental Structure," in H. Hochman and G. Peterson, eds., *Redistribution Through Public Choice* (New York: Columbia University Press, 1974), pp. 43–92.

[5]De Tocqueville, p. 168.

exchange for full federal assumption of the costs and administrative responsibility for Medicaid (which provides health care for low-income households). All of these programs are currently shared by the federal government and the states on a matching basis, with the federal share ranging from 50 to 77 percent.

2. A "turnback" to the states and localities of a variety of existing federal programs in the areas of education and training, social services, transportation, and community development.

3. The consolidation into more broadly defined "block" grants of a large number of specific categorical grant programs. Proposed block grants include child welfare, training and employment, rental rehabilitation, welfare administration, vocational and adult education, education for the handicapped, and rehabilitative services.

4. The creation of a "Federalism trust fund" from which the federal government would earmark the revenues from certain excise taxes and the windfall profits tax on oil for use by the states. This fund will eventually be phased out and will disappear after 1991 leaving the states the option of imposing their own excises to replace these funds or, alternatively, of cutting their spending.

This set of proposals reflects the administration's contention that the federal government has intervened in matters in which it has no legitimate business. In particular, the evolution of an elaborate system of categorical grants (with existing federal grant programs in excess of 500 distinct entities) has produced an intergovernmental fiscal system of "bewildering complexity." It is the view of the President, as expressed in his State of the Union message, that "this massive Federal grant-making system has distorted State and local decisions and usurped State and local functions." The thrust of the New Federalism is thus a move toward devolution, a move to disengage the federal government from its involvement in a broad range of domestic programs. As Governor Babbitt of Arizona has stated, "Congress ought to be worrying about arms control and defense instead of potholes in the streets. We might just have both an increased chance of survival and better streets."

The Administration's View of Fiscal Federalism

On first examination of the administration's proposals against the backdrop of our economic guidelines for the assignment of functions, there is one striking discrepancy: the proposed shift to the state and local sector of full responsibility for AFDC and Food Stamps. In fact, it is hard to find any rationale for the proposed swap of AFDC and

THE NEW FEDERALISM

Food Stamps for full funding of Medicaid. Assistance to the poor is one area where federal support seems essential. This has been recognized by economists and political scientists of both parties. Richard Nathan, former assistant director of OMB and a. Republican who generally supports the movement toward decentralization and the use of block grants, argues:

> The best long-run answer is to have the policies for transfer payments made at the national level, with the Federal government providing equalized grant-in-aid payments to state governments which administer some of these payments. . . . [Unrestricted grants to states for welfare] would isolate the most controversial and vulnerable group of welfare recipients. It could result in competition by the states whereby some states would hold down benefits and tighten eligibility standards in ways that could eventually result in higher concentrations of the poor in the states with the most adequate welfare benefits. . . . The fact that people and jobs move in a free society is the underlying reason why the burden of financing welfare benefits should be shared on an equitable basis by the society as a whole.[6]

In short, this is one facet of the New Federalism that involves a fundamental misunderstanding of the appropriate roles of different levels of governments – a misunderstanding that may well undermine efforts to provide adequately for the poor. The likely response at the state and local level will be a scaling down of such assistance; Senator Moynihan, putting it more strongly, sees it as effectively "abolishing" AFDC. While the administration's dissatisfaction with the deficiencies of existing welfare programs is easy to understand, it is crucial to recognize at the same time that the appropriate response is reform of these programs at the *federal* level, not the abdication of federal responsibility for assistance to the nation's poor.[7] A far more sensible "swap" is the one suggested by the National Governor's Association and the National Council of State Legislatures: full state responsibility for roads, police, and schools in exchange for federal assumption of welfare.

[6]Claude E. Barfield, *Rethinking Federalism* (Washington, D.C.: American Enterprise Institute, 1981), p. 71.

[7]A case for decentralization of public assistance to the poor has been made on the political grounds that federal programs are subject to "irresistible pressures" for redistribution. State and local government responsibility for this function, so the argument goes, is essential to hold these programs in check. The thrust of this argument, however, appears to be undercut by recent experience: Real levels of federally supported welfare programs have declined substantially over the past decade. Measured in constant dollars, the average monthly AFDC benefit, for example, declined by 56 percent between 1969 and 1980. Ibid., pp.72–3.

The administration's case for clarification and decentralization of "allocative functions" rests on firmer ground. The uncoordinated evolution of categorical grant programs has resulted in an enormously complex and overlapping system of intergovernmental grants that is badly in need of reform. The legitimacy of each of these programs on economic grounds must rest on the existence of a compelling national interest that transcends the concerns of state and local decision-makers. Undoubtedly, many existing categorical grant programs could not pass this test. It is, however, beyond the scope of this paper to examine these programs case-by-case to determine which among them can satisfy this criterion. Instead, I shall turn more broadly to the administration's proposals for grant consolidation and turnback as the basic mechanisms for the transition to the New Federalism. I begin with some background on the design of intergovernmental grants-in-aid.

The Economics of Intergovernmental Grants[8]

From an economic perspective, a system of intergovernmental grants has three objectives:

1. The encouragement of those state and local activities (e.g., basic research) whose benefits extend beyond jurisdictional borders;

2. The "equalization of fiscal capacity" to permit each jurisdiction to provide satisfactory levels of key public services with a level of fiscal effort that is not discernibly greater than that in other jurisdictions;

3. The establishment of a more efficient and equitable tax system for the public sector as a whole through some degree of revenue sharing (which effectively substitutes federal tax revenues for those from more distorting and regressive state-local forms of taxation).

It is important to recognize that these goals require quite different types of grants. To encourage certain programs with benefits on a national scale, the federal granting authority must adopt specific categorical grants that are carefully targeted on the individual activity. This calls typically for some form of matching grant that reduces the cost of the program to the recipient and thereby creates an incentive for its expansion. In contrast, equalizing grants and revenue sharing are not intended, in principle, to stimulate expenditures on specific programs (or in general). These objectives require unconditional or "lump-sum" grants that come to the recipient with no

---

[8]For a systematic analysis of the economic role of intergovernmental grants, see Oates, *Fiscal Federalism*, chap. 3.

THE NEW FEDERALISM

strings attached. In summary, we should expect a properly designed system of intergovernmental grants to include matching-grant programs that would encourage increased outputs where substantial "spillover benefits" exist and unconditional grants with larger allocations directed to those states or localities with relatively small tax bases.

As noted earlier, the New Federalism places heavy reliance on another form of grant: block grants.[9] The administration proposes to consolidate many narrowly defined categorical grant programs into block grants under which the federal aid is authorized for a broad range of activities within which the recipient chooses how to use the funds. The chief characteristic of block grants is the budgetary discretion they allow the recipient; state and local agencies would identify problems, design programs, and allocate monies within the broadly defined functional areas of the block grants.

Political scientist Michael Reagan contends that block grants represent a "reasonable compromise between the values of categorical grants and shared revenues" and that "such grants may be a useful way of centralizing policy while decentralizing administration and permitting considerable local choice and decision making on particular programs."[10] This description is, however, a bit misleading. An economic perspective suggests that in terms of their effects, block grants are typically equivalent to revenue sharing. Because of the "fungibility" of funds, block grants are effectively lump-sum monies; in general, there are no real (or binding) constraints on their use. Suppose, for example, that someone gives me $100 per month to spend on food. It is a simple matter, if I want to use these funds for other purposes, to substitute the grant for $100 of my own income that I would otherwise have spent on food consumption. I can then use the $100 for whatever I please so that it is as if the funds came with no strings attached. Likewise, block grants to state and local governments can easily replace state-local revenues that would have been used for these programs; the grant funds are thus effectively available for other programs or for state-local tax relief.

The one qualification to this equivalence condition is that block grants can constrain state and local budgetary decisions in the case where the grant exceeds the total that the recipients would have chosen to spend in the broad functional area of the grant. While this may occasionally occur, it must surely be the exception rather than the rule, particularly if the recipient exercises any budgetary inge-

[9]Barfield presents a useful discussion of the recent experience with block grants.
[10]*The New Federalism* (New York: Oxford University Press, 1975), p. 63.

nuity. The basic point, then, is that block grants should be viewed as essentially equivalent to revenue sharing. This is not to say that they are undesirable, but only that they should be seen for what they are.

The Effects of the New Federalism on the State-Local Sector

The proposed grant consolidation and turnbacks of programs to the states and localities might be thought to stimulate budgetary activity at these levels as state-local agencies step in to fill the formerly federal role in providing various services. Closer study, I think, suggests otherwise. In particular, the evidence indicates that existing federal grant programs have induced a significant budgetary response at state and local levels; the restructuring of the grant system will, I shall argue, eliminate much of this stimulus with a substantial contractionary impact on state and local budgets.

First, the consolidation of categorical grant programs into block grants (even if the dollar level of grant monies were unchanged, which they are not) would lessen the stimulative impact of the federal grant system on state-local expenditure. Economic theory, supported by a number of empirical studies, finds that categorical, matching grants induce a significantly larger budgetary response than nonmatching, lump-sum aid.[11] Matching grants for specific programs not only provide funds but, at the same time, lower the unit cost or price of the supported services and limit opportunities for the funds to leak into state or local tax relief. The empirical estimates, moreover, suggest that the magnitude of this stimulative effect is quite large, much larger than the effect of unconditional grants on state and local spending. Thus, the shift in the structure of the intergovernmental grant system away from categorical to block grants should, in itself, reduce the expansionary impact of federal grants on state-local budgets.[12]

Second, the eventual turnback of programs, along with sources of funding, is likely to have a net contractionary effect. The argument

---

[11]For a useful survey of the empirical work on the budgetary effects of intergovernmental grants, see Edward M. Gramlich. "Intergovernmental Grants: A Review of the Empirical Literature," in Oates, ed., *The Political Economy of Fiscal Federalism* (Lexington, Mass.: Heath-Lexington, 1977), pp. 214–240.

[12]This reduction in the stimulative effect of grants will probably be cushioned somewhat in the transition period by the existing clientele for the categorical-grant programs. States and localities may find, in the short run, that they expend a larger fraction of block-grant monies than purely unconditional funds to meet the expectations of certain groups who previously received support under the categorical programs. See Barfield, chap. 4.

THE NEW FEDERALISM

here is a bit more subtle and intriguing. Consider, for example, the elimination of a broad block grant for education accompanied by a reduction of the federal taxes that support this grant. The analysis from the preceding section suggests that we can regard the block grant monies as essentially unrestricted funds. The implication is that the loss of grant funds to a state or local jurisdiction is equivalent to a reduction in its revenue sharing allocation. At the same time, however, federal taxes are being cut so that (neglecting distributional effects) the jurisdiction's tax base is being increased by the same amount. The turnback exercise effectively takes unrestricted funds away with one hand and gives them back with the other.

From this perspective, one might conclude that turnbacks would have no net effect on state-local budgets. The implicit assumption here is that a dollar of unrestricted grant funds to a local jurisdiction should have the same effect on local spending as a dollar increase in private income. This seems reasonable, since in either case the disposable income of the community has increased by the same sum. It is not hard to demonstrate this equivalence formally; the theoretical literature shows that, subject to certain conditions, a lump-sum intergovernmental grant to a community is fully equivalent in all its effects to a federal tax cut directly to the individuals in the community.[13] This proposition is known among public-finance specialists as the "veil hypothesis" (i.e., an unconditional intergovernmental grant is a "veil" for a federal tax cut).

Empirical work has not, however, in this instance, confirmed the theory.[14] Instead, various studies of the effects of nonmatching aid find that unrestricted intergovernmental grants have a significantly more expansionary impact on state and local spending than do equivalent increases in private disposable incomes. This finding is known in the literature as the "flypaper effect" (i.e., money sticks where it hits). Moreover, it has been of considerable interest among public-finance scholars and has led to a lively exchange involving the development of competing theories and of further empirical work. Assuming that there is something to the flypaper effect, it follows that the budgetary impact of a reduction in block (unrestricted) grants accompanied dollar-for-dollar by federal tax cuts will not net out to zero; the contractionary effect of the reduced grants will more than offset

---

[13]D. Bradford and Oates, "The Analysis of Revenue Sharing in a New Approach to Collective Fiscal Decisions." *Quarterly Journal of Economics* 85 (August 1971): 416–39.

[14]See Gramlich.

the stimulus from increased private disposable income.[15] The implication of this proposition is that state and local governments will not increase their own levels of taxes sufficiently to offset fully the loss of grant revenues.

The bottom line is that both the consolidation of categorical grants into block grants and the turnback of grant programs and tax bases to state and local governments should work in the direction of a reduced stimulus to state-local expenditure. I should expect only a small fraction of the cutbacks in existing federal grant support to be replaced by increases in state and local taxation. Finally, I want to emphasize here that I am *not* arguing that this is necessarily an undesirable outcome. Whether state and local spending is, at present, excessive or deficient involves another set of issues. My intent here is purely descriptive: to predict the effect of the New Federalism programs (for ill or good) on the size of state-local budgets.

Urban Assistance: The Enterprise Zone Program

Although not specifically a part of the New Federalism, the recent administration proposal for the creation of enterprise zones to aid recovery of "the decaying areas of America's inner cities and rural towns" is relevant to intergovernmental fiscal efforts. The concept, which originated in Great Britain and has gained considerable support in the U.S. Congress, calls for the designation of specific zones for the application of special economic incentives to encourage new business investment.

The rationale for the zone approach to urban recovery has a number of facets. First, there is an economic efficiency argument involving neighborhood externalities. The argument envisions a continuing process of urban decay in which the closing and departure of firms and the associated loss of jobs and abandonment of buildings create a progressively more unfavorable environment for existing firms and any prospective new business enterprise. There is, in short, a kind of vicious circle that leads to a process of cumulative deterioration. To reverse this process requires special measures that endow the area with particular attractions for business in the expectation that the advent of new firms will eventually change the economic environment of the area and give the recovery a self-sustaining character. Second, there is an equity argument. The economic decay of center cities has left many of the urban poor without access to nearby jobs

---

[15]For a useful collection of studies exploring the flypaper effect and related issues, see P. Mieszkowski and W. Oakland, *Fiscal Federalism and Grants-in-Aid* (Washington, D.C.: The Urban Institute, 1979).

THE NEW FEDERALISM

at appropriate skill levels. Enterprise zones, it is argued, can bring such jobs to depressed areas (and may well be cheaper than the income transfers needed to support the poor and unemployed).

On March 23, 1982, President Reagan presented the specifics of his Enterprise Zone Tax Act to Congress. In his words, "The idea is to create a productive, free-market environment in economically-depressed areas by reducing taxes, regulations and other government burdens on economic activity." The major elements of the proposed program are:

1. Tax reductions and credits including a three- or five-percent investment tax credit for capital investments in personal property in an enterprise zone, a 10-percent tax credit for the construction or rehabilitation of commercial, industrial, or rental housing structures within a zone, tax credits for employers for new hirings in a zone (with an increased credit if the new employees are "disadvantaged individuals" when hired), elimination of capital-gains taxes, and certain other tax breaks;

2. Regulatory relief (largely unspecified but *not* including suspension of the minimum wage) at federal, state, and local levels;

3. Improved local services;

4. Involvement in the programs of neighborhood organizations.

The proposal has very little to say about the last three components of the program. This is, in part, because much of the initiative is to come from state and local levels. "Consistent with the Administration's policy of Federalism," Reagan said, "the Federal Government will not dictate to state and local governments what they must contribute to the zones. The program is designed for creative and innovative experiments by state and local governments within the zone areas." State and local authorities would nominate zones in a competitive application process; the Secretary of HUD would in turn select from the applications up to 25 zones in each of three years. The life of these zones would be determined by the nominating government, with a maximum duration of the federal incentives of 20 years plus a four-year phase-out period.

Does the Enterprise Zone program possess the potential for an economic rejuvenation of decayed inner-city areas? In addressing this question, it is important to recognize the limited character of the proposed program. The measures will apply only to certain designated zones in those cities (or "rural towns") which make application for support and whose applications are selected by the Secretary of HUD. This is not a broad-based program directing resources to all depressed urban areas. As Representatives Jack Kemp (R-N.Y.) and

Robert Garcia (D-N.Y.) said of their version of the bill: "It is no panacea. Neither is it intended as a substitute for other urban proposals. It is simply a relatively low-cost attempt to try something new, at a time when we can't turn our backs on any new approaches to unemployment and economic decay."[16] So the question must be whether or not enterprise zones can succeed in their more modest objective of stimulating economic development in selected areas.

This is not an easy question to answer in part because the program in each zone would have a distinctive character determined by the respective state and local authorities. However, there are a number of reasons for believing the potential of enterprise zones to be quite limited.

1. The basic premise of the program is that the choice of location for business investment is reasonably responsive to fiscal incentives. There is not much evidence to support this proposition. A number of economists have examined locational patterns of new investment in relation to fiscal differentials and haven't been able to find much.[17] This work is far from conclusive, but it would be fair to say, I think, that tax differentials do not seem to exert a substantial impact on business location.[18]

2. To the extent that certain firms are on the "margin," they may be induced to locate in a new enterprise zone. However, a large fraction of such businesses are likely already to be committed to the city in question; consequently, they may decide to locate in the zone instead of elsewhere in the city. In such instances, the program will simply rearrange economic activity within the city with little overall impact.

3. Some critics have emphasized that the program fails to address the crucial issue of making available new capital for investment in the zones. One survey of small urban businesses found their most pressing concern to be the shortage of available business capital

---

[16]"Enterprise Zone Strategy Keys on Senate," *Baltimore Sun,* April 5, 1982, p. A1.

[17]For a good survey of this body of research, see Oakland, "Local Taxes and Intraurban Industrial Location: A Survey," in G. Break, ed., *Metropolitan Financing and Growth Management Policies: Principles and Practice* (Madison: University of Wisconsin Press, 1978), pp. 13–30.

[18]In contrast, there is evidence that suggests considerable mobility of households in response to differentials in local services and taxes. One strand of this evidence is the finding of "capitalization" – the demonstrated willingness of individuals to pay more to live in jurisdictions with better services and lower taxes. See, for example, Oates, "The Effects of Property Taxes and Local Public Spending on Property Values: An Empirical Study of Tax Capitalization and the Tiebout Hypothesis." *Journal of Political Economy* 77 (November-December 1969): 957–71. A second line of work has detected

The New Federalism

manifested in high interest rates.[19] This, of course, is largely a matter of the existing state of the national economy.

4. What is perhaps more basic are the underlying obstacles to economic growth in depressed urban areas: crime, poor work habits, and a general air of demoralization. It seems unlikely that the proposed system of zones, relying heavily on tax credits, can convince large numbers of small businesses that new ventures in deteriorated urban neighborhoods are economically viable. This is not necessarily to condemn the proposed program, for it is obviously no simple matter to eradicate these fundamental obstacles to economic revitalization. It should, however, serve to temper our expectations.

5. Finally, it is worth noting the magnitude of the proposed spending on the program: $124 to $310 million in the first year. One professed objective of enterprise zones is to offset in part some of the effects of the Accelerated Cost Recovery System (ACRS), a part of the tax bill passed last summer, that apparently will benefit primarily the Sunbelt and suburbs. But the ACRS provisions are expected to cost the Treasury some $50 to $60 billion per year. It is hard to believe that a program the size of the administration's enterprise zones can go very far in offsetting the geographical impacts of ACRS or, more generally, in making a real dent in the problems faced by the older central cities.

Conclusion

It is time for a reexamination of the U.S. federal system with particular attention to the clarification of the responsibilities of the different levels of government and a long overdue restructuring of the intergovernmental grant system. The evolution of American federalism in recent decades has exhibited a distinctly helter-skelter character with a resulting maze of overlapping intergovernmental programs and blurring of functions. The administration's concern with a return to "first principles," involving a withdrawal of the federal government from excessive involvement in many basically state-local matters, is to be commended.

---

the movement over time of households away from fiscally disadvantaged communities to those providing net fiscal benefits. See J. R. Aronson and E. Schwartz, "Financing Public Goods and the Distribution of Population in a System of Local Governments," *National Tax Journal* 26 (June 1973): 137–60.

[19]"Enterprise Zones Proposal is Criticized," *Wall Street Journal*, April 12, 1982, p. 25.

CATO JOURNAL

At the same time, the more one probes into the specifics of the New Federalism, the more one becomes aware of the troubling absence of any vision or outline of the proper structure of our federal system. The administration has not provided any real guidelines for making the distinction among federal, state, and local responsibilities. There is, for example, no apparent principle underlying the proposed swap of welfare programs for Medicaid. Moreover, the attempt to shift the basic responsibility for income-maintenance programs to the state and local levels is, I believe, fundamentally misguided and puts in jeopardy the prospects of the nation's poor.

A further manifestation of this absence of vision is evident in the administration's approach to the consolidation of grant programs. While such consolidation is surely justified in many instances, it is not to be pursued indiscriminately. Many categorical grant programs have a sound rationale and perform an important function in terms of encouraging state and local activity on matters in which there exists a broader national interest. In such cases, a narrow program, carefully targeted on a quite specific objective and providing aid conditional on its use to promote that objective, is appropriate. To push such programs under the umbrella of block grants effectively undermines their role. What is needed is a careful assessment, program-by-program, to determine which categorical grant programs are the proper subject for consolidation (or extinction) and which have a legitimate role to play in our intergovernmental system – not a headlong rush into the consolidation of all accessible categoricals.

A return to "first principles" may well be desirable, but we do need some sense of what those principles are.

1 Decentralization in the Public Sector: An Empirical Study of State and Local Government

John Joseph Wallis and Wallace E. Oates

1.1 Introduction

Decentralized choice in the public sector (as in the private sector) provides an opportunity to increase economic welfare by tailoring levels of consumption to the preferences of smaller, more homogeneous groups. More centralized decisions typically involve relatively uniform levels of consumption that circumscribe the diversity of outputs needed to accommodate differences in tastes. The existing literature in local public finance has explored the normative theory of decentralization in substantial depth. The important Tiebout model, for example, describes the way in which mobile consumers through their location decisions can make use of decentralized choice in the public sector to enhance the efficiency of resource allocation.

The purpose of this paper is to explore empirically the extent and variation in fiscal decentralization in the state and local sector in the United States. The state-local sector exhibits wide variation in the relative roles of state and local government both over time and across states. In 1902, local governments accounted for 82 percent of the tax revenues in the state-local sector; by 1982, this had fallen to 43 percent.

John Joseph Wallis is assistant professor of economics at the University of Maryland and a faculty research fellow of the National Bureau of Economic Research. Wallace E. Oates is professor of economics at the University of Maryland, where he is also a member of the Bureau of Business and Economic Research.

We are grateful to our discussant, James Hines, and to the other participants of the NBER Conference on Fiscal Federalism for some very helpful comments on an earlier draft of this paper. We also thank our colleague Harry Kelejian for his counsel on some econometric issues. For their assistance in the assembling of our large data set, we are deeply indebted to Mark Eiswerth, Christopher Graves, Deborah Shiley, and Calvin Timmerman. Finally, we express our appreciation to the NBER for the support of this research.

6   John Joseph Wallis and Wallace E. Oates

Likewise, wide variations in the extent of fiscal decentralization are evident among states. In 1981, for example, state government spending in New York accounted for only 28 percent of total state-local expenditures in contrast to Vermont, where the state government share of spending was 60 percent.

In this paper, we shall investigate the extent to which the existing theory of decentralized fiscal choice can explain the observed patterns in the structure of the state-local sector both over time and across states. Our approach is to set forth the conditions that would enhance the potential welfare gains from a more decentralized public sector and then to see if the presence of these conditions is, in fact, associated with greater fiscal decentralization. Using a large panel data set of the U.S. state-local sector reaching back to 1902, we explore econometrically the variation both over time and across states in various measures of fiscal centralization.

In the first part of the paper we provide a historical overview of the trends in fiscal centralization during the twentieth century. A pervasive tendency toward centralization in the state-local "fisc" is evident; there are also some interesting regional differences with historical roots. In the second section, we discuss the circumstances that enhance the potential welfare gains from fiscal decentralization and formulate some specific testable hypotheses concerning the determinants of the optimal degree of decentralization. The third section then presents the findings from our econometric analysis, where we make use of the error-components approach to our panel data set to test the hypotheses. The final section of the paper offers some reflections on likely future tendencies in the centralization of the state-local sector. In addition, we include an appendix that describes our data base.

1.2   Trends in Fiscal Centralization in the State and Local Sector during the Twentieth Century

We begin our investigation of fiscal centralization with an overview of the trends in the vertical structure of the state and local sector during the present century. At the outset, we acknowledge the difficulty of developing a fully satisfactory measure of the extent of decentralization (see Oates 1972, 196–98). Available data essentially limit us to fiscal measures, and, following earlier work, we will use the fiscal share of the state government in the state-local sector as our measure of fiscal centralization.

Even this does not resolve all the ambiguities, since we can construct fiscal "centralization ratios" (i.e., the state share in the state-local fisc) on either an expenditure or revenue basis. Should we measure the relative importance of a level of government by the share of public revenues that it raises or by its share of public expenditures? The basic issue here is how to treat intergovernmental transfers of revenues. If we use a revenue measure, we attribute such funds to the grantor. This seems sensible if the grantor prescribes to a significant extent the use of the funds. However, where such funds are transferred unconditionally (say, under a revenue-sharing program) so that the grantor is simply a revenue-collection agent for the recipient. it may make more sense to attribute the funds to the transfer recipient. Since grants of both kinds are widely used in the public sector. we shall not opt for one measure over the other; instead we shall present fiscal centralization ratios in both revenue and expenditure terms and note where the two measures generate divergent results.

Table 1.1 presents the state and local government shares in public expenditure for selected years.[1] These are the respective shares in "direct expenditure" (that is, in disbursements to final recipients of government payments) so that intergovernmental transfers of funds are attributed to the recipient level of government. The most striking feature of table 1.1 is the dramatic increase in fiscal centralization that it reveals over the current century. The state share of state and local spending was only 12.4 percent in 1902; by 1982, this figure had risen to 40.5 percent. On closer inspection, however, the table reveals an interesting feature of the process of centralization: nearly all of this process seems to have taken place in the first half of the century. By 1952, the state share had risen to 35 percent (in fact, in 1950 this share was 39 percent). Since 1950 the state share in state and local sector expenditure has grown only very slightly.

What accounts for this trend toward centralization? There are logically three ways in which changes in these shares can occur: the services that states perform may have grown in fiscal terms relative to

Table 1.1   State and Local Government Shares in State–Local
             Expenditures for Selected Years (in percentages)

Year	State Share	Local Share
1902	12.4	87.6
1913	13.2	86.8
1922	19.2	80.8
1932	24.1	75.9
1942	32.6	67.4
1952	35.0	65.0
1962	36.1	63.9
1972	38.1	61.9
1982	40.5	59.5

Source: The figures from which these percentages were computed come from Tax Foundation. Inc., *Facts and Figures on Government Finance*. 23d biennial ed., (New York: Tax Foundation, Inc., 1986), Table D1, p. d3.

those of local governments; there may have been a shifting of services from local to state governments; or certain new services may have been introduced with a disproportionate assignment of these new services to the state government level. A closer investigation indicates that the explanation is largely a matter of the last of these alternatives: the state-local sector was called upon to provide a number of new services in the first half of the century with state governments playing the more important role. In particular, state governments over this period entered into the provision of highways, higher education, public welfare, and various retirement and unemployment compensation programs that account for the bulk of the expansion in the state share. For highways, for example, state governments in the aggregate spent only $4 million in 1902; with the advent of the automobile, state level expenditures rose to $2.56 billion by 1952. This represents an increase in the state share of total state and local spending on highways from 2.0 percent in 1902 to 55 percent in 1952. The relative role of state government in education likewise exhibits a striking expansion. In 1902 we find state governments in the aggregate spending only $17 million on education; by 1952 this figure has become $1.49 billion. This represents an increase in the state share of educational spending from 7 percent in 1902 to 18 percent in 1952. The major portion of this spending is for public higher education in which state governments have taken the lead.

Similarly, state governments in the first half of the century greatly expanded their efforts in the provision of public welfare support. Aggregate spending by state governments on public welfare grew from $10 million in 1902 to $1.4 billion by 1952, representing an increase in the state share of public welfare expenditures from 27 percent in 1902 to 51 percent in 1952. Much of this growth, incidentally, took place during the New Deal years when the federal government relied heavily on state governments for the operation of relief programs (see Wallis 1984, 1987). Finally, there was a rapid expansion of state insurance trust fund expenditures, including unemployment compensation and retirement benefits (again associated with the New Deal), from virtually zero in 1902 to $1.4 billion in 1952.

We thus find that the centralizing trend in state and local expenditures is largely a phenomenon of the first half of the century and represents an expansion of state governments into the provision of several major new public services. State governments, in fact, played a very minor fiscal role at the turn of the century, but in the ensuing 50 years they became an equal fiscal partner in the state and local sector. This expansion of the relative role of the states would seem not to be purely politically motivated; there is a sound economic case for state provision of the services that expanded so rapidly in this period. The need for a highway system to link localities within a state clearly calls for a level of government transcending that with a purely local orientation. Likewise, the development of a viable system of higher education reaching out beyond major urban centers requires a supra-local presence. And, finally, as has been argued in the pubic finance literature (e.g., Oates 1972), there are serious constraints on the ability of local governments to provide assistance to the poor; the need for programs at higher levels of government for poor relief is widely recognized.

If we examine the trends in fiscal centralization from the perspective of revenues rather than expenditures, we find roughly the same picture except that levels of centralization are generally a bit higher for revenues than for expenditures. Table 1.2 reports state and local shares in revenues from own sources. The major difference between tables 1.1 and 1.2 is that the latter attributes intergovernmental revenues to the level of government that is the source (not the recipient) of the funds. Using a revenue measure of fiscal centralization, we find again a quite dramatic trend toward fiscal centralization. The state share of state-local revenues from own sources was only 17.6 percent in 1902; by 1982 this had risen to 56.8 percent. Thus, state governments shifted from being a relatively minor partner in the fund-raising function of the state and local sector at the beginning of the century to becoming the major partner by 1982. Once again, we find that the bulk of this centralizing process took place in the first half of the century; by 1952, the state's share in state and local revenues was already over 50 percent. Since midcentury, there has been some further centralization of revenues, but the trend has slowed significantly. This has been accompanied by a continuing increase in the reliance on state intergovernmental grants to local governments. Table 1.3 documents this trend with figures indicating the fraction of local revenues coming from intergovernmental transfers; the rise in this figure over the first half of the century has continued since 1950.

Table 1.2   State and Local Government Shares in State–Local Revenues from Own Sources for Selected Years (in percentages)

Year	State Share	Local Share
1902	17.6	82.4
1913	17.8	82.2
1922	24.4	75.6
1932	29.7	70.3
1942	48.9	51.1
1952	50.4	49.6
1962	48.9	51.1
1972	52.9	47.1
1982	56.8	43.2

Source: **Same as Table 1.1.**

10   **John Joseph Wallis and Wallace E. Oates**

Table 1.3   Intergovernmental Transfers as a Percentage of Local Government
                  Revenues for Selected Years

1902	6.6
1913	6.0
1922	8.3
1932	14.3
1942	27.8
1952	31.6
1962	30.6
1972	37.7
1982	41.5

Source: Tax Foundation, *Facts and Figures,* Table F14, p. f19.

The fiscal evolution of the state and local sector thus reveals a very
striking tendency toward centralization in both spending and revenues
over the first half of the century. This trend has moderated since 1950,
however, with only a very slight increase in the state share of fiscal
activity since then.

In addition to a strong secular trend toward a more centralized state
and local sector, there is also a persistent and interesting historical
pattern of centralization across regions. The southern regions of the
country in 1902 had much more concentrated public sectors than did
the other regions of the nation. Table 1.4 presents our fiscal centrali-

Table 1.4   Fiscal Concentration Measures by Region, by Year — 1902 to 1982

Region	Revenues/Expenditures				
	1902	1922	1942	1962	1982
New England	0.195	0.259	0.494	0.468	0.591
	0.191	0.237	0.450	0.454	0.523
Mid-Atlantic	0.159	0.194	0.455	0.405	0.526
	0.131	0.198	0.338	0.282	0.358
East North Central	0.155	0.187	0.517	0.441	0.539
	0.139	0.194	0.333	0.298	0.384
West North Central	0.172	0.209	0.448	0.432	0.546
	0.165	0.221	0.357	0.386	0.425
South Atlantic	0.284	0.311	0.620	0.604	0.612
	0.268	0.305	0.487	0.421	0.452
East South Central	0.281	0.284	0.597	0.584	0.619
	0.273	0.281	0.429	0.473	0.481
West South Central	0.248	0.272	0.629	0.612	0.605
	0.241	0.255	0.466	0.472	0.446
Mountain	0.246	0.335	0.529	0.534	0.583
	0.238	0.307	0.441	0.430	0.411
Pacific	0.179	0.241	0.571	0.515	0.570
	0.186	0.260	0.430	0.379	0.396

Note: First row for each region is revenue measure; second row for each region is
expenditure measure.

zation measures for both expenditures and revenues for twenty year intervals from 1902 to 1982. In 1902 state governments in the South Atlantic and East South Central regions accounted for roughly twice as much of the state-local fisc as did state governments in the Mid-Atlantic or East North Central regions; other regions fell between these two extremes. While regional differences have narrowed with time, the southern regions still remained slightly more centralized in 1982.

These regional differences may reflect to some extent the variation in the underlying economic, social, and demographic factors that we discuss in the next section. There are, however, strong historical differences in the structure of the state-local sector that must be kept in mind. Colonial land laws were particularly important. Although both the southern and northern colonies began under the same Virginia Company charter, the two regions developed distinctly different ways of establishing private property rights in land. In Virginia and surrounding colonies, an individual was allowed to decide which specific parcel of land he would take title to. People took their 50-acre head rights, for example, in the best bottomland available, leaving hilltops and scrub land to the colonial government.

In the New England colonies, under the joint influence of the Virginia Company charter and the Massachusetts Bay Colony charter, the colonial government generally made large grants of land to towns. These grants were typically ten miles square and were made to an already existing group of prospective townsmen. The colonial land grant was to the town, not to individuals, and the town council then distributed lands to the members of the community (occasionally selling land directly). This method of land distribution accounts for (perhaps it would be better to say "was endogenous with") the importance of community leaders and institutions like the local minister and the church, as well as for the vigor of the typical New England town meeting.

The New England method of distributing land led naturally to a very active local political life, and it created local governments which had, from the very beginning, considerable real assets at their disposal. In contrast, the process of distributing land in the South did very little to encourage local governments. In many areas large land owners were the effective government, and local agreement to levy taxes on themselves would only occur on issues on which there was considerable agreement. Indeed, the effects of land policy are still visible on the maps of southern states today. The numerous small counties and tortured boundary lines follow the borders of the existing private property distribution at the time the counties were formed. This contrasts sharply with the geometric precision of New England townships.

The compromise between northern, southern, and other interests that led to the Northwest Ordinances of 1785 and 1789 created a method for establishing private property rights over federal lands in the Old

Northwest and eventually the trans-Mississippi West that followed the New England model in geometry and the southern model in individuality: land was sold in rectangular plots, but sold directly to individuals. And, importantly, the ordinances retained the New England principle of providing for the support of local government by allotting fixed amounts of land for the support of schools and other public functions.

The result of this historical development was relatively strong local governments in the northern and western regions of the country and relatively weak local governments in the southern regions. These regional differences persisted well into the twentieth century. Unlike the trend toward centralization (most of which had taken place by mid-century), the near equalization of fiscal centralization ratios across regions appears to be a phenomenon of the latter half of the century. Centralization ratios take a sharp jump upwards between 1922 and 1942, but they retain their pattern of regional differences into the 1960s.

1.3   The Economics of Decentralization in the Public Sector: Toward Some Testable Hypotheses

The decentralized provision of public services provides a means to increase the level of economic welfare by differentiating levels of public outputs according to the demands of local constituencies. The magnitude of the potential gains from such decentralization depends upon the variation in the optimal levels of public outputs across jurisdictions. If the optimal level of output varies little from one jurisdiction to another, then the welfare losses from providing a uniform level of output of public services across all jurisdictions will tend to be relatively small. The case for decentralized provision will, in such instances, be less compelling than where desired outputs vary widely from one area to another.[2]

The general approach in this study will be to identify the conditions that enhance the welfare gains from decentralization and then to see (in the next section) if these conditions can "explain" in econometric terms the observed variation in fiscal decentralization in the state and local sector both over time and across states. The primary determinants of the optimal degree of fiscal decentralization encompass three classes of variables:

1. Conditions relating to the land area of the state, the size of its population, and the geographical distribution of the population
2. The level of income and wealth in the state
3. The extent of diversity of tastes for public outputs and their geographical distribution among the population

We shall consider each of these classes of determinants in turn and see what they imply in terms of testable hypotheses.

The size of the state both in terms of population and land area has potentially important implications for the optimal degree of decentralization. That is, in certain ways, a fairly obvious point. A large jurisdiction with a sizeable population offers more opportunities for welfare-enhancing decentralization. As John Stuart Mill observed over a century ago in his tract on *Representative Government*, "There is a limit to the extent of country which can advantageously be governed, or even whose government can be conveniently superintended, from a single centre." This immediately suggests

Hypothesis 1: The larger the size of a state in terms of land area, the less centralized, other things equal, should be its public sector.

However, there is a bit more to the economics of size and geography. Many public services have important economies of scale with respect to population size. For services with important dimensions of "publicness" (i.e., where units of output can be consumed by additional persons without reducing the level of consumption of anyone else), cost per unit of services *per person* varies inversely with the size of the population. In relatively small states, population size at decentralized levels may simply be insufficiently large to exhaust the available economies of scale. In such instances, it may be more economical to provide these services at the state rather than the local level. This suggests

Hypothesis 2: The larger the population of the state, other things equal, the less centralized should be its public sector.

More than simply aggregate population size is at issue here. The way the population of a state is distributed among its local jurisdictions is of central importance for the optimal degree of decentralization. The point is that to take advantage of existing economies of scale with respect to population at the local level requires a certain concentration of economic units. Certain public outputs (including things like zoos, museums, and various specialized services) involve significant indivisibilities; the first "unit" of output of such goods may require a substantial expenditure. Even if all persons have similar demand functions for such a good, it does not become efficient for a locality to provide the good until the sum of the individual demands exceeds its cost. In short, the range of services provided at the local level will depend on the extent of the concentration of the population in urban areas.

In an intriguing study of one metropolitan area, Schmandt and Stephens (1960) found that the number of distinct "subfunctions" (or particular services) that were provided in a municipality was strongly and positively associated with population size. The larger a local jurisdiction, the greater the range of services it provides. This suggests that if the population of a state is thinly spread throughout its land area, there will be a relatively small role for local government. In contrast, the concentration of population in urban areas will make it economically desirable for the local sector to provide a wider range of services.

Hypothesis 3: The larger the fraction of a state's population residing in urban areas, the less centralized, other things equal, should be the state and local sector.

The second set of considerations influencing fiscal decentralization involves the level of income and wealth in the state. Higher levels of income seem to have two effects on the extent of decentralization— effects that work in opposite directions. First, it has been observed in a number of empirical studies (Martin and Lewis 1956; Oates 1972; Kee 1977; Oates 1985; Bahl and Nath 1986) that the higher-income, developed countries have much more decentralized public sectors than do the poorer, developing countries. In one of these studies using data for the mid-1970s, Oates (1985) finds that for a sample of 18 industrialized nations, the mean central government share of total public expenditure is .65; for the corresponding sample of 25 developing countries, the central share is .89. Higher-income countries seem to have a much stronger tendency toward (or history of) decentralization in the public sector. Several explanations have been suggested for this pervasive finding. Wheare (1964), for example, contends that decentralization is expensive and that a country must be relatively affluent to adopt a relatively decentralized form of government. Alternatively, Martin and Lewis (1956) suggest that centralization is necessary in the early stages of development to economize on scarce administrative talent.

This particular line of argument, however, does not seem relevant to a study of the state and local sector in the United States, for the finding of a significant negative relationship between per capita income and fiscal decentralization is limited to comparisons of developed and developing countries. Where the sample is limited to higher-income, developed countries, the relationship between income and decentralization disappears (see Kee 1977; Oates 1985). This suggests that among the states within the U.S., which all fall within the "developed" classification on a world scale, this "income effect" on decentralization is unlikely to be of importance.

There is, however, a second way in which the level of income can influence the extent of fiscal decentralization. It has been observed that the propensity to engage in income redistribution has a relatively high income elasticity. Wealthier polities tend to provide much more in the way of transfers (as a fraction of total income) to lower-income (and other) groups. Local governments tend to be notably circumscribed in their capacity to redistribute income to poor economic units because of the mobility of potential recipients (and sources) across local jurisdictions (see, e.g., Brown and Oates, 1987). For this and other reasons, programs aimed at assisting the poor tend to be more centralized than those involving direct services. On these grounds we might expect higher-income states, other things equal, to have more centralized state and local sectors.

Hypothesis 4: The higher the level of per capita income in a state, the more centralized, other things equal, should be its public sector, as a result of a higher level of involvement in redistributive programs.

The third set of considerations relating to fiscal decentralization encompasses the effects of variations in tastes and demands for public services. The general idea here is a straightforward and seemingly unambiguous one: the greater the diversity of tastes and demands among economic units, the more likely, other things being equal, will be significant differences in the optimal levels of outputs across local jurisdictions. This suggests that we seek some proxy variables for taste and demand differences for public services.

We expect the demand for public (like private) goods typically to vary positively with income; thus, one determinant of the variation in demand should be the degree of inequality in the distribution of income. This suggests that the value of the Gini coefficient will be positively associated with the variation in the demand for public services.

Hypothesis 5: The more unequal the distribution of income, the less centralized, other things equal, should be the state and local sector.

Other proxy measures for the variation in demand for public services are less clear. We expect various socioeconomic differences in the population to manifest themselves in varying demands for public services. Variation in such things as the age distribution of the population, racial composition, and religious affiliations may well contribute to an increased diversity in demands for publically provided services. There may exist, for example, a certain life-cycle pattern to demand for public services with younger households with children present exhibiting a higher demand for things like public education than older households. Or, to take another possible case, states with a substantial mixture of religious groups, some of which provide their own schools, may tend to have widely varying demands for public education. While all this admittedly requires closer examination, we take as a "working hypothesis"

Hypothesis 6: States exhibiting more in the way of diversity as indicated by socioeconomic indicators should tend to have, other things equal, more decentralized public sectors.

This last set of considerations relating to the extent of differences in demands for public services is subject to one important qualification. In order for the variation in demand for local services among the population of a state to manifest itself in the form of welfare gains from increased decentralization, there must be some tendency for people with similar demands to be grouped together in local jurisdictions. If the intrastate diversity in individual demands is mirrored in each local jurisdiction, then there will be little in the way of differences in demands aggregated at the local level. It is where individuals separate themselves into groups with relatively homogeneous demands for public services (as in the Tiebout model) that the welfare gains from fiscal decentralization reflect the diversity of household demands. This suggests a further reason for expecting the optimal degree of decentralization to vary directly with the extent of urbanization within a state. It is within metropolitan areas where individuals can conveniently work in one jurisdiction (the central city) and live in another (a suburban community) that the opportunity for sorting of households in residential communities according to demands for local services has its greatest potential.

As will be discussed in the following section, our measures of socioeconomic diversity are rather naive. The two measures available over the entire sample period are the population living on farms and the ethnic composition of the population.[3] Our ''homogeneity'' measure is simply $(PC - .5)^2$, where PC is the percentage of the population that is white or (under the alternative definition) living on farms. This variable takes on its maximum possible value of $\frac{1}{4}$ for a completely homogenous population and declines to a minimum possible value of zero for a population that is evenly divided between the two groups. This measure is admittedly crude, but we hope that it captures the essential point of the hypothesis.

Historically, however, simply the proportion of farmers and that of whites in the population have also been important determinants of public policy. Farmers are a diverse lot, but their late nineteenth-and early twentieth-century political goals can be subsumed under the common label of ''populism.'' While supporting a fairly wide range of social and economic reforms, the populists stood firmly behind the notions that a small government was better than a large one and that local governments were better than more centralized governments. Agrarian elements, reformer or otherwise, were also leery of the ''city,'' and states with farm majorities often apportioned state legislative districts to give rural areas disproportionate representation. The net effect of having a large share of the population living on farms is not altogether clear: farmers were against large cities which would tend to promote a more centralized state-local fisc, but they also supported smaller and more decentralized governments as a general principle. As the following section will show, accounting for the share of farmers in the population is important econometrically, even if we do not have a clearcut theoretical prior on the sign of the variable.

The percentage white variable is unavoidably connected with historically centralized southern governments and with a difficulty in interpreting how race relations would affect the structure of government in the South. Since Southern states have historically been more centralized, we expect that

Hypothesis 7: States in the southern region of the country will, other things equal, have more centralized public sectors.

Since the percentage white is considerably lower in most southern states than elsewhere, simply including the percentage white will pick up a "southern" effect. We try to control for this with a dummy variable, but a more complicated problem remains. In many states, especially in the South, a large part of the black population was denied the right to vote until the 1960s. We do not know whether the enforcement of laws (or more informal measures) designed to control and coerce a substantial part of the community requires a more or less centralized government. We also do not know whether the granting of black suffrage would have led to a movement for more or less centralized government; it might have encouraged decentralization as black majorities in local government attempted to use their newly obtained political power in those governments over which they had the most control. As we shall see, it appears as though the level of the black population, as well as our diversity measures, may be an important determinant of the degree of centralization.[4]

1.4 An Econometric Study of Fiscal Decentralization

To test our set of hypotheses on fiscal decentralization, we shall make use of a large panel data set on the state and local sector that we have assembled in the course of a broader historical study of U.S. government finance. Drawing on the U.S. *Census of Governments* and various other sources, we have collected data on state and local governments and on other relevant socioeconomic variables at roughly decade intervals beginning in 1902. We thus have nine sets of cross-sectional observations on the 48 contiguous states that include data on expenditures, revenues, and tax receipts for state government and for local governments in each state. For a description of our data base, we refer the reader to the appendix at the end of this paper.

With this panel data set, we can explore both changes over time and differences among states in the extent of fiscal decentralization. For this purpose, we have adopted the error-components technique for the estimation of our regression equations. Using the error-components estimator, our general approach to the testing of our various hypotheses takes the form:

(1) $$C_{it} = a + bX_{it} + cZ_{it} + s_i + t_t + e_{it},$$

where C_{it} is our measure of fiscal centralization (i.e., the state share of state-local spending or revenues), X_{it} is a vector of control variables, Z_{it} is the vector of variables representing our hypotheses, s_i is a state-specific disturbance term, t_t is a time-specific disturbance term, and e_{it} is the normal disturbance term with zero expected mean. Part of the appeal of the error-components approach is that it allows us to separate out an effect that is specific to each state in our sample and also to each time period. The remaining component of the disturbance term is the usual random error term with zero mean.

We begin the econometric analysis by presenting the simple regression equations involving our measures of fiscal centralization and each of the variables chosen to test one of our hypotheses. We are unable unfortunately to test all the hypotheses we set out in the preceding section because of limitations on our data. We have measures for each state and time period on land area, population size, urbanized population, and per capita income. This allows us to test hypotheses one through four. We do not, however, have data on the distribution of income so that we are unable to test hypothesis five.[5] Next, we have a set of socioeconomic variables from which we will create proxies for variations in tastes for public services so that we can explore hypothesis six. And, finally, the use of a dummy variable for southern states will provide a test of hypothesis seven.

The results of the simple regressions appear in table 1.5. Each row of the table reports the results of the univariate error-components regressions for one of our proposed explanatory variables; the first two columns indicate the results using the state share of total state-local expenditures as the dependent variable, and the second two columns report the estimated equation with the state share of total state and local revenues as the dependent variable. The first set of hypotheses, numbers one through three, relate to the size and urbanization of the state. Here we find that the simple regressions provide support for two of the three hypotheses. The size of the state (measured in terms of population) and the extent of urbanization both have the hypothesized negative coefficients, and these coefficients are statistically significant at the .01 level regardless of whether the expenditure or revenue variable is employed to measure fiscal centralization. Size as measured by land area, although it has the hypothesized sign, is not statistically significant.[6]

Hypothesis four proposes a positive relationship between fiscal centralization and the level of per capita income. In the univariate regression, however, we find an inverse association. [More on this shortly.] To explore hypothesis six concerning variation in tastes, we have used two proxies for the homogeneity of the state's population. As noted earlier, the measures are the squares of the difference between .5 and

Table 1.5   Simple Univariate Error-Components Regressions, Fiscal
Concentration Measure on Selection of Independent Variables
(Absolute t-Statistics)

	Expenditures		Revenues	
	Constant (1)	Coefficient (2)	Constant (3)	Coefficient (4)
LAND AREA	0.3622	−1.94E−07	0.4309	−7.38E−08
	(10.3)***	(.90)	(7.7)***	(.34)
POPULATION	0.3802	−1.01E−05	0.4392	−4.3E−06
	(12.4)***	(5.9)***	(9.0)***	(2.5)***
PERCENTAGE	0.4587	−0.2147	0.4956	−0.1371
URBAN	(15.2)***	(6.7)***	(11.7)***	(4.3)***
PER CAPITA	0.3853	−1.9E−05	0.476	−2.71E−05
INCOME	(11.7)***	(1.54)	(10.5)***	(2.06)**
HOMOGENEITY	0.3816	−0.3009	0.4517	−0.2428
FARM	(13.6)***	(3.3)***	(10.5)***	(2.8)***
HOMOGENEITY	0.3849	−0.2075	0.4865	−0.3602
WHITE	(10.6)***	(2.13)**	(8.6)***	(4.0)***
PERCENTAGE	0.3396	0.0442	0.4265	−0.0008
FARM	(13.8)***	(1.21)	(11.3)***	(.02)
PERCENTAGE	0.4962	−0.1642	0.6003	−0.1958
WHITE	(8.5)***	(2.9)***	(8.5)***	(3.8)***

Notes: Every row represents two univariate regressions. In columns (1) and (2) the
constant and coefficent are from a regression of the percentage of total state and local
expenditures undertaken at the state level, regressed on the individual independent
variables. In columns (3) and (4) the constant and coefficent are from a regression of
the percentage of total state and local revenues undertaken at the state level, regressed
on the individual independent variables.
N = 432 for all regressions
*** = 1% significance level
** = 5% significance level
* = 10% significance level

the percentage white or the percentage residing on farms. A state with
50 percent of its population living on farms, for example, would be as
diverse as possible, and the farm homogeneity variable would, in this
instance, equal zero. We find in table 1.5 that the univariate results
support neither version of hypothesis six: the estimated coefficient on
both the farm and white homogeneity variables is negative and statistically significant in both equations, indicating that more homogeneous
populations are associated with more decentralized governments.

The percentage white variable has a significantly negative association
with fiscal centralization, which probably reflects the southern effect.
The percentage of the population living on farms does not exhibit a
significant association with centralization (with opposite signs for the
revenue and expenditure equations).

While the univariate equations are of some interest, a multiple-regression model containing a set of control variables is obviously needed to provide a more reliable test of the various hypotheses. We present in table 1.6 the results of our error-components multiple-regression analysis. The first two columns indicate the estimated coefficients for the equation using the expenditure measure of fiscal centralization, while the second two columns report the results using the revenue definition for the fiscal centralization variable. The multivariate tests for the first three hypotheses confirm the univariate findings: the extent of fiscal centralization is significantly and negatively related to the size of the population and the percentage urban, but is not significantly associated with land area. Larger states in terms of population and states whose population is more highly urbanized tend to have more decentralized fiscal systems.

Table 1.6   Error-Components Regressions, Fiscal Concentration Measure on Selection of Independent Variables (absolute t-statistics)

	Expenditures		Revenues	
	(1)	(2)	(3)	(4)
LAND AREA	$-2.05E-07$	$-1.37E-07$	$-6.13E-08$	$-1.21E-08$
	(1.3)	(.87)	(.37)	(.07)
POPULATION	$-9.30E-06$	$-7.02E-06$	$-5.48E-06$	$-3.37E-06$
	(5.2)***	(3.9)***	(3.1)***	(1.87)*
PERCENTAGE	-0.1966	-0.2917	-0.0783	-0.1933
URBAN	(4.7)***	(6.2)***	(1.9)*	(4.15)***
PER CAPITA	$2.39E-05$	$3.58E-05$	$3.01E-06$	$1.62E-05$
INCOME	(1.76)*	(2.5)***	(.20)	(1.09)
HOMOGENEITY	-0.045	-0.1707	-0.0092	-0.2134
FARM	(.41)	(1.48)	(.08)	(1.89)*
HOMOGENEITY	-0.1628	0.5812	-0.3573	-0.0331
WHITE	(1.81)*	(2.11)**	(3.8)***	(.12)
PERCENTAGE	—	-0.2284	—	-0.2477
FARM		(4.3)***		(4.7)***
PERCENTAGE	—	-0.4305	—	-0.1748
WHITE		(2.9)***		(1.19)
SOUTHERN	—	0.0377	—	0.0416
DUMMY		(1.67)*		(1.84)*
Constant	0.4686	0.8073	0.5411	0.7343
	(13.3)***	(7.5)***	(11.8)***	(6.7)***

Notes: The dependent variable in columns (1) and (2) is the concentration measure for expenditures and in columns (3) and (4) is the concentration measure for revenues.

N = 432 for all regressions.

*** = 1% significance level.

** = 5% significance level.

* = 10% significance level.

When we come to the income variable, however, the results differ from the univariate cases: for the multivariate equations, the estimated coefficient on per capita income possesses the hypothesized positive sign and is statistically significant in the expenditure equation. Higher income states thus exhibit a tendency toward more centralized state and local sectors (at least in terms of the expenditure measure of centralization).[7]

The estimated coefficients for the southern dummy variable are positive (as hypothesized) and statistically significant. Simply being a southern state seems to explain roughly a third of the difference in fiscal centralization between southern and northeastern states. However, the results for the socioeconomic variables are more difficult to interpret. The estimated coefficients on our homogeneity variables, both percentage white and farm, are extremely sensitive to the specification of the equation, and we hesitate to place much confidence in these estimates. The coefficient on the farm homogeneity variable is negative in all four equations, which runs counter to hypothesis six. There is another intrepretation of this variable in conjunction with the percentage farm variable in equations (2) and (4) in table 1.6. Having more farmers appears to produce a more decentralized government, but at a decreasing rate. Or, what may be the more appropriate way to phrase that statement in the American historical context: having fewer farmers (as has happened over time) leads to a more centralized government, and does so at an increasing rate. This effect is quite interesting in light of the strong negative effect that urbanization exerts on centralization, as it indicates that we cannot simply think of percentage farm and percentage urban as proxies for one another.

The racial homogeneity variable has the predicted positive sign in equation (2) and is statistically significant. But it is negative in the other three equations in Table 1.6. The estimated coefficient for percentage white is negative in both instances, but statistically significant only in equation (2). We find these results difficult to interpret. Taken at face value, the results in equation (2) indicate that a larger white population results in greater decentralization but at a diminishing rate. The white "decentralization effect" is increasingly offset by the "diversity effect" as percentage white rises toward 100 percent.

Finally, we thought it would be of interest to compare our results for the error-components analysis covering the entire period of eighty years with the set of cross-sectional multiple-regression equations for each decade. We present in table 1.7 the estimated cross-sectional equations for each of our observed years (using ordinary least squares). The estimated equations use the expenditure definition of the dependent variable.[8] While the overall results correspond roughly to our earlier

22   John Joseph Wallis and Wallace E. Oates

Table 1.7   OLS Regressions. Fiscal Concentration Measure on Selection of Independent Variables by Year, 1902 to 1982 (absolute t-statistic)

	1902	1913	1922	1932	1942
LAND AREA	4.09E−08	−1.14E−07	−2.06E−08	−2.10E−07	−3.84E−07
	(1.99)*	(.37)	(.07)	(.79)	(1.36)
POPULATION	−1.08E−05	−8.38E−06	−1.27E−04	−9.96E−06	−3.66E−06
	(1.93)*	(1.29)	(2.22)**	(1.85)*	(.65)
PERCENTAGE URBAN	−0.2139	−0.3637	−0.0922	−0.3881	−0.6506
	(2.03)**	(2.64)**	(.66)	(2.47)**	(3.55)***
PER CAPITA INCOME	−5.27E−05	−1.10E−04	7.04E−05	6.98E−05	−2.41E−05
	(1.05)	(1.41)	(.84)	(1.28)	(.44)
HOMOGENEITY FARM	0.2753	0.5569	−0.2164	−0.1137	0.7401
	(1.15)	(1.61)	(.56)	(.24)	(1.22)
HOMOGENEITY WHITE	0.8875	−0.154	−1.404	−0.3403	−0.8996
	(2.01)*	(.23)	(1.83)*	(.38)	(.89)
PERCENTAGE FARM	0.2356	−0.2117	−0.0988	−0.1183	−0.3778
	(2.31)**	(1.15)	(.51)	(.57)	(1.30)
PERCENTAGE WHITE	−0.6444	0.147	0.5052	0.0436	0.5309
	(3.61)***	(.49)	(1.31)	(.09)	(.92)
SOUTHERN DUMMY	0.0261	−0.043	−0.025	0.0371	0.0359
	(.64)	(.79)	(.52)	(.75)	(.70)
Constant	0.8056	0.4787	0.1031	0.5157	0.5139
	(6.5)***	(2.12)**	(.35)	(1.49)	(1.18)
R_2	0.67	0.35	0.37	0.60	0.46

findings, a cursory examination of the table indicates that the results vary considerably from one period to the next; the estimated coefficients on many of the variables exhibit substantial changes in their magnitude and the values of their *t*-statistics from one period to the next. The population and percentage urban variables, however, are consistently negative (with only one exception) and often statistically significant.

In summary, our econometric results, while admittedly somewhat mixed, do provide support for several of the hypotheses. We find that the extent of fiscal centralization varies inversely and significantly with both population size and urbanization (although not significantly with land area). In addition, we have found a positive relationship (at least in the multivariate error-components analysis) between fiscal centralization and the level of per capita income. This is consistent with the view that higher-income states will have a more pronounced inclination to engage in redistributive activities which tend to have a disproportionately large role for the state government. As suggested by the historical discussion, we have found that southern states (at least until quite recently) have relatively centralized state and local fiscs. Finally, we obtained quite mixed (and often puzzling) results with our racial

Table 1.7   (continued)

	1952	1962	1972	1982
LAND	−3.01E−07	2.25E−07	−9.90E−08	−2.70E−07
	(1.07)	(1.04)	(.44)	(1.33)
POPULATION	−5.97E−06	−9.55E−06	−5.77E−06	−4.80E−06
	(1.15)	(3.19)***	(2.18)**	(2.15)**
PERCENTAGE	−0.8729	−0.4959	−0.1905	−0.1493
URBAN	(3.8)***	(3.42)***	(1.56)	(1.29)
PER CAPITA	1.62E−05	−3.68E−05	−8.45E−05	−2.65E−05
INCOME	(.35)	(.94)	(2.39)**	(.97)
HOMOGENEITY	1.467	1.396	3.297	11.201
FARM	(1.61)	(1.24)	(1.81)*	(2.37)**
HOMOGENEITY	−0.9271	0.0621	0.4963	−0.2163
WHITE	(.74)	(.05)	(.39)	(.16)
PERCENTAGE	−0.1491	0.33	2.037	9.262
FARM	(.29)	(.45)	(1.48)	(2.32)**
PERCENTAGE	0.7064	0.0631	0.0424	0.2931
WHITE	(.93)	(.09)	(.05)	(.33)
SOUTHERN	0.0697	0.0291	0.0493	0.0276
DUMMY	(1.35)	(.78)	(1.49)	(1.00)
Constant	0.277	0.4959	−0.0389	−2.3211
	(.48)	(.98)	(.06)	(1.74)*
R^2	0.53	0.66	0.66	0.54

Notes: The dependent variable in all regressions is the state share of combined state and local expenditures.

N = 48 for all regressions.

*** = 1% significance.

** = 5% significance.

* = 10% significance.

and farm variables. Although they often have significant explanatory power in the regression equations, they do not provide clear support for hypothesis six and present formidable problems of interpretation.

1.5   Some Reflections on Future Trends in Fiscal Centralization

As we have seen, the twentieth century has been a period over which the state and local sector has exhibited a strong tendency toward increased fiscal centralization. Is this a trend that is likely to continue? This is not an easy question to answer, but we would like to offer some thoughts. At the turn of the present century, the fiscal role of state governments was a very modest one. However, various developments brought an increased demand for important new public services, notably highways, higher education, and public assistance programs, that were appropriately placed in the domain of state government. As a result, the fiscal share of state government in the state and local sector rose dramatically. But, as we saw, this rise in the extent of fiscal centralization was primarily a phenomenon of the first half of the century. The trend toward further fiscal centralization has slowed dramatically (if not ceased altogether). From this perspective, it would appear that the forces behind the trend toward centralization are largely history now; without some new thrust for state-level intervention, there would seem to be little reason to expect further centralization of the state and local sector.

On closer examination, there appear to be some such centralizing forces still at work—at least to a modest degree. The primary force is a continuing concern with so-called fiscal equalization: the more equal access of all socioeconomic groups to "satisfactory" levels of public services. This concern (although by no means new) has been reinforced by court decisions on public education and various restrictions on local finances, and is no doubt partly responsible for the continuing tendency toward heavier reliance on intergovernmental aid to local governments. Equalizing grants from the states have provided a means for reducing the fiscal disparities between wealthier and poorer localities.

At the same time, there are some reasons to expect the potential welfare gains from decentralized finance to remain substantial and perhaps to grow over time. A basic mechanism for the realization of these gains is the mobility of individuals, permitting the formation of communities that are relatively homogeneous in their demands for local services. The development of metropolitan areas in which individuals work in one locality (perhaps the central city) but reside in a nearby residential community provides a setting well suited to the realization of the gains from local finance. Rising incomes, improved transportation, and the increasing mobility of individuals would suggest that the potential gains from decentralization should remain substantial.

Our overall econometric results point to these divergent forces. If population and urbanization continue to grow, this will create pressures for more decentralized government. However, the positive effect of income growth on fiscal centralization should continue; indeed the concern with equalization may be the manifestation of a kind of income effect. But the other major source of centralization, the declining number of farmers, cannot be expected to contribute much to centralization in the future.

There are thus forces at work, some of which favor increased centralization, but others of which increase the relative gains from decentralized finance. Any prediction of outcomes is thus extremely precarious. However, we would venture the conjecture that the local sector is unlikely, at least in terms of expenditure responsibilities, to experience much further diminution in its relative fiscal role over the next few decades. The local provision of services promises important welfare gains that will not go unnoticed.

Appendix

The variables used in this paper are taken from a variety of Commerce Department sources and are, for the most part, exactly what they seem. Problems arose occasionally from gaps in the available series. This appendix describes how the gaps where bridged.

The fiscal variables, revenues and expenditures by state for state and local governments, were taken from the decennial Census of Governments. This census was taken in 1902, 1913, 1922, 1932, 1942, 1962, 1972, and 1982 (with additional censuses taken in 1927, 1957, 1967, and 1977). A census was contemplated, but not taken, in 1952. Coverage of local governments in the 1902, 1913, and 1922 censuses varied slightly. And the 1922 census did not include a complete enumeration of local government expenditures. These gaps were filled by several interpolation techniques.

The 1902 census of governments recorded complete information on public revenues and expenditures for all levels of government.[9] The 1913 Census of Governments included all governments except for places with population less than 2,500.[10] The 1922 Census of Governments included information on receipts for all levels of government, and expenditures for state governments only.[11]

To account for the exclusion of governments in places with less than 2,500 population, we utilized the breakdown of government expenditures by population size in the 1902 census. The 1902 returns reported fiscal totals for cities with population of 8,000 to 25,000 and all minor subdivisions. The 1913 Census reported fiscal totals for all cities with population of 2,500 to 8,000 but for no smaller units. Both censuses reported totals for larger cities and counties. We calculated revenues and expenditures of minor subdivisions (cities with under 8,000 population) as a percentage of revenues and expenditures for cities with over 8,000 population and counties in 1902. Then revenues and expenditures for cities with over 8,000 population and counties in 1913 were multiplied by the 1902 shares to generate an estimate of "all minor subdivision" revenues and expenditures for 1913.

The revenue data for 1922 were fairly complete. We were able to collect total revenue and expenditure data for state governments, as well as local tax revenues and local revenue from state grants. The census department estimated a nationwide total for local revenues in 1922 at $4,148 million.[12] We assumed that the ratio of local nongrant total revenues to tax revenues was the same in each state as it had been in 1913, and calculated an estimated nongrant total revenue figure for 1922. The estimated nationwide total was slightly higher than the census estimate, and therefore every state was adjusted by a common factor (.927469) to bring our total revenues in line with the census total. Finally, we estimated local expenditure by assuming that the ratio of expenditures to revenues in each state was the same as the nationwide estimates made by the census.[13]

Complete state level data were available for 1953, but no local data were collected. Information on local revenues was collected in 1953 and that information was used to construct estimates of local revenues and expenditures for 1952. Specifically, the census department estimated that nationwide local revenues in 1952 were .91 of the total local revenue in 1953. We simply adjusted the 1953 revenue figures by .91 to obtain our 1952 estimates. The census also estimated that local expenditures in 1952 were 1.2 times greater than revenues, and we calculated local expenditures by multiplying our revenue estimate by 1.2.

The control variables where comparatively easy to assemble. From *Historical Statistics* it was possible to collect population, land size, racial composition, and urban population for each decade. Note that the census data refer to census years (years ending in 0), while the financial variables refer to the relevant Census of Government years. The one variable that caused a problem was per capita income.

Per capita income is available in *Historical Statistics* from 1929 on. Before 1929 the state level income estimates of Richard Easterlin (1957) are available for the years 1900 and 1920. Nationwide GNP per capita was $246 in 1900, $382 in 1910, and $860 in 1920. Of the total growth in income between 1900 and 1920, therefore, .2215 occurred between 1900 and 1910. We took 22.15 percent of the income growth in each state between 1900 and 1920, and added it to the 1900 income figure from Easterlin to estimate per-capita income in each state for 1910.

Notes

1. The years are mainly those during which there was a Census of Governments in the United States (see the appendix).
2. For a more rigorous treatment of the determinants of the optimal degree of decentralization, see Oates (1972, appendix to chapter 2).
3. We also have information on the age structure of the population, but including variables on age structure had no measurable effects on the results; these variables were not statistically significant in the regression analysis.
4. Including a measure of the share of whites in the population along with our racial homogeneity variable in the same equation raises some tricky issues

of interpretation. There is the question of whether this specification is any different than one which enters the white share variable in a nonlinear form with both linear and square terms. If one believes that the homogeneity of the population (as measured by the squared deviation from one-half of the fraction of the population that is white) influences fiscal centralization, then the specification including both PC and $(PC - .5)^2$ is appropriate. However, this is admittedly a restrictive specification; in particular, it imposes a symmetry condition on the effects of homogeneity (i.e., 55 percent white has the same effect as 45 percent white). If our specification is not the correct one, then of course there may well be some confounding of measured effects between the share and homogeneity variables. We have examined some other (and more complicated) specifications, but they have not altered the main empirical findings in the paper (these results are available from the authors). The interpretation of the homogeneity measure depends upon the particular specification, but not always in a way that is easily characterized. Since the results for these variables are quite sensitive to specification, we are reluctant to place much weight on them in this paper. But as the results in the next section indicate, there does seem to be something here that merits further investigation. This discussion applies as well to our treatment of the farm variables, where we include in the regression equations measures of both the share of the farm population and a farm homogeneity variable.

5. In a cross-sectional study of fiscal decentralization using data for 1969–70, Giertz (1976) finds that the Gini coefficient is positively and significantly associated with the extent of fiscal centralization, suggesting that a higher degree of inequality in the distribution of income is associated with a more centralized state and local sector. This finding runs counter to our hypothesis five. Giertz argues that this result reflects the greater need for income redistribution in states with more inequality.

6. In an earlier cross-sectional study using data for 1962, Litvack and Oates (1970) likewise found population size and percentage urban to be negatively and significantly associated with fiscal centralization in the state and local sector. Giertz (1976) found, in addition, a negative and significant relationship between fiscal centralization and land area.

7. Giertz (1976) found such a relationship in his cross-sectional study.

8. The results using the revenue version of the dependent variable do not differ in any important ways from those reported in table 1.7.

9. U.S. Bureau of the Census (1907). Receipt and Expenditure data taken from Table 10, pp. 982–93.

10. U.S. Bureau of the Census (1914). Receipt and expenditure data for states taken from Table 6, pp. 36–37, Table 8, pp. 40–41, Table 10, pp. 44–45; for counties Table 3, pp. 122–23 and Table 5, pp. 210–11; for incorporated places Table 3, pp. 462–69 and Table 5, pp. 560–67.

11. U.S. Bureau of the Census (1924). Receipts for local governments taken from Table 1, pp. 12–16. Receipts and expenditures taken from Table 2, p. 17, Table 3, pp. 52–53, and Table 4, p. 54.

12. The census estimates for local finances were based on information gathered by the census from a sample of large cities and scattered data collected by the census bureau. Estimates of local government finances were built up from these partial samples. We have used these estimates to fill in missing data in 1922 and in 1952.

13. Local Expenditures = 1.101013 · Local Revenues

References

Bahl, R. W., and S. Nath. 1986. Public expenditure decentralization in developing countries. *Environment and Planning C: Government and Policy* 4:405–18.

Brown, Charles C., and Wallace E. Oates. 1987. Assistance to the poor in a federal system. *Journal of Public Economics* 32:307-30.

Easterlin, Richard A. 1957. State income estimates. In *Population, redistribution, and economic growth, United States, 1870–1950, vol. 1,* ed. Everett Lee. Philadelphia: American Philosophical Society.

Giertz, J. Fred. 1976. Decentralization at the state and local level: An empirical analysis. *National Tax Journal* 29:201–10.

Kee, Woo Sik. 1977. Fiscal decentralization and economic development. *Public Finance Quarterly* 5:79–97.

Litvack, James M., and Wallace E. Oates. 1970. Group size and the output of public goods: Theory and an application to state-local finance in the United States. *Public Finance* 25:42–60.

Martin, Alison, and W. Arthur Lewis. 1956. Patterns of public revenue and expenditure. *Manchester School of Economic and Social Studies* 24:203–44.

Oates, Wallace E. 1972. *Fiscal federalism.* New York: Harcourt, Brace, Jovanovich.

———. 1985. Searching for leviathan: An empirical study. *American Economic Review* 75:748–57.

Schmandt, H. J., and G. R. Stephens. 1960. Measuring municipal output. *National Tax Journal* 13:369–75.

U.S. Bureau of the Census. 1907. *Wealth, debt, and taxation.* Washington, D.C.: U.S. Government Printing Office.

U.S. Bureau of the Census. 1914. *Wealth, debt, and taxation.* Washington D.C.: U.S. Government Printing Office.

U.S. Bureau of the Census. 1924. *Wealth, debt, and taxation.* Washington D.C.: U.S. Government Printing Office.

U.S. Bureau of the Census. 1935. *Financial statistics of state and local governments.* Washington, D.C.: U.S. Government Printing Office.

U.S. Bureau of the Census. 1948. *Revised summary of state and local government finances in 1942.* State and Local Special Studies no. 26. Washington, D.C.: U.S. Government Printing Office.

U.S. Bureau of the Census. 1954. *State government finances.* Washington, D.C.: U.S. Government Printing Office.

U.S. Bureau of the Census. 1964. *Census of governments, 1962.* Vol. 4, no. 4. Washington, D.C.: U.S. Government Printing Office.

U.S. Bureau of the Census. 1974. *Census of governments, 1972.* Vol. 4, no. 5. Washington, D.C.: U.S. Government Printing Office.

U.S. Bureau of the Census. 1984. *Census of governments, 1982.* Vol. 4, no. 5. Washington, D.C.: U.S. Government Printing Office.

Wallis, John Joseph. 1984. Birth of the old federalism. *Journal of Economic History* 94:139–60.

———1987. The political economy of new deal fiscal federalism. Unpublished manuscript.

Wheare, Kenneth C. 1964. *Federal government.* 4th ed. London: Oxford University Press.

PART III

INTER-GOVERNMENTAL GRANTS AND REVENUE SHARING

[8]

THE ANALYSIS OF REVENUE SHARING IN A NEW APPROACH TO COLLECTIVE FISCAL DECISIONS *

David F. Bradford and Wallace E. Oates

In spite of the widespread sharing of revenues by central governments with provincial, state, and local public units in a number of countries, there exists little formal analysis of the allocative and distributive effects of these programs. Proponents of revenue sharing in the United States [1] refer to a "fiscal mismatch" between the federal and state-local governments; the ability to generate revenues (particularly in terms of an elastic tax base), they contend, is disproportionately under the control of the federal government, while expenditure "needs" have become increasingly urgent at state-local levels. The solution to this problem is "the regular distribution of a specified portion of the federal income tax to the states primarily on the basis of population and with few strings attached." [2]

While one can recognize the gravity of the fiscal problems besetting many state and local governments, the existing literature on revenue sharing cannot help but prove somewhat puzzling to students of public finance. We are familiar in theoretical terms with the effects of unconditional, lump sum grants to individual economic units, but the question of the effects of such grants to a collectivity remains unanswered. Are unconditional intergovernmental grants equivalent to a set of lump sum grants directly to the individual members of the collectivity? If so, revenue sharing is simply an implicit reduction in federal personal taxes. Or does revenue sharing have effects on public outputs and disposable incomes that cannot be duplicated through a cut in federal taxes?

* We are indebted to the Ford Foundation for support of this work, and in particular, are grateful to Richard Cornwall. Joseph Pechman. Carl Shoup, and the members of the Committee on Urban Public Economics for many helpful comments on earlier drafts of this paper.

1. See, for example, Walter Heller and Joseph Pechman, "Questions and Answers on Revenue Sharing," Brookings Reprint 135 (Washington, D.C., 1967).

2. *Ibid.*, p. 2.

Previous analyses of intergovernmental grants have been unable to provide answers to these questions, because they typically treat governmental units as if they were individual consumers equipped with indifference curves with the familiar properties.[3] Since, however, intergovernmental grants are not grants to individuals but rather grants to groups of people, this analytic approach is clearly inappropriate. What is needed is a theoretical framework that incorporates explicitly the political process, by which we mean the process of collective choice through which the recipients of the grant determine their response to the increment to the public treasury.

In this paper, we present a new approach to the study of the economic behavior of collectivities, one that places a central emphasis on the structure of political decision-making institutions. In Section I, we set forth the model with which we propose to describe revenue sharing and its effects on the individuals receiving the funds. Using this model, we show in Sections II and III that, in two simple and familiar models of budget determination — the Lindahl model and the system of simple majority rule with fixed tax shares — revenue sharing is precisely equivalent, in terms of *both* its allocative and distributive effects, to a reduction of central government taxes of a specified incidence. In Section IV, we begin to explore the generality of this result in terms of a new method of formalizing the properties of political decision systems. We describe in this section a set of sufficient conditions on the political process to assure the equivalence of revenue sharing to a reduction in central government personal taxes. Although these conditions are fulfilled by the simple, illustrative Lindahl and majority rule models, they are not dependent on any particular connection between individual preferences and collective choices. Rather they are properties that could in principle be observed directly from the behavior of collectivities, much as individual indifference maps are in principle observable by revealed-preference techniques.

We find, moreover, in Section V that there are plausible circumstances under which the sufficient conditions and the equivalence between revenue sharing and lump sum grants to individual citizens do not hold. For example, special forms of majority rule in the constitution of the receiving government may result in outcomes being obtainable through grants to the collectivity that could not be generated by the political process following individual grants to its

---

3. See, for example, an excellent paper by J. Wilde and the references cited therein: "The Expenditure Effects of Grant-in-Aid Programs," *National Tax Journal*, Vol. 21 (Sept. 1968), pp. 340–48.

citizens. We argue in this section that the sources of these differences between grants directly to citizens and grants to their government may have important implications for the desirability of a program of revenue sharing. Section VI examines briefly the implications for our conclusions of tax competition among jurisdictions and of the introduction of fiscal effort clauses into the revenue-sharing formula, and Section VII contains some concluding remarks. Finally, in the Appendix we present a formal proof of the equivalence theorem described in Section IV.

I. The Analytic Framework

To isolate the issues of interest to us, we confine our attention to a model world of "fiscal clubs." We assume initially that each club has a single collective activity, which may be thought of as the provision of a public good for joint consumption by the members of the club. There is, in addition, a single private good that the members consume. A "state of the club" is completely described by a vector $[y_1, y_2, \cdots, y_n, g]$, whose first n components indicate the claims of the n members of the club to the private good and whose last component, g, indicates the level of provision of the public good. The set of feasible states of the club is constrained by the requirement that no one have a negative allotment of private goods ("disposable income") and by a relation that specifies the maximum level of the collective activity attainable, given the total quantity of the private good available for distribution. We assume initially that the public good and the private good can be traded off on a constant cost basis, and choose the units so that this conversion is one-for-one.[4]

For any club, the feasible state that actually occurs is a matter of politics, formal or informal. Most feasible states will not be political equilibria. In all likelihood, for example, the state in which everyone has the same amount of the private good but where no public good is provided will be altered by political activity into some other state in which a positive level of the collective activity is undertaken. Similarly, a state in which one individual has a

4. The conversion might be thought of as occurring through production internal to the club, or, alternatively, by exchange in a large market. We should point out that much of the simplification adopted here is purely for expository purposes. In particular, the logic of the argument is compatible with a world of many private and public goods and of more complicated production-exchange relationships. These extensions are developed in the Appendix.

huge command over the private good and all other individuals possess virtually nothing will generally be modified, perhaps through the political process of revolution, into a state with a somewhat more egalitarian distribution of disposable income. The essential point is that, given the endowments of the members, their relative bargaining skills, information costs, etc., and the set of alternative feasible states, the vector of disposable incomes and the level of the collective activity are *simultaneously determined* by the political process.

We can characterize revenue sharing in our model world as a disturbance of equilibrium. An agency external to the club alters the state of the club by making it a gift of a specified sum; we might imagine the immediate effect to be an increment to the level of the club's collective activity. The new state is, of course, a member of a larger set of feasible alternatives than the original one, but there is no reason to expect it to be a political equilibrium within that enlarged set. The political process will in general bring about further changes, ultimately producing a new equilibrium state.

In this paper, we pose the question whether the new equilibrium state resulting from the gift to the club could be reached following a quite different initial disturbance, namely, a set of grants to the individual members of the club that totals to the same amount as the revenue-sharing grant to the collectivity. This will immediately be recognized as the question of whether revenue sharing is identical in its effects to a specific program of central government personal tax reductions or rebates. We should emphasize that the thesis we are examining is *not* that revenue sharing is equivalent in its effects to, say, an x percent across-the-board cut in federal taxes, or to any other program of federal tax reduction as normally conceived. Rather, we are exploring the conditions under which the ultimate state attained with revenue sharing is identical in every detail (i.e., in terms of the disposable income of each individual and the level of output of the public good) to that resulting from a grant of, say, $10 to Mr. 1, $7 to Mr. 2, etc., where these grants may bear no relation to any politically feasible set of individual grants actually attainable through tax reduction by the central government.

Incidentally, as we shall show later, it is not difficult to describe a political process for which this equivalence does not hold. In the next two sections, however, we show that this equivalence does obtain under reasonable conditions in two simple models of collective budget determination: the Lindahl procedure and majority rule with fixed tax shares. These simple cases serve to clarify the nature of the proposition and to motivate our speculations about its plausibility in more complex political systems.

II. Revenue Sharing in a Lindahl Model

The Lindahl mechanism of collective budget determination can be thought of as the analogue in a world with collective goods to a Walrasian *tâtonnement* in the competitive equilibrium theory of private goods.[5] In the latter, individuals in the system treat successive price vectors called out by the auctioneer as final, indicating the amounts of the various goods and services that they wish to demand and supply at those prices. For collective goods, the "auctioneer-politician" calls out successive sharing formulas. More specifically, he calls out for each individual i a tax share h_i, which indicates the fraction of the cost per unit of the public good that the ith person will have to pay through the sacrifice of units of the private good. Tentatively taking this "price" per unit of the public good as fixed, each individual indicates the number of units he would like to see provided. The auctioneer then varies tax shares until the number of units of the public good demanded by all the members of the club is the same. This is the equilibrium quantity, which is financed by taxing each member according to his indicated tax share.

The position of a particular member of the club under a Lindahl equilibrium is depicted in Figure I. With a "before-tax" income of $0A$ and a tax share of h (which equals the slope of AB), the line

5. Useful discussions of the Lindahl process are available in L. Johansen, "Some Notes on the Lindahl Theory of Determination of Public Expenditure," *International Economic Review*, Vol. 4 (Sept. 1963), pp. 346–58. and *Public Economics* (Chicago: Rand McNally, 1965); J. Head, "Lindahl's Theory of the Budget," *Finanzarchiv*, Vol. 23 (Oct. 1964), pp. 421–54; and H. Aaron and M. McGuire, "Efficiency and Equity in the Optimal Supply of a Public Good," *Review of Economics and Statistics*, Vol. 51 (Feb. 1969), pp. 31–39. Foley derives a theorem for Lindahl equilibria in a world with public goods that parallels precisely the fundamental theorem of welfare economics in a world with only private goods (D. Foley, "Resource Allocation and the Public Sector," *Yale Economic Essays*, Vol 7 (Spring 1967), pp. 45–73). For a general analysis, including a description of the historical development of the Lindahl model, see R. Musgrave, *The Theory of Public Finance* (New York: McGraw-Hill, 1959), Ch. 4. and P. Samuelson, "Pure Theory of Public Expenditure and Taxation," in J. Margolis and H. Guitton, eds., *Public Economics* (London: MacMillan, 1969), pp. 98–123. The shortcomings of the Lindahl model as a description of actual budget determination are well known. In particular, as many writers have pointed out, there is an incentive for the individual to understate his true preferences so as to induce others to pay a larger share of the costs of the public good. Such behavior will in general prevent the attainment of the Lindahl solution. However, because of its familiarity and "nice" properties, we have found it very useful for pedagogical purposes to explore the effects of revenue sharing in a Lindahl framework.

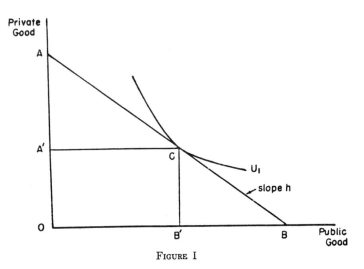

FIGURE I

segment AB indicates the level of consumption of the private good
that will be available to the member for each alternative level of
provision of the collective good. The individual is assumed to have
a preference relation of the usual sort defined over bundles of private and public goods. Given his pretax income and tax share, his
chosen level of provision of the public good will be his most preferred bundle along AB, shown in Figure I as point C, with public
good provision $0B'$ and after-tax income $0A'$. Since this position
was assumed to be one of Lindahl equilibrium, the corresponding
diagrams for all other citizens would display the same desired provision of the public good; however, before- and after-tax incomes and
tax shares will generally be different for each citizen.

Consider now the nature of the new Lindahl equilibrium that
will obtain if the club as a collectivity receives a gift of $B'G$ units
of the public good (see Figure II). The Lindahl "auction" process,
instead of beginning with each member on his vertical axis, now com-
mences with everyone having the same disposable income as in the
previous equilibrium but with the collective activity at least tentatively set at a level $B'G$ units above its previous equilibrium level.
The process now determines a new equilibrium level of provision
of the public good and set of tax shares. For our typical individual
in Figure II, the Lindahl process, following the gift to the club,
begins at point D. At an announced tax share h', he confronts a
hypothetical choice among the alternative bundles of private and
public goods indicated by the straight line $A''B''$ passing through

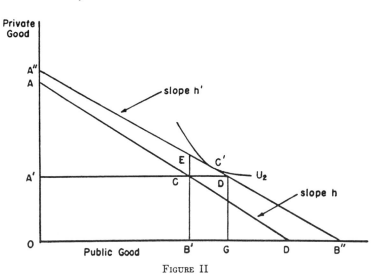

FIGURE II

D with slope *h'*. Suppose that from among these points the individual prefers *C'*; if *h'* is an equilibrium tax share, a set of shares for the other club members has been found such that they all are in agreement on the level of provision of the public good implied by *C'*.

In the new political equilibrium in the case depicted in Figure II, the level of the collective activity exceeds that prevailing before the revenue-sharing program, but by an amount less than the full sum of the grant. This implies that members' disposable income is correspondingly increased. Before turning to our central proposition, we might point out the formal fact that the effect of the grant could conceivably be an absolute reduction in the provision of the public good, or an increase by an amount exceeding the grant, depending on the preference maps of the members. This simply says that the public good may be an inferior good, a good with a very high income elasticity of demand, or somewhere in between.

We now turn to the question of whether the gift to the club may be considered as equivalent to a set of gifts to the individual members. On the assumption that each individual has a single most preferred level of the collective activity for his equilibrium tax share, a glance at Figure II enables us to see this equivalence. If, instead of making a grant to the club, the central agency had given *CE* of the private good to our typical individual, then, confronted with tax share *h'*, he would have chosen among precisely the same alternative combinations of public and private goods, with C' his desired outcome. With corresponding amounts (i.e., $B'G$ times the individual's tax share) given to other members and with each again confronted with the postgift tax share previously derived, precisely the same Lindahl equilibrium would emerge. Moreover, such a set of gifts to the members of the club costs the central agency exactly the same sum as the gift to the club. By simple geometry, distance CE equals $(h' \cdot B'G)$; since the tax shares add to one, summing this quantity of the private good over all the members yields a total gift of the private good of $B'G$.

It is important to emphasize that what has been shown here for the case of the Lindahl method of budget determination is that revenue sharing is equivalent to a highly specific program of individual tax reduction by the central government, *not* simply in the sense that the programs generate the same provision of public good by the club, for in addition they generate *precisely* the same after-tax income for each member. That is, they result in precisely the same vector describing the state of the club.

III. Revenue Sharing and Majority Rule

Critics have objected that the Lindahl model is an unsatisfactory example of collective decision making because it is unrealistic, especially in ignoring the problem of inducing citizens to reveal their demands for public services when their taxes depend directly upon this variable. Furthermore, it may be thought that our result is somehow dependent upon the special optimality characteristics of the Lindahl solution. Later in the paper, we describe a set of properties of budget determination systems that are sufficient to assure this result, properties that are both plausible and unrelated to any optimality conditions. Before proceeding to the more general analysis, however, it is useful to show that the same conclusions hold for a familiar collective decision rule that does not in general generate optimal outcomes: simple majority rule.

Although majority rule as a political process of budget determination has a certain appeal as being more "realistic" than the Lindahl rule, it requires more restrictions on the admissible outcomes of the process to assure determinacy. The central difficulty is that the "game" of determining the distribution of income does not have a solution under majority rule when all possible assignments of posttax income to citizens are considered allowable. While a majority can assure itself of the entire "pie," those in the excluded minority will always be able to offer a subset of the winners even greater rewards for joining a new majority.[6] While the Lindahl rule will generate a "solution" consisting of a government budget plus individual tax shares, majority rule will not, therefore, reach a stable outcome unless some restrictions are placed on the values of these variables. We consider here the case in which individual tax shares are taken as fixed in advance; the level of the club's budget then becomes the sole variable to be determined by the political process under majority rule.[7] That is, alternative pairs of levels of provision of the public good are put to the voting test until one is found that at least $(n/2 + 1)$ of the members prefer to any other.

In Figure III line AB, with slope h, shows the consumption alternatives in terms of the private and public goods for an indi-

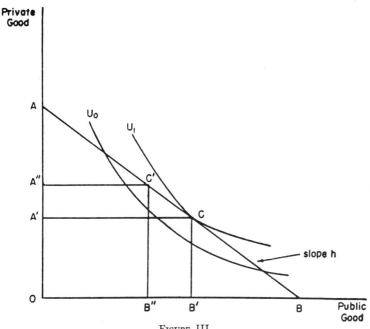

FIGURE III

6. This proposition has been analyzed formally by Benjamin Ward, "Majority Rule and Allocation," *Journal of Conflict Resolution*, Vol. 5 (Dec. 1961), pp. 379–89.

7. Duncan Foley has explored the possibility of stable outcomes under several different types of restrictions on tax shares (*op. cit.*). Foley, however, takes the level of the budget as fixed in his analysis.

vidual who has pretax income 0*A* and is assigned tax share *h*. Under the assumption that each person's preference structure generates indifference curves of the usual shape, every member's preference relation among club budget levels will be single-peaked. The individual represented in Figure III, for example, prefers budget level 0*B'* to all others. Furthermore, of any two proposed budgets less than 0*B'* he prefers the larger, while of any two greater than 0*B'* he prefers the smaller. In this situation, the well-known theorem of Duncan Black informs us that the equilibrium level of provision of the collective good is the median peak (i.e., the median of the members' most preferred budgets).[8] Note in addition that, since tax shares are fixed in advance, this majority rule process does not in general lead to a Pareto optimal level of provision of the public good.[9] This equilibrium budget level might be 0*B''*, in Figure III, which would place our typical club member at point *C'* with after-tax income 0*A''*.

Figure IV, derived in much the same way as was Figure II, illustrates the member's situation after his club has received a gift of *B''G* units of the public good. Since his tax share is assumed

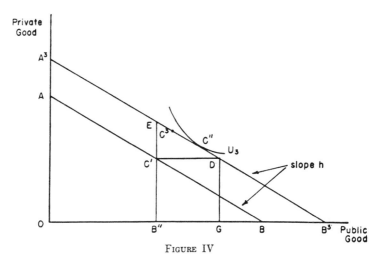

FIGURE IV

8. D. Black, "On the Rationale of Group Decision Making," *Journal of Political Economy*, Vol. 56 (Feb. 1948), pp. 23–34.
9. Since Black's analysis only considers a one-dimensional set of alternatives, our discussion of the case of majority rule, unlike that of the Lindahl mechanism, does not generalize directly into a world with many public goods. Tullock has made some headway toward generalizing Black's results (G. Tullock, "The General Irrelevance of the General Impossibility Theorem," this *Journal*, Vol. 81 (May 1967), pp. 327–52).

fixed in advance, the effect of the gift is to shift uniformly outward the locus of possible alternative bundles of private and public goods. The new set of alternatives lies along the straight line A^3B^3, with slope h, passing through D. The most preferred outcome of the member depicted is labeled C'', where the abscissa of C'' is the new peak of his preference structure over club budgets. Majority rule selects the median of such peaks, perhaps the abscissa of C^3, as the equilibrium level of provision of the public good, and our club member receives the bundle of private and public goods implied by C^3.

Could the external authority have achieved the same state of the club by a program of gifts directly to the members? Once again, the answer is apparent from an examination of Figure IV. Following a grant of $C'E$ of the private good (and assuming that he keeps the same assigned tax share, h), the member confronts the same alternatives that he does after the gift to the club; his preferences over these alternatives are unchanged, and in particular his preferred or "peak" level of provision of the public good is the same. Consequently, a set of grants to the members of the club where the ith member receives $h_i \cdot B''G$ (where h_i is his tax share) will generate precisely the same state of the club as the grant of $B''G$ of the public good to the collectivity.

Before we turn to a discussion of our efforts to generalize the results of these simple analyses, it may be worthwhile pointing out the approach they suggest to the measurement of the distributive effects of revenue sharing. The implicit gift to the individual involved in a gift of $0G$ to the club, in both the models considered, is $(h \cdot 0G)$, where h is the individual's tax share in the *new* equilibrium. Roughly speaking, the gift to the individual is the increment in taxes he would experience if the club expanded its budget, without the gift, by the amount $0G$. We must say "roughly" because (a) it is difficult to contrive a rigorous concept of a tax increment that would not be generated by the political process in fact, and (b) the tax share really needed is that prevailing in the new equilibrium. However, if we can devise some sensible approximations to the *marginal* tax shares of different classes of individuals, we can make some reasonable estimates of the net distributional effect of the adoption of a revenue-sharing program as contrasted to various patterns of reductions in federal taxes.

IV. REVENUE SHARING IN A MORE GENERAL FRAMEWORK

An interesting result of the preceding analysis is that, under two quite different types of collective decision-making rules, precisely the same conclusions concerning the nature of the effects of revenue sharing emerge: revenue sharing is in both cases equivalent to gifts directly to the members of the club. And even more specifically, we were able to show under both systems that gifts to the club were equivalent to a distribution of the total sum among the members such that each member's gift is proportional to his tax share. This immediately raises the issue of how general these results are. What characteristic of these collective decision-making rules is it that gives rise to this common outcome?

In the Appendix of this paper, we attempt to develop a more general analysis of this issue. The analytic framework is generalized in two ways. First, the definition of a state of the club is expanded to allow for any number of distinct collective activities. A state of the club is thus defined by a specification of the disposable incomes of the n members, of the levels of each of m collective activities, and of the cash balance of the club (which, of course, is only a particular collective activity). Second, no "constant cost" assumptions are made; instead it is simply assumed that there is at any time a given set of possible states of the club called the "feasible set." Although the intuitive motivation for this feasible set is the production possibility set of standard theory, we require only the restrictions that the set is closed and bounded, that no one be assigned a negative disposable income, and that any state attainable by redistribution of the total disposable income of a feasible state is itself feasible.

The notion of a political process is also put in a more generalized form. Specifically, we conceive of a political process as a mapping that indicates for any initial feasible state the set of possible ultimate political equilibria. The problem of the general analysis is then to describe the sorts of mappings for which our conclusion continues to hold that revenue sharing is precisely equivalent to a specific program of grants to individuals. That is, we seek to describe sufficient conditions on a political process to assure this result.

In the Appendix, we prove formally the sufficiency of one set of four conditions. They are:

(1) the mapping representing the political process is single-valued;

(2) the mapping is continuous;

(3) for a given feasible set, no two *distinct* equilibrium states exist for which it is true that in one everyone has a disposable income greater than or equal to his disposable income in the other; and

(4) if an individual has zero disposable income initially, he should not attain a greater disposable income via the political process than he would if in the initial state the collective cash balance were higher (with the other initial collective activities held the same).

Condition (1) is a kind of "determinacy condition." It says that, if you understood completely all the complexities of a club's political system, you could predict accurately the final state that would be reached from any initial state. This rules out randomness in the political process, although we consider it likely that analogous conditions to the four given ones would suffice to assure the validity of a similar theorem in a model that systematically incorporates uncertainty.

Condition (2) rules out threshold effects. It says that small changes in initial conditions will not generate abruptly large changes in political equilibrium, and might therefore be called the "no-revolution condition."

It may have been noticed that nothing has been said about the responsiveness of the political system to the preferences of the members. Nowhere have we mentioned maximizing behavior by the individual members, much less by the collectivity. And in fact, all of our conditions could be fulfilled by political processes completely unconnected with the members' preferences. However, we do require a property that we believe political processs highly responsive to individual preferences are likely to have, and that is condition (3). We therefore, with some hesitation, call it a "responsiveness condition." It says, in a sense, that the pattern of collective activities chosen by the club is not the result of whim. Some idea of its force is suggested by the things it rules out. It implies, for example, that there are no *politically feasible* ways to provide the collective service vector more cheaply for everyone than the way actually realized in any particular equilibrium (although there may be cheaper ways feasible under a different distribution of the tax burden). Moreover, it rules out "indifference": if the set of collective activities in an equilibrium state is disturbed in some feasible way — say, the level of police protection increased and the level of fire protection decreased — while leaving the disposable incomes of the members unchanged, then the resulting state is not a political equilibrium. Similarly, if the amount spent on collective activities in an equilibrium is changed with the change being financed by an increase (or decrease, as appropriate) in *everyone's* disposable income, the resulting state is not a political equilibrium. Note that it does *not* say, in either of these cases, that the political process will tend to restore the original state; it simply says that the state will be further changed from its initial disturbance.

Condition (4) is the "it doesn't pay to be poor" condition. It says that, if you start off with zero income, you will not do better than you would *if initially* the club were providing the same levels of collective services *and* more money were in the collective cash balance. Since this condition does seem essential for our result, it obviously is not trivial, and it may have hidden implications that we have not yet discovered. However, on its face it does not seem unreasonable.[1]

These four conditions are sufficient to assure the equivalence of revenue sharing and a particular pattern of gifts (central government tax cuts) to members. We find the conditions interesting not only because we think it plausible that they are approximately true in many cases, but also because there are identifiable situations where they are false, and where our equivalence conclusion does not hold. (Note, however, that we have not proved that failure of our conditions implies failure of the equivalence conclusion; we prove sufficiency, not necessity.)

The four conditions are not implausible ones. Conditions (1) and (2), making allowances for uncertainty, information costs, and time, seem tame enough. Condition (3), however, is both key to the results and somewhat more questionable. A little experimenting will convince the reader that it holds (as do (1) and (2), and (4) by default) in the simple political systems examined in the previous sections providing that individual members have strictly convex preferences.[2] Its applicability to the real world, however, depends upon the view that the results ruled out by condition (3), as discussed above, are properly excludable, say, for Princeton Borough, or the State of New Jersey. While we find condition (3) acceptable in many cases, there are clear examples where it is not

---

1. As Professor William Vickrey has pointed out to us, condition (4) can be made apparently even more innocuous by reducing the bound of "zero disposable income" to any finite negative number, since all that we require for the theorem is a lower bound to the set. We remain concerned, however, that, even in this form, it may have some implications we do not yet appreciate.

2. Note that the phrase, "for a given feasible set," must be taken seriously in this and other experiments. This means that the fact that an increase in all budgets might lead to no increase in the public good, only increases in disposable income, in either the Lindahl or majority-rule models does not violate condition (3), since these changes involve alterations to the feasible set. Condition (3) is perhaps weaker than may be first supposed.

fulfilled. These and other exceptions to the equivalence conclusion are discussed in the next section.

We should also point out that we have found it difficult to generalize the result, true for the simple models, that the gift to a member, which is identical in effect to the gift to the club, is equal to his tax share times the total amount of the gift to the club. This is because the concept of tax share in more general models is not well defined. To find the procedures for computing the equivalent gifts to individuals in more general models, which is precisely the problem of estimating equivalent gifts empirically under the assumption that our theorem is true of the real world, is a problem awaiting further work.

V. When Revenue Sharing Differs from Income Redistribution

We distinguish two sorts of cases in which the equivalence conclusion does not hold. In the first class are cases of the failure of condition (3), and, generalizing from the examples we can think of, we call this "failure by institutional structure." In the other class, the problem is more fundamental; the failure of equivalence arises from the invalidity of the modeling of the political process as a determinate mapping, given the set of feasible states. The cases we have constructed of this sort justify calling this "failure by learning or habit."

The first class may be illustrated by an extreme example. Suppose that Princeton Borough is forbidden by higher authority, say the state constitution, from collecting more than some fixed amount in taxes, perhaps based on the town's acreage. And suppose that the "real" equilibrium budget is significantly in excess of this amount, so that the town is continually spending its limit. In this situation, it may well be possible to find a combination of reduction in *all* citizens' incomes and increase in the town budget that would not be changed by the town's political process. This contradicts condition (3), and it is not difficult to see that the equivalence conclusion is likely to fail as well.

Much less extreme examples give similar results; in particular, no constraint by higher authority is needed to produce them. To take such a case, suppose that Princeton's own bylaws (amendable by a two-thirds majority) require a two-thirds majority approval of any property tax rate in excess of 3 percent, with lesser tax assessments requiring only a simple majority approval. Suppose further that seven-twelfths of the voters would approve a budget in excess of that which can be financed by the 3 percent tax. In this case also, it is not difficult to imagine a reduction in the incomes of all citizens, accompanied by an increase in town spending, such that the resulting situation is stable under the political process, since it could only be altered by a reduction in the property tax rate, preventable by a simple majority. Here again we have failure of condition (3); failure of the equivalence conclusion could certainly also be shown.

Clearly, the last example of violation of condition (3) is not farfetched, and even the first example may not be too far from describing the situation of some city governments. This suggests that a rationale for revenue sharing could be constructed on the basis of interest in the higher government in circumventing such structural characteristics of the lower-level governments as those described. The implications of this point of departure for sharing formulas (and for other specifics of revenue-sharing plans) appear to be a promising and interesting subject for further research.[3]

The second class of failures of the equivalence conclusion involves dynamic elements. In his textbook on public finance, Otto Eckstein points out: "An old program is a good program. Once it has existed for a period, a program generates its own clientele, both inside and outside the government, which has a vested interest in its continuance."[4] This could be interpreted to mean that the mapping that represents the choice from the set of alternative feasible states, given any starting point, itself depends upon the history of the system prior to the starting point. This phenomenon is akin to that of changing tastes in ordinary economic theory and could certainly upset the equivalence conclusion. A special case might be a sort of fiscal illusion whereby citizens don't know, and can't correctly imagine, the consequences of some proposed collective action. If they had experienced it, they would choose it; if not, they would reject it. If the sequence of events following revenue sharing should involve some experience with this action, the choice generated by the political process from a *given* starting point out of a *given* feasible set might well be different from that which would occur in the absence of that experience. As does the first class, the second

3. An obvious question that must be addressed in such an analysis is that of the functions of such structural features. James Buchanan has suggested some possible answers (*The Demand and Supply of Public Goods,* Chicago: Rand McNally, 1968).

4. O. Eckstein, *Public Finance,* 2nd ed. (Englewood Cliffs, N.J.: Prentice-Hall, 1967), p. 33.

class of failures of the equivalence conclusion might support a revenue-sharing program, and closer analysis of it would certainly be desirable.

VI. A System with Many Clubs

The analysis to this point has been conducted wholly in terms of revenue sharing by an external agency with a single, isolated group of individuals. When, however, we expand the system to include many fiscal clubs and allow mobility of individuals among clubs, the possibility arises of a new phenomenon, which may have implications both for resource use and for the distribution of income: competition among clubs for members. It has been argued by some advocates of revenue sharing that decentralized levels of government, engaged in competition to attract not only new residents but also additional business investment, are reluctant to raise tax rates for fear of discouraging potential entrants; such tax competition, so the argument goes, leads systematically to less than efficient levels of provision of the public services consumed in these jurisdictions. A program of revenue sharing, the advocates suggest, will help to resolve this problem by providing additional funds and thereby stimulating levels of expenditures on the public services provided by subcentral levels of government.[5]

It seems to us, however, that the extension of the analysis to a system with many clubs does not alter the substance of our earlier conclusions. There are, for example, real grounds on which to question the proposition that there in fact exists pervasive tax competition that leads to a systematic underprovision of state and local public services.[6] However, even if this contention is true, even if in our model all fiscal clubs hold their levels of provision of public goods below the desired level for fear of discouraging potential

5. See, for example, W. Heller, *New Dimensions of Political Economy* (Cambridge: Harvard University Press, 1966), p. 126.

6. Since potential residents (members) presumably consider fiscal benefits as well as costs in making choices, a jurisdiction (club) might, for example, have greater success in expanding its membership by extending, rather than contracting, levels of provision of public goods relative to what they would have been in the absence of competition. For an empirical study of 53 suburban communities in New Jersey, which suggests that the quality of local public schools, as well as local tax rates, influences significantly the location decisions of at least some families, see W. Oates, "The Effects of Property Taxes and Local Public Spending on Property Values: An Empirical Study of Tax Capitalization and the Tiebout Hypothesis," *Journal of Political Economy*, Vol. 77 (Nov./Dec. 1969), pp. 957–71. An interesting theoretical analysis of the formation of fiscal clubs is contained in J. Buchanan, "An Economic Theory of Clubs," *Economica*, Vol. 32 (Feb. 1965), pp. 1–14.

members by excessive tax bills, it does not follow that a revenue-sharing program will correct the situation.

To provide an incentive to expand the provision of public services to efficient levels, what is needed is a program that reduces, *at the margin*, the effective price of public services to the club. Some type of conditional, matching-grant program, for example, by which the external fiscal authority pays a certain proportion of the cost per unit of the public service will reduce the price of a unit of the good to the club's membership. Under a revenue-sharing program, in contrast, the price of an additional unit remains unchanged, and there is good reason to expect any existing tax competition to continue with the resulting subefficient levels of public output. As James Wilde has put it, "The introduction of an [unconditional] aid program can be expected to result in a tax competition as fierce as ever, though carried on at a lower level of local tax rates than previously." [7]

For this reason, revenue sharing in its pure form (i.e., as a wholly unconditional grant) is not the appropriate program to resolve inefficiencies stemming from tax competition among jurisdictions. Although, as we suggested in the preceding section, revenue sharing may under certain circumstances have more than just distributive effects, it does not provide the sort of systematic incentive for the expanded output of public services that would appear necessary to offset the effects of any existing tax competition. It is interesting in this regard that several proponents of revenue sharing, in their concern that federal assistance should provide a stimulus to the output of public services, have recommended the inclusion of a "fiscal effort" term in the revenue-sharing formula. Typically, the proposal is that the grant to a particular jurisdiction vary directly with the proportion of its income that the jurisdiction raises in tax revenues. Such a provision clearly does introduce a price effect into a revenue-sharing program; for each extra dollar the jurisdiction spends (through its own increased taxation), the size of the grant it receives from the central government is increased by some fraction of a dollar. A dollar of increased public expenditure thus costs the residents of the jurisdiction less than a dollar.

For this reason, the inclusion of a fiscal effort term in the revenue-sharing formula does destroy the formal equivalence of revenue sharing with a set of lump sum grants directly to the individual members of a club; it means a reduced price per unit of the public service to the club and in general higher levels of public outputs.

7. Wilde, *op. cit.*, p. 346.

It is possible, however, under some circumstances for a fiscal effort provision to lead to rather curious results. It can, for example, actually penalize a club or jurisdiction that, because of some institutional constraint (e.g., legal ceilings on property tax rates), is unable to increase its revenues. In this instance, other jurisdictions that respond with an increase in their own levels of taxation can realize a larger portion of the available shared revenues, thereby leaving a relatively smaller grant for the constrained collectivity.[8]

VII. CONCLUDING REMARKS

Using an analytic framework designed to describe models of collective choice, we have found in this paper that, for a reasonably broad class of processes of collective decision making, revenue sharing is precisely equivalent to a specific set of lump sum grants directly to the individual members of the collectivity. We found, however, that there are also a number of not implausible circumstances under which the equivalence theorem does not hold and for which revenue sharing may allow the realization of outcomes not attainable under any set of grants to individuals. An evaluation of the likelihood of these exceptions to the theorem is, we think, a matter of importance for the evaluation of revenue-sharing programs and a particularly promising area for further research.

Finally, we simply point out that, in assessing the empirical plausibility of the equivalence condition, it must be recognized that any actual revenue sharing will take place in a growing system, one in which for a number of reasons state and local budgets are probably going to rise fast enough to call for increases in tax rates (as well as revenues).[9] Equivalence (or approximate equivalence) does not require in this environment that states and localities cut their tax rates as a consequence of revenue sharing; it may imply only that they will not raise them as rapidly as otherwise.

8. The analytic framework developed in this paper also appears applicable to the study of intergovernmental grants with price effects; in particular, matching grants to a collectivity are, under appropriate conditions, presumably equivalent to some specific set of expenditure subsidies to individuals. This is a matter we are currently exploring.
9. For example, William Baumol has argued that an inevitable bias in technical progress will make state-local government activities ever more expensive relative to manufactured goods ("Macroeconomics of Unbalanced Growth: Anatomy of Urban Crisis," *American Economic Review*, Vol. 57 (June 1967), pp. 415–26). Some evidence on this is available in D. Bradford, R. Malt, and W. Oates, "The Rising Cost of Local Public Services: Some Evidence and Reflections," *National Tax Journal*, Vol. 22 (June 1969), pp. 185–202.

APPENDIX: A GENERAL THEOREM

Let S be the set of feasible states of the club. A typical element s of S is an $(n + m + 1)$-dimensional vector whose first n components, s_i $(i = 1, \ldots, n)$, specify the private good claims, y_i (the "disposable incomes"), of the n members, whose next m components, s_{n+j} $(j = 1, \ldots, m)$, indicate the levels, g_j, of operation of m collective activities, and whose $(n + m + 1)$ st component indicates the level, G, of the collective cash balance. The set S is determined by the resources available to the club and by the production and exchange relationships that determine how the private good can be transformed into the different collective goods. It is assumed that S is closed and bounded, that disposable incomes must be nonnegative, and that a state attainable from a feasible state by redistribution of its disposable income is itself feasible.[1] Symbolically, if $s \epsilon S$, then

$$s_i \geq 0, \quad i = 1, \ldots, n$$

and

$$s_j' = s_j \quad j = n + 1, \ldots, n + m + 1,$$
$$s_i' \geq 0 \quad i = 1, \ldots, n$$
$$\sum_{i=1}^{n} s_i' \leq \sum_{i=1}^{n} s_i$$
$$\rightarrow s' \epsilon S.$$

It is further assumed that collective activities are not costless or are, at best, free. Let $Y(g_1, \ldots, g_m, G)$ be the set of all distributions of disposable income obtainable in S, given government activities $g_1, \ldots, g_m$ and collective cash balance G. Then the last assumption can be formulated as the requirement that, for $\epsilon_1, \ldots, \epsilon_{m+1} \geq 0$, $Y(g_1 - \epsilon_1, \ldots, g_m - \epsilon_m, G - \epsilon_{m+1})$, if defined, contains $Y(g_1, \ldots, g_m, G)$. Figure V shows a typical feasible set in the two-person, one-public service case, assuming fixed collective cash balance, G.

We represent a political process for the club by a mapping, p_S, from S into the set of subsets of S, such that $p_S(s)$ is a set containing the possible ultimate equilibrium states in S that might be reached by the political process, given s as a "starting point." The political process, p_S, is thus a set-valued function of state vectors. If s is itself an equilibrium vector, $p_S(s) = \{s\}$; s is mapped into itself by political process.[2]

Of special interest to us are the restrictions that one must place on this rather general model of collective budget determination in order to be able to demonstrate a proposition about the equivalence

1. It would probably be possible to relax the last part of this restriction to say that the set of possible states having any given vector of collective services and collective cash balance is convex.

2. One might describe as a "constitution" the mapping from the set of all possible sets of feasible states to the set of possible political processes, $\{S\} \rightarrow \{p_S\}$.

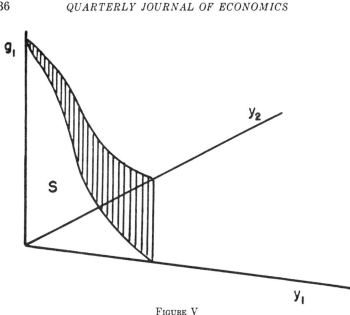

Figure V
The feasible set. S, holding collective cash balance at G, is enclosed by the shaded surface and the planes of the axes.

of revenue sharing to a program of income redistributions, as we have done in the simple cases examined in the text. We have found four assumptions about p_S to be sufficient for this:

ASSUMPTION 1. *To any initial state corresponds exactly one ultimate equilibrium state.*

In the text we described this assumption somewhat unrigorously as the single valuedness of the political process. Because of this assumption we can treat p_S as a vector-valued function of state vectors (though it is, strictly, a set-valued function); $p_S(s)$ is an element of S. If s is an equilibrium state, $p_S(s) = s$.

ASSUMPTION 2. *p_S is continuous.*

ASSUMPTION 3. *If s is an equilibrium state under p_S, and $s' \epsilon S$, $s' \neq s$ gives no less disposable income to all citizens ($s_i' > s_i$, $i = 1, \ldots, n$), then s' is not an equilibrium under p_S.*

The fourth assumption concerns families of subsets of S. Let $S(g_1, \ldots, g_m, G)$ refer to the set of all elements of S having the specified levels of government activities and the specified collective cash balance, and consider the family of such sets defined as G varies from zero to some maximum.

ASSUMPTION 4. *If $s \epsilon S(g_1, \ldots, g_m, G)$ and, for some $i \leq n$, $s_i = 0$, and $s' \epsilon S(g_1, \ldots, g_m, G')$, $G' > G$, then $p_S(s)_i \leq p_S(s')_i$.*

The meaning of these assumptions was discussed in the text. We can now state:

THEOREM. *Given A1–A4, if* $G < G'$ *and* $s' \epsilon S(g_1, \ldots, g_m, G')$, *then there exists* $s \epsilon S(g_1, \ldots, g_m, G)$ *such that* $p_S(s) = p_S(s') \equiv x$.

Before proceeding to a proof of the theorem we should indicate how it implies the equivalence conclusion. It is assumed that, since revenue sharing in its pure form does not affect the technology of producing public services or the terms of trade under which they are purchased, the set of feasible states is the same, no matter how the gift is made to the club — be it to the club's collective cash balance or to the individual citizen. The initial effect of a gift to the club is an increment to the club's cash balance; this new state is further transformed by the political process. The theorem says that among the states in the same feasible set with the same initial government services but with the pre–revenue-sharing cash balance, is a state that maps into exactly the same state as is attained as a result of revenue sharing. That is, the same final outcome can be produced by a gift directly to citizens.

Proof. The idea of the proof is very simple and recalls proofs of existence theorems in competitive equilibrium theory. Suppose we "try out" an arbitrary element of $S(g_1, \ldots, g_m, \check{G})$ (to simplify the notation we call this set henceforth simply $S(G)$) to see whether it maps into x under p_S. If, say, individual i ends up with too much disposable income on this trial, the natural next step would be to pick a new starting point in $S(G)$ that gives individual i somewhat less disposable income than the original trial vector. The initial disposable incomes of the other citizens are similarly adjusted. All we need to show is that there definitely is at least one element of $S(G)$ that does not need any adjustment, since A3 says that if two equilibria in S have the same disposable income components they are identical. (This oversimplifies slightly. Since it is against the rules to reduce the disposable income of someone who starts with zero, assumption A4 is needed to make sure this will not be required.)

The proof employs the Brouwer fixed-point theorem, which states that a continuous mapping from a closed and bounded convex set in Euclidean space into itself has a fixed point (i.e., there is a point that is mapped into itself by the function). Having shown $S(G)$ to be closed, bounded, and convex, we define a function that maps any element of $S(G)$ which does *not* lead via the political process to x as an equilibrium into a different element of $S(G)$, so that if this function maps that element into itself, then that element of $S(G)$ does generate the political equilibrium s. This "correction" process will be seen to be continuous, and hence such a fixed point must exist, establishing the theorem.

(1) $S(G)$ is closed, bounded, and convex. $S(G)$ consists of all elements of S with a certain specified collective activities vector and specified cash balance, G. Since it is also assumed that any distribution of a given total disposable income is possible (including distributions summing to less than the given total), clearly $S(G)$ is convex. Since S is bounded, so must be $S(G)$. Furthermore,

$S(G)$ is closed, for suppose a sequence of elements of $S(G)$ converges to a limit. Since S is closed the limit point is in S; since all elements of $S(G)$ have the same government services components and collective cash balance, so must the limit point. But then the limit point must be in $S(G)$, by definition of $S(G)$. It follows that there is a maximum aggregate disposable income in $S(G)$; call it $y^*(G)$.

(2) We first take care of a pathological case. If $y^*(G) = 0$, by the assumption about the costliness of government activities and cash balances, $y^*(G') = 0$. This means that $S(G')$ and $S(G)$ each contain a single element, s' and s, respectively, in which no one has a positive disposable income. Then, by A4, $p_s(s)_i \leq p_s(s')_i$, $i = 1$, $\ldots$, n. Then, by A3, $p_s(s) = p_s(s')$.

(3) If $y^*(G) > 0$, define the "correction mapping" in a series of steps. First, define the function f from $S(G)$ into Euclidean n-space:

$$f(s)_i = \max\{s_i + x_i - p_s(s)_i, 0\}, i = 1, \ldots, n;$$

then the mapping g from $S(G)$ into the real line:

$$g(s) = \max\left\{ \sum_{i=1}^{n} f(s)_i, y^*(G) \right\};$$

then the mapping h from $S(G)$ into Euclidean $(n + m + 1)$-space:

$$h(s)_i = \frac{y^*(G)}{g(s)} \cdot f(s)_i, \qquad i = 1, \ldots, n$$

$$h(s)_{n+j} = g_j, \qquad j = 1, \ldots, m$$

$$h(s)_{n+m+1} = G.$$

We must show that h is a continuous mapping into $S(G)$. Since all the component functions are continuous, so is h. Since $f(s)_i$ is constrained to be nonnegative, the first n components of h are nonnegative; i.e., the disposable incomes are nonnegative, as required. That the sum of the first n components of h is no greater than $y^*(G)$ is assured by the scaling factor $y^*(G)/g(s)$. Finally, the m government activity components of h and the collective cash balance are at those levels by which $S(G)$ is defined.

(4) Since h is a continuous mapping from $S(G)$ into $S(G)$, by Brouwer's theorem, it has a fixed point. We must now show that if s is such a fixed point, $p_s(s) = x$. If $s_i > 0$, $f(s)_i > 0$, and so $f(s)_i = s_i + x_i - p_s(s)_i$. Thus $h(s)_i = s_i$ implies

$$\frac{y^*(G)}{g(s)} (s_i + x_i - p_s(s)_i) = s_i;$$

$$x_i - p_s(s)_i = \left(\frac{g(s)}{y^*(G)} - 1 \right) s_i.$$

Since, by construction, $\dfrac{g(s)}{y^*(G)} \geq 1$, this implies $x_i - p_s(s)_i \geq 0$.

If $s_i = 0$, $f(s)_i = 0$, and so $x_i - p_S(s)_i \leq 0$. But, by A4, $p_S(s)_i \leq x_i$; hence $x_i - p_S(s)_i = 0$. Hence we have, for $i = 1, \ldots, n$,

$$x_i - p_S(s)_i \geq 0.$$

By A3, this implies $x_i = p_S(s)_i$, $i = 1, \ldots, n + m + 1$.

Q.E.D.

PRINCETON UNIVERSITY

Towards a Predictive Theory of Intergovernmental Grants*

By David F. Bradford *and* Wallace E. Oates
Princeton University

Until quite recently, theoretical analyses of the impact of intergovernmental grants on public expenditures have run either implicitly or explicitly in terms of the familiar theory of individual choice.[1] The recipient of the grant is typically viewed in effect as an individual decision maker with preference patterns of the usual sort defined over private and public goods. Within this theoretical structure, a number of propositions have been developed including, for example, the conclusion that, dollar-for-dollar, a matching grant will induce a greater expansion in spending on the public good than will a lump-sum, unconditional grant.

The difficulty with this analysis, as we all have been well aware, is that this is not the appropriate theoretical framework for the study of intergovernmental grants. Such grants are not grants to individuals; they are grants to groups of people. This means that the effects of these grants depend upon the process by which the group makes collective decisions. A real theory of intergovernmental grants must, for this reason, be one which takes explicitly into account the political process through which the collectivity determines its levels of spending upon public goods.

* The authors are grateful for a number of helpful comments to the participants in economics seminars at McMaster University and at Rutgers University. In addition, they are indebted to the Ford Foundation whose support has greatly facilitated this study.

[1] For an excellent presentation using this approach, see James Wilde.

In one recent paper, Goetz and McKnew have shown for a special case that it is conceivable that lump-sum grants can have a greater stimulative impact on public spending than an equal-dollar matching grant. Using a rather complicated model in which the collectivity decides separately on the aggregate level of public spending and on the mix of public programs, they show that, if individual preferences bear a particular kind of relation to one another, simple majority voting will lead to greater public expenditure in response to a lump-sum grant than to a matching grant of the same amount.

Whether this special case is likely to occur with any frequency is another matter, but, at any rate, it is clear that one can concoct particular instances in which a process of collective decision making will lead to results which are at variance with the conclusions which follow from the model of individual choice. Our purpose in this paper is to try to explore somewhat more systematically the effects of these two types of intergovernmental grants.

The question arises whether there are interesting classes of collective decision processes for which the comparative effects of the two types of intergovernmental grants can be predicted. In an earlier paper on revenue-sharing (Bradford and Oates), we have constructed a framework for conceptualizing collective budget determination which offers the possibility of dealing systematically with the effects of intergovernmental grants under varying sets of assumptions about the nature of political processes and the range of political possibilities. In that paper, we examined the case of lump-sum grants to collectivities, and we succeeded in distinguishing a class of political processes under which such grants are equivalent (both in terms of their allocative and distributive effects) to a set of grants directly to the individual members of the collectivity. In this paper, we explore the application of this same approach to a comparison of the effects of lump-sum and matching grants to political units.

In section I, we provide a brief recapitulation of the theory of intergovernmental grants in terms of the standard model of individual choice. This, as it turns out, proves to be of some value for the case of collective choice as well. Section II describes the conceptual framework for analyzing processes of collective choice that we developed in our earlier paper and indicates the relevance of the basic theorem proved there to the problem under study here. In section III, we use this framework to analyze the allocative and distributive effects of lump-sum and of matching intergovernmental grants where the collectivity makes its fiscal decisions by simple majority rule. In particular, we prove that, under simple majority rule with fixed tax shares and a single public good, a matching grant will always lead to a larger public expenditure than will a lump-sum grant of the same amount. In conclusion in section IV, we speculate on the prospects for generalizing this result.

I. *Intergovernmental Grants in a Model of Individual Choice*

In this approach, the recipient of the grant is typically assumed to be an individual decision maker with convex preferences defined over quantities of a private

good and a public good as in Figure 1.[2] To simplify the analysis we assume that units of both goods are chosen such that the price of the public good in terms of the private good is unity.

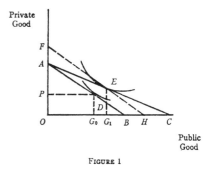

FIGURE 1

Subject to a pre-grant budget constraint of AB, the community selects an output of the public good of OG_0 which leaves OP to be consumed in the form of the private good. Assume next that the community is the recipient of a matching-grant program; the central government, for example, might agree to share the cost of providing the local public good by funding a specified percentage of the community's expenditure on the good. In terms of Figure 1, such a grant pivots the community's budget constraint outward about the point A to reflect what is now in effect a lower unit price of the public good to the local community. As a result, provision of the public good in Figure 1 rises to OG_1, and the community receives a grant of DE.

Suppose, however, that instead of a matching grant of DE, the grantor chose to give the community a lump-sum grant of the same amount. Such a grant would

[2] Alternatively, one might assume that Figure 1 represents community indifference curves. The difficulties associated with such curves are such, however, as to render them of dubious value, particularly for predicting the effects of government grants.

shift the community's budget constraint outward to FH but would not alter the relative prices of the private and public goods. Moreover, it is clear from Figure 1 that the matching grant would induce a smaller increase in spending on the public good than would the matching grant; since FH passes through E but is steeper than AC, it follows, given normal convexity properties of the preference map, that the tangency of FH with an indifference curve must lie to the left of E. Or, in economic terms, the lump-sum grant induces more expenditure on the public good because it not only enriches the community (i.e., has an income effect), but in addition reduces the price of the public good to the recipient (i.e., has a substitution effect). In the individual model, a matching grant thus possesses a greater stimulating effect on public spending than does a lump-sum grant of the same amount. We now turn to a reconsideration of the properties of these grants in a framework with explicit collective decision making.

II. *The Analytic Structure*

For simplicity, we will at this point continue to use a model in which there is a single pure public good, a single private good, and a given and constant price of each where the units of these goods are defined such that the price of the public good in terms of the private good is unity. We need next to describe in conceptual terms the local community and its political process. Briefly, we represent what we will call the *state of the community* by a vector $[y_1, y_2, \cdots y_n, g]$, whose first n components indicate the disposable incomes (or claims to the private good) of each of the n members of the community and whose last component, g, is the number of units of the public good. The set of *feasible states* of the collectivity represents the community's budget constraint; for each total quantity of the private good available for distribu-

tion among the members of the community, the boundary of this set indicates the maximum level of provision of the public good attainable.

Not all feasible states for the community, however, will be political equilibria. A state, for example, in which all the community's resources were used for provision of the public good would probably generate political pressures which would lead to another state in which members of the community would consume a positive quantity of the private good. In this framework, we can view the *political process* (or the rule for collective decision making) as the mechanism through which one feasible state is transformed into another (possibly itself). *For a given set of feasible states*, a political process thus defines for each initial feasible state the resulting equilibrium state; it is a mapping which indicates how the political process transforms each state of the community into an equilibrium state. Note in particular that, starting from a given feasible state, the political process simultaneously determines *both* the level of output of the public good and the disposable income of each member of the community.

From this perspective, we can characterize a grant to the community as a disturbance to the existing equilibrium state and a change in the feasible set. We could think of the grant as initially taking the form of an increment to the level of provision of the public good. However, this new state, which is itself a member of an enlarged set of feasible states, will not in general represent a political equilibrium. It will itself typically be transformed by the political process into a new equilibrium state.

We have found it extremely useful for analytic purposes to explore one particular question relating to the response of the community to a grant program. Specifically, we ask—in the case of each grant to the community as a whole—*if there is some particular way the grantor might have distributed the grant funds directly to the individual members of the community so that precisely the same equilibrium state of the community would result.* If this is the case, we can show that a particular intergovernmental grant is precisely equivalent, both in terms of its ultimate impact on the provision of the public good and on the disposable income of each member of the community, to a set of grants made directly to the individuals themselves.

We find (not surprisingly) that the answer to this question depends upon the properties of the political process. In our earlier paper, we developed a proposition for lump-sum grants which may be described briefly as follows. Assume that a grant program to a community acts in the first instance to increase some collective activity (where "holding a cash balance in the public treasury" counts as a collective activity). In contrast, assume that each of the set of grant programs to individuals which duplicates the effective set of possibilities (i.e., the feasible set) generated by the grant to the collectivity, has the initial effect of simply increasing individual disposable incomes, leaving the levels of the local government activities unchanged.[3] Then, our proposition states that, under a set of suitable conditions on the political process (conditions discussed at length in our earlier paper), there is a program of grants to individuals which leads via the political process to precisely the same equilibrium state of the community as does the grant to the collectivity.[4]

[3] We could be comparing, for example, a grant of $1 million to a local government which initially simply increases local public revenues to a set of grants directly to the individual members of the community where the sum of these latter grants is $1 million.

[4] It is interesting that the proof of this proposition does not require that there exist any particular relationship between individual preferences and collective choice.

In the most general case, it is not possible to derive the precise character of this program of individual grants. However, in particular cases in which the political process is specified in some detail (as we will show in the next section), this can be done. Finally, and directly to the point of our study here, we have found that for certain cases, we can link individual preferences and the implicit set of individual grants through the political process in a manner which allows us to predict the effects of changes in the form of the grant on the collective choice. And it is to this issue we turn now.

III. *Intergovernmental Grants and Simple Majority Rule*

An important example in which we can employ our analytic framework to examine in some detail the effects of different programs of intergovernmental grants is the case where the community makes its collective fiscal decision by simple majority rule. More specifically, we will take as our model a community in which each individual's tax *share* is known and fixed and in which the level of provision of the public good is determined by a simple majority voting rule. By this we mean that the community votes on alternative pairs of provision of the public good until one is found which at least $((n/2)+1)$ members of the community prefer to any other. This model could represent, for example, a local school district which finances its expenditures through a local property tax and which employs majority voting to determine the annual school budget. In this instance, each individual's tax share is defined by the assessed value of his property divided by the total assessed value of taxable property within the district. His tax bill is then determined by the product of his tax share and the size of the school budget selected by the electorate.

In Figure 2, we indicate the position of

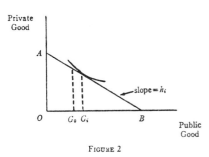

FIGURE 2

any individual (say the ith) member of the community. Since by construction the price per unit of the public good in terms of the private good is unity, the slope of his budget constraint, AB, is equal to his tax share, h_i (i.e., the "tax-price" to him of a unit of the public good). Assuming that each person's preference map exhibits indifference curves of the usual shape, it follows that the preferences of each member of the community for the public good will be single-peaked. In terms of Figure 2 where OG_i is the individual's most preferred level of provision of the public good, this means that, between any two levels of the public good greater than OG_i, he prefers the smaller of the two (i.e., the one closer to OG_i). Similarly, for any two budgets less than OG_i, he prefers the larger. With preferences which satisfy this property of single-peakedness, the theorem of Duncan Black states that, under simple majority rule, the equilibrium budget is the median peak. or in other words, the median of the most-preferred levels of provision of the public good. This means that, aside from the individual who possesses the median peak, the equilibrium public budget will not be that budget which is most preferred by any given member of the community. In Figure 2, for example, the equilibrium budget, say OG_0, will in general differ from the individual's most preferred budget, OG_i.

Let us now disturb the political equi-

librium represented in Figure 2 by the introduction of a grant program to the community. We consider first the case of a lump-sum grant to the collectivity. Assume that the central government provides the community with an unconditional grant of a specified sum. In Figure 3, if the grant were $EH = BD$, this would imply that, if each member of the community were to maintain his level of consumption of the private good at its previous equilibrium level, the output of the public good could increase to OG_1, or by the full amount of the grant. The full range, how-

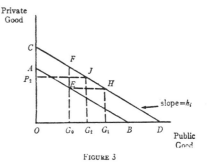

FIGURE 3

ever, of alternative bundles of private and public goods available to the ith individual is indicated by the new budget constraint, CD, and it is unlikely that the point H will represent a new political equilibrium. Suppose instead that, using majority rule, the community decides to increase the public budget to OG_2 so as to increase also consumption of the private good. In Figure 3, point J by assumption thus indicates the new equilibrium provision of the public good and the level of private consumption, OP_2, of individual i.

We now ask if, instead of using an intergovernmental grant, the grantor could have generated the identical equilibrium state of the community by parcelling out the grant funds directly to the individual members of the community. The answer is yes. If, for example, the central government had given person i in Figure 3 a lump-sum grant of EF, this individual would have had precisely the same budget constraint, CD, as in the case of the grant of EH to the collectivity. With the same budget constraint and a given preference map, his array of preferences for public budgets and hence his voting pattern would be exactly the same in the two cases.

Note next that $(EF) = h_i(EH)$, the grant to each individual, which from his position is equivalent to the grant to the collectivity, is equal to the product of his tax share and the intergovernmental grant. Moreover, since the tax shares (the h_i) sum to one, it follows that the sum of the grants to the individuals equals the amount of the original grant to the collectivity. This means that, if the central government simply divides up the grant monies among the individuals in proportion to each person's *local* tax share, precisely the same state of the community results as if the total of the grant funds were given to the public treasury of the community. A lump-sum grant to a community in this model is, therefore, an implicit set of grants to the members of the community where each individual's grant is proportional to his local tax share.

Consider next the case of a matching grant to the community. In Figure 4 with AB again possessing slope h_i and representing the individual's pre-grant budget constraint and with G_0 the original equilibrium public budget, the grant pivots the individual's budget line about point A to AC. Note that the slope of AC is $[h_i(1-m)]$, where m is the fraction of the unit cost of the public good funded by the grantor. If, for example, the grantor adopted a 1:1 matching grant, this would imply that $m = \frac{1}{2}$, or that the effective tax-price to the individual is now:

$$h_i(1 - m) = h_i(1 - \tfrac{1}{2}) = \tfrac{1}{2}h_i.$$

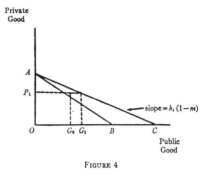

FIGURE 4

A matching grant to the community thus reduces the tax-price per unit to each taxpayer by the fraction m. As a result of the grant, the community will, by majority rule, select a new level of provision of the public good which we indicate by G_1 in Figure 4. In this particular case, our i^{th} person ends up consuming OG_1 of the public good and OP_1 of the private good.

It is easy in this case to see how the central government could have generated this same equilibrium state of the community by dealing directly with the individual members rather than by a matching intergovernmental grant. In particular, suppose that the central government refunded directly to each individual the fraction m of his local tax payment. Or, perhaps more realistically, the central government might allow the ith individual a credit of (mT_i) against his tax bill from the central government, where T_i is the ith person's local tax bill. In either case, the effect on each individual in the community would be identical to that resulting from an intergovernmental matching grant where the central government funded the fraction m of the local budget. In all these cases, the resulting budget constraint for each individual and hence his voting pattern would be the same. It is thus clear that the median peak of preferred budgets would be OG_1 in Figure 4 for all these alternatives. Within our model of simple majority voting with fixed tax shares, an intergovernmental matching grant in which the grantor pays x percent of the local expenditure on the public good is therefore precisely equivalent both in terms of its effect on the public budget and on the disposable income of each person in the community to a refund to each individual of x percent of his local tax bill.

On the basis of the preceeding analysis, we are now in a position to compare the effects of equal-size matching and lump-sum grants on the level of the public budget. Consider first in Figure 5 the effects on the ith person of a matching-grant program to the community where the fraction m again represents the grantor's

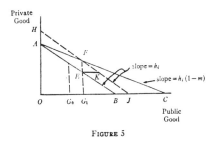

Private
Good
H
A
F
slope $= h_i$
E K
slope $= h_i(1-m)$
O G_0 G_1 B J C
Public
Good

FIGURE 5

share of local public expenditures and which results in an increase in public spending from OG_0 to OG_1. In this case the implicit grant to the ith individual (i.e., the rebate on his local taxes that he would have received from the central government under a program equivalent to the matching grant) is the distance EF. The grant to the community would thus equal $\Sigma(EF_i)$, which (as indicated earlier) is the distance EK.

Suppose next that, instead of a matching grant to the community, the central government chose to make a lump-sum intergovernmental grant of this same sum, EK. From our earlier analysis, it is clear

that this would be precisely equivalent to a set of lump-sum grants directly to the individuals in the community such that the size of each person's grant is proportional to his local tax share; in Figure 5, for example, the ith individual would receive a lump-sum grant of EF. This would shift the individual's budget line up by the distance EF to the new budget line HJ. We can now see that in this model, lump-sum and matching intergovernmental grants of the same total sum have precisely the same implicit pattern of grants to the individual members of the community: they both imply a distribution of the grant funds among individuals in proportion to each individual's local tax share. The difference is that the matching grant has a price effect as well as an income effect, whereas the lump-sum grant results only in an income effect.

With the result, we can now prove that under simple majority rule with fixed tax shares, a matching intergovernmental grant will always produce a larger expenditure on the public good than will a lump-sum grant of the same amount. On first glance, it might appear that we could simply invoke the analysis of grants in the model of individual choice and argue that the ith individual will always prefer a larger public budget under the intergovernmental matching grant than under a lump-sum grant of the same size because the matching-grant has a favorable price effect in addition to an income effect. Since, therefore, all persons prefer a larger public budget, the median of the most-preferred budgets will obviously also be larger. This, however, is not quite true.

This argument is valid for the median voter. In this case, the equilibrium local budget is his most preferred budget so that, under the matching grant in Figure 5, he would have an indifference curve tangent to AC at this point, F. The argument from the model of individual choice clearly is applicable in this instance; a lump-sum grant to him of *EF* (or, equivalently, an intergovernmental lump-sum grant of *EK*) would lead him to a most-preferred provision of the public good which is smaller than that under the matching-grant program.

Consider next, however, the case in Figure 6 where an individual's most-preferred budget under the matching grant is indicated by point *M*, a budget which is less than that of the median voter. In this instance, it is possible that this person

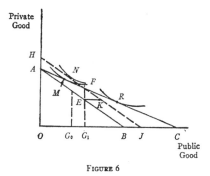

Private
Good

H
A N
              F
M R
     E K

O G_0 G_1 B J C
                                    Public
                                    Good

FIGURE 6

could prefer a larger budget (e.g., that indicated by point *N*) if the community received a lump-sum grant of *EK* than under the matching-grant program. This *can* occur because the individual's implied grant, *EF*, under the lump-sum intergovernmental grant exceeds the implicit sum he would receive under *his* most-preferred budget under the matching grant. In this case, the added income effect of the larger implicit lump-sum grant may be stronger than the substitution effect of the *hypothetical* matching grant. Note, however, and this is crucial to the argument, that, although such a person's most-preferred budget *may* be larger under the lump-sum intergovernmental grant, it will *never* be as large as the equilibrium budget under the matching grant. It is clear from

the geometry in Figure 6 that the tangency of an indifference curve with a budget line under the lump-sum grant must always occur on a curve which is higher than that which passes through *M*, and this means that the point *N* must always lie to the left of *F*.

We have shown, therefore, that all voters with most-preferred public budgets less than the median under the matching grant will continue to vote for budgets under the lump-sum grant which are smaller than the equilibrium budget under the original matching grant. Since the model of individual choice shows that the median voter under the matching grant will himself prefer a smaller budget under the lump-sum grant, it follows that the median of the most-preferred public budgets will be smaller under a lump-sum intergovernmental grant than with a matching-grant program of the same amount. It is, incidentally, easy to see that people who prefer relatively large budgets under the matching grant (e.g., like point *R* in Figure 6) will generally prefer smaller budgets under the lump-sum grant. For these individuals, the most-preferred budget under the matching grant implies a larger income effect than the lump-sum grant, as well as the price effect.

IV. *Some Further Thoughts*

In Section III, we were able to employ our analytic framework to reach some specific conclusions concerning the allocative and distributive effects of intergovernmental matching and lump-sum grants for the case of simple majority rule with fixed tax shares. While we feel that these results are of some interest in themselves, they are obviously quite limited in a number of respects. Besides applying to a single collective decision rule, they are derived in a model which assumes convexity of preferences, a single public good, etc.

This raises the issue of the extent of the generality of these results. We might mention that, although we have decided not to burden the reader with another special case, we have been able to prove that the results derived in section III also follow for the case of the Lindahl budget-determination model under the assumption that the collective activity is a normal good. Aside from this, however, we can report only somewhat uneven progress in our attempts to generalize these propositions concerning lump-sum and matching grants.

In our earlier paper, we were able to demonstrate the basic theorem of the existence of a set of individual lump-sum grants which is equivalent to a lump-sum grant to the collectivity as a whole for a fairly broad class of collective decision processes in which there are any number of collective goods and in which there are virtually no restrictions on the properties of individual preferences. The same formal analysis implies that, for this same broad class of political processes, there exists a set of tax credits to individuals and lump-sum redistributive payments within the community which would duplicate the allocative and distributive effects of any particular intergovernmental matching-grant program.

These propositions concern political choices within a *given* set of alternative states. The principal concern of this paper, on the other hand, is the comparison of choices made under different sets of feasible states, a comparison of the choice made among the alternatives available under a matching grant with that made from the different set of states possible under a lump-sum grant. The restrictions which we placed upon the political process in our earlier paper seem, we feel, both plausible and not obviously equivalent to the conclusions expressed in the propositions. However, to compare outcomes in different feasible sets requires further assumptions about the political process, and it remains an open question whether there are reasonable and interesting restrictions which will ensure in general the result derived for the particular case in this paper.

REFERENCES

D. Black, "On the Rationale of Group Decision Making," *J. of Pol. Econ.*, Feb. 1948, *56*, 23–34.

D. Bradford and W. Oates, "The Analysis of Revenue-Sharing in a New Approach to Collective Fiscal Decisions," to appear in a forthcoming issue of the *Quart. J. Econ.*

C. J. Goetz and C. R. McKnew, Jr., "Paradoxical Results in a Public Choice Model of Alternative Government Grant Forms," in *The Theory of Public Choice: Essays in Application,* J. M. Buchanan and R. S. Tollison, eds. (Ann Arbor: University of Michigan Press, forthcoming).

J. Wilde, "The Expenditure Effects of Grant-in-Aid Programs," *Nat. Tax J.*, Sept. 1968, *21*, 340–8.

[10]

LUMP-SUM INTERGOVERNMENTAL GRANTS HAVE PRICE EFFECTS

Wallace E. Oates

This paper seeks to resolve an emerging inconsistency: the existing theory of intergovernmental grants suggests that unconditional grants have only income effects, with the implication that they will provide only a modest stimulus to budgetary expansion, while empirical studies find a much greater expansionary impact than can be rationalized in terms of a pure increase in income. This apparent inconsistency is of some importance, for it obscures the perspective we should take on basic programs, such as federal revenue-sharing and certain state grants to local authorities. If, for example, the theory is correct, then revenue-sharing becomes simply a veil for a federal tax cut to individuals. Several years ago, Bradford and Oates produced a set of sufficient conditions for an unconditional intergovernmental grant to be fully equivalent, in both its allocative and its distributive effects, to a set of lump-sum grants made directly to the individuals who constitute the collectivity. This proposition, although hedged by a number of important restrictions, seemed fairly powerful and compelling. In particular, it suggested that an additional dollar of

ACKNOWLEDGMENT. I am grateful to David Bradford, Sharon Bernstein Megdal, Kenneth Rosen, and the members of COUPE for a number of helpful comments on an earlier draft of this paper. Financial support for this research was provided through a grant to the Princeton University Economics Department from the Sloan Foundation. Wallace E. Oates, Princeton University.

lump-sum grants to a government should have roughly the same expansionary impact on public expenditure as a dollar increase in the private income of that jurisdiction.

However, empirical work indicates otherwise. In a recent survey of empirical studies of intergovernmental grants, Gramlich (1977) concludes that the "work to this point strongly suggests that revenue-sharing is not a veil for tax cuts—that it does make an appreciable difference in the pattern of expenditures whether the federal government disburses untied aid to state and local governments or makes untied tax cuts benefiting individuals" (p. 230). Although the findings vary considerably among studies, they nearly all imply a marginal propensity to spend from lump-sum grants well in excess of the $.05 to $.10 range of estimated responses in state-local public expenditure to a one dollar increase in private income. The Gramlich and Galper study (1973), for example, estimates that an additional dollar of unconditional aid to state and local governments induces, on average, a 43 cent increase in their spending. Gramlich observes, "The results are so striking that the field could well use more theory . . . on whether and under what conditions the standard indifference-curve, utility maximization analysis had better give way to a variant more cognizant of political realities" (p. 230).[1]

This paper is a direct response to Gramlich's challenge. It sets forth a simple model of local budgetary choice consisting of output-maximizing local officials constrained by voter preferences. The model generates what is at first sight a rather surprising phenomenon: lump-sum intergovernmental grants have the effect of simply reducing the price of local output (resulting in a movement along the demand curve). In contrast, an increase in private income shifts the demand curve in the usual way. I have deliberately kept the model extremely simple (but, I think, fairly realistic within these limits) to focus on this fundamental asymmetry, for it is this kind of asymmetry that is implied by the empirical evidence.

---

1. An alternative response to this apparent inconsistency between theory and measured behavior is embodied in the intriguing paper in this volume by Howard Chernick. Chernick contends that at least certain forms of nonmatching grants have quite important incentive effects. More specifically, grant administrators, through negotiation, seek (and typically obtain) a substantial commitment of resources from recipients to supplement whatever aid is given. This suggests that much of what has been treated as lump-sum grants for purposes of empirical analysis may, in fact, have important *implicit* matching provisions.

The Model

In brief, the model[2] postulates that local government seeks to maximize output. One can envision a local school board that attempts to expand the curriculum in local schools and to enrich its quality. The local authority must, however, "sell" its program and the associated budget to the electorate. The demand functions of the electorate thus become a constraint on the determination of the local budget. In particular, I shall employ the standard median-voter proposition in the following way: local officials set output at the highest level consistent with the demand of the median voter. To motivate this assumption, consider again a local school board which presents to the electorate a proposed budget on which voters must indicate their approval or disapproval by a simple yes or no. If the proposed budget is rejected, then a process is set in motion (perhaps, but not necessarily, involving a subsequent vote) which will result in a somewhat reduced level of expenditure. In this case, all those who wish a budget equal to, or larger than, that proposed by the school board will vote yes. Those who prefer a smaller budget may vote no with the prospect of a lower level of spending and taxes. The school board, to guarantee itself of majority support for its proposal, sets its budget equal to the median of the voters' preferred budgets. A proposal in excess of this runs the risk of rejection.[3]

Voters make their decisions on the basis of two pieces of information: the level of output (Q) and the associated tax liability (T), which implies that voters know only the tax-price (Q/T), not necessarily the true cost, of providing the proposed level of services. Imagine once again the local school board taking to the voters an annual proposal for a program of school services and a property-tax levy to finance the program. What happens in this model is that intergovernmental grants allow the local authority to provide a given

---

2. The model developed in this section is quite similar in spirit to that in Courant et al. in this volume. The magnitudes of the implied responses to grants are, however, quite different.

3. More formally, the "reversion level" to which the budget adjusts in the event of rejection is of crucial importance. If, for example, a rejection of the board's proposal entails a drastic cut, some of those who would have preferred a budget only slightly less than that on the ballot may vote yes. Thus, somewhat paradoxically, a very low reversion level may permit local authorities to get assent to a larger budget than otherwise. For a careful treatment of all this, see Romer and Rosenthal (1977).

FISCAL FEDERALISM AND GRANTS-IN-AID

level of services at a lower tax-price to the voters; this is the source of the price effect.

Somewhat more formally, the model can be expressed in terms of the following system of six equations:

$$B = Q \tag{1}$$

$$B = T + R_o \tag{2}$$

$$P = \frac{B - R}{B} = \frac{T}{Q} \tag{3}$$

$$Q_d = Y_o{}^\alpha P_m{}^\beta \tag{4}$$

$$P_m = \gamma P \tag{5}$$

$$Q_s = Q_d, \tag{6}$$

where:

B = Total public expenditure on the service,
Q = Level of output of the service (subscripts d and s refer to quantity demanded and quantity supplied),
T = Locally raised tax revenues,
R_o = Intergovernmental grants received (exogenously determined),
P = Tax-price per unit of output (where subscript m refers to the tax-price of the median voter),
Y_o = Level of private income (exogenously determined).

Equation (1) states that the size of the budget is equal to the level of output; here I assume that output is provided at constant cost with units defined so that cost per unit is one.[4] Equation (2) indicates that whatever part of the budget is not financed by (exogenously determined) intergovernmental revenues must be met by local tax receipts. Equation (3) defines the tax-price to the community; note that the community's *perceived* price is the *average* tax cost per unit. (More on this soon.) In (4), I assume a simple multiplicative demand function, where the individual voter's demand function for the public

---

4. For purposes of the analysis here, I shall simply assume that local officials provide public services at minimum cost. Alternatively, one could posit that the constant cost per unit includes an element of waste or "fat" in the budget. Either interpretation will generate the asymmetry that is the central concern of this paper.

service depends upon his (given) level of income and his tax-price. The demand function in (4) is that of the median voter who is the point of reference for the analysis; his tax-price, P_m, is assumed in (5) to be some predetermined fraction of P, the tax-price to the community. Finally, equation (6) embodies the assumption of output maximization by local officials: it says that these officials set output at the maximum level that voters can be sure to support by pushing the budget to the largest size consistent with a guarantee of majority assent (i.e., the median of the most preferred budgets). The model consists of six equations and six unknowns and will, in general, produce a solution when private income and intergovernmental grants are given.

Figure 1 depicts this solution. Let D_m represent the demand curve of the median voter. In the case where intergovernmental grants are zero, the tax-price to the median voter is represented by a straight line with a vertical intercept equal to γP_m. Note the effect of a positive lump-sum intergovernmental grant: it shifts γP_m to $\gamma P_m'$ by lowering the tax-price of output. The result is that we move along the

Figure 1

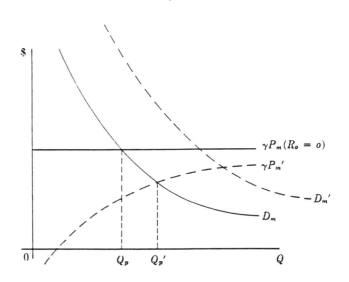

demand curve to a higher level of output, Q_p'.[5] The asymmetry between lump-sum grants and increases in private income is immediately apparent. Increases in income shift the demand curve outward (as illustrated by D_m'), while grants lower the price to the taxpayer-voter and produce a downward movement along his demand curve.

It is, incidentally, unclear whether a one-dollar increase in grants will lead to less, the same, or more public spending than a one-dollar increase in private income. That depends on the price and income elasticities of demand. If we differentiate the system for B with respect to Y and R, we find that:

$$\frac{dB}{dR} = \frac{-\beta T^{-1}}{F} \tag{7}$$

$$\frac{dB}{dY} = \frac{\alpha Y^{-1}}{F} \tag{8}$$

where: $F = \dfrac{1 - \beta(R/T)}{B}$.

For (7) to exceed (8), we require that:

$$\frac{-\beta}{\alpha} > \frac{T}{Y} \tag{9}$$

(i.e., that the ratio of absolute value of the price elasticity of demand to the income elasticity of demand exceed local taxes as a fraction of private income). Existing elasticity estimates (see, for example, Bergstrom and Goodman, 1973) for local services suggest that the value of the left-hand side of (9) is on the order of one-half, which well exceeds the value of the right-hand side. Inserting some typical values for the parameters and variables into (7) and (8), I calculated that $dB/dR \approx .4$ and $dB/dY \approx .1$ which are quite close to actual estimates.

---

5. An admitted difficulty with the analysis is that we have no guarantee that the same person in the before and after situations will be the median voter. It is, thus, not quite legitimate to assume that we are moving along one individual's demand curve, although this may still represent a reasonable approximation. One set of conditions sufficient to guarantee that the median voter doesn't change is that all voters have the same underlying preference functions, that output is financed by a proportional or progressive income tax, and that alterations in the distribution of income are not so large as to change the rank ordering of incomes. This is obviously a very restrictive set of conditions.

None of these computations, of course, should be taken very seriously in such a simplified model. Nevertheless, it's always encouraging to see one's model generate plausible results.

Fiscal Illusion and Voter Behavior

One aspect of this formulation requires further comment. It might appear from equation (6) that the existence of an output-maximizing local authority is superfluous to the model; since the equilibrium output is that demanded by the median voter, it would seem that a voting model is all that is needed. This, however, is not quite true. In fact, the local government uses the grant funds to deceive voters (who possess less-than-complete information about the true cost of output) into agreeing to an excessively high level of output. The marginal cost of output *to the electorate* is unity so that the median voter would prefer, in figure 1, an output of Q_p, irrespective of whether there are grant funds available or not.[6] But what the electorate sees is not a price of unity, but rather a tax-price equal to the fraction of total costs covered by local tax collections; the voter thus uses an average tax-price (which is less than the true marginal cost to him) to decide on levels of output. There is a kind of fiscal illusion in the model, which the local authority operates to its advantage by generating a higher level of services than the electorate would really desire if it had accurate cost information.

This clarifies somewhat the source of the asymmetry in the collective-choice mechanism. Increases in personal incomes to the members of a community are not equivalent, in terms of their budgetary effects, to an equal increase in lump-sum intergovernmental revenues because, although they may generate the same true budget constraint, they do not result in the same *perceived* budget constraint. In general, voter choices will depend on the particular form in which their increase in resources comes.

REFERENCES

Bergstrom, T., and Goodman, R. 1973. Private Demands for Public Goods. *American Economic Review* 63: 280–96.

---

6. This ignores any income effects associated with the grant (which is probably an appropriate assumption, since grant funds disbursed by a higher level of government must be financed by taxes). For a treatment which incorporates explicitly the cost of the grants, see Courant et al.

Bradford, D., and Oates, W. 1971. The Analysis of Revenue Sharing in a New Approach to Collective Fiscal Decisions. *Quarterly Journal of Economics*, 85: 416–39.

Chernick, H. The Economics of Bureaucratic Behavior: An Application to the Allocation of Federal Project Grants. This volume.

Courant, P.; Gramlich, E.; and Rubinfeld, D. The Stimulative Effects of Intergovernmental Grants: Or Why Money Sticks Where It Hits. This volume.

Gramlich, E. 1977. Intergovernmental Grants: A Review of the Empirical Literature. In W. Oates, ed., *The Political Economy of Fiscal Federalism.* Lexington, Mass.: Lexington Books, 219–40.

Gramlich, E., and Galper, H. 1973. State and Local Fiscal Behavior and Federal Grant Policy. *Brookings Papers on Economic Activity* 1: 15–58.

Romer, T., and Rosenthal, H. 1977. Bureaucrats vs. Voters: On the Political Economy of Resource Allocation by Direct Democracy. Unpublished manuscript.

[11]

THE ROLE OF INTERGOVERNMENTAL GRANTS IN THE U.S. ECONOMY WITH SPECIAL ATTENTION TO COUNTERCYCLICAL POLICY

By Wallace E. Oates*

CONTENTS

Under a federal system of government, the public sector is not a single, monolithic decision-making structure; it is, rather, a highly fragmented collection of agents working in the context of a constitution which outlines (often only very roughly) the scope of independent responsibilities and powers of the different levels of government. In the abstract, we can envision each level of the public sector setting about its own business; Lord Bryce, late in the nineteenth century, described a federal system in terms of ". . . a great factory wherein two sets of machinery are at work, their revolving wheels apparently intermixed, their bands crossing one another, yet each doing its own work without touching or hampering the other." [1]

In practice, however, federal systems have evolved in sharp contrast to the Bryce conception. We live in an age of "cooperative federalism" in which the activities of different levels of government are enmeshed to a very high degree. The objective and responsibilities of Federal, State, and local governments overlap and their operations impinge upon one another to such an extent that it is simply impossible to set forth autonomous or independent functions for the various governmental levels. Instead, the central problem becomes one of integrating budgetary and other decisions of different public units into a coherent and, to the degree possible, a consistent set of policies.

*University of Maryland.
[1] Lord Bryce, "The American Commonwealth" (New York: Macmillan, 1896), p. 325.

It is largely from this perspective that intergovernmental grants have come to play a central role in the fiscal structure of nearly all federal governments. Such grants have proved to be a highly flexible fiscal instrument with which one level of government can provide both inducements and assistance to another in a way that promotes the objectives of the public sector as a whole. There remain compelling advantages, for example, for retaining a large measure of fiscal discretion at highly decentralized levels of government; State and local governments are in a position to tailor their programs to the particular needs and preferences of their own constituencies. At the same time, the Federal Government has its own set of allocative and distributive responsibilities and priorities. But rather than preempt State and local choice (which is often unconstitutional, as well as unwise), the Federal Government can induce State and local officials to take account of the national interest through a set of grants that provides direct fiscal incentives for expanding those activities that confer benefits on the rest of the Nation (or, alternatively, to curtail those that have detrimental external effects).

Intergovernmental grants thus constitute a powerful policy tool for the integration of decisions by different levels of government. As such, it is not too surprising to find that these grants have exhibited a dramatic historical growth. In the United States, for example, Federal grants to State and local governments totalled about $2½ billion in 1950 (about 5½ percent of Federal expenditures); by 1977 these grants had reached over $60 billion (approximately 15 percent of total Federal outlays).

This paper explores the role for intergovernmental grants both in theory and practice. Part I examines, first, what the principles of economics suggest for the appropriate employment of such grants, and second, the actual range of uses and the growth of intergovernmental grants in the United States. As such, Part I is intended to provide an overview of the potential and actual roles of intergovernmental grants in the United States; it calls attention to some of the basic issues in the design of these grants, but does not attempt a careful assessment of individual grant programs. Part II is a more detailed study of the particular and relatively recent use of grants as a tool of macroeconomic stabilization policy. Drawing both on U.S. experience and that of other federal countries, Part II explores the need for and the potential of intergovernmental grants as an addition to the Federal government's set of countercyclical policy instruments. Finally, Part III evaluates the role of grants with a special eye to their future deployment in the U.S. economy.

I. Intergovernmental Grants: An Overview

The public sector as a whole has a range of different responsibilities: Corrections in the allocation of the economy's resources in instances where market choices generate significant distortions; the redistribution of income in accord with society's view of an equitable income distribution; the stabilization of the economy at high levels of employment with reasonable price stability; and the attainment of an acceptable rate of economic growth. In the pursuit of each of these objectives, the Federal government (and the States as well) has employed a variety of forms of intergovernmental grants. This raises the issue of the appropriate form of grant to achieve a specific goal, an issue on which the basic principles of economics can shed some light. Part I thus begins with a brief examination of the general principles of grant design.

A. External Effects Across Jurisdictions: A Role for Matching Grants

An important potential source of distortions in allocative decisions exists whenever the choices of one individual or group of individuals impinge significantly on the welfare of others in the absence of any payment mechanism. The classic example in economics is that of the factory spewing forth smoke which imposes external costs on the neighboring laundry. In this case, the decisionmaker (the factory owner) has no incentive to take account of the costs (or benefits) that he or she generates for third parties so that these economic choices fail to incorporate the full range of social costs or benefits that are relevant to the decision.[2] The likely consequence is a distorted pattern of resource use with excessive levels of activities generating external costs and inappropriately low levels of those that produce spillover benefits.

External effects are not limited to decisions by private consumers or firms. The programs adopted by one local or State government may have important implications for the welfare of residents of other jurisdictions. A good system of roads in one locality, for example, provides services for travelers from elsewhere. Likewise, research activities in the hospitals funded in one State may produce new treatment or cures of widespread interest. In such instances, we can hardly expect the State or locality to draw on its own resources to expand the activity to levels for which outsiders would be willing to pay if some payment mechanism existed. From the perspective of the Federal Government, such myopic decisions on the part of States and localities are a matter of serious concern for programs where external effects are important.

As a representative of the national interest, the Federal Government could in principle respond by simply taking over the whole function and thereby "internalizing" all the relevant costs and benefits. Oftentimes this response is simply unconstitutional or for other reasons politically infeasible. But even were it a viable alternative, this is frequently a case where the cure may be worse than the disease. The decentralized provision of public services offers some quite compelling advantages for the efficient use of resources. Most important, a State or local government is in a position to fashion its programs closely in accordance with the particular tastes of its constituency. Were the central government to take over the service and establish, say, uniform levels of output across all jurisdictions, quite significant welfare losses would be a likely result. There are nearly always important welfare-enhancing forces associated with allowing individuals or small groups of

² In certain instances where the affected parties are able to come together and negotiate an agreement, Ronald Coase has shown that voluntary private decisions can yield an efficient outcome. See his "The Problem of Social Cost," Journal of Law and Economics, 3 (October 1960), pp. 1–44. However, the Coase resolution of externalities relies on a number of quite restrictive assumptions such as low transactions costs and an absence of strategic behavior: these considerations suggest that its relevance is limited to cases involving only a very small number of participants. On this matter, see William Baumol and Wallace Oates, The Theory of Environmental Policy (Englewood Cliffs, N.J.: Prentice-Hall, 1975), Chapter 2.

334

individuals to determine their own most appropriate levels of services instead of having them imposed from the center.[3]

Rather than preempting State-local outputs of services involving external effects across jurisdictions, the Federal Government can resort to intergovernmental grants to influence State-local choices. In particular, the Federal Government can provide a direct fiscal inducement to State and local officials to expand specific activities through a properly designed system of grants. The form of these grants is of central importance. For example[4] to encourage expansion of a particular service (like medical research) requires the use of a conditional grant, not simply an unconditional or lump-sum transfer of funds; that is, the funds must be earmarked for the intended purpose. But more than this, the grantor must ensure that the recipient is not in a position simply to substitute the grant monies for its own revenues such that there is no net effect on the level of the activity. Note that, even if a grant is conditional in the sense that the recipient is required to use the monies for a prescribed function or program, it does not follow that the grant will induce an increase in spending for the function relative to that which would have been forthcoming in the absence of the grant. For example, particularly in periods of rising budgets, a locality which receives a grant to expand local police services can use these funds to cover planned budgetary increments that would otherwise have been financed with its own revenues; the grant funds would then effectively be available for other programs or, alternatively, for local tax cuts. In short, this fungibility of grant funds may allow States and localities to use conditional grants in the same way that they would employ monies with no strings attached, thereby frustrating the intent of the Federal grant program.[4]

The proper form of grant in the presence of external benefits is a matching grant, under which the Federal Government agrees to pay some fraction of the unit cost of the recipient. Under 1:1 matching, for example, the State or locality receives $1 in grant monies for each $1 it expends from its own funds. Note that such a grant effectively cuts in half the cost of the prescribed State-local services to the State or locality. Moreover, the only way the recipient can increase its grant monies is by expanding its own spending. Unlike a block grant for some specified purpose, the matching grant has a "price effect" which provides a direct inducement to an expansion of the service. In theory, the matching terms should reflect the magnitude of the spillover effect; if, for example, $2 of local expenditure generate $1 of benefits for residents of other jurisdictions, then the Federal share should be one-third or 1:2 matching. This would effectively "internalize" the external benefits. In practice, it may be difficult to determine with any precision the exact shares of local and external benefits, but the analysis does at least provide some guidelines. It suggests that, where the purpose of the grant program is to en-

---

[3] One attempt to compute some (admittedly rough) estimates of the welfare losses associated with imposing uniform levels of school expenditures across all jurisdictions generated some quite sizable magnitudes; the estimates indicated that, on average, the transfer of a dollar of spending from one school district to another involved a deadweight loss of about 50 cents (i.e., the expenditure of the additional dollar in the recipient jurisdiction was valued at 50 cents less than its loss in the school district where it was previously spent). See David Bradford and Wallace Oates, "Suburban Exploitation of Central Cities and Governmental Structure," in Harold Hochman and George Peterson, eds., "Redistribution Through Public Choice" (New York: Columbia University Press, 1974), pp. 43-90.

[4] For a more formal treatment of all this, see Wallace E. Oates, "Fiscal Federalism" (New York: Harcourt Brace Jovanovich, 1972), Chapter 3. A case in which this is not true is where the state or locality would have expended none of its own funds (or at least less than the sum of the grant) on the grant-aided program. So called demonstration grants may thus induce expenditures which would not have taken place without **Federal assistance.**

courage state and local provision of particular services that confer benefits elsewhere in the Nation, the appropriate instrument is the matching grant.[5] Moreover, where the spillover benefits are regarded as large compared to local benefits, the Federal Government should offer relatively benerous matching terms (and conversely).

B. Equalization of Fiscal Capacity: A Role for Unconditional Grants

In addition to improved resource allocation, federal systems of government have typically placed an extensive reliance on intergovernmental grants for equity reasons. The basic rationale for these grants stems from perceived geographical inequities in fiscal well-being; those jurisdictions with relatively large tax bases and a population that requires comparatively little in the way of social services are in a position to provide adequate service levels with significantly lower tax rates than elsewhere. Central governments in dozens of countries have responded to these geographic fiscal differentials with equalizing grants whose objective is to remove, or at least to narrow, the differentials.[6] The stated purpose of the grants usually runs n terms of establishing a fiscal environment in which each jurisdiction (e.g., State or locality) can provide a 'satisfactory' level of key public services with a "fiscal effort" that is not discernibly greater than that in other jurisdictions. To achieve this goal, the central government typically bases the allocation of grant funds on the measured "need" and fiscal capacity of the decentralized units of government so that jurisdictions with populations requiring large public expenditures and with comparatively small tax bases receive proportionately larger sums.

Two points concerning equalizing grants are worthy of special emphasis. First, note that the proper grant form in this case is an unconditional (lump sum) grant. The intent of the grant is to equalize fiscal capability; it is not to stimulate public spending. From this perspective, it would be inappropriate to employ a matching grant which would effectively lower the marginal cost of services to each jurisdiction and thereby directly encourage increased expenditure. Fiscal equalization implies grants to jurisdictions that vary with need and fiscal capacity, but are invariant to the fiscal response of the recipient.

Second, while equalizing grants may serve to reduce fiscal differentials among jurisdictions, they are not an effective device for achieving the socially desired distribution of income among individuals. Although such grants will typically channel funds (on net) to poorer areas, they are very clumsy instruments for redistributive purposes. Most low income areas will have some wealthy residents and, likewise, high income jurisdictions usually contain some poor individuals so that transfers from rich to poor areas through the medium of equalizing grants are bound to have some perverse redistributive dimensions.

---

[5] These grants, incidentally, should involve "open-end matching:" that is, the matching terms should be available to the recipient whatever level of spending is selected. If the matching shuts off at some level of State or local expenditure on the program, the grant no longer has a price effect and may become equivalent in its effects to a purely unconditional, lump-sum grant. The use of closed-end matching could be justified, in principle, if external benefits decline significantly at high program levels or, more pragmatically, in terms of a budget constraint on the grantor. But the general presumption is in favor of open-end matching grants. On this, see Oates, "Fiscal Federalism," Chapter 3.

[6] For a careful examination of equalizing grants and their use in federal countries, see Russell L. Mathews, "Fiscal Equalization in a Federal System" (Canberra: Centre for Research in Federal Financial Relations, 1974).

Unconditional equalizing grants are not a substitute for a national program to achieve an equitable distribution of income among individuals.

C. Taxation and Revenue Sharing

A third important rationale for intergovernmental grants is the establishment of an efficient and fair system of taxation for the public sector as a whole. There exists the sense, backed by some evidence, that the Federal tax system is on net a more just and less distorting structure than the tax system of State and local governments. The Federal income tax, for example, is probably a good deal more progressive in terms of its incidence than State-local income, sales, and property taxes.[7]

Moreover, taxes at more decentralized levels of government have greater potential for distorting the flow of resources in the economy. To take one example, the supply of capital to the economy as a whole may not be very responsive to moderate levels of Federal taxation. At State and local levels, however, similar taxes may chase capital from high-tax to low-tax jurisdictions resulting in real inefficiencies in resource allocation and consequent reduced output. The relatively high mobility of both goods and people across State or local boundaries suggests much more sensitivity to fiscal differentials than at the national level (a sensitivity which State and local officials are well aware of).

In addition, with a little ingenuity, States and localities are often able to shift a substantial portion of their tax burden onto residents of other jurisdictions. The taxation of certain production activities in one jurisdiction, for instance, may result in higher prices that are paid largely by outsiders. As one illustration, the burden of value-added taxation of the auto industry by the State of Michigan probably falls predominately on purchasers of new automobiles throughout the Nation. Likewise, areas which draw heavy tourist populations frequently meet much of their local tax needs through substantial excise taxes on hotel and restaurant bills. These are not, incidentally, isolated examples: Charles McLure has estimated that, on average, State governments in the United States are able to "export" approximately 20 to 25 percent of their taxes onto residents of other States.[8]

The thrust of the argument is that it is considerably more difficult to design an efficient and equitable tax system at the State-local level than at the Federal level. People and goods can move away from high-tax jurisdictions and thereby introduce both serious distortions in the allocation of resources and unintended distributional results. The Federal government, in contrast, has a greater scope for reliance on progressive taxation and can avoid, through a national uniformity of tax rates, the distortions in resource allocation generated by State-local tax differentials. Moreover, a greater reliance on centralized taxation can also provide some economies of scale in tax administration. Data for the United States indicate that the administrative costs of

[7] For a good summary of the evidence on the incidence of various taxes in the United States, see Joseph A. Pechman and Benjamin A. Okner, "Who Bears the Tax Burden?" (Washington, D.C.: The Brookings Institution, 1974). As Pechman and Okner make clear, any conclusions on overall tax incidence must be hedged by a number of important qualifications.

[8] C. McLure, "The Interstate Exporting of State and Local Taxes: Estimates for 1962," "National Tax Journal," 23 (1970), pp. 206–213.

the Federal individual income tax amount to only about one-half of one-percent of revenues; at the State level, these costs for income or sales taxation are typically on the order of 1 to 2 percent of revenues.[9]

This suggests that we might improve the equity and efficiency characteristics of the Federal-State-local tax system as a whole by shifting more of the taxation function onto the central government. At the same time, however, we have stressed that there are important reasons for retaining State and local discretion over the size and composition of their expenditures. One way to accomplish these two objectives is through revenue sharing. From this perspective, revenue sharing is a mechanism through which Federal taxation can be substituted for State-local taxes. The Federal Government acts, to some extent, as a tax-collection agent for the States and localities: it collects tax revenues in excess of its own needs and distributes this excess in lump-sum form to State and local treasuries. Note that the appropriate form for these grants is as unconditional monies. It is of the greatest importance that State and local jurisdictions pay their own way at the margin; to promote fiscally responsible choices, it is essential that each jurisdiction bears the cost of any decisions to expand levels of State or local services.

We thus have two potential roles for unconditional grants: Fiscal equalization and an improved overall system of taxation. At a pragmatic level, there is no reason why the Federal Government cannot pursue both of these objectives at the same time through a system of unconditional grants (revenue sharing) in which the size of the per capita grant varies with the fiscal characteristics of the jurisdiction.

THE GROWING RELIANCE ON INTERGOVERNMENTAL TRANSFERS

The continuing growth in the size and complexity of the public sector has brought with it a rapid expansion in the use of intergovernmental grants. Such transfers provide a policy tool capable of promoting a number of quite different and important government objectives, and this has not gone unnoticed. Table 1 provides some aggregate data that document this striking growth: Federal grants to State and local governments have increased from about $2.5 billion in 1950 to almost $63 billion in 1978. This represents an annual compound rate of expansion of 12.7 percent, which is well in excess of the rate of growth of Federal outlays so that these grants have come to account for an increasingly large percentage of Federal spending. About 15 percent of Federal expenditures now take the form of grants-in-aid to States and localities.[10] On the receiving end, table 1 indicates that

---

[9] Joseph Pechman, "Federal Tax Policy," Revised Edition (Washington, D.C.: Brookings Institution, 1971), p. 53; James Maxwell, "Financing State and Local Governments," Revised Edition (Washington, D.C.: Brookings Institution, 1969), p. 102.

[10] This rapid expansion in intergovernmental transfers is not limited to the United States; it has happened in most other federal (and nonfederal) countries as well. In a comparative study of fiscal systems, Werner W. Pommerehne found over the period 1950-70 quite large increases in central-government transfers to other governments in Canada, France, West Germany, Switzerland, and the United Kingdom. See his, "Quantitiative Aspects of Federalism: A Study of Six Countries," in W. E. Oates, editor, "The Political Economy of Fiscal Federalism" (Lexington, Mass.: Heath-Lexington, 1977), pp. 336-337.

State governments have come to rely more substantially on Federal assistance; States now obtain close to one-fourth of their revenues from Federal grants.

TABLE 1.—GROWTH IN INTERGOVERNMENTAL GRANTS IN THE UNITED STATES

[Dollar amounts in millions for selected fiscal years]

	Federal grants-in-aid to State and local governments (1)	Federal grants as a percentage of total Federal outlays [1] (2)	Federal grants to States as a percentage of total State revenues (3)	State aid to local government [2] (4)	Federal grants directly to local government (5)	Grants received by local government as a percentage of total local revenues [3] (6)
1950	$2,486	5.8	16.4	$4,217	$211	27.5
1960	6,974	7.6	19.4	9,522	592	27.2
1965	11,029	9.3	20.2	14,010	1,155	28.4
1970	21,857	11.1	21.6	26,920	2,605	33.1
1971	26,146	12.4	23.4	31,081	3,391	34.1
1972	31,253	13.5	23.8	35,143	4,551	34.0
1973	39,256	15.9	24.2	39,963	7,903	37.1
1974	41,820	15.5	22.5	44,553	10,199	38.2
1975	47,054	15.4	23.4	51,068	10,906	38.8
1976	55,589	15.2	22.7	56,169	13,576	39.1
1977	62,575	15.2	22.5	60,311	16,637	39.2

[1] Total Federal outlays as measured under the Unified Budget.
[2] State aid includes substantial amounts of Federal aid that is channeled through State governments to localities.
[3] Grant revenues include payments from both the Federal and State governments.

Sources: The data (either presented directly or used to calculate percentages) for years prior to 1976 are from Tax Foundation, Inc., "Facts and Figures on Government Finance," 19th biennial edition, 1977 (New York, 1977), tables 57, 110, 134, 147, 185; for 1976 and 1977, data are from Bureau of the Census, "Governmental Finances in 1975–76," table 5, and "Governmental Finances in 1976–77," table 5.

Likewise, local governments, which receive aid both from Federal grants and from their respective States, have become increasingly reliant on intergovernmental transfers. Table 1 indicates that in the aggregate State grants to local governments have risen from about $4 billion in 1950 to over $60 billion in 1977; similarly, Federal grants directly to local jurisdictions have grown rapidly from less than $1 billion in 1950 to over $16 billion in 1977. The relative size of the Federal and State contributions to the localities is, incidentally, a little misleading; several grant programs channel funds from the Federal Government to localities through the States, and these monies appear in official figures as State grants to local government. Regardless of the specific source, local governments now depend on intergovernmental grants for almost 40 percent of their total revenues.

Moreover, these transfers support a wide variety of public programs. Table 2 indicates the breakdown of Federal grants by categories of aid for fiscal year 1977. Note, in particular, the diversity of purposes for grant funds. A substantial chunk (about one-fourth) of Federal intergovernmental transfers goes for public welfare. There is a sound rationale for this. It is difficult for States and especially localities to engage in aggressive redistributive programs to help lower-income households. A particular jurisdiction that adopts high taxes on the wealthy with comparatively generous support for the poor creates a powerful set of incentives for migration that will encourage an influx of low-income beneficiaries and an outflow of the well-to-do. Such potential mobility across State and local borders constitutes a real constraint on the scope for redistributive fiscal activity at decentralized levels of government. This suggests that the Federal Government must assume a primary responsibility for public redistributive programs; the Federal Government has, in fact, used intergovernmental transfers extensively for this purpose.

339

TABLE 2.—*Federal Intergovernmental Expenditure,*[1] *1976–77*

	Millions
Education	$10, 205
Grants-in-aid	8, 339
Elementary and secondary education	2, 302
School lunch and school milk program	2, 144
Human development	1, 564
Maintenance and operation of schools	696
Occupational, vocational, and adult education	660
Emergency school assistance	238
Education for the handicapped	118
Work incentive training	99
Other grants-in-aid	518
Payments for services	1, 866
Scientific research and development	1, 840
Tuition payments	26
Public welfare	19, 520
Medical assistance (medicaid)	9, 829
Maintenance assistance	6, 337
Social services, N.E.C.[2]	2, 405
Special supplemental food programs (WIC)	279
Food stamp program	250
Work incentives, N.E.C.[2]	242
Other	178
Health and hospitals	2, 353
Health services administration	720
Alcohol, Drug Abuse, and Mental Health Administration	471
Health Resources Administration, N.E.C[2]	410
National Institutes of Health	294
Environmental Pollution Abatement and Control	191
Other	267
General revenue sharing	6, 764
Highways	6, 173
Natural resources	969
Housing and urban renewal	2, 914
Air transportation	381
Social Insurance Administration	1, 532
Other and combined	22, 238
Unemployment compensation for Federal Employees, ex-servicemen, and temporary extended benefits	5, 213
Labor and manpower, N.E.C.[2]	4, 747
Waste treatment facilities	4, 052
Community planning and development	2, 207
Urban mass transportation	1, 891
Antirecession fiscal assistance	1, 694
Law Enforcement Assistance Administration	684
Civil Defense and Disaster Relief	287
Federal contribution to District of Columbia	281
Programs for the Aging	203
Promotion of science, research, libraries and museums	177
Payments in lieu of taxes	168
Other	634
Total Federal intergovernmental expenditure	73, 045

[1] Federal intergovernmental expenditure includes, in addition to pure grants, Federal payments for certain services from State and local government so that the total of these expenditures exceeds somewhat the figure for Federal grants-in-aid for fiscal year 1977 that appears in Table 1.
[2] N.E.C. means "Not Elsewhere Classified."

Source: Bureau of the Census, "Governmental Finances in 1976–77", Tables 10 and 12.

340

We noted earlier the role for these transfers to provide a stimulus for State-local programs that confer benefits on residents of other areas. Federal grants for highways and for various educational activities are good examples of grants for this purpose: the U.S. population as a whole has an important interest both in a good system of national roadways and in an educated electorate. Intergovernmental grants provide a mechanism for higher level governments to represent the broader concern through budgetary incentives.

In addition, the Federal Government instituted in 1972 a system of revenue sharing with State and local governments. Although the revenue-sharing formulae are quite complex, the program amounts roughly to a set of unconditional grants to the States and localities on a per capita basis.[11] Over the longer run as indicated earlier, revenue sharing is essentially a substitution of Federal taxation for State-local revenues with the objective of an improvement of the efficiency and equity characteristics of the overall tax structure.

Aside from revenue sharing, the Federal Government in the United States (in contrast to many other countries) has relied almost exclusively on conditional grants. These grants usually involve some kind of cost sharing between the Federal agency and the recipient State or locality, which typically takes one of two forms: An explicit grant formula that specifies the respective shares of the grantor and recipient or an application and negotiation procedure for a particular "project grant" under which the State or local share is determined in the grant process itself. In both instances, the Federal Government has typically included equalizing elements by providing more generous matching terms to jurisdictions with a lesser fiscal capacity. This is accomplished under grant formulae through "variable matching grants" in which the fiscal circumstances of the jurisdictions enter into the formula that determines the Federal matching share; under project grants the Federal administrator takes local fiscal capacity into consideration in determining the local contribution.[12] Formula grants, incidentally, are the major grant instrument in the Federal intergovernmental transfer system: one study found that formula grants account for about two-thirds of the dollar total of Federal grants to State and local governments: formula grants, moreover, go primarily to the States. In contrast, the Federal Government has employed project grants mainly for transfers to local governments; project grants make up about one-fifth of the dollar total of Federal intergovernmental transfers.[13]

This brief overview suggests that economic analysis can go some distance in providing a rationale for the Federal grant system. However, the discussion to this point has been in highly aggregative terms; closer examination of Federal transfers to State and local governments reveals a number of anomalies. This should not be surprising, for the design and enactment of grant programs is, in

---

[11] Revenue sharing does have some modest equalizing features. For a careful analysis of the formulae, see Robert Reischauer, "General Revenue Sharing: The Program's Incentives," in W. E. Oates, editor, "Financing the New Federalism" (Baltimore: Johns Hopkins University Press for Resources for the Future, 1975), pp. 40–87.

[12] For an excellent analysis of how project grants work, see Howard Chernick, "The Economics of Bureaucratic Behavior: An Application to the Allocation of Federal Project Grants," in Peter Mieszkowski and William Oakland, editors, "Fiscal Federalism and Grants-in-Aid" (Washington, D.C.: Urban Institute, 1979), pp. 81–103.

[13] See Advisory Commission on Intergovernmental Relations, "Federal Grants: Their Effects on State-Local Expenditures, Employment Levels, Wage Rates" (Washington, D.C.: ACIR, Feb. 1977, A–61). This study uses data for 1972.

part, the result of an interaction of Governors, mayors, and various special interest groups with Federal legislators. Such interaction is frequently characterized by a tension between the grant administrator's desire to restrict the scope for use of funds to realize the grantor's objectives and the recipient's efforts to minimize any strings attached to the monies. The form of the grant program that finally emerges must reflect, to some extent, the nature of the resulting compromise.

With this in mind, it is interesting to return at least briefly to the structure of the Federal grant system and explore a bit further the extent to which this structure appears consistent with our economic principles of grant design. We have noted as a primary justification for intergovernmental grants the existence of external benefits across governmental jurisdictions for a range of State-local services including such things as highways and educational programs. For such programs, the analysis prescribes a system of open-ended matching grants where the respective matching shares reflect (at least roughly) the extent of the spillover benefits. From this perspective, certain characteristics of the Federal grant system are quite puzzling. Most Federal matching grants are close-ended—with the major exceptions being Federal grants for public assistance and Medicaid.

This implies that, at the margin, the States and localities that have reached maximum funding are receiving no inducement to take into account the spillover benefits that their fiscal decisions generate. Moreover, it appears difficult to justify the actual matching shares under a number of programs by the extent of external benefits. The Federal share, for example, for interstate highways has been 90 percent of construction costs; it seems unlikely that 90 percent of the value of the interstate highways passing through a particular State would accrue to out-of-State drivers. To an even greater degree, the benefits from sewage waste-treatment systems are largely local; there may exist in some instances, significant external effects involving neighboring jurisdictions, but hardly enough to rationalize the existing Federal share of 75 percent of construction costs. More generally, a study by the Advisory Commission on Intergovernmental Relations reveals that most Federal grant programs require either low (less than 50 percent) or no matching on the part of the recipient State or local government; programs requiring high matching (over 50 percent from the recipient) appear to account for only about 5 percent of Federal grant monies.[14] It seems likely that for many programs external benefits themselves are inadequate to justify the magnitude of the Federal share.[15]

The tendency over the past decades has been toward the consolidation of specific programs into larger block grants to the States and localities with the funds distributed by formula. This movement to

---

[14] ACIR. "Federal Grants," pp. 26–28.

[15] In addition to the issue of the matching share itself, other elements in grant design can have a profound impact upon the effectiveness of a particular grant program. As one illustration, we return to the Federal subsidy program for waste-treatment plants to reduce water pollution, under which the Federal Government has provided several billion dollars for the construction of new waste-treatment facilities. As various studies have shown, the failure to link the grants directly to their intended purpose—the reduction of water pollution—has seriously undercut their efficacy. In particular, the subsidies support only a specific technology—waste treatment—even where a less costly and more effective alternative exists. Moreover, by subsidizing only the construction of treatment plants, the program has provided no incentive for the efficient operation of these facilities; one study found that in over half the plants studied services were substandard either because of poor operating procedures or because the plants were not designed to treat the waste load delivered to them. On this, see Allen V. Kneese and Charles L. Schultze, "Pollution, Prices, and Public Policy" (Washington, D.C.: The Brookings Institution, 1975), Chapter 3.

grant consolidation has much appeal. In particular, it has simplified the Federal grant system somewhat by replacing a maze of sometimes overlapping and conflicting individual programs with a single grant of funds to support a fairly wide range of State and local services. In this way, such block grants permit the recipient much greater discretion in the use of the monies so that State and local officials can allocate their available resources more closely in line with thier own priorities. At the same time, it must be recognized that block grants provide virtually no economic incentives for uses of funds for particular services or functions. Since they entail no open-ended matching requirements, these grants do not affect the marginal costs of providing public services to the respective State or locality. As we stressed earlier, the fundibility of grant funds makes conditional block grants, in principle, equivalent to purely unconditional transfers of funds. For this reason, they are not a suitable policy instrument for resolving distortions in the provision of public services associated with external benefits or costs.

In the evaluation of Federal grant programs, it is essential (in addition to observing general principles) to measure the impact of the programs on the decisions, budgetary and otherwise, of State and local officials. There has been some effort in this direction, although our understanding of the effects of Federal grants is, at best, quite spotty. Despite the considerable variation in the particular estimates from one study to the next, research findings, on the whole, suggest that Federal grants have had a substantial stimulative impact on State and local expenditures; grant monies have not been used simply to substitute for State-local tax revenues.[16] Moreover, the evidence supports our expectation that conditional grants generate a larger expenditure response (dollar-for-dollar) than do purely unconditional transfers, with high Federal matching providing a greater stimulus than low matching.

While these general results are consistent with our theoretical expectations, there is another aspect of the findings that is somewhat more intriguing: The extent of budgetary expansion appears, in some instances, to be surprisingly large. Consider, for example, the case of a purely unconditional grant to a local community. Since such grants contain no explicit incentives for budgetary expansion, we might expect the members of the community to treat these monies as a kind of windfall supplement to their wealth or income. In principle, it shouldn't really matter that the monies flow into the local government treasury; if local officials are responsive to the preferences of their constituencies, it should make little difference whether the grant goes to the local government or directly into the pockets of the local residents. In short, it seems reasonable to expect the effect of an unconditional intergovernmental grant to be (at least roughly) equivalent to a set of unconditional grants to the people themselves. From this perspective, an unconditional intergovernmental grant is simply a veil for a Federal tax cut directly to individuals.[17]

[16] For useful surveys of the empirical work on the budgetary impact of intergovernmental grants. see Edward M. Gramlish. "Intergovernmental Grants: A Review of the Empirical Literature." in W. Oates. education. "The Political Economy of Fiscal Federalism" (Lexington, Mass.: Heath-Lexington. 1977). pp. 219–240; and ACIR. Federal Grants."
[17] For a formal presentation of the veil hypothesis, see David F. Bradford and Wallace E. Oates. "The Analysis of Revenue Sharing in a New Approach to Collective Fiscal Decisions," "Quarterly Journal of Economics," 85 (August, 1971), pp. 416–439.

343

The implication of the "veil hypothesis" is that the additional local public spending generated by a dollar of lump-sum grants to the local government should be approximately the same as the incremental public expenditure resulting from a one-dollar increase in private income in the jurisdiction. In both cases, aggregate income in the jurisdiction has risen by a dollar so that the desired increase in public spending should be (roughly) the same. However, existing empirical work suggests that this is not the case. In particular, if the present size of the State-local sector is any guide to desired marginal adjustments, one might look for increases in private income to induce additional State-local expenditure on the order of 10 to 15 cents per dollar of additional income. The evidence indicates, however, that the stimulative effect of unconditional intergovernmental transfers is much larger than this—closer to a figure of 50 cents on the dollar. Lump-sum Federal grants to the States and localities do not appear to be equivalent in their budgetary effects to a cut in Federal income taxes.[18]

Although our understanding of the workings of intergovernmenta¹ grants is far from complete, economic analysis does provide a numbe. of important insights. In particular, the discussion indicates that the Federal Government has found these grants an attractive policy tool for the pursuit of a diverse set of objectives: The encouragement of State-local programs which also service the broader national interest, the promotion of an improved distribution of income, and the establishment of a more efficient and equitable tax system. However, to accomplish their intended objectives at the least cost to society as a whole, individual grant programs must take the proper form; they must provide the appropriate incentives for State and local decision-makers. It is clear that, from this perspective, a number of Federal grant programs have serious deficiencies. The careful application of our principles of grant design together with evidence of the response to particular types of fiscal incentives can make a valuable contribution to the removal of these deficiencies and to the evolution of a structure of intergovernmental transfers that effectively promotes our allocational and distributional objectives.

More recently, the Federal Government has expressed interest in the potential of intergovernmental grants as a macro-stabilization tool. This issue, to which we next turn, is a central concern of this paper.

II. Intergovernmental Grants for Countercyclical Purposes

The "Economic Stimulus Package of 1977" (consisting of Anti-Recession Fiscal Assistance, local public works, and public service employment under titles II and VI of the Comprehensive Employment and Training Act) represents the culmination of recent interest in the United States in intergovernmental grants as a device for assisting in the maintenance of the economy at high levels of employment with reasonable stability of prices. This set of programs provides

---

[18] The evidence on the apparently large stimulative impact of unconditional grants comes from a number of sources including various econometric studies and an actual monitoring of the U.S. revenue sharing program. There are, however, important qualifications attached to these results such that they should not be regarded by any means as the last word on the subject. For descriptions of these findings, see E. Gramlich, "Intergovernmental Grants: A Review . . . ," and Richard P. Nathan, Charles F. Adams, Jr., and Associates, "Revenue Sharing: The Second Round" (Washington, D.C.: The Brookings Institution, 1977). For a useful collection of papers exploring this whole issue, see Peter Mieszkowski and William Oakland, editors, "Fiscal Federalism and Grants-in-Aid" (Washington, D.C.: Urban Institute, forthcoming).

344

a variety of Federal assistance to State and local governments including supplementary revenue-sharing funds in times of recession and grant monies specifically earmarked for local public works or public service employment. In each instance, the magnitude of the grant funds is tied explicitly to the state of the economy (both national and local).

Proposals for countercyclical intergovernmental assistance in the United States have a considerable history, which is both interesting and instructive in its own right. In the 1940's Alvin Hansen and Harvey Perloff argued that State and local fiscal activity had been (and, in the absence of major reform could be expected to be) highly destablizing.[19] Looking back over the preceding decades of the 1920's and 1930's, they called attention to the perverse fiscal behavior of State and local governments:

> The taxing, borrowing, and spending activities of the State and local governments collectively have typically run counter to an economically sound fiscal policy. These governmental units have usually followed the swings of the business cycle, from crest to trough, spending and building in prosperity periods and contracting their activities during depression. In the boom of the late twenties, they added to the disposable income of the community, and bid up prices and building costs in large-scale construction activities. In the depressed thirties, the fiscal policies of these governments exerted a deflationary rather than an expansionary effect on the economy: expenditures, and especially construction outlays, were severely reduced, borrowing was restricted, and taxes weighing on consumption were substantially increased.[20]

Their explanation of this behavior is a straightforward and, on the surface at least, a fairly compelling one. Most State and local governments operate subject to some sort of legally required balanced budget (for current expenses). When the national economy goes into recession, their tax revenues level off or even decline. The balanced-budget constraint then forces State and local officials to cut spending and/or raise tax rates to eliminate the potential deficit. In consequence, State and local fiscal activity accentuates the swings in the level of economic activity.

This view of State-local budgetary behavior has become known as the "fiscal-perversity" hypothesis. To deal with the problem, Hansen and Perloff suggested some budgetary reforms which would allow State and local governments to build up financial reserves in good times that could be drawn upon to maintain spending in times of recession. In addition, they explicitly recommended that the Federal Government initiate special grants to the states and localities for expanded public construction programs during recessionary periods because "Only the Federal Government is in a position to manage adequately the interrelated problems involved in carrying out a positive and flexible countercyclical policy." [21] They reasoned that, since there typically exists considerable flexibility in the timing of construction projects, it would make sense to use this flexibility for countercyclical purposes by encouraging more capital spending when slack exists in the economy. This would be accomplished by making special Federal grant funds available at such times to State and local governments.

---

[19] Alvin H. Hansen and Harvey S. Perloff, "State and Local Finance in the National Economy" (New York: Norton, 1944), ch. 4.
[20] *Ibid.*, p. 49.
[21] *Ibid.*, p. 199.

What the discussion makes clear is that the case for the Hansen-Perloff proposal (and, likewise, for current measures for countercyclical fiscal assistance) depends on two distinct premises:

(1) State and local governments tend to behave in a fiscally destabilizing fashion over the course of the business cycle; and

(2) Federal grants to State and local governments that vary inversely with the level of aggregate economic activity in the economy can, to some significant degree, reverse or at least neutralize this perverse pattern of behavior.

Both of these premises are empirical propositions on which we have some evidence both in terms of U.S. experience and that in other federal countries as well. A careful consideration of this evidence should tell us a good deal about the potential effectiveness of intergovernmental grants as a countercyclical policy tool.

A. Cyclical Budgetary Behavior of State-Local Governments

One must first examine the historical record of State-local fiscal activity to see if it supports the fiscal perversity hypothesis. Have State and local governments in fact followed a destabilizing course of fiscal behavior?

Robert Rafuse undertook the first careful study of this issue in an examination of the post World War II period.[22] Exploring the period from 1946 to 1964, Rafuse found that State and local budgetary behavior was dominated by one feature: Continued and dramatic growth regardless of the condition of the national economy. State-local spending and taxes increased steadily through periods of boom and recession alike. From the perspective of the downswing, this was most encouraging. Rafuse concludes that "These [State and local] governments have been a significant factor in moderating the seriousness of the postwar recessions and in promoting recovery." [23] In particular his estimates indicate that, in the aggregate, State-local fiscal behavior reduced the magnitude of the contraction in the economy in every one of the four postwar recessions he examined. In the 1960–61 downswing, for example, Rafuse estimates that the decline in GNP of $2.7 billion from the second quarter of 1960 to the first quarter of 1961 would have been in excess of $6 billion in the absence of the stabilizing fiscal influence of the State-local sector.

Of course, the obverse of this is that continuing State-local budgetary expansion did contribute to the overheating of the economy during periods of excess demand. However, the record for the two decades following the conclusion of World War II does not appear consistent with the fiscal-perversity hypothesis; State and local governments were not over these years a systematically destabilizing force in the economy.

Before looking at the more recent record, it may prove useful at this juncture to stop and ask where (assuming the Rafuse findings to be correct) Hansen and Perloff might have gone wrong. Three points are particularly relevant:

(1) The automatic response of State-local budgets to cyclical movements in the economy tends, on balance, to be stabilizing. As the

---

[22] "Cyclical Behavior of State-Local Finances," in Richard A. Musgrave, ed., "Essays in Fiscal Federalism" (Washington, D.C.: The Brookings Institution, 1965), pp. 63–121.
[23] *Ibid.*, p. 118.

346

economy contracts, for example, tax receipts tend to decline thereby cushioning the fall in consumers' disposable incomes. At the same time, certain expenditures including those associated with unemployment benefits are on the rise which further shores up private purchasing power.

(2) If State and local fiscal behavior is to be destabilizing (on net), the source must be in the discretionary response of public officials to the changing state of the economy. In particular, the fiscal-perversity hypothesis posits a response of increased tax rates and decreased discretionary expenditures to the potential budgetary deficit created by the contraction in the economy. Such a discretionary response may occur, but it need not. If State and local officials have adequate financial reserves, they may simply ride out difficult times by drawing on these reserves without raising taxes or cutting spending; the reserves can then be replenished during the succeeding expansion. It is not clear a priori which view closely approximates actual budgetary patterns, but it does suggest that a close examination of the cyclical behavior of State and local holdings of financial assets should provide some useful evidence. Note, moreover, that even if there is some "perverse" discretionary response of the Hansen-Perloff variety it must more than offset the automatic features of State-local fiscal systems to render the overall effect destabilizing.

(3) Most of the preceding discussion focuses on operating budgets. However, a major category of State and local expenditure which is not heavily dependent on current revenues is new construction. The bulk of capital spending by States and localities is financed by the issue of long-term debt. There is a sound rationale for this form of finance: since capital structures provide services to the various (and changing) residents of a jurisdiction over a long period, it makes sense to spread out the payments for these services over the useful life of the facility, rather than to place the whole burden on current residents through tax finance.

More recent State-local fiscal experience provides some useful evidence on all this. In particular, the Advisory Commission on Intergovernmental Relations (ACIR) published in 1978 its findings on the cyclical patterns of State-local budgets.[24] Using a number of different measures of fiscal activity, the ACIR study examines State-local spending and revenues over the four upswings and contractions in the U.S. economy from 1958 to 1977. The ACIR findings reinforce the Rafuse conclusions. Table 3 summarizes these results for rates of growth of expenditures, revenues, and surpluses. Note that, in each of the four contractions, State-local spending grew more rapidly than revenues so that, in the aggregate, the change in the surplus was negative. Conversely, during expansions, receipts grew faster than expenditures thereby pushing State-local budgets in the direction of a larger surplus. Like Rafuse, the ACIR found that the State-local sector has exerted, on net, a stabilizing influence on the national economy.

[24] "Countercyclical Aid and Economic Stabilization" (Washington, D.C.: U.S.G.P.O., December 1978).

347

TABLE 3.—STATE-LOCAL FISCAL BEHAVIOR: AVERAGE QUARTERLY RATES OF GROWTH OF EXPENDITURES, RE-
CEIPTS, AND SURPLUSES, 1957-77

	Average quarterly rate of growth in percent		Surplus (average quarterly change, billions)
	Expenditures [1]	Receipts	
DURING RECESSIONS			
Contraction [2] (peak-trough):			
1957: III–1958: I	2.9	1.7	−$0.55
1960: I–1960: IV	2.1	1.9	−.10
1969: III–1970: IV	3.2	2.8	−.46
1973: IV–1975: I	3.3	2.6	−1.32
DURING EXPANSIONS			
Expansion [2] (trough-peak):			
1958: I–1960: I	1.5	2.4	.34
1960: IV–1969: III	2.4	2.5	.08
1970: IV–1973: IV	2.5	2.9	.80
1975: I–1977: I	1.8	2.9	2.95

[1] Total expenditures, receipts, and surplus were used to compute the above, hence Federal aid and trust fund amounts are included.
[2] Peak and trough quarters used are for real GNP, as identified by the U.S. Department of Commerce, Bureau of Economic Analysis (BEA).

Source: Advisory Commission on Intergovernmental Relations, "Countercyclical Aid and Economic Stabilization (Washington, D.C.: U.S.G.P.O., December 1978), p. 6.

In addition to these summary measures of fiscal activity, Edward M. Gramlich of the University of Michigan conducted a careful econometric investigation of State-local budgetary behavior.[25] Gramlich constructed a comprehensive model of State-local budgetary activity in which fiscal officials maximize an objective function subject to a set of budgetary constraints. The distinguishing feature of the model is its focus on asset stocks (including both physical capital and financial assets) as key decision variables. Gramlich used quarterly data from 1954 through 1977 to estimate the parameters of the model. What emerges from this study is a view of State-local fiscal behavior that contrasts sharply with the Hansen-Perloff perspective. In particular, Gramlich finds that changes in the stock of financial assets absorb the lion's share of cyclical movements in the budget. Using the estimated model in a simulation exercise to evaluate the impact of the 1975 recession on the State-local sector, he finds that the recession induced only a quite small reduction in spending; although tax receipts fell substantially, State-local officials apparently absorbed this reduction in the form of a smaller budgetary surplus. In short, the Gramlich results suggest that State and local governments are not prone to the destabilizing kind of fiscal behavior envisioned in the fiscal perversity hypothesis.

[25] See his "State and Local Budgets, the Day After It Rained: Why is the Surplus So High?," Brookings Papers on Economic Activity, 1 (1978), pp. 191–214; and "State and Local Budget Surpluses and the Effect of Federal Macroeconomic Policies," A Study for the Joint Economic Committee of the U.S. Congress (Washington, D.C.: U.S. Government Printing Office, January 12, 1979).

348

The Gramlich findings receive some additional support from another study of State-local fiscal activity by Frank Jones and Mark Weisler.[26] Looking at the 1970's, they find (as expected) a pronounced *automatic* countercyclical effect in State and local budgets; during years of rising unemployment, the state of the economy itself induced increased spending and held back growth in tax revenues to a significant extent. Predictably, the discretionary response in State-local budgets was typically (but not always) in the opposite direction, but for most years the automatic effects dominated so that, *on net*, State and local fiscal activity has been counter-rather than pro-cyclical.[27]

More generally, Jones and Weisler examine econometrically the financial behavior of State-local government from 1955 to 1976. Like Gramlich, they find that the accumulation of financial assets by State-local governments is inversely related to the state of the economy: during periods of rapidly rising real GNP, State and local officials build up financial stocks; during harder times, they draw on them (or borrow).[28] In short, the State-local sector relies on financial adjustments to absorb cyclical budgetary influences so as to insulate, to some degree at least, expenditure programs from cyclical forces.

In addition, the Jones and Weisler regression equations indicate that State and local capital spending is significantly countercyclical. From 1955 to 1976, State-local expenditures both on new structures and for durable equipment exhibited an inverse relationship with the percentage change in real GNP. This, as noted earlier, is really not too surprising: during periods of slack in the economy, credit is readily available on comparatively easy terms so that these are attractive times for State-local governments to issue long-term debt and initiate previously planned capital projects.

The picture that emerges from the evidence this paper draws together suggests that the State-local sector has not been a destabilizing force in the U.S. economy; if anything, it seems to have been moderately stabilizing. The record, therefore, does not appear to support Hansen and Perloff's fiscal-perversity hypothesis. It is interesting to recall that the Hansen-Perloff view drew largely on the fiscal behavior of State and local government in the Great Depression of the 1930's. During this extraordinary episode in U.S. economic history, the State-local sector contributed to the severity of the economic decline by raising taxes and cutting spending. The time pattern of this response however, is quite intriguing. Using E. Cary Brown's measures of a weighted full-employment surplus,[29] the data indicate that over the first four years of the Depression, State and local government actually behaved in a fiscally supportive manner in the sense of adding positively to the level of aggregate demand. It was only after 1934

[26] "Cyclical Variations in State and Local Government Financial Behavior and Capital Expenditures," "Proceedings of the Seventieth Annual Conference on Taxation," National Tax Association—Tax Institute of America (Columbus, Ohio, 1978), pp. 78–87.

[27] There are, incidentally, some difficult conceptual and empirical problems in separating discretionary from automatic changes in the budget. Jones and Weisler use the conventional full-employment budget surplus as their benchmark for this distinction. For some reservations on all this, see Edward M. Gramlich, "Comments on Vogel's ' The Responsiveness of State and Local Receipts to Changes in Economic Activity: Extending the Concept of the Full Employment Budget,' " "Studies in Price Stability and Economic Growth, Papers Nos. 6 and 7, The Impact of Inflation on the Full Employment Budget," Joint Economic Committee, U.S. Congress (Washington, D.C.: U.S. Government Printing Office, June 30, 1975).

[28] Somewhat more precisely, their equations indicate that, on average, various categories of State-local borrowing are negatively related to the percentage change in real GNP: the *t*-statistics, however, are not sufficiently large to permit great confidence in these particular results.

[29] "Fiscal Policy in the 'Thirties:' A Reappraisal," "American Economic Review" 46 (December 1956), pp. 857–879.

349

that the State-local sector became a net drag on the economy. This suggests an interesting view: Over the course of the usual ups and downs in the economy, the State-local sector seems not to accentuate cyclical swings (and, if anything, to be modestly countercyclical); but over an *extended* period of major contraction, State and local governments, as they exhaust their normal reserves, will be forced to adopt restrictive budgetary measures to meet fiscal constraints. The implication appears to be that the State-local sector may need some sort of disaster insurance to prevent procyclical activity in cases of real economic collapse, but not continual support over the normal swings in the economy.

B. *The Effects of Intergovernmental Grants on the Cyclical Pattern of State-Local Expenditure*

The evidence from the United States does not support the first premise of the case for countercyclical fiscal assistance. But what about the second? What can one say about the likely impact of counter-cyclical grants on the temporal pattern of State-local expenditure? Even if the State-local sector has been a moderately stabilizing force in the economy, it is possible that anticyclical grants could make State and local government yet more stabilizing.

As far as the United States is concerned, there is little to go on because of the virtual absence of experience with such grants prior to the 1976–77 legislation. The one attempt to answer this question is Gramlich's simulations of his model of the State-local sector.[30]

In particular, Gramlich used his model to estimate the response in State and local expenditure to the three types of Federal aid included in the Economic Stimulus Program; these include essentially un-conditional grants under Anti-Recession Fiscal Assistance, funding for capital projects under the local public works program, and monies for job creation under Titles II and VI of CETA. His estimates are quite striking: they suggest that, in the very short run, only a mini-scule portion of any grant funds will find their way into increased expenditure *or* tax relief. In the case of countercyclical revenue sharing, for example, Gramlich finds that, in the first quarter following the grant, only 3 percent of the funds will go into increased spending and only 6 percent will be used for tax reduction. The remainder (over 90 percent) will be absorbed into increased financial stocks.

This is a particularly disturbing result. If, for example, State and local governments did not use countercyclical aid to increase their expenditures but instead cut State-local taxes, at least the additional grant funds would have effects roughly like a Federal tax cut; they would increase disposable income and stumulate, to some extent, private expenditure. If, however, the grant monies simply go into a larger State-local surplus, they will exert hardly any effect on the level of aggregate demand. The Congressional Budget Office, for one, has expressed concern over the likely effectiveness of countercyclical revenue sharing for just this reason.[31]

Note that these results do not imply that intergovernmental grants have only minor effects on State-local expenditure. As we say in

[30] See papers cited in footnote 25, especially the JEC paper.
[31] Congressional Budget Office. "Countercyclical Uses of Federal Grant Programs (Washington, D.C.: U.S. Government Printing Office, November 1978), p. 37.

350

Part I, a wide body of evidence suggests that these grants have quite sizable stimulative effects.[32] The issue here is one of timing. Gramlich's results indicate that the short-run effects are minimal; over the longer haul, as State-local financial stocks accumulate, more of the grant funds flow into increased spending and reduced State-local taxes. But, of course, it is the short run that is important for macrostabilization policy, and, from this perspective, Gramlich's estimates cast serious doubt on the countercyclical potential of intergovernmental grants in the United States. The time lag in the impact of these grants appears too long for stabilization purposes.

C. Fiscal Experience in Other Federal Countries

The impact of decentralized levels of government on the cyclical behavior of the economy has been a matter of serious concern in other federal nations. In each case, the central government has assumed a primary responsibility for macrostabilization policy, but the fear has been that central countercyclical measures will be offset, partially or totally, by destabilizing budgetary activity at decentralized levels such that the public sector as a whole will not achieve the desired fiscal stance over the course of the upswings and downswings in the level of aggregate economic activity. A survey of research and of actual policy in other federal countries may therefore provide further insights.

There has been some research in Canada on the issue of the actual pattern of provincial and municipal fiscal activity. In particular, Robinson and Courchene, looking at the period 1952–65, tried to determine if provincial and municipal budgetary movements had been pro- or anti-cyclical.[33] Their findings are not too different from those in the United States. In short, they find that provincial and municipal government, taken as a whole, has exerted a stabilizing effect on the Canadian economy. In a series of regression equations, they find that from 1952 to 1965 a rise in the unemployment rate (or, alternatively, a fall in the ratio of actual to potential GNP) reduced significantly the aggregate surplus in provincial-municipal budgets. Although the fiscal swings at the provincial-municipal level have not been as strongly countercyclical as those of the Federal budget, they have at least been in the right direction. The source of this fiscal behavior is interesting. Undertaking some disaggregation, Robinson and Courchene found that municipal budgetary activity has, on average, been essentially neutral with regard to cyclical movements in the economy; neither municipal revenues nor spending show much in the way of fiscal sensitivity to the state of the economy. In contrast, provincial revenues exhibit pronounced anti-cyclical swings with revenues declining in recession and rising in the upswing; the authors note some tendency for provincial spending to be procyclical, but this is more than offset by changes in revenues. In summary, the Robinson-Courchene study suggests that in Canada, as in the United States, the evidence does not provide much support for the fiscal-perversity hypothesis.

---

[32] For a survey of the empirical work on the stimulative effects of intergovernmental grants, see Gramlich. "Intergovernmental Grants: A Review of the Empirical Literature," in W. Oates, editor, "The Political Economy of Fiscal Federalism" (Lexington, Mass.: Health-Lexington, 1977), pp. 219–240.
[33] T. R. Robinson and T. J. Courchene, "Fiscal Federalism and Economic Stability: An Examination of Multi-Level Public Finances in Canada, 1952–65," Canadian Journal of Economics, 2 (May 1969), pp. 165–189.

This finding receives further support from a more detailed study of the cyclical patterns of budgetary activity in a single province; Douglas Auld, using a weighted-budget measure to examine the fiscal record of the Ontario provincial government found, on the whole, a stabilizing pattern of budgetary response to the state of the economy;[34] there was ". . . little evidence of a consistent 'perverse' effect."[35]

In contrast to the Canadian experience, there is some evidence of destabilizing fiscal behavior by State and local governments in the Federal Republic of Germany.[36] Moreover, and this is of particular interest here, the Federal Government in West Germany has attempted to modify this behavior through the use of both tied and unconditional grants to the States. The effects of these programs may shed some further light on the potential of intergovernmental grants for macrostabilization purposes.

Concern developed over the 1960's in West Germany with the observed procyclical character of State and local capital spending (which accounts for over three-fourths of total public investment); local investment expenditures in particular grew rapidly in booms and declined considerably in recessions thereby accentuating cyclical forces in the economy. The Federal Government, however, is constitutionally prohibited from giving aid directly to local governments; all such monies must go through the States. Inasmuch as grant funds themselves had exhibited a slightly procyclical pattern (since they were tied to tax revenues), an explicit attempt was made in the 1966–67 recession to supplement the usual grant flows; in particular, the Federal Government expanded its tied grants to the States for local investment programs by 23½ percent. State grants to local governments, however, increased by only about 2 percent. For one major program, public provision of low-cost housing, the Federal Government increased its grants to the States from 250 million DM in 1966 to 1,560 million DM in 1967; the response of the States was to reduce their own contributions for this program from 3,890 million DM to 2,510 million DM. In short, the States reduced their expenditure "mark-for-mark" with the increase in monies from the Federal Government. Total public expenditure for the program actually declined from 1966 to 1967!

More generally, Jack Knott examined the grant receipts and investment expenditures for each of the eight regular States from 1966 to 1971.[37] The results are quite suggestive. In four of the States, investment grants to local governments exhibited a pronounced procyclical pattern: they declined absolutely during the 1966–67 recession and then expanded rapidly during the 1969–71 boom at about a 20 percent annual rate. In contrast, the other four States pursued a more countercyclical course; in these States grants grew rapidly (at an annual rate

[34] Douglas A. L. Auld, "Counter-Cyclical Budget Effects in Ontario: Some Preliminary Evidence," Canadian Tax Journal (March–April, 1975), pp. 173–183.
[35] *Ibid.*, p. 181.
[36] On the Germany experience, see Jack H. Knott, "Stabilization Policy, Grants-in-Aid, and the Federal System in Western Germany," in W. E. Oates, editor, "The Political Economy of Fiscal Federalism" (Lexington, Mass.: Heath-Lexington, 1977), pp. 75–92; Knott, "Accommodating Purposes: Fiscal and Budgetary Policy in West Germany" (Berlin: International Institute of Management, April 1978); P. Bernd Spahn, editor, "Principles of Federal Policy Coordination in the Federal Republic of Germany: Basic Issues and Annotated Legislation" (Canberra: Centre for Research on Federal Financial Relations, The Australian National University, 1978).
[37] "Stabilization Policy, . . . ," pp. 82–87.

352

of roughly 15 percent) during the recession and then slowed their rate of growth in the subsequent period of economic expansion. When, however, Knott looked at local public investment expenditures in these groups of states, he found only modest differences. For both groups, local investment spending was procyclical: expenditures fell absolutely in the recession and rose significantly in the boom. Despite the quite striking differences in State grant policy with four States adopting procyclical grant policies and the other four following an anticyclical pattern of grant disbursements, local investment expenditures were strongly destabilizing in all groups.[38]

The German experience thus appears to contrast with that in the United States and Canada in that State-local fiscal behavior in Germany has significantly accentuated the swings in levels of macroeconomic activity. The existing evidence, however, does not suggest that the Federal Government has been able to make effective use of intergovernmental grants to reverse this pattern of State-local budgetary behavior.

D. Further Thoughts on the Design and Use of Countercyclical Grants

In addition to the timing of grants, their *form* is important. Since the intent of countercylcical aid is to alter the temporal pattern of State-local expenditures, grant funds should take a form that discourages fiscal substitution and that offers a direct inducement to spending. From this perspective, unconditional, lump-sum assistance is the least effective type of aid, for it leaves recipients free to do whatever they wish with the monies. To stimulate State-local spending in recessions and dampen it in booms, Federal programs should tie grant funds to State-local expenditure decisions. The most direct way to accomplish this (as discussed in Part I) is through matching requirements. In a recession, for example, the Federal Government could implement new matching-grant programs and/or offer more generous matching terms for additional expenditures under certain existing programs. In this way, the States and localities could obtain these Federal grant funds only through budgetary expansion on the prescribed programs; they could not simply substitute the grant monies for their own revenues (or add the funds to their surplus).[39]

This suggests, moreover, that programs suitable for countercyclical assistance must possess an inherent flexibility. In particular, social service programs, many of which provide basic support for lower income families, are ill suited to cyclical variations in levels of Federal assistance; the disruptive effects could be quite painful. Following the Hansen-Perloff proposal of the 1940's, the Congressional Budget Office contends that an attractive candidate for countercyclical aid is capital construction grants.[40] Federal grants for the construction

---

[38] It is the case, however, that during the 1966–67 recession, local public investment fell somewhat more in that group of States where State categorical grants for investment declined. It may be that the grants prevented local expenditures from falling by as much as they would have otherwise. Even were this the case, Knott surmises that, "Even a fairly large program accounting for almost 50 percent of local investments cannot guarantee an anticyclical local-government spending policy." (p. 86)

[39] None of the current countercyclical programs in the United States requires matching. The Congressional Budget Office has called attention to this, but offers some reservations about matching requirements because, ". . . some grantees might be deterred from accepting the Federal funds because of the difficulty of raising the required matching money during a recession." (Countercyclical Uses of Federal Grant Programs, op. cit., p. 41.) The CBO suggests some other methods for limiting fiscal substitution such as earmarking of grant funds. Also see the CBO study for an assessment of the issues of "triggering" and "targeting" of grant funds—mechanisms for automatically turning the grant programs on and off over the cycle and for determining the distribution of the funds among jurisdictions.

[40] *Ibid.*, Ch. 6.

of highways or mass-transit facilities, for example, could be varied countercyclically to encourage an enlarged effort during periods of recession and reduced expenditure in times of expansion. The focusing of countercyclical aid on construction grants offers two important advantages. First, since large construction grants are often for specific projects that the recipient government would not have otherwise undertaken, there are very limited opportuntities for fiscal substitution; States and localities will, in general, be unable to use the grant funds to displace their own revenues. Second, many capital projects, like the construction of highways, have considerable flexibility; they can be speeded up or slowed down somewhat without serious disruption to the program.

This latter issue, however, does point up a fundamental problem in the use of grants (and particularly of categorical aid) for countercyclical purposes. Existing expenditure programs have their own rationale in terms of the allocative and distributive priorities of the various agents in the public sector. Their proper execution, moreover, typically requires a certain amount of planning and timing. To adapt these programs to countercyclical ends is not without cost. It is not a simple or costless matter, for example, to increase the flow of resources to highway construction and then to lay off workers and release other inputs in precise conformity with swings in the level of macroeconomic activity.[41] And to the extent this is achieved, it is bound to come at some expense to other public objectives. In brief, the attempt to regulate the flow of State-local spending for specific programs for macrostabilization purposes requires some loss in terms of the effectiveness of the programs on other criteria.

One could argue that, instead of discontinuities in State-local programs, countercyclical aid promises to stabilize budgets by providing additional funds at precisely those times when State and local tax collections are suffering from an economic downturn. From this perspective, Federal countercyclical grants could serve what the Congressional Budget Office has called a "fiscal stabilization" function; they could even out the flows of State-local revenues relative to changes in fiscal "needs." The difficulty there is that macrostabilization policy may, under certain circumstances, require flows of Federal aid that are quire different from those needed for fiscal stabilization. For example, during a period of inflation:

> Fiscal stabilization . . ., regardless of whether the inflation coincides with excess aggregate demand, may require an increase in grants to compensate for increased costs. Service provision demands a steady flow of resources in order that careful program development and implementation can occur and that vital activities not be disrupted.[42]

In short, macroeconomic stabilization and fiscal stabilization are not entirely consistent objectives in terms of their implications for Federal grant policy.

Perhaps more important, to the extent that Federal countercyclical assistance is successful in evening out flows of revenues to State and local governments, this aid may simply relieve State-local

---

[41] For a careful study that explores the difficulties inherent in the use of highway programs for countercyclical ends, see Ann Friedlaender, "The Federal Highway Program as a Public Works Tool," in Albert Ando et al., eds., "Studies in Economic Stabilization" (Washington, D.C.: The Brookings Institution 1968), pp. 61–116.

[42] Congressional Budget Office, "Countercyclical Uses of Federal Grant Programs," p. ix.

354

officials of the need to make their own provision for cyclical forces on the budget. The earlier-cited evidence on State and local fiscal behavior suggests that, at least in the aggregate, the State-local sector has done a fairly decent job of building up stocks of financial assets during periods of expansion and drawing on those reserves to maintain spending during economic downturns. If Federal countercyclical grants were available, State-local officials might no longer find it necessary to maintain their own reserves. If this were to happen, Federal grants would have little macroeconomic impact; their primary effect would be to increase State and local dependence on the Federal treasury.

III. Reflections on the Evolution of Federal Grants Past and Future

As has been shown, the Federal grant system in the United States has not been static; it has undergone a continuing process of change both in size and structure. From a modest collection of programs and level of expenditures in 1950, it has grown rapidly to occupy a major place in the Federal budget. This has resulted both from the expansion of older programs and the addition of new ones. In the early 1950's, these grants consisted primarily of transfers to individuals under public assistance programs such as Aid to Families with Dependent Children (AFDC) and Old Age Assistance. The late 1950's brought the addition of the interstate highway program followed by grants for sewage treatment plants and support for other capital projects. Public assistance continued to grow with new programs such as Medicaid. And in the 1970's came General Revenue Sharing, consisting basically of unconditional transfers of funds to State and local governments. These examples, of course, are simply a few of the major developments in the grant system; as table 2 shows, the range of programs and the categories of support under existing Federal grants constitute an enormously complex structure of assistance. In light of this continuing evolution, this paper concludes with an exploration of some of the issues that have figured (and will continue to figure) in the deliberations and decisions concerning the form and extent of Federal intergovernmental grants.

A. The Grant System and Macroeconomic Stabilization

A major fiscal innovation of the 1970's has been the attempt to adapt various parts of the Federal grant system, including revenue sharing, to support Federal countercyclical policy. The findings in this paper, although admittedly based on quite limited evidence, point toward a pessimistic conclusion on this particular thrust of grant policy: existing empirical work on federal fiscal systems both here and abroad does not indicate much potential for Federal grants as a countercyclical policy tool. First, the State-local sector in the United States has not been, as some had thought, a historically destabilizing force in the economy; on the contrary, the budgetary patterns of State and local governments have, in the main, taken an anticyclical form. Second, the capacity of the Federal Government to have a significant short-run impact on State-local spending and taxes seems, at best, very limited. State and local governments (in the aggregate at least) appear to handle their finances over the business cycle fairly well. Federal grants do affect their fiscal behavior, but only with a substantial time lag. The suggestion of studies, like that of Gramlich's, is that there may exist important parallels between the permanent-income hypothesis of individual spending behavior and the fiscal activities of State and local government. In particular, like individuals, State and local officials appear to pay little attention to purely temporary increases or decreases in receipts in making current budgetary decisions.

This is not to say that revenue sharing is an ineffective program. As Part I indicated, the grant system has a range of allocative and distributive objectives, and there are good reasons to believe that revenue sharing can make some valuable contributions to their realization. But the attempt to extend revenue sharing (and other grant programs) to include countercyclical elements does not appear very promising.

B. *The Grant System and Income Equalization*

In addition to its allocative and stabilization functions, the public sector has an acknowledged responsibility of promoting a more socially desirable distribution of income. This has taken the form, in part, of a set of transfer programs with funds targeted for low-income households. The development and structure of the U.S. system of income transfers is the subject of another study in this collection by Sheldon Danziger, et al.,[43] and a few of their findings are of interest here. In particular, their analysis reveals that, over the period 1965–76, the percentage of persons with pretransfer incomes below the poverty line declined hardly at all (from about 21.3 percent to 21.0 percent); moreover, this figure has actually risen during the 1970's from 18.8 percent in 1970 to 21.0 in 1976. Transfer programs, including both those that operate through Federal grants to States and localities and those that are direct Federal transfers to individuals, have had a real impact. The Danziger-Haveman-Plotnick estimates suggest that, in terms of posttransfer income, the incidence of poverty among persons has fallen from 15.6 percent in 1965 to 11.8 percent in 1976, a fall of roughly 25 percent in posttransfer poverty incidence. Moreover, after further adjustments for the underreporting of incomes, the payment of Federal income and payroll taxes, and the receipt of in-kind transfers, they estimate that the percentage of persons with incomes below the poverty line has fallen from 12.1 percent to 6.5 percent, a reduction of the poverty population by close to one-half. The intriguing and important finding is that growth in the economy itself appears not to have made much contribution to the real incomes of the poor; the source of real progress in the reduction of poverty over the past 15 years is the expansion in public transfer programs.[44]

In light of these findings, one might expect that Federal grants would exhibit a strongly income-equalizing pattern among States with more funds per capita going to the lower-income States. This would also be consistent with the goal of fiscal equalization that was examined in Part I of this paper. In fact, this is not exactly the case. Rudolph

---

[43] Sheldon Danziger, Robert Haveman, and Robert Plotnick, "The U.S. Income Transfer System: An Analysis of Its Structure and Impact," in this volume.
[44] This result is admittedly dependent, in part, on the choice of 1976 as the end point.

Penner found (see table 4) that the five poorest States in the United States receive only slightly more than average in Federal grants per capita; moreover, the five richest States also receive above-average totals of per capita grants.[45] This was true both in 1967 and 1975, but by 1975, the average per capita grant income in the five richest States had come to exceed that in the five poorest States.

Perhaps all this should not be too surprising. There are a great many grant programs with diverse allocative and distributive purposes that are obscured in the aggregate. What is true as Penner observes, is that the Federal grant system has something for everyone.

TABLE 4.—GRANTS PER CAPITA AND GRANTS AS A PERCENTAGE OF PERSONAL INCOME IN THE 5 RICHEST AND 5 POOREST STATES, 1967 AND 1975

	Grants as percent of personal income	Grants per capita
5 richest States, 1967:		
Connecticut	1.6	$62
New York	1.8	70
Illinois	1.5	56
California	3.2	118
New Jersey	1.3	48
Average, 5 richest	2.1	80
National average	2.5	78
5 poorest States, 1967:		
Mississippi	4.7	90
Arkansas	4.6	97
Alabama	4.0	87
South Carolina	2.7	59
West Virginia	4.4	103
Average, 5 poorest	4.0	85
National average	2.5	78
5 richest States, 1975:		
Connecticut	2.8	190
Delaware	3.4	226
Illinois	2.9	196
New Jersey	2.9	191
New York	4.2	276
Average, 5 richest	3.5	230
National average	3.8	221
5 poorest States, 1975:		
Mississippi	6.1	246
Arkansas	5.0	220
New Mexico	6.7	299
South Carolina	4.4	199
Alabama	4.9	223
Average, 5 poorest	5.2	229
National average	3.8	221

Source: Rudolph G. Penner, "Reforming the Grants System."

C. On Allocational Objectives and Grant Design

In addition to redistributive goals, many Federal grant programs have as their fundamental intention to induce certain responses from the States and localities; in our discussion of external effects, we noted the use of grants to encourage specific activities that confer benefits across jurisdictional boundaries. From this perspective, the design of individual grant programs is of paramount importance; such programs will not succeed in generating the intended response unless they provide the proper incentives to the recipients. This point deserves heavy

[45] "Reforming the Grants System," in Peter Mieszkowski and William Oakland, editors, "Fiscal Federalism and Grants-in-Aid." Note, however, the large variation among the five States in each category.

emphasis: it is not enough simply to channel funds to State and local agencies; the form of the grant must be such as to induce the desired budgetary (or other) outcome.

Moreover, as emphasized in Part I, this can be quite a subtle matter. Under a wide variety of circumstances, grant recipients can easily convert conditional grants into unconditional monies in the sense that the ultimate impact of a given conditional grant is identical to that which would have occurred had the funds come with no strings attached. Furthermore, such outcomes are not easy to detect: the only observable behavior is the pattern of fiscal response that the recipient chose after receiving the grant; it is hard to know exactly what would have happened in the absence of the grant (or if the grant had been unconditional rather than conditional). All is not, of course, lost; one can make inferences about these effects from a variety of evidence including econometric analyses. But, because of the fundibility of grant funds, it is not easy, and the findings are typically shrouded in some uncertainty.

In Part I we explored the importance of matching requirements as an inducement for fiscal expansion. Matching, in addition to making external funds available, generates a price effect by reducing the effective cost of the service to the State or locality. If the Federal Government were seeking to encourage the expansion of a number of particular State and local activities, we would expect to find a variety of grant programs, each with a narrowly defined scope and with either explicit or implicit matching provisions.

It is interesting in this regard that the 1960's were years of a proliferation of relatively specific Federal grant programs. In contrast, there were strong forces in the 1970's to stem this trend, first, through the consolidation of many individual programs into block grants providing funds for broadly defined functions and, second, through the introduction of revenue sharing. This was in part a reaction to the troublesome complexity of the emerging grant system, but also to some sense that the Federal Government was encroaching on State and local prerogatives.[46] The shift in the direction of block grants and revenue sharing indicates a movement in the Federal grant system away from direct influence on individual State-local services and toward a substitution of Federal revenues for State and local taxes. The Federal Government is, in effect, altering somewhat the structure of the tax system as a whole, and exerting less leverage on State and local provision of particular services.

What all this portends for the future is not very clear. But it does suggest that we must look hard at both the rationale for and the design of our grant programs. In particular, it is crucial that for each program we first establish explicitly the basis for Federal intervention and its objectives, and, second, that we design the grant program to achieve those objectives. Effective grant design requires both that the Federal Government adopt the proper form of grant and determine the grant parameters (e.g., matching shares) so that the program will generate its intended response from the recipients.

---

[46] There was also evidence that some of these programs were badly designed and were having unanticipated (and undesired) effects.

PART IV

THE PROVISION
OF LOCAL PUBLIC
GOODS

National Tax Journal

Volume XXII, No. 2   June 1969

THE RISING COST OF LOCAL PUBLIC SERVICES: SOME EVIDENCE AND REFLECTIONS

D. F. BRADFORD, R. A. MALT, AND W. E. OATES [*]

IN THE past two decades in this country, we have witnessed a rapid expansion in spending by local government. From 1948 to 1966, local government expenditures rose from $13.4 billion to $60.7 billion, which represents an annual compound rate of increase of close to 9 per cent. Some increase in public spending is to be expected: in a country with an expanding population and rising real income, the public sector has naturally been called upon to provide a larger quantity and improved quality of services. But an expansion of the magnitude of the increase in local-government spending, well in excess of the overall increase in national income, does merit further investigation.

To some observers, this rapid rise in local public expenditures, particularly in the large cities, is simply the result of inept and, in some cases, corrupt administration by local government. Richard Whalen, for example, suggests that recent budgets in New York City are indicative of the "atrocious" performance of city government:

[*] Bradford and Oates are assistant professors at Princeton University. Malt is lecturer in economics, Tel Aviv University. The authors are indebted to several people for critical readings of earlier versions of the paper, especially to R. G. Hollister, whose comments led to the writing of the section on measuring public output. In addition, they are grateful to the Ford Foundation for support facilitating completion of this study.

The plain fact is that municipal spending is out of control and the world's richest city lives in a state of chronic bankruptcy [7, p. 101].

In spite of the opaque language, the Mayor's budget message expresses a tragedy as poignant as any dramatist might contrive. We are told, in effect, that certain fantastic expenditures will grow more fantastic; that they simply cannot be controlled nor can alternatives be devised [7, p. 107].

Ineptness however, can hardly explain the nearly universal phenomenon of rapid secular growth of state and local budgets. The evidence does suggest that, in addition to the need for a larger "bundle" of public services, steadily rising costs have exerted real fiscal pressures on local governments, especially in the big cities. William Baumol [2], in fact, has argued recently that the bulk of the services provided by city governments are services for which increases in productivity are inherently very difficult to achieve; teachers, for instance, are not easily replaced by machines. Baumol contends that the character of the technology of producing these services prevents city governments from offsetting rising wages and salaries with cost-saving innovations, and that as a result the unit costs of these services have risen at a relatively rapid rate. In contrast to Baumol's explanation, others attribute rising costs in the public sector to the absence of competitive forces,

forces which, if present, would induce the introduction of more efficient techniques of production.

How important are rising costs in explaining the rapid expansion in local public spending? As those who have studied output and costs in the public sector are well aware, the problem of measuring the unit costs of public services is a formidable one.[1] One must identify units of outputs and inputs in a way which can be rendered operational; this in itself is no easy task. Our aim in undertaking this study was to see what (if anything) can be said, on the basis of available data, about the trend over time in the unit costs of local public services. Although we find that we can make only few rigorous inferences from the data, we feel that this paper can serve two purposes. First, we will present some data and observations on the rate of increase of costs for a variety of locally produced public services, data which suggest strongly that rapidly rising unit costs, by any reasonable definition, have been a major source of fiscal pressure on local governments. Second, we hope that the study has some value both in terms of illuminating further the nature of the problem of measuring units of public output and in suggesting the kinds of data which would be required to provide a sound basis for measuring trends in productivity for these services.

It is essential that we define conceptually at the outset what we mean by a unit of output of a public service. When one examines the various measures of public output which have been advanced in the study of this problem, it becomes clear that often the authors are talking about quite different things. There exist real ambiguities about just what one means by public output (or the output of any good for that matter), and it is of central importance that we make clear what it is that we want to measure.

[1] For a useful survey of the work on measuring units and costs of public output, see Werner Hirsch [4].

Units of Public Output

A number of rather subtle problems in the measurement of output, to some extent common to all commodities, arise in especially acute form in the case of public output. In this section we look closely at one of these: we attempt to spell out carefully the distinction between the services directly produced (which we call "D-output") and the thing or things of primary interest to the citizen-consumer (termed "C-output").

Let I represent a vector of inputs in the production of a public good. Various types and combinations of labor, capital equipment, *etc.*, as expressed in the vector I, map through a production function into a vector D of "directly produced" goods or services. In the case of police services, for example, the components of I would presumably consist of such inputs as men, cars, and communications systems; the resulting vector D of direct outputs might include as components the number of city blocks provided with a specified degree of surveillance (by patrolmen on foot or automobile patrols), the number of blocks provided with readily available police-officer reserves, the number of intersections provided with traffic control, and so on.[2]

[2] The vector I does not in general map into a unique vector D. As a highly simplified example, assume that D has only two components: a specified level of police surveillance or the direction of traffic at intersections. A given input vector might be capable of providing 50 blocks with police surveillance or alternatively 100 intersections with direct traffic control, or yet further a number of combinations of the two. For a given I, we thus have the additional problem of selecting that D from the available alternatives which provides the most desired pattern of consumption of these services. Differing qualities of a service would in this framework be treated as distinct services. One component of D, for instance, might consist of the number of blocks for which a high level of police surveillance is provided, while another component would indicate the number of blocks receiving a low degree of surveillance. There would obviously exist a tradeoff between these levels of surveillance as between the other functions of the police department.

When the citizen votes on a police budget, however, he is primarily interested, not in the vector D, but rather in such things as the degree of safety from criminal activity and the smoothness and rapidity of the flow of traffic. And these depend only in part on D. To confine ourselves to this complication alone, let us suppose that these "matters of concern" to the consumer can be described by a vector which registers in every citizen's utility function along with the quantities of private goods he consumes. This vector is, moreover, completely determined by the vector D and by certain environmental variables, such as the "propensity to riot" in the community and the driving habits of local residents. Let C be such a vector. In the case of police services, the components of C might be the probabilities that a citizen will not be subjected to specified sorts of accidents or criminal acts during the year. According to the assumptions just made, we can express an individual's preferences in the form:

$$(1) \qquad U = U(C, Z),$$

where Z is a vector representing the level of provision of other public goods and of the quantities of private goods consumed by the individual, and where

$$(2) \qquad C_k = f_k(D, E),$$

with E a vector of environmental variables and f_k a function indicating the degree of safety of the k'th sort felt by the individual in environment E enjoying directly produced police services D.[3]

[3] Even this represents an oversimplification. It is quite likely that the "degree of safety" (as expressed in the vector C) resulting from a given vector D will differ among individuals. The probability of being assaulted may, for instance, be greater for a night watchman than for a file clerk. In this case where the vector C is "individual specific," we would have to write the utility function of citizen i as:

$$U^i = U^i (C^i, Z^i)$$

where

$$C_k^i = f_k^i (D, E).$$

Notice that, in terms of these definitions, we can make sense of a scalar multiple of only the vector D. We can, for example, reasonably inquire as to the increase in inputs needed to provide $2D$ (e.g., to double the number of city blocks provided with a specified degree of surveillance). If this can be accomplished with a less than doubling of the amount of inputs, economies of scale in "direct output" could be said to exist. In contrast, since the components of C may consist of such things as the probabilities of avoiding various sorts of accidents or assaults, it is not possible to talk meaningfully about scalar multiples of C. What we can examine, however, is the cost of making C available to an increased number of persons. In this second sense, "economies of scale" are present if C, for instance, can be provided for twice as many consumers without doubling the quantities of inputs.[4]

It is important for our purposes to distinguish between these two concepts of output, because the trends in their cost may be quite different. The changing environmental characteristics in the cities, for example, suggest that in recent years the cost (per capita) of providing city residents with specified levels of safety (i.e., a given C-vector) has probably risen much more rapidly than the cost of maintaining police patrols at a certain frequency (i.e., a given D-vector). Moreover, the data suitable for measuring the cost of one vector is largely irrelevant for the other: the trend in certain insurance premiums, for instance, may provide a reasonable guide to changes in existing levels of safety; such premiums, however,

---

This means that we cannot talk about a single vector C for all consumers. We can, however, still make the distinction between C- and D-concepts of output, and this is what is important for our purposes.

[4] In the case of a pure public good, the cost of extending consumption of the good to yet another consumer is by definition zero. This represents the polar case of "economies of scale" as regards the C-concept of output.

tell little about the cost of maintaining patrols over a certain number of city blocks.

This distinction may be illustrated as well for the case of goods which are not in themselves "final" in even the sense in which police services are: the services of educational institutions, for example, enter the production of human capital, which is itself employed in further production processes. Let I now be a vector of inputs (*e.g.*, teacher days, books, *etc.*) in the production of education, and let D measure the "direct output" (*e.g.*, pupil-lessons in arithmetic, pupil-lessons in geography, school plays, *etc.*). Employing the human-capital approach, we might argue that the purpose of education is the development of certain skills on the part of pupils; in this framework, we can interpret the vector C as measuring the degree of achievement of this objective (with components such as the student's scores on various tests which measure his mastery of skills). Even treating the acquisition of skills as solely of pecuniary interest, the value of a specified C-output will depend in turn upon the other factors of production available and on the existing technology of production. Let Q stand for the output per man obtainable from a worker with the "quantities of skills" designated by C:

$$(3) \qquad Q = Q(C, Z),$$

where Z is taken to represent available quantities per man of other factors of production. Just as, in their previous incarnation, the relationship between D and C depended upon the environment, so here

$$(4) \qquad C_k = g_k(D, E),$$

where, in this case, E might describe the "basic intelligence" of pupils, home backgrounds, and neighborhood conditions. Here again, it is easy to confuse output measures in the nature of C's (test performance, reading and writing ability), with others in the nature of D's (hours of instruction of various kinds); acquired skills are not equivalent to the number of years spent in school. It is interesting in this connection that most recent work in the economics of education and, to some extent in the economics of health services has jumped both steps by dealing with the capitalized value of future output (or internal rates of return) yielded by expenditures on these services.

In view of the foregoing discussion, it is not surprising that considerable ambiguity surrounds the notion of "unit costs" of public outputs. Even when the distinction between the D- and C-concepts of output is carefully drawn and maintained, a multi-dimensional vector of output remains, with variations over time and space in the relative sizes of components: the perennial problem of quality change. When expenditure figures have been adjusted in some sense for scale, the "unit" of which one then knows the cost is rather like an automobile—very different in 1968 from what it was in 1930.

In the following sections, we have assembled cost and expenditure data on a variety of local-government functions upon the basis of which we attempt to make inferences concerning the likely trend of unit costs for the D- (and sometimes also the C-) concept of output. Because satisfactory measures of outputs corresponding to existing data are not available, we have not hesitated to make intuitive judgments, although since all figures are shown, the reader can easily substitute his own guesses. Although there do exist unresolved problems about the trend in unit costs, the evidence does point more unambiguously to one general conclusion: in the areas we have studied, we find that local governments have not been able to offset the rising costs of inputs, notably manpower, by cutting back on the use of these inputs through significant cost-saving advances in techniques of production. Improvements in quality of output have certainly occurred, but they seem if anything to have stimulated rather than reduced levels of public spending.

The remainder of the paper consists of brief studies of costs in public elementary and secondary education, health and hospital care, police and fire protection, and some reflections on the "unit costs" of welfare services. As Table I indicates, expenditures on these services together accounted for 63 per cent of local-government general public expenditures in the metropolitan areas of the United States in 1962. By far the largest single item in these budgets is education, and to this we turn first.

TABLE I

The Division of Local-Government General Public Expenditures in U.S. Standard Metropolitan Statistical Areas (1962)

Education	42%	Interest on debt	4%
Highways	8%	Administration .	4%
		Housing and Urban Renewal	4%
Public Welfare.	7%		
Sanitation	6%	Fire Protection.	3%
Health and Hospitals ...	6%	Parks and Recreation ..	3%
Police	5%	Miscellaneous .	9%

Source: George F. Break, *Intergovernmental Fiscal Relations in the United States*, Washington, D.C.: The Brookings Institution, 1967, p. 170.

Education [5]

Our primary concern in this section is with the *D*-concept of output, with the trend in costs of providing a given number of students with instruction of a specified kind (*e.g.*, a certain number of "standard" geography lessons). We have arranged the data on education in such a way that, if *D*-output had been constant, all increases in costs would have resulted from rising input prices. Satisfactory measures of output are not available. Nevertheless, the information we have assembled on per-pupil inputs and costs in public elementary and secondary

[5] We are indebted to the members of the Research Division of the National Education Association for their assistance in obtaining needed data.

education suggest to us a much more rapid increase in costs than is likely to have occurred in output. At any rate, these data indicate clearly that rapidly rising expenditures *per student* account for a major portion of the increase in school budgets.

In Table II, we find that the salaries of city public-school teachers have increased, as would be expected, with the general rise in per-capita incomes in the U.S. economy. The increase in recent decades has in fact been quite rapid, almost 5 per cent per annum in the postwar period.

Technological advances might have partially offset this rise in teachers' salaries through the introduction of less costly techniques of educating pupils. However, if such technological advances have occurred, they have been dominated by other factors. Table III indicates that current costs per pupil day in public elementary and secondary schools have risen continuously and dramatically in the present century. In the post-war period (1947-67), these costs have increased at a rate of 6.7 per cent per year, even *more* rapidly than the rise in teachers' salaries.[6]

It is interesting to note that over the period 1947-66 the wholesale price index, a measure of the money cost of producing farm and industrial output, rose by 1.4 per cent per year. The statistics in Table III say that the number of units of the WPI bundle of goods which must be given up for a pupil-day of public-school instruction rose about 5.3 per cent per

[6] The figures in Table III do not allow for the growing proportion of pupils in secondary schools, where cost per pupil is significantly higher (roughly 50 per cent more). However, a crude adjustment to the series in Table III, which weights pupils in grades 9 to 12 and elementary pupils (*i.e.*, kindergarten to 8th grade) in the ratio of 3 to 2, suggests that this factor is not of great importance. The adjustment yielded an annual rate of increase of current costs per pupil day of 4.8 per cent for 1900-67 and 6.7 per cent (no change) for 1947-67.

TABLE II

INDEX OF AVERAGE ANNUAL SALARIES OF CITY PUBLIC SCHOOL TEACHERS
(1957-59 = 100)

1925	37	1947	55	
1927	38	1949	67	
1929	40	1951	71	
1931	41	1953	81	Annual Rate of Increase:
1933	38	1955	87	(Compounded)
1935	37	1957	96	
1937	39	1959	104	1925-1965 3.2%
1939	41	1961	113	1947-1965 4.8%
1941	42	1963	121	
1943	44	1965	128	
1945	48			

Source: *City Public School Teachers, 1925-65,* Bulletin #1504, U.S. Department of Labor, Bureau of Labor Statistics, May, 1966, pp. 24, 35.

TABLE III

CURRENT COSTS PER PUPIL-DAY IN U.S. PUBLIC SCHOOLS

1900	$ .12	1955	$1.51	
1910	.18	1956	1.67	
1920	.33	1957	1.69	
1930	.50	1958	1.85	
1940	.50	1959	1.94	Annual Rate of Increase:
1946	.77	1960	2.13	(Compounded)
1947	.86	1961	2.20	
1948	1.02	1962	2.37	1900-1967 5.0%
1949	1.11	1963	2.42	1947-1967 6.7%
1950	1.18	1964	2.57	
1951	1.26	1965	2.70	
1952	1.39	1966	2.93	
1953	1.35	1967	3.15	
1954	1.48			

Source: These figures were calculated by multiplying average daily school attendance for each year by the average number of days in the school year to give a number of pupil days figure. This last number was then divided into the annual current expenditure on public elementary and secondary education to give the current cost per pupil day. The sources of the data for these calculations are *Status and Trends: Vital Statistics, Education, and Public Finance,* Research Division, National Education Association, Report R13, August 1959, pp. 11, 22; *Estimates of School Statistics, 1966-67,* Research Division, National Education Association, Report R20, 1966, pp. 10, 20; and U.S. Department of Health, Education, and Welfare, *Statistics of State School Systems,* 1963-4, Washington, 1967, p. 21. There were a few gaps in the data for the average length of the school term. For these years, we used interpolations of the available data.

annum over the period 1947-67. The relative cost of education per pupil day has thus increased very rapidly in recent times.[7]

[7] Because our investigation was inspired by Baumol's contention that the technology of producing public output is stagnant especially relative to manufacturing technology, we have chosen to compare the rate of growth of our various measures of unit dollar costs of public outputs with the rate of growth of the wholesale price index, an index relatively low in service components. The difference between these growth rates tells us the rate of growth of the unit cost of the good in question in terms

A real improvement in educational programs has no doubt taken place in this same period; students today receive in general superior training to that of earlier years; and the massive urbanization of the society has certainly led to a shift of students from low to high per-pupil-expenditure areas, probably with significantly improved schooling the result. Ad-

of units of the composite bundle of goods used as a basis for the WPI. Since we display the original dollar figures and dollar growth rates, the reader is free to substitute alternative "numeraires."

mitting the difficulty of documenting the fact, it seems to us unlikely, however, that the technology by which a teacher produces a "geography-lesson-equivalent" has advanced at a rate comparable to the rate of increase of teacher compensation, or that the "geography-lesson equivalents" transmitted to a student have increased at a rate comparable to expenditure per-student. The evidence thus appears to suggest strongly that rapidly rising unit costs have, in fact, characterized the public-education "industry" in the United States in recent decades.

What the data do indicate unambiguously is that the cost of the bundle of inputs combined with a pupil day in the production of human capital has risen at a rapid rate in the post-war period. Pupil-teacher ratios have declined slightly in this period (from 27.8 pupils per teacher in 1948 to 25.7 in 1966),[8] but our rough calculations suggest that this alone can account for less than ½ of one per cent per annum in the rise in costs per pupil day. It is evident that the rapid rise in the salaries of teachers and administrators has been a major contributor to the great expansion in school budgets. Much has been made of the impact of the post World War II "baby boom" on the costs of our educational programs, but the truth appears to be that local governments would probably have been subject to real budgetary pressures even if the school-age population had not been expanding.[9]

It is interesting to speculate on the sources of this apparently significant increase in unit costs in public education. As noted earlier, Baumol would attribute the rise in unit costs to the technological character of the education industry. The personal interaction between pupil and teacher is generally regarded as a basic part of educational programs; there is, therefore, good reason to believe that it is more difficult to replace teachers by machines than in the manufacturing sector, where labor is not, by the nature of the output, such an integral part of the production process. As a result, as wages and salaries rise through the economy with the growth in per-capita incomes, one might well expect an increase in the relative cost of educational services because of a relatively slow increase in productivity.

One can, however, advance other hypotheses to explain this phenomenon. A rise in the relative cost of educational services could, for example, result from a movement along the production-possibilities frontier.[10] Assuming a frontier with the usual "bowed-out" shape, we would expect the opportunity cost of an additional unit of education to rise as a larger proportion of the resources in the economy is employed in providing educational services. That education has grown relative to the rest of the economy is beyond dispute; over the period of 1948-67, for example, the number of public-school teachers more than doubled, while the civilian labor force increased by less than 30 per cent. As a result, the transfer of

---

[8] Same sources as Table I: see NEA Reports R13 (pp. 9, 15) and R20 (p. 13). It is incidentally by no means clear that this reduction in the number of pupils per teacher has contributed significantly to the quality of education. The Coleman Report, for example, finds little correlation between pupil-teacher ratios and levels of achievement by students.

[9] One qualification is necessary here. It may well be that the rapid growth in the number of pupils, resulting in an increased demand for teachers, led to a more rapid rise in teachers' salaries than would otherwise have taken place. In this way, the expansion in the absolute number of pupils may have contributed to the rise in costs per pupil.

[10] The Baumol hypothesis concerns *shifts* in this frontier. If we were to put education on the horizontal axis and all other goods on the vertical axis, assuming for simplicity a linear frontier, Baumol's contention would be that technical advance for other goods has continually shifted up the intercept on the vertical axis, while the intercept on the education axis has remained unchanged (or increased relatively little). Thus, the slope of the production-possibilities frontier would increase over time, which would imply a rising opportunity cost of educational services.

resources into the labor-intensive education "industry" could conceivably have contributed to some extent to a rise in relative costs in education.[11] This expansion may not have been the only factor which has tended to bid up the prices of resources required in relatively large amounts in education. It is likely, in addition, that there has been a relative expansion in other labor-intensive industries which compete directly for the same inputs used in education. In particular, growth in the demand for commodities and services requiring a relatively large input of personnel with advanced training has tended to raise the prices of these inputs.

Incidentally, since training is the major output, as well as a major input of the educational process, the factor demand shift just mentioned, which has raised the unit cost of education, has also signalled a rise in the value of output obtainable from human capital. The fact that studies of the rate of return on investment in human capital have not uncovered any marked trend suggests that the advance of the value in production of a unit of education may have kept pace with the rise in its unit cost.[12]

It may also be the case that rising costs of public education are simply the result of inefficiency in the public sector. It is probably true that incentives to innovate and use resources effectively are not as strong in the government as in private industry; thus, the failure to realize gains in productivity in public education could stem from the absence of competitive

forces.[13] Although one would probably be reluctant to describe private educational institutions as paradigms of free enterprise, we would expect, if this hypothesis is true, to find that pupil costs have risen less rapidly in private schools. Data on the cost of private education are difficult to come by, but we have located some fragmentary evidence. The Treasurers of three of the leading private secondary schools in the East provided us with time series on costs per pupil over the period 1947-66. In all three cases, the annual increase in current costs per pupil was 4.2 per cent. Although this figure is somewhat below the increase in costs in the public schools, it does include expenses for room and board for which the rise in costs is presumably considerably less than instructional costs. This would suggest that costs of instruction have probably risen at a rate well above the overall increase in costs. In a recent study of parochial schools, Fr. Ernest Bartell [1] found that current costs per pupil in the elementary schools in the dioceses of Youngstown, Ohio, and San Francisco, California, rose at more than 6 per cent annually over the period 1958-63, a figure slightly in excess of the increase in costs in the public schools over this period. On balance, it appears that current instructional costs in nonpublic schools have also risen much more rap-

[11] This argument appears in a slightly different guise in footnote 9. Incidentally, the convexity of the production-possibilities frontier does not require that different units of factor inputs be of varying quality or adaptability, but only that there exist differences of factor intensities among industries. For a proof of this point, see G. D. N. Worswick [8].

[12] We wish to thank R. Hollister for pointing out to us this important fact.

[13] Werner Hirsch [4, p. 486] has suggested that local governments may frequently be constrained from attaining the least-cost combination of factor inputs. The reluctance of local electorates to approve (and wide-spread limitations on) local bond issues to finance capital-expenditure programs may often mean that local officials must adopt more labor-intensive techniques of production than would otherwise be desired. In a dynamic framework, this may imply for our purposes that lagging productivity in the provision of local public services results in part from the inability of local governments to obtain the authority to acquire new and more efficient capital equipment and structures.

idly than the wholesale price index, at a rate roughly comparable to that in the public schools.

One critic has suggested that lagging productivity in education is probably the result of a powerful interest group, namely professional educators who have blocked cost-reducing innovation. This possibility is most difficult to evaluate; however, for this to be the whole of the story, it is necessary for this group to have "frozen" the technology of education at some point in the distant past, for only this could account for a rate of increase in the cost per pupil-day equal to the rise in factor prices. Furthermore, even if this hypothesis is true, it offers small comfort unless there exists a real prospect for altering the system.

In summary, the picture we get of primary and secondary education is one of an industry in which costs of inputs have risen rapidly and in which the bundle of physical inputs combined with each pupil has increased slightly. As a result, there has occurred a continuous and striking expansion in expenditures per pupil of the order of 7 per cent per annum in the post-war period. There have certainly been real improvements in the quality of educational programs, but we would doubt that output (if we had a reasonable measure of it) per dollar of input has grown at a rate anything like the rate of increase in costs. Education is in all likelihood an industry where rising unit costs explain a very large portion of the rise in spending. We might point out further that, while the improvement in the quality of educational programs should be a source of real satisfaction, it does not offer much comfort from the standpoint of school budgets. Rising salaries of teachers and administrators, in the past and in the foreseeable future, translate themselves into increased cost per pupil, and, unless there are some radical developments in teaching methods by which we can economize on the use of skilled teachers, this is a trend which we would expect to persist in the future.

Health and Hospitals [14]

The problems confronting an assessment of cost trends in public health and hospital services are at least as severe as those in education: methods and quality of treatment for various diseases have in many cases altered radically in recent decades so that defining units of output and consumption is extremely difficult. We can, nevertheless, at least conceptualize the provision of health and hospital services in terms of the scheme described earlier. The components of the I-vector would now consist of medical personnel, beds, medicines, surgical equipment, *etc.* A given I would then map into a vector D, whose components would indicate the number of (potential) treatments for various maladies (*e.g.*, a certain number of flu shots, appendectomy operations, and so on). The consumer, however, is less concerned with the treatment itself than with his cure from the disease; a flu-shot, for instance, is not equivalent to avoiding a case of influenza. The C-vector is thus best associated with the dimensions of the individual's state of health and as such is jointly determined by available health treatment (D) and by a number of exogenous variables reflected in the vector E (e.g., the age of the residents, past accidents, and the presence or absence of epidemics). Like the degree of safety from criminal acts, the state of health of the members of a community depends on several environmental variables as well as on the quantity and scope of available health treatment.

It is clear that both the mix and quality of treatment have changed significantly over time so that (as in the case of education) we cannot evaluate directly the change in costs over time of a specified vector D. There have clearly

[14] We are indebted to Herman M. Somers and Charles Berry of Princeton University for helpful comments on this section of the paper.

taken place important technological advances in methods of treatment, but the available data suggest that, *from the standpoint of local public budgets*, other factors have more than offset any possible cost savings from improved techniques of medical treatment. Over the period 1955-64 total public expenditures for health and medical services more than doubled; the increase was from $4.4 billion (or $26.5 per capita) in 1955 to $9.0 billion (or $46.9 per capita) in 1964.[15] This represents an annual rate of increase in per capita expenditure of over 6½ per cent. It is difficult, however, to determine accurately just how much of this increase resulted from (1) a larger quantity of health and medical services, (2) a higher quality of services, and (3) higher unit costs. We do, nevertheless, have some information which suggests that for a major component of public health services, namely care in general hospitals, increases in unit costs have been quite important.

Hospital care appears to provide a clear example of rising costs resulting, at least in part, from lagging productivity. The basic task is to provide room and board in a clean environment and the services of nurses and other skilled attendants. While it may be possible to achieve some productivity advances in supporting services (through perhaps a more extensive delegation of specialized tasks to semi-skilled workers) one would expect these advances to be quantitatively unimportant. This problem has been recognized in several quarters. Herbert Klarman, for example, points out that:

> In most industries increases in wages are not fully translated into higher prices, since part of the higher cost of input can be absorbed through increased productivity. Hospitals, by contrast, have but limited potentialities for achieving gains in productivity. The New York State Board of Charities (now Social Welfare) recognized this fact more than 30 years ago,

15 See source for Table IV, page 25.

as have many economists who have reflected on hospital cost [3, p. 237].

Turning to the available cost information, we find that the data provide support for the argument that productivity advances in hospital care have lagged. Table IV shows the trends in Hospital Daily Service Charges from 1935 to 1963. This index, which covers the charge to full-pay adult in-patients for room and board, routine nursing care, and minor medical and surgical supplies, isolates clearly the basic elements of hospital care. Over the entire period covered, the daily charge for hospital care increased at an annual compound rate of 6.5 per cent; over this same period, the wholesale price index shows an annual growth rate of 3.0 per cent. In the post-war period, the rise has been even more dramatic: an annual rate of growth 7.4 per cent (compared to a 1.3 per cent annual rise in wholesale prices). The charge to patients for hospital care has clearly risen much more rapidly than the general level of costs throughout the economy.[16]

There is, moreover, evidence that these increases in the daily service charge to patients reflect a general rise in the costs of hospital care, a rise which is also present in public expenditures for hospital services. In a recent study of general hospitals in New York City, Klarman [3, pp. 227-248] found a very rapid rise in expenditures for hospital care. Of interest here is Klarman's discovery that between 1934 and 1957 cost per patient-day rose from $5.26 to $26.40, an annual compound rate of increase of 7.3 per cent. This increase in patient-day cost accounts for 94 per cent of the rise in expenditures for in-patients over this period. After in-

16 Of course, the charge to patients does not necessarily equal the cost of the services rendered, and it is likely that average-cost pricing practices result in patient charges which reflect the relative expansion of medical research in hospitals and the costs of esoteric (and expensive) special equipment. The latter elements are more properly associated with quality improvements.

TABLE IV

INDEX OF HOSPITAL DAILY SERVICE CHARGE (1957-59 = 100)

1935	23.8	1951	64.1		
1939	25.3	1952	70.4		
1940	25.4	1953	74.8		
1941	25.9	1954	79.2		
1942	28.0	1955	83.0	Annual Rate of Increase:	
1943	30.2	1956	87.5	(Compounded)	
1944	31.5	1957	94.5		
1945	32.5	1958	99.9	1935-1963	6.5%
1946	37.0	1959	105.5	1947-1963	7.4%
1947	44.1	1960	112.7		
1948	51.5	1961	121.3		
1949	55.7	1962	129.8		
1950	57.8	1963	138.0		

Source: U.S. Department of Health, Education and Welfare, *Health, Education, and Welfare Trends,* 1964 edition, Part I, page 22.

TABLE V

EMPLOYMENT, EXPENSES, AND AVERAGE LENGTH OF STAY IN STATE AND LOCAL GOVERNMENT SHORT-TERM GENERAL AND OTHER SPECIAL HOSPITALS, 1946-65.

Year-End	Personnel per 100 patients [a]	Payroll per patient day	Total Expense per patient day	Average Length of stay in days
1946	129	$ 4.58	$ 7.39	11.4
1948	136	6.20	10.27	11.0
1950	149	7.80	12.56	10.7
1952	153	9.63	15.37	10.7
1954	175	12.66	19.34	9.9
1956	195	14.46	22.08	9.4
1958	206	16.51	25.82	9.0
1960	215	19.47	29.43	8.8
1961	227	20.75	32.27	8.8
1962	232	22.69	34.45	8.5
1963	237	23.57	36.19	8.5
1964	236	25.05	38.57	8.5
1965	234	27.17	41.84	8.5

[a] Personnel data for 1954 and thereafter include full-time personnel plus full-time equivalents of part-time personnel; previously the figures were for full-time personnel only. From 1952 onward, residents, interns, and students are excluded.
Source: *Hospitals,* Guide Issue, August 1, 1966, Vol. 40, Part 2, p. 439.

vestigating the sources of these cost increases, Klarman concludes that "Medical advances, insofar as they are reflected in the ancillary services of the hospital, account for less than one-fourth of the dollar increase in patient-day cost in the 1950's" [3, p. 247]. The most important cause, Klarman suggests, is the "lag in productivity gains" [3, p. 248].

The statistics covering State and Local Government Short-Term and Other Special Hospitals presented in Table V provide further evidence of the rise in unit costs, although they do suggest some significant improvements in the quality of care. Between 1946 and 1965, average total expenses per patient day rose without interruption from $7.39 to $41.84, an annual compound rate of increase of 9.6 per cent. Payroll expenses increased at an annual rate of 9.8 per cent, from $4.58 to $27.17 per patient day, during the same period. It is important to recognize that these figures are based on *all* expenses including the *total* payroll of hospitals; they incorporate the great expansion of services beyond the room-and-board function. We find here that hospital personnel per 100 patients nearly doubled, rising from 129 in 1946 to 234 in 1965.[17] A crude adjustment for these changes may be made by assuming that increases in personnel per patient and a corresponding fraction of total expenses constitute pure quality improvements. If we thus "deflate" the total expense per patient day in 1965 by multiplying by 129/234, unit costs over the period would have increased from $7.39 to $23.07, a still quite substantial annual rate of increase of 6.2 per cent.

Hospital care is, however, but one component of the vector D, and it is quite possible that productivity gains are achievable when this input is combined with its complementary factors. An example might appear to be the reduction in the average length of stay in the hospital. The average duration per visit for in-patient care in State and Local Government General and Specific Hospitals declined from 11.4 days in 1946 to 8.5 days in 1965 (see Table V). Statistics covering all general and specific hospitals in the nation show a reduction from 15.3 days in 1931 to 9.3 in 1962.[18] The cost-saving implications of this trend should not, however, be taken for granted. In the first place, this reduction in average stay in the hospital cannot offset the whole of the increase in patient-day costs. While the average length of stay declined by about one-third over 1936-62, the index of hospital daily services charges for this period increased over five times in money terms and more than doubled in real terms. Second, it isn't clear to what extent the reduction in duration of patient stay can be attributed to rising productivity in medical care. Less aggregated statistics would reveal the extent to which changes in the reasons for hospital admis-

[17] Some portion of this shift is attributable to the change in the definition of the series in 1954 to include full-time equivalents for part-time workers.

[18] Same source as for Table IV, p. 28.

sions explain the shortened duration of stay. A large increase in the number of one-day visits for physical examinations, for example, could reduce this statistic. Herman Somers has pointed out to us that there has been a tendency, under the influence of hospitalization-insurance programs, to substitute hospital service for such services as physician house-calls. Further, though according to Somers unlikely, some of the reduction may have resulted from economizing on the use of hospital services to offset the higher price. To this extent, the reduction in length of stay may actually reflect a deterioration in the care received per visit.

As to changes in the overall costs of treating various illnesses, reliable information is most difficult to come by. Anne Scitovsky [6] has recently completed the most careful study of this problem, a study which involved a systematic survey of historical medical records for five types of medical treatment (acute appendicitis, maternity care, otitis media in children, cancer of the breast, and fracture of the forearm). Mrs. Scitovsky found that over the period 1951-2 to 1964-5 the increase in average costs of treatment for these "illnesses" ranged from 68 per cent to 106 per cent, a rate of increase of somewhat less than the rise in costs of hospital care but still well above the increase in the *WPI*. We stress that these figures incorporate the many technical improvements in the treatment of these diseases. What this does suggest, however, is that technical advance in health and hospital services has not been of a cost-saving character. Mrs. Scitovsky, in her study, concluded that "If forced to make a guess, we would say that the net effect of changes in treatment, at least over the past 14 years, has been to raise costs, and hence that the medical care price index, if it had taken account of such changes, would have shown a greater rise than it did" [6, p. 1194].

In summary, it appears that public health and hospital care (like public education) has been an area where rising unit costs have been a major contributor to the increase in local public spending. As with education, there have no doubt taken place important improvements in technology, but these advances as a whole do not seem to have been of a cost-reducing nature: they have resulted in higher quality services, but not at less cost. Desirable as such progress is, we should recognize at the same time that, rather than easing the pressures on local budgets, these advances appear to have had the opposite effect of stimulating additional public spending.

Police and Fire Protection

The available information on per-capita expenditures and employment for police and fire protection suggests that rising costs of inputs have been a major source of the increase in expenditures for these functions. In addition, the continuing urbanization of U.S. society appears to have generated a need for a larger quantity of inputs (per capita) simply to maintain existing levels of safety.

While increasing use is made of sophisticated capital equipment in the provision of police and fire protection (e.g., advanced communication systems, improved fire trucks, and so on), the fact is that the major part of spending for both functions is for manpower. Allen Manvel has found that "Salaries and wages make up the bulk of local government expenditure for these protective services—about seven-eighths of all policing costs and four-fifths of fire protection expenditure" [5, p. 36]. Of course, the fact that payments for labor absorb such a large share of police and fire budgets does not mean that there is a fixed relationship between labor input and output, however measured. The non-labor portion of the budget could be purchasing ever-improving equipment and thereby continually lowering the unit cost of police and fire protection.

If this is the case, however, citizens must have been purchasing a rapidly growing output of police and fire services (at least of our *D*-concept of output) since the turn of the century. Table VI shows per-capita local-government expenditures on police and fire protection from 1902 through 1966. Over the entire period, per-capita expenditure on police protection has risen at an average annual compound rate of 4.7 per cent and on fire protection at 4.2 per cent. During this period the wholesale price index rose at an average annual compound rate of 1.9 per cent. As would be expected, annual rates of increase in the post-World War II period (1946-66) were even more rapid; the figure for police is 7.1 per cent, and for fire 6.2 per cent. In contrast, the wholesale price index over this period rose at an average rate of 2.4 per cent.

Are these increases in per-capita spending the result of rising unit costs or do they simply indicate a growing per-capita output of the services? This is a difficult question to answer, but the evidence appears to suggest that rising costs have probably been quantitatively the more important of the two sources of increasing spending. In view of the preponderance of labor inputs in the provision of these services, we examined the aggregate employment data for the police and fire functions and found that the number of police and fire personnel per-capita has increased, but only modestly (relative to the rise in costs) in recent years. In cities with populations of 50,000 or more, for example, police employment (full-time equivalents) per 10,000 population increased from 20.6 in 1952 to 23.9 in 1963, while the corresponding fire-protection employment grew from 14.8 to 16.3 per 10,000 population over these same years.[19] If we "deflate" the per-capita expenditure series in Table VI by the increases in police and fire per-

[19] U.S. Bureau of the Census, *City Employment in 1952* and *City Employment in 1963*, (Government Employment Series).

TABLE VI
LOCAL-GOVERNMENT EXPENDITURES (PER-CAPITA) ON POLICE AND FIRE
PROTECTION IN THE UNITED STATES

	Police	Fire		Police	Fire
1902	$ .63	$ .51	1953	$ 5.81	$3.78
1913	.91	.78	1954	6.20	4.05
1922	1.69	1.44	1955	6.64	4.22
1927	2.21	1.71	1956	7.01	4.41
1932	2.43	1.68	1957	7.57	4.75
1934	2.18	1.50	1958	8.06	5.04
1936	2.30	1.60	1959	8.37	5.16
1938	2.53	1.78	1960	8.96	5.53
1940	2.51	1.78	1961	9.59	5.94
1942	2.64	1.76	1962	9.97	6.05
1944	2.81	1.89	1963	10.50	6.33
1946	3.10	2.10	1964	10.72	6.38
1948	3.96	2.78	1965	11.36	6.74
1950	4.57	3.23	1966	12.21	7.02
1952	5.35	3.76			

Annual Rate of Increase:
(Compounded)

	Police	Fire
1902-1966	4.7%	4.2%
1946-1966	7.1%	6.2%
1950-1966	6.3%	5.0%

Sources: The data for aggregate local-government expenditures on police and fire protection and for the resident population of the United States for 1902-62 are from the U.S. Bureau of the Census, *Historical Statistics of the United States, Colonial Times to 1957* and *Continuation to 1962 and Revisions.* For Fiscal years 1963-66, the expenditure data are available in the Bureau of the Census' annual publication, *Governmental Finances.* Estimates of the U.S. resident population for these years are contained in the *Current Population Reports* of the Bureau of the Census.

sonnel, we find that expenditure per capita for public police protection has grown at an annual rate of 4.7 per cent over 1952-63, while per-capita spending on fire protection for these years has risen at 4.0 per cent per annum (as compared to rates of 6.1 per cent and 4.8 per cent in the absence of this "deflation"). We stress again that our data concern costs and quantities of inputs; certainly technical advances in the provision of these services have occurred so that these inputs provide better quality services than in earlier years. We doubt, however, that such improvements have taken place at a rate comparable to that of the increase in per-capita spending for these functions. We are thus inclined to believe that rapidly rising unit costs are here again an important contributor to the swift increase in spending by local governments in this country.

Further examination suggests that the increases that have occurred in inputs per capita for these services are probably in large measure the result of the growing urbanization of U.S. society. In terms of what we have called the C-concept of output (in this case the "level of safety"), one might think that increasing urbanization would allow some economies of scale, or perhaps more accurately, economies of agglomeration. Concentration of populations might, for instance, make it possible to provide the service of maintaining a fire crew within five minutes of each resident more cheaply on a per-capita basis. On the other hand, large concentrations of people increase the possible number of interactions among persons of the sort which result in a need for police and fire protection. Baumol makes this point, when he argues that the aggregate extent of many kinds of external diseconomies increases as the square of the population in an area [2,

TABLE VII

CITY FIRE PROTECTION AND POLICE EMPLOYMENT PER 10,000 POPULATION,
BY CITY SIZE, 1954 AND 1963

Full Time Equivalent Employment Per 10,000 Population by Function		Population Group 1963				
	over 1,000,000	500,000 to 999,999	300,000 to 499,999	200,000 to 299,999	100,000 to 199,999	50,000 to 99,999
Police	33.2	25.9	19.6	19.5	18.7	17.5
Fire Protection	15.1	17.4	15.4	18.3	17.5	16.1

		1954			
		over 1,000,000	250,000 to 999.999	100,000 to 299,999	25,000 to 99,999
Police		26.3	21.9	18.4	16.8
Fire Protection		13.1	16.4	17.1	15.5

Sources: U.S. Bureau of the Census' *City Employment in 1954* and *City Employment in 1963*, (Government Employment Series).

TABLE VIII

CITY-GOVERNMENT EXPENDITURES (PER-CAPITA) ON POLICE AND FIRE
PROTECTION FOR FOUR U.S. CITIES
(Fiscal Years 1951 and 1966)

	1951		1966	
	Police	Fire	Police	Fire
New York	$10.90	$6.42	$36.46	$16.95
St. Louis	10.54	4.85	32.08	13.04
San Francisco	10.88	9.98	28.22	24.41
Philadelphia	10.07	6.56	23.26	9.74
Average	10.60	6.95	30.01	16.04

Annual Rate of Increase:
(Compounded)
(1951 to 1966)

	Police	Fire
New York	8.4%	6.7%
St. Louis	7.7%	6.8%
San Francisco	6.6%	6.1%
Philadelphia	5.7%	2.7%
Average	7.2%	5.7%

Sources: Population and expenditure data for fiscal year 1951 are available in the U.S. Bureau of the Census, *Compendium of City Government Finances in 1951.* Aggregate expenditure figures for fiscal year 1966 are from the Census Bureau's *City Government Finances in 1965-66.* Population estimates for 1965 for these cities are contained in the U. S. Bureau of the Census, *Current Population Reports,* Population Estimates, Estimates of the Population of Standard Metropolitan Statistical Areas: July 1, 1965, Series P-25, no. 371, 1967.

p. 424]. This effect tends to raise the cost (per capita) of maintaining a given level of the *C*-concept of output, the level of safety enjoyed by a resident.

To examine this aspect of police and fire services, we turned to the available data on employment by city size and found that police manpower (per-capita) is much higher in the large cities than in the small ones. This information is summarized in Table VII. In contrast, Table VII indicates that fire-fighting forces tend to rise roughly in proportion to population.[20] One interesting feature of this Table is the suggestion that, except for the very largest cities, the number of police and fire personnel per capita for each city size remained relatively stable from the 1950's to the early 1960's. This would imply that much of the observed increase in aggregate employment per capita can be explained by the shift of people to more densely populated areas where presumably a larger "D-vector" is required to provide a given level of safety.

Finally in another attempt to control for the effect of urbanization on the figures in Table VI, and because we are particularly interested in the situation in urban areas, we assembled in Table VIII per-capita city-government expenditures on police and fire protection in four large U.S. cities in 1951 and 1966. The sample was selected largely on the basis of easy availability of data. The average annual compound rate of increase in these statistics over the period was greater than the all-local government figures (from Table VI) for three of the four cities, as was the rate of increase in the average per-capita expenditure in the four cities taken together. Perhaps even more interesting than the comparison of rates of growth is the contrast in the absolute levels of expenditure per capita. In view of the employment statistics in Table VII, it is not too surprising to find that in 1966 the average per-capita expenditure in the four cities was about 2½ times the all-local-government average in both police and fire protection categories. The

[20] Not shown, although supported by data from the same source, is the fact that very small cities, under 25,000 population, employ substantially fewer firemen per capita than larger cities. In 1954, for instance, in cities with populations between 10,000 and 25,000, fire-protection employment per 10,000 residents averaged 10.4, while for cities between 25,000 and 100,000 this average was 15.5.

major cities in this country thus appear both to spend much more per capita on police and fire services than smaller cities and to have had a higher rate of growth in per-capita spending for these functions.

Public Welfare

The provision of public-welfare support to needy individuals may take the form of services of various sorts, especially the services of social workers, or of direct money transfers, and is most typically a combination of the two. To judge from the opinions of experts and the complaints of welfare workers, one could probably realize substantial economies in the delivery of direct services both through streamlining record keeping and reducing the volume of existing records which now apparently absorb a great deal of social workers' time. In terms of the cost of serving one welfare recipient, however, such streamlining (important as it is) might well represent a one-time efficiency improvement, as the possibilities for increasing the output of services per case worker beyond this point would appear limited. The cost of providing a constant level of welfare services to a constant welfare-receiving population would from this point tend to rise in step with the general increase in wages and salaries in the economy.

It is more difficult to make sense of a "unit cost" for the direct transfer-payment aspect of welfare services. A dollar input of money for direct transfer payments generates a dollar of payments received, and in this sense unit costs of this dimension of welfare programs do remain constant. There is, however, a further consideration which suggests that a constant (real) level of welfare payments is not likely to be adequate: the relative character of poverty. As standards of living rise in society, the poverty line also has a natural tendency to rise.

If we were to adopt a wholly relative definition of poverty in the context of an unchanging "natural" relative distribution of income, the welfare budget (for a constant population) would grow at exactly the same rate as the general rise in wage and salary income. For the poor (e.g., those below the twentieth percentile) to retain their same *share* of disposable income, welfare payments would in this case have to grow along with the level of aggregate income. It is interesting that in this particular case we get the same increase in "unit costs" as in the case of a constant-quality public service for which input prices rise at the average rate as for the economy as a whole and for which there is zero technical progress: unit costs rise at the same rate as wages and salaries in the rest of the economy.

Welfare budgets of the large cities in the United States have grown particularly rapidly. The central cities have long served as at least a temporary destination for poor, often ill-educated immigrants from rural areas in this country and from abroad. This immigration, coupled with the flight of the middle class to the suburbs, has resulted in severe financial difficulties for many cities. New York City, for example, now has over 900,000 persons (roughly 10 per cent of its population) on the welfare roles and devotes approximately 20 per cent of the city budget to welfare programs (as compared to an average of only 7 per cent for all local governments in metropolitan areas). Suburban, residential communities have largely escaped the problem, leaving the task of providing for welfare cases to the governments of the big cities. In several instances, state governments have provided some assistance. However, the magnitude and character of the welfare problem have led many observers to the conclusion that both the administration and financing of welfare programs be made the responsibility of the federal government.

Summary and Conclusions

Our original purpose in undertaking this study was to evaluate the hypothesis advanced by Baumol and others of a relatively static technology in the production of local public services, a phenomenon which is claimed to have resulted in cumulative increases in the relative cost of providing these public services and has thereby contributed directly to the fiscal distress of local government (especially in the big cities). Like other investigators of output in the public sector, we encountered serious problems in determining the trends in the unit costs of these services over time because of the difficulty of isolating measures of output. As we show in the first section of this paper, there exist real conceptual (as well as empirical) ambiguities in determining units of output.

The cost and expenditure series which we have assembled suggest, we think, that rising unit costs have been a major (probably the single most important) source of recent increases in local public budgets. We found that, during the period since World War II, current cost per pupil day in public elementary and secondary schools, expenditure per patient day in public hospitals, and per-capita spending on police and on fire protection (where these series were adjusted where possible to eliminate the effects of increased quantities of inputs) have risen at annual compound rates of roughly 5 to 7 per cent (as compared to an annual increase in total local-government spending of almost 9 per cent). In all these instances real improvements in the quality of the services provided have occurred so that these series do not in this sense represent a genuine measure of unit costs. It does, however, appear that in many instances improvements in technology, while leading to superior services (e.g., have not been of a cost-reducing form. As a result, these advances have not in general allowed local governments to offset the rising prices of inputs through utilizing fewer units. The data suggest in addition that for some services (e.g., police and fire protection) the pressures of high and rising costs have been much more intense on the governments of the large, central cities than on smaller, suburban municipal governments.

In addition, the historical record together with some further reflections indicate to us that local (especially large city) governments can probably expect that costs will continue to rise cumulatively and at a more rapid rate than those in the rest of the economy, even if there is no increase either in the quantity or quality of the services provided. Increasing expenditures appears to be the price of simply standing still. Any programs designed to expand the quantity of existing services to meet the needs of an expanding population or any attempts to improve the quality of these public services mean additional expenditures over and above those resulting from the seemingly inexorable rise in costs per unit of output.

REFERENCES

1. Bartell, E., *Costs and Benefits of Catholic Elementary and Secondary Schools*, South Bend, Indiana, 1967.
2. Baumol, W., "Macroeconomics of Unbalanced Growth: The Anatomy of Urban Crisis," *Am. Econ. Rev.*, June 1967, 57, 415-26.
3. *The Economics of Health and Medical Care*, Ann Arbor, 1964.
4. Hirsch, W., "The Supply of Urban Public Services," in H. Perloff and L. Wingo, eds., *Issues in Urban Economics*, Baltimore, 1968, 477-526.
5. Manvel, A., "Changing Patterns of Local Urban Expenditure," in H. Schaller, ed., *Public Expenditure Decisions in the Urban Community*, Washington, 1963, 19-36.
6. Scitovsky, A., "Changes in the Costs of Treatment of Selected Illnesses, 1951-65," *Am. Econ. Rev.*, Dec. 1967, 57, 1182-95.
7. Whalen, R., *A City Destroying Itself*, New York, 1965.
8. Worswick, G., "The Convexity of the Production Possibilities Frontier," *Econ. Jour.*, Dec. 1967, 67, 748-50.

[13]

GROUP SIZE AND THE OUTPUT OF PUBLIC GOODS: THEORY AND AN APPLICATION TO STATE-LOCAL FINANCE IN THE UNITED STATES

by

JAMES M. LITVACK and WALLACE E. OATES *

I. INTRODUCTION

The purposes of this paper are first to explore the relationship between the Pareto-efficient level of output of a public good and the size of the group which consumes the good, and second to use this theoretical framework to analyze the degree of fiscal centralization in state-local finance in the United States. Since, as Bowen [2, p. 177] and others have shown, the derivation of the demand for a public good involves the vertical summation of individual demand curves, we would expect that enlarging the size of the group would lead to a greater demand and hence an increased output of the good. This, we will show, is typically (but not necessarily) the case for a "pure" public good. Viewing the problem in a slightly different way, we can see that an increase in the number of consumers' is precisely equivalent to a fall in the price of the good to each consumer. Therefore, unless a negative income effect outweighs the substitution effect (i.e., the case of the Giffen good), the efficient level of output will increase with the size of the group consuming the good. When, however, we extend the simple model to the case of "im-

* The authors are respectively Lecturer and Assistant Professor of Economics at Princeton University. They are grateful to William Baumol, David Bradford, Vernon Dixon, Shlomo Malt, Ross Marcou, Uwe Reinhardt, and the members of the Graduate Research Seminar at Princeton University for many helpful comments on earlier drafts of this paper. Needless to say, the responsibility for any errors in the final product rests solely with the authors. In addition we are indebted to the Ford Foundation whose support greatly facilitated the completion of this study.

pure" public goods, we find that costs of congestion will offset to some extent the savings which result from spreading the costs of output over a larger number of consumers. In this more general case, an increase in the size of the group of consumers may result in a rise or fall in the "price" of the good to the individual consumer.

By making certain assumptions concerning the price elasticities of demand for public goods and the relative "purity" of the goods provided by different levels of government, we proceed in the latter part of the paper to apply the theoretical framework to an examination of the degree of fiscal centralization in state-local finance in the United States. Here we find that a simple model based on the theory in the earlier sections can "explain" most of the variation in the degree of fiscal centralization among the states in this country.

II. GROUP SIZE AND THE EFFICIENT OUTPUT OF A PURE PUBLIC GOOD

Consider first a group of individuals in an economy which provides two goods, a pure private good (Y) and a pure Samuelsonian public good (X). We can represent the utility function of the ith person as:

$$(1) \qquad u_i = u_i\,(y_i, x)$$

where y_i is the quantity of the private good he consumes. By assumption, everyone in the group consumes the same quantity of X; moreover, additional consumers can join the group and thereby consume X without diminishing the quantity consumed by existing members. As Samuelson [9] and Musgrave [7, Chapter 4] have shown, to achieve Pareto efficiency requires that the output of X be expanded to the point where the sum of individual marginal rates of substitution (hereafter MRS) for the good equals its marginal cost. Symbolically, we have that:

$$(2) \qquad \sum_{i=1}^{n} \frac{\partial u_i/\partial x}{\partial u_i/\partial y_i} = \frac{\partial g/\partial x}{\partial g/\partial y}$$

where $g(y, x) = 0$ defines the budget constraint and where n is the number of consumers in the group. [1]

[1] We assume that the usual second-order conditions for the utility functions and budget constraint are satisfied.

To keep matters in the simplest terms, assume for now that all individuals have identical preference patterns and equal levels of income and that the output of public goods is financed by an equal cost-sharing agreement among all the individuals in the group. We can in this way proceed in terms of a "representative man". If we assume further that public goods are produced under conditions of constant cost, we can simplify (2) to:

$$(3) \qquad ns = c_0, \; (i.e., s = c_0/n)$$

where:

n = number of consumers in the group,

$s = s(y_i, x)$ = MRS for X in terms of Y for each individual,

c_0 = marginal cost of X in terms of Y (assumed constant).

Equation (3) indicates that, at the efficient level of output, the cost or "price" to each consumer of a marginal unit of X (i.e., his share of the marginal cost in terms of Y) must equal his MRS for the public good. It is worth noting at this point the obvious analogy between (3) and the efficiency condition for the output of a private good. In the latter case, the individual's MRS is itself equal to marginal cost, which under competitive conditions equals the price of the good. In (3) we can by analogy equate the "price" of the public good to the individual consumer with c_0/n. [2]

From this point of view, it is easy to see what the effect of increasing the size of the group of consumers will be on the efficient level of output of the public good (X). Increasing n in (3) is equivalent to decreasing the cost or price of a unit of X to the consumer. [3] So long as X is not a Giffen good, it is therefore clear that a rise in n will lead to an expansion in the efficient level of output of X. In addition, it follows that the expenditure per capita on X at the efficient level of output will rise if individual demands for X are price

[2] We should stress that when we refer to c_0/n as the "price" of a unit of the public good to the individual consumer, we do not mean to imply that the consumer can buy a unit of the good by paying that sum. The analysis is concerned with comparing Pareto-efficient levels of output of a public good for different sizes of groups of consumers. Assuming equal cost-sharing, we use "price" to refer to the payment per unit of output that each individual *would* make if the Pareto-efficient level of output were provided.

[3] It is assumed here that new members of the group are identical in terms of tastes and income with existing members. This would imply that a rise in n results in a proportionate increase in the budget constraint $g(y, x) = 0$.

elastic, or will fall if the demands of individuals for X are price inelastic. In the latter case, although the output of X will typically rise, the resulting increase in the total cost of providing X will be more than offset by having a larger number of consumers among whom to share the cost. [4]

If we continue to associate c_0/n with the price of X *(i.e., p_x)* to the individual consumer, we find that the rate of change of price with respect to n, namely *(dp_x / dn)*. diminishes as n increases.

Since

(4) $$p_x = \frac{c_0}{n}$$

differentiation of (4) yields:

(5) $$dp_x / dn = -c_0 \left[\frac{1}{n^2} \right]$$

The rational for this result (which will prove useful later) is quite straightforward: the addition of a person to a very small group will obviously result in a much bigger reduction in the share of a given tax bill for each person than if an additional person joins a group which is already of size one million. In the latter case the impact will be negligible.

The analysis to this point has proceeded under a set of highly restrictive assumptions, the implications of which themselves need examination. Suppose, for example, that individuals no longer possess identical tastes and levels of income. In this case, equation (2) will not in general simplify to (3). If we divide through (2) by n, we will find now that the MRS of some individuals exceeds their share of the marginal cost of x, while for others $s_i < c_0/n$. Note, however, that so long as new members of the group share the cost of X, the general thrust of the argument is still valid: increasing n in effect reduces the price of the public good to existing members and will typically lead to a rise in the efficient level of output of the public good. Looked at in another way, the reduction in c_0/n implies that re-establishment of the efficient level of output of X necessitates a

---

[4] One could conceivably use this approach to infer the price elasticity of demand for various public goods. If larger groups of consumers are associated with a smaller expenditure per capita on the good, the demand would presumably be price inelastic (and vice-versa).

fall in the average of the individual MRS's (*i.e., in* $\Sigma s/n$). To reduce the MRS of individuals in the group will in general require an increase in the output of X. [5]

Of more interest is the case where the public good is no longer pure. Since public goods in practice always contain some elements of impurity, it is worth considering just how the output and expenditure on impure public goods is likely to vary with the size of the group of consumers.

III. GROUP SIZE AND IMPURE PUBLIC GOODS

The term "impure public good" refers here to a good which all consume in common, but for which the level of utility of the individual depends not only on the level of output of the good, but also on the size of the group which consumes these units of output. Impure public goods are typically characterized by costs of congestion: after some point the addition of yet another person to the group reduces the level of consumption of the good of the other members. We can express this formally with the utility function:

(6) $u_i = u_i \, (y_i, \hat{x})$, where $\hat{x} = h(x,n)$ with $\partial\hat{x}/\partial x > 0$ and $\partial\hat{x}/\partial n < 0$

If $\hat{x}$, for example, indicates the speed at which one can safely drive an automobile between two specified points, the value of $\hat{x}$ depends both on the quality of the system of roads connecting the two points (x) and on the number of drivers using these roads (n). As n becomes large, traffic congestion sets in, and the time required to make the journey increases (*i.e.*, $\hat{x}$ declines). Similarly, the level of protection $(\hat{x})$ provided for each individual by a given policy force (x) depends on the number of persons (n) for whom surveillance and other police services must be provided.

Let us return to the simple model originally postulated (with persons of identical tastes and incomes, constant costs of production of X, and an equal cost-sharing scheme) and make only one change:

[5] This might not be the case if the entry of new members induced a radical alteration in the cost-sharing scheme for the financing of X. If this alteration led to significant changes in the distribution of income in favor of those with relatively low demands for X, it is conceivable that Σ MRS could decline without an increase (or even with a fall) in the output of the public good. This would, one would guess, be a rather unlikely case.

X is now assumed to be an impure public good. Since the individual's utility function now includes $\hat{x}$ (instead of simply x), we need to develop a cost function for $\hat{x}$ in order to relate benefits to costs. To simplify this problem, we assume that:

(7) $\hat{x} = (1/\alpha) \, x$, where $\alpha = w(n)$ with $d\alpha/dn > 0$ for n
             above some threshold value

This implies that, for a given n, the marginal cost of $\hat{x}$ is simply equal to αc_o, where c_o is the (assumed constant) marginal cost of x. As n increases, however, α will (after some point) begin to rise, which reflects the presence of costs of congestion. A higher n means that it takes more x to generate a given output of $\hat{x}$. In terms of our earlier example, as the number of drivers between two points increases, additional lanes (*i.e.*, more x) will be required to prevent an increase in the amount of time needed for the trip (*i.e.*, a fall in $\hat{x}$).

Our efficiency condition, which specifies that the sum of the individual MRS's should equal marginal cost, now becomes:

(8) $ns = \alpha c_o,$ or $s = (\alpha c_o)/n$

At the Pareto-efficient level of output of $\hat{x}$, each individual's MRS will again equal his share of the marginal cost of $\hat{x}$. If we treat $(\alpha c_o/n)$ as the price of a unit of $\hat{x}$ to the consumer, it is immediately clear from (7) and (8) that an increase in n need no longer lead to a fall in the price of the public good. As n increases, so does α; whether $p_{\hat{x}}$ rises or falls with n therefore depends on the increase in α relative to that in n. The point is that, in the case of impure public goods, an additional consumer has two effects on the price of the good to existing consumers. First, as in the case of the pure public good, he assumes part of the cost of providing the good and thereby tends to reduce the price to the other individuals. In addition, however, he now adds to the level of congestion so that more units of x are required to provide a given output of $\hat{x}$. The effect of an additional consumer on $p_{\hat{x}}$ may therefore be either effect of an additional consumer on p_x may therefore be either positive or negative depending on the relative strength of these two effects.

More specifically, we find through differentiation that:

$$(9) \qquad dp_{\hat{x}}/dn = \frac{c_0 n \, (d\alpha/dn) - \alpha c_0}{n^2} - \frac{c_0}{n} \left[(d\alpha/dn) - (\alpha/n) \right]$$

The effect of changes in n on the price of the public good thus depends on the nature of the function which relates α to n. The evidence available on this matter plus some further reflection suggests that typically, for relatively small groups, $p_{\hat{x}}$ is likely to fall as n grows, but that, as the group of consumers becomes larger, $(dp_{\hat{x}}/dn)$ is likely to change sign and become positive. For relatively small groups, additional consumers can usually be accomodated without imposing significant congestion costs; it reduces no-one's welfare, for example, to allow another motorist on an underutilized road. Moreover, where n is small, we saw in equation (7) that the cost savings conferred by additional consumers in terms of sharing the tax bill tend to be greater than when n is large. As a result, we might expect that, for small values of n, an additional individual will, through his tax payment, add more to the welfare of others than he subtracts in terms of costs of congestion. In terms of (9), the argument is that, when n is small, $(d\alpha/dn)$ is very small so that $(dp_{\hat{x}}/dn)$ is likely to be negative.

As n becomes large, however, marginal congestion costs tend to increase and eventually are likely to swamp the opposing effect. The available evidence on motor traffic, for example, suggests that once costs of congestion set in on a given roadway (as, for example, during rush hours in most U.S. metropolitan areas), the costs imposed by additional drivers increase quite rapidly; in fact these studies indicate that marginal congestion costs rise roughly exponentially with the number of motorists. [6] In (9), this implies that, after some point, $(d\alpha/dn)$ will increase rapidly with n and will become larger than (α/n) (at which point α/n will also begin to rise). From there on, the effect of further entrants will be to push up the price of the public good. The analysis therefore suggests that, if we begin with $n = 1$ and then allow n to increase, $p_{\hat{x}}$ will typically fall

---

[6] Our colleague Uwe Reinhardt has explained to us the rationale for this result, A car requires a certain amount of space between itself and other cars to travel safely at a given speed. This space increases roughly with the square of the speed. Once the total required space of the automobiles on a road equals the length of the road (or sooner in the more realistic case where cars are not distributed evenly over the road), speed must therefore diminish more than proportionately to the increase in the number of users. For some evidence of this, see [11, Part III].

for some period and then at some point will reverse itself and begin to rise as costs of congestion come to outweigh the effect of spreading the tax bill over a larger number of consumers. [7] With this as background, we will in the remainder of the paper attempt to illustrate a way in which this theoretical structure can be used to gain insight into a specific problem in U.S. state-local finance.

IV. FISCAL CENTRALIZATION IN U.S. STATE-LOCAL FINANCE: A FRAMEWORK FOR ANALYSIS

The degree of fiscal centralization in an economy typically refers to the extent to which fiscal decision-making and control are in the hands of the central government. As a measure of this phenomenon, we will use the so-called "centralization ratio", the percentage of total public spending undertaken by the central government. The problem is to explain the source of the variation in centralization ratios among the various states. [8] Why, for example, in 1962 did the state government in New York undertake only 22 % of total state-local spending, while in Vermont the corresponding figure was 60 %?

It appears that much of this variation in the relative size of the budget of the state government stems from differences in the way the outputs of the public services provided by state and by local governments respond to an increase in both the size and the concentration of the population. As a result, the theoretical treatment in the preceding sections of the paper, a treatment which stressed both the savings per capita from spreading the tax bill among a larger number of consumers and the possibility of associated con-

---

[7] James Buchanan [4] has demonstrated that to determine the optimal-size group to utilize a given facility requires that additional members be admitted to the "club" until the marginal congestion cost equals the new member's share of the cost of the facility. In terms of our formulation of the problem, Buchanan's proposition is that the opimal-size group is that for which p_x^* is a minimum.

Since the units for this study are the individual state economies, the term central government must be understood to refer to the central government in each state, or, in other words, the state government. Decentralized levels of the public sector include the various local governments in each state. From this perspective, the degree of fiscal centralization refers to the percentage of state-local public expenditure which is undertaken by the state government.

gestion costs, seems to have direct relevance to the empirical problem at hand. Before constructing a model, however, it will prove useful to explore more systematically the potential sources of variation in the extent of fiscal centralization.

There are three possible causes of intereconomy differences in the degree of fiscal centralization of the public sector. First, functions or services provided by one level of government in one economy may be the responsibility of another level of government elsewhere. A government in which education is provided at the central level will obviously tend to be more highly centralized than one in which the responsibility for public education is vested in local governments. Second, even if across all economies there exists an identical allocation of functions among levels of government, centralization ratios may still vary if there is a differing relative expenditure on these functions. A country, for example, with an unusually large fraction of its resources devoted to national defense will tend to have a relatively high degree of fiscal centralization. Third and last, services provided in the public sector in one economy may not be provided publicly at all in others. Two economies whose public sectors are identical in all other respects will have differing centralization ratios if in one local governments provide certain recreational facilities, while in the other all such facilities are produced in the private sector.

In building a model to explain variations in fiscal centralization, the relative emphasis to be placed on these three sources of variation depends on the problem at hand. If there exist among the various economies striking differences in the character of the populations, in the state of technology, and in various social and political institutions, one might expect real differences in the allocation of functions among levels of government. In a country, for instance, where there are radical differences in ethnic and cultural variables, one would not be surprised to find the educational system more decentralized in order to provide desired diversity in educational programs. For an analysis of fiscal centralization within the United States, however, differences of these types are probably less important. As a result, when looking at the public sectors in the various states, we find that the division of functions between state and local governments is typically quite similar from state to state. State governments in nearly all cases assume primary responsibility for providing a system of highways within the state and for offering a program of

public higher education. Local governments, in contrast, are responsible for public primary and secondary education, local police and
fire protection, and a host of other services of interest primarily to
local residents. In consequence, it seems clear that a model designed
to explain interstate variations in centralization ratios must look
mainly to factors influencing the level of spending on these various
services and the range of services provided.

In this spirit, consider the following (admittedly highly simplified)
model. The central governments (in this case the state governments)
in the various economies are assumed to provide positive levels of
outputs of a specified set of public goods, goods which approach the
pure end of the public goods' spectrum and for which the demands
of consumers are price inelastic. In contrast to the central government, local governments in this model provide a varying mix of
impure public goods, goods whose consumption is limited to persons
within the locality and which are subject to significant costs of congestion. We assume, moreover, that the demand for local public
goods is also price inelastic.

What can we say about the relative degree of fiscal centralization
in these economies? If we assume that governments at all levels provide
(at least roughly) Pareto-efficient levels of output, we can reach
some conclusions on this matter. One point is immediately clear:
assuming similar cost functions, expenditure per capita by the central
government will vary inversely with the size of the population.
Since by assumption congestion costs are relatively unimportant for
goods provided by the central government, our earlier theoretical
discussion suggests that an expansion of the population will lead to
a fall in the "price" of the good to the individual consumer. Since,
moreover, the demands of consumers are postulated to be price inelastic, we would expect the expenditure per capita on these goods
to decline as the population grows.

The size of the population and, even more important, its concentration in the various localities will tend to have the opposite effect
on spending by local governments. This tendency results from
two types of economic forces. First, a heavy concentration of a relatively large population into a few localities will result in high levels
of congestion costs. As suggested in the preceding section, as n becomes large, the price of impure public goods is likely to rise as
congestion costs will come to more than offset the gains from
expanding the number of taxpayers. Since the demands for public

goods in this model are price inelastic, we would anticipate that expenditure per capita by local governments on these goods would increase as the population becomes highly concentrated in urban areas.

Second, an increased concentration of a population into a fewer number of localities makes it efficient for local governments to provide a wider *range* of public services. Even if all persons have similar demand functions for a particular local public good, it does not become efficient to provide the good until the sum of the individual demands exceeds the cost of the project. The point is that for many publicly provided goods there are important indivisibilities; the first "unit" of output in these cases may require a substantial expenditure, and it will not be worthwhile to provide the good until n is sufficiently large that $ns > c_0$ for the initial unit of the good. What all this implies is that we would expect local public expenditures per capita in densely populated localities to exceed that in more sparsely populated communities both because of higher levels of spending per capita on those services provided in all communities and because of a greater number of services provided publicly in the more densely populated areas.

The model thus suggests that expenditure per capita by the central government should vary inversely with the size of the population, while a higher concentration of the population is likely to result in increased spending per capita at the local level. This would imply that the degree of fiscal centralization should bear an inverse relationship both to the size and the concentration of the population.

V. CENTRALIZATION IN STATE-LOCAL FINANCE: SOME EMPIRICAL RESULTS

To test the explanatory power of the model developed in the preceding section, we will examine next the interstate variation in centralization ratios (*i.e.*, state government spending as a percentage of state-local expenditures). It is clear at the outset that the model represents a very great simplification of the actual structure of state-local finance in this country, but it does, we believe, capture some basic tendencies in this fiscal structure. The largest item of direct expenditure by state governments is the construction and maintenance of highways to link metropolitan and rural areas in the state with each other and with those in other states. While state highways obviously are not pure public goods, they do typically exhibit significant economies of scale in consumption. In general, it does not cost a great deal more to connect two cities of one million persons each with a highway adequate for safe, high-speed travel than to provide a highway with a similar capability and covering the same distance between two cities of 100,000 persons each. Expenditure per capita will naturally be greater in the less populous state where there are fewer persons to share the cost. In view of this and of the fundamental importance to a state of a well-developed system of highways, a model which assumes that state governments provide relatively pure public goods with price-inelastic demands may represent a reasonable approximation to the actual state of affairs. [9]

At the local level, the model indicates that public spending per head should rise as a given population is crowded into more densely populated communities both because of higher spending resulting from increased costs of congestion and because of a wider range of services provided publicly. In this regard, William Baumol[1] has argued that, as the size of the population grows, external diseconomies (costs of congestion) tend to increase even more than proportionately as a result of the increased scope for personal interaction. The evidence does appear to support Baumol's contention: we find, for example, that the larger, more densely populated cities in this country employ more, not less, policemen per 10,000 persons and still appear to have substantially higher crime rates [See (3)]. This can be interpreted in terms of equation (8) to mean that, as n rises in densely populated localities, α increases so rapidly that the price of a given level of protection from crime to the in-

[9] In this connection, Shlomo Malt [6, p. 126], in a detailed study of the relationship between fiscal and demographic variables using 1962 data, found a simple correlation coefficient between state and local spending per capita on highways and population size of —.40. Malt also found a negative correlation (*i.e.*, —.27) between population size and spending per capita on the other major item in the budgets of state governments, namely expenditures for public higher education. The source of this relationship is not altogether clear. The work of Seymour Harris [5], for example, does not suggest the presence of important economies of scale in higher education (although this is a very tricky thing to measure). It may be that this relationship stems (at least in part) from the fact that several of the larger states in this country (*e.g.*, Massachusetts, Pennsylvania) have extensive, well developed systems of private higher education which have reduced the need in these states for public colleges and universities.

dividual actually increases. In addition, more highly populated municipalities do appear to provide a greater number of public services: Schmandt and Stephens [10], in a study of 550 different public services provided by municipalities in Milwaukee County, found that the size of the population of the municipality was the best predictor of the number of goods and services provided publicly. For these reasons, the model constructed in the preceding section of this paper, while admittedly representing a major simplification, does provide, we think, some insights into the determinants of the degree of fiscal centralization. At any rate, it does appear worthwhile to explore a bit more systematically the ability of such a model to explain empirically the interstate variations in the degree of fiscal centralization.

The regression equations presented in Table I suggest that population size and concentration variables can "explain" most of the interstate variation in centralization ratios. Equation (I.1) indicates that the degree of fiscal centralization is, as expected, inversely related to the size of the population. The relationship is in fact quite a strong one: the population variable alone explains close to one half of the variation in centralization ratios. Equation (I.2) includes, in addition to population size, the percent of the population living in metropolitan areas [*i.e.*, within Standard Metropolitan Statistical Areas (SMSA's)] to serve as a measure of the concentration of the population in each state. This is also statistically significant and has the anticipated sign. The population size and concentration variables thus produce results consistent with the theoretical treatment of fiscal centralization and are quite powerful in that together they account for well over half of the interstate variation in centralization ratios. [10] Equation (I.3) simply adds to (I.2) a regional dummy variable for those states in the southern part of the country, and (I.4) includes dummy variables placing the states in the four Census regions in the United States. Equation (I.3) indicates that, even after standardizing for the effects of population size and concentration, states in the southern region of the country tend to have a higher degree of fiscal centralization.

Equations (I.5) and (I.6) suggest further that the model presented in the paper can provide a rationale for the observed results. In (I.5)

[10] Using 1957 data, Pryor [8] also found that centralization ratios in U.S. state-local finance are inversely related to population size; he does not, however offer an explanation for this relationship.

TABLE I

Regression Equations

[Note: Numbers in parenthesis are values of the *t*-statistic]

	Constant	*In P*	*U*	*S*	*E*	*C*	*R*²
	Dependent Variable: State Expenditures as a Percentage of State-Local Spending						
I.1)	87 (11)	−6.0 (−6.0)					.44
I.2)	90 (13)	−4.3 (−4.4)	−.3 (−4.0)				.59
I.3)	91 (14)	−5.3 (−5.6)	−.2 (−2.5)	5.9 (3.0)			.66
I.4)	90 (15)	−4.5 (−4.3)	−.2 (−3.3)	4.2 (1.6)	2.5 (1.0)	−3.8 (−1.5)	.70

	Constant	*In P*	*R*²
	Dependent Variable: State-Government Expenditure Per Capita (Dollars)		
I.5)	346 (13)	−28 (−8.0)	.58

	Constant	*U*	*R*²
	Dependent Variable: Local-Government Expenditure Per Capita (Dollars)		
I.6)	57 (2.3)	2.2 (5.6)	.40

where:

In P = Natural log of the population (000's)
 U = Percent of population living within metropolitan areas (within SMSA's)
 S = Dummy variable for Southern Region (U.S. Bureau of Census Definition)
 E = Dummy variable for Northeast Region (U.S. Bureau of Census Definition)
 C = Dummy variable for Northcentral Region   (U.S.Bur. of Census Definition)

Sources: The centralization ratios (*i.e.*; state direct general expenditures as a percentage of state-local general expenditures) are from the Bureau of the Census, *1962 Census of Governments,* Vol. IV, No. 4, p. 66. Intergovernmental transfers under this classification are treated as expenditures by the recipient government. On page 63 of this same volume are estimates for each state of per capita general expenditures by state-local governments. To divide this figure between state and local governments, we multiplied per capita state-local general expenditure for each state by the state's centralization ratio. The data on population and percent of population living in SMSA's are for 1960 and were taken from the Bureau of the Census, *Pocket Data Book, U.S.A.* 1967.

we find that expenditures per capita by state governments bear a significantly inverse relationship to the size of the population. It is interesting in this connection that the log form of the population variable has a far stronger correlation with per capita spending by state governments than does the simple numerical value of the population variable (*i.e.*, an R^2 of .58 as compared to an R^2 of only .29 in the latter case). This is consistent with the earlier theoretical result in equation (5), which suggests that the cost savings per capita from a given absolute increase in the size of the population becomes less important as the population becomes larger. Equation (I.6) in Table I indicates, moreover, that spending per capita by local governments is positively and significantly related to the percent of the population living in metropolitan areas. [11] These influences when combined quite naturally result in centralization ratios which are inversely related both to the size and the concentration of the population.

We stress, in concluding this study, that our empirical results are intended primarily to illustrate one way in which the theoretical structure developed in this paper can be used to understand actual fiscal phenomena. There is, however, certainly much more to explaining variations in the degree of fiscal centralization than appears here (in terms, for example, of some differences in the assignment of fiscal responsibility for certain activities such as public-welfare programs). We do believe, however, that the determinants of the degree of fiscal centralization suggested by our theoretical treatment are of real importance, and we present these empirical findings in support of this contention.

VI. SUMMARY AND CONCLUSIONS

In terms of a simple model with a pure public good, increasing the size of the group which consumes the good is equivalent to reducing its "price" to each individual. As a result, the efficient level of output (unless it is a Giffen good) will vary directly with the size of the group of consumers. If, moreover, individual demands for the

---

[11] Malt [6, p. 126] found positive and higly significant simple correlations between the percent of the population in urban areas and per capita state and local spending on the following predominately local functions: local schools, health and hospitals, police, fire, and sewage/sanitation.

public good are price elastic, it follows that the efficient level of spending per capita, as well as the number of units of output, will also rise with group size. If the public good is "impure" (*i.e.*, subject to costs of congestion), an increase in the group size may lead either to a rise or fall in the price of the good to the consumer, for in this case the costs of congestion imposed by additional consumers will work to offset the savings per capita resulting from having a larger number of persons to share the cost of the good. The analysis suggests that, as the size of the group of consumers grows, the price of impure public goods will typically decline initially but then will reverse itself and begin to rise as congestion costs come to dominate the price-reducing effects of increasing the number of taxpayers.

The latter part of this paper consisted of an application of the theory to an explanation of interstate variations in fiscal centralization in the United States. We constructed a model in which the central government (here the state government) was assumed to provide outputs of relatively pure public goods for which the demand is price inelastic, and in which local governments provide a variable menu of highly impure public goods with price-inelastic demands. The implication of this model is that the degree of fiscal centralization should vary inversely with both the size and the concentration of the population in each state. The empirical results suggest that the model possesses considerable explanatory power, as a population-size variable and a variable indicating the percent of the population living in metropolitan areas were able to "explain" over half of the variation among the states in the degree of fiscal centralization.

REFERENCES

[1] W. Baumol, "Macroeconomics of Unbalanced Growth: The Anatomy of Urban Crisis", *Amer. Econ. Rev.*, June 1967, *42*, 415—26.

[2] H. Bowen, *Toward Social Economy*, New York 1948.

[3] D. Bradford, R. Malt, and W. Oates, "The Rising Cost of Local Public Services: Some Evidence and Reflections", June 1969, *22*, 185—202.

[4] J. Buchanan, "An Economic Theory of Clubs", *Economica*, Feb. 1955, *32*, 1—14.

[5] S. Harris, *Higher Education: Resources and Finance*, New York 1962.

[6] S. Malt, *Population and the Fisc: The Impact of Demographic Change on Public Expenditures and Revenues*, Ph. D. dissertation, Princeton Univ., 1967.

[7] R. Musgrave, *The Theory of Public Finance*, New York 1959.

[8] F. Pryor, "Elements of a Positive Theory of Public Expenditure", *Finanzarchiv*, Dec. 1967, *26*, 405—30.

58   JAMES M. LITVACK and WALLACE E. OATES

[9] P. Samuelson, "The Pure Theory of Public Expenditure", *Rev. Econ. Stat.*, Nov. 1954, *36*, 387—9.

[10] H. Schmandt and G. Stephens, "Measuring Municipal Output", *Nat. Tax Jour,*, Dec. 1960, *12*, 369—75.

[11] U.S. Dept. of Commerce, Bureau of Roads, *Highway Capacity Manual*, Washington 1950.

TAILLE D'UN GROUPE ET PRODUCTION DE BIENS PUBLICS: LA THEORIE ET UNE APPLICATION AUX FINANCES LOCALES ET DES ETATS AUX ETATS-UNIS

par

JAMES M. LITVACK et WALLACE E. OATES

RESUME

Cette étude a pour but tout d'abord d'approfondir la relation entre le niveau d'efficience parétien relatif à la production d'un bien public et la taille du groupe qui consomme ce bien, et ensuite d'utiliser cette base théorique pour analyser le degré de centralisation fiscale dans les finances locales et des Etats aux Etats-Unis.

En termes de modèle simple avec un bien public „pur", on montre qu'un accroissement dans la taille du groupe consommateur du bien équivaut à un abaissement de son „prix" pour chaque individu pris en particulier. En fin de compte, le niveau d'efficience de production (à moins qu'il s'agisse d'un bien „Griffen") variera directement avec la taille du groupe de consommateurs. Si, de plus, les demandes des particuliers pour le bien public sont élastiques au prix, il s'ensuit que le niveau d'efficience de dépense par tête, aussi bien que le nombre d'unités de production, augmenteront également avec la taille du groupe. Si le bien public n'est „pas pur" (c'est-à-dire sujet à des coûts de saturation) un accroissement dans la taille du groupe peut entraîner soit une augmentation, soit une chute du prix fiscal du bien pour le consommateur car dans ce cas les coûts de saturation imposés par les consommateurs supplémentaires auront pour effet de compenser les épargnes par tête résultant de ce qu'un plus grand nombre de personnes se partagent le coût du bien. L'analyse suggère que, lorsque la taille du groupe de consommateurs croît, le prix des biens publics „non purs" diminuera initialement en tout état de cause, mais qu'ensuite il se renversera de lui-même et commencera à augmenter à mesure que les coûts de saturation en viendront à supplanter les effets de réduction de prix dûs au nombre de plus en plus important de contribuables.

La seconde moitié de l'étude a trait à une application de la théorie à une explication des variations entre Etats dans la centralisation fiscale aux Etats-Unis. Nous construisons un modèle dans lequel le gouvernement de l'Etat (c'est-à-dire le gouvernement central dans chaque Etat) fournit par hypothèse les biens publics relativement ,,purs" pour lesquels la demande est inélastique au prix, et dans lequel également les gouvernements locaux fournissent un ensemble variable de biens publics essentiellement ,,non purs" avec des demandes inélastiques au prix. On déduit de ce modèle que le degré de centralisation fiscale, mesuré par la part du gouvernement de l'Etat dans les dépenses locales et des Etats, devrait varier inversement à la fois avec le taille et la concentration de la population dans chaque Etat. Les résultats empiriques tendent à démontrer que le modèle possède un très grand pouvoir explicatif, en ce sens qu'une variable relative à la taille de la population et une variable indiquant le pourcentage de la population vivant dans une zone urbaine peuvent ,,expliquer" plus de la moitié de la variation entre Etats dans le degré de centralisation fiscale.

BEVÖLKERUNGSGRÖSSE UND PRODUKTION EINES ÖFFENTLICHEN GUTES: THEORIE UND EINE ANWENDUNG AUF DIE STAATS- UND GEMEINDE- FINANZEN IN DEN USA

von

JAMES M. LITVACK und WALLACE E. OATES

ZUSAMMENFASSUNG

In diesem Artikel wird zunächst das Verhältnis zwischen dem Pareto-optimalen Produktionsniveau eines öffentlichen Gutes und der Größe der Bevölkerungsgruppe untersucht, die dieses Gut verbraucht; dieser theoretische Rahmen wird dann zur Analyse des Grades der finanzpolitischen Konzentration der Staats- und Gemeindefinanzen in den USA benutzt.

Mit Hilfe eines einfachen Modells mit einem „echten" öffentlichen Gut wird gezeigt, daß eine Vergrößerung der Bevölkerungsgruppe, die dieses Gut verbraucht, einer Senkung seines „Preises" für jeden einzelnen gleichkommt. Das bedeutet, daß sich das Pareto-optimale Produktionsniveau (sofern es sich nicht um ein Giffen-Gut handelt) in direktem Verhältnis zu der Größe der Verbrauchergruppe ändert. Wenn darüber hinaus die Einzelnachfrage nach dem öffentlichen Gut preiselastisch ist, so ergibt sich daraus, daß das Effizienzniveau der Pro-Kopf-Ausgaben sowie die Anzahl der Produktionseinheiten ebenfalls mit der Zahl der Verbraucher steigen. Wenn das öffentliche Gut ein „unechtes" ist (d.h. wenn bei Überschreiten der Kapazitätsgrenze zusätzliche Kosten — „congestions costs" — auftreten), kann eine Vergrößerung der Verbrauchergruppe sowohl zu einer Erhöhung als auch zu einer Senkung des Preises dieses Gutes für den Verbraucher führen; denn in diesem Fall haben die durch zusätzliche Verbraucher bedingten Zusatzkosten die Tendenz, die Pro-Kopf-Ersparnisse überzukompensieren, die dadurch entstehen, daß sich die Kosten für das Gut auf einen größeren Personenkreis verteilen. Die Analyse ergibt, daß mit der Vergrößerung der Verbrauchergruppe der Preis für „unechte" öffentliche Güter charakteristischerweise zunächst fällt, dann jedoch zu steigen beginnt, weil die Zusatzkosten die preisreduzierenden Wirkungen der Vergrößerung der Zahl der Steuerzahler übersteigen.

Im zweiten Teil des Artikels wird die oben entwickelte Theorie dazu benutzt, die Unterschiede im Grad der finanzpolitischen Zentralisation zwischen den Einzelstaaten in den USA zu erklären. Es wird ein Modell konstruiert, in dem der Staat (d.h. die Zentralregierung in jedem Staat) für die Produktion relativ „echter" öffentlicher Güter sorgt, deren Nachfrage preisunelastisch ist, und in dem die Gemeinden eine unterschiedliche Skala überwiegend „unechter" öffentlicher Güter anbieten, deren Nachfrage preisunelastisch ist. Dieses Modell läßt den Schluß zu, daß der Grad der finanzpolitischen Zentralisation, gemessen an dem Anteil des Staates an den Gesamtausgaben, umgekehrt proportional zu der Größe und der Dichte der Bevölkerung in jedem Staat ist. Die empirischen Ergebnisse zeigen, daß das Modell beträchtliche Erklärungskraft besitzt, da eine Variable für die Größe der Bevölkerung und eine Variable für den Prozentsatz der in großstädtischen Ballungsräumen lebenden Bevölkerung es gestatten, mehr als die Hälfte des Unterschieds im finanzpolitischen Zentralisationsgrad zwischen den einzelnen Staaten zu erklären.

[14]

Suburban Exploitation of Central Cities and Governmental Structure

————◆————

DAVID F. BRADFORD AND
WALLACE E. OATES

The fiscal difficulties of the central cities and, in fact, the whole host of social and economic problems that contribute to our so-called urban crisis are largely the result, according to some observers, of a systematic "exploitation" of the cities by residents of suburban municipalities. The precise form this exploitation takes is often not made explicit, but at any rate the assertion is that the suburbanites are in large measure to blame for the deterioration in the quality of life in the cities.

The term "exploitation" typically refers to an "unjust relationship" between one individual (or group of individuals) and another. It is therefore a normative concept and can take on a precise operational meaning only when a just relationship is defined. Unfortunately, there seems to be no generally accepted definition of such a relationship between residents of cities and suburbs, with the result that exploitation of central cities by their suburbs has been given a number of different interpretations.

In some of the public-finance literature, for example, the term has been used to describe a process in which suburban commuters utilize the public services provided by the cities but then return home to their residential communities to pay (at least the bulk of)

David F. Bradford and Wallace E. Oates are members of the Department of Economics at Princeton University. They are grateful to Robert Aten, Theodore Bergstrom; Lester Chandler, Bruce Hamilton, and Daniel Hamermesh for a number of extremely helpful comments on an earlier draft of this paper.

their local taxes. The suburbanites thus exploit the central-city residents who must. willy-nilly. support public services for the commuters in order to have any themselves. This we shall call the "narrow" public-finance version of the exploitation thesis.

In the writings of more popular commentators on the plight of American cities. however. quite another set of issues dominates the discussion. Here the sin of the suburbanites is said to be their clustering in homogeneous settlements from which the poor are "walled-out" by zoning and other devices. there to enjoy public-service standards higher than those maintained in the central city while paying less in local taxes. This situation describes exploitation of the central city, and more generally of the poor. in a rather odd sense. It appears that the tax instruments available to local governments. taken together with the package of services normally provided by them and with the rules for local political procedures. tend to produce local public budgets that are somewhat redistributive toward the poorer residents of the jurisdiction.[1] A local governmental system that allows formation of jurisdictions uniform in income composition thus allows the upper-income families of a metropolitan area to avoid "exploitation" by the poorer families of the area. By taking away their ability to exploit the rich through the local fiscal system. the suburban governmental system exploits the poor!

Whichever of these notions of exploitation is accepted. there is little doubt that the system wherein public services are provided by relatively small and autonomous local-government jurisdictions in the suburbs has important implications for the distribution of welfare when compared to the obvious alternative of a unified metropolitan jurisdiction or the transfer of public functions to even higher (state or federal) levels of government. Particularly in view of the California and New Jersey court decisions that the finance of public schools through local property taxes is incompatible with the equal service provisions of the state constitutions. there is a pressing need for analyses of the distributive and allocative effects of the enlargement of fiscal jurisdictions.

The latter issue of the economic effects of fiscal consolidation is the central concern of this study. Rather than attempting to provide a definition and an examination of exploitation in some particular sense, we prefer to study the effects of alternative forms of governmental and fiscal structure on the distribution of income and uses of resources in metropolitan areas and to leave the reader to draw his own conclusions about the forms and extent of exploitation implied by these alternatives.

Before turning to our central issue, however, we shall in Section I examine the current state of knowledge about what we have termed the narrow public-finance view of exploitation. In Section II we review the way the current system of local public finance operates. In preparation for the analysis to follow, we lay particular stress here on the pressure toward the formation of income-homogeneous fiscal units. In the next two sections (Sections III and IV), which contain the most important material in the paper, we attempt to analyze the implications for the distribution of welfare of the choice between the current, fragmented system of local government and a unified metropolitan-wide government of some sort. Section III contains an analysis of the long-run equilibrium differences we might expect, and Section IV an analysis of the redistribution resulting from the transition from the current system to our model of a unified system. Section V presents a brief summary and some concluding remarks. Throughout we have tried, wherever possible, to provide quantitative, as well as qualitative, evidence and conclusions.

I. THE NARROW PUBLIC-FINANCE EXPLOITATION THESIS

Some twenty years ago Amos Hawley found that local public spending per capita in 76 cities, each with a population in excess of 100,000, showed a positive correlation to the proportion of the population in the metropolitan area living outside the central city. From this finding Hawley concluded that central cities were being exploited by the suburbs in the sense that residents of the cities "...are carrying the financial burden of an elaborate and costly service installation, i.e., the central city, which is used daily by a noncontributing population in some instances more than twice the size of the contributing population."[2] Hawley used 1940 data for his

46 *David F. Bradford and Wallace E. Oates*

study. A number of later studies using more recent fiscal and population figures. notably studies by Harvey Brazer and Julius Margolis. found this same type of empirical relationship, but these authors were far more cautious about drawing the type of inference Hawley drew from this phenomenon.[3] In particular. it is clear that suburban commuters do make some positive contributions to the fiscal well-being of the city. Many cities, such as Philadelphia. Detroit. and New York, have local income or wage taxes levied on income earned in the city. In addition, most cities levy sales taxes and, in some cases, a variety of user charges, including such things as tolls on bridges and tunnels leading into the city. Less directly, but perhaps at least as important, the use of city facilities by a greater number of suburban residents may increase the level of economic activity in the city and thereby enhance city property values with a corresponding stimulus to city receipts from property taxation. In fact. residential suburbs have been known to claim that the cities take advantage of them by reaping the tax benefits from a high concentration of commercial-industrial property. whereas the suburbs must service the population (particularly the heavy expense of providing public education). The existence of a positive correlation between central-city expenditures per capita and the fraction of the population living in the suburbs is not convincing evidence for the exploitation thesis. The suburban commuters may even more than pay for the extra costs of the public services that the city must provide.

A few studies have been undertaken to attempt to settle this issue by measuring both the fiscal contribution and the fiscal costs that suburban residents bring to the city. The approach has typically been to allocate the costs of city services on a per capita basis between city and suburban users of city services and to estimate the fiscal receipts to the city that come from the pockets of suburban residents. The difference between costs imposed and revenues generated by suburban users of city services is then calculated. Such studies have generally found little in the way of fiscal exploitation one way or the other. William Neenan. for example. notes the findings of James Banovetz in a study of the Twin Cities metropolitan area. Banovetz's results indicate that "...no conclusive evidence can be found to support charges that either the core cities of Minneapolis and St. Paul or their suburbs in Hennepin or Ramsey Counties, respectively, are subsidizing the other to any appreciable extent."[4]

Neenan himself is the author of a recent study of suburban exploitation in the Detroit metropolitan area.[5] In comprehensiveness of services included and in the care with which measurements of service flows are carried out, Neenan's analysis probably represents about the best that can be done. We shall therefore review briefly his procedures and findings.

Neenan's approach differs from that of earlier studies. Rather than simply allocating costs on a per capita basis, he develops indices of "willingness-to-pay." Assuming the benefits (that is, the willingness to pay) to vary proportionately with income, Neenan allocates the benefits from city services among city and suburban residents according to their relative income levels. An example may be helpful here. Suppose that the cost per visit (total cost per number of visits) of operating the city's museum is one dollar. If a suburban resident has twice the level of income as that of a city resident, Neenan would attribute a benefit of two dollars per visit to the suburban user of the city museum and a benefit of only one dollar to a city resident. Since, in Neenan's sample of seven suburban communities, income levels in the suburbs are generally higher than those of city residents, this approach naturally has the effect of placing a relatively high value on city services consumed by suburbanites.

Neenan's procedure is biased in two ways toward a finding of positive exploitation. First, because of higher suburban incomes, his technique generates a value of city services to all users that exceeds their cost; thus a suburbanite may well pay the costs he imposes on city residents and yet realize a "consumer surplus" when these costs are compared to his willingness-to-pay. But Neenan assumes that the suburban resident "exploits" the city if he does not contribute to the city treasury the full benefits from any city services he consumes. This is somewhat like saying that the purchaser of a commodity exploits the seller because he gets more in satisfaction than he gives up in terms of his payment (that is, he realizes a consumer surplus). Now surely an ethical question exists as to how these

48 *David F. Bradford and Wallace E. Oates*

"gains-from-trade" should be allocated between city dwellers and suburbanites. but it does seem somewhat questionable to insist. as Neenan in effect does. that they should all accrue to the residents of the city.[6] It would seem to make just as much sense to argue that city residents should be fully compensated for the costs imposed by suburban users of city services. but that there is no compelling reason why they should receive payments in excess of these costs. At any rate. Neenan's approach is surely favorable to obtaining results indicating suburban exploitation of the city.

Second. it should be noted that the particular assumption made by Neenan. namely. valuation proportional to income. does not seem to be derivable from any more fundamental assumptions about the underlying demand functions. Figure 1 illustrates what happens to the total valuation of a given output as income varies for the simple case where demand is linear and unit income elastic.[7] At output G_1. a doubling of income leads to considerably less than a doubling of total valuation (as measured by the areas under the demand curves). As a little experimentation should convince the reader. as long as we are operating in a region in which the lower-income citizen positively values increments in G (that is. to the left of G_2). no income elasticity would be large enough to produce a doubling of total valuation with a doubling of income. if the underlying demand curves are linear. All this says is that it is difficult to know whether Neenan's particular assumption is reasonable or not: we suspect that his willingness-to-pay factor is high.[8]

In spite of these procedures. which favor the exploitation thesis. Neenan finds it to be of minor quantitative significance. The net subsidy from Detroit to the seven suburban communities ranges from $1.73 per capita to $12.58 per capita. with a median value of only $6.78. This compares with an average level of local spending per capita in the United States in 1966 (the year of Neenan's data) of roughly $200. Neenan's study. like the others. thus suggests that the narrow public-finance version of the suburban exploitation thesis is of little moment.

Moreover. it seems to us that these types of studies do not confront directly certain far more fundamental and important issues

FIGURE 1

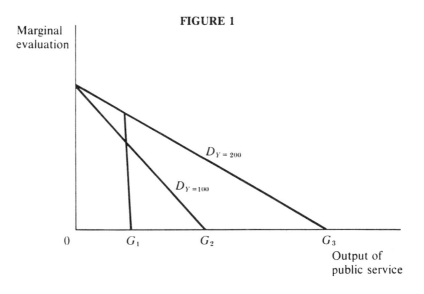

Marginal
evaluation

$D_{Y=200}$

$D_{Y=100}$

0 G_1 G_2 G_3

Output of
public service

concerning the fiscal structure of metropolitan areas. In particular, we see three broad sorts of questions that specialists in public finance would want to ask about urban fiscal organization:

1. How does the efficiency of the provision of public services and the allocation of activities in metropolitan areas vary with alternative governmental structures?

2. If the residents of one jurisdiction within the area (say, the current residents of the central city) were interested simply in maximizing their own real wealth, what expenditure and taxing or pricing policies should the government of that particular jurisdiction adopt?

3. How does the distribution of wealth or welfare (or, more conventionally, the distribution of income) observed within urban areas under current governmental structures compare with that which would exist under alternative organizations of the local public sector?

One might think that the existence of measured exploitation, such as that found by Neenan, provides *prima facie* evidence that the allocation of resources to public activity in the metropolitan area is inefficient, at least relative to some sort of ideal organization. Unfortunately, this conclusion is not valid. Once a zoo has been con-

50 *David F. Bradford and Wallace E. Oates*

structed, the cost of allowing extra visitors is sure to be less than the average of all costs, including capital costs. If it is priced at marginal cost, the jurisdiction operating the zoo will be shown on Neenan's analysis to be exploited by visitors from outside that jurisdiction, who cover the marginal, but not the average, cost they "impose." This would be the result even if the zoo were constructed to efficient scale and in the presence of efficiency in every aspect of the urban economy. It is true, of course, that if any facility is used to a significant degree by individuals from outside the sponsoring jurisdiction, and if increases in capacity benefit all (for example, by reducing congestion) in a way that cannot be effectively priced, there is a presumption that "too little" capacity will be purchased. However, measured exploitation tells us nothing about the presence of such inefficiencies or about the extent of possible gains from eliminating them, even judged against a nonoperational ideal standard.

A more practical issue is whether central cities, or other jurisdictions viewed as selfish collectives, are doing all they can for their members. James Buchanan has pointed out that it may make sense for a central city to adopt apparently regressive policies in order to retain *some* of the surplus generated by upper-income residents in the provision of a public good.[9] One can generalize this and ask what policies will maximize the welfare of the existing citizens (or of some specified subgroup of citizens), taking into account the possibility of exploiting the residents of other jurisdictions (à la the optimal tariff). An obviously interesting further question is how the equilibrium of a system of such competing jurisdictions is likely to look when judged by efficiency criteria (and again the analogy of tariff wars in international trade is suggestive). In any case, the existence of measured exploitation tells us nothing about where to look for "profitable" policy changes from the point of view of the central city, nor can it even be taken as evidence that the central city is not already following an optimal strategy.

It appears that studies of suburban exploitation are fundamentally concerned with issues of income distribution. Ultimately the studies seem to say, not that the metropolitan area's organization is inefficient, not that the central city is doing less well by its citizens than it might, but simply that too big a piece of the benefits is going to the rich suburbs. Our reservations regarding these studies viewed in this light are, first, that they do not specify the alternative system against which outcomes in the existing urban structure are to be tested and, second, that they have focused on only one aspect, and probably a quantitatively insignificant one, of the way in which metropolitan governmental structure influences both the city-suburb and the rich-poor income distribution. As we indicated in the introductory section, local public budgets appear to have a redistributive potential, the force of which is much muted by the availability of a suburban structure permitting "specialization" by income class. In the following sections we begin to explore the ways in which the income distribution that results differs from that which would obtain if metroplitan areas were unified fiscal jurisdictions.

II. REVIEW OF THE OPERATION
OF THE CURRENT SYSTEM

Let us define the Current System as an institutional structure for providing a substantial portion of public services in metropolitan areas by autonomous local fiscal units, each with taxing and zoning powers.[10] What we wish to stress here is the pressure in the Current System toward a set of jurisdictions uniform in income or wealth composition. This stems in part from the tendency, already noted, for local public budgets to be somewhat redistributive from wealthier to poorer members of the fiscal unit.

We should perhaps be somewhat more precise. What appears to be the case is that wealthier members of a large mixed-wealth population can gain by forming a separate fiscal unit. There are *two* sorts of economic reasons for this, only one of them having to do with the redistributive character of public budgets; the other stems from systematic variations in demand for public services with levels of income. Charles Tiebout was the first to explore systematically the way the availability of many alternative local governmental units allowed for diversity of tastes for publicly provided services.[11] Tiebout argued that an equilibrum residential location pattern in such a system would be efficient in the sense that it would not be possible to change the assignment of people to communities. the mix of services provided in any community. or the distribution of private goods in such a way as to make someone better off. with no one worse off.

Among the various aspects of the Current System that did not receive explicit treatment in Tiebout's analysis is the available set of financng instruments and institutions for political choice. When one recognizes that the taxes available to local governments tend to be strongly wealth correlated and. more particularly. tend to assign higher shares of tax burdens to those with the *relatively* higher wealth within communities. it is clear that there is added to the taste-variation element (which itself tends to produce income-homogeneous jurisdictions in response to higher demands for various public services from higher-income households) a further. possibly quite significant. pecuniary force toward income homogenization of suburban communities.

In the absence of control over entry to the community. however. this would appear to be a recipe for musical chairs. with the well-to-do coalescing into units that then become extremely attractive to anyone less wealthy. who would fall toward the bottom of the income distribution in the wealthy community and hence bear a relatively small tax burden. Add to this picture the political choice mechanism of majority rule within communities so that the composition of the public-service package cannot be controlled by the original members of the group. and one has a set of strong forces working against the stability of equilibria characterized by highly income-homogeneous suburban communities.

In an ingenious analysis Bruce W. Hamilton has shown how local zoning power can bring order to this system.[12] The predominant source of local governmental revenues is the property tax. By requiring minimum purchases of housing services. communities can essentially confine entrants to the community to those who will generate at least as much incremental tax revenue as they do incremental costs in the public budget. Taking the ideal case. Hamilton assumes local governments can put a precise floor under the value of real estate owned. and hence the taxes paid. by any net additional members. Since those purchasing more than the minimum amount of housing pay more taxes than those at the floor, there is a pressure toward the formation of differentiated communities until, "in the limit," one observes a set of communities homogeneous in housing consumption. The remarkable attribute of this solution noted by Hamilton is that it converts the property tax into an ideal benefit tax. A family wishing to consume its desired level of housing, but more public services, moves to another community with the same zoning requirement but providing the higher service level. The increment in the family's tax bill will just equal the increment in costs imposed on the new community. Moreover, in this situation the tax on housing services is free of deadweight loss. Because of the diversity of housing-public service combinations available, it is possible for a family (by moving, it must be noted) to buy more housing without paying more tax, while continuing to receive a given bundle of public services. Furthermore, the outcome may be expected to be stable. There is no possibility for migrants to increase their public services without paying more in taxes, and no reason to expect shifts in majorities that will alter the bundle offered by a given community, since those with different preferences will have no incentive to enter in the first place.

There are, of course, many differences between the model sketched out above and the actual suburban governmental system. However, much the most important element not yet introduced (it is introduced by Hamilton) is the presence in the system of one, large, jurisdiction that, in the nature of things, cannot become an income-uniform unit: the central city. By virtue of its history, size, and economic function, it can hardly be imagined to be composed of any uniform income group.

In the model described there will be in any jurisdiction with a wide spread of income levels a steady pressure on those at the upper end of the distribution to emigrate to income-homogeneous suburbs. In the logic of the model the central city is the odd man out, and one would expect, in the absence of compensating advantages to the upper-income families, to find the central city inhabited only by the poorest families in the metropolitan area.

The idea of central cities as "holders of the bag" is, of course, not a new one and may be found, for example, in the description by Edgar Hoover and Raymond Vernon of the process of migration of middle-income and upper-income classes and of industry and jobs from the central cities to increasingly accessible surrounding suburban communities.[13] Certainly consistent with this picture are the data contained in the various government censuses conducted over the last thirty years. Especially in the older metropolitan areas, one typically finds absolute losses in population in the central city, rapid growth in the population of suburban communities, growing disparities in relative levels of income between central city and suburban residents, a shift in the racial composition of the central city with a growing proportion of economically disadvantaged minority groups, rising tax rates in the cities relative to those in the suburbs, and a continuing shift of the relative share of economic activity to the suburbs. All this is well known and empirically substantiated.

The relationship between this process and the governmental structure of urbanized areas has not, however, been carefully spelled out. The Current System tends to reinforce the other pressures toward suburbanization of upper-income families and toward income homogenization of the suburbs. It may be asked whether these phenomena, and the role of the Current System in generating them, are necessarily a bad thing. There are two important reasons, one widely recognized the other hardly discussed at all, for thinking they might be.

The first reason is that income segregation is a force perpetuating income differences in the sense that a person's being born into a poor community seems to increase his chance of being a poor adult. This in itself is likely to be seen as offensive. In addition, as will be argued below, income segregation not only influences who will be poor but also probably increases the variance of the income distribution.

The second reason concerns the pressure toward suburbanization in the Current System. Cities presumably increase productivity as the result of economies of agglomeration; an excessive centrifugal force thus leads to a reduction in wealth. Taken by itself, the Current System appears to generate such an effect. Whether one must be concerned about this depends upon whether there would be too

254   *Studies in Fiscal Federalism*

Suburban Exploitation of Central Cities   **55**

little or just the right amount of agglomeration were the influences of the governmental structure neutralized. and upon whether those influences are quantatively significant. What is involved here is a second-best situation. The suburban sector in the idealized version of the Current System operates with perfect efficiency. whereas the central city is seen as inherently incapable of the sort of benefit taxation that would enable it to be efficient in the same sense. Much as the presence of an incurable monopoly may require deviations from competitive behavior in other sectors to achieve second-best efficiency. the presence of an incurable central city may require interference with an apparently efficiency-enhancing suburban system.

The quantitative importance of the suggested ill effects of income segregation and of excessive suburbanization of upper-income families as well as the quantitative significance of the governmental structure in inducing these outcomes are far from clear. Nor is it obvious how valuable. on the other hand. are the efficiency advantages of the Current System. In the next section we discuss these issues further and attempt to pull together such quantitative evidence as is now available.

III. THE LONG-RUN DISTRIBUTION
OF WELFARE UNDER A UNIFIED
FISCAL STRUCTURE

In this section we want to investigate how the distribution of welfare in a system in which public services of entire metropolitan areas are administered and financed by single authorities (be they metropolitan governments or. perhaps. state governments) would compare with that under the Current System. For this purpose we assume that the Unified System (by which we shall mean a consolidated fiscal jurisdiction encompassing at least the whole metropolitan area) is in long-run equilibrium in the sense that all adjustments of location. composition of public services. etc.. have been made. In this context there is obviously no reason to be concerned with the distribution of welfare between central city and suburban residents per se. Rather. we shall ask the following kinds of questions: Which classes of individuals. in terms of personal characteristics of productivity. taste. etc.. will be better off and which worse off (and by how much) under the Unified System as compared to the Current System? How might the overall size distribution of income vary with governmental structure? And finally. in terms of economic efficiency. in which system is the "potential welfare" greater? That is. if we had the proverbial lump-sum. optimal redistribution taking place. which system would make people better off?

To reach any sort of reasonably precise conclusions we must make some specific assumptions concerning the fiscal structure under the Current and Unified Systems. To facilitate the analysis both in this section and in the next. we shall postulate that the federal government carries on the same set of redistributive programs and other activities in both systems. As outlined in the preceding section. we take the Current System to be one in which local public services are financed primarily by local real property taxes with levels of expenditures and tax rates determined in the main by each jurisdiction within the metropolitan area. In contrast. under the Unified System we assume that decisions concerning levels of spendng on public services are determined on (at least) a metropolitan-wide basis and are financed by a tax system with a uniform set of rates applicable to the entire area. For much of the analysis. we shall assume a central role for a metropolitan-area property tax. This obviously need not be the case. In fact. one of the attractions of a Unified System is presumably the potential for a greater reliance on other (possibly more progressive and efficient) forms of taxation. We shall offer a few observations on this. but the reader should have little difficulty in modifying the analysis to account for alternative revenue structures under the Unified System.

Income Redistribution from Rich to Poor

We look first at the differences in the size distribution of real income under the Current and Unified Systems. The difficulties inherent in locating the incidence of taxes and imputing the benefits of public-expenditure programs can give us little confidence in any precise calculations of fiscal incidence. However. it is possible. we think. to reach some qualitative (and a few rough quantitative) judgments on the basis of what we see as a shortcoming in most existing studies of fiscal incidence. In one of the best-known and most comprehensive of these studies W. Irwin Gillespie allocated both the fiscal benefits and the tax costs of public programs among income classes for public programs at all levels of government in the United States for 1960.[14] For state-local fiscal programs Gillespie found a redistribution in favor of those families with incomes under $5,000 (increasing their money incomes by roughly 30 percent) and little or no redistribution among families with incomes in excess of this figure.[15] What is interesting for our purposes is that these estimates were generated largely by applying general assumptions about the incidence of various taxes and expenditures to state and local aggregates. Gillespie reasons, for example, that the benefits from expenditures on primary and secondary education can be allocated among students by simply dividing aggregate spending by the number of pupils. But this fails to recognize (as we shall see in the next section) that expenditure per pupil is typically significantly higher in richer than in poorer areas under the Current System.

In fact, Gillespie's estimates may come closer to approximating fiscal incidence under our Unified System than under the Current System. Consider, for example, the extreme case in which all public services are provided locally and complete income segregation has taken place. Then, clearly, there will be no redistributive effects generated by the state-local fiscal system. The other extreme is the Unified System with similar expenditure patterns and tax rates across the whole metropolitan area; here "average" fiscal incidence by income class (which seems to be closer to what Gillespie is measuring) would presumably be a reasonable measure of actual patterns. The Current System lies somewhere between the two polar cases. There has been some, probably substantial, income segregation. However, its extent has been limited by, among other forces, the necessarily income-integrated character of central cities. Furthermore, state governments do provide a substantial portion of public services and raise even more of the revenue within their boundaries.

Taken together these observations suggest that, as far as redistribution through the fiscal system is concerned, changing from the Current to a Unified System will result in a redistribution of income from the wealthy to the poor. However, the resulting pattern of fiscal incidence may resemble more closely Gillespie's measurements for the existing system, rather than more pronounced pro-poor fiscal effects. The potential for redistribution is, of course, greater in the Unified System should political forces favor more progressive tax-expenditure packages.

Possibly more important than the change in income distribution via the fiscal system could be the change resulting from reduced income segregation. We have no quantitative evidence to offer on this issue, however, and raise it mainly in the hope of encouraging empirical work. The influence of income segregation on the variance of the income distribution may be illustrated by a simple, if admittedly extreme, example. Imagine that an adult's productivity is purely a function of the average productivity of those in the community of his birth. In this case, equalizing the average productivity in communities would lead in one generation to fully equalized productivities of individuals.

Efficiency Differences Favoring the Current System

The thrust of the Tiebout analysis is that the Current System has some desirable efficiency properties, and, as we discussed earlier, Hamilton's extension of this theory to include the property tax and residential zoning reinforces these characteristics. An equilibrium in this idealized version of the Current System is efficient, not only in the sense that a Pareto-optimal amount of public services is offered in each community and no reshuffling of families among communities (possibly accompanied by side payments) could make everyone better off but also in having a tax system with no deadweight losses.

The latter advantage may not be trivial. A real-estate tax rate of 3.0 percent amounts to an excise tax on housing of roughly 25 percent. A wedge of this magnitude between the marginal cost and marginal valuation of housing could well have a substantial influence on housing choices and leave a significant opportunity for gain from the purchase of additional housing at the existing equilibrium. Assume, for example, that the price elasticity of demand for housing is unity.[16] The elimination of a 25 percent excise tax on a commodity with a unit price elasticity of demand and consuming 25 percent of the household's budget generates a net gain equal to roughly 1 percent of the household's income. The ability of the Current System to neutralize the deadweight loss of the real property tax as applied to residential housing would thus appear to be a significant advantage.

However, some factors tend to work against the importance of this characteristic of the Current System. First, the variety and number of suburban communities are small compared to the magnitudes that would be required to reach the level of efficiency implied by complete elimination of the deadweight loss. There is still substantial variation in income and housing consumption within communities. and we can safely presume that there are many property owners confronting decisions to enlarge or otherwise alter their properties. a margin at which the deadweight loss of the property tax remains. Second. several policies of the federal government. especially the freedom from income tax of the implicit rent from owner-occupied housing and the deductibility from taxable income of local property taxes, tend to offset the distorting effects of the property tax. particularly in the suburbs and particularly as applied to wealthier households with relatively high marginal tax rates under the federal income tax. Third. as we have pointed out. the Current System does not eliminate the deadweight loss associated with the real property tax in central cities. where. incidentally. the tax rates tend to be substantially higher than in the suburbs. Thus the potential welfare advantage of the Current System in terms of reducing the deadweight loss due to the property tax in housing must be regarded. we would judge. as small. Moreover. we should again note the possibility under a Unified System of a tax structure relying less heavily on property taxes and. as a result. perhaps generating less in deadweight losses.

A more serious matter may be the sacrifice of the other sort of efficiency in a Tiebout world. The choice of public services by a community in this model amounts to exactly the same thing as the choice of a consumption bundle by an individual household. We take it that under a Unified System there will be strong pressure to provide. in

60 *David F. Bradford and Wallace E. Oates*

some sense, the same public services to all households, whereas under the Current System households make a choice between private and public expenditure and among compositions thereof by choosing their residential community appropriately. The efficiency advantage of the Current System is similar to that of a market system over a system involving equal division of some set of private commodities among all households. The quantitative extent of this efficiency gain depends upon the degree of difference in the demands for public services among communities in the Current System and the price elasticity of demand (or. more precisely, the elasticity of the marginal valuation of those services with respect to changes in their levels).[17]

To develop a feeling for the potential quantitative importance of this welfare gain from the Current System, we have chosen to examine local public expenditures for primary and secondary education. This choice was dictated by the relatively large magnitude of these expenditures in local public budgets, by the availability of reasonably good data, and, especially, by the current importance for public policy of the issue of equalizing educational expenditures.

For purposes of empirical estimates (both in this section and later), we have chosen a group of central cities and suburban communities in New Jersey. With its extremely heavy emphasis on local finance, high degree of fiscal fragmentation, and preponderant reliance on local property taxes. New Jersey appears to represent about as good an approximation to our Current System as we are likely to find. Our sample includes the five central cities and a group of fifty-three residential communities in the eight counties in Northeastern New Jersey that are included in the Census definition of the New York Standard Consolidated Area.[18] This area encompasses three Standard Metropolitan Statistical Areas (SMSAs): Newark. Jersey City, and Paterson-Clifton-Passaic, and two additional counties: Middlesex and Somerset, an area that in 1960 had a population of almost 4 million. Let us call this empirical counterpart to the Current System the New Jersey Metropolitan Area (NJMA), and its government as a Unified System the New Jersey Metropolitan Government (NJMG). For the most part we rely on 1960 data, for which we have comprehensive demographic and fiscal information. but we also have available for some categories roughly comparable figures for 1970.

The public service that we examine here is measured by expenditure per pupil in public schools: in fact. we shall assume that "expenditure per pupil" is a public good in the Samuelson sense within each community.[19] Within our sample. expenditure per pupil in the school year 1959-1960 varied from $295 to $547. with an average value of $413 over the whole set of communities. There is thus a substantial variation among communities in the chosen level of provision of this public good. a matter that we shall examine further in Section IV.

Our procedure will be to estimate the loss in efficiency that would have resulted from enforcing a uniform level of expenditure per pupil of $413 (the mean value of spending across the sample) throughout the NJMA in 1959-1960.[20] To make this estimate. we require a marginal valuation function for expenditure per pupil. Specifically. let us assume that each individual has the demand function

$$(1) \qquad\qquad E = AY^{\alpha}P^{\beta}$$

where E is expenditure per pupil. Y is his family income. P is the "price" of an additional dollar of spending per student. and A, α. and β are constants. Then. for given values of E and Y, P is the value to that family of a one-dollar increase in per pupil expenditure. Solving (1) for P yields

$$(2) \qquad\qquad P = \left(\frac{E}{A} Y^{-\alpha} \right)^{1/\beta}$$

This relationship is of the form

$$(3) \qquad\qquad P = BE^{1/\beta}Y^{\gamma}$$

where

$$B = \left(\frac{1}{A} \right)^{1/\beta}, \; \gamma = -\frac{\alpha}{\beta}$$

62 *David F. Bradford and Wallace E. Oates*

If we assume these parameters in the demand function to be the same for everyone, the aggregate marginal value of a one-dollar change in per pupil expenditure for the n members of the community is

$$(4) \qquad \sum_{i=1}^{n} P_i = \sum_{i=1}^{n} BE^{1/\beta} Y_i^{\gamma}$$

The marginal cost of expenditure per pupil is simply n_s, the number of pupils in the community.[21] If the community undertakes the efficient level of spending per pupil, we would thus have that

$$(5) \qquad \sum_{i=1}^{n} P_i = BE^{1/\beta} \left(\sum_{i=1}^{n} Y_i^{\gamma} \right) = n_s$$

We can greatly simplify our procedure with one final assumption that each community is homogeneous in income so that every family in a given community in 1960 possessed the median family income for that community. Then (5) becomes

$$(6) \qquad nBE^{1/\beta} Y^{\gamma} = n_s$$

where Y is the median family income for the community in 1960. If we solve (6) for E and put the equation in log form, we get:

$$(7) \qquad \log E = -\beta \log B + \beta \log \left(\frac{n_s}{n} \right) - \gamma\beta \log Y$$

Using our cross-section of 53 suburban communities. we estimated equation (7) by ordinary least squares and obtained:

$$(8) \qquad \log E = 4.0 - 0.36 \log \left(\frac{n_s}{n} \right) + 0.65 \log Y$$
$$\qquad (16.0) \quad (5.6) \qquad\qquad (7.7)$$

where the numbers in parentheses are the absolute values of the t-statistics for the respective coefficients and where $R^2 = .57$.[22] The estimated coefficients of the variables are all significantly different from zero at a 99 percent level of confidence and possess the anticipated signs. Using these regression results. we can go back and compute estimated values for our key parameters where we find that:

$$\beta = -0.36 \qquad\qquad \log B = -\frac{1}{\beta}(4.0) = 11.10$$

$$\gamma = -\frac{1}{\beta}(0.65) = 1.80 \qquad\qquad B = 65{,}840$$

$$\alpha = -(\beta\gamma) = 0.65 \qquad\qquad A = 55.5$$

We recall from equation (1) that β and α can be interpreted respectively as the price and income elasticities of demand for per-pupil expenditure.[23] Note how small is the price elasticity, implying the potential for substantial efficiency losses in the Unified System.

Using these estimated values for our parameters, along with our information on expenditure levels and changes in expenditure per pupil, we can calculate the valuations of changes in per pupil expenditure in each of our fifty-three suburban communities. If we take a linear approximation to the change in marginal valuation (that is, a linear approximation to the demand curves over the relevant range), we can substantially simplify our calculations. The value at the margin to the community of an additional dollar devoted to increasing the educational expenditure is exactly one dollar. The value of such a marginal dollar at a level of expenditure per pupil differing from the initial level by an amount ΔE is thus

(9)
$$\frac{P'}{n_s} \approx \left(n_s + \frac{\partial P}{\partial E} \cdot \Delta E\right)/n_s$$

where P is interpreted as the community marginal evaluation of expenditure per pupil (6), and P' is the community marginal evaluation after the change, ΔE. Differentiating the left-hand side of (6) and making use of the equilibrium condition, $P = n_s$, we have

(10)
$$\frac{\partial P}{\partial E} = \frac{P}{\beta E} = \frac{1}{\beta}\left(\frac{n_s}{E}\right)$$

so that the value of a marginal dollar of expenditure at the new level is

(11)
$$\frac{P'}{n_s} \approx 1 + \frac{1}{\beta}\left(\frac{\Delta E}{E}\right)$$

By the usual consumers' surplus arguments, the approximate value per dollar of a sum used to bring about a change ΔE in per pupil expenditure is

(12)
$$\frac{1}{2}\left(\frac{P' + P}{n_s}\right) \approx \left[1 + \frac{1}{2\beta}\left(\frac{\Delta E}{E}\right)\right]$$

We used this expression to obtain an estimate of the deadweight loss that would occur if the total amount spent on education in our sample of communities was so redistributed as to equalize the expenditure per pupil at the average level of $413. Given the range of initial spending levels, this implied increases ranging up to 40 percent and decreases to 25 percent for the communities in our sample.

After calculating the change in educational spending for each community, we used (12) to compute the value of these sums as viewed by the members of communities themselves. Since, by assumption, marginal valuation equaled marginal cost at the original level of expenditure per pupil, communities in which per pupil expenditure increased valued the amounts gained at less than the dollar amounts involved, whereas communities suffering a reduction in expenditure per pupil valued the loss in spending in excess of the actual dollar amount. The absolute values of these differences are the deadweight losses. Finally, we compared the mean value of these aggregate losses across communities to the mean of the absolute value of the change in educational expenditures. In short, this is the average deadweight loss as a percentage of the average change in expenditures.

For those communities that would have realized an increase in expenditure per pupil, this figure is about 35 percent. This figure indicates that each additional dollar of expenditure received by those jurisdictions that were net gainers was valued, on average, at only about $0.65; conversely, the computations indicate that dollars transferred away from the school budgets of communities were valued at an average of about $1.15 each. These estimates are obviously quite large; they suggest that, subject to our assumptions, the transfer of a dollar of school spending from one community to another under our hypothetical 1960 program for NJMA would have involved a mean deadweight loss of $0.15 for the contributor and $0.35 for the recipient, or a total deadweight loss of roughly $0.50.

Such large estimates suggest that losses of efficiency in this form should be carefully considered in any choice between the Current System and a Unified System. However, we would urge caution in the interpretation of these particular findings. We have made highly simplifying assumptions to estimate the price elasticity of demand for expenditure per pupil and to calculate our measure of inefficiency. Furthermore, the particular service under study, education, is one that might well be used to argue in favor of a Unified System, since it is believed by many to involve substantial spillover benefits.[24] Several recent court decisions, for instance, could be interpreted as taking this point of view. It is interesting that other local services, including garbage collection, recreational facilities, and fire protection, are not so frequently cited as generating spillover benefits, although, in a highly mobile society, almost any local service clearly has some external effects and for certain services, such as police protection, they may be quite important.

Efficiency-Enhancing Characteristics
of the Unified System

The most obvious advantage in terms of economic efficiency of a Unified System is its potential for internalizing the spillover effects associated with public budgetary decisions of the many independent communities in the Current System. However, to give a reasonable assessment of the Unified System as an internalizer is a difficult task, particularly since there exist alternative techniques (involving communication and negotiations among communities) to achieve this objective. To attempt to evaluate this source of increased efficiency seemed to lead us too far afield so that we will do no more here than simply note its possible importance.

There is, however, another respect in which the Unified System may promote economic efficiency relative to the Current System. In our discussion of the operation of the Current System, we stressed its tendency toward "excessive" income segregation and especially the "excessive" incentives to suburbanization resulting from the central city's necessarily income-integrated character. In this section we want to investigate whether, in the complex of forces producing the suburbanization of upper-income families, those arising from the governmental structure are of measurable significance. The answer to this question is obviously of great importance, for it has direct implications for the potential of alterations in local fiscal organization or policies to influence decisions of households and business firms and thus the economic characteristics of metropolitan areas.

Evidence that would enable us to answer this question is scarce, although there is some. Richard Muth, for example, notes that the tendency for cities to spread out as they increase in population size is stronger than can be accounted for by the differential housing-supply response predicted by his estimated relationships.[25] Although he offers some other possible explanations, it is certainly conceivable that this could result from an increase in the number of local jurisdictions from which to choose as the absolute population of the metropolitan area grows; this would presumably strengthen the centrifugal force we have described. Muth finds in addition that "the lower the average income level of the central city relative to its suburbs, the smaller is the central city's population and the larger is the land area occupied by the urbanized area," a result that can be explained in terms of the local fiscal structure.[26]

Bruce Hamilton has also found some corroboration of his model of choice of community. We have already described the implication of his analysis that the real property tax in the suburbs does not impose any deadweight loss. In the central city, however, this deadweight loss will remain. Put another way, the property tax is, in effect, ignored in choosing the amount of housing to consume in the suburbs (since the tax depends only on the amount of public service the household chooses to buy, a choice it makes by its selection of community), but it will influence the housing choice in the central city. This implies an observable difference in housing demand functions between central city and suburbs, a difference that Hamilton finds supported by econometric evidence.[27]

More direct evidence is presented by Bradford and Kelejian, who estimate relationships predicting the residential division of poor and rich families between the central city and suburbs.[28] Their econometric model includes variables designed to measure the net benefit of the central-city fiscal system relative to that of the alternative suburban fiscal system to the middle class and poor. Although the presumptive bias in this case is against the variables used, they are found to have statistically significant explanatory power. In an illustrative calculation of the influence of these variables, an "average" city was constructed and its government given an increase of transfers from higher levels of government from 20 to 50 percent of the city's total expenditure. The result was an increase of the fraction of the imaginary urbanized area's middle-class families living in the central city from 60 to 72 percent.

This result actually understates the impact of the illustrative policy on the structure of the urbanized area implied by the Bradford-Kelejian model. They find the income distribution of the central city itself to be a very important determinant of the location of middle-class residents, who show a marked tendency to flee poverty in the central city. This influence is found to operate with a much longer lag than the "direct" fiscal effect, and hence it did not affect the outcome of the example. Over a longer period, however, the "favorable" effect on the central-city income distribution would reinforce the shift of middle-class families back to the central city.

Feedback phenomena such as this seem bound to magnify, perhaps greatly, the dispersive effect of the current fiscal structure of urban areas. As upper-income families move out, the incentive increases for their employers to move out. Central-city amenities involving increasing returns to scale and catering to wealthier families —theaters, clubs, etc. — become uneconomical, reducing the city's attraction. The story could be spun out at length, although that would be a weak substitute for some solid quantitative knowledge (little of which is available) about these phenomena. The point to be emphasized is that it seems possible in principle that relatively small direct effects working against the central city could cause very large shifts in outcomes, and it may be very difficult to distinguish between a high income elasticity of demand for suburban space and a large systemic response in reduced urban amenity to a small initial shift in the relative fiscal surplus of middle-class families in the central city. It thus seems plausible that the fiscal organization under the Current System has played an important role in the process of suburbanization, although the extent of its effect is still not very clear.

Income Segregation under the Unified System

Although we have stressed the fiscal inducements for the formation of income-homogenized communities under the Current System, it by no means follows that such tendencies would be entirely absent under a Unified System. In fact, there is little doubt that, even if our metropolitan areas had been consolidated fiscal jurisdictions throughout their history, we would still observe a substantial degree of residential segregation by income class. This view is supported by an examination of the large fiscal units with which we have been familiar—the central cities themselves.

Here one is struck by the fact that, in spite of fiscal unification, the quality of the public services (particularly schools, cleanliness, and protection from crime) vary widely in different sections of the same city. Certain public schools are known in most cities to be better than others and some areas safer in which to walk. The quality of amenities varies considerably even within these unified fiscal districts.

This phenomenon can be better understood if we make a careful distinction between inputs and outputs of public services. For this purpose we draw upon a conceptual framework (similar to that used by others) that R. A. Malt and we developed in an earlier paper.[29] There we differentiated between what we called "*D*-output," or services directly produced, and "*C*-output," the level (or quality) of public services actually consumed by individuals.

To be more systematic, let I be a vector of inputs in the production of public services. In the case of schools, for example, this vector might consist of number of teachers, schoolrooms, or books. The vector I maps through a production function into a vector D of "directly produced" services. To return to education, D could consist of providing a given number of students with instruction of a specified kind (for example, a certain number of "standard" mathematics lessons). If we were concerned with protection from criminal acts, we might associate D with certain levels of surveillance, such as traffic control activity, resulting from an input *I* of men, cars, communications systems, and so on.

An individual, however, is presumably interested in the level of services consumed: he is interested in the quality of the schools his and other children attend and in the degree of protection from crime he actually receives. And these are determined only in part by *D*. They depend also on a number of other variables that describe the "environment" in which the direct outputs are provided. A specified degree of surveillance, for example, will provide a higher level of protection from crime in an area where there are few prone to commit criminal acts than in an area where this "propensity" is much higher. Likewise, as we have learned from the Coleman Report and other studies, the education a student receives depends largely on a number of variables, such as the characteristics of his schoolmates, that have little to do with the vector of public inputs into the school system.

More formally, the argument is that we can express an individual's utility function in the form

(13) $$U = U(C_1, C_2, \ldots C_n, Z)$$

where *Z* is a vector representing the level of his private-goods consumption and C_i is his level of consumption of the ith public service. In turn, we have

(14) $$C_i = f_i(D_i, E)$$

which indicates that the level of public services consumed depends both on D_i, the level of services produced (a function of inputs), and on *E*, a vector indicating the environmental characteristics of the area in which the service is provided.

With this background, let us return to our observation of the considerable variation in the quality of public services within cities themselves. This stems largely, we would guess, from the fact that fiscal unification tends to generate pressures more for uniformity in inputs than for outputs of public services. With the same set of tax rates applicable to the jurisdiction as a whole, one area, for example, is likely to protest loudly if the level of expenditure per pupil in the schools serving its children falls significantly below that in another part of the city. The discussion surrounding some of the recent court decisions has also been largely "input-oriented." In the California case. for example. the central point seems to have been that variations in the size of the tax base per pupil led to lower spending and hence inferior schools in poorer districts. There remains. however. the further issue. admittedly a difficult one to handle. that equality in expenditure per pupil by no means implies an equal quality of schools.

As a rough approximation. let us then visualize a city with a uniform tax structure and an identical vector of inputs for all public services in all sections of the city. It seems clear that we would expect to find in such a city variations in the quality of services consumed. the C-vector. because of differences in the environmental characteristics in the various parts of the city. More specifically. we would expect a clustering of the relatively wealthy in more costly residences. serving to provide an environment (an E-vector) favorable to a higher-quality package of public services. Wealthier neighborhoods will have better schools. even with the same expenditure per pupil. because of the characteristics of the pupils themselves and their families. Likewise. such sections will generally be cleaner and safer places to live than poorer areas of the city. Thus. in spite of the same tax structures and service inputs. we find that the quality of public services is likely to be significantly higher in wealthy than in poor parts of the city.

An interesting implication of this result would seem to be that the "tax price" of public services would actually be lower in these wealthier sections of the city because the same tax rate yields a higher quality of public services consumed. a "bigger" C-vector. This. however. need not be the case. Local services have typically been financed by income-related taxes. like the property tax. so that those living in higher-valued dwellings pay more in taxes. Moreover. to the extent that any favorable "fiscal" differential remains. it will tend to be capitalized into higher rents.

What we have here is an example of an economy of agglomeration analytically identical to that which occurs when. say. garment makers locate near one another. The mechanism sustaining this configuration is the willingness of those benefiting from the agglomeration to outbid others for the site. A curious question arises here, however. What is it that prevents poor people from outbidding rich people for sites near other rich people? The sheer price of the real estate is not a fully adequate explanation, as there are many examples of poor people occupying, in high density, expensive sites. The answer to the question may be that the consumption services involved typically are demanded with a high-income elasticity. We may here have the principle underlying the fact that rich people tend to form suburban communities, and garment-makers do not.) Or it may be that formal or informal zoning techniques are used, or "gentlemen's" agreements of one sort or another.[30]

In addition, as Wilbur Thompson has pointed out: "The wealthier urban households tend to cluster for many reasons unrelated to local public finance .... More commonly, income segragation is socially based as families choose their neighbors by using income as an index of desirable personal and social characteristics, and housing value as the surrogate for the unknown income."[31]

The thrust of these arguments, then, is to weaken somewhat the expectation of gains in economies of integration in a Unified System. The "natural" forces of relatively cheap housing inducing concentrations of poor people in central cities and of the tendency of wealthier families to reside in income-specialized neighborhoods even within a fiscal jurisdiction make it likely that in a Unified System, as in the Current System, cities would still have become sites of serious social and fiscal problems. But fiscal consolidation should have made these problems somewhat less intense and have provided a framework better suited to coping with them.

IV. IN THE LONG RUN WE ARE ALL DEAD

In the previous section we were primarily concerned with the long-run equilibrium properties of two structures for providing public services in urban areas: the Current System and the Unified System. Of equal interest, however, is the nature of the redistribution of welfare that would take place as a consequence of a shift from the Current System to the Unified System.

As before. we must make some simplifying assumptions about the existing system and some specifications concerning the sort of Unified System to which the hypothetical transition is to be made. For purposes of our analysis. we shall assume that under the Current System all local public services are financed by local real property taxes with levels of expenditures and tax rates determined independently by each jurisdiction within the metropolitan area. With the shift to a Unified Jurisdiction. we assume that all financing becomes centralized with revenues still raised by a tax on real property but with a uniform rate applicable to all property in the jurisdiction. Within this framework. we shall initially perform two sets of conceptual experiments. First. we postulate that expenditures per capita throughout the metropolitan area remain unchanged and examine the redistributive effects of substituting an area-wide property tax for the differing tax rates existing under the Current System. Incidentally. once this "baseline" analysis is established. the reader should have little difficulty in analyzing the implications of alternative financing schemes. such as a shift away from property taxation to increased reliance on an income tax. In our second group of experiments we shall hold constant the aggregate level of revenues and expenditures for the metropolitan area as a whole. but assume that. under the Unified Jurisdiction. expenditures per capita (or per pupil in the schools) are equalized across all sections of the metropolitan area. This will allow us to examine the redistributive effects of shifts in expenditure patterns as we move from the Current System to our hypothesized Unified Jurisdiction. We shall. in this part of the study. place a special emphasis on expenditures for public education in view both of their relatively large magnitude and their current importance for public policy. The analysis will consider the effects of this shift in the short run in which the stock of housing and structures is assumed fixed and. to a lesser extent. some of the longer-run changes that we might expect.

The most obvious shortcoming of this approach is the failure to integrate the tax and expenditure sides of the budget in the context of the new governmental system so as to take account of the effects of

TABLE 1

Equalized Tax Rates for Central Cities (1960)

Newark	4.94%
Jersey City	5.85
Paterson	3.91
Clifton	2.03
Passaic	3.53

Source: Morris Beck, *Property Taxation and Urban
Land Use in Northeastern New Jersey* (Washington,
D.C.: Urban Land Institute, 1963), Appendix B.

this change in fiscal structure on the aggregate levels of expenditures and receipts themselves. We shall, however, offer some observations later on this matter, where we shall argue that this should not alter greatly the general character of the results we obtain from our earlier experiments.

To generate empirical estimates of the various redistributive effects, we shall use the same sample of five central cities and fifty-three suburban municipalities in Northeastern New Jersey that we described and used for estimation purposes in the preceding section. Our procedure will thus be to take the New Jersey Metropolitan Area (NJMA) and study the patterns of income redistribution associated with a shift from the Current System to "the" New Jersey Metropolitan Government (NJMG). As earlier, we shall rely heavily on 1960 data, but will in most cases be able to provide some at least roughly comparable estimates for 1970.

Turning to our first experiment, we take the equalized or "true" value of taxable property in 1960 for the NJMA as a whole and simply divide it into the property-tax revenues collected by all local jurisdictions in the area for that year to determine what uniform metropolitan rate would have generated this aggregate level of receipts.[32] This rate for the Unified Jurisdiction is 3.03 percent. It is apparent from Table 1 that aside from Clifton this would have implied a substantial reduction in property-tax rates for the central cities. In particular, for the two largest cities — Newark and Jersey City — the reduction in tax rates would have been close to 40 and 50 percent, respectively. In contrast, the mean tax rate in 1960 for our sample of suburban communities was 2.53 percent. A shift to a Unified Jurisdic-

74 *David F. Bradford and Wallace E. Oates*

tion would thus have raised the tax rate on the property of a "typical" suburbanite in the NJMA from 2.53 to 3.03 percent, or an increase of about 20 percent.

What can we say about the redistributive implications of these results? In the short run, the most important point to note is that this shift consists of a redistribution of wealth among property owners. The preceding calculations would therefore suggest, on average, a redistribution away from suburban property owners to those in the central cities. If we assume that the typical suburbanite owns his own home and use the mean value of an owner-occupied home in our sample of suburban communities of $19,000, a first approximation would be that his property-tax bill for 1960 would haven risen from about $475 to 570.[33]

However, this calculation overlooks an important effect: the impact of the change in the tax rate on the value of the property. The amount of wealth redistribution away from a landlord is simply the capitalized value of the change in his annual taxes or, in income dimensions, the annual tax change itself. The most obvious manner of estimating the latter is simply to multiply the original value of the property by the increase in the property-tax rate, as we have just done above. However, this is presumably an overestimate, since the increase in tax rate (holding government services constant) will tend to reduce the market price of the property. If we consider the market value, V, of a property generating a before-tax net rental flow of R dollars annually to be $V = R/(i + t)$, where i is the appropriate discount rate and t the property-tax rate, then the value of the property after a (ceteris paribus) change in the tax rate to t^* will be $V(i + t) / (i + t^*)$. The naive method of estimating the change in taxes ignores this fact. However, it is not difficult to show that the naive estimate need only be multiplied by a correction factor of $i/(i + t^*)$ to yield an estimate that incorporates the capitalization of the change in the tax rate.[34]

To apply this result, we must make a guess as to the correct rate of discount. Since the above argument treats gross rents as constant, a defensible procedure probably only in real terms, the discount rate we should use is a real rate, say, something between 4 and 8 percent. Since t^* in our case is 3 percent, this corresponds to a range in

$i/(i + t^*)$ from 0.57 to 0.73. For purposes of our rough calculations we have taken $i= 6$ percent, so that the estimated tax changes used in the remainder of this section are obtained by multiplying the naive version by 0.67. The reader with other ideas about the discount rate will have little difficulty readjusting our results.

The data presented earlier on changes in tax rates indicate that a shift to a Unified System would induce a redistribution on average from owners of suburban property to owners of property in the central cities. Taking $19,000 as the value of our typical suburban residence, we find, under the assumption of full capitalization at 6 percent, that an increase in the property-tax rate from $2\frac{1}{2}$ to 3 percent would reduce the value of this typical property to slightly more than $18,000. This represents a transfer of wealth away from the suburban property owner to owners of central-city property of approximately $1,000 in the form of an increase in the annual tax bill from $475 (0.025 × $19,000) to roughly $540 (0.03 × $18,000).

In the city, where a much larger fraction of the housing stock consists of rental units, the short-run benefits from reduced tax receipts would accrue primarily to landlords; this would presumably do little for the poor in the cities since they are predominantly renters. On the other hand, a significant fall in tax rates in the cities should make some contribution in the long run both to the construction of new rental units and the maintenance of existing ones with resulting reductions in levels of rents; it should also encourage business firms to locate (or at least remain) in the city, thereby creating more jobs easily accessible to the city poor. To get a very rough idea of the possible long-run impact on city rents, we took the median rent in each of our five central cities for 1960, estimated the reduction in the property-tax payment on that unit after the creation of the NJMG (using the figures from Table 1), and then simply assumed this reduction to be passed forward fully in terms of lower rents to occupants.[35] The results are presented in Table 2. At least for Newark and Jersey City, the fall in rents would have been substantial (respectively, roughly $100 and $130 annually); they are somewhat more modest for the others. However, these are no doubt overestimates, since they assume full shifting to tenants and make no allowance for the loss in deductions under the federal-income tax;

TABLE 2

Median Rents in Central Cities (1960)

	Actual	*Under NJMG with Shifting*
Newark	$77	$69
Jersey City	71	60
Paterson	75	72
Clifton	84	89
Passaic	69	67

moreover, for the city poor, the change is exaggerated since their initial level of rent would typically be less than the median rent for the city as a whole.

What turned out to be at least as interesting and somewhat more surprising was an analysis of the redistributive effects of the introduction of NJMG among the suburban communities themselves. The variation among these municipalities is quite striking and, moreover, bears little relationship to levels of income. The effective tax rates within this sample vary all the way from 1.59 to 5.45 percent so that the introduction of a uniform metropolitan tax rate would in many instances generate large changes in local tax bills. To see by how much these changes would redistribute income from richer to poorer communities, we first simply regressed the change in the tax rate for each community (that is, 3.03 percent minus the actual 1960 rate in the community) against median family income (1959) and found

(15)
$$\Delta t = 0.05 + 0.07Y \qquad R^2 = 0.03$$
$$\quad (0.1) \quad (1.3)$$

where Δt = change in tax rate $(\overline{\Delta t} = 0.5)$

Y = median family income (in thousands of dollars, $\overline{Y} = \$8.3$)

N = 53 (number of observations)

and where the numbers in parentheses are the absolute values of the t-statistics for the respective coefficients.[36] We see that, although the sign of the income variable is positive as expected, it is not significantly different from zero. which is reflected in the equation's ability to explain only a minute fraction of the change in tax rates.

To pursue this matter a bit further. we also examined the relationship between the change in the size of the typical tax bill in each community and median family income. To facilitate this calculation. we simply assumed that the median-income family in each community lived in the median-valued. owner-occupied dwelling. The naive estimate of the change in the tax payment, T_i', for the typical resident in the ith community, therefore is

(16)
$$\Delta T_i' = (\Delta t_i)V_i$$

where V_i is the median value of an owner-occupied dwelling in municipality i.[37] Applying our correction factor to obtain $\Delta T_i = 0.67 \Delta T_i'$ and regressing the change in tax bill on median income we get

(17)
$$\Delta T = 58 + 15Y \qquad R^2 = 0.12$$
$$(1.1) \quad (2.6)$$

In equation (17) the income variable is statistically significant and suggests that. on average. an increase of \$1.000 in median family income is associated with a rise of about \$15 in property-tax payments. The relationship. however. is extremely weak. This is evident when we examine some of the communities in the sample. There were. for instance. seven communities in the group of fifty-three with median family incomes in excess of \$10.000. Of these seven "richest" communities. two had tax rates under the Current System of 3.01 and 3.02. respectively. and hence experienced virtually no change in tax rates and hence tax bills after our creation of the NJMG. A third community in this group experienced an increase in tax rate slightly less than the mean change for the sample as a whole. This means that. of the seven communities with the highest median family income. three would have had rises in their tax rates and two increases in their tax bills far less than the average for the sample as a whole.

In summary. the results of our tax experiment under the creation of NJMG suggest a redistribution of income in the short run away from property owners in the suburbs as a group to owners of property in the cities with some longer-run effects probably filtering down to renters in the city. In addition, the shift to the NJMG would generate a considerable redistribution of income among residents of the suburbs, ranging from changes in tax payments for a typical resident in each of our sample of municipalities from +$226 to −$226. And this does not allow for redistributive effects within communities. These redistributive effects among suburbs would seem at best to be only very weakly income related. It thus appears that, at least in the short run, the introduction of a metropolitan-wide tax on real property would redistribute income in nontrivial sums but in a rather haphazard way.

We turn now to our second set of experiments involving equalizing expenditures across the NJMA. We examine first spending on public schools. Our procedure here (similar to that earlier) is to assume that aggregate expenditures on public education are the same under the Current System and under NJMG. However, we postulate that, with the creation of NJMG, expenditure per pupil is equated in all school districts and shall examine the shifts in spending per pupil that such an equalization would imply.

If we take total current spending on public elementary and high-school education in NJMG in the school year 1959–1960 and divide by the weighted enrollment, we find that expenditure per student under NJMG would have been $413. Table 3 indicates actual expenditure per weighted pupil in 1959-1960 in the five central cities in the sample. We find that the introduction of NJMG would have generated some increase in educational spending in three cities. However, the changes would appear, on the whole, to be fairly modest. In the two largest cities, expenditure per pupil would have remained unchanged in Jersey City and would have risen by less than 10 percent in Newark. For our sample of suburbs as a whole, the mean value of expenditure per student was $418; there would thus have taken place, on average, only a very small shift in educational spending from the suburbs to the cities.

Once again the most striking effect is to be found in the redistribution of expenditures among the suburban municipalities. Expenditure per pupil within our sample varied from $295 to $547, which implies a change in spending per student ranging from +$118 (an

TABLE 3

Current Expenditure Per Weighted
Pupil (1959–1960)

Newark	$381
Jersey City	413
Paterson	377
Clifton	360
Passaic	414

increase of 40 percent) to -$134 (a reduction of about 25 percent). Aside from these extremes, an inspection of the results reveals tht there would be quite significant changes in spending on schools for a large number of communities within the sample. In contrast to our tax changes. these alterations in expenditure per pupil are strongly related to income. The regression equation (18) indicates that, for

$$(18) \qquad E = 174 + 22Y \qquad R^2 = 0.34$$
$$(4.9) \quad (5.1)$$

each increment of $1.000 to median family income. a "typical" community spends an additional $22 annually per pupil. Equalizing current spending per pupil in the NJMA would thus have tended to raise this figure in poorer municipalities and lower it in high-income jurisdictions.

Turning to spending for functions other than education. we find that it is by no means clear that consolidation would have worked in favor of the cities. One of the reasons that cities have higher tax rates than suburban communities is that they provide a wider range of public services. In an important study of the Milwaukee metropolitan area. H. Schmandt and G. Stephens found that larger jurisdictions in terms of population provided a far greater number of services in the public sector than did smaller jurisdictions.[38] It is frequently the case. for example. that smaller suburban communities leave the job of trash and garbage removal to private firms or that fire protection is provided by a volunteer fire department. In contrast. if metropolitan areas were unified fiscal districts. we should expect pressures to assure that services provided publicly in one part of the metropoltan area would generally be provided publicly elsewhere; in all likelihood, there would thus be more public services provided in the suburbs, part of the cost of which would fall on city residents. This would not necessarily be true for all services. It might still make sense, for example, to have a single publicly provided zoo in the central city that would serve the residents of all the metropolitan area. Nevertheless, we should expect some narrowing in the range of services provided publicly between cities and suburbs relative to that existing under the Current System.

Substantial city-suburb expenditure differentials for noneducational functions do in fact exist in the NJMA. Table 4 shows current municipal spending per capita on all functions other than schools and debt service for our five central cities in 1960. At least for the two largest central cities, current expenditure on nonschool functions greatly exceeds $52, which is the mean value of this variable for our sample of suburban municipalities. The difference, incidentally, is only in small part attributable to higher welfare payments in Newark and Jersey City. A far larger part of the differential reflects higher spending on such things as police, fire protection, and hospital services.[39] Among the suburbs themselves, we find that spending on these functions bears a small, but significant, positive relationship to income so that a leveling of spending across suburban municipalities would be, on average, modestly income equalizing. There would, however, be numerous exceptions to this.[40]

The overall picture that emerges from our study is that the replacement of the Current System in the NJMA by a Unified Jurisdiction in 1960 would have resulted in a fall in property-tax rates in the central cities and a rise in the average tax rate in the suburbs. However, we found wide variations in the changes among the suburbs and no strong indication that, on the whole, these changes would systematically benefit either the rich or the poor. On the expenditure side, equalizing current expenditure per pupil would have resulted in modest increases in spending in most cities but a more radical alteration among the suburbs, with expenditure per pupil typically rising in low-income communities and falling in higher-income municipalities. Spending on noneducational functions would, in contrast, have fallen significantly in the cities and risen somewhat

TABLE 4

Expenditure per Capita on Municipal Functions
Other than Schools and Debt Service (1960)

Newark	$110
Jersey City	128
Paterson	65
Clifton	50
Passaic	75

Source: *Twenty-Third Annual Report of the Division
of Local Government,* State of New Jersey, 1960.

in the suburbs, with the distribution of the increase among suburban communities varying inversely, in most cases, with income.

It is appropriate at this point to re-examine briefly our rather unrealistic assumption of unchanged spending and revenues with the introduction of a Unified Jurisdiction. In our judgment, aggregate spending on most functions would probably rise. It is difficult to believe, for example, that with existing commitments a large number of suburban communities would be able to make substantial cuts in their school budgets. Rather, we should expect to see a "leveling upward" in expenditure per pupil so that increases in spending would significantly outweigh reductions. This in fact appears to have taken place in Toronto. In a study of the effects of introducing a metropolitan government on educational spending, Gail Cook found that "Before federation (1951) there was no significant difference between the expenditures of the Toronto municipalities and the control municipalities.... After federation (1961) the Toronto municipalities expenditures on education were significantly higher than those of the control municipalities."[41] Similarly for noneducational functions, we should predict rising expenditures, in part as we have noted, because of the increase in the range of services provided publicly in the suburbs. This would mean higher tax rates and spending than envisioned in our experiments, but note that the pattern of relative changes between city and suburbs and among the suburbs themselves would still be essentially the same as described in the preceding analysis.

TABLE 5

Equalized Tax Rates for Central Cities (1970)

Newark	6.39%
Jersey City	6.40
Paterson	5.23
Clifton	2.38
Passaic	4.00

Source: Robinson V. Cahill, et al., Superior Court of New Jersey Law Division, Hudson County Docket No. L-18704-69 (Jan. 28, 1972), Appendix A.

The empirical study in this section has been based upon data for 1960. This raises the question of how the metropolitan finances have changed over the last decade. On the basis of the information we have been able to assemble, we find that the general picture is much the same as in 1960 except that some of the differentials we noted earlier seem to have increased in magnitude. Table 5, for example, indicates that effective property-tax rates in the central cities (with the exception of Clifton) have risen to extremely high levels. However, tax rates in suburban municipalities have also increased dramatically; the mean of the county averages of municipal tax rates for our eight counties had reached 3.67 percent by 1970.[42] This no doubt overstates somewhat the increase in suburban tax rates since the cities are included in these averages, but it is clear that rates in the suburbs have risen rapidly, perhaps proportionately almost as much as those in the cities. Even if this is true, however, the absolute gap between property-tax rates in the cities and those in the suburbs in NJMA has almost certainly widened substantially over the past decade. The institution of a NJMG would thus appear, on the tax side, to have a somewhat greater redistributive effect in favor of the cities than in 1960.

On the expenditure side, we find that spending on schools also increased rapidly over the decade. Table 6 shows the current expense per pupil for 1971-1972 for our five cities.[43] These figures compare with an unweighted average of current expenses per pupil in the eight counties of $1,084.[44] As in 1960, expenditure per pupil

TABLE 6

Current Expense Per Pupil (1971–1972)

Newark	$1121
Jersey City	897
Paterson	857
Clifton	961
Passaic	928

Source: Same as Table 5.

in the cities (with the notable exception of Newark) is somewhat below that for the suburban communities as a whole. A perusal of the data indicates, however, that, as in 1960, there are wide variations in school spending among suburban districts, with many districts spending considerably less per pupil than the cities.

Likewise, spending on (noneducational) municipal functions has increased greatly since 1960. Table 7 (as compared to Table 4) indicates that nonschool spending per capita more than doubled over the decade in our five central cities. However, expenditure per capita on these functions also more than doubled, on average, in our sample of suburban municipalities, rising from a mean value of $52 in 1960 to a mean of $134 in 1970.[45] Thus the relative levels of expenditure between the cities and suburbs remained roughly the same, although the absolute differential obviously increased substantially. There is again a wide variation in expenditure per capita among the suburbs, although no suburban community in the sample spent as much as either Newark or Jersey City.

TABLE 7

Expenditure per Capita on Municipal Functions (1970)

Newark	$279
Jersey City	292
Paterson	184
Clifton	146
Passaic	160

Source: *Third-Annual Report of the Division of Local Finance, 1970, State of New Jersey, September, 1971.*

84 *David F. Bradford and Wallace E. Oates*

V. SUMMARY AND CONCLUDING REMARKS

Our reading of the evidence suggests that suburban exploitation of central cities interpreted as the failure of suburbanites to bear their fair share of the costs of city services is typically of minor quantitative importance. What is of greater significance and interest for the distribution and levels of welfare among residents of metropolitan areas is the choice of governmental structure. The Current System of providing public services relies heavily on independent fiscal decisions by a multitude of small jurisdictions using the property tax as a primary source of revenues. Alternatively. we can envision a Unified System encompassing (at least) the entire metropolitan area with expenditure decisions being made on an area-wide basis to be financed by a property (or other form of) tax(es). where a single rate structure would apply to the entire jurisdiction.[46] We may distinguish two sets of issues: those having to do with the long-run equilibrium differences between the Current System and a unified metropolitan government. and those concerned with the transition from one system to the other.

In the long run we should expect a somewhat more egalitarian distribution of income under a unified fiscal structure than under the Current System. We are not. however. convinced that the difference would be very great unless the Unified System involved a basic shift away from property taxes to more progressive forms of taxation. or unless the secondary effects of reduced income segregation on individual productivity differences proved important.

On efficiency grounds there are arguments in favor of both alternatives. The Current System offers families a wider scope of choice in terms of combinations of private and public services. For education. our evidence suggests that this choice is widely exercised and highly valued. Arguing against the Current System (in addition to interjurisdictional externalities) is its excessive pressure toward the formation of wealth- or income-homogeneous communities. and correspondingly its excessive tendency for suburbanization of upper-income families. Just how different the two systems would look in this respect is difficult to predict. since there are "natural" forces favoring income segregation (genuine or perceived economies of agglo-meration) as well as the "artificial" fiscal forces. However, the central city would almost certainly have a significantly higher proportion of wealthy families under a Unified System. Empirical evidence on the social value of this difference is badly needed.

Turning to the transition from the Current System to a plausible sort of Unified System, we found, for our sample of New Jersey cities and suburban communities, that this would redistribute wealth in some unexpected and rather haphazard ways. On the tax side, the effect of shifting to an area-wide real property tax would redistribute wealth principally among landlords with the effects on others, via changes in the supply of housing and other structures, being difficult to predict and occurring only after the rather long lags involved in such supply changes. We do not know much about the wealth distribution of landlords in the central city, where a large proportion of families are renters. In the suburbs we know a little about landlord wealth, since we know median family income and the median value of owner-occupied homes in each community. Within the suburbs there would be substantial redistribution, but the change in tax bills would be only weakly and nonprogressively related to income. Since, in addition, there is presumably nontrivial income variation within suburban communities, the redistribution may be even more erratic than our estimates suggest.

On the expenditure side, in the case of a shift to a uniform level of expenditure per pupil in public schools, the redistribution would tend more clearly to be from rich to poor, although hardly at all from suburb to city residents. Shifting to a uniform expenditure per capita on noneducational functions would be slightly redistributive from rich to poor in the suburbs. It is most unlikely that equalization would be carried this far between city and suburb, but to the extent it was carried, and to the extent that unification meant the extension of central-city services to the suburbs, this equalization would work very much to the disadvantage of central-city residents.

It is rather difficult to draw any sweeping conclusions from all this. The picture is cloudy, and its features as presently discernible do not point to a clearly superior governmental structure for urban

86   *David F. Bradford and Wallace E. Oates*

areas. Of course we cannot expect empirical evidence alone to dictate the choice, but it is obvious that more and better quantitative studies of the sorts of phenomena discussed in this paper would be extremely valuable.

NOTES

[1] In his comprehensive study of the redistributive effects of governmental budgets, W. Irwin Gillespie found that, in the United States for 1960, state-local budgets were redistributive in favor of families with incomes under $5,000. See his "Effect of Public Expenditures on the Distribution of Income," in R. A. Musgrave, ed., *Essays in Fiscal Federalism* (Washington, D.C.: Brookings Institution, 1965), pp. 164-66.

[2] Amos Hawley, "Metropolitan Population and Municipal Government Expenditures in Central Cities," *Journal of Social Issues* (1951), p. 107.

[3] Harvey Brazer, *City Expenditures in the Unites States* (New York: National Bureau of Economic Research, 1959); Julius Margolis, "Metropolitan Finance Problems: Territories, Functions, and Growth," in James Buchanan, ed., *Public Finances: Needs, Sources, and Utilization* (Princeton: Princeton University Press, 1961), pp. 229-93.

[4] William Neenan, "Suburban-Central City Exploitation Thesis: One City's Tale," *National Tax Journal* (June, 1970), p. 119.

[5] *Ibid.*, pp. 117-39.

[6] In one Detroit suburb, Grosse Point Park, Neenan in fact finds that the residents contribute more in revenues to Detroit than they impose on the city in terms of costs, but yet "exploit" the city because these payments fall short of their measured willingness-to-pay.

[7] We assume here that these are "income-compensated" demand curves, so they indicate the marginal valuation of each additional unit of output.

[8] It may be objected that linear compensated demand curves are too special a case to cast doubt on Neenan's weighting. Let us examine a more transparent example: the case of homothetic individual preferences defined over alternative bundles of a private good X and a public good G, which we represent by the utility function $U(X, G)$. Consider a particular bundle of the two goods: (X_0, G_0); this would generate a level of utility $U(X_0, G_0)$. We determine next an increment to the quantity of X, which would precisely compensate the individual for the loss of G_0. We would thus have

$$U(X_0 + \Delta X, 0) = U(X_0, G_0)$$

Let us define the total valuation of the public good, $V_g(X_0, G_0)$, as equal to ΔX. We can then write:

$$U[X_0 + V_g(X_0, G_0), 0] = U(X_0, G_0)$$

Homothetic preferences imply that, for positive t,

$$U[t(X_0 + V_g(X_0, G_0)), 0] = U(tX_0, tG_0)$$

from which it is clear that $V_g(tX,tG) = tV_g(X,G)$; total valuation is a linear homogeneous function. Thus, for this case total valuation is doubled by doubling the quantities of both the private and public goods. Doubling the quantity of the private good alone less than doubles the total valuation of the public good.

[9]James M. Buchanan, "Principles of Urban Fiscal Strategy," *Public Choice* (Fall, 1971), pp. 1-16.

[10]For an insightful overview of the characteristics of this system see Julius Margolis,"Metropolitan Finance Problems."

[11]Charles Tiebout, "A Pure Theory of Local Expenditures," *Journal of Political Economy* (October, 1956), pp. 416-24.

[12]Bruce W. Hamilton, "The Impact of Zoning and Property Taxes on Urban Structure and Housing Markets," Ph.D. dissertation, Princeton University, 1972.

[13]Edgar Hoover and Raymond Vernon, *Anatomy of a Metropolis* (Cambridge: Harvard University Press, 1959).

[14]W. Irwin Gillespie, "Effect of Public Expenditures."

[15]The redistribution toward the poor, incidentally, resulted from a "sharply 'pro-poor' expedenture schedule [which] outweighs a 'pro-rich' tax schedule," *ibid.*, p. 165.

[16]This seems a reasonable estimate. See Richard Muth, *Cities and Housing* (Chicago: University of Chicago Press, 1969), p. 69, and Frank deLeeuw, "The Demand for Housing: A Review of Cross-Section Evidence," *Review of Economics and Statistics* (February, 1971), pp. 1-10.

[17]For a detailed theoretical treatment of this issue, including a discussion of the measurement of such efficiency losses, see Wallace E. Oates, *Fiscal Federalism* (New York: Harcourt Brace Jovanovich, 1972), ch. 2.

[18]For a listing and description of the suburban communities in the sample and the sources of data, see Oates, "The Effects of Property Taxes and Local Public Spending on Property Values: An Empirical Study of Tax Capitalization and the Tiebout Hypothesis," *Journal of Political Economy* (November-December 1969), pp. 957-71

[19]To allow for the increased cost associated with education at higher grade levels, the figures used are expenditure per weighted pupil. For a description of the weighting scheme, see Oates, "The Effects of Property Taxes," p. 962. This procedure, incidentally, typically results in a figure for expenditure per pupil that is slightly less than that where no weighting is employed.

[20]We are ignoring at this point the important possibility of inter-jurisdictional external effects associated with local education, a matter to which we shall return later.

[21]We shall assume that this cost is borne by the residents of the community. With financing by a local property tax, this would imply either an absence of commercial-industrial property or that such property is owned by residents of the community. The bulk of the real property in most of the suburban communities in our sample is residential.

[22]We have not attempted here to be very thorough or rigorous in setting forth our conceptual structure. For a very careful investigation of sufficient conditions to assure the appropriateness of our approach, and for further empirical results, see the paper by Theodore Bergstrom and Robert Goodman, "Private Demands for Public Goods," *The American Economic Review* (June, 1973), pp. 280-96.

88   *David F. Bradford and Wallace E. Oates*

[23]These price and income elasticities are, incidentally, remarkably close to those used by Robin Barlow. Barlow used estimates of -0.34 and 0.64, respectively, which he took from a cross-section study of Detroit communities by Gensemer. The price variable in the Gensemer study, defined somewhat differently from ours, was the percentage of taxable property classified as nonindustrial. See Barlow, "Efficiency Aspects of Local School Finance," *Journal of Political Economy* (September-October 1970), pp. 1028-40.

[24]See, for example, Burton Weisbrod, *External Benefits of Public Education* (Princeton, N.J.: Industrial Relations Section, 1964). Even in the absence of external effects, local collective-decision procedures may result in subefficient levels of spending on education as suggested by Robin Barlow's study, "Efficiency Aspects of Local School Finance." Finally, from another viewpoint, some might object that this whole approach is inappropriate, since education is a kind of Musgrave "merit good."

[25]Richard Muth, *Cities and Housing*, pp. 317-18.

[26]*Ibid.*, p. 329.

[27]To the extent that the "tax-price" for public services among suburban communities with similar housing opportunities does vary, the differences are likely to become capitalized so as to equalize the attractiveness of the alternative communities of residence. Some empirical work seems to support this contention; see, for example, Oates, "The Effect of Property Taxes."

[28]David F. Bradford and Harry H. Kelejian, "An Econometric Model of the Flight to the Suburbs," *Journal of Political Economy* (May/June 1973), pp. 566-89.

[29]See Bradford, Malt, and Oates, "The Rising Cost of Local Public Services: Some Evidence and Reflections," *National Tax Journal* (June, 1969), 185-202.

[30]Fiscal consolidation, incidentally, does not necessarily imply the absence of local zoning authority. In some central cities, such as Baltimore, for example, particular sections of the city are empowered to enact regulations (e.g., minimum lot sizes) concerning land-use patterns within their districts.

[31]*A Preface to Urban Economics* (Baltimore: Johns Hopkins Press, 1965), p. 128.

[32]The data required for this calculation were taken from the *Annual Report of the Division of Taxation, 1960,* Department of the Treasury, State of New Jersey, p. 52.

[33]The great bulk of housing units among this group of communities was, incidentally, owner occupied. Also, to be a bit more precise, our estimated value of a "typical" suburban property is the mean value of the median values of owner-occupied dwellings in the 53 suburban municipalities rounded off to the nearest thousand; the actual mean was $19,200.

[34]Assuming complete capitalization of property taxes, the market value of a property yielding a gross annual rent of R (forever) is

$$V = \frac{R}{(i + t)}$$

where the notation is the same as in the text. The annual tax bill is, of course, tV. When the tax rate is increased to t^*, we took as our naive estimate of the increase in the tax bill ($\Delta T'$) simply

$$\Delta T' = (t^* - t) \, V = (t^* - t)\frac{R}{(i + t)}$$

If, however, we take account of the fall in the value of the property we have

$$\Delta T = t^* V^* - t V$$

where V^* is market value following the capitalization of the tax increase. We can express this as

$$\Delta T = t^* \left[\frac{R}{(i + t^*)} \right] - t \left[\frac{R}{(i + t)} \right]$$

$$= R \left[\frac{i(t^* - t)}{(i + t^*)(i + t)} \right]$$

We can convert the naive estimate. $\Delta T'$, into ΔT by simply multiplying the former by the correction factor $[i/(i + t^*)]$.

[35]These estimates were constructed by using (like Muth. *Cities and Housing*, p. 137), a gross-rent multiplier of 100. The rent was multiplied by 100 to obtain an estimate of the market value of the unit to which the change in the tax rate was applied to generate our naive estimate of the alteration in the tax bill. This was then multiplied by 0.67 to take account of the increase in property values generated by the decrease in the tax rate.

[36]There is, incidentally, substantial variation in median family income among this group of municipalities ranging from $5,900 to over $14,000.

[37]This is probably not too bad an assumption for our purposes. Most dwelling units in these communities are, as noted earlier, owner occupied. Moreover, the simple correlation coefficient between Y and V is in excess of 0.9, and, in regressions of V on Y, the addition of variables reflecting the distribution of income did not significantly affect the outcome.

[38]H. Schmandt and G. Stephens, "Measuring Municipal Output," *National Tax Journal* (December, 1960), pp. 369-375.

[39]Although some of this differential reflects a larger number of services provided in the cities, it may also result in part from the fact that a higher level of spending (or inputs) per capita may be necessary in the cities to obtain a given quality of output. In terms of our analytic framework, the E-vector in the city relative to that in the suburbs may require a larger input of directly produced services (the D-vector) in order, for example, to provide a given level of protection from criminal acts. As Norton Long observes about the cities, "The direct dollar cost of law enforcement is large, but not nearly so large as the cost of its failure to produce the product—security—which is its manifest function." See his "The City as Reservation." *The Public Interest* (Fall, 1971), p. 31.

[40]A regression of spending for noneducational functions on median family income in our sample of 53 suburban communities indicated that a rise of $1,000 in family income was associated, on average, with an increase of $3.40 per capita in expenditure.

[41]Gail Cook, "Effect of Metropolitan Government on Resource Allocation: The Case of Education in Toronto," Institute for the Quantitative Analysis of Social and Economic Policy, University of Toronto, Working Paper 7207 (April, 1972), p. 10.

90 *David F. Bradford and Wallace E. Oates*

[42]Robinson V. Cahill et al., Superior Court of New Jersey Law Division. Hudson County Docket No. L-18704-69 (Jan. 28, 1972), Appendix A.

[43]The figures in Table 6 are not based on weighted enrollments but are simply current expenditure divided by the total number of students in grades kindergarten through twelve in the public schools. This should not, we judge, affect the comparability of these figures within our set of jurisdictions very significantly.

[44]To be precise, this figure was derived by taking a simple average of the eight county averages of current expense per pupil. The source is the same as that for Tables 5 and 6.

[45]*Third-Annual Report of the Division of Local Finance, 1970,* State of New Jersey, September, 1971.

[46]We have in this paper limited the analysis essentially to two alternatives: extreme fragmentation or complete unification. Obviously, there is a myriad of other possible organizations of the public sector, and no doubt an optimal structure would involve differing size jurisdictions for providing various public services. However, at least for an initial exploration of the effects of governmental structure on resource allocation and the distribution of income, we think it has probably been more useful to see how much we can say about these polar cases.

[15]

The Use of Local Zoning Ordinances to Regulate Population Flows and the Quality of Local Services

WALLACE E. OATES

Department of Economics, Princeton University,
Princeton, N.J., U.S.A.

1. Introduction

The central argument of this paper is that the use of local zoning ordinances to control the entry both of people and business firms represent a primary policy instrument by which suburban communities in the United States regulate the quality of certain key local public services. The recent economic literature on zoning has placed a heavy emphasis on fiscal incentives: it contends that local exclusionary practices have aimed at preventing the entry of relatively low-income households (and/or large families) who do not "pay their way" in the sense that the public-service demands they make on local schools and other public facilities are greater than their relatively meager contribution to the local treasury.

While there is, no doubt, considerable truth to the fiscal view of zoning, I have come to believe that of at least equal importance is the role of zoning in the determination of the quality of local services. The basic point is simply that the level of local services depends not only on the inputs into the local public sector in the narrow budgetary sense, but also on the people and businesses that make up the community. In more technical terms, the production functions for local public services contain, as independent variables, both local government inputs of labor and capital and the characteristics of the local population and industry. In addition to zoning for purely fiscal reasons, it is thus my contention that local officials use exclusionary devices to control this latter set of "inputs" into the production function for local services. This I will call "public-goods zoning" to distinguish it from the more conventional treatments of "fiscal zoning" in the existing literature.[1]

When seen from this perspective, the critical role of local zoning regulations, and

---

[1] The term "public-goods zoning" was introduced in an earlier paper (Mills and Oates, 1975).

the jealousy with which they are guarded by local officials are not hard to understand. If, as I believe, there is a comparatively limited capacity to improve the quality of the most important local services through the public budget, then it is hardly surprising to find local communities turning to the other major policy instrument at their disposal.

In the first section of this paper, I will present a conceptual framework for understanding the interaction of population flows and local services in the urban public economy. This will develop the rationale for local zoning as a response to various real and pecuniary forces at work in the metropolitan system. In the second part, I turn to the estimation of production functions for two of the most critical local services: the quality of local schools and the level of public safety. In both cases, I will examine how measures of the *outputs* of these services depend on public-sector inputs and on other key "environmental" variables. The concluding section then explores the troublesome implications of the analysis, implications which pose a serious dilemma between the satisfaction of individual goals and certain democractic ideals.

2. Conceptual Framework

2.1. The Tiebout Model

Much of the recent economic analyses of the workings of the local public sector takes as its point of departure the model advanced some 20 years ago by Charles Tiebout (1956). The Tiebout model envisions a world of mobile consumers who "shop" among a large number of communities offering varying levels of public services and select, as a community of residence, a locality with a service level corresponding to their demands. The resulting solution closely parallels the market solution for private goods.

> Just as the consumer may be visualized as walking to a private market place to buy his goods, the prices of which are set, we place him in the position of walking to a community where the prices (taxes) of community services are set. Both trips take the consumer to market. There is no way in which the consumer can avoid revealing his preferences in a spatial economy. Spatial mobility provides the local public-goods counterpart to the private market's shopping trip. (p. 422)

Moreover, by "voting with their feet," consumers reveal their tastes for local services and promote an efficient allocation of resources within the public sector.

The model, however, is based on a number of heroic assumptions and some curious omissions. It is quite striking, for example, that a model which purports to describe individual location decisions in response to fiscal variables is wholly nonspatial in character and makes hardly any mention of local taxation! In addition, Tiebout's view of completely footloose and perfectly informed consumers (unconstrained by place of work or friends), who make a location decision solely on fiscal criteria, seems to verge on the absurd.

Nevertheless, when seen in a less extreme light, the Tiebout model points to some important tendencies inherent in the modern urban economy. Perfect, frictionless mobility, for example, may not be necessary for Tiebout forces to operate. Census data indicate that the average family does, in fact, move surprisingly frequently ; in the U.S., the 1970 Census showed that only about one-half of the families sampled were living in the same house as in 1965. The vast majority of these moves are certainly not motivated primarily by fiscal considerations; a change in job location or family status is far more likely to provide the stimulus. But once the individual (for whatever reason) undertakes the search for a new residence, he is likely to take into account the availability of local services; his choice of a community may then depend on such things as the quality of local schools and the level of public safety. Particularly in the modern metropolitan economy, an individual who works in the central city can typically choose among a large number of suburban residential communities offering a wide variety of levels of local services.

In spite of its rather unrealistic assumptions, the Tiebout model may still provide a tolerably accurate description of urban fiscal behavior. There is, in fact, a growing body of evidence that suggests this to be the case; these findings indicate that the quality of local services do exert an influence on individual location decisions.[2]

2.2. Income Segregation and Fiscal Zoning

For purposes of this study, I want to focus attention on one important facet of the Tiebout solution: the tendency toward the formation of communities that are relatively homogeneous in income.[3] The Tiebout model involves a "sorting out process" in which individuals with similar demands for local services locate together. Since we might generally expect the demand for local services to exhibit a positive income elasticity, this in itself should encourage a tendency toward segregation by income. However, there is a second inducement to income segregation implicit in the use of income-related taxes (such as property taxes) to finance local services. High-income residents in a particular community have a fiscal incentive to exclude those with lower incomes, since the latter will make only a relatively small contribution to the local treasury. We thus have both a taste element and a pecuniary incentive operating in the local public sector to produce a system of communities that are relatively homogeneous in income.

This "segregation solution" has some interesting implications. First, note how

---

[2] See, for example, Oates (1969).
[3] This discussion draws heavily on Bradford and Oates (1974).

it removes the potential for any income redistribution through local budgets. Even though communities employ income-related taxes (such as property or personal income taxes), no redistribution whatsoever occurs in the limiting case of perfect income segregation, since everyone in a particular community has the same income.

A second intriguing aspect of this outcome is its apparent instability. It will generally be in the interest of a relatively poor individual to locate in a high-income community, where at the existing tax rate he will get a partial free ride from the larger tax payments of his neighbors. We can thus envision a process in which wealthy households establish a community with high levels of public outputs only to find themselves "invaded" by lower-income families seeking the pecuniary advantages of the large tax base—a continuing game of hide-and-seek with no stable solution.[4]

How do we bring stability into this world? One answer is through zoning ordinances: higher-income communities may adopt exclusionary zoning regulations specifically to keep out poorer families (especially those with children). Such ordinances may typically require a minimum lot size and, perhaps, certain housing characteristics to ensure that only a wealthy family can afford to purchase or build a house. Zoning regulations thus constitute a policy instrument to achieve a stable composition of the local community.

Until recently there has been little formal economic analysis of zoning activities. In general, there seemed to be some presumption that the use of local property taxation generates certain inefficiencies or distortions in the local housing market (as well as in local decisions concerning public services), and that the introduction of zoning impediments to mobility among local jurisdictions probably makes things even worse. However, Hamilton (1975) has demonstrated that this need not be the case. In fact, the Hamilton model shows that a system of many communities, each using property taxation and zoning ordinances which specify a minimum value for local houses, effectively converts the property tax into a pure benefit tax and restores all the efficiency properties of the Tiebout solution.

Briefly, the Hamilton argument runs as follows. By requiring minimum purchases of housing services, communities can essentially confine entrants to the community to those who will generate at least as much incremental tax revenue as they do incremental costs in the public budget. Taking the ideal case, Hamilton assumes local governments can put a precise floor under the value of real estate owned, and hence the taxes paid, by any net additional members. Since those purchasing more than the minimum amount of housing pay more taxes than those at the floor, there is a pressure toward the formation of differentiated communities until, "in the limit," one observes a set of communities homogeneous in housing consumption. The remarkable attribute of this solution is that it converts the property tax into an

[4] For a formal analysis of the stability properties of the Tiebout model under different forms of local taxation, see Wheaton (1975).

ideal benefit tax. A family wishing to consume its desired level of housing. but more public services. moves to another community with the same zoning requirement but providing the higher service level. The increment in the family's tax bill will just equal the increment in costs imposed on the new community. Moreover. in this situation the tax on housing services is free of deadweight loss. Because of the diversity of housing–public service combinations available. it is possible for a family (by moving. it must be noted) to buy more housing without paying more tax. while continuing to receive a given bundle of public services. Furthermore. the outcome may be expected to be stable. There is no possibility for migrants to increase their public services without paying more in taxes. and no reason to expect shifts in majorities that will alter the bundle offered by a given community. since those with different preferences will have no incentive to enter in the first place.

The type of zoning visualized in the preceding discussion is a form of *fiscal* zoning: its objective is to prevent the entry of households who will not pay their "fair share" of the local budget. However. if we examine more closely the process of providing local services. we find that a second critical role for zoning ordinances is the determination of local service levels themselves.

2.3. Public-Goods Zoning

Implicit in the preceding analysis has been a relatively simple view of the provision of local services. Tiebout assumes that. for any given level of output. there is an optimal (least-cost per capita) community size. The idea is that. after some point. local services are subject to costs of congestion; yet further residents will. at this point. reduce the level of the service that is consumed jointly by all members of the community. The optimal-size community can be defined as that for which the cost of congestion imposed by the marginal resident is equal to his local tax bill.[5] At this point. he just offsets the costs he imposes on existing residents by the tax-savings he provides them. This will be the group size for which the specified level of output of the local service can be provided at the least cost per head. Tiebout thus sees zoning as a technique for achieving the optimal community size.

What this view overlooks is that the characteristics of the individuals of the community are themselves a critical determinant of the level of local services. Consider. for example. the provision of public safety. For a given input of police services through the public budget. the degree of safety on the streets will be higher the less prone are the members of the community to engage in criminal activity. Likewise. the more able and highly motivated are the pupils in a specified school facility. the higher will be their levels of achievement. This suggests a somewhat more complex

---

[5] This assumes a rising marginal cost of congestion. For a more formal treatment of this problem. see Buchanan (1965).

view of the provision of local services in which the members of the community are themselves inputs into the production function. Moreover, it suggests that zoning may be used to control both the size *and* composition of the local community.

This phenomenon can be better understood if we make a careful distinction between inputs and outputs of public services. For this purpose I draw upon a conceptual framework developed in an earlier paper (Bradford, Malt and Oates, 1969). There we differentiated between what we called "*D*-output," or services directly produced, and "*C*-output," the level (or quality) of public services actually consumed by individuals.

To be more systematic, let *I* be a vector of inputs in the production of public services. In the case of schools, for example, this vector might have as its elements the number of teachers, schoolrooms, and books. The vector *I* maps through a production function into a vector *D* of "directly produced" services. To return to education, *D* could consist of providing a given number of students with instruction of a specified kind (for example, a certain number of "standard" mathematics lessons). If we were concerned with protection from criminal acts, we might associate *D* with certain levels of surveillance, such as traffic control activity, resulting from an input *I* of men, cars, communications systems, and so on.

An individual, however, is presumably interested in the level of services consumed; he is interested in the quality of the schools his and other children attend and in the degree of protection from crime he actually receives. These are determined only in part by *D*. They depend also on a number of other variables that describe the "environment" in which the direct outputs are provided. A specified degree of surveillance, for example, will provide a higher level of protection from crime in an area where there are few prone to commit criminal acts than in an area where this "propensity" is much higher. Likewise, as we have learned from the Coleman Report and other studies, the education a student receives depends largely on a number of variables, such as the characteristics of his schoolmates, that have little to do with the vector of public inputs into the school system.

More formally, the argument is that we can express an individual's utility function in the form

$$U = U(C_1, C_2, \ldots, C_n, Z) \tag{1}$$

where Z is a vector representing the level of his private-goods consumption, and C_i is his level of consumption of the ith public service. In turn, we have

$$C_i = f_i(D_i, E) \tag{2}$$

which indicates that the level of public services consumed depends both on D_i, the level of directly produced services (a function of inputs), and on E, a vector indicating the environmental characteristics of the area in which the service is provided.

It is this vector E that is of central interest here. My contention is that among the most important elements of E are the characteristics of the people themselves. The most direct (and, I feel sure, the least expensive) way to consume high levels of certain local services is to assemble a community of families whose "propensities" are conducive to a high quality of local outputs.

Some admittedly rather casual empiricism suggests to me that the local services that matter most are: 1) the quality of local public schools; 2) the degree of public safety; and 3) the "aesthetic" character of the community. For each of these collectively consumed services, the input of the people themselves is of major importance.[6] Bright and highly motivated pupils mean good schools; law-abiding citizens result in safe streets; and a population of substantial means will typically provide an attractive environment.

There is, of course, no wholly reliable measure of whether or not a particular individual or family will, in fact, contribute positively or, alternatively, detract from the quality of local services. However, in the absence of detailed individual knowledge (and, perhaps, because the real reasons are neither legally nor socially acceptable), people fall back on socioeconomic characteristics as a rough guide. As Thompson (1965) has pointed out:

> More commonly, income segregation is socially based as families choose their neighbors by using income as an index of desirable personal and social characteristics, and housing value as the surrogate for the unknown income.

The thrust of the argument is that local public-goods zoning is an instrument for setting off a population whose individual characteristics reinforce one another in the provision of high-quality local services. And this typically means segregation by socioeconomic class. Note that public-goods zoning, although different in intent, can imply much the same sort of behavior as fiscal zoning; both can function to exclude households from lower socioeconomic groups, in the first case to maintain high-quality local services and in the second to prevent increased tax bills for existing residents. In the Appendix, I explore somewhat more systematically both of these incentives for local zoning ordinances.

3. Estimation of Production Functions

If this view of the urban public sector is basically a correct one, we would expect to find that levels of *outputs* of local services vary significantly and systematically

---

[6] The nature and extent of commercial-industrial property is also of significance, in particular for the aesthetic dimension of local services. I will not, however, treat the issue of business firms in this paper. For a provocative study of environmental quality and the fiscal benefits from increased local tax revenues, see Fischel (1975).

with the socioeconomic characteristics of the community. In this section. I will present some findings on this matter from the state of New Jersey for two key local services: public education and levels of public safety.

3.1. On the Determination of Educational Achievement

The first major source of empirical support for this view of education was the Coleman Report (1966). Analyzing a nationwide body of educational data. Coleman and his associates concluded that the socioeconomic characteristics of a pupil and his classmates were the predominant determinants of his educational achievement; school inputs were found to be inconsequential. However. subsequent studies showed the Coleman statistical analyses to be extremely crude and the conclusions, in some instances. quite suspect.[7]

Nevertheless. subsequent empirical work has certainly not called into question the fundamental importance of socioeconomic factors in the determination of scholastic achievement. One survey of the production-function literature (Averch, 1972) reports that: "The socioeconomic status of a student's family and community is consistently related to his educational outcome." The findings on school inputs are a good deal more ambiguous. Most studies report only modest effects, if any, of school resources on educational achievement. However, a few studies have found some sizeable effects. Hanushek (1972), for example, in a recent multiple-regression study of 471 elementary schools drawn from several states, discovered a positive and substantial relationship between both teachers' scores on a verbal test and their years of teaching experience, on the one hand, and their pupils' scores on verbal and math examinations, on the other. The use of other measures such as expenditure per pupil. pupil-teacher ratio, and library books per pupil has rarely produced results of any significance.

One recent and unpublished study. by Sosne (1975) at Princeton. of test scores in public schools in New Jersey has once again validated the importance of socio-economic variables. while finding virtually no significant association between the scores and any school-input variables. Sosne analyzed statistically the scores on two tests—reading and math achievement tests—that were administered to all New Jersey fourth graders in 1972 as part of the New Jersey Educational Assessment Program. Using a sample of 141 school districts. he regressed the mean test score for each district on several different sets of socioeconomic and school-input variables. As measures of school resources. he experimented with some 28 variables including everything from expenditures per pupil and pupil-teacher ratios to library books per pupil and mean teacher degree. In no instances was he able to find a systematic relationship between test scores and any of the measures of school inputs. On the

See. in particular. Bowles and Levin (1968) and Hanushek and Kain (1972).

TABLE 1
Regression Equations on School Achievement[*]

$R = 46 + 0.001Y + 0.002E$	$R^2 = 0.51$	(1)
$\quad\quad (6.7) \quad (0.6)$		
$M = 38 + 0.0007Y - 0.002E$	$R^2 = 0.36$	(2)
$\quad\quad (5.7) \quad (0.7)$		
$R = 54 + 0.001Y - 0.002E + 0.2D - 0.3T$	$R^2 = 0.51$	(3)
$\quad\quad (6.5) \quad (0.3) \quad (0.1) \quad (0.9)$		
$M = 42 + 0.0007Y - 0.004E + 0.1D - 0.1T$	$R^2 = 0.37$	(4)
$\quad\quad (5.8) \quad (0.9) \quad (0.0) \quad (0.6)$		

[*] The numbers in parentheses below the estimated coefficients are the absolute values of the t-statistic. The number of observations for all the equations is 141.

R mean score on reading achievement test (1972):

M mean score on math achievement test (1972):

Y median family income in thousands of dollars (1969):

E expenditure per pupil (1971-72):

D mean teacher degree (1972):

T pupil-teacher ratio (1972).

other hand, the basic socioeconomic variables showed a consistently high degree of explanatory power.

In Table 1, I present a few of Sosne's regression equations which are typical of his results. For both the mean reading (R) and math (M) scores. median family income (Y) in the district is highly significant, while none of the school-input variables (expenditure per pupil (E), mean teacher degree (D), and pupil-teacher ratio (T)) display much in the way of explanatory power. An additional $1,000 of median family income is associated, on average, with an increased score of one point on the reading achievement test, where the mean over the entire sample was 59.6.[8] In other equations Sosne employed, instead of median family income, a "social class index" incorporating information on both the levels and dispersion of family incomes in the district and on years of schooling among the adult population. This also was highly correlated with district test scores. In summary, the New Jersey school test scores exhibit a strong association with basic socioeconomic variables, but no systematic relationship with measures of school inputs.

3.2. Some Findings on Public Safety

The empirical literature on the determinants of crime rates is somewhat more sparse than that on educational attainment. but some does exist. Like the studies

[8] District mean scores on the reading test ranged from 37.4 to 71.5 correct answers per pupil with a mean of 59.6 and a standard deviation of 5.9.

of education, the findings tend to confirm the basic importance of the characteristics of the population in determining the frequency of acts of crime. In particular, two recent cross-sectional studies of urban crime rates in the United States (McPheters and Stronge, 1974; Pogue, 1975) report strong statistical associations between reported crime rates and the levels of certain "environmental" variables (including, for example, measures of affluence and the age composition of the population). They do not, however, agree on the importance of police inputs: one study finds no relationship whatsoever, while the other reports a significant effect of police expenditures on crime activity.

There are some serious problems in the use of *reported* crimes as a measure of the existing level of public safety. In particular, it is well established that reported figures do not bear a one-to-one relationship with actual crimes. However, several recent studies, which compare survey findings with official estimates of the incidence of crime, find high correlations between the two. Although official figures may embody serious reporting errors, such errors appear to be fairly systematic so that they may not invalidate comparisons of crime rates across cities. [9]

To supplement the findings on educational attainment in New Jersey schools, I want to present some preliminary statistical results on crime rates in New Jersey localities. My procedure was to take as a sample all the municipalities and cities with populations in excess of 10,000 (in 1970) in a single metropolitan complex in order to minimize variation from purely geographical differences. In particular, the sample consists of all such local jurisdictions in northeastern New Jersey within the New York Standard Consolidated Area; this definition produced a sample of 127 localities.

The dependent variable for the study is a crime index provided by the State of New Jersey. This index is essentially the sum of reported crimes of certain specified types divided by the population of the municipality. [10] It is thus a measure of criminal acts per capita.

Table 2 reports the results of regressing this crime index (C) on a set of socio-economic and police-input variables. The measure of resources devoted to police protection is police employment per capita (L). In equation (1), we find that crime levels exhibit a statistically significant relationship with median family income and the percentage of the population in the 18 to 24 years range; the higher the level of family income, the lower, on average, is the crime index. Although the coefficient of the police-employment variable has the expected negative sign, it is not significantly different from zero. Equation (2) indicates that, if we use as our proxy for socio-economic level the percentage of families with incomes below the poverty line (instead of median family income), the equation explains a substantially larger fraction of the variation in the dependent variable. The incidence of crimes is con-

---

[9] For an assessment of this issue, see Skogan (1974).

[10] See State of New Jersey, *Uniform Crime Report, 1973.*

TABLE 2

Regression Equations on Crime Levels*

$C = 3.778 - 0.2Y + 17.6A - 11.0L$ $R^2 = 0.23$ (OLS)		(1)
(3.4) (2.9) (3.2) (0.5) (OLS)		
$C = \ \ 998 + 295P + 12.0A - 21.2L$ $R^2 = 0.39$		(2)
(2.3) (6.6) (2.5) (1.0)		
$C = 4.158 - 0.2Y + 17.5A - 66.7L$ (TSLS)		(3)
(2.9) (2.7) (3.1) (0.5)		
$C = 1.493 + 373P + 12.0A - 297.6L$ (TSLS)		(4)
(2.1) (4.6) (1.6) (1.9)		

* The numbers in parentheses below the estimated coefficients are the absolute values of the t-statistic. The number of observations for all equations is 127

    C crime index for 1973:

    Y median family income in thousands of dollars (1969):

    A percentage of the population between ages 18 and 24 (1970):

    P percentage of families with incomes below the poverty line (1969):

    L police employees per capita (1973).

siderably higher in communities with a relatively large fraction of low-income families.

The results in equations (1) and (2) are. however. suspect. These equations were estimated by ordinary least squares (OLS). but it seems clear that the police-input variable is not exogenous. In particular. the level of police employment no doubt itself depends on levels of criminal activity: police activity is. in part. a response to levels of crime. This suggests that the estimates in equations (1) and (2) are probably subject to simultaneous-equation bias. To deal with this. I re-estimated (1) and (2) using two-stage least squares (TSLS).[11] The results appear in Table 2 as equations (3) and (4). The findings are essentially the same as with OLS with one important exception: in equation (4). the coefficient of the police-employment variable is now statistically significant using a one-tail test at the 0.5 level. We now have a basic ambiguity. If we use median family income as our measure of the socioeconomic level of the community. we cannot reject the null hypothesis of a zero coefficient on the police-input variable. In contrast. if we use instead the percentage of families below the poverty line. we can reject the null hypothesis at a 0.05 level of significance in favor of the alternative that more police personnel per capita result in a reduced

---

[11] To purge the endogenous variable (L) of its presumed correlation with the disturbance term. I used the following additional instrumental variables in the first stage: the crime index in 1972. population size. population density. the percentage change in population from 1960 to 1970. and the value of commercial and industrial property per capita.

incidence of crime. In both cases, however, the socioeconomic variables exhibit a significant association with the crime index.[12]

3.3. Some Reflections on the Statistical Results

The empirical findings presented in this paper are admittedly of a preliminary and somewhat crude character. Rather than some reduced-form regressions of levels of output, it would be far more desirable to work from fully specified structural models which describe the interactions among variables in the determination of levels of educational achievement and of crime. Nevertheless, tentative though they may be, the results for New Jersey point consistently to the systematic importance of basic socioeconomic variables as determinants of the quality of local services. In contrast, I have been unable to find much unambiguous evidence on the effects of budgetary inputs. I do not, incidentally, doubt that some such effects exist. Improved educational facilities and more comprehensive police surveillance surely have some impact on levels of services. However, the evidence seems to suggest that these effects are dwarfed in importance by the characteristics of the population itself.

Even if all this is true, it does not prove that local zoning ordinances have in fact been designed to regulate the quality of local services. Exclusionary zoning can be explained in purely fiscal terms: communities admit only the relatively affluent in order to generate a large tax base and keep tax rates low. It is interesting in this regard that some of the recent judicial decisions attacking local land-use regulations have chosen to ignore the issue of local zoning as a means to exclude certain "sorts" of people and have instead focused on the legality of exclusionary policies to reap fiscal benefits.[13] Since both types of motivation lead to much the same kind of zoning policy, it has proved unnecessary to go beyond the purely fiscal explanation. In short, there is a real problem of collinearity in distinguishing between the extent of fiscal and of public-goods zoning.[14]

---

[12] Another rather intriguing bit of evidence comes from a controlled experiment with police patrols in Kansas City. Over the one-year period October 1, 1972, to September 30, 1973, the Kansas City police divided a 35-mile area of the city into sections, some of which were provided with no patrol cars, others with one car, and the remaining with 4 to 5 patrol cars. At the end of the year of experimentation, analysts found virtually no changes in levels of reported crimes in any of the areas. This finding was further substantiated by extensive victimization surveys. In brief, the Kansas City police could find no relationship between crime levels and the number of police patrols. See the *New York Times*, November 11, 1973, Section I, page 5.

[13] See, for example, the potentially revolutionary Mount Laurel case in New Jersey. In this case, the State Supreme Court accepted the township's contention that its zoning ordinances were not intended to exclude prospective residents on the basis of "... believed social incompatibility." The Court instead declared Mount Laurel's *fiscal*-zoning practices unconstitutional on the grounds that they fail to take into account the regional needs of low- and moderate-income families.

[14] It would be useful to try to circumvent the collinearity problem by finding cases which clearly represent one form of zoning to the exclusion of the other. Such cases, however, are not easy to come by.

Nevertheless, the statistical evidence on levels of educational attainment and public safety does suggest a strong motivation for public-goods zoning. If the socio-economic characteristics of the population are primary determinants of the quality of local services, then there exists a real incentive to regulate admission to the community in order to promote a high level of local public outputs. There is, moreover, a considerable amount of more impressionistic evidence that points to a widespread use of public-goods zoning. One recent survey of suburban municipal leaders in New Jersey found that 66.4% cited "social and racial conflict" or "community hostility" as being the chief impact of low- and moderate-cost subsidized housing on the municipality, while only 21.3% identified fiscal problems as the chief impact.[15] There is, I feel sure, a good deal more to local zoning policies than just keeping down local tax rates.

4. Implications of the Analysis

In the concluding section, I want to explore briefly some of the policy implications of public-goods zoning. In particular, the view of zoning and of the provision of local services advanced in this paper has important consequences for the concern with equal access to public services. The court decisions, for example, on school finance in the United States have questioned the use of local property taxation to finance public schools, because variations in local tax bases appear to generate wide differences in expenditure per pupil, with resulting unequal educational opportunities. The thrust of some of these decisions has been toward the development of a system of school finance that will come closer to equalizing resources per pupil.

If, however, the perspective of this paper on the "production function" for these services is correct, the present approach to achieving equal service levels is likely to be largely futile. We may attain more equality in inputs, but this may have only modest effects on differentials in outputs. In fact, we are already accumulating evidence that suggests precisely this. One recent report from Hawaii, where the state pays all the school bills and where no community is allowed to levy additional taxes for schools, indicates marked differentials in achievement-test scores in mathematics and reading; these differentials indicate the same type of relationship to family background, etc., as they do elsewhere in the country.[16]

If our concern is truly with equal availability of public services (or even with

---

One example is building codes which seek to limit the number of bedrooms in such a way as to discourage the entry of families with schoolchildren. This is presumably a form of fiscal zoning designed to hold down the level of the local school budget.

[15] New Jersey County and Municipal Government Study Commission (1974).

[16] "Equal School Aid No Panacea in Hawaii," *New York Times*, Wednesday, July 30, 1975, p. 39.

equal *capacity* to attain specified service levels), it is becoming increasingly clear that equalizing the resource or tax base among local jurisdictions is not an adequate solution. The implication of the basic argument of this paper is that if, for example, we were to set out to equalize the "tax-price" of local public services (like school achievement and public safety) across all localities, we would have to vary the resources per capita inversely with the "level of productivity" for these services. Poorer jurisdictions would, in general, require more (potential) spending per pupil and larger law-enforcement budgets per capita than wealthier localities. Moreover, my conjecture is that the achievement of equality defined in terms of outputs (or equal choice among output levels) might well require enormous (and politically infeasible) differentials in inputs, at least for some services like perhaps education and public safety.

This last possibility suggests that continuing inequality in certain basic services may, for all practical purposes, be a necessary consequence of a system which relies heavily on local finance and permits a substantial degree of geographic segregation by socioeconomic class. If this be true, we would then seem to face a choice between the existing system with its basic reliance on decentralized choice (and an inherent inequality in services) and a more centralized public sector which would encourage a restructuring of locational patterns to ensure a much greater diversity among local populations.[17] The compromise, toward which we seem to be moving, is one in which a substantial emphasis on local choice remains, but where there are transfers of funds (in some instances of only modest sums) from wealthier to poorer jurisdictions through the intervention of higher levels of government. I find it difficult to conceive, however, that this "solution" (although it may represent the only attainable one in political terms) can ever result in anything like equalized levels of local services. What all this does imply is a basic conflict between certain fundamental democratic values: equality versus decentralized choice.

Acknowledgment

The author is grateful to Lester Chandler, Edwin Mills, and Harvey Rosen for their most helpful comments, to Linda Martin and Jeffrey Sosne for their excellent assistance, and to the Alfred P. Sloan Foundation for support.

Appendix

In this appendix, I want to examine more systematically the incentives for both fiscal and public-goods zoning in an analytical framework in which local communities

[17] This latter alternative is obviously an extremely complex one with basic political dimensions: we have seen already, for example, the response to one attempt to generate greater heterogeneity: school busing.

finance public outputs through income-related taxes, and in which population characteristics themselves enter the production function for local outputs.

To simplify the analysis, I will assume that all individuals possess identical utility functions:

$$U = U(C, Z) \tag{A1}$$

where C is the level of the local public good, and Z is the consumption of a single private good. Individuals differ, however, in level of income. In particular, there are two types of people: rich people with incomes Y_R, and poor persons with an income level of Y_P. Moreover, each individual's level of income is independent of his choice of C. (In a spatial setting, this amounts to assuming that income does not depend on residential location.) The individual seeks to maximize his utility (A1) subject to the budget constraint:

$$Y_R(\text{or } Y_P) = Z + T \tag{A2}$$

where T is his tax bill, and where the price of Z is set at unity. Note that T is not fixed: each person determines T by his choice of a local jurisdiction.

As in the Tiebout model, I will assume that each community provides a given level of output of the local public service which it finances through local taxation. The provision of local services, however, depends not only on inputs through the public budget, but on the characteristics of the population. In particular, I will simply postulate that, other things being equal, the level of output of the local service varies directly with the fraction of the population that consists of high-income individuals. The production function for the ith community is

$$C_i = C_i(I_i, R_i/N_i) \tag{A3}$$

where I_i is the level of direct inputs per capita for provision of the service, R_i is the number of high-income individuals residing in the ith local jurisdiction, and N_i is its total population. Note that (A3) implies that a community, in providing local services, must employ more inputs to maintain a prescribed service level if the fraction of high-income residents is reduced. Inputs and the proportion of high-income persons are substitutes in the production of the local public service.

The size of the public budget (B_i) is

$$B_i = N_i I_i p \tag{A4}$$

where p is the price of a unit of inputs (assumed to be the same for all localities). I will further assume that this budget is financed through a local income tax where the tax rate (t_i) must be

$$t_i = \frac{B_i}{\Sigma(Y_R R_i + Y_P P_i)} \tag{A5}$$

where P_i is the number of low-income persons in community i. This. incidentally, gives the following form to the individual's budget constraint:

$$Y_R \text{ (or } Y_P) = Z + t_i Y_R \text{ (or } Y_P) \qquad (A6)$$

The most important implication of this formulation of the local finance problem is the externalities inherent in the individual's choice of a community. When an additional person joins the local jurisdiction. he typically alters the utility levels of existing residents through two different channels: his direct impact on the service level and his influence on the tax base and rate. Consider. for example, a community with both high-income and low-income residents. The entrance of a new high-income resident brings with it two utility-enhancing effects for existing community members: for a given level of inputs per capita. the level of the local service rises. and the tax rate falls. Conversely, the arrival of new low-income individuals tends to depress the service level and raise the tax rate. Abstracting for the moment from problems of congestion. it would clearly be in the interest of the community to encourage the entry of high-income persons and to impede that of the poor.

These incentives are quite straightforward and obvious. It is of some interest. however, to enquire further as to likely equilibrium solutions in such a system. As a first case, suppose that there exists complete (costless) mobility for all individuals with no local zoning regulations *and* no problems of congestion.* It's hard to see how there could be an equilibrium under these circumstances. If a group of high-income individuals formed a community to provide high levels of service outputs at relatively low cost. there would be an immediate incentive for lower-income persons to enter the jurisdiction to enjoy both the higher "productivity" of local services and their lower tax-price. This case would seem to involve an endless game of hide-and-seek in which the rich seek to form new communities away from the poor only to find the latter in rapid pursuit.** (See Wheaton (1975) for a formal demonstration of this.)

If, however, there exist restrictions on community size, either of a rigid, fixed sort or through costs of congestion. the analysis alters substantially. As a second case. suppose that there are places in each community for only n persons. where n is significantly less than the total population of either rich or poor people. In this instance, it is possible to visualize an equilibrium solution involving total segregation

---

* There is. in one sense. already congestion of one sort in the model since the level of the public service. C_i, depends on inputs *per capita*; more people with no change in aggregate inputs means a lower I_i and. hence. C_i. By absence of congestion here. I mean that a larger population size does not reduce C_i for any given I_i.

** Even were we to envision a situation in which the fraction of rich people were the same in all communities. this would still not represent an equilibrium. for any high-income person could raise his utility level by locating elsewhere (even in one of the already existing communities. but preferably in a new locality).

by income maintained by differentials in land prices. Although a lower-income individual would prefer, other things being equal, to reside in a rich community, other things will no longer be equal. In particular, the higher demand for locations in wealthy communities will bid up the price of residences there. The wealthy can, in this case, maintain their income-homogeneous community through the high land-prices which will discourage entry by the poor. Note, however, that high-income individuals will, to some extent at least, pay for the fiscal advantages they enjoy in the form of high (explicit or implicit) rents, since the positive fiscal differential will tend to become capitalized into the value of local property.

In practice, the number of places in a local community is obviously not fixed; the size of the local population depends upon the intensity of land use. Although there may exist some costs of congestion, it is not, in general, possible for the wealthy to rely on "natural" barriers to entry to exclude the poor. Even where land values are relatively high, lower-income individuals may turn to high-density housing to economize on living costs, while realizing the benefits from the local public sector.

What all this implies is that higher-income people will have an incentive to seek out an explicit policy tool with which to exclude the poor. The most effective device would, of course, be the capacity to discriminate among potential entrants by income level. In the absence of such an "admission test," local zoning ordinances may provide a reasonably effective exclusion mechanism. In particular, since the demand for housing appears quite highly correlated with income (de Leeuw, 1971) the residents of a particular community may be able to approximate fairly closely the desired community composition by establishing a carefully designed set of regulations on the characteristics of local housing. In this way, they can have a community with a relatively large tax base on the one hand, and with a comparatively efficient provision of local services on the other. In brief, the result is both high-quality services and low tax rates for the wealthy.

Finally, it may be worth asking whether or not the "segregation" solution which emerges as the limiting outcome in the zoning model is Pareto-efficient. We noted in the text that both the Tiebout and the Hamilton models (the latter incorporates fiscal zoning) generate Pareto-efficient outcomes. However, my conjecture is that, for the model developed in this appendix, the solution may (but need not) be an efficient one. The answer depends, at least in part, on the production function for local services. Suppose, for example, that in equation (A3) the output of public services (for a given level of inputs, I) rises quite rapidly as the proportion of wealthy goes from zero to relatively small values, but then increases only very slightly for yet further increments to this fraction (that is, a few high-income persons make a big difference to the productivity of the local public sector but, after that, additional wealthy people make little difference). In this instance, it is quite conceivable that the Pareto-efficient solution would be one which spread the wealthy individuals around the various communities so as to enhance the productivity of local services.

This kind of solution, incidentally, would be quite unlikely in the model presented in this appendix, for it would seem to require some sort of side-payments by which low-income individuals could induce some wealthy individuals to reside in their community.* In contrast, if the production function were such that the productivity gains from a larger fraction of high-income residents increased rapidly at the margin with the size of this fraction, then the efficient solution might well involve complete income segregation. The introduction of the characteristics of the population into the production function for local services would thus appear to have some important implications for the efficient, as well as for the equilibrium, configuration of outputs and location.

References

AVERCH, H., ET. AL., *How Effective is Schooling? A Critical Review and Synthesis of Research Findings.* The Rand Corporation, Santa Monica, 1972.

BOWLES, S. and H. LEVIN, "The Determinant of Scholastic Achievement: An Appraisal of Some Recent Evidence." *The Journal of Human Resources* 8:3–24 (Winter 1968).

BRADFORD, D., R. MALT and W. OATES, "The Rising Cost of Local Public Services: Some Evidence and Reflections," *National Tax Journal* 22:185–202 (June 1969).

BRADFORD, D. and W. OATES, "Suburban Exploitation of Central Cities and Governmental Structure," in *Redistribution Through Public Choice* (H. HOCHMAN and G. PETERSON, eds.). New York, 1974, pp. 43–90.

BUCHANAN, J., "An Economic Theory of Clubs," *Economica* 32:1–14 (February 1965).

BUCHANAN, J., "Principles of Urban Fiscal Strategy," *Public Choice* 11:1–16 (Fall, 1971).

COLEMAN, J., et al., *Equality of Educational Opportunity.* Washington, 1966.

DE LEEUW, F., "The Demand for Housing: A Review of the Cross-Section Evidence." *Review of Economics and Statistics* 53:1–10 (February 1971).

FISCHEL, W., "Fiscal and Environmental Considerations in the Location of Firms in Suburban Communities," in *Fiscal Zoning and Land Use Controls* (E. MILLS and W. OATES, eds.). Lexington, Mass., 1975, pp. 119–174.

HAMILTON, B., "Zoning and Property Taxation in a System of Local Governments," *Urban Studies* 12:205–211 (June 1975).

HANUSHEK, E., *Education and Race: An Analysis of the Educational Production Process.* Lexington, Mass., 1972.

HANUSHEK, E. and J. KAIN, "On the Value of Equality of Educational Opportunity," in *On Equality of Educational Opportunity* (F. MOSTELLER and D. MOYNIHAN, eds.). New York, 1972, pp. 116–145.

MCPHETERS, L. and W. STRONGE, "Law Enforcement Expenditures and Urban Crime." *National Tax Journal* 27:633–644 (Dec. 1974).

* Buchanan (1971) has developed a similar argument for a reduced tax burden on the well-to-do to stop the exodus of the wealthy and middle-class from the center of cities.

MILLS, E., and W. OATES, eds., *Fiscal Zoning and Land Use Controls*. Lexington, Mass., 1975.

New Jersey County and Municipal Government Study Commission. *Housing and Suburbs: Fiscal and Social Impact of Multifamily Development*. Trenton, N.J., 1974.

OATES, W., "The Effects of Property Taxes and Local Public Spending on Property Values: An Empirical Study of Tax Capitalization and the Tiebout Hypothesis," *Journal of Political Economy* 77:957–971 (Nov.–Dec. 1969).

POGUE, T., "Effect of Police Expenditure on Crime Rates: Some Evidence," *Public Finance Quarterly* 3:14–44 (Jan. 1975).

SKOGAN, W., "The Validity of Official Crime Statistics: An Empirical Investigation," *Social Science Quarterly* 55:25–38 (June 1974).

SOSNE, J., *The Relationship of Expenditures and Performance in New Jersey Schools*. Princeton, N.J., 1975.

State of New Jersey, *Uniform Crime Reports. 1973*. Trenton, N.J., 1974.

TIEBOUT, C., "A Pure Theory of Local Expenditures," *Journal of Political Economy* 64: 416–424 (Oct. 1956).

THOMPSON, W., *A Preface to Urban Economics*. Baltimore, 1965.

WHEATON, W., "Consumer Mobility and Community Tax Bases: The Financing of Local Public Goods," *Journal of Public Economics* 4:377–384 (Nov. 1975).

[16]

On Local Finance and the Tiebout Model

By Wallace E. Oates*

Much of the recent research on the local public sector takes as its point of departure the Tiebout model of local finance in which individual households seek out a community of residence that provides a fiscal bundle closely approximating their demands for local services. A central theme of this literature is the efficiency-enhancing properties of the Tiebout solution. In the "pure" case, it is a straightforward matter to show that a system, in which mobile consumers "shop" among a large group of local jurisdictions that offer a sufficiently diverse set of local public goods at a "tax-price" equal to marginal cost, will generate a Pareto-efficient outcome. The result is, in fact, a close analog to the private-market solution, for, as Charles Tiebout pointed out, "Spatial mobility provides the local public-goods counterpart to the private market's shopping trip.... Just as the consumer may be visualized as walking to a private market place to buy his goods, the prices of which are set, we place him in the position of walking to a community where the prices (taxes) of community services are set" (p. 422).

The pure model, however, involves a set of assumptions so patently unrealistic as to verge on the outrageous. In particular, Tiebout assumed a world of footloose consumers, who move costlessly among local jurisdictions in response *solely* to fiscal considerations; the Tiebout household is unconstrained by travel costs to a location of employment or by any other nonfiscal ties to a given locality. Moreover, access to each local jurisdiction in the system must be available at a tax-price equal to the cost of servicing the marginal consumer.

While the model thus generates some appealing sorts of results, the demands it makes on the nature of consumer behavior and

institutional structure are formidable to say the least. The issue is whether or not the local sector in the real world is sufficiently "Tiebout-like" in its structure and operation to permit the use of the model for purposes of prediction *and* prescription.

This is a hard question. As the earlier quotation from Tiebout suggests, it is not too dissimilar from asking, "Is the private sector of the U.S. economy competitive?" As we know, there is not a simple answer to this query. For some analytical purposes (perhaps, for a broad view of the incidence of certain general forms of taxation) the answer may be yes; for others (as, for example, an antitrust investigation of a particular industry) the answer may well be no. Likewise, we are not likely to reach a definitive, general answer to the question of whether or not the local public sector is *sufficiently* Tiebout-like; the response will depend on the specific problem for which this query has relevance.

Nevertheless, there has been a considerable empirical (as well as theoretical) effort over the past fifteen years that explores the workings of the local sector from a Tiebout perspective. I wish in Section I to offer some brief observations on this work before proceeding in Section II to the issue of local production functions.

I

At the most basic level, we can simply look to see if, as a necessary condition for the operation of the Tiebout process, there exists enough diversity in the local sector to permit the kind of sorting out according to demands for local services that is envisioned in the model. Casual observation suggests an affirmative response, at least for most large metropolitan areas in the United States: a newly arriving household, for example, with a place of employment in the central city will typically have a wide range

*Bureau of Business and Economic Research, and department of economics, University of Maryland.

of suburban communities from which to select a residence. In a more systematic study of this issue, William Fischel presents a quite fragmented view of the typical suburban sector with a multitude of local jurisdictions exercizing both fiscal and zoning powers, and in which the concentration ratio (the land area encompassed by the four largest suburban governments) is relatively low. Enough competitors appear to exist for the process to work; however, as Dennis Epple and Allan Zelenitz (among others) have argued recently, sheer numbers, while constraining the choice of local officials, are not sufficient to ensure competitive outcomes in the local sector.

Another strand of empirical work involves a long series of capitalization studies that have examined the impact of local amenities and taxes on property values. Although the studies vary widely in choice and definition of variables (for example, output versus expenditure measures of amenities) and specific findings, the results on balance suggest strongly that fiscal differentials across neighboring jurisdictions tend to become capitalized into property values. The interpretation of this apparently straightforward result has turned out to be quite complex. On one issue, there is a consensus: capitalization of fiscal differentials is consistent with the view that consumers "shop" among local communities. People (not surprisingly) appear willing to pay more to live in jurisdictions that provide, in particular, such amenities as superior schools and greater safety from crime. The empirical literature thus provides some support for the operation of the "demand side" of the Tiebout model.

On the supply side, matters are less clear. Several authors (Bruce Hamilton, 1976b; Matthew Edel and Elliott Sclar; Epple, Zelenitz, and Michael Visscher) have pointed out that *full*-Tiebout equilibrium would imply an absence of any capitalization: with a perfectly elastic supply of local communities, the benefits from higher levels of amenities would be precisely offset by the associated increase in local tax bills. However, this "strong version" of the Tiebout model surely stretches reality. If we introduce some restrictions on the supply of communities (see Mark Pauly or Mahlon Straszheim) or certain forms of voting behavior on the part of residents (John Yinger), a "modified" Tiebout equilibrium will, in most instances, exhibit capitalization. Moreover, in these latter "weak versions" of the Tiebout model, the outcomes are no longer so clearly efficiency enhancing. In short, there appear no clear, unambiguous inferences to be made from the findings of capitalization of fiscal differentials as regards the efficient functioning of the local sector.

Exploring another implication of the Tiebout hypothesis in a recent and provocative study of several hundred towns in Pennsylvania, Howard Pack and Janet Pack have concluded that individuals within communities exhibit far too much variation in their demands for local services to be consistent with a Tiebout-like process. This is a tricky issue. First, Pack and Pack use income as a proxy for the (unobservable) demand for local services; income is, no doubt, positively correlated with demand but not perfectly so—even if demand were perfectly homogeneous in a town, we would expect to find a nonzero variation in household income. Second, and more fundamental, is the nature of the test. How much variation is too much to be consistent with a Tiebout world? The problem is that the null and alternative hypotheses are unclear. We might pose as the null hypothesis that the intracommunity variance in demand is at least as large as the variance in the metropolitan population as a whole; the Tiebout hypothesis would surely pass this test at a high level of confidence. This is admittedly a rather weak test, but at least one with a sound conceptual basis.

The efficiency properties of the Tiebout model also depend on marginal-cost pricing: the marginal resident must pay a fee equal to the cost of extending the local service to include his consumption. Tiebout assumed, in this regard, that the local service is subject to costs of congestion. Empirical demand studies (see, for example, Theodore Bergstrom and Robert Goodman) have tended to support this result: these studies find, in general, that they cannot reject the null hypothesis of a constant marginal cost for an additional consumer. While this is consistent with the Tiebout view, the mechanism of finance is more troublesome. Tiebout himself was not very explicit on this; he hardly mentions local taxation. However, most localities do not place a central reliance on user fees; they employ a variety of revenue sources, often relying heavily on property taxation. The introduction of property taxation links inextricably the issues of efficiency in local services *and* in housing markets. Hamilton (1975) has shown that the Tiebout model can be extended to a framework in which localities make use of property taxation *and* of a zoning ordinance that specifies a minimum level of housing consumption. While the Hamilton model generates a Pareto-efficient outcome, it makes even greater demands on reality than Tiebout: the Hamilton equilibrium entails communities that are homogeneous *both* in demands for local services and housing consumption.

Moreover, when we introduce further complications in terms of renters (who, many demand studies tell us, seem to believe that they pay lower taxes than owner-occupants), commercial-industrial property which assumes part of the local tax burden, and various intergovernmental grants, the precise link between the tax bill of the marginal consumer and the incremental cost of local services is broken. On this point, Pack and Pack cite a wide variation in housing values within communities, which they take as *prima facie* evidence that tax-prices vary substantially among residents; some of this variation may be offset through capitalization, but, if so, it comes at the expense of introducing inefficiencies into local housing markets (Hamilton, 1976a). In brief, it is unclear how closely the effective tax-price facing a potential resident reflects the marginal cost of local services.

II

While the Tiebout literature has at least addressed the issues examined in Section I, it has virtually ignored what I see as a central problem in local finance: the nature of the production function for local services. As noted earlier, Tiebout envisioned the provision of local services to be subject to costs of congestion; more specifically, he postulated a U-shaped cost curve with respect to community size, the low point of which served to define optimal community size. Most of the subsequent literature has simplified matters even further by taking the cost per person of a given level of local services to be constant with respect to community size; by assuming identical production functions across communities and with an appropriate selection of units, output in each jurisdiction becomes identical with expenditure per capita. While this procedure simplifies the analysis, it overlooks an issue with quite profound and troublesome implications for public policy.

My contention is that, for certain key local services such as education, public safety, and environmental quality, the production function contains as arguments not only the usual direct inputs of labor and capital, but also the characteristics of the individuals who comprise the community. For public safety, for example, a given input of police services will be associated with a higher degree of safety on the streets the less prone are the members of the community to engage in crime. Likewise, the more able and highly motivated are the pupils in a certain school, the higher will be levels of achievement.

Somewhat more formally (following David Bradford, R. A. Malt, and Oates), let I represent a vector of direct inputs into the production of local services. For schools, for example, this vector could have as elements the number (and quality) of teachers, schoolrooms, and books. The vector I maps into a vector D of "directly produced" services. For education, D might consist of providing a given number of students with a certain kind of instruction (for example, a specified series of "standard" mathematical lessons). In the case of public safety, we might associate these directly produced services with particular levels of surveillance.

However, what concerns the residents of the community is not the elements of D, but levels of final consumption: the quality of the schools in terms of student achievement, the degree of safety on the streets, and the physical attractiveness of neighborhoods. But these final outputs depend only in part on direct public inputs. For any given I vector, the quality of local schools will be better the more able are students; similarly, the level of public safety will be higher, *ceteris paribus*, the more law-abiding are residents.

In more formal terms, we can express the individual's utility function as $U = U(C_1, C_2,....,C_n, Z)$ where C_i is the level of consumption (final output) of the ith local service and Z is a composite private good. In turn, the production functions for the C_i are of the general form: $C_i = C_i(D_i, E)$ where D_i is the vector of directly produced services (a function of I) and E is a vector whose elements are the characteristics of the residents of the community.

My central concern here is with the role of the vector E in determining final outputs of local services. There is plenty of evidence of its importance. The Coleman report and subsequent empirical work attest to the overriding weight of the characteristics of pupils and their families in explaining levels of achievement in local schools. Likewise, population characteristics are typically the major explanatory variables in equations seeking to explain crime rates (see Oates). There is, I believe, little doubt over the moment of the elements of the E vector.

Moreover, this perspective on local production functions has two provocative policy implications. First, it points to an important role for local zoning ordinances as a means for regulating outputs of local services. The existing local-finance literature views the central function of zoning as basically that of excluding lower-income households that will not make a contribution to the local treasury commensurate with their share of budgetary costs. Exclusionary measures to this purpose constitute "fiscal zoning" (see Hamilton, 1975). The contention here is that local zoning regulations can also serve, if admittedly imperfectly, as a mechanism for controlling the composition of the local population so as to enhance the quality of

local services; this is "public-goods zoning." Moreover, it may well be the case that, for services like education and public safety, the variables comprising the E vector dwarf in importance the budgetary inputs of the I vector. There may be only a comparatively limited capacity to improve the quality of the most important local services through the public budget. From this perspective, it is not hard to understand the jealousy with which local officials regard their zoning prerogatives. Zoning may be the one policy instrument they have to exert some control over the more important variables determining final outputs of local services. While this view may raise some thorny issues of social justice with difficult, and perhaps uncertain, normative implications, I would suggest at the same time that it does possess some positive explanatory power.

The second implication of this formulation of local production functions concerns the efficiency properties of the Tiebout model (see the appendix to Oates). In particular, matters become a good deal more complicated. Note that, in this framework, residents of a community are *both* consumers of and inputs into the local services in their jurisdiction. *In consequence efficiency in consumption and in production become inseparable problems.* The sorts of issues that arise in this context are perhaps best suggested by a provocative example. The importance of peer-group effects in schooling are well documented. However, in an intriguing econometric study drawing on an unusually rich body of data, Vernon Henderson, Peter Mieszkowski, and Yvon Sauvageau found for their sample that the peer-group effect (as measured by the mean IQ of the class in which a particular student is placed) is not only extremely important in determining achievement, but is non-linear: "The achievement of individual students rises with an improvement in the average quality of their classroom situations, but the increment in achievement decreases with the level of average class quality" (pp. 97–98).

The implication of this result is that a mixing of weak and strong students will improve the performance of the overall student population. This will, however, run counter to the interests of the more able students. Note also that it suggests an outcome that can easily be at variance with the sorting out of households according to demands for local services. There may, in this instance, be real tradeoffs both between efficiency in consumption and in production and also among the well-being of different individuals. More generally, the problem is that the efficient consumption of local services will typically require, along Tiebout lines, relatively homogeneous populations within each jurisdiction, while efficiency in production *may*, as in our example, point to considerably more heterogeneity.

The explicit recognition that the quality of local services depends on community composition as well as budgetary inputs admittedly complicates significantly the theory of local finance. However, the issues here have important implications both for the efficiency and equity aspects of public policy. In particular, I don't see how we can truly come to terms with such major concerns as the reform of school finance to provide equal educational opportunity from a perspective that focuses on variations in expenditure per pupil.

III

Both the literature surveyed in Section I and my discussion of local production functions in Section II suggest that the local public sector exhibits certain "imperfections" when measured against a standard of perfect economic efficiency. While this raises certain troublesome *and* intriguing issues concerning the actual workings of the local sector, we should be careful not to overreact to all this and effectively "throw out the baby with the bathwater." The Tiebout model does, I believe, generate some important *descriptive* insights; I have noted earlier the evidence supporting the operation of the demand side of the model—people appear to consider fiscal variables in their selection of a jurisdiction of residence. Moreover, in spite of the various imperfections of the system, the existence of choice among communities offering varying outputs of local services surely has some im-

portant efficiency-enhancing properties. Individual households not only have some discretion over their consumption of these services, but the competitive aspects of the provision of local services encourage a certain responsiveness to consumer tastes and put some pressure on local officials to seek out reasonably cost-effective techniques of production. While competition among local jurisdictions may not completely eliminate the potential for self-serving behavior among local officials, it surely does limit significantly the scope for such behavior (see Epple and Zelenitz).

REFERENCES

T. **Bergstrom and R. Goodman,** "Private Demands for Public Goods," *Amer. Econ. Rev.,* June 1973, *63,* 280–96.

D. **Bradford, R. Malt, and W. Oates,** "The Rising Cost of Local Public Services: Some Evidence and Reflections," *Nat. Tax J.,* June 1969, *22,* 185–202.

M. **Edel and E. Sclar,** "Taxes, Spending, and Property Values: Supply Adjustment in a Tiebout-Oates Model," *J. Polit. Econ.,* Sept./Oct. 1974, *82,* 941–54.

D. **Epple and A. Zelenitz,** "Competition Among Jurisdictions and the Monopoly Power of Government," disc. paper no. 79/1, Tulane Univ. 1979.

_____, _____, **and M. Visscher,** "A Search for Testable Implications of the Tiebout Hypothesis," *J. Polit. Econ.,* June 1978, *86,* 405–25.

W. **Fischel,** "Is Local Government Structure in Large Urbanized Areas Monopolistic or Competitive?," unpublished paper, Mar. 1980.

B. **Hamilton,** "Zoning and Property Taxation in a System of Local Governments," *Urban Studies,* June 1975, *12,* 205–11.

_____, (1976a) "Capitalization of Intrajurisdictional Differences in Local Tax Prices," *Amer. Econ., Rev.,* Dec. 1976, *66,* 743–53.

_____, (1976b) "The Effects of Property Taxes and Local Public Spending on Property Values: A Theoretical Comment," *J. Polit. Econ.,* June 1976, *84,* 647–50.

V. Henderson, P. Mieszkowski, and Y. Sauvageau, "Peer Group Effects and Educational Production Functions," *J. Public Econ.*, Aug. 1978, *10*, 97–106.

W. Oates, "The Use of Local Zoning Ordinances to Regulate Population Flows and the Quality of Local Services," in Orley Ashenfelter and Wallace Oates, eds., *Essays in Labor Market Analysis*, New York 1977, 201–19.

H. Pack and J. Pack, "Metropolitan Fragmentation and Local Public Expenditures," *Nat. Tax J.*, Dec. 1978, *31*, 349–62.

M. Pauly, "A Model of Local Government Expenditure and Tax Capitalization," *J. Public Econ.*, Oct. 1976, *6*, 231–42.

M. Straszheim, "Extensions in the Theory of Capitalization of Local Public Goods and Tax Liabilities," unpublished paper, 1980.

C. Tiebout, "A Pure Theory of Local Expenditures," *J. Polit. Econ.*, Oct. 1956, *64*, 416–24.

J. Yinger, "Capitalization and the Theory of Local Public Finance," disc. paper D80–7, Kennedy School of Government, Harvard Univ., July 1980.

[17]

On the Measurement of Congestion in the Provision of Local Public Goods

WALLACE E. OATES*

Department of Economics and Bureau of Business and Economic Research, University of Maryland, College Park, Maryland 20742

Received January 16, 1986; revised August 5, 1986

This paper contends that a measurement problem (the "zoo effect") has led to upwardly biased estimates of the degree to which local public goods are subject to congestion. The suggestion is that the observed positive correlation between public expenditure and population size reflects in large measure the wider range of services provided in more populous jurisdictions—not simply a high propensity of these goods to become congested. © 1988 Academic Press, Inc.

Just over a decade ago, seminal papers by Borcherding and Deacon [3] and Bergstrom and Goodman [1] initiated a large econometric literature on the estimation of demand functions for local public goods. In addition to generating estimates of price and income elasticities of demand, the specifications used in this literature have produced an intriguing finding: a measure of the congestion or crowding characteristics of these goods.

The standard approach in these studies involves the estimation of a multiplicative demand function that contains as one of its arguments a variable for the size of population of the community. From the estimated coefficient for this variable and the estimated price elasticity, one can compute a "congestion parameter" that measures the extent of crowding associated with increasing the size of the group that consumes the good. More specifically, the relationship between consumption and population size in these studies takes the form $Z^* = ZN^{-\gamma}$, where Z indicates the number of units of the service provided in the locality, N is population size, Z^* is the level of the good consumed by an individual in the jurisdiction (i.e., the variable that enters his utility function), and γ is the congestion parameter. If Z were a pure public good, γ would take on a value of zero;

*This paper was written during a sabbatical leave at Resources for the Future. I am grateful to RFF and to the Sloan Foundation for their support of this work. I also thank Henry Aaron, Theodore Bergstrom, Jan Brueckner, Bruce Hamilton, Douglas Holtz-Eakin, Ray Kopp, Carolyn Lynch, Melville McMillan, Robert Schwab, Perry Shapiro, and an anonymous referee for some very helpful comments on an earlier draft of this paper.

progressively larger values for γ reflect a larger crowding effect with $\gamma = 1$ indicating "congestion" equivalent to that for a private good.

The econometric literature provides estimates of γ for a range of local public services. While these estimates exhibit some diversity, the thrust of the evidence suggests that most local public goods exhibit a high degree of congestion. Most studies find point estimates for γ in the range of unity or, in some instances, even higher. Typically, these estimates and their associated standard errors are such that one can reject the null hypothesis, H_0: $\gamma = 0$, but cannot reject H_0: $\gamma = 1$. The view that has emerged from this literature is, therefore, that local public goods are "quasi-private" goods.

This is a striking finding, for it suggests that the services provided in the local public sector do not have the usual publicness properties that we associate with collective goods. Moreover, it has given rise to a number of interesting and conflicting interpretations. For example, taking this result at face value, Bergstrom and Goodman [1] in their original paper ask "Why, if there are not increasing returns in the municipal provision of the goods and services which we study, is their provision in the public domain" (p. 293).[1] This finding has thus been used to question the allocation of functions to the public sector. Alternatively, Borcherding *et al.* [2] suggest that this result is indicative of bureaucratic forces to increase the size of the budget. They argue that bureaucratic power is likely to be positively correlated with population size so that the relationship between spending and population size can be explained through Niskanen-type behavior rather than the congestion properties of the goods themselves. As Niskanen [11] summarizes the matter.

> We are left with the somewhat ambiguous conclusion that the services supplied by state and local governments are either (1) public, but that the economies of collective supply are appropriated by monopoly governments and bureaus in the form of overspending and/or (2) private and divisible at the margin of the existing scale of government jurisdictions, in which case there is no obvious reason for governmental supply. In either case, the observed results do not appear consistent with the simple models of responsive governments and efficient production (p. 633).

---

[1] Bergstrom and Goodman [1] offer two possible answers to their own question. First, they conjecture that there may exist substantial scale economies for cities of smaller size than those that they consider in their study. Second, there may exist "social reasons" for the public provision of certain services. Following up on the first of these, McMillan *et al.* [8] estimated congestion parameters for a sample of relatively small jurisdictions consisting of municipalities with populations under 10,000. They found values for γ significantly below unity for the three local services that they study. However, an attempt to replicate their findings by Edwards [5] with another sample of small jurisdictions was not successful. Mueller [10] offers yet another explanation. He contends, quite correctly it seems to me, that certain services, although perhaps subject to crowding, need to be provided publicly because of their nonexclusion characteristics. It may not be possible, for example, to provide police services efficiently through private contracting between households and suppliers because of external effects.

There are, however, a number of problems with the procedure used in the literature to measure congestion in local public goods. For one, as Edwards [5] and McKinney [7] have pointed out, the posited congestion relationship discussed earlier is restrictive. As an examination of the requisite derivatives reveals, the form of the congestion relationship used in the literature implies decreasing marginal costs of congestion.[2] Edwards [5] has recently employed a less restrictive polynomial formulation of the congestion relationship that allows for either increasing or decreasing marginal congestion and finds that it (marginally) outperforms the standard specification. Moreover, his point estimates for the polynomial relationship imply a considerable degree of publicness for the local services he examines.

The point that I wish to make in this paper is a simpler and more straightforward one. I will suggest that the congestion finding emerging from this literature is the likely result of a measurement problem—the "zoo effect," as I call it. This effect imparts an upward (and, I suspect, quite substantial) bias to the estimator for the congestion parameter. Consequently, we cannot, I shall argue, take the existing econometric literature on demand functions for local public goods as persuasive evidence either of the "quasi-private" nature of these goods or of bureaucratic budget-maximizing behavior.

1. POPULATION SIZE AND THE RANGE OF LOCAL SERVICES

My point of departure is an intriguing paper published some 25 years ago by Schmandt and Stephens [12]. In that piece entitled "Measuring Municipal Output," the authors studied the provision of local services by measuring outputs, not in terms of levels of spending or inputs, but by the number of distinct "subfunctions" provided in the municipality. For example, they measured the level of police services, not by expenditures on police protection, but by the number of particular activities (e.g., foot and motorcycle patrol, criminal investigation, manual traffic control, etc.) available in the community. Police protection was, in this way, broken down into 65 subfunctions or activities. The number of subfunctions for all local services in their study totaled 550. The dependent variable in their study was simply the numerical total of these subfunctions provided in each municipality. Such a dependent variable is, of course, subject to an array of objections.

---

[2]With $Z^* = ZN^{-\gamma}$, we obtain:

$$(\partial Z^*/\partial N) = -\gamma ZN^{-(\gamma-1)} < 0, \quad \text{and} \quad (\partial^2 Z^*/\partial N^2) = \gamma(\gamma+1)ZN^{-(\gamma-2)} > 0$$

for positive values of γ.

But, for my purposes here, the Schmandt and Stephens study produced an illuminating insight. They found that the number of subfunctions provided in a municipality was positively and strongly correlated with the size of the population.[3]

This finding seems reasonable (Litvack and Oates [6]). The point can be made clearly in terms of a simple, hypothetical case. Suppose that the annual cost of a municipal zoo is $1 million. Suppose further that the willingness to pay of each individual for "zoo services" is $1 per annum. If local fiscal choices are made efficiently, we would expect to find jurisdictions with populations in excess of 1 million providing zoos, while jurisdictions with populations under 1 million would not deem it worthwhile to have a zoo. My example obviously involves enormous simplification: fixed zoo size, equal willingness to pay, the failure to consider costs of congestion, etc. But it makes the basic point. For many public goods (or "subfunctions"), there are important indivisibilities. The first "unit" of output for such goods may require a substantial expenditure such that it does not become desirable to provide the good until population reaches a certain critical size—the size for which the sum of the marginal rates of substitution equals (or exceeds) the cost of the first unit. We would thus expect, as Schmandt and Stephens [12] found, that more populous jurisdictions would provide a wider *range* of local public services.

The implication of this finding for the existing estimates of congestion should be clear. The suggestion is that the observed positive relationship between population size and expenditure on local public services (like police protection or parks and services) may be largely the result, not of crowding, but of the increased range of services provided in larger jurisdictions. Thus, existing estimates of congestion, by failing to recognize that the consumption bundle itself varies with population size, are likely to contain an upward bias. The nature of this bias is evident from a more systematic consideration of the "zoo effect."

2. UPWARDLY BIASED ESTIMATES OF CONGESTION

Let us consider a class of local activities that I call "Parks and Recreation" and that has two components:

(1) Local playgrounds (Z_1) that are provided by all jurisdictions, and

---

[3]As an anonymous referee pointed out to me, there may be "a recording problem when accounting for subfunctions performed in providing local services. Larger jurisdictions are more likely than small ones to have readily identifiable programs or specific budget allocations relating to such subfunctions. Following your police example, patrols, criminal investigation, and traffic control may be readily distinguishable in large municipalities while in small municipalities they may not all be accounted for separately even though local police actually perform these duties."

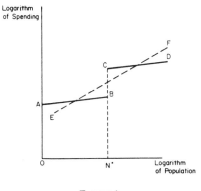

FIGURE 1

(2) zoos (Z_2) that are provided only by jurisdictions where population exceeds some critical level, N^*. We thus have:

$Z_1^* = Z_1 N^{-\gamma}$,   where $Z_1 > 0$ for all jurisdictions
$Z_2^* = Z_2 N^{-\gamma}$,   where $Z_2 = 0$ for jurisdictions with $N \leq N^*$, and
                $Z_2 > 0$ for jurisdictions with $N > N^*$.

I assume for simplicity that γ is the same for both goods. When econometric studies of local services are conducted, this distinction between Z_1 and Z_2 is not made; instead, such studies use aggregate expenditure data—that is, spending on the whole class of activities "Parks and Recreation."

The nature of the problem is apparent in Fig. 1. Ignoring the disturbance term, we would observe a relationship between the logarithms of expenditure and population size as depicted by the discontinuous curve ABCD. The slope of the segments *AB* and *CD* indicates the population elasticity of spending on each of the two local services; this I shall denote as α. There is a discontinuity at N^*, since jurisdictions with $N > N^*$ provide zoos as well as local playgrounds. However, if we ignore this distinction and simply estimate a log–linear relationship between spending on the whole class of activities and population size using the observed points along the two line segments, we obtain an estimated curve like the dotted line EF. Whereas the true population elasticity for the provision of each local service, α, is the slope of the line segments AB and CD, our estimated elasticity is the slope of EF—an upwardly biased estimate.[4] Since the congestion parameter, γ, is

---

[4] Theodore Bergstrom has pointed out that, if we do not impose a log–linear specification, a better approximation to the discontinuous relationship in Fig. 1 would be some kind of S-shaped curve for which the argument for an upwardly biased congestion parameter is not so clear. The existing literature, however, relies virtually exclusively on the log–linear specification.

a positive linear transformation of the population elasticity, α, it too is upwardly biased.[5]

The hypothetical case here is extreme. involving a single well-defined discontinuity in the expenditure function. In fact, each broad class of local services encompasses many components, more of which are provided as population size increases. We could embed the "zoo effect" in a more general framework by positing a continuous relationship of the form,

$$E = f(L, R),$$

where E is the level of expenditure in the community on a class of services, L is the level of individual services, and R is the range of services provided.[6] Since both L and R depend on population, we have

$$L = g(N) \quad \text{and} \quad R = h(N),$$

where $g'(N)$ and $h'(N)$ are both positive. Taking the total derivative, we obtain

$$dE/dN = (\partial E/\partial L)(dL/dN) + (\partial E/\partial R)(dR/dN),$$

where both terms on the right-hand side of the equation are positive. If we understand these variables to be measured in logarithmic terms, we have for

---

[5] More specifically, the functional form employed in the existing literature implies that

$$\gamma = \alpha/(\beta + 1),$$

where γ is the congestion parameter. α is the population elasticity of spending, and β is the price elasticity of demand. For $\beta > -1$ (which most studies find), γ is a positive linear function of α. There is a bit more to this matter. As Ray Kopp has pointed out to me. the zoo effect also biases the estimator for the price elasticity of demand. β. As tax price falls (as a result, say, of a larger commercial–industrial tax base), some of the expansion in spending is directed to new subfunctions; not all of it goes to existing activities. By assuming that all spending for a particular function is for a single activity, existing studies thus overestimate the price responsiveness of demand for individual subfunctions. This bias would appear to reinforce that of the population elasticity parameter on γ. the congestion parameter, as both tend to produce overestimates of γ.

[6] L relates to the level of inputs in the provision of local services; as such. it reflects the Z's in the consumption–population relationship discussed in the text. More precisely. L could be interpreted as a "representative" level of inputs for those services provided at a positive level. The partial relationship between E and L would thus indicate how expenditure varies with service levels with the range of services held constant.

the population elasticity of expenditure for the *level* of local services,

$$\alpha = (\partial E/\partial L)(dL/dN) = (dE/dN) - (\partial E/\partial R)(dR/dN),$$

where the last term embodies the zoo effect. But the specification and aggregation procedures used in the existing literature produce estimates, not of α, but of dE/dN. By ignoring the term reflecting the range of services provided (i.e., the zoo effect), these studies generate upwardly biased estimates of the population elasticity for the level of particular activities and, thus, for the congestion parameter.

3. SOME CONCLUDING REMARKS ON EMPIRICAL TESTING

I have tried in this paper to establish a *prima facie* case for the presence of an upward bias in existing estimates of the degree of congestion in local public goods. Testing for the presence of this bias and estimating its magnitude are needed to establish its empirical significance. These steps will not be easy. Although the empirical phase of this work goes beyond the scope of this paper, I wish to offer some thoughts on empirical approaches to these issues. Three general approaches suggest themselves. The first involves the use of independent evidence on the extent to which the range of services increases with population size for particular classes of local services. Suppose that we had reason to believe that certain classes of services (or functions) exhibited a marked variation in the range of services across communities of different size, while other classes of services showed little such variation. Then we might use as a crude test for the presence of the zoo effect a comparison of estimated congestion coefficients among these classes of services. If the zoo effect were important, we would expect to find that the estimated congestion coefficient would be larger for classes of services where the range of services displayed greater increases with population size. I call this a crude test, for among other things it would ignore the other sources of variation in the congestion characteristics of the various services. To implement this approach would require independent estimates of how the range of services varies with population, and I know of no ready sources of such evidence. Schmandt and Stephens [12] provide some information on this in the form of rank order correlation coefficients between the number of subfunctions and population size for several classes of local services. They found the highest rank order correlation coefficient between "subfunctions" and population size for police protection, followed by general government, fire protection, refuse disposal, and public schools in that order. For schools, for example, one might expect that there is somewhat less variation in the range of activities provided. But even for education, Schmandt and Stephens enumerated 74 distinct activities and found a positive and statistically significant association between the number of activities and the number of pupils in the school district. For all these reasons. I suspect that this first approach is not promising.[7]

The Schmandt and Stephens [12] study did, incidentally, provide one suggestive bit of evidence on scale effects. As I have noted, they found a strong positive correlation between the range of services and population size. But, in addition, they found a small negative, but statistically insignificant, correlation between population size and per capita local expenditure. This suggests that larger communities were able to consume a wider range of local services for the same level of expenditure per capita. These findings are thus consistent with the existence of some degree of publicness in local services. We cannot push this too hard, however, since there is no control for the quality of individual services. It is conceivable that while the range of services increases with population size, it comes at the expense of the quality of individual services.[8]

A second approach would involve the use of disaggregated expenditure data. In the extreme, suppose that we could obtain data on individual services so that there would be no aggregation issues to complicate matters. Then the estimated congestion coefficients would be uncontaminated by scale effects associated with a varying range of services. However, our ability to get such data seems doubtful. To return to the homely example in the paper, suppose that we had obtained separate expenditure data on local playgrounds and on zoos instead of aggregated data on "parks and recreation." We might feel that estimates of congestion based on these disaggregated data would provide more accurate measures of the congestion properties of these local services; at least they would not be biased by the fact that certain small communities did not provide zoos. While there is something to this, it remains true that even the subfunctions on which we might obtain data will still probably contain some "range effects." For example, zoos come in different sizes, and it may require a very large

---

[7] Douglas Holtz-Eakin has indicated to me that, using a panel data set from his dissertation, he has estimated congestion parameters for certain local services, first, using deviations from means across jurisdictions and, second, using deviations from means over time within jurisdictions. In the cross sectional analysis, he obtained estimates of roughly unity (like the existing literature), but for the time–series analysis, he found much lower values (in the 0.3–0.5 range) for the congestion parameter. His conjecture is that the range of services is likely to exhibit much greater variation across jurisdictions than over time within a jurisdiction. If this is true, then the higher parameter estimates from the cross sectional data may well reflect the zoo effect.

[8] Alternatively, an increased range of services may enhance quality. An anonymous referee has suggested that there may be important "complementarities" among local services so that as the range of services expands, productivity is increased for yet other services. In addition, larger jurisdictions may be able to acquire public officials with superior "credentials," again reflecting scale effects from spreading the costs over a large population.

population to make it worthwhile to acquire certain expensive animals (like pandas?). In fact, as this example suggests, it may not always be easy at the empirical level to distinguish between the level and range of services. Thus, while we might expect estimates of congestion based on more disaggregated data to be relatively less contaminated by the zoo effect (and thus smaller if the zoo effect is important), such results could probably be taken only as suggestive, for there would remain problems of interpretation.

A third approach, and perhaps the most appealing one, is to seek other measures of output that are not contaminated by the zoo effect. In an interesting application of this approach, Brueckner [4] uses communities' fire insurance ratings as a measure of output for municipal fire protection services. He finds that in contrast to the expenditure studies, his results indicate that fire protection exhibits a substantial degree of "publicness." Using a different approach, McMillan *et al.* [9] employed "fire protection rating" as a control variable in their regression equations explaining municipal expenditures on fire protection in a sample of Ontario municipalities; they found that the presence of this variable to control for the quality of output resulted in a reduced estimate of the congestion parameter. These results are suggestive, but the problem is that such measures of output are not easy to come by for other local services.[9]

In sum, empirical study of the congestion properties of local services is not going to be an easy matter. There are a number of effects that need to be disentangled, and the data required for this unravelling of effects does not appear to be readily available.[10] But until such work is done, we must maintain a healthy skepticism concerning existing estimates. I suspect that local services are a good deal more "public" in nature than these estimates indicate.[11]

[9] Bruce Hamilton has suggested an alternative approach involving the use of property values. If larger jurisdictions provide a wider range of outputs reflecting scale effects, then the benefits from these additional services ought to be capitalized into local property values. In a multiple-regression equation that explains differentials in property values across communities, we would then expect to find that, in addition to per capita spending on local services, the size of the community (perhaps interacting in some form with spending) should have a positive effect on property values.

[10] As noted earlier, the increase in local spending associated with larger communities may reflect not the technology of providing local services, but the enhanced bureaucratic powers in larger jurisdictions. To test this hypothesis would require the introduction of some measure of bureaucratic power that would effectively separate out the "bureaucratic effect" from the other roles of the population variable.

[11] This paper has focused solely on the implications of the zoo effect for the measurement of the congestion properties of local services. However, Henry Aaron points out that the zoo effect may well have some interesting normative implications for governmental structure. The spreading of costs over a larger population can provide an incentive for the unification of smaller jurisdictions into larger units. Such unification can be comprehensive or can take the form of "special districts" for the provision of those services for which such economies exist.

REFERENCES

1. T. C. Bergstrom and R. P. Goodman, Private demands for public goods, *Amer. Econom. Rev.*, **63**, 280–296 (1973).
2. T. E. Borcherding, W. C. Bush, and R. M. Spann, The effects on public spending of the divisibility of public outputs in consumption, bureaucratic power, and the size of the tax-sharing group, *in* "Budgets and Bureaucrats" (T. E. Borcherding, Ed.), Duke Univ. Press, Durham, NC (1977).
3. T. E. Borcherding and R. T. Deacon, The demand for the services of non-federal governments, *Amer. Econom. Rev.*, **62**, 891–901 (1972).
4. J. K. Brueckner, Congested public goods: The case of fire protection, *J. Public Econom.*, **15**, 45–58 (1981).
5. J. H. Y. Edwards, "Congestion Function Specification and the Publicness of Goods Provided by Local Governments," unpublished doctoral dissertation, University of Maryland (1985).
6. J. M. Litvack and W. E. Oates, Group size and the output of public goods: Theory and an application to state–local finance in the United States, *Public Finance*, **25**, 42–62 (1970).
7. S. McKinney, "The Membership Margin and the Median Voter," unpublished paper (1985).
8. M. L. McMillan, W. R. Wilson, and L. M. Arthur, The publicness of local public goods: Evidence from Ontario municipalities, *Canad. J. Econom.*, **14**, 596–608 (1981).
9. M. L. McMillan, W. R. Wilson, and L. M. Arthur, "A Note on the Publicness of Local Public Goods," unpublished paper (1980).
10. D. C. Mueller, "Public Choice," Cambridge Univ. Press, London/New York (1979).
11. W. A. Niskanen, Bureaucrats and Politicians, *J. Law Econom.*, **18**, 617–659 (1975).
12. H. J. Schmandt and G. R. Stephens, Measuring municipal output, *Natl. Tax J.*, **13**, 369–375 (1960).

[18]

ECONOMIC COMPETITION AMONG JURISDICTIONS: EFFICIENCY ENHANCING OR DISTORTION INDUCING?

Wallace E. OATES and Robert M. SCHWAB*

University of Maryland, College Park, MD 20742, USA

Received March 1987, revised version received February 1988

This paper explores the normative implications of competition among 'local' jurisdictions to attract new industry and income. Within a neoclassical framework, we examine how local officials set two policy variables, a tax (or subsidy) rate on mobile capital and a standard for local environmental quality, to induce more capital to enter the jurisdiction in order to raise wages. The analysis suggests that, for jurisdictions homogeneous in workers, local choices under simple-majority rule will be socially optimal; such jurisdictions select a zero tax rate on capital and set a standard for local environmental quality such that marginal willingness-to-pay equals the marginal social costs of a cleaner environment. However, in cases where jurisdictions are not homogeneous or where, for various reasons, they set a positive tax rate on capital, distortions arise not only in local fiscal decisions, but also in local environmental choices.

1. Introduction

The literature on local public finance contains two sharply contrasting themes. The first views interjurisdictional competition as a beneficent force that, similar to its role in the private sector, compels public agents to make efficient decisions. The cornerstone of this position is the famous Tiebout model (1956) in which individual households choose among jurisdictions in much the same way that they choose among sellers of private goods: an efficient provision of local public goods results from this process of 'voting with one's feet'. Likewise, in the more recent Leviathan literature that views government as a revenue-maximizing entity, competition among jurisdictions is seen as a powerful constraint on the undesirable expansionary tendencies of the public sector. Brennan and Buchanan (1980), for example, argue that

*Oates is also a member of the Bureau of Business and Economic Research, University of Maryland. Both authors were visiting scholars at Resources for the Future while much of this research was done. We are grateful to the National Science Foundation, the Sloan Foundation, and Resources for the Future for their support of this research. For helpful comments on an earlier draft, we thank William Baumol, Paul Courant, William Fischel, Marvin Frankel, Edward Gramlich, Bruce Hamilton, Robert Lee, Michael Luger, Therese McGuire, Peter Mieszkowski, Peter Murrell, Arvind Panigariya, Paul Portney, John Quigley, Daniel Rubinfeld, John Wilson, George Zodrow, the participants in the Sloan Workshop in Urban Public Economics at the University of Maryland and two anonymous referees.

0047-2727/88/$3.50 © 1988, Elsevier Science Publishers B.V. (North-Holland)

competition among governments in the context of the 'interjurisdictional mobility of persons in pursuit of "fiscal gains" can offer partial or possibly complete substitutes for explicit fiscal constraints on the taxing power' (p. 184). Competition, by these arguments, can serve its welfare-enhancing 'disciplinary' function in the public, as well as the private, sector.

However, a second body of literature contends that interjurisdictional competition is a source of distortion in public choices. The general theme here is that in their pursuit of new industry and jobs, state and local officials will hold down taxes and other sources of costs to households and particularly to business enterprise to such an extent that public outputs will be provided at suboptimal levels. There are several strands to this line of argument. One focuses on 'tax competition' and contends that incentives to attract business investment will keep tax rates below levels needed to finance efficient levels of public services [Oates (1972, pp. 142–143)]. As Break (1967) has put it,

> The trouble is that state and local governments have been engaged for some time in an increasingly active competition among themselves for new business.... In such an environment government officials do not lightly propose increases in their own tax rates that go much beyond those prevailing in nearby states or in any area with similar natural attractions for industry.... Active tax competition, in short, tends to produce either a generally low level of state-local tax effort or a state-local tax structure with strong regressive features. (pp. 23–24).

Such 'cut-throat competition', as the ACIR (1981, p. 10) observes, has given rise to proposals for federal intervention to 'save the states from themselves'.

Cumberland (1979, 1981) has developed a second strand of the competition argument; it is his contention that local setting of standards for environmental quality would be subject to 'destructive interregional competition'. In their eagerness to attract new business and create jobs, state and local authorities, Cumberland argues, are likely to compete with one another by relaxing standards for environmental quality so as to reduce costs for prospective business firms. Cumberland concludes that national (minimum) standards for environmental quality are needed to prevent the excessive degradation of the environment that would result from state or local standard setting.

The distortion arguments are not, however, fully convincing. If existing residents care about public outputs (including environmental quality), and presumably they do, then tax or standard competition to attract economic activity imposes real costs on the citizenry. It is not at all clear that such competition is likely to extend to levels that ultimately result in suboptimal public outputs. Stigler (1957), for example, has contended that 'Competition of communities offers not obstacles but opportunities to various communities to choose the type and scale of government functions they wish' (p. 216). Nevertheless, the possibility of 'destructive competition' surely seems plausible and, in consequence, makes observers (like Cumberland) justifiably reticent to vest responsibility for setting environmental standards at state or local levels.

Part of the difficulty is that there exists little systematic analysis of these distortionary forms of interjurisdictional competition from which we can reach normative conclusions about local policy decisions.[1] The discussion is typically informal, often times anecdotal, and does not establish any soundly grounded results. Consequently, one may be geniunely disturbed by the possibly detrimental effects of tax and standard competition, but have little sense as to their likely importance.

It is our purpose in this paper to develop a simple model of interjurisdictional competition that can provide some insights into the basic normative issue. Using a standard kind of neoclassical model of production in tandem with a median-voter procedure for making local public decisions, we construct a model in which individual communities select both a tax rate on capital and a level of local environmental quality. We begin with a basic model of homogeneous 'worker' jurisdictions in which we find that simple-majority rule generates socially optimal decisions as regards both the taxation of capital and the setting of environmental standards. We then extend the model in two different ways. We introduce first a positive tax rate on capital that can have its source either in various realistic constraints on the choice of tax instruments or in a Niskanen-type of local government behavior; here we find outcomes involving not only fiscal distortions but also excessive degradation of the local environment. The second extension entails the introduction of mixed communities with both wage-earners and non-wage-earners. In this setting, the interests of the two groups within the community diverge, and the median-voter outcome is no longer socially optimal (unless some rather unlikely sorts of cooperation take place).

As this Introduction suggests, one of the interesting features of the model is that it incorporates into the decision process two distinct sources of interjurisdictional competition: local taxation and the choice of environmental standards. As the analysis will show, the joint determination of these two policy variables within a community can involve some intriguing interrelationships between revenue and environmental considerations.

2. The basic model

In this section we set forth a simple model that we believe captures the

[1] There is some recent theoretical work on tax competition. See, in particular, Mintz and Tulkens (1986), Wilson (1985, 1986), and Zodrow and Mieszkowski (1983, 1986).

spirit of interjurisdictional competition. In the model, jurisdictions compete for a mobile stock of capital by lowering taxes and relaxing environmental standards that would otherwise deflect capital elsewhere. In return for an increased capital stock, residents receive higher incomes in the form of higher wages. The community must, however, weigh the benefits of higher wages against the cost of forgone tax revenues and lower environmental quality.

We envision with a large number (say n) of local jurisdications, where the jurisdictions are sufficiently large that:

(i) individuals live and work in the same jurisdiction, and

(ii) pollution generated in one jurisdiction does not spill-over into another.

Suppose that each of these n jurisdictions produces a private good, Q, that is sold in a national market. Production requires capital, K, labor, L, and polluting waste emissions, E, where we treat E as a non-purchased input. We posit further than the production function exhibits constant returns to scale and possesses all of the nice curvature properties of a standard neo-classical production function.

An important part of the model is the specification of local environmental policy and the way in which it impinges on local productive activity. We shall assume that the local government sets a standard for local environmental quality: it specifies, for example, that the concentration of pollutants in the environment shall not exceed some physical quantity. This standard then translates into a limitation on the aggregate level of waste emissions in the locality. The local environmental authority thus effectively determines $\sum E$ for the jurisdiction. We will assume further that this aggregate is allocated among firms according to some measure of their level of productive activity. More precisely, we posit that a firm's allowable emissions are directly proportional to its labor force. Environmental policy thus determines the emissions–labor ratio, α, in the jurisdiction.[2] If we define k to be the capital–labor ratio, we can write the production function for a particular jurisdiction as:[3]

$$Q = F(K, L, E)$$
$$= Lf(k, \alpha). \tag{1}$$

[2]There are obviously other ways in which one could specify the form of local environmental policy. The form we have chosen, in addition to seeming reasonable, facilitates the analysis. As will become evident, it allows us to capture the effects of environmental policy both on environmental quality and on the production of output in terms of a single parameter, α, that enters both the production and utility functions. It is not inconsistent, incidentally, for α to correspond both to a particular level of aggregate emissions and to a specific emissions–labor ratio, for (as we will note shortly) the labor input in a jurisdiction is taken to be fixed. Finally, we stress that none of the basic results of the paper changes if communities use certain other policy tools such as Pigouvian taxes on emissions rather than the command and control strategy we have assumed here. See Oates and Schwab (1987) for a discussion of this point.

[3]For notational simplicity, we shall not employ a superscript to denote a particular jurisdiction, although the functions are understood to be jurisdiction-specific.

While the production function exhibits constant returns to scale in all inputs, the nature of environmental policy allows firms to act as though there were constant returns to scale in just the purchased inputs, capital and labor. If a firm doubles its input of labor, it is allowed to double emissions; therefore, a doubling of capital and labor implies a doubling of all inputs and, hence, output. In equilibrium, we will then observe firms that are of finite (though indeterminate) size earning zero profits.

Throughout the paper we use subscripts to denote partial derivatives, and we therefore write the marginal products of capital, emissions, and labor as f_k, f_α, and $(f - kf_k - \alpha f_\alpha)$. We assume that marginal products are diminishing and that increases in α raise the marginal product of capital; f_{kk} and $f_{\alpha\alpha}$ are therefore negative and $f_{k\alpha}$ is positive.

We also assume that there is a fixed stock of capital in this society which is perfectly mobile (at least in the long run) across jurisdictions. This capital is distributed so as to maximize its earnings, which implies that the return to capital, net of any local taxes, will be equated across jurisdictions.[4] All of the communities are small in the sense that they treat this rate of return as a parameter. This is analogous to an assumption of perfect competition in product markets; just as perfectly competitive firms believe they have no influence on price and therefore behave as price-takers, these competitive communities take the rate of return on capital as given.[5] The community raises tax revenues by levying a tax of t dollars on each unit of capital; per capita tax revenue T is then tk.[6] Capital receives its marginal product f_k, and therefore given some rate of return r available in other jurisdictions, the local stock of capital will adjust so that

$$f_k - t = r. \tag{2}$$

Labor, in contrast, is perfectly immobile.[7] We assume initially that each

---

[4] We assume that the ownership of capital in this society has been determined exogenously. There is no requirement in the model that people necessarily own capital in their community; capital is traded in a national market.

[5] For a model more in the spirit of 'imperfect competition' in which there is explicit interaction between the policy decisions of two competing jurisdictions, see Mintz and Tulkens (1986).

[6] We can extend the model by introducing local public goods that provide services to capital such as roads and police and fire protection. Suppose that each unit of capital requires services which cost s dollars. If the tax rate on capital is t', then we can think of t as the difference between t' and s (i.e. as the tax on capital in excess of the cost of services consumed by capital). t, incidentally, can be negative in which case it would indicate a unit subsidy to capital.

[7] We assume labor to be immobile for two reasons. First (and most obvious), it greatly simplifies the analysis. And, second, it seems an appropriate assumption in view of the policy problem under study. More specifically, we are considering the decisions of a given population as they relate to the inflow and outflow of business investments that generate 'local' income. The analysis thus focuses on how existing residents view the effect of their collective choices on interjurisdictional movements of capital. However, as we have shown in Oates and Schwab (1987), all of the basic results in this paper emerge from a model in which labor is perfectly mobile and the size of each community is fixed. We thank Robert Lee for raising the mobility issue with us.

community consists of individuals identical in both tastes and productive capacity and whose pattern of residence across jurisdictions is 'historically determined'. Each individual puts in a fixed period of work (e.g. a 40-hour week). The labor market is perfectly competitive, and the real wage w equals the gains from hiring an additional worker. w is then the sum of (i) the marginal product of labor, and (ii) the additional output stemming from the increase in permitted emissions, αf_α; under constant returns to scale, w then equals $(f - kf_k)$.

Each of the identical residents receives utility from consumption c and from the local level of environmental quality. Since environmental quality depends on the local choice of α, we can write

$$u = u(c, \alpha), \tag{3}$$

where u is a quasi-concave function that is increasing in c, but decreasing in α (i.e. α is a 'bad', and therefore u_α is negative).

Each resident's income consists of an exogenous component y, wages w, and tax revenues T collected from capital.[8] The budget constraint for any representative individual then requires:

$$c = y + w + T$$

$$= y + (f - kf_k) + tk. \tag{4}$$

Note that an individual has two roles here. First, he is a consumer, seeking in the usual way to maximize utility over a bundle of goods and services that includes a local public good, environmental quality.[9] And, second, he supplies labor for productive purposes in return for his income. From the latter perspective, residents have a clear incentive to encourage the entry of more capital as a means to increasing their wages. But this jurisdiction must compete against other jurisdictions. To attract capital, the community must reduce taxes on capital (which lowers income and, therefore, indirectly lowers utility) and/or relax environmental standards (which lowers utility directly). These are the tradeoffs inherent in interjurisdictional competition.

---

[8] It is easiest to think of the tax revenues from capital simply being distributed on an equal per-capita basis to the residents of the community; this is how we shall treat these revenues. Alternatively (and equivalently), we could envision these revenues as being employed to finance outputs of various local public goods with a corresponding reduction in local tax payments by residents.

[9] For simplicity, we have not, at this juncture, incorporated into the model the rest of the public sector. Instead, we simply assume that, behind the scenes, the local government provides efficient quantities of the various local public goods which it finances through the imposition of lump-sum taxes. We return to this matter later.

2.1. The median-voter outcome

The interesting normative issue here is whether there is any systematic tendency for residents to choose other than optimal values for α and t. To address this issue, we must specify a collective-choice rule for the determination of these two policy parameters and then compare the outcome under this rule to the socially optimal outcome. For this purpose, we adopt in this section the widely used median-voter model as the mechanism for determining α and t. Since all individuals within a jurisdiction are in every respect identical, we can determine the median-voter outcome by maximizing the utility of any representative consumer.[10] Formally, the median-voter model requires the maximization of the utility function in eq. (3) subject to the budget constraint in (4) and the constraint on the rate of return in (2).

The first-order conditions for the solution to this problem are:

$$u_c = \lambda_1, \tag{5a}$$

$$u_\alpha = \lambda_1 f_\alpha - (\lambda_2 - \lambda_1 k) f_{k\alpha}, \tag{5b}$$

$$\lambda_1 t = (\lambda_1 k - \lambda_2) f_{kk}, \tag{5c}$$

$$\lambda_2 = \lambda_1 k, \tag{5d}$$

where λ_1 is the Lagrange multiplier associated with the budget constraint and λ_2 is the Lagrange multiplier associated with the constraint on the rate of return. From these conditions, we find that maximization requires:

$$t = 0, \tag{6a}$$

$$-u_\alpha/u_c = f_\alpha. \tag{6b}$$

Eq. (6a) indicates that the community should set the tax rate on capital exactly equal to zero. It should neither try to attract capital by offering a subsidy ($t < 0$), nor try to raise any revenue by taxing capital ($t > 0$).[11] Eq. (6b) says that the community should choose a combination of consumption and environmental standards such that its marginal rate of substitution between the two is equal to f_α, the 'marginal product of the environment'.

[10] With identical persons, we could just as well invoke a beneficent local official who chooses the parameters of public policy so as to maximize the welfare of the residents of the jurisdiction.

[11] If capital requires local public services (see footnote 6), then (6a) would indicate that the community should set a tax on capital which exactly covers the cost of those services. Where head taxes are available. Zodrow and Mieszkowski (1983) also find that a tax rate of zero on capital is optimal.

We offer the following interpretation of these results. The rate of return constraint implies that we can write the community's budget constraint:

$$c = y + (f - kf_k) + (f_k - r)k$$

$$= y + (f - rk). \tag{4'}$$

Wage and tax income are thus always equal to the surplus which remains after output has been sold and capital receives its market-determined rate of return. The community is much like a perfectly competitive firm that has a fixed quantity of labor but can vary its capital. Like such a firm, the community maximizes its net income by choosing a capital stock such that the marginal product of capital, f_k, equals its price, r. But if f_k equals r, then the tax rate, t, must be zero; the community thus takes all its surplus in the form of wages and none as tax revenues.

We can gain further insight into the setting of environmental policy as described in eq. (6b) by considering the impact of a small change in α on consumption. From the budget constraint, the change in consumption is the sum of the change in the wage and the change in tax revenues. We thus see that environmental policy has two distinct effects on consumption: a 'wage effect' and a 'fiscal effect'.

Consider first the wage effect. Differentiation of the wage equation shows that a tightening of environmental policy taking the form of a decrease in α of $d\alpha$ would reduce wages by $(f_\alpha - kf_{k\alpha}) d\alpha$ if the capital stock remained constant. This is the direct effect. Tightening environmental policy, however, must cause the capital stock to fall in order to maintain the rate of return r, and therefore the wage rate falls further. If the change in the capital stock is dk, then this additional change in w must be $-(kf_{kk}) dk$; total differentiation of eq. (2) shows that dk must equal $-(f_{k\alpha}/f_{kk}) d\alpha$, and therefore the indirect effect of tightening environmental standards is a fall in the wage of $kf_{k\alpha} d\alpha$. The sum of the indirect and direct effects of a decrease in α on the wage is thus $f_\alpha d\alpha$. This is the wage effect of environmental policy.

Now consider the fiscal effect. The change in tax revenue, dT, is $t\,dk$. From the discussion above, dk is $-(f_{k\alpha}/f_{kk}) d\alpha$, and therefore the fiscal effect of environmental policy must be $-t(f_{k\alpha}/f_{kk}) d\alpha$.

The total effect of a decrease in α on consumption is then:

$$dc = dw + dT$$

$$= f_\alpha d\alpha - t(f_{k\alpha}/f_{kk}) d\alpha. \tag{7}$$

However, if the tax rate has been set equal to zero, the fiscal effect vanishes; the change in consumption, in this case, is simply equal to the change in the wage, $f_\alpha\,d\alpha$. Maximizing behavior thus implies that the community will set α so that the change in wage income equals the marginal willingness-to-pay for environmental quality, $-u_\alpha/u_c$. But the change in wage income, as we see from (7) with $t=0$, is precisely equal to the increment in output associated with a marginal change in environmental policy. Since the wage effect equals the 'output effect' of a marginal change in α, we find in (6b) that local environmental decisions are such that the marginal willingness-to-pay for environmental quality equals the 'marginal product' of the environment.

It is important to stress that the determination of the environmental standard and the tax rate on capital are closely intertwined. In particular, if the tax rate (for whatever reason) is non-zero, then the marginal rate of substitution will no longer equal the marginal product of the environment, since in that case the fiscal effect will not vanish. We return to this issue in section 3 of the paper.

2.2. Efficiency in the basic model

We know that perfect competition among firms leads to efficiency; we wish to know if competition among communities also fosters efficiency. Efficiency requires that we maximize the utility of a representative consumer in one community subject to three constraints: (i) we allow a representative consumer in every other community to reach a specified level of utility (which may vary across communities), (ii) aggregate production in the society equals aggregate consumption, and (iii) we allocate society's stock of capital among the n communities. The necessary conditions for the solution to this problem require:

$$-u_\alpha^i/u_c^i = f_\alpha^i, \quad i = 1, 2, \dots, n, \tag{8a}$$

$$f_k^i = f_k^j, \quad i, j = 1, 2, \dots, n. \tag{8b}$$

where the superscripts refer to communities.

As we argued above, if eq. (8a) did not hold in some community, then it would be possible to change α and consumption in that community so as to increase welfare; if (8b) did not hold, it would be possible to increase aggregate output by moving capital from a community where the marginal product of capital is low to a community where it is high.[12]

It is clear that these conditions will be satisfied under the basic model we have described. The aggregate demand for capital at some rate of return r is the horizontal summation of the communities' demand curves. The market will clear at a rate of return r^* which equates aggregate demand and

---

[12] Note that since environmental quality is a non-traded good, it is not necessary that the marginal product of the environment or the marginal rate of substitution between consumption and the environment be equal across communities.

society's fixed stock of capital. We showed that all communities would set a tax rate of zero, and therefore the marginal product of capital in all communities will be r^*, satisfying (8b). We also showed that if each community maximizes the utility of a representative consumer, then it will equate the marginal rate of substitution between c and α and the slope of the consumption possibility curve, thereby satisfying (8a). In our basic model, competition among jurisdictions is thus conducive to efficient outcomes.

We can offer the following interpretation of these results. We showed above that the marginal private cost of improving environmental quality (measured in terms of forgone consumption) must be f_α, inasmuch as f_α is the change in the wage and there is no fiscal effect of environmental policy when the tax rate is set at its optimal level of zero. We also showed that the community maximizes utility by equating the marginal private cost of improving environmental quality and marginal private benefit. But clearly, f_α is also the marginal social cost of tightening standards, since f_α represents society's forgone consumption. Thus, utility-maximizing behavior promotes efficiency in this model because society's and the community's evaluation of the costs and benefits of environmental policy are identical.[13]

3. The interaction between tax and environmental policies

We showed above that if communities set the optimal tax on capital of zero, then competition would lead jurisdictions to establish efficient standards for environmental quality. As we discuss below, however, communities may choose to tax or subsidize capital for a variety of reasons. In this section of the paper we examine the choice of environmental policy when tax policy has not been set optimally.

3.1. Capital taxation as a 'second-best' tax

Communities may be forced to tax capital if they are unable to finance local public goods by imposing a non-distorting tax such as a head tax; fiscal constraints may thus result in the adoption of a levy on capital as a 'second-best' tax. Recently, Wilson (1986), Zodrow and Mieszkowski (1986), and Wildasin (1986) have shown that communities will underprovide local public goods if they must rely on a tax on capital. The argument is basically as follows. Communities realize that as they raise the tax rate to finance the

---

[13]Given our assumption that jurisdictions are sufficiently large that pollution created in one jurisdiction does not spill-over into another, there is no divergence between the marginal private benefit and marginal social benefit of reducing pollution. If there exist any interjurisdictional externalities occasioned by the transport of pollution from one community to another, then (for the usual sorts of reasons) local choice will not generate a socially optimal outcome. For an excellent general treatment of a variety of interjurisdictional externalities, see Gordon (1983).

local public good, they will drive out capital. Thus, they raise the tax rate only to the point at which the cost of the public good, including the negative effects of a smaller capital stock, equals the benefits. But as Wildasin (1986) explains, the social cost of local public goods is less than the private cost, since capital that leaves one community will be deflected to another. Thus, underprovision of local public goods arises, because communities fail to take into account the beneficial externalities they confer on other communities.

Our purpose in this section is to show that the taxation of capital also distorts the choice of environmental standards. One way to establish this point is to introduce a local public good explicitly into the median-voter model developed in section 2 of the paper; in the presence of such a good, tax revenues must be positive. We present such an expanded model in the appendix. But we can also make our basic point somewhat more simply.

Suppose the community has chosen some positive tax rate t. We might then ask what level of environmental policy α the community should choose in order to maximize $u(c, \alpha)$ subject to the rate of return constraint in (2) and the budget constraint in (4). The analog to eq. (6b) for this problem is

$$-u_\alpha/u_c = f_\alpha - t(f_{k\alpha}/f_{kk}). \tag{9}$$

It is clear in (9) that the social benefit from improving the environment, $-u_\alpha/u_c$, will exceed social cost, f_α, inasmuch as all of the terms on the right-hand side are positive except f_{kk}; therefore, environmental quality is set at an inefficiently low level. This contrasts with our earlier result where we found that social costs and benefits would be equal if the community chose the optimal tax rate of zero.

The interpretation is straightforward. From the discussion of eq. (7), it is clear that the first term on the right-hand side of (9) is the wage effect of environmental policy and that the second term is the fiscal effect. Thus, (9) shows that the community will continue to tighten environmental standards to the point that willingness to sacrifice the composite good equals the *sum* of lost wages and forgone tax revenues. The lost wages, as shown above, are equal to lost output (i.e. the wage effect equals the output effect); the forgone tax revenues (the fiscal effect) thus represent a wedge between the private and social cost of improving the environment.

3.2. An alternative model of public choice

We can get a result similar to that in the preceding section without actually constraining the community to tax capital. Instead, we can invoke the spirit of some of the recent public-choice literature which posits that government agencies have their own set of concerns in the political arena that typically are not in complete harmony with the interests of their constituents. One common hypothesis [with Niskanen (1977) as its source] is that bureaucrats seek to maximize their budgets. Salary, perquisites of office, reputation, power, and the capacity to award patronage typically rise as the agency's budget expands.

In the Niskanen spirit, we thus specify a government objective function, g, which has two arguments: revenues from the taxation of capital T (which are equal to tk) and the utility of a representative voter:

$$g = g[T, u(c, \alpha)], \tag{10}$$

where we would expect the partial derivatives of g with respect to T and u to be positive. We include the utility of voters since government, even if its central concern is to maximize its own welfare, cannot entirely ignore the well-being of its constituents. We thus envision a government which must balance its desire to realize the benefits of higher taxes today against the possibility that the voters will 'turn the rascals out' tomorrow.

It is not difficult to show that the maximization of this objective function subject to the community's budget constraint and the constraint on the rate of return on capital implies that government will set a positive tax rate on capital and that the marginal social benefit of further improving the environment will exceed marginal social cost, i.e. environmental quality will be set at an inefficiently low level. The intuition behind these results is straightforward. The Niskanen public agent derives utility from increased tax revenues. This provides an incentive to entice capital into the jurisdiction with lax environmental standards so as to increase the tax base. Thus environmental policy again has a fiscal effect as it provides a further means by which the bureaucrat can generate additional tax revenue, and this fiscal effect leads to excessive local pollution.

3.3. Efficiency under distorting taxes on capital

Our analysis of the interaction between tax and environmental policies suggests that it is important to pay close attention to the notion of efficiency. We argued above that if an omnipotent planner faced only the three constraints we described, then, as shown in (8a), this planner would choose an environmental standard for each community such that $-u^i_\alpha/u^i_c$ equals f^i_α. It is not true, however, that (8a) is the efficiency condition for the choice of an environmental standard in the presence of distorting local taxes on capital.[14]

To see this point, consider the special case where the society consists of

---

[14] We thank an anonymous referee for bringing this issue to our attention and working out its implications.

only two communities. Suppose we wish to maximize the utility of community 1 residents subject to the constraints that we allow community 2 residents to reach some given level of utility, that consumption equal production, and that we allocate society's fixed stock of capital between the two communities; a fourth constraint requires that there be a wedge between the marginal product of capital in the two communities of $(t^1 - t^2)$. The solution to this probem requires:

$$-u_\alpha^1/u_c^1 = f_\alpha^1 - (t^1 - t^2)[f_{k\alpha}^1/(f_{kk}^1 + \mu f_{kk}^2)], \qquad (11)$$

where μ is the ratio of the number of workers in the two communities, L^1/L^2.

Clearly, if $(t^1 - t^2)$ were zero, then (11) reduces to (8a). If this wedge is positive, however, then efficiency requires the marginal social benefit from reducing pollution in community 1, $-u_\alpha^1/u_c^1$, to exceed the marginal product of the environment in 1, f_z^1. The explanation is as follows. If the environmental standard in 1 were relxed, capital would flow from 2 to 1 in order to maintain the wedge between the marginal product of capital in the two communities. Aggregate output would rise by the product of the difference in marginal products and the flow of capital. Efficiency requires us to loosen the standard in 1 to the point that the marginal social loss from increased pollution equals the gain in output. Thus, communities that set high tax rates should set relatively lax environmental standards to offset the distortions introduced by fiscal policy.

4. Another extension of the basic model: Environmentalists vs. advocates of economic growth

While we believe that our simple model captures the spirit of interjurisdictional competition, there is an important intrajurisdictional dimension to such behavior that cannot be addressed in a model with a homogeneous population. In particular, several empirical studies stress that the 'environmental–jobs' tradeoff often involves an intense conflict of interest among different constituencies within the local community. There are frequently conservationist groups whose opposition to economic development and the associated environmental degradation runs directly counter to the interests of those whose employment and income depend on the entry of new industry. Deacon and Shapiro (1975), for example, in a study of voting behavior on a conservationist measure in California, found a significant propensity for 'laborers and construction craftsmen' to oppose the conservation act, reflecting presumably their preference for economic development and new jobs. Likewise, in a study of a pulp-mill referendum in New Hampshire, Fischel (1979) found systematic tendencies for 'laborers' to favor the mill and for 'professionals' to oppose it. This suggests that we extend the model to encompass individuals with different circumstances and interests, and observe how this affects local decisions on public outputs and taxes.

To put the results in the sharpest perspective, we return to our basic model and introduce one new element. We assume that the community now contains two types of people. The first type are, like before, wage-earners; for them, the presence of more capital implies a higher wage rate, and, hence, an increase in income. In contrast, the other subset consists of individuals who have no wage income. Members of this second group have an exogenous component of income supplemented by their share of revenues from the taxation of capital. There thus arises a potential conflict of interest between the two groups in the community: workers, L, have an incentive to encourage the influx of capital as a source of higher wage income, while non-wage-earners, N, without this incentive are likely to be more concerned with the environmental deterioration that can accompany an increased stock of capital. The two groups are unlikely to see eye-to-eye on the tradeoff between environmental quality and jobs. We shall characterize outcomes in such a divided community for two distinct cases: a worker majority and a non-worker majority.

4.1. Worker-majority outcome

Let us assume first that the group of workers constitutes the majority (i.e. $L > N$) and that, under median-voter rule, this group enforces its will on the community as a whole. Assuming (as before) that workers are homogeneous in every way, we need simply maximize the utility of a representative worker subject to the relevant constraints. On first inspection, this would seem to pose an identical problem to that in our initial model. However, this is not quite so; there is an important difference with significant implications for the outcome. In particular, the presence of non-wage-earners introduces an asymmetry affecting wage income, but not the division of tax revenues. Instead of eq. (4), the budget constraint for the representative worker becomes:

$$c = y^l + w + T$$

$$= y^l + f - kf_k + \theta tk, \tag{4''}$$

where $\theta = L/(N+L)$ and y^l is per-capita exogenous income for wage-earners. In the last term on the RHS of (4''), we now have the parameter θ, reflecting the (equal) division of tax revenues among non-wage-earners as well as workers. The presence of θ results in certain changes in the first-order conditions; in place of (5a) through (5d), we now find that

$$u_c^l = \lambda_1, \tag{5a'}$$

$$u_\alpha^l = -\lambda_1 f_\alpha - (\lambda_2 - \lambda_1 k) f_{k\alpha}, \tag{5b'}$$

$$\lambda_1 t = \frac{1}{\theta}(\lambda_1 k - \lambda_2) f_{kk}, \tag{5c'}$$

$$\lambda_2 = \lambda_1 \theta k, \tag{5d'}$$

with the parameter θ entering into (5c') and (5d').

By suitable rearrangement, we find that utility maximization of the subset of workers requires [instead of (6a) and (6b) as earlier] that

$$t = \left(\frac{1-\theta}{\theta}\right) k f_{kk}, \tag{6a'}$$

$$\frac{-u_\alpha^l}{u_c^l} = f_\alpha - \theta t \frac{f_{k\alpha}}{f_{kk}}. \tag{6b'}$$

In contrast to our earlier results, workers no longer desire a zero tax rate on capital; in fact, (6a') is unambiguously negative, indicating that the worker-determined outcome implies a subsidy to capital. The rationale for this result is clear. Workers reap all the gains from the increased wage income associated with a larger capital stock, but they no not bear the full cost of the subsidy to capital – some of the cost of the subsidy falls on non-wage-earners. Thus, a small change, dt, from zero in a negative direction yields an increase in wages (that although equal to the subsidy to capital) exceeds the part of the subsidy subscribed by the group of workers.

Similarly, we find a change in moving from (6b) to (6b'); workers, in a sense, now prefer a somewhat higher level of environmental quality as their marginal rate of substitution is now less than f_α. This result reflects the fiscal effect of environmental policy; since t is negative, workers must take into account their share of higher subsidy payments if they choose to increase α. Workers therefore find it in their interest to raise wages by subsidizing capital directly rather than by relaxing environmental standards.

4.2. Non-wage-earners in the majority

Our second case involving a majority of non-wage-earners (i.e. $N > L$) is more straightforward, since the tradeoff for these individuals is simply between environmental quality and revenues from the taxation of capital. Here we maximize the utility of a representative non-wage-earner subject to the relevant constraints – that is, we maximize (3) subject to (2) and the applicable budget constraint:

$$c = y^n + \theta t k, \tag{4'''}$$

where y^n is an exogenously-determined component of income. By suitable manipulation of the first-order conditions, we obtain:

$$t = -k f_{kk}, \tag{6a''}$$

$$\frac{-u_\alpha^n}{u_c^n} = \frac{-\theta t f_{k\alpha}}{f_{kk}}. \tag{6b''}$$

In contrast to (6a') for the workers, (6a'') is unambiguously positive: non-wage-earners desire a positive tax on capital. Eq. (6b'') embodies a pure 'fiscal effect' in the choice of environmental standards; it indicates that the MRS of non-wage-earners for environmental quality should be set equal to the marginal fiscal gains per capita from the taxation of capital. These two conditions, incidentally, imply a kind of Laffer-curve effect: if we hold α constant, we see that the derived tax rate on capital is such that the change in revenues from the tax is zero. To see this, let $T = \theta k t =$ per-capita revenues from the taxation of capital. Then,

$$dT = \theta(k dt + t dk). \tag{12}$$

From our return-on-capital constraint, $(f_k - t) = r$, we obtain $f_{kk} dk = dt$. Substituting this and (6a'') into eq. (12), we find that:

$$dT = \theta(k f_{kk} dk - k f_{kk} dk) = 0. \tag{13}$$

The results for our two special cases of worker-majority rule and a non-wage-earner majority make two basic points. First, the desired policies of the two groups clearly differ. Workers wish to subsidize capital in order to augment their wage income, while non-wage-earners, in contrast, want to tax capital as a source of revenues. Likewise, the two groups will prefer different levels of local environmental quality; there is some presumption that wage-earners will opt for a lower level of environmental quality (i.e. a higher value of α) than will non-wage-earners, although we have not been able to demonstrate this as a general result.[15]

[15] Eqs. (6a') and (6b') together imply that the wage-earner's marginal rate of substitution of consumption for environmental quality will be $(f_\alpha - k f_{k\alpha}) + \theta k f_{k\alpha}$; similarly, (6a'') and (6b'') imply that non-wage-earner's MRS will be $\theta k f_{k\alpha}$. $(f_\alpha - k f_{k\alpha})$ is the derivative of the wage rate with respect to α and is presumably positive. It does not seem possible, however, to determine whether the term common to both will take on a larger value in the wage-earner or non-wage-earner equation; we can establish that θ (by definition) is larger in the wage-earner case, but there seems to be no such general claim concerning the relative value of k and $f_{k\alpha}$. The terms that we can sign thus point to a higher MRS for wage-earners and suggest that wage-earners will choose a lower level of environmental quality. But this result is clearly not general; this would require a number of further assumptions regarding the preference functions and levels of relative income.

Second, it is evident that the outcome under a majority of either group is not socially optimal. The conditions for the maximization of social welfare are, as we saw earlier, satisfied by the median-voter outcome for a system of homogeneous jurisdictions of wage-earners. But if the jurisdictions are divided between workers and non-wage-earners, not only will there be a divergence of desired policies within each community, but the median-voter outcome will not, in either case, be an economically efficient one.[16]

In concluding this section, we would note that although we have framed the conflict of interests as involving environmentalists versus growth advocates, we have not assumed that there are any systematic differences in preferences between the two groups. One might, for example, postulate that certain groups possess utility functions that place a greater weight on environmental amenities than do those of others. However, it is not necessary to make such a distinction to provide a source for such conflicts of interest. In this section, the divergence of interests has its source solely in differing economic circumstances: the income of one group depends on the local stock of capital, while that of the other does not. The tension between the two groups thus represents a special case of a more general phenomenon under which one group attempts to use the fiscal system in order to 'exploit' the other. Workers attempt to saddle non-wage-earners with subsidies to capital that raises wages, while the latter group seeks to tax capital so as to enhance local revenues at the expense of wages. This model may, incidentally, have some explanatory power. As we have seen, the subsidization of capital makes little sense in our basic model with a homogeneous population. Yet we know that states and localities often engage in vigorous efforts to attract new business capital. Perhaps this is best understood as an effort of certain interest groups to further their ends at the expense of the remainder of the populace.

5. Summary and concluding remarks

To summarize our results, we present in table 1 the outcomes for our basic model of homogeneous jurisdictions of workers $[\theta = L/(L+N) = 1]$, for our

---

[16]The inefficiencies that characterize either outcome indicate that there are potential 'gains-from-trade' between the two groups in the setting of policy, since both of our majority-rule outcomes lie inside the utility-possibilities frontier. If there were some mechanism to reach a 'cooperative' solution, welfare gains would be possible. It is a straightforward matter to describe such a cooperative outcome by solving for the Pareto-efficiency conditions for the community as a whole. Such an exercise demonstrates that the cooperative solution involves zero taxation of capital and a Samuelsonian condition for the level of environmental quality. These conditions (like those for our basic model) satisfy the social optimality conditions for the system as a whole. It is not easy, however, to envision a mechanism to facilitate such cooperative action. There may in some instances exist other issues so that some kind of log-rolling maneuver may permit an approximation to the cooperative outcome. But, more generally, there do not seem to exist institutions to accommodate the necessary bargains.

Table 1

Summary of results.

Case	Tax rate	Marginal rate of substitution
$\theta = 1$	$t = 0$	$-\dfrac{u_z}{u_c} = f_z$
Tax-constrained	$t > 0$	$-\dfrac{u_z}{u_c} = f_z - t\dfrac{f_{kz}}{f_{kk}}$
Niskanen	$t > 0$	$-\dfrac{u_z}{u_c} = f_z + kf_{kz}\dfrac{g_T}{g_u u_c}$
$1/2 < \theta < 1$	$t = \left(\dfrac{1-\theta}{\theta}\right)kf_{kk} < 0$	$-\dfrac{u_z^l}{u_c^l} = f_z - t\theta\dfrac{f_{kz}}{f_{kk}}$
$0 < \theta < 1/2$	$t = -kf_{kk} > 0$	$-\dfrac{u_z^n}{u_c^n} = -t\theta\dfrac{f_{kz}}{f_{kk}}$

tax-constrained case, for our Niskanen model with revenue maximization, and for our two cases involving mixed jurisdictions. The homogeneous case generates a socially optimal outcome, while the remaining cases do not.

The results of the analysis are admittedly somewhat mixed, but they do have some interesting implications. For instances of relatively homogeneous communities where the benefits and costs of public programs are clearly understood and where public decisions reflect the well-being of the jurisdiction's residents, the analysis indicates that outcomes will tend to be roughly efficient. Such communities will tend to select both incentives for new industry and standards for local environmental quality that are socially optimal. In this regard Fischel (1975) demonstrated some years ago that, in a simple framework in which firms pay communities an entrance fee in compensation for environmental damage, a socially efficient allocation of firms and environmental quality results. Our basic model in a sense replicates Fischel's results, although the mechanism for compensation in our model – a higher wage – is somewhat different from the direct payment in the Fischel model. Nevertheless, it achieves the same result. In our basic model, interjurisdictional competition is efficiency-enhancing.

As we have seen, however, there are three distinct sources of potential distortion in local decision-making. First, if the jurisdiction does not have access to efficient tax instruments – if, as in our analysis, it is constrained to tax capital – then distortions occur in both fiscal and environmental decisions. More specifically, communities, because of the fiscal effects associated with environmental decisions, will opt for a socially excessive level of pollution. Second, if public decisions deviate from the will of the electorate (as in our Niskanen model), then efficient outcomes, not surprisingly, are not to be expected. In particular, we found that (as in the tax-constrained case) revenue-maximizing behavior will lead to excessive taxation of capital and suboptimal environmental quality in the jurisdiction. And third, conflicts of interest within a heterogeneous community can also introduce distortions into public decisions. Depending on which group gets the upper hand, such conflict can result in either the taxation or the subsidization of capital with consequent inefficiencies in decisions on environmental amenities.

In concluding the paper, there are two further issues that we wish to raise. The first concerns the meaning of the term 'local' in the analysis. We have used this term in a rather imprecise way to refer to units for decentralized decision-making. But the question arises as to the sorts of units to which the analysis would presumably be applicable. We can offer a few observations on this. It is clear that the units cannot typically be the smallest units of local government such as municipalities within a metropolitan area. As we noted earlier, the jurisdictions in our model are sufficiently large that residents live and work within their boundaries and that pollution generated in the area does not spill across these boundaries. This would suggest that the units suitable for decentralized choice under this framework would have to be at least as large as metropolitan areas and perhaps, in some instances, larger – state boundaries might, for certain pollutants and commuting patterns, provide the best approximation. At any rate our analysis clearly does not refer to the standard Tiebout kind of community where individuals may work in a jurisdiction other than that in which they reside. What is involved here are larger jurisdictions: metropolitan areas or perhaps even states or regions.

Second, our colleague Peter Murrell has raised a troublesome issue that we have not attempted to incorporate into the formal analysis: the well-being of future generations. Certain dimensions of environmental quality, if degraded by current generations, are not easily restored later. The development of wilderness areas and the creation of certain forms of long-lived, hazardous wastes come quickly to mind. The issue here is that the concern for future generations is, in one important sense, more difficult to incorporate in local policy decisions than at the national level. In particular, the well-being of one's own progeny is unlikely to depend in important ways on environmental decisions within one's present locality. An individual's children and their offspring will probably live elsewhere so that their 'environmental heritage' under a system of local decision-making will be determined by others. This may well result in a form of myopia under local standard-setting that leads to socially suboptimal levels of environmental quality for one's descendants. In principal, at least, more centralized decision-making should serve to 'internalize' these concerns and provide better representation of the interests of those yet to come. This is, however, a complicated matter. As William Fischel and Bruce Hamilton have pointed out to us, in a setting of mobile individuals, the phenomenon of capitalization would provide some protection for the interests of future generations. Decisions that lead to degradation of the local environment at some later date will be reflected in reduced current property values. Capitalization of future streams of benefits and costs can thus compel even myopic decision-makers to take cognizance of the future.

Appendix

In this appendix we explicitly incorporate a local public good into our median-voter model. Let z be per-capita consumption of the public good which the community purchases at a price p, and continue to let c be a composite private good which serves as the numeraire. Suppose, initially, that the community can finance the local public good with a combination of head taxes and taxes on capital. The first-order conditions for a welfare maximum in this problem require: (i) the community must set the tax rate on capital equal to zero and thus finance the public good entirely through the head tax; (ii) the marginal rate of substitution between α and c must equal f_α; and (iii) the marginal rate of substitution between z and c must equal p. The first two of these conditions are consistent with the discussion in section 2 of the paper; the third is not surprising.

Now suppose that we rule out the use of the head tax and require that the public good be financed entirely by taxing capital; this is, we require:

$$pz = tk. \tag{A.1}$$

The problem then becomes: maximize $u(c, z, \alpha)$ subject to the private budget constraint, the government budget constraint in (A.1), and the rate of return constraint in (2). Let γ_1, γ_2 and γ_3 be the Lagrange multipliers associated with these constraints. Then the first-order conditions for this problem require:

$$u_c = \gamma_1, \tag{A.2}$$

$$u_z = \gamma_2 p, \tag{A.3}$$

$$\gamma_2 t = -f_{kk}[\gamma_3 - \gamma_1 k], \tag{A.4}$$

$$\gamma_3 - \gamma_2 k = 0, \tag{A.5}$$

$$u_\alpha = -\gamma_1 f_\alpha - f_{k\alpha}[\gamma_3 - \gamma_1 k]. \tag{A.6}$$

Assuming the community chooses a positive level of z, t must be positive. Given that t is positive and f_{kk} is negative, (A.4) implies that $(\gamma_3 - \gamma_1 k)$ must be positive. If $(\gamma_3 - \gamma_1 k)$ is positive, then (A.5) requires that γ_2 must be greater than γ_1; (A.2) and (A.3) then imply that the marginal rate of substitution between the private good will exceed the price of the public good, i.e. the public good will be underprovided. This result is consistent with those in the Wilson (1986), Zodrow and Mieszkowski (1986), and Wildasin (1986) papers.

Combining the first-order conditions shows that the community will choose a level of environmental quality such that:

$$-u_a/u_c = f_a - t(f_{ka}/f_{kk})(u_z/u_c)/p. \tag{A.7}$$

The community's marginal willingness-to-pay for better environmental quality is greater than f_a, and therefore the community sets an inefficiently low environmental standard. As in the simpler model presented in the text, the source of the inefficiency is the fiscal effect of environmental policy, $-t(f_{ka}/f_{kk})$; the community relaxes standards in pursuit of greater tax revenues as well as higher wages.

References

Advisory Commission on Intergovernmental Relations, 1981, Regional growth: Interstate tax competition (ACIR, Washington, DC).

Break, George F., 1967, Intergovernmental fiscal relations in the United States (The Brookings Institution, Washington, DC).

Brennan, Geoffrey and James Buchanan, 1980, The power to tax: Analytical foundations of a fiscal constitution (Cambridge University Press, Cambridge and New York).

Cumberland, John H., 1979, Interregional pollution spillovers and consistency of environmental policy, in: H. Siebert, et al., eds., Regional environmental policy: The economic issues (New York University Press, New York) 255–281.

Cumberland, John H., 1981, Efficiency and equity in interregional environmental management, Review of Regional Studies, No. 2, 1–9.

Deacon, Robert and Perry Shapiro, 1975, Private preference for collective goods revealed through voting on referenda, American Economic Review 65, 943–955.

Fischel, William A., 1975, Fiscal and environmental considerations in the location of firms in suburban communities, in: E. Mills and W. Oates, eds., Fiscal zoning and land use controls (D.C. Heath, Lexington, MA) 119–174.

Fischel, William A., 1979, Determinants of voting on environmental quality: A study of a New Hampshire pulp mill referendum, Journal of Environmental Economics and Management 6, 107–118.

Gordon, Roger, 1983, An optimal taxation approach to fiscal federalism, Quarterly Journal of Economics 97, 567–586.

Mintz, Jack and Henry Tulkens, 1986, Commodity tax competition between member states of a federation: Equilibrium and efficiency, Journal of Public Economics 29, 133–172.

Niskanen, Jr., William, 1977, Bureaucracy and representative government (Aldine, Chicago).

Oates, Wallace E., 1972, Fiscal federalism (Harcourt Brace Jovanovich, New York).

Oates, Wallace E. and Robert M. Schwab, 1987, Pricing instruments for environmental protection: The problems of cross-media pollution, interjurisdictional competition and intergenerational effects, Unpublished paper (University of Maryland, College Park).

Stigler, George, 1957, The tenable range of functions of local government, in: Joint Economic Committee, U.S. Congress, Federal Expenditure Policy for Economic Growth and Stability (U.S. Government Printing Office, Washington, DC) 213–219.

Tiebout, Charles M., 1956, A pure theory of local expenditures, Journal of Political Economy 64, 416–424.

Wildasin, David E., 1986, Interjurisdictional capital mobility: Fiscal externality and a corrective subsidy, Unpublished paper (University of Indiana, Bloomington, Indiana).

Wilson, John D., 1985, Optimal property taxation in the presence of interregional capital mobility, Journal of Urban Economics 17, 73–89.

Wilson, John D., 1986, A theory of interregional tax competition, Journal of Urban Economics 19, 356–370.

Zodrow, George R. and Peter Mieszkowski, 1983, The incidence of the property tax: The benefit view versus the new view, in: G. Zodrow, ed., Local provision of public services: The Tiebout model after twenty-five years (Academic Press, New York) 109–129.

Zodrow, George R. and Peter Mieszkowski, 1986, Pigou, Tiebout, property taxation and the under-provision of local public goods, Journal of Urban Economics 19, 296–315.

PART V

CAPITALIZATION AND LOCAL FINANCE

The Effects of Property Taxes and Local Public Spending on Property Values: An Empirical Study of Tax Capitalization and the Tiebout Hypothesis

Wallace E. Oates

Princeton University

The purpose of this paper is to present some empirical findings on a problem for which we presently possess only the scantest of evidence: the effects of local public budgets on property values in the community. There do exist several studies of the incidence of property taxes, the mainstay of local revenue systems in the United States, but in nearly all cases these studies are based on assumptions concerning the degree to which the tax on various components of property is capitalized. We have, however, little hard empirical evidence indicating whether property taxes are in fact capitalized and, if so, to what extent.[1] This deficiency might not seem very serious if we had a single, compelling theory of the shifting and incidence of property taxes, a theory which suggested a definite solution to the problem. The truth, however, is that the theory of the shifting of property taxes points to a wide range of possibilities: under some circumstances the whole of the tax may be reflected in a reduced rental income (and hence lower property values) for landlords, while in other situations the tax may result primarily in increased rents to tenants, with little impact on the market value of property.

Some years ago in this journal, Tiebout (1956) developed a formal model involving consumer location in accord with preferences for local public goods and services. He suggested that at least at a theoretical level we can envision a system in which we get something resembling a market solution to the production and consumption of local public goods. Very simply, Tiebout's world is one in which the consumer "shops" among different

I am indebted to the Ford Foundation for support of this work and, in addition, am grateful to William Baumol, David Bradford, Lester Chandler, Thomas Frederick, James Heckman, John Heinberg, E. Philip Howrey, Harry Kelejian, James Litvack, and the members of the graduate seminar at Princeton University for many extremely helpful comments on earlier drafts of this paper.

[1] The paucity of empirical work on this problem is readily apparent from Netzer's survey of the evidence in his comprehensive study of the property tax (1966, chap. 3).

communities offering varying packages of local public services and selects as a residence the community which offers the tax-expenditure program best suited to his tastes. The obstacles to such consumer mobility (including job commitments and family ties) are obviously great; as a result several economists have expressed serious reservations as to the likely explanatory power of the Tiebout model. On the other hand, with the growing urbanization of society, there is some reason to believe that the Tiebout hypothesis may be relevant to the real world: individuals working in a central city frequently have a wide choice of suburban communities in which to reside, and the quality of the local public schools, for instance, may be of real importance in the choice of a community of residence. If this is true, the outputs of public services (as well as taxes) should influence the attraction of a community to potential residents and should thereby affect local property values.

The first section of this paper develops briefly the conceptual framework for examining the effects of property taxes and local expenditure programs on property values. This will provide the background for an empirical study involving fifty-three residential communities in northeastern New Jersey. The results of the study, which suggest the direction of the effects of tax and expenditure programs on local property values, together with rough estimates of orders of magnitude, have, I believe, some interesting implications for local-government finance.

Local Public Budgets and the Tiebout Model

There exists an extensive literature on the theory of the shifting of property taxes, a literature which points to the probable effects of property taxes on the value of land and structures.[2] The traditional or "classical" theory suggests (subject to numerous qualifications) that the part of the tax falling on the land would, since the income from land is a pure economic rent, be absorbed by the land owner (that is, this part of the tax would be capitalized in the form of reduced property values). In contrast, the portion of the tax applicable to structures would in the long run be "shifted" forward to purchasers, as the tax would depress the net return on investment in the construction industry and would thereby result in a diminished stock of structures in future periods.

This literature, however, deals largely with the case of a single tax rate applicable to all land and structures. If, in contrast, we consider a system (as is the case in the United States and several other countries) in which localities have varying tax rates and offer differing levels of output of public services, a quite different approach and set of conclusions suggest

---

[2] For an excellent critical survey of the theories of the shifting and incidence of the property tax, see Simon (1943).

themselves. In terms of the Tiebout model, we can conceive of a utility-maximizing consumer who weighs the benefits stemming from the program of local public services against the cost of his tax liability and chooses as a residence that locality which provides him with the greatest surplus of benefits over costs. From this standpoint, the individual's tax liability (that is, the value of his house and lot multiplied by the property tax rate) becomes the price of entry into the community, the price of consuming the local output of public services. It is the present value of the future stream of benefits from the public services *relative* to the present value of future tax payments that is in this case important.

This general-equilibrium approach to the problem implies that, if a community increases its property tax rate in order to expand its output of public services, *net* rental income (actual or imputed) to property owners need not decline and may well increase.[3] Moreover, this suggests a way to determine whether the Tiebout hypothesis of consumer location in accordance with preferences for local budgetary programs has any relevance to actual behavior. If consumers, in their choice of locality of residence, do consider the available program of public services, we would expect to find that, other things being equal (including tax rates), gross rents (actual or imputed) and therefore property values would be higher in a community the more attractive its package of public goods. Individual families, desiring to consume higher levels of public output, would presumably tend to bid up property values in communities with high-quality programs of public services. As Bickerdike noted, "Some things, such as lighting and cleaning of streets, are advantages visible to the eye; they may be taken into account when a man is choosing a house, though they are apt to be forgotten when the rate-collector calls" (1902, p. 476). In contrast, if local expenditure programs have no impact at all on locational decisions, we would not expect local property values to depend on spending variables, for in this case the demand and supply for local property would presumably be independent of these programs. The next section of this paper is an attempt to see if we can discern empirically the effects (or absence of effects) of local property taxes and public expenditures on local property values and, if so,

---

[3] A superb treatment of the incidence of property taxes is to be found in appendix G of Marshall's *Principles of Economics* (1948). Marshall is careful to distinguish between the case of a national property tax and a system of local taxes on property. Contrasting "onerous rates" (those which yield no compensating benefits) with "remunerative rates" (those which confer benefits on those who pay them), Marshall argues that for local rates "onerous taxes on site values tend to be deducted from the rental which the owner, or lessee, receives: and they are accordingly deducted, in so far as they can be foreseen, from the ground rent which a builder, or anyone else, is willing to pay for a building lease. Such local rates as are remunerative, are in the long run paid by the occupier, but are no real burden to him" (1948, p. 797). Marshall notes further that "such rates [remunerative], ably and honestly administered, may confer a net benefit on those who pay them; and an increase in them may attract population and industry instead of repelling it" (1948, p. 794).

whether we can get some rough approximations concerning the relative strength of the two effects.

An Empirical Study

The study consists of a cross-sectional analysis of a sample of communities with the aim of determining, other things being equal, the relationship between property values and local property taxes and expenditures. The problem (as usual in these kinds of experiments) is that within a sample of communities other things are not equal. It therefore becomes necessary to specify the other determinants of local property values and then to attempt to hold these constant while observing the partial relationship among the variables of concern. In addition to the level of property tax rates and the output of public services, one would expect the value of residences in a particular community to depend on a number of other variables. First, within a metropolitan area, the accessibility of the community to the central city should be of importance. Since the central city is the primary source of employment in the area, individuals should, other things being equal, prefer living close to the city to minimize the cost in both time and money of traveling to their place of employment (and to make the leisure activities of the city more accessible). Therefore, *ceteris paribus*, we would expect property values to vary inversely with distance from the central city.

Second, the character of the residences themselves is an obvious determinant of value. Large houses in an excellent state of repair and in a pleasant location will tend to sell at higher prices than smaller, run-down residences in unattractive areas. For this study, I will thus assume that the value of dwellings in a particular community depends upon the physical characteristics of the residences and area, on the proximity of the community to the central city, on the property tax rate, and on the level of output of public services in the locality. The sample under study consists of a group of fifty-three municipalities in northeastern New Jersey, all of which are located within the New York metropolitan region.[4] To maintain some semblance of homogeneity, the sample is limited to "residential" communities. A residential community is defined as one with an employment-residence ratio of less than 100 (that is, a municipality in which a larger number of residents go outside the community to their place of employment than come into the community to work from other places of residence).

The next task is to locate operational measures of the variables. As an index of proximity to the central city, I have used simply the linear distance of the municipality from midtown Manhattan. The physical characteristics of the property, including the attractiveness of the neighbor-

---

[4] For a description of the sample of communities and of the sources of data, see the Appendixes.

hood as a place of residence, are more difficult to quantify. Some data are available on the quality of the housing stock in each community (U.S. Bureau of the Census 1963). As a measure of size, the study employs the median number of rooms per dwelling. To measure the age (and presumably to some extent the state of repair) of the housing stock, I have used as an independent variable the percentage of the houses in the community built since 1950. However, this still leaves unconsidered the various intangible characteristics of a house: its physical charm or beauty and the attractiveness of the particular neighborhood or community as a place to live. As a proxy variable for these intangibles, the study uses family income. Wealthier families will presumably select higher-quality residences—better houses in more desirable neighborhoods. The median family income of the community therefore represents a measure of the intangible features of the houses in the community.

In the choice of fiscal variables, one cannot use the nominal property tax rate because the wide variation in assessment ratios across communities implies that the actual rate at which communities tax property is not likely to bear a systematic relationship to the nominal rate. Instead, I have used the "effective" tax rate (that is, the nominal rate times the assessment ratio), which should provide a better measure of the true rate at which property is taxed in the locality.[5] The major problem in the selection of variables is determining a reasonable index of output for local public services. Those who have worked in this area are familiar with the difficulties in obtaining operational measures of output in the public sector. Frequently the only feasible proxy for public output is some measure of inputs. Per capita public expenditure immediately suggests itself; further reflection, however, suggests that this is likely to be a rather unsatisfactory measure of the level or quality of output. Public spending per capita in two communities may vary, for example, as a result of differing relative sizes of the school population; a community with a relatively large number of children will, other things being equal, have to spend more per capita to provide a school system of the same quality as another community with an older age distribution of the population. And these variations in spending may have nothing to do with the quality of public output provided.[6]

[5] Official assessment ratios for each community are determined by the state of New Jersey for use in the school-aid equalization program. These ratios are arrived at by comparing the actual prices at which individual homes in the various communities are bought and sold with the value at which these homes are assessed for tax purposes. In 1960 assessment ratios ranged all the way from 11 percent to 104 percent. In the regressions, I have used a simple average of effective tax rates for each community over the period 1956–60, which serves to smooth out any aberrations resulting from an unrepresentative sample of homes sold in a particular year. See Beck (1963, p. 44).

[6] In the actual regression runs, the coefficient of the per capita public-expenditure variable was not significantly different from zero.

By far the largest single item in local public budgets (and no doubt the most important to families with children) is primary and secondary education. Again no direct measure of output is available, but comprehensive data on inputs, more precisely on costs, are published annually. I have, as a result, used expenditure per pupil as a proxy variable for the level of output of educational services. While this is by no means a perfect variable for my purposes (in part because it neglects the noneducational public services provided locally), there is some reason to expect that, for a group of residential communities in the same section of a metropolitan area, the quality of local school systems should vary directly with expenditure per pupil.[7] If this is the case and if (as the Tiebout model suggests) individuals consider the quality of local public services in making locational decisions, we would expect to find that, other things being equal (including tax rates) across communities, an increased expenditure per pupil should result in higher property values.

Using the multiple-regression technique, my procedure was to regress the median value of owner-occupied dwellings (including house and lot) in the various communities on the median number of rooms per house, the percentage of houses constructed since 1950, median family income, the distance in miles from Manhattan, the annual expenditure per pupil in the public schools, the effective property tax rate, and the percentage of families in the community with an income of less than $3,000 per year.[8] The inclusion of the last variable, the percentage of low-income families, is necessitated by the character of the data. Poorer families are more likely to reside in rental dwellings than wealthier families in suburban com-

---

[7] Kiesling (1967), in a recent study of a sample of school districts in the state of New York, had only modest success with a per pupil expenditure variable in explaining the level of achievement as measured by the test scores of pupils in the sample districts. It may still be the case, however, that *perceived* benefits in terms of smaller classes, better libraries, etc., are closely related to expenditure per pupil, and that this is what counts in terms of the evaluation of different schools by parents. For purposes of determining whether individuals consider the benefits from public services in selecting a community of residence, expenditure per pupil may for this reason be a satisfactory variable. In computing expenditure per pupil, I (like Kiesling) used a weighted average of enrollments to take account of the increased cost of pupils at higher grade levels. Following Kiesling and incorporating information from New Jersey sources, I employed the following weights to determine a "weighted pupil enrollment" for each school district: kindergarten pupils = .5, elementary school pupils (grades 1–8) = 1, secondary school pupils (grades 9–12) = 1.25, special pupils (mentally retarded, etc.) = 2. Expenditure per pupil for each school district was then calculated by dividing the weighted enrollment into the annual current costs of the district. See Appendix B for data sources.

[8] The dependent variable in the analysis is the median value of single-unit, owner-occupied dwellings (including the value of both house and lot) in the community which is provided in the *1960 Census of Housing* (U.S. Bureau of the Census 1963). The value of residences is based upon appraisals by owners and may, as a result, be subject to considerable error. However, the typical or average value for residences in a municipality seems to be reasonably accurate. Kish and Lansing (1954), for example, found that the difference between the mean of appraisers' and owners' estimates for over 500 residences was only $350.

munities. In consequence, in a community with a relatively large number of low-income families, median family income will tend to understate significantly the actual median income of homeowners. And it is this latter figure which is needed for the study, since we are trying to explain the median value of owner-occupied dwellings. We would therefore expect the median value of owner-occupied houses to be higher relative to median family income in the community as a whole for those municipalities where a relatively large number of low-income families reside.

Before presenting the regressions, it is important to stress that the variation in the dependent variable, the value of owner-occupied dwellings, is likely to be quite substantial in the presence of capitalization of the tax. If, for example, we consider two identical houses in two identical communities, where both dwellings have an expected life of forty years and rent for $2,000 annually, the difference in the market value of the houses, if one were subject to a 4 percent property tax and the other to a 2 percent tax, would be in excess of $5,000 if the tax were fully capitalized.[9] As a result, we are not likely to be faced with the difficult task of isolating minute differences in property values, differences which could easily be obscured by minor imperfections in the explanatory variables.

Employing ordinary least squares (OLSQ), equation (1) indicates that, with other things constant, property values bear a significant negative relationship to the property tax rate and a significant positive association with expenditure per pupil.[10]

[9] For property of a finite life, in this case forty years, we have:

$$V = \sum_{i=1}^{40} \frac{Y_n}{(1 + r)^i} = \sum_{i=1}^{40} \frac{(Y - tV)}{(1 + r)^i}, \tag{N1}$$

where V = market value of the property, Y = gross annual rental income, Y_n = net (after tax) rental income, r = rate of discount. Solving for V, we get:

$$V = \frac{Y\left[\sum_{i=1}^{40} \frac{1}{(1 + r)^i}\right]}{1 + t\left[\sum_{i=1}^{40} \frac{1}{(1 + r)^i}\right]}. \tag{N2}$$

Using a rate of discount of 5 percent, the difference cited in the text is calculated from the expression:

$$V = \frac{\$2,000m}{(1 + .02m)} - \frac{\$2,000m}{(1 + .04m)} = \$25,550 - \$20,350 = \$5,200,$$

where:

$$m = \sum_{i=1}^{40} \frac{1}{(1 + .05)^i} = 17.1591.$$

[10] The tax, expenditure, and distance variables are employed in log form, which somewhat enhances their explanatory power. This would appear to make sense. As suggested by equation (N2) in the preceding footnote, we would not expect property values to vary linearly with the absolute level of the tax rate; rather, the higher the tax rate, the smaller should be the impact of a given absolute change in the rate. Similarly, we might expect that additional expenditures per pupil would tend to yield

$$V = -21 - 3.6 \log T + 3.2 \log E - 1.4 \log M + 1.7R$$
$$(2.4) \quad (4.1) \qquad (2.1) \qquad (4.8) \qquad (4.1)$$

$$+ .05N + 1.5Y + .3P \quad (1)$$
$$(3.9) \qquad (8.9) \quad (3.6)$$

[Note: The numbers in parentheses are the absolute values of the t-statistic for the coefficients. All the coefficients are statistically significant at a 5 percent level of significance.]

$$R^2 = .93,$$

where V = median home value in thousands of dollars (1960); $\log T$ = natural log of the effective percentage tax rate (the rate used is a simple average of effective rates over the years 1956–60); $\log E$ = natural log of annual current expenditures per pupil in dollars (1960–61); $\log M$ = natural log of the linear distance in miles of the community from midtown Manhattan; R = median number of rooms per owner-occupied house (1960); N = percentage of houses built since 1950 (1960); Y = median family income in thousands of dollars (1959); P = percentage of families in the community with an annual income of less than \$3,000 (1959). These results thus appear to suggest some capitalization of the tax and appear consistent with the Tiebout hypothesis.

Some further thought, however, suggests good reason to be suspicious of the results in equation (1). One could make a good case for the argument that the negative association between tax rates and home values stems from a dependence of tax rates on property values (rather than the reverse). Given the level of public spending, the higher the property values in a community, the lower are the tax rates needed to generate the revenues to finance the program. A more complete model would have to include another equation in which the tax rate is treated as a dependent variable, presumably as a function of the level of local public spending, the size of the tax base, and the extent of public issues of debt (if any). Moreover, the level of spending per pupil in the local public school system probably also depends to some extent on the wealth and income in the community.

What all this means is that equation (1) may well contain some simultaneous-equation bias, since the supposed independent variables, the tax rate and expenditure per pupil, probably depend to some extent on the

---

successively diminishing increments of benefits. Finally, a log form for the distance variable seems reasonable, since being an additional mile from the central city would presumably be more important to someone who was quite close to the city than to an individual who was already twenty miles away. I also experimented with two other variables from the *1960 Census of Housing* (U.S. Bureau of the Census 1963), variables which one might expect to influence the value of owner-occupied houses in a community: the "homeowner vacancy rate" and the percentage of owner-occupied units deemed "sound" by the census takers. Neither variable, however, was statistically significant or had any appreciable effects on the results.

dependent variable, home values. If this is true, the coefficients of log T and log E in equation (1) will be correlated with the error term, and the results in equation (1) may be spurious. To provide a more reliable test of the capitalization and Tiebout hypotheses, I reestimated equation (1) using two-stage least squares (TSLS).[11] The TSLS version appears as equation (2).

$$V = -29 - 3.6 \log T + 4.9 \log E - 1.3 \log M + 1.6R$$
$$\quad (2.3) \quad (3.1) \quad\quad (2.1) \quad\quad (4.0) \quad\quad (3.6)$$

$$+ .06N + 1.5Y + .3P \quad (2)$$
$$(3.9) \quad (7.7) \quad (3.1)$$

$$R^2 = .93.$$

The results in equation (2) differ little from those in equation (1) except that the coefficient on the public-expenditure variable is somewhat larger. It is interesting to try to get some idea of the orders of magnitude implied by the coefficients of the tax and expenditure variables. Equation (2) indicates that (with public output held constant) an increase in local property tax rates from 2 percent to 3 percent will reduce the market value of a house by about $1,500.[12] Considering a typical house with a market value of $20,000 and an expected life of forty years, and using a rate of discount of 5 percent, full capitalization of the increase in the tax would imply a reduction in value to about $17,740.[13] Equation (2) thus suggests

[11] To "purge" the tax and expenditure variables of their correlation with the error term, it is necessary to derive "predicted" tax and spending variables by regressing log T and log E on the other independent variables in equation (1) and on some additional predetermined variables. These new predicted variables are then used to reestimate equation (1). On this procedure, see, for example, Johnston (1963, chap. 9). The additional predetermined variables employed in generating the new tax and expenditure variables were: the median number of years of school completed by males of age twenty-five or more, population density, percentage of dwellings owner-occupied, the percentage of change in population from 1950 to 1960, the percentage of the population enrolled in public elementary and secondary schools, a dummy variable with a value of one for those communities in Hudson County and a value of zero for municipalities in other counties, and the value of commercial and industrial property per resident. In the complete model, these variables would appear as exogenous variables in other equations which determine the levels of tax rates and public expenditures.

[12] The mean value of the effective property tax rate for the sample of communities is 2.4 percent.

[13] The capitalized value of the house is calculated with the use of equation (N2) in footnote 9. The first step is to employ equation (N2) to determine the value of the annual rent, Y:

$$\$20,000 = \frac{Ym}{1 + .02m} \quad \text{yields} \quad Y = \$1,566, \quad (N3)$$

where

$$m = \sum_{i=1}^{40} \frac{1}{(1 + .05)^i} = 17.1591.$$

(Continued)

that a substantial portion of the tax increase, approximately two-thirds (that is, \$1,500/\$2,260) in this case, is being capitalized in the form of depressed property values.[14]

In addition, by assuming typical values of the variables, it is possible to get some feeling for the relative strength of the tax and expenditure variables. For this purpose, consider the following experiment. Assume that the community is composed of identical homes, each worth \$20,000 and each housing one public school pupil. Assume next that the community decides to raise its effective property tax rate from 2 percent to 3 percent to provide a balanced expansion in spending on all locally provided services. Since roughly half of the local public budget goes into education, this implies that expenditure per pupil in the school system will rise by \$100 (that is, \$20,000 [.01/2]). Again using typical values of the variables, assume that this allows spending per pupil to rise from \$350 per annum to \$450. Plugging these values into equation (2), one finds that the impact of the tax increase is to reduce the value of each house by \$1,500. On the other hand, the increase in expenditure per pupil from \$350 to \$450 pushes house values up by roughly \$1,200. Equation (2) thus suggests that the half of the budget increase going into the school system almost in itself offsets the depressive effects of the higher taxes on home values. This makes no allowance for the presumed positive impact on property values of the improved quality of other locally provided services. If we had considered a rise in tax rates for the sole purpose of improving the quality of the school system, equation (2) would (for average values of the variables) suggest that the effect on property values of the benefits from the improved services would more than offset the depressive influence of higher property taxes. The evidence therefore suggests that the benefits forthcoming from the primary service provided by local government, the public school system, do in fact exert a positive influence on local property values; better schools, other things being equal, appear to enhance the value of

---

Then, using this equation again with the computed value of Y and a tax rate of 3 percent, we find the value to be:

$$V = \frac{\$1,566m}{1 + .03m} = \$17,739.$$

The mean value of an owner-occupied house in the sample is \$19,200.

[14] Ridker and Henning (1967) have recently studied the determination of residential property values in the St. Louis metropolitan area. Using 1960 census data, they find important some of the same variables I have used in this study. Although they did not employ any property-tax or public-spending variables, the authors did include a dummy variable to distinguish between census tracts in Illinois and Missouri. Property taxes are significantly higher in Illinois than in Missouri, and Ridker and Henning found that, other things being equal, property in the St. Louis metropolitan area is of higher value if it is located in Missouri rather than in Illinois. Their results thus also suggest some capitalization of local property taxes.

local residential property. One clearly should not place too much stock in the precise outcome of the example just considered; rather, the results should be regarded as indicating no more than orders of magnitude. In this light, equation (2) suggests that the impact of increased benefits on property values from an expansion in spending on the local school system approximately offsets the depressive effects of the higher taxes required to finance the expanded program. If property values do provide a reasonably accurate reflection of the benefits from local public services, these results would seem to suggest that these communities have, on the average, expanded public spending to the point where (very roughly) the benefits from an additional unit of output equal marginal cost.

While the benefits from better schools may cancel out the effects on residential property values of higher taxes, equation (2) does imply that increases in property tax rates *unaccompanied* by an expanded program of public services will depress local property values. This is important for comparing the effects of property taxes across communities; it means, for example, that if one community (because of houses of lower value or as a result of a relatively large population of children) levies higher tax rates than a neighboring municipality in order to provide the *same* quality of public services, property values in the former community will be depressed relative to those in the adjacent community where tax rates are lower. Consumers thus appear to some extent to "shop" for public services. If one community can provide a given program of public services more "cheaply" (that is, with lower tax *rates*) than another, at least some individuals appear willing to pay more to live there.

Before concluding this study, I should comment briefly on some problems inherent in the approach adopted and on deficiencies in the available data. Most studies of the effects of taxes (for example, the shifting of the corporation income tax) have relied upon time-series data to isolate the effects over time on relevant variables of changes in tax rates. In contrast, I have in this paper adopted cross-sectional techniques. This latter approach would appear best suited to the problem under investigation: we are asking what effect a change in tax rates and/or expenditures has on the equilibrium value of residential property. The problem is thus one of comparative statics for which cross-sectional estimation is the appropriate technique. Implicit in the use of cross-sectional regression analysis is the assumption that the observations do in fact represent points of equilibrium. This, of course, is seldom if ever strictly true and, especially where an adjustment period of some length is likely, it is possible that the results may be distorted to some extent (Kuh 1959; Grunfeld 1961). It could be, for example, that the negative association we have observed between property taxes and home values is primarily a short-run phenomenon, which would disappear over a longer period of time. Unfortunately, there are not available time-series data to investigate the nature of the adjustment process. Ultimately, however, time-series studies of the adjustment process would provide a valuable supplement to cross-sectional studies of the effects of local taxes.

Finally, I should recognize explicitly (as the reader no doubt already has) the imprecision of several of the operational measures of the variables. This, along with the problems inherent in the use of simultaneous-equation estimation techniques, suggests that some caution is in order concerning the degree of reliability that we can attribute to the results.

Summary and Conclusions

This paper reports the findings of a cross-sectional study of the effects of local property taxes and local expenditure programs on property values. Using the two-stage least-squares estimation technique in an attempt to circumvent the likely presence of some simultaneous-equation bias, the regression equation indicates that local property values bear a significant negative relationship to the effective tax rate and a significant positive correlation with expenditure per pupil in the public schools. The size of the coefficients suggests that, for an increase in property taxes unaccompanied by an increase in the output of local public services, the bulk of the rise in taxes will be capitalized in the form of reduced property values. On the other hand, if a community increases its tax rates and employs the receipts to improve its school system, the coefficients indicate that the increased benefits from the expenditure side of the budget will roughly offset (or perhaps even more than offset) the depressive effect of the higher tax rates on local property values.

These results appear consistent with a model of the Tiebout variety in which rational consumers weigh (to some extent at least) the benefits from local public services against the cost of their tax liability in choosing a community of residence: people do appear willing to pay more to live in a community which provides a high-quality program of public services (or in a community which provides the same program of public services with lower tax rates).

Appendix A

Notes on the Sample of Communities

The group of communities used in the empirical study consists of all residential New Jersey municipalities of population size 10,000–50,000 (according to the 1960 Census of Population) in the New York metropolitan region with the exception of those in Monmouth County. This county was omitted from the outset because it includes a large number of beach-resort communities with seasonal residences. For a definition of the New York metropolitan region, see Hoover and Vernon (1962, p. 8). By residential community is meant a municipality with an employment-residence ratio of less than 100 according to *The Municipal Year Book 1963* (1963, table 3). This procedure produced a group of fifty-three municipalities which were included in the study and are listed below.

Bergen County	*Essex County*	*Morris County*
Bergenfield	Maplewood	Madison
Cliffside Park	Millburn	Parsippany-Troy Hills
Dumont	Montclair	
East Paterson	Nutley	*Passaic County*
Fair Lawn	Orange	Hawthorne
Fort Lee	South Orange	Totowa
Garfield	Verona	Wayne
Glen Rock	West Orange	
Hasbrouck Heights		*Somerset County*
Lodi	*Hudson County*	Bound Brook
Lyndhurst	Secaucus	North Plainfield
Maywood	Weehawken	Somerville
New Milford	West New York	
North Arlington		
Palisades Park	*Middlesex County*	*Union County*
Ridgefield Park	Edison	Cranford
Ridgewood	Highland Park	New Providence
River Edge	Metuchen	Roselle
Rutherford	Middlesex	Roselle Park
Teaneck	South Plainfield	Summit
Tenafly	South River	Westfield
Waldwick		

Appendix B

Sources of Data

The sources of data for the variables used in the estimations are as follows:

VARIABLE	SOURCE
1. Median value of owner-occupied dwellings	Census of Housing, 1960
2. Median number of rooms per owner-occupied dwelling . . .	Census of Housing, 1960
3. Population	Census of Population, 1960
4. Median number of years of school completed by males of age twenty-five and over	Census of Population, 1960
5. Effective property tax rates . . .	Beck (1963)
6. Value of commercial and industrial property per resident	Beck (1963)
7. Population density	Beck (1963)
8. Median family income	Beck (1963)
9. Percentage of dwellings built since 1950	*Municipal Yearbook, 1963*
10. Percentage of dwellings owner-occupied	*Municipal Yearbook, 1963*

Variable	Source
11. Percentage of population with family incomes under \$3,000 .	*Municipal Yearbook, 1963*
12. Percentage change in population from 1950 to 1960	*Municipal Yearbook, 1963*
13. Linear distance in miles from midtown Manhattan (that is, Fifth Avenue and 34th Street) . . .	Measured in *Rand McNally Road Atlas,* 43d ed. (1967)
14. Municipal expenditure data . . .	*Twenty-Third Annual Report of the Division of Local Government,* State of New Jersey, 1960
15. School district enrollment and expenditure data	*Tenth Annual Report of the Commission of Education, Financial Statistics of School Districts,* School Year 1960–61, State of New Jersey

References

Beck, M. *Property Taxation and Urban Land Use in Northeastern New Jersey.* Urban Land Institute Research Monograph 7. Washington: Urban Land Institute, 1963.

Bickerdike, C. "Taxation of Site Values." *Econ. J.* 12 (December 1902):472–84. Reprinted in American Economic Association, *Readings in the Economics of Taxation* (Homewood, Ill.: Irwin, 1959), pp. 377–88.

Grunfeld, Y. "The Interpretation of Cross-Section Estimates in a Dynamic Model." *Econometrica* 29 (July 1961):397–404.

Hoover, E., and Vernon, R. *Anatomy of a Metropolis.* New York: Doubleday, 1962.

Johnston, J. *Econometric Methods.* New York: McGraw-Hill, 1963.

Kiesling, H. "Measuring a Local Government Service: A Study of School Districts in New York State." *Rev. Econ. and Statis.* 49 (August 1967): 356–67.

Kish, L., and Lansing, J. "Response Errors in Estimating the Value of Homes." *J. American Statis. Assoc.* 49 (September 1954):520–38.

Kuh, E. "The Validity of Cross-Sectionally Estimated Behavior Equations in Time Series Applications." *Econometrica* 27 (April 1959):197–214.

Marshall, A. *Principles of Economics.* 8th ed. New York: MacMillan, 1948.

Netzer, D. *Economics of the Property Tax.* Washington: Brookings Institution, 1966.

Nolting, O., and Arnold, D., eds. *The Municipal Year Book 1963,* vol. 30. Chicago: The International City Managers' Association, 1963.

Ridker, R., and Henning, J. J. "The Determinants of Residential Property Values with Special Reference to Air Pollution." *Rev. Econ. and Statis.* 49 (May 1967):246–57.

Simon, H. "The Incidence of a Tax on Urban Real Property." *Q.J.E.* 57 (May 1943):398–421. Reprinted in American Economic Association, *Readings in the Economics of Taxation* (Homewood, Ill.: Richard D. Irwin, 1959), pp. 416–35.

Tiebout, C. "A Pure Theory of Local Expenditures." *J.P.E.* 64 (October 1956): 416–24.

U.S. Bureau of the Census. *1960 Census of Housing.* Vol. 7, pt. 6. Washington: Government Printing Office, 1963.

[20]

The Effects of Property Taxes and Local Public Spending on Property Values: A Reply and Yet Further Results

Wallace E. Oates

Princeton University

In addition to presenting some findings of his own, Henry Pollakowski contends that my earlier empirical study (1969) of local public budgets and property values suffers from misspecification on two different counts and from an improper use of two-state least-squares estimation. I want to consider each of these points in turn.

First, Pollakowski is quite legitimately disturbed by the fact that the reduced-form equation I estimated contained a variable representing only one of the public services, namely primary and secondary education, that is provided by local governments in New Jersey (although it is the case that this accounts for roughly two-thirds of municipal spending among the communities in my sample).[1] The logic of a Tiebout-type model suggests that residents of a community should have some concern for the levels of other public services as well and that, as a result, these outputs too might influence local property values. In addition, levels of spending on other public functions surely do affect local tax rates so that we would expect differentials in such spending across communities to be correlated with local rates of property taxation. Therefore this omission will, as Pollakowski indicates, probably result in biased estimates of the coefficients of my earlier equation.

To correct for this likely bias, it is necessary to reestimate the equation incorporating variables representing levels of output of other public services. As those who have worked on these problems know, it is extremely difficult to develop reliable operational measures of levels of output of most public services. The only readily available measures typically relate to spending, although, as we are all aware, expenditures can be a very unsatisfactory proxy for the level of service actually provided.[2] It may be, however, that across a group of residential municipalities in the same general section of a metropolitan area levels of expenditure may represent a reasonable measure of output.

[1] This same criticism, incidentally, has been advanced by Charles Upton (1970) and by Robert Coen and Brian Powell (1972).

[2] For one discussion of the conceptual problems inherent in such measures, see Bradford, Malt, and Oates (1969).

At any rate, to deal with this problem I have reestimated a revised form of my earlier equation in which the sole difference in specification is the addition to the equation, as an independent variable, of municipal spending per capita in 1960 (in dollars) on all functions other than local public schools and debt service.[3] This variable, which I label Z, is intended to serve as a proxy for the level of provision of all municipal public services other than schools. Using the same sample of communities and body of data as in my earlier study, estimation by ordinary least squares (OLSQ) now generates the equation[4]

$$V = -26 - 4.2 \log T + 3.6 \log E - 1.2 \log M + 1.4R + 0.06N$$
$$\quad (3.0) \quad (4.6) \qquad (2.4) \qquad (4.3) \qquad (3.2) \quad (4.3)$$

$$+ \ 1.5Y + 0.3P + 1.5 \log Z \qquad\qquad\qquad\qquad\qquad (1)$$
$$\quad (8.6) \quad (3.1) \quad (1.9)$$

$$N = 53 \qquad R^2 = .94.$$

(The numbers in parentheses are the absolute values of the t-statistic for the estimated coefficients. Using a one-tail test, all coefficients are statistically significant at a 95 percent level of confidence.)

The addition of Z to the equation has two notable effects on the results. First, the spending variable is itself significant and exhibits the anticipated sign, which is consistent with the hypothesis that public services other than schools do exert some influence on local property values. Second, the absolute value of the estimated coefficient of the tax variable is increased somewhat. This may reflect the significant positive correlation that exists between T and Z, with the result that the omission of Z in my earlier paper may have understated the degree of capitalization of the property tax.

The results in equation (1) are, however, suspect because of the likely dependence of the tax and the two expenditure variables on the dependent variable, V. A complete model would include both an equation in which the tax variable is a function of variables indicating levels of expenditure and the tax base (including V) and equations for expenditures on public services in which spending would depend on levels of wealth and tax rates, as well as other variables. This suggests that, since T, E, and Z depend on V, equation (1) will be subject to simultaneous-equation bias. Following my procedure in my earlier paper, I reestimated equation (1)

[3] This information is provided in the *Twenty-third Annual Report of the Division of Local Government (1960)*, State of New Jersey, Department of the Treasury. This figure includes local spending on such services as police and fire protection, streets and roads, health and welfare services, libraries, parks and playgrounds, etc.

[4] For the definition of each of the variables, see either my earlier paper or Pollakowski's preceding comment.

using two-stage least squares (TSLS) and treating T, E, and Z as endogenous variables. Using the same set of predetermined variables as earlier yielded

$$V = -35 - 5.0 \log T + 4.8 \log E - 1.1 \log M + 1.1R + 0.06N$$
$$\quad\;\; (2.7) \quad (3.8) \qquad\;\; (2.1) \qquad\qquad (3.4) \qquad\qquad (2.2) \qquad (4.2)$$

$$+ 1.4Y + 0.2P + 2.7 \log Z \qquad\qquad\qquad\qquad\qquad (2)$$
$$\;\; (7.1) \quad (2.4) \quad\; (2.2)$$

$$N = 53 \qquad R^2 = .93.$$

The results in equation (2) are similar to those in (1) except that the coefficients of both the tax (T) and nonschool spending (Z) variables increase in absolute value. Whereas the estimated tax coefficient in my earlier paper (i.e., -3.6) suggested the capitalization of roughly two-thirds of tax differentials,[5] the point estimate of the coefficient in (2) now indicates, for typical values of the variables, roughly full capitalization of property-tax differentials across the communities in the sample.

This brings us to Pollakowski's critique of my use of TSLS, which I frankly do not find very persuasive. The variables which I chose to use as predetermined variables are those which (among others) would enter as independent variables in the equations explaining tax rates and levels of public expenditure.[6] They are, within my system, exogenous variables and, as such, I have no reason to believe that they are correlated with the disturbance term. Pollakowski argues, rather curiously it seems to me, that several of these variables (e.g., level of educational attainment) are likely to be correlated with the disturbance term because they are themselves correlated with variables, such as air pollution, which were erroneously (?) omitted from the original equation. Thus, his objection seems fundamentally to be again one of misspecification of the original equation. I do find all this a bit far-fetched. After all, practically everything in the world depends at least in some remote way on everything else, and it is the economist's job to separate out the quantitatively important functional relationships. At any rate, it seems to me that the burden of proof rests on Pollakowski to produce a more plausible specification than mine which invalidates my particular application of TSLS. This he has not done.

Moreover, I am unconvinced by Pollakowski's argument that the income variable (Y) should not appear in the equation. The variables R (median number of rooms per house) and N (average age of houses) serve as proxy variables for the physical characteristics of houses in each

---

[5] See the conceptual experiment on pp. 965–66 in that paper.

[6] For example, expenditure per pupil will surely be a function of the level of educational attainment of the adult members of the community.

community. What I need is something further to reflect the intangible attributes of a community that make it a more or less attractive place in which to reside. Income seems to me a reasonable proxy for these attributes, since wealthier families will presumably select residences in the more attractive communities. In fact, Ridker and Henning (whom Pollakowski cites) use a form of the income variable for just this purpose. In their equation, like mine, it serves "as a proxy for the housing and neighborhood characteristics that have not been included in this study" (1967, p. 251). This surely strikes me as a more reasonable variable for this purpose than Pollakowski's choice of B (the percentage of houses having more than one bathroom) in his own study.

However, it is true, as Pollakowski shows, that the results of these types of studies do exhibit considerable sensitivity to the specification of the equation; this does suggest that these results should be viewed with some reservations. It indicates, moreover, that, complicated as the problem is, we need to continue work on the development of structural models of metropolitan residential and commercial location from which we can derive the equations we want to estimate. The estimation of reduced-form equations in the absence of such fully specified general-equilibrium models is admittedly a second-best procedure. It is interesting, however, that, in spite of the formidable theoretical and empirical problems involved, a number of recent cross-sectional and time-series studies have found evidence of the capitalization of local fiscal differentials.[7] All this should, perhaps, come as no great surprise; it is what we would expect on the basis of rational economic behavior.

I want finally to make an observation on the sorts of inferences we can make from these findings. It is not legitimate to conclude from this that we in fact live in a Tiebout world in which each family seeks out the mix of public services it most prefers at the lowest "tax price" and locates accordingly so that we generate a fully efficient solution in the sense that each family gets the bundle of local services it most desires, subject to its budget constraint. Such a normative conclusion need not follow from the findings of capitalization. What does seem to be implied is that there are at least some families who are sensitive to fiscal differentials. All that is required for capitalization to occur is that there be a sufficient number of families who do take fiscal variables into consideration so that any differential fiscal benefits (positive or negative) among communities in the same general area are offset (roughly) through adjustments in the value of local property. If this is true, it means that models of the Tiebout type do possess positive or predictive power in evaluating the effects of various local fiscal programs. Just how efficient the outcome is remains, however,

[7] See, for example, Smith (1970), Orr (1968), Heinberg and Oates (1970); there is also some as yet unpublished work with similar findings.

a matter of real uncertainty, particularly when we extend the analysis to encompass the entire metropolitan area, including the central city.[8]

References

Bradford, D.; Malt, R.; and Oates, W. "The Rising Cost of Local Public Services: Some Evidence and Reflections." *Nat. Tax J.* 22 (June 1969): 185–202.

Coen, R., and Powell, B. "Theory and Measurement of the Incidence of Differential Property Taxes on Rental Housing." *Nat. Tax J.* 25 (June 1972): 211–16.

Hamilton, B. "The Impact of Zoning and Property Taxes on Urban Structure and Housing Markets." Ph.D. dissertation, Princeton Univ., 1972.

Heinberg, J., and Oates, W. "The Incidence of Differential Property Taxes on Urban Housing." *Nat. Tax J.* 23 (March 1970): 92–98.

Oates, W. "The Effects of Property Taxes and Local Public Spending on Property Values: An Empirical Study of Tax Capitalization and the Tiebout Hypothesis." *J.P.E.* 77 (November/December 1969): 957–71.

Orr, L. "The Incidence of Differential Property Taxes on Urban Housing." *Nat. Tax J.* 21 (September 1968): 253–62.

Ridker, R., and Henning, J. "The Determinants of Residential Property Values with Special Reference to Air Pollution." *Rev. Econ. and Statis.* 49 (May 1967): 246–57.

Smith, R. S. "Property Tax Capitalization in San Francisco." *Nat. Tax J.* 23 (June 1970): 177–93.

Upton, C. "The Provision of Local Public Goods: The Tiebout Hypothesis." Mimeographed. 1970.

---

[8] This may be giving away a little too much. As Bruce Hamilton (1972, p. 77) has pointed out recently, with capitalization of variations in service levels and tax rates, to say that a family does not respond to fiscal differentials implies that the family is insensitive to differences in the price of housing across communities. For example, a family which does not care about the quality of local schools (i.e., has a low demand for public education) can purchase a dwelling of a given quality for a lesser price in a low-expenditure community (with the tax rate held constant).

21

Reprinted from
NATIONAL TAX JOURNAL
March, 1970, Vol. XXIII, No. 1

THE INCIDENCE OF DIFFERENTIAL PROPERTY TAXES ON URBAN HOUSING: A COMMENT AND SOME FURTHER EVIDENCE

J. D. HEINBERG AND W. E. OATES [*]

THERE HAS BEEN a recent revival of interest in the venerable issue of the shifting and incidence of the property tax, including a recent study in this Journal by Larry L. Orr [4]. Orr's main conclusion, based on theoretical analysis and empirical evidence drawn from a multiple-regression study of 31 communities in the Boston area, is that a "substantial portion" of property taxes on the improvement component of urban rental housing is borne by property owners — as opposed to occupants. More specifically, he contends that the incidence of property-tax differentials among communities is on the owners [4, p. 254].

In this comment, we will not take strong issue with Orr's theoretical model, although its relaxation of the assumption of a perfectly elastic supply of improvements is not (as he himself admits) particularly novel. What does concern us are the procedures which he employs to test the theory. We will argue that incorrect operational definitions of certain key variables, the inclusion of at least one inappropriate observation, and the likely presence of simultaneous-equation bias cast serious doubt on his regression results and the derived conclusions. In a final section, we present an alternative method of examining the incidence of

[*] The authors are respectively member of Research Staff of the Urban Institute and Assistant Professor of Economics at Princeton University. We are indebted to Larry Orr for making available to us the data he used in his study and to Gary Watts for his assistance with the computations. In addition, we are grateful to the Ford Foundation for support which facilitated the completion of this study.

property taxes on urban housing along with some empirical results which, in our view, are more defensible.

Problems in Orr's Empirical Test

To determine empirically the incidence of property-tax differentials, Orr regresses a rent variable on an equalized property-tax rate and a set of additional independent variables which presumably account for the non-tax influences on the level of rents. He finds that, holding other things constant, his rent variable is not significantly correlated with the level of property-tax rates. This Orr interprets as indicating that higher taxes do not result in higher rents; therefore, these tax differentials presumably fall on property owners, not on tenants.

Upon first inspecting Orr's results, we were struck by the fact that his key independent variable does not appear to be a reliable measure of the tax rate applicable to rental housing. Orr's tax variable is the equalized rate on *single-family* homes. It is well known, however, that single-family homes are mainly owner-occupied, while rental units are predominately contained in multi-family structures. This fact would be of little concern if one could assume no significant differences in assessment ratios of single-family and multi-family housing in the Boston area. But this is not the case, as was shown rather conclusively in this Journal in an extensive study of 1962 sales-assessment ratios in Boston by Oldman and Aaron [3]. They found an assessment ratio for single-family structures of .36, as compared, for example, to a ratio of

.53 for structures containing from three to five apartments [3, p. 40-41]. Since assessment ratios for different classes of dwellings are not the same and almost surely vary in relative terms among the communities in the sample, it would seem likely that Orr's tax variable does not provide a reasonable measure of the level of taxation of rental units.[1] For this reason alone, it is hardly surprising that the tax variable is not significantly correlated with the level of rents in Orr's regression equation.

After further consideration, we also found ourselves dissatisfied with Orr's operational definitions of certain other variables, and, upon making what seemed to us the appropriate adjustments, we reached some rather disturbing alterations in his results. To clarify the issue, it is useful to review briefly his statistical procedures. Specifically, Orr regressed the median gross rent per room (R) in the sample communities on average land values (X_1), a dummy variable indicating private or public provision of water and sewage facilities (X_2), an index of accessibility to centers of employment (Y_1), condition of housing units (Y_2), differentials in annual expenditures per pupil in the public schools (Y_3), and on effective tax rates (t). His regression results appear as equation (1) in Table I.

We feel that there are two obvious and important errors in the measurement of these variables. First, Orr uses, as his measure of R, median gross rent divided by the median number of rooms in *all* housing units. The proper denominator,

however, is median number of rooms in renter-occupied housing units *only* $(R°)$. Similarly, he employs for Y_2 the fraction of *all* housing units dilapidated or deteriorating, rather than the fraction of renter-occupied units in this structural condition $(Y°_2)$. The apparent reason for the use of these imprecise measures is that they were available for all 31 communities, whereas the proper data can be obtained for only 24 communities in the sample.[2] The size and condition of all housing units in a community may, however, bear little resemblance to these same characteristics for rental housing alone. This takes on a central importance when one recognizes that in several of Orr's communities rental units make up only a small portion of the total housing stock (e.g., only 5 per cent in one municipality). It therefore seemed better to us to work with the smaller sample for which the proper data are available.

To insure that Orr's results are not changed substantially by employing this smaller sample, we reproduced his regression using the subset of 24; it appears as equation (2) in Table I. The overall pattern of estimated coefficients, t-statistics and R^2 is quite similar to that in the original regression.[3]

Our next step was to determine the impact on Orr's results of substituting $R°$ and $Y°_2$ for his R and Y_2. The results

---

[1] We were unable to find any evidence that the State of Massachusetts conducted competent equalization studies or carefully supervised all local assessment procedures in Orr's sample period (around 1960). Sazama's study of 1962 equalized property-tax rates in large central cities, including Boston, indicated that no current ratio was available for Boston, and that the last good equalization study had been made by the Massachusetts legislature in 1955 [5, p. 153]. This hardly seems a favorable climate for uniformities in local practices.

[2] The communities in Orr's sample for which $R°$ and $Y°_2$ are not available are Andover, Hingham, Holbrook, Lynnfield, Norfolk, Rockland, and Westwood. In fact, data on R and Y_2 are not available for these communities in [6], the source cited by Orr. They were supplied to us through personal correspondence by Orr. The sources of data on $R°$ and $Y°_2$ are given in Table I.

[3] The only variables for which estimated coefficients and t-ratios change appreciably are the structural-condition variable and the dummy for public services: both are reduced in size and significance. The latter is easily explained by the fact that four of the five towns for which the variable took on the value of "one" were among those deleted from the sample.

TABLE I

REGRESSION EQUATIONS: RENTS PER ROOM ON SELECTED INDEPENDENT VARIABLES

Equation	Dependent variables	Sample size	Constant term	Land values X_1	Public services X_2	Accessibility Y_1	Structural condition Y_2	Education expenditures Y_3	Taxes	R²
1	R	31	14.1* (17.7)	.059* (2.0)	1.74* (3.1)	.123* (3.7)	-11.40* (-1.8)	.007** (1.5)	.211 (0.6)	.759
2	R	24	15.1* (20.4)	.060* (2.2)	0.66 (0.7)	.116* (4.3)	-5.03 (-0.7)	.007* (1.8)	-.240 (-0.6)	.835
3	R*	24	22.1* (12.2)	.072 (1.1)	-2.47 (-0.8)	.050 (0.7)	Y_2^* -0.48 (0.0)	.011 (1.0)	-1.26* (-1.8)	.473
4	R*	23	23.1* (10.9)	.015 (0.2)	-2.54 (-0.9)	.113 (1.2)	1.57 (0.1)	.014 (1.2)	-1.60* (-2.1)	.498

Figures in parentheses are estimated t-statistics for the coefficients.
* Significant at 95 per cent level of confidence (one-tail test).
** Significant at 90 per cent level of confidence (one-tail test).
Source: R, X₁, X₂, Y₁, Y₂, Y₃, t — data were obtained through personal correspondance with Larry L. Orr.
   R* — Median gross rent per renter-occupied housing unit, from [6], Tables 17, 21, 24.
       Median room number per renter-occupied housing unit, from [6], Tables 13, 19, 23.
   Y₂* Fraction of rental units dilapidated or deteriorating, from [6], Tables 12, 18, 22.

of this substitution, as seen in equation (3) in Table I, are disturbing to say the least. None of Orr's independent variables is any longer significant except the tax variable which has a *negative* sign. This would imply that an increase in tax rates, other things equal, causes a *reduction* in rents. This result is inconsistent with any reasonable theoretical expectation: non-shifting implies no effect on rents and shifting implies a positive effect.

In selecting a group of communities for further study, we felt it advisable to make one last adjustment, namely to drop Boston itself from the sample. As the central city in the metropolitan area, it is hardly comparable in size or other characteristics to the suburban communities which constitute the remainder of the sample.[4] For sake of completeness, we include as equation (4) in Table I a regression run on this group of 23 communities with our substitution of R° and Y°_2 for Orr's R and Y_2. The results are essentially the same as those in equation (3).

Finally, we want to emphasize that, even if Orr's model were perfectly specified and all operational variables were perfect measures of their theoretical counterparts, there would still be good reason to be uneasy over his results. The problem is that several of Orr's independent variables are in fact determined at least in part by his dependent variable — the level of rents. Land values, for example, surely depend to some extent on the income from rental units. Moreover, the tax rate itself depends upon the value of rental (as well as of owner-occupied) property: the higher are property values, the lower need be the tax *rates* to finance a given program of public expenditures. Where such a "reverse line" of causation is present, the independent variables in

the analysis are correlated with the error term resulting in biased estimates of the coefficients. This would suggest the use of an estimation technique designed to deal with the problem of simultaneous-equation bias.[5]

We conclude that Orr's empirical test does not offer a reliable basis for determining the incidence of differential property taxes on the improvement component of rental housing. The likelihood that the property-tax variable is a highly imprecise measure of the rate at which rental property is taxed, the use of inappropriate measures of the size and condition of *rental* housing, and possible bias of the estimated coefficients resulting from the use of ordinary least squares all suggest that Orr's results must be viewed with serious reservations.

Some Further Empirical Results

In this section of the paper, we attempt to rework Orr's study in such a way as to meet the objections we have raised. Our empirical results do not, however, provide a direct answer to the question examined by Orr: whether property-tax differentials on *rental* housing are borne by tenants or owners. Indeed, for reasons discussed earlier, we see no feasible way to answer this question based on existing data. Our results do indicate tax capitalization, but, as will become clear, it is capitalization of a somewhat different sort than that suggested by Orr.

Since Orr's property-tax rates apply to single-family dwellings, a study of incidence using these rates can only examine their impact on the value of owner-occupied dwellings rather than their effects on rental units. For this reason, we replaced Orr's dependent variable, the rent variable, with the median value of owner-occupied dwellings in each community. We then regressed this variable on the equalized tax rate and a set of additional variables (similar to

---

[4] An argument similar to the one for Boston could perhaps be raised against including its dense, close-in suburbs with large stocks of old rental housing (e.g., Brookline, Cambridge, Somerville), but we will not push this point further.

[5] For a rigorous treatment of this whole issue, see, for example, Johnston [1, Chapter 9].

those used by Orr) to account for the other determinants of property values. Following Orr, we assume that the value of dwelling units in any particular community depends on the quality of the dwellings themselves, the proximity of the community to sources of employment, and on the existing levels of public services and tax rates. If differentials in local property taxes are in fact capitalized, we would expect an inverse relationship between the value of dwelling units and the tax rate: higher taxes would (other things equal) make these units less attractive and would thereby depress their market value.[6]

Using ordinary least squares (OLSQ) and the sample of 23 communities discussed earlier, we reach the following results:

(5) $V = -26 - 5.2 \log t + .005Y_3$
$\qquad (3.1) (2.6) \qquad (0.6)$
$\qquad\qquad\qquad + 7.4R + .07N + .06Y_1$
$\qquad\qquad\qquad (6.5) \quad (2.0) \quad (1.1)$

[Note: the numbers in parentheses are the absolute values of the t-statistic for the coefficient.]

$R^2 = .93$

where:

V = Median value of owner-occupied dwellings in thousands of $ (1960)
Log t = Natural log of Orr's equalized percentage property-tax rate
Y_3 = Orr's expenditure per pupil in public schools in $ (1960-61)

[6] More precisely, if t is the property-tax rate, r the rate of discount, Y the annual (imputed) rent, V the value of the property, and n the life of the asset, we have in the event of complete capitalization that:

$$V = \frac{-Y}{(1 + mt)}$$

where $\quad m = \sum_{i=1}^{n} \frac{1}{(1 + r)^i}$

From this expression, it is clear that an increase in t will induce a fall in V. This expression is derived in Oates [2].

R = Median number of rooms per owner-occupied dwelling (1960)
N = Per cent of houses built since 1950 (1960)
Y_1 = Orr's accessibility variable which measures the proximity of the community to sources of employment.

The variables R and N, measures of the size and age of the housing stock, are intended as proxy variables for the quality of dwelling units in the community; both are statistically significant at a 95 per cent level of confidence and have the expected sign. In contrast, Orr's accessibility variable (Y_1), which attempts to measure proximity to jobs, is not significant although it does have the anticipated sign. Of primary interest is the tax variable (Log t), the natural logarithm of the equalized tax rate. We find that tax rates bear a significant and negative relationship to the value of owner-occupied dwellings, which is consistent with the hypothesis of (at least partial) capitalization of the tax. Finally, a variable to measure the level of output of public education services is not here significant.[7]

As we suggested earlier, however, one must be uneasy about equation (5) because of the likely presence of simultaneous-equation bias. In an attempt to circumvent this difficulty, we re-estimated equation (5) using two-stage least squares

[7] The data on the tax, expenditure per pupil, and accessibility variables were supplied us by Orr; the median number of rooms per owner-occupied dwelling is from the 1960 Census of Housing, Tables 13, 19 and 23; and the per cent of houses built since 1950 appears in the Municipal Yearbook, 1963 edition, Table III. As an alternative to Orr's accessibility variable, we tried using simply the linear distance of the community from downtown Boston; while this variable had the expected negative sign, it likewise was not statistically significant. Finally, we point out that the tax variable has greater explanatory power when used in log form; this incidentally is what one would expect from the formula in footnote 6.

(TSLS).[8] We find in equation (6) that in this case the TSLS results are very similar

$$(6)\quad V = -19 - 6.0 \text{ Log } t + .015Y_3$$
$$\qquad\quad (1.9)\,(2.5)\qquad\quad (1.4)$$
$$\qquad\qquad\qquad\quad + 6.3R + .09N + .08Y_1$$
$$\qquad\qquad\qquad\quad\;\; (4.6)\quad (2.1)\quad (1.3)$$
$$\quad R^2 = .92$$

to those obtained using OLSQ. In particular, the coefficient of the tax variable is still negative and significant. We might note also that the coefficient of the other fiscal variable, expenditure per pupil in the public schools, possesses the expected sign and is considerably larger here than in (5); it is not, however, significantly different from its value in (5) and, using a one-tail test, is significantly different from zero only at a 90 per cent level of confidence.[9]

[8] We treated both the tax rate and expenditure per pupil variables, which clearly depend to some extent on property values, as endogenous. In addition to the remaining independent variables in (6), we used the following as exogenous variables: per cent of dwelling units owner-occupied (1960), population size (1960), percentage population growth (1950 to 1960), population density (1960), median family income (1959), percentage of families with incomes less than $3,000 (1959), the median number of school years completed by males of age 25 years and over (1960), and the per cent of pupils enrolled in private schools (1960). The sources of these data are as follows: per cent of dwellings owner-occupied from the *1960 Census of Housing*, HC (1) No. 23, Massachusetts; per cent growth in population and population density from the *County and City Data Book*, 1967; per cent of pupils enrolled in private schools from the *Municipal Yearbook*, 1963 edition; and the remaining data from the *1960 Census of Population*, PC (1) 23C, Massachusetts. For a description of TSLS (which involves purging the suspect variables in (5) of their correlation with the error term by regressing them on a set of exogenous variables), see Johnston [1, Chapter 9].

[9] One of the authors [Oates, 2] has made a similar study of the effects of property taxes and educational expenditures on local property values in 53 surburban municipalities in northeastern New Jersey. The results for the New Jersey sample bear some resemblance to those in equation (6). In particular, the coefficients

We can use equation (6) along with some typical values of the variables to get a rough idea of just how large a portion of the tax differentials among the communities is being capitalized in the form of reduced property values. Equation (6) indicates that an increase in property-tax rates from 3 per cent to 4 per cent will, other things equal, result in a fall in the value of an average dwelling of roughly $1,700. If we consider a dwelling with an expected remaining life of 40 years and a current market value of $17,000 (the average market value for our sample), we find that complete capitalization of this increase in the tax rate implies a decline in the value of the property to about $15,300, or a decline of roughly $1,700.[10] Equation (6) thus suggests that on the average the whole of the tax differentials among the communities is capitalized; in comparing two otherwise identical communities, owners of property in the high-tax locality would therefore appear to absorb the entire impact of the higher taxes.[11]

of both an equalized property-tax variable and a variable measuring expenditure per pupil in public schools were statistically significant and possessed the same signs as in (6).

[10] To reach this figure, we make use of the expression in footnote 6. Using this expression first to determine the value of Y, we have, assuming a rate of discount of 5 per cent and a tax rate initially of 3 per cent that:

$$\$17,000 = \frac{mY}{(1 + .03m)}$$

$$\text{where } m = \sum_{i=1}^{40} \frac{1}{(1.05)^i} = 17.16$$

This yields $Y = \$1,500$. We next assume a rise in t to $t = .04$, and, re-employing this formula, we have:

$$V = \frac{(17.16)\,(\$1,500)}{1 + (.04)\,(17.16)} = \$15,300.$$

[11] We have not tried (as did Orr) to separate the value of the structure from that of the land. This is a very tricky undertaking; it is not clear to us that simply including an independent variable (which incidentally is obviously not in this case independent) reflecting local land

We stress, however, that this does not mean that an increase in municipal property-tax rates to finance improved public services will necessarily depress local property values. For purposes of illustration, assume that the coefficient of the expenditure per pupil variable in (6) is in fact an accurate measure of the extent to which an improved program of public education (resulting from increased spending per pupil) enhances local property values. For simplicity, assume further that the community is composed of families each of which contains one public-school pupil and each of which resides in a dwelling with a market value of $17,000. In this case, an increase in local property-tax rates from 3 per cent to 4 per cent will generate additional revenues of $170 per family. Assume that one half of the increased revenues goes into public schools,[12] so that expenditure per pupil rises by $85. The coefficient of Y_3 in equation (6) implies that the increased attractiveness of local public schools resulting from this program will in itself generate a rise in local property values of about $1,300, which will off-set most of the depressive effect (i.e., –$1,700) of the higher taxes. The point is that, when considering a budgetary

values effects this separation. As it turns out; this is not for our purposes really necessary, since our results suggest that the whole of the tax differentials (those parts that fall on the land and on the structures) is capitalized. On another matter, one might regard the capitalization issue as irrelevant in the case of owner-occupied housing since the owner and tenant are one in the same. The issue, however, becomes one of great importance when it comes time to sell one's house, for capitalization of the tax implies a reduction in the market value of the property.

[12] For Massachusetts in 1962, Orr points out that 42 per cent of local revenues were devoted to education [4, p. 260].

change in a single community, one must evaluate the effects on property values operating through both the tax and the expenditure sides of the budget.[13]

Our study thus suggests that differentials in local property-tax rates on *owner-occupied* housing are capitalized. While this result is, we believe, interesting in its own right, we acknowledge that it cannot be used in any obvious way to make reliable inferences about the incidence of property taxes on rental housing. We feel, however, that this is all that can be derived with any confidence from the available data.

REFERENCES

[1] J. Johnston, *Econometric Methods,* New York, 1963.
[2] W. Oates, "The Effects of Property Taxes and Local Public Spending on Property Values: An Empirical Study of Tax Capitalization and the Tiebout Hypothesis." *The Journal of Political Economy,* 77 (Nov./Dec. 1969), pp. 957-971.
[3] O. Oldman and H. Aaron, "Assessment-Sales Ratios under the Boston Property Tax," *National Tax Journal, 18,* (March 1965), pp. 36-49.
[4] L. Orr, "The Incidence of Differential Property Taxes on Urban Housing," *National Tax Journal, 21,* (Sept. 1968), pp. 253-62.
[5] G. Sazama, "Equalization of Property Taxes for the Nation's Largest Central Cities," *National Tax Journal,* 18 (June 1965), pp. 151-74.
[6] U.S. Bureau of the Census, *U.S. Census of Housing: 1960,* Vol. I, Part IV; Washington 1963.

[13] These results are again similar to those reached by Oates in his study of northeastern New Jersey. The coefficients of the fiscal variables in the New Jersey regression equation also suggest that, *ceteris paribus,* the bulk of property-tax differentials are capitalized, but that for a given community, the depressive effects of higher taxes on local property values are (roughly) fully offset by the positive impact of increased spending per pupil.

PART VI

PUBLIC CHOICE AND FISCAL FEDERALISM

22

6 "Automatic" Increases in Tax Revenues—The Effect on the Size of the Public Budget

WALLACE E. OATES*

This chapter addresses what has become a commonplace assertion concerning the fiscal difficulties of state and local governments: the inability of these governments to meet their rapidly expanding budgetary needs because of the relatively low income elasticity of their revenue systems. The argument typically runs as follows. Because of rising relative costs of most public services and the growing demand for these services as incomes expand, the budgets of state and local governments necessary to keep pace with the demand for public outputs increase more than proportionately with aggregate personal income. Most state and local tax structures, however, possess an income elasticity not much in excess of unity, so that revenue "needs" grow more rapidly than do actual revenues at existing tax rates. This shortfall is sometimes described as a "revenue gap," implying that political obstacles to raising tax rates and introducing new sources of revenues are likely to result in an underprovision of public services.

* Professor of Economics, Princeton University.

I am very grateful to William Baumol, Ray Fair, Stephen Goldfeld, James Ohls, Richard Quandt, and Michelle White for their comments on an earlier draft of this paper. In addition, I want to acknowledge the invaluable assistance of Judith Hawkes and John Murray with the empirical work and the expert help of Rosemary Little in locating the necessary data. For support of this study, I am indebted to the National Science Foundation.

The proposed solution to the problem is to make available to state and local governments more income-elastic sources of funding to close, at least partially, these revenue gaps. Such proposals have figured as central arguments, first, in the case for revenue sharing, and, second, in movements for reform of state and local tax systems themselves. Early in the push for revenue sharing, Walter Heller contended that, "At the Federal level, economic growth and a powerful tax system, interacting under modern fiscal management, generate new revenues faster than they generate new demands on the Federal purse. But at the state–local level, the situation is reversed. Under the whiplash of prosperity, responsibilities are outstripping revenues."[1]

Similarly, in the literature on state–local tax reform, one encounters with some regularity conclusions like those expressed by the New Jersey Tax Policy Committee, a body appointed by former Governor William Cahill to assess the New Jersey tax system and to make recommendations.

> The inelastic nature of New Jersey's state tax system means inevitable recurrent fiscal crises as revenue gaps open up. The expedients of the past can no longer be relied upon to close these gaps. Exploiting the same tax sources cannot cope with the projected growth in expenditures and provide the funds required to reform the tax structure. . . .
>
> If the "mix" of the tax system were changed to rely more heavily on income-elastic taxes, this would minimize the need for raising rates. The total tax burdens would be unchanged, but the need for recurrent legislative intervention would be diminished.[2]

I do not want to overstate the case. Obviously, revenue sharing and tax reform have had other fundamental objectives, such as a more equitable distribution of the tax burden. Nevertheless, I think it is fair to say that the goal of increasing the income elasticity of state–local sources of revenues has figured importantly in these programs.

One author, James Buchanan, has attributed an almost cosmic importance to the issue. Buchanan argues that, "with the adoption of the Sixteenth Amendment to the Constitution, the central government was granted access to the single fiscal weapon that was to remake the whole national fiscal pattern."[3] For, as Buchanan has indicated elsewhere, "In a period of rapidly increasing national product, that tax institution charac-

[1] See Heller, *New Dimensions of Political Economy* (Cambridge, Mass.: Harvard University Press, 1966), p. 118.

[2] *Summary of the Report of the New Jersey Tax Policy Committee* (Trenton: Feb. 23, 1972), pp. 2–3.

[3] See Buchanan, "Financing a Viable Federalism," in Harry L. Johnson, ed., *State and Local Tax Problems* (Knoxville: University of Tennessee Press, 1969), p. 5.

terized by the highest elasticity will tend, other things equal, to generate the largest volume of public spending."[4]

This last statement is a precise formulation of the hypothesis that I want to investigate here, and I stress that it is a hypothesis. It has served as an unexamined assumption in the sorts of discussions cited earlier. However, it is an empirical proposition, and, although it possesses a certain pragmatic plausibility, I will suggest in the next section that its validity, on a priori grounds, is far from clear. In fact, on one interpretation, it can be seen to imply some very curious and suspect behavior on the part of individual taxpayers. The later sections of the chapter consist of a set of empirical studies of state and local finances designed to answer the following question. Over the decade 1960-70 (a period of intense fiscal pressure on state and local governments), did those governments with more income-elastic revenue systems exhibit a comparatively large expansion in expenditures? I will also explore some international data bearing on this thesis as it relates to the growth of the public sector as a whole.

On the Income Elasticity of the Revenue System

First, I want to explore somewhat more systematically the proposition that the growth in public expenditure depends on the income elasticity of the revenue system. In terms of rational economic behavior, this seems a very peculiar assertion. We would expect that individual demands for public services would be based upon tastes, levels of income, and the cost of these services. With a given cost-sharing scheme (or set of tax shares), we could then determine the pattern of individual demands at some moment in time.

But why should people care about the income elasticity of the tax structure? What the proposition under study seems to imply is that people will not object to increases in public expenditure if they can be funded with no increases in tax rates (that is, from increments to revenues resulting solely from growth in income), but they will not support an expanded public budget if it requires a rise in tax rates. This suggests what people care about is not their tax *bill*, but rather their tax *rate*. Viewed this way, the hypothesis simply is not consistent with our conventional description of rational behavior; it implies that consumer-taxpayers are subject to a kind of "fiscal illusion."

---

[4] See Buchanan, *Public Finance in Democratic Process* (Chapel Hill: University of North Carolina Press, 1967), p. 65. Michael Reagan appears to share Buchanan's view: "Not least among the reasons for federal dominance of the revenue picture is the superior *elasticity* of the income tax, which gives it a considerable political advantage. . . ." See Reagan, *The New Federalism* (New York: Oxford University Press, 1972), p. 38.

A simple view of individual rationality, therefore, does not support the basic proposition. If people want a higher level of public services, they should presumably be willing to support the extended budget whether it is financed by an expansion in the tax base at given rates or by higher rates applied to a static base. The tax bill is what matters to the rational taxpayer. It is worth noting here that, over the decade of the 1960s, the remarkable expansion in state–local public spending was financed largely from new levies consisting both of higher tax rates and the imposition of new forms of taxes. As Walter Heller and Joseph Pechman have pointed out, "Between 1959 and 1967, every state but one raised rates or adopted a major new tax; there were 230 rate increases and 19 new tax adoptions in this period."[5] On the face of it, there seem to be good reasons to be skeptical of the importance of an elastic tax structure for the level of public expenditure.

What kind of a case can we muster in support of the proposition? Somewhat surprisingly, hardly anyone[6] has really bothered to justify the hypothesis; it is typically put forward simply as an assertion of unquestioned validity. One encounters a few vague, unsatisfactory statements like that of L. L. Ecker-Racz, "The people can afford higher taxes if only they would agree to the need. Instead they have an instinctive aversion to taxes for reasons none of us can be sure about. Public officials, interested in political longevity, in electoral support, feel obliged to heed the people's voice and echo their complaints."[7]

To try to make some sense of the hypothesis, we can go either (or, perhaps, both) of two routes. The first simply argues that this is a matter on which consumer-taxpayers do in fact act irrationally. There is a "faulty perception" on the part of the individual who regards an extra dollar of taxes as more costly to him if it results from a higher tax rate than from a more elastic base. At least over some range of tax liabilities, he suffers from a very direct sort of fiscal illusion. Richard Wagner, for example, advances this explanation:

> There also exists a large body of casual evidence supporting the existence of faulty fiscal perception. Whenever a legislative assembly considers changes in

---

[5] See Heller and Pechman, "Questions and Answers on Revenue Sharing," in *Revenue Sharing and Its Alternatives: What Future for Fiscal Federalism?*, Hearings before the Subcommittee on Fiscal Policy of the Joint Economic Committee (1967), pp. 11–17; reprinted in *Studies in Government Finance Reprints*, Brookings Institution Reprint No. 135, p. 10.

[6] The one important exception, to my knowledge, is Richard Wagner.

[7] See Ecker-Racz, *The Politics and Economics of State–Local Finance* (Englewood Cliffs, N.J.: Prentice-Hall, 1970), p. 197. This comment is in the context of a discussion of the growth of fiscal "needs" and revenues, and the elasticity of the tax structure.

tax rates, tortuous discussion takes place and considerable publicity is given to the deliberations. Yet no similar agonizing takes place over the continual, automatic increase in tax rates that is produced by progressivity in the national tax structure. Everyone is aware of a consciously enacted tax surcharge; a similar surcharge is enacted each year when income grows under progressive taxation, but many taxpayers remain unconscious of this surcharge.[8]

This is not, I think, an explanation to be dismissed lightly. There are other empirical studies which provide support for the presence of "illusory" behavior. William Branson and Alvin Klevorick, for example, have found the evidence on consumption behavior to be consistent with a model incorporating a money illusion: their findings indicate that in the short run, consumption expenditure depends not only on real income but also on a distributed-lag term involving the level of prices.[9]

Nevertheless, although this line of argument possesses a certain plausibility, I (along with most economists, I suspect) am uncomfortable with a hypothesis founded solely on irrational behavior. It is tempting to take an alternative tack to see if there are not some elements in the system of collective choice (that is, political mechanism) which can account for the supposed phenomenon. Perhaps the process through which individual tastes become translated into public budgets contains a set of incentives or costs that can explain the expansionary implications of a more income-elastic revenue system. In this case, the so-called fiscal illusion may be a property of the political mechanism and may yet be consistent with rational individual behavior.

One possible explanation can be found in the *transactions costs* associated with changes in tax rates. Richard Wagner has also made this case:

> As viewed by legislators, the cost of thus changing tax structures may exceed the benefits, in which case the required change in relative tax collections will not occur. Such legislative behavior may be interpreted as a form of habitual behavior, and may very well be rational. There is a cost incurred in failing to routinize many types of activity—the value of the resources consumed in examining the consequences of the alternative choices, in this case, choices among possible tax structures. If the costs incurred by continual reexamination exceed the benefits received from taking more timely actions, habitual behavior is efficient—it is the least inefficient of the attainable alternatives.[10]

---

[8] See Wagner, *The Fiscal Organization of American Federalism* (Chicago: Markham, 1971), p. 87.

[9] Branson and Klevorick, "Money Illusion and the Aggregate Consumption Function," *American Economic Review*, vol. 59 (December 1969), pp. 832–849).

[10] Wagner, "The Fiscal Organization," pp. 85–86.

The New Jersey Tax Policy Committee may have had a similar point in mind when they argued that a more income-elastic tax structure would diminish "the need for recurrent legislative intervention."[11]

While there may be some truth to this contention. I have real reservations as to its likely importance. The resource costs of legislative action are, I should guess, relatively small compared to the benefits of meeting the service demands on the public sector. (In fact, there may be, on net, benefits from a regular reevaluation of spending *and* tax rates, like that, for example, which takes place with the annual budget referendum in many school districts; such processes require a periodic reconsideration of the level and composition of the public budget in the explicit context of the level of taxes.) I should be surprised if the costs of legislative action were sufficient to prevent significant realignments of the budget deemed desirable by the public. What may be true, as Wagner suggests, is that the need for adjustment in tax rates introduces some delays into the process. Thus, although I doubt that over the longer haul such transactions costs are likely to have much effect on the budget, there may be some short-run effects. The interesting question here, as for many other economic issues, may be, How long is the short run? More attention will be paid to this question in the empirical work which follows.

Aside from legislative transactions costs, the income elasticity of the tax structure may influence the budget because of taxpayer ignorance (*not* irrationality). As Anthony Downs has argued, it may be fully rational for the taxpayer–voter to be uninformed about the public budget.[12] Since the probability that an individual's vote will influence the outcome of a given state or local election is for most purposes negligible, it may not be in his interest to absorb the "costs" of becoming informed, or even of voting for that matter. "Ignorance of politics is not a result of unpatriotic apathy; rather it is a highly rational response to the facts of political life in a large democracy."[13]

The fiscal illusion (or "faulty fiscal perception" as Wagner called it earlier) need not, therefore, imply irrational behavior by taxpayer–voters. Because of the information costs inherent in determining the implicit "surcharge" resulting from rising income, the individual may not bother to make himself aware of the rise in his tax bill. In contrast, he can hardly help noticing the political turmoil and publicity that normally accompany a legislative action to increase tax rates. The information costs are, in this

---

[11] *Summary of the Report*, p. 3.

[12] Downs, "An Economic Theory of Political Action in a Democracy," *Journal of Political Economy*, vol. 65 (April 1957), pp. 135–150.

[13] Ibid., p. 147.

instance, very low; the daily perusal of the newspaper or other news media will call the increase to his attention. From the perspective of the politician, this fact suggests that he can, in effect, hide the costs of a larger budget from the taxpayer if he can finance it by an implicit surcharge from a growing tax base; if he must call attention to the higher taxes by a legislated increase in tax rates, he will have to incur some loss of taxpayer–voter support.

Again, this line of argument possesses a certain plausibility. I would be reluctant to push it too hard, however, for the logical implication is that if the tax system were sufficiently income-elastic, the public sector over time could come to absorb virtually all the taxpayer's income with no opposition. Pushed to its extreme, the argument is absurd. Nevertheless, it may yet be true that *over some range of tax bills* the fiscal illusion is operative.

With this as background, we turn in the next three sections to a series of empirical tests of the hypothesis that a higher income elasticity of the tax structure provides a positive stimulus to the growth of public spending. In the next two sections, we will examine the relationship between the change in expenditure for state governments and for a sample of local governments, respectively, and the elasticity of the tax structure over the period 1960–70. In a later section, I provide some additional, but admittedly highly conjectural, evidence using international cross-sectional data.

Growth in Spending by State Governments, 1960–70

The decade 1960–70 was one of extraordinary increases in state–local budgets; in the aggregate, state–local spending grew from a level of $52 billion in 1960 to $131 billion in 1970 (an average annual rate of increase of about 9 percent as compared with an average annual increase of roughly 6.5 percent in money GNP). The state and local public sector was indeed one of the economy's leading "growth industries" during the sixties. If a relatively inelastic tax structure acts as a constraint on state–local spending, this should be a period during which this constraint would be readily evident.

In this section, I will examine the growth in spending by state governments from 1960 to 1970 to see if, other things equal, those state governments with more income-elastic tax systems did in fact experience comparatively large increases in expenditure. The method of analysis is as follows. First, I postulate an expenditure function for state governments of the form:

(1) $$G_{it} = \alpha_0 + \alpha_1 V_{it} + \alpha_2 R_{it} + \alpha_3 S_{it} + u_{it},$$

where

> G_{it} = per capita general expenditure of the ith state government in
> year t
> V_{it} = socioeconomic determinants of public spending (a vector of
> socioeconomic variables) for state i in year t
> R_{it} = federal grants per capita to the ith state government in year t
> S_{it} = percentage of state–local spending in state i during year t that
> is undertaken by the state government
> u_{it} = the disturbance term.

The rationale for most of these variables is pretty obvious. The variable S_{it}, for example, serves as a measure of the division of fiscal functions between the state and the local governments in each state. A relatively large value of S indicates a comparatively major role for the state government which, other things equal, should be reflected in a higher level of expenditure per capita.

Our concern, however, is with the growth in spending from 1960 to 1970. This we can express by simply subtracting the expenditure function for 1970 from that for 1960 to obtain:

$$(2) \qquad \Delta G_i = G_{i1970} - G_{i1960}$$
$$= \alpha_1(V_{i1970} - V_{i1960}) + \alpha_2(R_{i1970} - R_{i1960})$$
$$+ \alpha_3(S_{i1970} - S_{i1960}) + (u_{i1970} - u_{i1960}).$$

The hypothesis is that, in addition to the determinants of the growth in spending specified in equation 2, the income elasticity of the tax structure also influences the extent of the increase. To test this, I will add a measure of the tax elasticity to equation 2. We then proceed to estimate the equation[14]:

$$(3) \quad \Delta G_i = a_0 + \alpha_1(V_{i1970} - V_{i1960}) + \alpha_2(R_{i1970} - R_{i1960})$$
$$+ \alpha_3(S_{i1970} - S_{i1960}) + \alpha_4 T_i + u_i^*,$$

where

> T_i = a measure of the income elasticity of the tax structure of the state
> government in state i
> u_i^* = the associated disturbance term.

A central concern is to determine a reliable operational measure of the elasticity of the state tax system. There is one set of estimates available

---

[14] While the formulation of the tax-elasticity hypothesis in equation 3 seems plausible, one would prefer a specification founded securely on a more compelling conceptual framework. For an exploration of this issue, see Appendix B.

from an external source. The Advisory Commission on Intergovernmental Relations (ACIR), in a report published in 1968, has provided an estimate for each state of the income elasticity of the state government's tax structure for 1967.[15] There are, however, a number of deficiencies in the ACIR estimates. For example, the estimates are based on only a fraction of the sources of each state's tax revenues; for some states, this is less than 60 percent. For purposes of this study, however, my most serious reservation is that the estimates are for a single year. What we need are measures of the tax elasticity for the decade 1960–70; where the ACIR variable is used in the equations that follow, we must, therefore, treat it as a proxy for tax elasticity for the decade. As such, it does not reflect either the timing of *changes* in the tax structure that occurred prior to 1967 or *any* effects of changes instituted after 1967. Incidentally, one interesting feature of the ACIR estimates is the considerable range in income elasticity that they indicate; the estimates extend from 0.7 for Nebraska to 1.4 for Oregon. This is encouraging, for it suggests substantial variation in the crucial independent variable.

To obtain more reliable measures of tax elasticity, I assembled fiscal histories of the forty-eight coterminous states over the decade, 1960–70. Existing estimates of the income elasticities of various state taxes indicate that far and away the most income-elastic is the individual income tax. Most estimates are in the range of 1.5 to 2.0; the ACIR suggests a "medium" estimate of 1.65. This compares to estimates of the income elasticity of general sales taxes of roughly unity. State corporate income taxes also exhibit a somewhat above-average income elasticity; the ACIR indicates a "medium" value of 1.2.[16]

This suggests that the extent of reliance on income taxation should provide a reasonable approximation to the relative elasticity of the tax structure. For this purpose, the comparative importance of the individual income tax should be the better measure. As noted above, state individual income taxes are, on average, much more income-elastic than corporation income taxes. Moreover, the individual income tax is typically a much larger component of state tax systems than are corporate income taxes: over the decade 1960–70, state governments, in the aggregate, collected 14 percent of their tax revenues from individual income taxes and only

[15] Advisory Commission on Intergovernmental Relations (ACIR), *Sources of Increased State Tax Collections: Economic Growth Vs. Political Choice*, Information Report M-41 (October 1968), table 7.

[16] For a summary of estimated income elasticities for various state and local taxes, see ACIR, *Federal–State Local Finances: Significant Features of Fiscal Federalism* (February 1974), table 173, p. 320; for the "medium" estimates see ACIR, *Sources of Increased State Tax Collections*, p. 3.

5.5 percent from taxes on corporation income. There is, incidentally, considerable variation in the degree of reliance on income taxation: there are a handful of states (Florida, Nevada, Ohio, Texas, Washington, and Wyoming) which generated no tax revenues from either individual or corporate income taxation during 1960–70, while at the other extreme the state of Oregon derived 47 percent of its tax revenues from the individual income tax alone and 57 percent from individual and corporation income taxes combined over this same period.

In the regression equations that follow, I will employ in succession the following different measures of the income elasticity of the state government tax system for 1960–70:

T_{Ai} = ACIR estimate of the income elasticity of the tax structure of ith state government for 1967

T_{Ii} = the sum of individual income tax receipts over the years 1960–70 as a percentage of the sum of total tax receipts over the same years for the ith state government

T_{Ci} = the sum of corporation income tax receipts (1960–70) as a percentage of total tax receipts (1960–70) for state i

$T_{Ti} = T_{Ii} + T_{Ci}$ = total income tax receipts as a percentage of total tax receipts for 1960–70 for state i.

I used each of these four tax variables in the process of estimating equation 3. The estimation also required making explicit the socioeconomic determinants of state government expenditure. I have used the following three variables:

Y_{it} = median family income in state i during year t

L_{it} = percentage of families in state i with incomes below the poverty line in year t

P_{it} = population size of state i in year t.

Table 1 summarizes the results obtained from estimating equation 3 by ordinary least squares (OLSQ). In Table 1, equation 1.1 employs the ACIR tax variable: although its sign is consistent with the hypothesized effect of tax elasticity, the standard error is sufficiently large that we cannot reject the null hypothesis of no effect at a .05 level of significance. In contrast, the individual income tax variable, T_I, is statistically significant in equation 1.2 of Table 1; this result does support the hypothesized positive effect of tax elasticity on the growth in public expenditure. As expected, the individual income tax variable appears to possess a more reliable effect on the growth of public spending than do corporation tax receipts.

There is good reason, however, to be suspicious of the results in Table 1, because there are some obvious systems problems inherent in the inter-

TABLE 1. Growth in State Government Expenditures, 1960–70 (OLSQ)

Equation	Constant	$(Y_{1970} - Y_{1960})$	$(L_{1970} - L_{1960})$	$(P_{1970} - P_{1960})$	$(R_{1970} - R_{1960})$	$(S_{1970} - S_{1960})$	T_A	T_I	T_C	T_T	R^2
(1.1)	−84 (1.3)	43 (3.4)	1.1 (0.9)	−16 (2.1)	2.1 (6.8)	−0.8 (0.7)	43 (1.5)				.64
(1.2)	−29 (0.5)	37 (3.1)	1.0 (0.8)	−15 (2.1)	2.0 (7.1)	−0.8 (0.7)		1.1 (2.9)			.69
(1.3)	−12 (0.2)	35 (2.5)	1.5 (1.2)	−18 (2.3)	2.0 (6.5)	−0.8 (0.7)			2.4 (1.9)		.65
(1.4)	−16 (0.3)	34 (2.8)	1.2 (1.0)	−15 (2.1)	2.0 (6.9)	−0.8 (0.7)				0.9 (3.0)	.69
(1.5)	−15 (0.2)	34 (2.6)	1.2 (1.0)	−15 (2.1)	2.0 (6.7)	−0.8 (0.7)		0.9 (2.3)	1.0 (0.8)		.69

Notes:
Dependent variable: ΔG = change in per capita expenditure by the state government, 1960–70.
N = 48 for all equations.
The numbers in parentheses below the estimated coefficients are the absolute values of the t statistic.

relationships among the variables. Two of the independent variables are clearly endogenous to the system as a whole. Intergovernmental grants are in part determined by the level of public expenditure, since under matching-grant programs, the funds received depend upon the level of spending selected by the recipient. The state share variable will also obviously depend upon the level of state government expenditure. This means that we must regard the variables $(R_{1970} - R_{1960})$ and $(S_{1970} - S_{1960})$ as endogenous to the complete system of equations: OLSQ can thus be expected to generate biased estimators of the coefficients in equation 3.

To provide a more reliable set of parameter estimates, I estimated the same set of equations by two-stage least squares; Table 2 indicates these results.[17] The general pattern of findings is quite similar to those obtained with OLSQ. In particular, the elasticity variable, T_I, which indicates the extent of reliance on individual income taxation, is significant at a .05 level under both methods of estimation. In both cases, the estimated coefficient is about unity. This suggests what I would judge to be a nontrivial, yet modest, effect on the growth in spending. As an illustration, the point estimates indicate that a state government which generated 35 percent of its revenues through individual income taxes would, other things equal, have experienced an expansion in spending per capita over 1960–70 of roughly $35 per capita more than a state which collected no revenues from this source. But this compares to a mean increase in state expenditure per capita of $228 for the decade. I think this can hardly be regarded as a really "large" effect.

The estimated coefficient for the ACIR tax variable, although positive in sign, remains statistically insignificant at a .05 level. Similar remarks also apply to the estimated coefficient of the tax elasticity variable defined in terms of corporation tax revenues. In sum, the evidence from state government fiscal experience in the decade 1960–70 does appear consistent with the basic hypothesis: state governments with more income-elastic tax structures did, other things equal, increase expenditure per capita by a greater amount than those with less elastic tax systems. The estimated magnitude of the effect does, however, appear to be of a modest order.

---

[17] To "purge" the endogenous grant and share variables of their presumed correlation with the disturbance term. I employed in the first stage a set of instrumental variables including, in addition to other independent variables in equations 1.1 through 1.5, the following: the percentage of the population under age eighteen, the percentage of the population over age sixty-five, the percentage of elementary and secondary pupils enrolled in nonpublic schools, the percentage of population that is black, acres of federally owned land per capita, miles of highway per capita, population density, and percentage of the population living in urban areas. These I regard as exogenous variables which would influence (directly or indirectly) the level of grants received and/or the state's share of state–local expenditures.

TABLE 2. Growth in State Government Expenditures, 1960-70 (TSLS)

Equation	Constant	$(Y_{1970} - Y_{1960})$	$(L_{1970} - L_{1960})$	$(P_{1970} - P_{1960})$	$(R_{1970} - R_{1960})$	$(S_{1970} - S_{1960})$	T_A	T_I	T_C	T_T
(2.1)	-145 (1.3)	54 (2.7)	0.5 (0.3)	-19 (2.1)	2.5 (3.6)	-1.2 (0.3)	34 (1.0)			
(2.2)	-102 (0.9)	49 (2.5)	0.4 (0.2)	-18 (2.1)	2.5 (3.8)	-1.2 (0.3)		1.0 (2.4)		
(2.3)	-63 (0.5)	44 (1.9)	1.4 (0.7)	-20 (2.3)	2.4 (3.2)	-2.2 (0.6)			2.0 (1.3)	
(2.4)	-77 (0.7)	44 (2.2)	0.9 (0.5)	-18 (2.2)	2.4 (3.6)	-1.7 (0.5)				0.9 (2.4)
(2.5)	-76 (0.6)	44 (2.0)	0.8 (0.4)	-17 (2.1)	2.4 (3.4)	-1.4 (0.4)		0.9 (2.1)	0.6 (0.4)	

Note: Dependent variable: ΔG = change in per capita expenditure by the state government, 1960-70. The numbers in parentheses below the estimated coefficients are to absolute values of the t statistic.

A few other findings from the regression equations in Tables 1 and 2 are noteworthy in passing. First, the parameter estimates suggest that inter-governmental grants have a large stimulative effect: for each extra dollar of grants received from the federal government, state governments exhibit an increase in spending of roughly $2.00 to $2.50. Second, the cross-sectional results point to an income elasticity of spending well in excess of unity: a state with a medium family income which rose $1,000 more than that of another state experienced, on average, a per capita increase in state government expenditure of about $40 to $50 more than the latter. Evaluated at the mean values of these variables, this implies an income elasticity of spending of approximately 1.5. Finally, it is interesting to note that population growth shows a consistent and significant negative association with the expansion in the budget. States apparently have not increased per capita spending at a pace commensurate with population growth.

Growth in Spending by City Governments, 1960–70

In addition to studying state governmental finances, I examined the fiscal experiences of a sample of thirty-three U.S. cities over this same decade of 1960–70. The well-documented fiscal difficulties of the cities during this period suggest at first glance that the constraints of an inelastic tax structure (if indeed such constraints exist) should have been at least as effective on city, as on state, budgetary growth.

To discern these effects, I ran essentially the same series of tests on increases in city expenditures as those reported for the states in the preceding section. My initial expectation was that these effects, even if operative, would be more difficult to uncover for the cities. First, cities typically place less reliance on income taxes than do the states (although there are a few striking exceptions); and second, to the extent that they do rely on income taxes, the taxes are normally a good deal less progressive than those of the states.[18] For both these reasons, the extent of reliance on income taxes probably does not reflect such substantial differences in tax elasticity for the cities as for the states. Moreover, during this decade many of the cities

---

[18] Most city income taxes are simply a flat percentage (for example, 0.5 or 1 percent) of taxable income with some level of exemption as the only source of progression. There are some exceptions: New York City, for example, possesses a progressive rate structure that in 1968 ranged from 0.4 percent on taxable income less than $1,000 to 2 percent on taxable income in excess of $30,000. State income taxes, in contrast, typically exhibit substantial progression. For a comprehensive description of the structure of individual state and city income taxes in 1968, see Advisory Commission on Intergovernmental Relations, *State and Local Finances, Significant Features 1966 to 1969* (November 1968), tables 35–42.

experienced a net outflow of population, including many middle-income and upper-income families, so that the expansion in the income tax base (even in per capita terms) was considerably less than at the state level.

The sample of thirty-three cities is, incidentally, not a random sample.[19] It draws on the larger cities in the United States and includes in particular all those sizable cities which made a significant use of income taxes; this was necessary to obtain a substantial variation in the tax variable. I should also mention that the Census of Governments does not provide any division between receipts from individual and corporate income taxes for the cities. The tax variable for the cities is simply total income taxes as a percentage of total tax revenues. Within the sample, this variable had a mean of 11.7 percent and ranged in value from 70 percent for Columbus, Ohio, to zero for twenty-one of the cities.

The regression results using OLSQ are reported in equation 4, where ΔX is the change in variable X from 1960–70; the variables $Y, L, P,$ and R are defined as earlier except that they now refer to city jurisdictions; S is again the state percentage of total state–local public expenditure, and T is income tax receipts as a percentage of total tax revenues.

$$(4) \qquad \Delta G = 121 - .03\Delta Y - 1.3\Delta L - .02\Delta P + 1.5\Delta R$$
$$ (1.5) \quad (1.3) \qquad (0.4) \qquad (0.3) \qquad (12.6)$$
$$+ 5.6\Delta S + 1.1T \qquad\qquad R^2 = .89$$
$$(2.5) \qquad (2.7) \qquad\qquad\quad N = 33$$

As for the states, the estimated equation is consistent with the hypothesis of a positive effect of tax elasticity on the growth in public spending. However, ΔR and ΔS are again clearly endogenous variables. Estimating the equation by TSLS yields[20]:

$$(5) \quad \Delta G = 125 - .03\Delta Y - 1.2\Delta L - .02\Delta P + 1.5\Delta R + 6.2\Delta S + 1.1T.$$
$$ (1.4) \quad (1.3) \qquad (0.4) \qquad (0.2) \qquad (8.8) \qquad (1.7) \qquad (2.7)$$

The results in equation 5 are quite similar to those in equation 4. In particular, the tax variable is still positive and significant at a .05 level. Curiously, the magnitude of the estimated coefficient is virtually identical with that for the states—about unity. This indicates that for each extra

---

[19] The list of cities appears in Appendix A.

[20] The additional instrumental variables used to estimate equation 5 were percentage of population under age eighteen, percentage change of fraction of population under age eighteen, percentage of nonwhite population, percentage change of fraction of nonwhite population, miles of highway per capita in the state, population density in the state, population density in the city, and percentage of population in the state residing in urban areas.

percent of tax revenues raised through income taxes, our "typical" city over 1960–70 would have generated an extra $1.00 increase in public spending per capita. Since the mean increase in expenditure per capita for the sample of cities is $147, this suggests a *relatively* larger budgetary effect than at the state level. The point estimate indicates that a city which collected one-half of its revenues from income taxes would have experienced a budgetary increase of about $50 more than a city with no income taxation, a differential of approximately one-third of the mean increase in city spending.

Also, like the findings for the states, equations 4 and 5 suggest a strong expansionary impact of intergovernmental grants; an additional dollar of grant revenues to the cities is associated, on average, with an increase in expenditure of about $1.50. There are, however, some anomalies in the results. The change in medium family income, for example, is negatively related (although not statistically significant) to the growth in spending.

Tax-Elasticity and the Size of the Public Sector: Some International Evidence

The evidence presented in this section is not intended to be taken very seriously. My primary interest is simply to point out that there is, in principle, no reason to restrict the tax elasticity hypothesis to state and local governments. As Buchanan's earlier comments suggest, it is certainly conceivable that the growth of the public sector as a whole may depend to some extent on the structure of the tax system.

Since I had an extensive body of international cross-sectional data readily available from an earlier study, I undertook some admittedly crude statistical work which bears on this proposition. I stress that these data did not permit the estimation of equations like those in the preceding sections, where the growth in public expenditure was regressed on the *changes* in the set of explanatory variables. Instead, I will present findings based on *levels* of variables, where the equation is of the general form:

$$(6) \qquad W_i = \alpha_0 + \alpha_1 V_i + \alpha_2 T_i + u_i,$$

where

W_i = total government revenues as a percentage of national income in country i

V_i = vector of socioeconomic variables in country i influencing the relative size of the public sector

T_i = measure of the income elasticity of country i's tax structure

u_i = disturbance term.

Equation 6 says that the relative *size* of the public sector depends on a set of variables, *V*, and a measure of tax elasticity, *T*. The presumption here is that *T* serves as a proxy for the historic level of the income elasticity of the country's tax system; if this elasticity has been comparatively high, then we would expect, other things equal, to find the country with a relatively large public sector.

Other studies have identified certain systematic influences on the relative size of the government sector.[21] The most powerful explanatory variable (as embodied in Wagner's "law") is the level of per capita income; wealthier societies typically possess a comparatively large "fisc." In addition, the degree of openness seems to have a systematic positive association with the governmental share of economic activity. For *V*, I will therefore employ measures of per capita income and the size of the foreign trade sector. A good measure of tax elasticity is hard to come by. We can, however, approximate the types of measures used in earlier sections with a variable provided in the International Bank for Reconstruction and Development's *World Tables:* direct taxes as a percentage of government general revenue. Direct taxes "comprise all taxes and surtaxes levied as a charge on the income of households and private nonprofit institutions (including contributions to social security); corporate income and excess profits taxes; and taxes on undistributed profits or on capital stock which are levied at regular intervals.[22] The tax variable can thus be roughly described as income taxes as a percentage of government revenues, and we would expect this to be positively related to the income elasticity of the tax system as a whole.

For a sample of fifty-seven countries,[23] the estimated equation is:

$$(7) \qquad W = 3.8 + .007Y + .15F + 0.3T \qquad\qquad R^2 = .64$$
$$(1.3)\quad (3.6)\quad\;\; (2.1)\quad\;\; (3.3)$$

where:

Y = gross domestic product (GDP) per capita in U.S. dollars for 1965
F = total exports as a percentage of GDP for 1965
W and T are defined as noted above (also for 1965).

---

[21] For a survey of these findings, see Kilman Shin, "International Difference in Tax Ratio," *Review of Economics and Statistics*, vol. 51 (May 1969), pp. 213–220.

[22] International Bank for Reconstruction and Development *World Table 6* (Washington, D.C.: IBRD, 1968), p. 1. The *World Tables* are a rich source of data assembled and distributed periodically by the research staff of the Economic Program Department of the IBRD.

[23] The sample consists of the fifty-eight countries listed in the data appendix to Wallace E. Oates, *Fiscal Federalism* (New York: Harcourt Brace Jovanovich, 1972), with the exception of the Malagasy Republic for which the data were incomplete.

The tax elasticity variable is highly significant: we can reject the null hypothesis of no association at a .01 level. In addition, the magnitude of the effect suggested by the point estimate of the coefficient is quite sizable: other things equal, an increase of 10 percentage points in the percentage of revenues raised by direct taxation is associated with a rise of 3 percentage points in tax revenues as a percentage of national income.

The absence of any very compelling case for the particular specification of the equation is admittedly unsettling. Nevertheless, the tax elasticity variable does possess considerable explanatory power. The evidence, crude as it is, from this international data is consistent with the findings for U.S. state and local governments: tax elasticity does appear to be positively related to the growth (or, in this case, the relative size) of the public budget.

Some Reflections and Conclusions

In concluding this study, I want to make four observations. First, there is one further possible source of bias in the results. For state and city governments, we found that over the decade 1960–70 the income elasticity of the tax structure did indeed display a positive association with the growth in public expenditure. This is certainly consistent with the basic hypothesis under study. Yet it is also conceivable that those states desiring a more rapid expansion in public outputs could have consciously constructed a more income-elastic revenue system to finance the anticipated budgetary growth. Or, in other words, one could argue that there is an element of taste reflected in the tax structure itself; more specifically the contention could be that, not only does tax elasticity influence the size of the budget, but planned increases in the budget also affect the income elasticity of the tax system. In fact, if one simply treats the tax-elasticity variable as endogenous in the TSLS estimations, the variable does in fact lose much of its explanatory power. This possibility suggests that the findings in this paper must be accepted with some caution.

Second, it is important to remember that the primary empirical support provided by this study comes from a single decade of rapid expansion in state and city budgets. The findings suggest that in the short run (in this case, ten years), a relatively inelastic tax structure may slow somewhat a process of very rapid growth in the public budget. It may yet be the case that over the longer haul the income elasticity of the tax system exerts little influence on the growth of the public sector. This latter issue remains unclear, although the international cross-sectional findings provide some tentative support for a long-run effect as well.

Third, Michelle White has called to my attention the limitations which result from confining the study of U.S. jurisdictions to states and large cities. In a letter to me, she suggests the hypothesis that ". . . there is more reluctance to raising tax rates at the state level and in large cities than in smaller governmental units such as school districts and townships. This may reflect the fact that increases in statewide taxes cause increased income redistribution so the middle class pay for more than they get. This is less true of local taxes."

Finally, I want to emphasize that this chapter is directed to the *empirical* question of whether or not tax elasticity influences the size of the public budget. I have deliberately avoided the issue of the *desirability* of income-elastic revenue systems. This latter normative problem is a complex one. One may argue that a higher income elasticity of the tax structure is needed to allow the state-local public sector to overcome some type of fiscal illusion in the political process and thereby provide "adequate" levels of public services. This kind of argument would certainly find widespread support among elected officials and legislators; increased tax elasticity provides for them a greater flexibility in budgetary operations. But it is just this sort of flexibility that one may wish to constrain. In fact, a good case can be made for opting for a relatively inelastic structure that will force frequent recourse to the electorate. In this way, the taxpayer-voter will more often have the opportunity to register his support or opposition to public programs in full view of their cost. This latter matter is, of course, a meaningful one only if the hypothesized budgetary effects of tax elasticity are in fact true. The findings in this study would, on balance, lend support to the view that such effects do exist, although they may not be quantitatively very large.

Appendix A

TABLE A.1 Sample of Cities

Atlanta	Memphis
Baltimore	Milwaukee
Birmingham	Minneapolis
Boston	Newark, N.J.
Buffalo	New Orleans
Chicago	New York
Cincinnati	Norfolk
Cleveland	Oklahoma City
Columbus, Ohio	Omaha
Dallas	Philadelphia
Denver	Phoenix
Detroit	Pittsburgh
Fort Worth	Saint Louis
Houston	Saint Paul
Indianapolis	San Antonio
Kansas City, Mo.	Toledo
Louisville	

Appendix B

The equation that I chose to estimate in the text is of an admittedly *ad hoc*, pragmatic character. It is not formally derived from an underlying model of political choice, but is rather a reduced-form expenditure function of the sort frequently encountered in the empirical literature in state and local finance. Its most useful property is its simplicity for purposes of estimation.

Here, I would like to report on, and explore further, some difficulties encountered in an attempt to specify and estimate a somewhat more appealing description of budgetary dynamics. In particular, the equation I employed in the text postulates that the (per capita) dollar increase in public expenditure over the chosen time period depends on changes in the values of key socioeconomic and fiscal variables and on the income elasticity of the tax structure. One disturbing aspect of this formulation is that it makes no provision for any displacements from desired levels of spending or explicit lags in the adjustment process; the specification, for instance, allows for no impact on budgetary growth of the particular value of G in the initial year (except as reflected through its alleged determinants).

To correct this deficiency, I tried to conceptualize the process of budgetary change so as to account explicitly for a lagged adjustment to the desired level of public expenditure. Let us postulate that at any time, t, there is a desired level of spending, G_i^*, which depends on a vector of socioeconomic variables, V_t, and a stochastic term, u_t, such that:

$$(B.1) \qquad G_{it}^* = \gamma_0 + \gamma_1 V_{it} + u_{it},$$

for the ith jurisdiction at time t. However, the actual level of expenditure, G_t, depends not only on the desired level, but on the level of spending in the preceding period, $G_{(t-1)}$. There is thus a process of adjustment from the previous size of the budget to that desired in the present period.

A useful way to introduce the impact of the income elasticity of the tax system is to visualize it as influencing the speed of adjustment of the budgetary process. During a decade when the desired budget is growing quite rapidly, we might expect a highly elastic tax structure to facilitate the expansion of public expenditure. Legislative action to raise tax rates or to introduce new sources of revenues is itself time consuming and costly so that an inelastic tax system exerts a kind of drag on budgetary growth. This suggests a formulation like the following:

$$(B.2) \qquad G_{it} = f(T_i)[G_{it}^* - G_{i(t-1)}] + v_{it}.$$

Equation B.2 specifies that the fraction of the adjustment of the budget from its *actual* level in period $(t - 1)$ to its *desired* level at time t is a function of the income elasticity of the tax system plus the influence of the stochastic disturbance term, v_{it}.

The next step was the search for a specific functional form for equation B.2 that would make sense analytically and would permit estimation. A straightforward and reasonable specification is:

(B.3) $G_{it} = [\beta_0 + \beta_1 T_i][G_{it}^* - G_{i(t-1)}] + v_{it}.$

The test of the hypothesis thus centers on the sign and statistical significance of the coefficient, β_1. If the income elasticity of the tax system is of importance in the process of budgetary adjustment, we would expect β_1 to be positive and significantly different from zero. Otherwise, the degree of adjustment will be indicated by β_0 alone. The null hypothesis, therefore, is $H_0: \beta_1 = 0$.

It is impossible to estimate equation B.3 directly, because G_{it}^* is not observable. However, by substituting the expression in equation A.1 for G_{it}^* in equation B.3, we obtain an equation consisting of observed variables and disturbance terms. This is the equation I undertook to estimate[24]:

(B.4) $G_{it} = [\beta_0 + \beta_1 T_i][\gamma_0 + \gamma_1 V_{it} - G_{i(t-1)}] + v_{it}.$

The econometric obstacles to estimating equation B.4 are quite formidable. First, the equation is nonlinear both in the variables and parameters. And, second, recall from the text that some of the variables in the vector, V_{it}, are themselves dependent on G_{it}, which introduces a simultaneous-equation bias into the parameter estimators. The price of introducing a more satisfactory conceptual formulation has thus been the creation of a very difficult estimation problem.

There are techniques for estimating an equation like equation B.4, where there are endogenous variables and nonlinearities in both the parameters and variables (although the full range of properties of the estimators is not yet known).[25] One approach is a two-stage procedure in which the first stage involves "approximately purging" the endogenous independent variables of their correlation with the disturbance term by regressing them on polynomial forms of the predetermined variables in the system. The calculated values of the endogenous variables are then substituted for the

---

[24] One simplification was necessary immediately. The presence of both u_{it} and v_{it} (and various cross-product terms involving them) made the equation impossible to estimate by any technique I could discover. I, therefore, made the further assumption that equation B.1 is an exact relationship, and simply discarded u_t from equation B.1.

[25] Stephen M. Goldfeld and Richard E. Quandt, *Nonlinear Methods in Econometrics* (Amsterdam: North Holland Publishing Co., 1972), chap. 8; and Takeshi Amemiya, "The Nonlinear Two-Stage Least-Squares Estimator," Stanford University, Department of Economics, working paper no. 25 (June 1973).

observed values. In the second stage, the values of the parameters are determined so as to minimize the sum of the squared deviations of the predicted values of the dependent variable from their observed values.

Unfortunately, my attempts to estimate equation B.4 by this two-stage procedure yielded nonsensical results; the values of the estimated parameters were far outside the bounds of any reasonable expectations. This may reflect an inappropriate specification of the process of budgetary adjustment, or, alternatively, some inadequacies of the estimation technique. At any rate, I feel at this juncture that the results reported in the text represent the most solid evidence that I can offer on the tax-elasticity hypothesis.

[23]

The Public Sector in Economics:
An Analytical Chameleon

*Wallace E. Oates**

It is both an honor and a pleasure to contribute to this volume in recognition of the wide-ranging and important work of Professor Horst Claus Recktenwald. Professor Recktenwald's contributions to economics are many, and they include a central concern with the subject of this essay: the role of the government sector. My interest here, however, is not so much with the public sector itself, as with the way in which economists view or «model» this sector. A striking feature of public economics over the past few decades is the emergence of several sharply contrasting perspectives on government. In this essay, I shall explore these alternatives in terms of their implications for our understanding of the public sector and the determination of public policy.

I. Alternative Approaches to the Analysis of the Public Sector

An examination of the literature of public economics over the last 30 years reveals three distinct conceptualizations of the public sector:

1. The «neoclassical» view of government envisions a basically beneficent entity that functions to correct distortions in resource allocation and to achieve the socially desired distribution of income. From this perspective, the sole objective of the public sector is to promote the social welfare through «optimal» interventions into the economy in instances of market failure and through policies to effect the needed redistribution of income.

2. In contrast, in voting models of the public sector, the preferences of the electorate determine the outcome. The standard model here is the widely used median-voter model based on the seminal work of Duncan Black (1958). Within this framework, the «equilibrium» outcome is the median of the most desired outcomes of the individual voters. This approach assigns to the public sector an essentially passive role: government policy simply carries out the «instructions» the electorate gives to public officials through the polling booth. As Brennan and Buchanan (1980) put it, «In these models, government is neither despotic nor benevolent; in a very real sense, «government», as such, does not exist» (p. 15).

* The author is grateful to Henry Aaron, Peter Coughlin, and Robert Schwab for helpful comments and to the Sloan Foundation for its support.

3. Under the third approach, the «bureaucracy» perspective, government agencies take a much more active role in economic decisions. However, the motivating force in these models is not the social welfare; public officials have their own sets of objectives that they pursue subject to the constraints imposed by the institutional setting. Niskanen (1971) has argued that the set of bureaucratic objectives can be subsumed under the single goal of budget maximization. In a more recent and extreme variant of this approach, Brennan and Buchanan (1980) conceptualize the entire public sector as a single entity, the «Leviathan», that strives single-mindedly to maximize the level of public revenues that it extracts from the economy. The bureaucratic models thus suggest outcomes whose properties are not so felicitous as the neoclassical view.

The latter two perspectives on the public sector have their origins in the burgeoning public-choice literature, which has as a primary objective the development of a realistic descriptive (or positive) analysis of the functioning of government. The contention of public-choice adherents is that the neoclassical perspective is not only naive, but dangerously misleading in terms of its policy implications. In the sections that follow, I shall explore this (and other) claims in an attempt to determine the potential contribution to our understanding of «public economics» of each of these models of the government sector. I shall proceed, first, by considering in some detail each of the three views of government, and, second, by examining the insights they provide into two policy issues: pollution control and fiscal limitations on public budgetary activity.

II. The Neoclassical View of Beneficent Public Policy

Neoclassical analysis typically employs a well defined and time-honored procedure. The analysis sets forth two problems: (1) the maximization of social welfare, and (2) the determination of the outcome from individual-maximizing behavior in the absence of public policy (or under a specified policy regime). This produces two sets of (first-order) conditions: one characterizes the socially optimal outcome and the other the «market» equilibrium. Where these outcomes diverge, the analysis proceeds to the specification of a set of policies that will alter the equilibrium such that it satisfies the social optimality conditions. This may entail the direct public provision of certain goods or services, or, alternatively, the introduction of a set of incentives (e.g. effluent fees) that will induce private decision-makers to alter their behavior in a welfare-enhancing manner.

A good example of this approach with a long and distinguished history is the treatment of externalities. Reaching back to Marshall and Pigou, economists have recognized the potential distortions in resource allocation where external effects are present. It is a straightforward matter to demonstrate that in the absence of Coasian bargaining, the market outcome will diverge from an economically efficient state. For the case of an external diseconomy like pollution, it is then easy to show that subject to certain conditions, the Pigouvian remedy of an effluent fee has the potential to remove this distortion and to sustain an efficient outcome [e.g. Baumol and Oates (1975, ch. 4)].

We shall consider the neoclassical treatment of externalities in more detail later, but, at this juncture, I would stress that one of the great virtues of the neoclassical procedure is that it provides us with the normative benchmark of an ideal welfare-maximizing outcome against which we can examine and assess predicted outcomes. Just how seriously we should take its specific policy prescriptions is another matter.

III. Voting Models of Collective Decisions

Our second class of public-sector models, voting models, has two major variants. The first, following Black (1958), envisions the actual participation of the entire collectivity in decision-making. Assuming that voters' preferences are single-peaked (and that there are an odd number of voters), it can be shown that there exists one alternative that is unique in the sense that it will defeat *any* other alternative in a pairwise choice. This alternative is the median of the most preferred outcomes of the individual voters; hence, the title of the «median-voter model.»

The second variant extends this result to encompass a two-party system of representative government. In his seminal paper, Downs (1957) shows that political competition among vote-maximizing politicians will generate an outcome that converges on the median-voter. A party that strays from the median of the preferred outcomes will lose votes by doing so. Thus, the median-voter model is by no means restricted to instances of referenda; its explanatory potential reaches as well to certain cases of representative government.

The median-voter result, however, is admittedly fragile. While single-peaked preferences, for example, are a defensible assumption for a single-dimensional «policy space», when we move to policy issues involving several dimensions, things quickly become more complicated. Only under severely restrictive conditions, for instance, can we guarantee the existence of a unique and stable equilibrium [e.g., Mueller (1979)]. Nonetheless, the median-voter model has been widely used in the public-finance literature for everything from formal theorems on intergovernmental grants [Bradford and Oates (1971)] to providing an analytical framework for the estimation of demand functions for local public goods [Bergstrom and Goodman (1973)].

The median-voter model serves primarily as a descriptive or positive model of public-sector behavior. Not surprisingly, since it relies on a one-person, one-vote procedure, the model does not, in general, lead to economically efficient outcomes. It requires a set of quite stringent conditions to insure that the median-voter equilibrium is Pareto-efficient. As Bergstrom (1979) has shown, a sufficient (but obviously very restrictive) condition for an efficient outcome is a symmetrically distributed pattern of individual demands about the median preferred level of output. Although the conditions for a coincidence of median-voter and efficient

47

outcomes are highly restrictive, it is yet quite plausible that the median-voter outcome will not diverge very greatly from the efficient solution. In fact, an appropriate design of the tax system can induce efficiency-enhancing voting behavior [Bergstrom (1979)]. In some of the recent public-choice literature, the median-voter outcome is even being referred to as the «competitive outcome» to contrast its relatively desirable properties with various bureaucratic sorts of public-sector behavior. It is to these more disturbing models of public-sector activity that we turn next.

IV. Bureaucratic Models of Government Behavior

The bureaucratic models of the public sector typically contain three ingredients:

(1) The specification of an objective function for public officials that does not coincide with the public interest. The Niskanen assumption of budget maximization, for example, is widely used in this literature.

(2) An assumption of asymmetrically distributed information. The Niskanen model is again seminal in this respect: it posits that the public agency knows and conceals certain important information. In particular, while the demand for public outputs may be (roughly) known, only the bureau knows its cost function which it deliberately misrepresents in order to make its case for the largest possible appropriation for its budget.

(3) An absence of effective competition. This is crucial. For even if the first two conditions were satisfied, effective political competition of the Downsian sort would eliminate the scope for wasteful behavior. Any attempt to ignore the social interest to pursue the agency's own objectives would give rise to opportunities for a political competitor to offer a more attractive alternative to the electorate.

With these three conditions in hand, it is easy to construct models of public-agency behavior that generate unhappy outcomes typically involving both excessive levels of public output and technical inefficiency in the provision of those outputs. In the Niskanen model, the mechanism for achieving these results is an excessively large budgetary request that the legislature (or other authority that approves the budget) cannot evaluate accurately. In other models involving public referenda on the budget, the agency exercises its «agenda-setting» prerogative in a way that induces the electorate to assent to something other than its most preferred outcome [See Romer and Rosenthal (1979) and Denzau, Mackey, and Weaver (1979)]. In the Romer and Rosenthal model, for example, the public agency takes advantage of a relatively unattractive alternative, the «reversion level» of the budget which obtains if the electorate rejects the agency's proposed budget. The proposed budget is larger than that most preferred by the median voter but still emerges victorious because it is preferred by the electorate to the only alternative: the relatively unappealing reversion level of public output.

A further, extreme variant of the bureaucratic approach is the striking and controversial Brennan and Buchanan model of Leviathan. Drawing by analogy on the traditional theory of monopoly in the private sector, they envision the entire public sector as a single monolithic agent that seeks systematically to exploit its citizenry through the maximization of the tax revenues that it extracts from the economy. Subject to the constitutional and other institutional constrains on its behavior, Leviathan designs its fiscal measures with one objective in mind: revenue maximization. A central issue in the design of the fiscal constitution becomes that of finding ways to constrain the revenue-raising activities of the «monster».

It remains to explore the insights that these various approaches to public-sector analysis can provide and to assess their usefulness and empirical validity. I approach this task next in terms of two specific issues.

V. The Regulation of Externalities: Pollution Control

As noted earlier, the neoclassical approach to public-sector analysis has provided economists both with a basic framework for thinking about the problem of externalities and with a concrete policy prescription. I will use pollution control as the prototype for an external diseconomy; for this class of externalities, the Pigouvian corrective takes the form of an effluent fee on polluting activities equal to marginal social damage.

The Pigouvian result is admittedly hedged by a number of important assumptions. Moreover, it makes large demands for information on the regulating authority; the determination of the optimal effluent fee requires knowledge not only of the social damage function, but also of the abatement cost functions of the sources of the pollution. In this regard, recent work has extended the analysis to instances of imperfect information and demonstrated a potential role for quantity instruments (such as marketable pollution permits) as an alternative to effluent fees [Weitzman (1974), Roberts and Spence (1976)]. It has also been shown that if individual decision-makers are confronted with a *schedule* of penalties reflecting the external costs associated with their activities, utility-maximizing behavior will lead to economically efficient choices [Collinge and Oates (1982)]. And this result requires no information on the abatement costs of the polluter.

Nevertheless, economists have not been very successful in persuading policy makers to adopt the Pigouvian prescription. Instead, regulatory agencies have typically opted for the more traditional command-and-control (CAC) mechanisms under which the regulator specifies specific abatement procedures for the control of pollution.

Why has the neoclassical policy prescription for pollution control proved so unpersuasive in the policy arena?[1] There are, I think, a number of reasons. First, economists have really not done a very good job in making clear to policy makers the rationale for a system of effluent fees. In a recent and systematic survey of a diverse group of legislative staff members and lobbyists in Washington who are directly concerned with environmental legislation, Kelman (1981) could not find a single person who could explain the economist's argument for the use of effluent

49

fees! Instead, individuals expressed their support for, or hostility to, fees in basic-ally ideological terms (e. g., «I trust the marketplace more than the bureaucracy» or that sources «shouldn't have a choice to pay and pollute»).

Second (and, I believe, more basic) is the failure of the neoclassical approach to consider how public-sector decisions are actually made. Neoclassical policy pre-scriptions come from the rarified atmosphere of pure welfare economics, not from a model of public-sector behavior. As public-choice economists have emphasized, the design of policy measures must take place in light of existing public institu-tions, not as if the public sector consisted of a benevolent, welfare-maximizing ruler.

From a public-choice perspective, it is much easier to understand why public officials have been wary of a heavy reliance on effluent fees. Not only have envi-ronmentalists often opposed such measures as unethical «licenses to pollute», but the sources of pollution themselves have been (and quite rightly) reluctant to subject themselves to another form of taxation. Buchanan and Tullock (1975) have noted that it may be quite rational for sources of pollution to prefer direct controls to a fee system, in spite of the potential savings in abatement costs that the latter promises. Under a system of effluent fees, polluters must bear the burden not only of control costs, but also of the fee payment for their residual waste discharges. And these effluent fee bills could be very large. One recent study [Palmer et al. (1980)] of the potential use of a fee system to restrict the emissions of certain halocarbons into the atmosphere estimates that aggregate abatement costs under a realistic CAC program of mandatory controls would total about $ 230 million; a system of fees resulting in a more efficient allocation of abatement activity among sources would reduce these costs to an estimated $ 110 million (a savings of roughly 50%). However, the effluent fees that sources would pay on their remaining emissions would total about $ 1,400 million! In spite of the substantial savings in abatement costs, Palmer et al. thus conclude that a system of fees would increase the total costs to polluters by a factor of six relative to a program of direct controls.[2] Studies of other pollutants [e.g., Seskin et al. (1983)] have reached similar findings, all of which suggests that sources may have good reasons to oppose systems of effluent fees.[3]

Buchanan and Tullock go on to argue that existing polluters may find further attractions in current CAC systems. Direct controls may effectively erect substan-tial barriers-to-entry into polluting industries. This occurs because CAC programs typically discriminate between existing and new firms: they frequently require far more stringent (and expensive) control procedures for new plants than for existing ones. In this way, existing firms may be able to use CAC measures to exclude entrants and thereby to cartelize their industry in a way that wouldn't have been possible in the absence of these control measures.

A positive theory of environmental policy thus requires us to push beyond the neoclassical analysis to consider the interests and interactions of the various parties in the policy-determination process. In particular, it reminds us that the most feasible policy measures are those that promise gains to these various parties-measures that represent Pareto improvements relative to the status quo.

From this perspective, environmental policy in the United States has, in two recent instances, moved in a most intriguing direction. As the economics literature has pointed out, the basic efficiency properties of a system of effluent fees can also be realized in terms of a system of marketable pollution permits (at least in a setting of perfect certainty). However, in contrast to a fee system, it is possible to design a system of marketable permits that minimizes the adverse impacts on the interested parties. In fact, under certain circumstances, McGartland and Oates (1983) show that using marketable permits, it is possible to move from an initial CAC equilibrium to a new outcome that both improves environmental quality and reduces costs to polluters.

A basic mechanism for achieving this result is an initial distribution of the permits free of charge to existing polluters with subsequent trades subject to a constraint that preserves environmental quality. This general approach to pollution control is embodied in two new U.S. programs: the Emissions Trading program for the control of air pollution and a system of «transferable discharge permits» (TDP) recently introduced in the State of Wisconsin for the management of water quality.[4] Under Emissions Trading, sources have the capacity to buy and sell entitlements to emit various air pollutants subject to provisions that protect air quality. Similarly, Wisconsin has introduced its new TDP system for the regulation of BOD discharges on certain rivers; sources can trade discharge permits providing that the predetermined water-quality standards are maintained.

Emissions Trading and the Wisconsin TDP program represent a potentially important policy innovation. They embody economic incentives in a way that both promotes cost-saving behavior in the aggregate and promises gains to the diverse parties involved in pollution control. It is much too early to herald these policy measures as the beginning of a broad movement for the adoption of economic incentives for environmental management. They represent, rather, two intriguing «experiments» with an innovative policy instrument; their future and ultimate impact is, at this juncture, uncertain.

But for my purposes here, these policy measures are of interest because they represent an important instance of a potentially fruitful union of the neoclassical approach with a public-choice awareness of policy determination. Public-choice economists, it seems to me, shouldn't ride too hard over the neoclassical approach to public economics. The neoclassical perspective can provide important insights into the nature of economic problems (like externalities) and can suggest potential policy correctives. Since, however, neoclassical analysis typically does not incorporate a positive framework of public-sector behavior, the determination of actual policy recommendations needs to reach beyond the formal welfare-analytic structure to incorporate public-choice elements.

VI. The Fiscal-Limitation Movement

Our second instance of public policy raises a very different set of issues. In fact, the fiscal-limitation movement would appear to make no sense at all in a neoclassical perspective. If a knowing and beneficent ruler introduced the policy measures needed to maximize social welfare, there would be no need for the electorate to introduce a set of constraints on budgetary behavior. The neoclassical approach cannot provide much assistance in understanding measures like Proposition 13 in California that places explicit limits on property-tax rates.

The focus here must be on our two public choice approaches to public-sector models. On first consideration, the fiscal-limitation «revolution» of the 1970's would seem to provide strong support for the bureaucratic perspective on government. Although the median-voter model does not, in general, produce efficient budgetary outcomes, there is no strong presumption that it should result systematically in excessive, rather than suboptimal, levels of public outputs.[5] In contrast, models in the bureaucratic spirit unambiguously point to overspending by public agencies. It would seem straightforward to interpret the fiscal-limitation measures of the 1970's in the United States as an attempt by the electorate to restrain the public-sector tendencies to budgetary excess.

Before pursuing this matter further, I want first to turn to the earlier distinction between two classes of bureaucratic models. The first group of models examines individual public agencies in terms of their own objective functions [Niskanen (1971), Romer and Rosenthal (1979a), etc.]. The second is the earlier-noted Leviathan model which contends that we can treat the public sector *as if* it were a huge, monolithic unit (e.g., a king) seeking to maximize the level of public revenues. Either of these classes of models produces outcomes exhibiting excessive public expenditure so that either can provide a plausible rationale for fiscal-limitation measures.

We need other «tests» to distinguish between the usefulness of these two types of models. On the face of it, the individual agency models are surely more realistic than Leviathan. The public sector in the modern industrialized countries of the west is a complex organization with vertical and horizontal divisions into levels of government and compartmentalized agencies that often possess considerable fiscal autonomy. The richness and intricacy of the modern government sector is obviously lost in the simplistic rubric of Leviathan. But this, of course, is not the whole of the matter. It is Brennan and Buchanan's contention that the admittedly simplified («as if») structure of the Leviathan model can capture some basic tendencies of the government sector.

This is, then, to some extent an empirical matter. There are, in fact, some operational empirical tests of Leviathan that distinguish it, I believe, from the other bureaucratic models. For one, the Leviathan model predicts that the monopolistic capacity of government to extract revenues from the economy will be larger in a more centralized public sector. Fiscal decentralization, as Brennan and Buchanan [(1980, p. 184)] emphasize, is a powerful constraint on Leviathan; the potential mobility of citizens among different taxing jurisdictions itself limits the ability of «local» governments to exploit their citizenry. This leads Brennan and Buchanan to predict that «total government intrusion into the economy should be smaller, *ceteris paribus*, the greater the extent to which taxes and expenditures are decentralized . . .» (1980, p. 185). Or, in other words, government should be bigger, other things equal, where it is more centralized.

Empirical tests of this proposition, however, do not support Leviathan. In a recent econometric study making use of both an international sample of countries and of state-local governments in the United States [Oates (1983c)], I could find no evidence of a positive association between the size of the government sector and the extent of fiscal centralization. If anything, the relationship seems more inclined in the opposite direction with greater centralization, other things equal, being associated with a smaller public sector.[6] Leviathan, it seems to me, is really not a very compelling model either at a conceptual level or in terms of its apparent explanatory power.

The individual-agency class of models must, however, be taken more seriously. Based upon plausible objective functions for individual decision-makers (or agencies), such models appear both reasonable *a priori* and capable of explaining the adoption of fiscal-limitation measures. But does the fiscal-limitation movement provide clear support for these models? In short, can we reasonably interpret Proposition 13 and the other budgetary constraints introduced in the 1970's as a response to the electorate's sense that government has become «too big»?

The answer to this question is, in fact, far from clear. The fiscal-limitation movement has been the subject of careful and intensive study. One strand of this work has tried to answer the question «What do the voters want?» Three quite good studies in different states [Citrin (1979), Courant, Gramlich, and Rubinfeld (1980), and Ladd and Wilson (1982)] all reached essentially the same finding: for most public programs, residents were generally satisfied with existing levels of services. In Michigan, for example, Courant et al. (1980) found that for every expenditure category save one, more survey respondents indicated a desire for higher levels of spending (to be supported by more taxes) than those wishing a reduction. The one exception is public welfare (i.e., basically programs for direct assistance to low-income households); for this one category of spending, there was broad support for budgetary cutbacks. The survey responses also suggest the perception of some waste in the public budget – the sense that modest reductions in spending can be absorbed without significant cuts in levels of basic services. But these studies do not point to a general feeling that government spending (at least at the state and local level where these measures have been introduced) is out of control and becoming much too large. It is noteworthy, in this regard, that the electorate in many states rejected proposed fiscal-limitation measures. In 1980, for instance, proposals similar in structure to Proposition 13 in California appeared on the ballot in five other states; all five proposals were defeated. For California, one can make a quite plausible case that the enactment of Proposition 13 was the result of some peculiar circumstances that had resulted in a dramatic shift in the tax structure toward increased reliance on property taxation [Levy (1979), Shapiro, Puryear and Ross (1979)]. From this perspective, Proposition 13 can be interpreted as a movement to eliminate the continuing escalation of taxation of residential

53

property and to restore the earlier balance between property taxation and other sources of revenue in California.

I do not want to overstate the case. The fiscal-limitation movement certainly did draw on some real sentiment in certain quarters against big government. But it is misleading, I believe, to interpret this movement as reflecting a broad consensus that the public sector has simply become too large relative to the desires of the electorate. Recent studies, moreover, suggest that the measures that were enacted in this period have apparently had little impact on levels of public spending [Oates (1983b), Esty (1983)].

The issue of the median voter versus bureaucratic models of public-sector behavior is thus far from resolved. A lively exchange is underway in the empirical literature in public economics providing evidence supporting one model over another. Romer and Rosenthal (1982), for example, find evidence from referenda on school budgets in the State of Oregon that supports their agenda-control model of bureaucratic behavior; more specifically, they find that, as predicted, the level of school spending varies inversely with the «reversion» level of expenditure. In contrast, Inman (1978) finds that he cannot reject statistically the basic assumption in the median-voter model.

A particularly intriguing test of the two models involves the widely observed «flypaper effect». The basic median-voter model predicts that the increment to public expenditure from an increase of one dollar in unrestricted intergovernmental receipts should be (roughly) the same as the increase in public spending associated with a one-dollar increase in private income. In both instances, the community's unrestricted resources are increased by the same sum. Since the impact on the community's budget constraint is the same, the resulting effect on public outputs should be identical.[7] However, many econometric studies find that this isn't so. These studies consistently find that the propensity for public spending to rise is higher per dollar of intergovernmental grants than per dollar of private income.[8] This is known as the «flypaper effect»-money sticks where it hits! This finding would, on the face of it, suggest that the public sector spends more from such grant revenues than the electorate wishes, thereby providing support for the bureaucratic class of models. In fact, several papers present bureaucratic types of models for the explicit purpose of explaining the flypaper effect [See Courant, Gramlich, and Rubinfeld (1979) and Oates (1979)].

However, once again, things are more complicated than at first they appear. Bruce Hamilton (1983) has recently shown that much of the flypaper effect can be explained in terms of a misspecification of the production function for local services. Taking another tack, Aaron (1984) argues that if the source of the grantor's funds (e.g., federal taxation) and its expenditures are explicitly incorporated into the analysis, then a wide range of potential effects of grants are consistent with a median-voter outcome. If, for example, the grantor cuts back the provision of certain public services to free up funds for the grant program, recipients may direct a substantial chunk of their grant monies into spending programs to restore service levels. Alternatively, if the grantor levies new taxes to generate grant funds, recipients may be more inclined to substitute the grant receipts for their own tax revenues. In yet a different approach to this issue, Jonathan Hamilton (1984) contends that the increasing marginal deadweight loss from taxation can account for the flypaper effect without any recourse to bureaucratic behavior.

Which approach best explains public-sector behavior, the median-voter model, the bureaucratic approach, or, perhaps, a new alternative yet to emerge, remains an open issue.[9] This is currently a lively and exciting area of research in public economics – and one that obviously has important implications for the design of fiscal institutions and budgetary policy. In particular, if political competition is a sufficiently strong and reliable force to make government decisions conform (at least roughly) to the will of the electorate, then we can allow a wide scope for public decisions on budgetary matters. If, however, the bureaucratic perspective is closer to the truth, the case for explicit constraints on public tax and expenditure decisions becomes compelling. We should not (as some have argued) introduce such constraints as a purely precautionary measure. As constraints, they may prevent us from doing things that we wish to do. But if the public sector is unresponsive to the preferences of the electorate, we may have little choice but to adopt such measures.

VII. Some Concluding Remarks

In recent decades, the public economics literature has introduced a rich and diverse set of models of public-sector activity. A primary objective in the public-choice dimension of this work has been the development of positive (or descriptive) models of government behavior. At this juncture in the evolution of this research, a central issue is the extent of the explanatory power of «competitive» models in the spirit of Downs versus the bureaucratic class of conceptualizations of public decision-making. And, as we saw in the preceding section, this issue has profound implications for the desired structure of the fiscal «constitution» and the determination of public policy. The «optimal» role of the government sector depends crucially on which of these views is the more accurate one.

At the same time, the neoclassical approach, light as it typically is on institutional content, still has much to offer. From the neoclassical literature, we can see the functioning of the economy against the admittedly idealized backdrop of a welfare-maximizing norm. This has its value in terms of providing insights into the nature of the economy and in *suggesting* potential forms of corrective policy. A deeper understanding of the actual functioning of the public sector is needed for the formulation of policy recommendations, but the neoclassical perspective remains one from which we can learn much.

Notes

1. At the policy level, the debate over effluent fees typically does not proceed in the unified Pigouvian framework. Policy decisions on environmental issues usually involve two-steps: the determination of a set of environmental quality targets (or standards) and a regulatory procedure for the attainment of these standards. From this perspective, the issue becomes that of using fees as an alternative to direct controls to achieve a set of "predetermined" standards of environmental quality. Baumol and Oates have called this the "charges and standards approach" (1975, Ch.10).
2. From the perspective of society, fee payments are simply a transfer payment from polluters to the public treasury; they are not a real social cost. But from the vantage point of sources, they are obviously a cost that reduces net income.
3. The issue here may be seen as involving the assignment of "property rights." The fee approach implicitly assigns the "ownership" of environmental resources to the general public and requires the users of these resources to make appropriate payments into the public treasury. The distribution of a limited number of permits without charge implies a kind of joint ownership of these resources between the public and the existing sources of emissions. The property rights associated with the permits are assigned to the sources. But the rights to any further use of the environment (as would occur in the absence of any controls) are denied to sources and hence are implicitly attributed to the general public.
4. See Oates (1983a) and O'Neil et al. (1983) for descriptions of these systems.
5. If demands for public outputs are strictly proportional to income, one can make a case that the median-voter outcome will tend to be less than the efficient level of output. With the usual skewed character of the income distribution, the mean level of income will exceed the median so that the median of the most preferred levels of output will fall short of that for which the sum of the MRS's equals marginal cost.
6. For most of the regression equations, the estimated coefficient on the fiscal-centralization variable was not statistically significant. For those cases where it was significant, it had a negative sign running counter to the prediction of the Leviathan model.
7. This is only approximately true, since the distribution of the increment to grants and to private income may differ, thereby giving rise to differential income effects. As Bradford and Oates (1971) show, for an x-dollar increase to unrestricted intergovernmental receipts, there is a *specific* distribution of these x-dollars in increments of private income that will generate an outcome precisely identical to that resulting from the grant.
8. For a useful survey of these findings, see Gramlich (1977).
9. For some further discussion of this, see Romer and Rosenthal. (1979b).

References

Aaron, H.: The Sticky Question of the Flypaper Effect, unpublished paper 1984.
Baumol, W. and W. Oates: *The Theory of Environmental Policy*, Englewood, Cliffs, N.J. 1975.
Bergstrom, T.: When Does Majority Rule Supply Public Goods Efficiently, *Scandinavian Journal of Economics*, 81 (1979), pp. 216–226.
Bergstrom, T. and R. Goodman: Private Demands for Public Goods, *American Economic Review*, 63 (1973), pp. 280–296.
Black, D.: *The Theory of Committees and Elections*, Cambridge 1958.

Bradford, D., and W. Oates: The Analysis of Revenue Sharing in a New Approach to Collective Fiscal Decisions, *Quarterly Journal of Economics*, 85 (1971), pp. 416–439.

Brennan, G. and J.M. Buchanan: *The Power to Tax: Analytical Foundations of a Fiscal Constitution*, Cambridge and New York 1980.

Buchanan, J.M. and G. Tullock: Polluters' Profits and Political Response: Direct Controls Versus Taxes, *American Economic Review*, 65 (1975), pp. 139–147.

Citrin, J.: Do People Want Something for Nothing: Public Opinion on Taxes and Government Spending, *National Tax Journal*, 32 (Supplement, June 1979), pp. 113–129.

Collinge, R. and W. Oates: Efficiency in Pollution Control in the Short and Long Runs: A System of Rental Emission Permits, *Canadian Journal of Economics*, 15 (1982), pp. 346–354.

Courant, P., E. Gramlich and D. Rubinfeld: The Stimulative Effects of Intergovernmental Grants: Or Why Money Sticks Where It Hits, in: P. Mieszkowski and W. Oakland (eds.), *Fiscal Federalism and Grants-in-Aid*, Washington, D.C. 1979, pp. 5–21.

Courant, P., E. Gramlich and D. Rubinfeld: Why Voters Support Tax Limitation Amendments: The Michigan Case, *National Tax Journal*, 33 (1980), pp. 1–20.

Denzau, A., R. Mackey and C. Weaver: Spending Limitations, Agenda Control, and Voters' Expectations, *National Tax Journal*, 32 (Supplement, June 1979), pp. 189–200.

Downs, A.: An Economic Theory of Political Action in a Democracy, *Journal of Political Economy*, 65 (1957), pp. 135–150.

Esty, R.: *The Effect of State Fiscal Caps on Expenditures*, unpublished Ph.D. dissertation, University of Maryland (1983).

Gramlich, E.: Intergovernmental Grants: A Review of the Empirical Literature, in: W. Oates (ed.), *The Political Economy of Fiscal Federalism*, Lexington, Mass. 1977, pp. 219–239.

Hamilton, B.: The Flypaper Effect and Other Anomalies, *Journal of Public Economics*, 22 (1983), pp. 347–361.

Hamilton, J.: The Flypaper Effect and the Deadweight Loss from Taxation, Charles Haywood Murphy Institute of Political Economy, Tulane University, Discussion Paper No. 84/3 (1984).

Inman, R.: Testing Political Economy's ‹As If› Proposition: Is the Median Voter Really Decisive?, *Public Choice*, 33 (1978), pp. 45–64.

Kelman, St.: *What Price Incentives? Economists and the Environment*, Boston 1981.

Ladd, H. and J. Wilson: Why Voters Support Tax Limitations: Evidence from Massachusetts Proposition 2-½, *National Tax Journal*, 35 (1982), pp. 121–148.

Levy, F.: On Understanding Proposition 13, *The Public Interest*, 56, (Summer 1979), pp. 66–89.

McGartland, A. and W. Oates: *Marketable Permits for the Prevention of Environmental Deterioration*, Department of Economics and Bureau of Business and Economic Research, Working Paper No. 83–11, University of Maryland 1983.

Mueller, D.: *Public Choice*, Cambridge 1979.

Niskanen, W.A., Jr.: *Bureaucracy and Representative Government*, Chicago 1971.

Oates, W.E.: Lump-Sum Intergovernmental Grants Have Price Effects, in: P. Mieszkowski and W. Oakland (eds.), *Fiscal Federalism and Grants-in-Aid*, Washington, D.C. 1979, pp. 23–30.

Oates, W.E.: *Economic Incentives for Environmental Management: The Recent U.S. Experience*, Background paper for the Organization for Economic Co-operation and Development (1983a).

Oates, W.E.: *Fiscal Limitations: An Assessment of the U.S. Experience*, I.U.I. Working Paper No. 90, Industrial Institute for Economic and Social Research, Stockholm (1983b).

Oates, W.E.: *Searching for Leviathan: An Empirical Study*, Department of Economics and

Bureau of Business and Economic Research, Working Paper 83-18, University of Maryland (1983c).

O'Neil, W., M. David, Ch. Moore and E. Joeres: Transferable Discharge Permits and Economic Efficiency: The Fox River, *Journal of Environmental Economics and Management*, 10 (1983), pp. 346-355.

Palmer, A. et al.: *Economic Implications of Regulating Chlorofluorocarbon Emissions from Nonaerosol Applications*, Santa Monica 1980.

Roberts, M. and M.: Spence, Effluent Charges and Licenses Under Uncertainty, *Journal of Public Economics*, 5 (1976), pp. 193-208.

Romer, Th. and H. Rosenthal: Bureaucrats Versus Voters: On the Political Economy of Resource Allocation by Direct Democracy, *Quarterly Journal of Economics* (1979a), pp. 562-587.

Romer, Th. and H. Rosenthal: The Elusive Median Voter, *Journal of Public Economics*, 12 (1979b), pp. 143-170.

Romer, Th. and H. Rosenthal: Median Voters or Budget Maximizers: Evidence from School Expenditure Referenda, *Economic Inquiry*, 20 (1982), pp. 556-578.

Seskin, E., R. Anderson, Jr. and R. Reid: An Empirical Analysis of Economic Strategies for Controlling Air Pollution, *Journal of Environmental Economics and Management*, 10 (1983), pp. 112-124.

Shapiro, P., D. Puryear and J. Ross: Tax Expenditure Limitation in Retrospect and in Prospect, *National Tax Journal*, 32 (Supplement, June 1979), pp. 1-10.

Weitzman, M.: Prices vs. Quantities, *Review of Economic Studies*, 41 (1974), pp. 477-491.

[24]

Searching for Leviathan: An Empirical Study

By WALLACE E. OATES*

Total government intrusion into the economy should be smaller, *ceteris paribus*, the greater the extent to which taxes and expenditures are decentralized....

[*Brennan and Buchanan*, 1980, p. 185]

In several papers and a recent book, Geoffrey Brennan and James Buchanan (1977, 1978, 1980) have put forth a striking and controversial view of the public sector. Drawing by analogy on the conventional theory of monopoly in the private sector, they envision a monolithic government that systematically seeks to exploit its citizenry through the maximization of the tax revenues that it extracts from the economy. From this perspective, they develop a fiscal constitution whose central purpose is to constrain "Leviathan" by limiting in various ways its access to tax and other fiscal instruments.

While the Leviathan hypothesis has been the source of lively debate and a wide range of policy proposals, it has not been the subject of much systematic empirical work or testing.[1] This is a matter of some importance since the policy implications of the Leviathan view are disturbing, to put it mildly. In particular, Brennan and Buchanan virtually

stand on their heads many of the basic theorems in public finance for an efficient and equitable tax system. If, in fact, the Leviathan view is an inaccurate depiction of the functioning of the public sector, the introduction of their policy proposals is likely to make a sorry mess of the fiscal system.

The Leviathan model does, however, have some straightforward implications for observable fiscal behavior. It is the purpose of this paper to examine one of these testable implications. Brennan and Buchanan stress that fiscal decentralization is itself a powerful constraint on Leviathan: competition among governments in the context of the "interjurisdictional mobility of persons in pursuit of 'fiscal gains' can offer partial or possibly complete substitutes for explicit fiscal constraints on the taxing power" (1980, p. 184). Such competition among governments in a federal system that places heavy reliance on "local" fiscal decisions will greatly limit the capacity of Leviathan to channel resources into the public sector. In short, as indicated by the epigraph to this paper, the Leviathan model implies that, other things equal, the size of the public sector should vary inversely with the extent of fiscal decentralization.[2]

Department of Economics and Bureau of Business and Economic Research, University of Maryland, College Park, MD 20742. I am grateful to Mark Eiswerth and Christopher Graves for their excellent assistance with the computations; to Jonathan Levin of the Government Finance Statistics Division of the International Monetary Fund for his invaluable help with the data; and to the Alfred P. Sloan Foundation for its support of this work. For helpful comments on an earlier draft, I thank Fred Abraham, Charles Brown, Bruce Hamilton, Harry Kelejian, Michael Luger, Edwin Mills, Richard Musgrave, Daniel Rubinfeld, Robert Schwab, and participants in the George Mason Public Choice Seminar and the Sloan Workshop in Urban Public Economics at the University of Maryland.

[1] For a critical appraisal of the Leviathan model, see Richard Musgrave (1981).

[2] As Musgrave has pointed out to me, other sorts of models besides Leviathan could produce such an outcome. He notes, in particular, the redistribution function. Under a highly decentralized public sector, there is likely to be comparatively little in the way of assistance to the poor for two reasons. First, sorting out along Tiebout lines will imply relatively income-homogeneous jurisdictions with little scope for redistribution from wealthy to poor *within* jurisdictions. And, second, the fear of attracting mobile poor with relatively generous support programs will tend to deter the adoption of such programs. All this suggests that the scope for public relief programs will be more circumscribed under a relatively decentralized fiscal system. This would lead us to expect comparatively larger budgets where the public sector is more centralized as a result of a greater demand for assistance to low-income households.

I. More on the Empirical Test

Brennan and Buchanan thus see a decentralized public sector as a mechanism for limiting the growth or size of government. But there is an alternative view. Suppose that instead of a monopolistic setting, competition among political parties produces an outcome that conforms fairly closely to the tastes of the citizenry—as under the conventional median-voter model. In such a competitive political environment, one would have no reason to expect a negative association between the size of public budgets and the degree of fiscal decentralization. In a centralized setting, the outcome would conform to the preferences of the "overall" median voter. If, in contrast, levels of output were set independently in each jurisdiction, the median voter in each locality would effectively choose the budget. It is impossible to determine whether the average level of output in the decentralized case would exceed or fall short of output under centralized decision making without knowing both the distribution of tastes and the location of the populace.[3]

In fact, one might argue for the competitive case that, *from a purely budgetary perspective*, increased fiscal decentralization would typically result in a higher level of government expenditure. Greater decentralization may result in the loss of certain "economies of scale" with a consequent increase in costs of administration. This, of course, need not imply an inferior outcome; the welfare gains from the tailoring of local budgets to local preferences and from the

wider range of choice available to mobile consumers may more than offset the additional administrative expenditures. The point is simply that fiscal decentralization may be relatively expensive in budgetary terms. Thus, a more competitive view of the functioning of the public sector would suggest, contrary to the Leviathan model, an absence of a positive association between government size and fiscal centralization with the possibility that this association might even be negative.

John Wallis, an American economic historian, has suggested to me an even stronger hypothesis. He contends that since individuals have more control over public decisions at the local than at the state or national level, they will wish to empower the public sector with a wider range of functions and responsibility where these activities are carried out at more localized levels of government. Based on his reading of American history, Wallis offers the conjecture that over time and across states, the state-local sector has tended to be larger, the more decentralized is fiscal decision making.

The resolution of this debate requires recourse to the actual facts of governmental structure and budgetary outcomes. A little over a decade ago in the context of a larger study, I undertook a cursory examination of the relationship between the size of government and the extent of fiscal decentralization, using a cross-sectional sample of 57 countries (1972, pp. 209–13). Regressing a measure of the size of the public sector (tax revenues as a fraction of national income) on a fiscal centralization ratio (i.e., central-government tax revenues as a percentage of total tax revenues), I found a strong and statistically significant negative association. Increased fiscal decentralization in this simple regression equation was associated with a *larger* government sector. However, after controlling for the effect of the level of income on the size of government (i.e., Wagner's "Law"), the relationship between the two variables of interest became much weaker: the sign remained negative but was not significantly different from zero at the usual confidence levels. This earlier work thus

---

[3]As Musgrave suggested to me, the result is likely to depend critically on the arrangement of preferences in the tails of the distribution. Suppose, for example, that the upper tail of the distribution of tastes stretches out quite far. This will have little impact on the outcome under centralized decision making, since the distribution of the tail has no effect on the median voter. Under a more decentralized system, however, these high demanders might reside together in a jurisdiction with an extraordinarily high level of output. Musgrave conjectures that the tail on the high side might be expected to be the more skewed so that, *ceteris paribus*, the budget is likely to be larger under decentralization.

does not support the Brennan-Buchanan model of Leviathan; in none of the statistical tests did the results suggest that fiscal decentralization was significantly associated with a relatively small public sector.

In view of the renewed interest in this issue, I turn in this paper to a more careful study of this relationship, making use of two quite different bodies of data. First, the International Monetary Fund (1982) has recently provided an extraordinarily rich set of information on public finances disaggregated by level of government. From this data, I have been able to assemble measures of the extent of fiscal centralization for a sample of 43 countries. The second sample is quite different: it consists of the state-local sector in each of the 48 contiguous states in the United States. For this second sample, I explore the association between the budgetary size of state and local government in each state and the degree of decentralization of the state-local "fisc."

Each of the two samples has its relative strengths and weaknesses for purposes of this study. The international sample encompasses much greater diversity in governmental structure and consequently provides considerably more variation in the variables of interest. There is, in a sense, more to work with here. However, this comes at some cost, for the state-local data are undoubtedly more reliable and comparable than those from different countries; there should, therefore, be less in the way of measurement error and differing classifications of budgetary items. Finally, there is the issue of the extent of fiscal mobility. There must typically exist greater mobility across state than national boundaries suggesting that fiscal decentralization, from the Brennan-Buchanan perspective, should enforce a greater fiscal "discipline" on state than on national governments. In short, the scope for state governments to extract "surplus" from their residents is probably less than for the central government. Nevertheless, state governments are surely in a much less constrained position than are the myriad of smaller local governments that compete with one another within a state's borders. The Leviathan model would thus predict that, other things equal,

those states with a more decentralized fiscal structure should have a smaller state-local sector.

The testing procedure will be to take as the null hypothesis the proposition that government size and the extent of decentralization bear no relation to one another. Since the various views discussed above suggest that the relationship between these two variables could be either negative or positive, it is appropriate to use a two-tailed test to determine if we can reject the null hypothesis in favor of the alternatives.

II. Empirical Results: The State-Local Sector

As a measure of the "size" of the public sector, the Leviathan view suggests that we focus on the level of tax revenue that the state extracts from the economy. Normalizing for the level of income, I take as the dependent variable for this part of the study aggregate state-local tax receipts in each state as a fraction of personal income (G). The appropriate measure of the extent of decentralization is less clear. In consequence, I have used three plausible indices of state-local decentralization. The first two are fiscal centralization ratios: the state share of state-local general revenues (R, a revenue measure) and the state share of state-local total expenditure (E, an expenditure measure). As a third and a nonfiscal index of decentralization, I have employed the absolute number of local government units in the state (L).[4] This variable is suggested by Brennan and Buchanan's observation that "the potential for fiscal exploitation varies inversely with the number of competing governmental units in the inclusive territory" (1980, p. 185).[5]

---

[4] I experimented with some variants of L involving the normalization of the number of local governments for land area and for population size. In these forms, its explanatory power was considerably reduced compared to its unnormalized form.

[5] In an interesting theoretical paper, Dennis Epple and Allan Zelenitz (1981) have explored the extent to which competition among local jurisdictions can limit the power of local governments to extract tax revenues from their residents. They find that increasing the number of local jurisdictions limits the scope for such taxation, but cannot eliminate it entirely.

VOL. 75 NO. 4   OATES: SEARCHING FOR LEVIATHAN   751

TABLE 1–SUMMARY STATISTICS

Variable	Mean	Maximum	Minimum	SD
G	.12	.18	.10	.02
R	.58	.78	.43	.08
E	.43	.59	.22	.08
L	1660	6620	120	1450

Note: G = total state-local tax receipts as a fraction of state personal income; R = state share of state-local general revenues; E = state share of state-local total expenditures; L = number of local government units; and SD = standard deviation.

TABLE 2—SPEARMAN RANK CORRELATION COEFFICIENT

Variable Pair	Correlation Coefficient	t-Statistic
G, R	− .22	1.50
G, E	− .25	1.73
G, L	− .06	0.41

Table 1 reports the basic summary statistics for the four variables. State-local tax revenues as a fraction of personal income (G) have a mean value of .12 and vary from a high of .18 for New York to a low of .10 for Ohio. There is considerable diversity in the extent of fiscal concentration: the centralization ratio for revenues (R), for example, varies from a maximum of .78 for New Mexico to a minimum of .43 for New Hampshire with a mean value of .58. Likewise. the number of local governments ranges from 6,620 in Illinois to only 120 in Rhode Island. The sources of the data are listed in the Appendix. I would note that the fiscal data come from the *1977 Census of Governments.* It seemed advisable to use a year prior to the "disturbances" introduced by the numerous measures enacted under the fiscal-limitation movement in the United States.

As a first and admittedly crude examination of the associations among these variables, I looked at the simple rank correlation between G and each of the three measures of state-local decentralization. While this fails to hold constant for the influence of other variables, it does give some sense of the simple relationship between the pairs of variables without imposing any a priori assumptions concerning the probability distribution of the population from which the sample was drawn. Table 2 reports the value of the Spearman rank correlation coefficient (Spearman's *rho*) between G and each of the decentralization measures and the associated *t*-statistic (Sidney Siegel, 1956, p. 202). The correlation between G and each of the fiscal centralization ratios is negative, indicating that a more centralized state-local sector

tends to be associated with a *smaller* state-local sector. Although the negative correlation runs counter to the prediction of the Leviathan model. the association is not sufficiently strong in either case to reject the null hypothesis of a zero correlation at a .05 significance level using a two-tailed test.[6] In contrast, the correlation between G and L, the number of local governments, has the negative sign implied by the Leviathan hypothesis; however, the relationship is very weak, and again we cannot reject the null hypothesis of a zero correlation. The simple rank correlations thus do not support the Leviathan model.

In an attempt to control for other variables that influence the size of the public sector, I move next to a multiple-regression analysis. In the absence of a fully specified model of the economy, I have resorted to a series of admittedly *ad hoc,* reduced-form equations using explanatory variables that other studies have found to be of significance in explaining the size of the government sector.[7] The regression analysis requires one further modification: since the dependent variable has a range limited to the zero-to-one interval, the basic assumptions of the regres-

[6]As an alternative testing procedure, I might have focused on the Brennan-Buchanan prediction of a positive relationship between G and the measure of fiscal centralization and taken it as the alternative to the null hypothesis of no relationship. This procedure would imply a one-tailed test of H_0 against H_1. However, as the regression results will make clear, this form of test would not alter the basic findings.

[7]Although I am unhappy with my inability to derive formally the equation to be estimated from a fully specified structural model. I would note that the dependent variable is the ratio of government revenues to personal income. The complete structural model would thus have to determine both the level of government budgetary activity and the level of private income—a formidable task.

TABLE 3—ESTIMATED REGRESSION EQUATIONS

(1R)	$G' = -1.8 - .004R$	$R^2 = .04$
	(11.5) (1.5)	
(1E)	$G' = -1.7 - .006E^*$	$R^2 = .10$
	(14.9) (2.2)	
(1L)	$G' = -2.0 + .5 \times 10^{-5}L$	$R^2 = .003$
	(59.2) (0.3)	
(2R)	$G' = -2.9 + .0001Y^* - .003P - .002U + .011^* - .006R$	$R^2 = .32$
	(8.7) (3.5) (0.4) (1.7) (2.8) (1.7)	
(2E)	$G' = -2.8 + .0001Y^* - .0002P - .002U + .008I - .004E$	$R^2 = .29$
	(6.6) (3.1) (0.0) (2.0) (1.9) (1.0)	
(2L)	$G' = -3.0 + .0001Y^* - .008P - .002U^* + .007I - .00002L$	$R^2 = .29$
	(9.2) (3.7) (1.0) (2.1) (1.8) (1.1)	

Note: The numbers in parentheses below the estimated coefficients are the absolute values of the t-statistic. An asterisk indicates that the estimated coefficient is statistically significant at the .05 level (using a two-tail test). U = percentage of state's population residing within Standard Metropolitan Statistical Areas (SMSA); P = population (in millions); Y = state personal income per capita; I = intergovernmental grants as a percentage of state-local general revenues.

sion model are not satisfied. To correct for this, I have used the logistic transformation to create a new dependent variable whose value can range over the whole set of real numbers (see, for example, Robert Pindyck and Daniel Rubinfeld, 1981, p. 287). Table 3 reports the findings for the transformed G (denoted G'). The results, incidentally, do not differ substantially from those if the transformation is not used.

The first three equations in Table 3 are the simple regressions of G' on each of the measures of decentralization. They are roughly consistent with the rank correlations, indicating negative associations of G' with R and E. The simple correlation with L is now positive but remains very weak. The next three equations attempt to control for the influence of other key variables on the size of the public sector. The level of per capita income (Y), for example, has a positive and significant association with the size of the public sector (consistent with earlier studies of Wagner's Law). Population size (P) exhibits a positive sign but is not significantly different from zero in any of the three equations. Next, the extent of urbanization (U) is negatively related to G' and is statistically significant in one of the three equations. Other things equal, the more urbanized a state, the smaller is its public sector, reflecting perhaps some economies in providing

services to more densely populated areas.[8] There exists a body of theoretical and econometric work suggesting that intergovernmental grants provide a significant stimulus to expenditures by the recipient. The findings here are consistent with this. The variable I, the percentage of state-local general revenues that comes from intergovernmental grants, has the expected positive coefficient and is statistically significant in equation ($2R$).

Of central interest here is the effect of including these control variables on the measured influence of the decentralization variables. The fiscal centralization ratios, R and E, retain their negative sign, but in neither case can we reject the null hypothesis of no association. The number of local governments L now has a negative sign (consistent with the Leviathan view) and a somewhat larger t-statistic, but we are likewise unable to reject the null hypothesis of no association at the .05 level. The results of the multiple-regression analysis do not appear to provide

[8] Rubinfeld has suggested that the negative and significant sign of the estimated coefficient of the urbanization variable could be interpreted as providing support for Leviathan. The contention is that in more highly urbanized areas, the Tiebout process of sorting can better work itself out. Thus, more highly urbanized states are likely, from this perspective, to be effectively more decentralized.

real support for either the view that decentralization constrains the size of the public sector or that it results in a more expansive government sector. I would note, moreover, that these findings seem quite robust. I experimented with several different specifications of the multiple-regression equation, including the use of some nonlinear transformations of the key variables. In a few instances, the fiscal centralization variables were both negative and statistically significant, providing some support for the Wallis hypothesis. But in no cases did I find any significant coefficients with the sign predicted by the Leviathan model.[9]

III. Empirical Results: The World Sample

The procedures for analyzing the data from my international sample of 43 countries are essentially the same as those for the state-local study. First I have computed the Spearman rank correlation coefficients between a revenue measure of government size and my measures of fiscal centralization. And second, I present estimates of regression equations using basically the same control variables as earlier. In addition to results for the world sample as a whole, I report the estimated equations for two subsamples: a group of 18 industrialized countries (so classified by the IMF) and the remaining 25 "developing" countries. As will become apparent shortly, there are some striking and important differences between the developing

[9] There is a further issue. Since some grant funds take a matching form, the level of public spending may influence the amount of intergovernmental grants-in-aid. Intergovernmental grants (I) thus may be taken to be an endogenous variable in the multiple-regression equations implying the presence of simultaneous-equation bias. Likewise, one can make a case for the endogeneity of the fiscal centralization ratios, R and E. To address this matter, I reestimated equations $(2R)$, $(2E)$, and $(2L)$ using the two-stage least squares procedure ($2SLS$) and treating I, R, and E as endogenous variables. In the $2SLS$ equations, the estimated coefficient for the grant variable remained positive but its t-statistic declined somewhat. The estimated coefficients of the centralization variables (R, E, and L) retained their negative signs but were not significantly different from zero.

TABLE 4—SUMMARY STATISTICS

Variable	Mean	Maximum	Minimum	SD
(a) World Sample ($N = 43$)				
G	.31	.57	.12	.13
R	.85	.99	.48	.14
E	.79	.99	.40	.18
(b) Industrial Countries ($N = 18$)				
G	.42	.57	.26	.09
R	.76	.96	.48	.15
E	.65	.92	.40	.16
(c) Developing Countries ($N = 25$)				
G	.22	.50	.12	.09
R	.92	.99	.71	.08
E	.89	.99	.63	.11

Note: G = total public revenues as a fraction of *GDP*; R = central government share of total government revenue; E = central government share of total public expenditure.

and industrialized countries in terms of both the size and structure of the public sector.

Table 4 presents the summary statistics for the world sample. The government-size variable G (here defined as total public revenues divided by gross domestic product) exhibits considerably more variation than in the set of state-local data. Tax revenues as a fraction of *GDP* have a mean value of .31 and range from a high of .57 in Sweden to a low of .12 in Bangledesh. For the international sample, I have only fiscal measures of the extent of centralization: R is the fraction of total general revenues going to the central government, and E is the fraction of total public expenditure attributable to the central government. For purposes of E, intergovernmental grants are excluded from the grantor's expenditures so that E is the central government's share of total disbursements. As Table 4 indicates, the extent of fiscal centralization ranges widely within the sample, reaching from almost complete centralization of .99 to a central government share of well under one-half.

Panels (b) and (c) of Table 4 reveal the dramatic differences between the typical industrialized and developing country. The industrialized countries exhibit both a much larger size of the public sector (a mean value of G of .42 compared to .22) and a far less centralized government sector (a mean of E

of .65 compared to .89). The developing countries are characterized by relatively small, but highly centralized, public sectors.

A listing of the data and their sources appears in the Appendix. I have used IMF data to construct the fiscal centralization ratios. From the IMF *Government Finance Statistics Yearbook* (1982), I included in this study every country for which I had reasonable assurance that the data encompassed all the relevant levels and units of government. I computed the centralization ratios for the most recent year for which data were available—1980 or 1981 in most cases—but reaching back as far as 1976 in a few instances. This produced the sample of 43 countries. Regarding the nonfiscal data, I have used as a measure of per capita income (in U.S. dollars) the recent estimates by Robert Summers et al. (1980) from the International Comparison Project of the United Nations.

Table 5 reports the rank correlation coefficients and associated *t*-statistics between G and R and between G and E for the entire world sample and for the two subsamples. For the entire set of 43 countries, the rank correlation between the size of the public sector and the extent of centralization is strongly and significantly negative. A relatively decentralized public sector is typically comparatively large. However, this result is misleading. It reflects the fact just noted that the poorer developing countries have small, centralized public sectors, while the industrialized countries have relatively large and decentralized governments. When we examine the coefficients for the two subsamples, we find that there is no longer a significant relationship between the variables. Within the subsamples, government size seems to have little relation to the degree of centralization in the public sector.

Turning next to the regression analysis in Table 6 (where again I make use of the logistic transformation of G, denoted G'), note first that the simple regressions $(1R)$ and $(1E)$ confirm the rank-correlation analysis. For the whole sample, G is negatively and significantly related to both R and E, but within each subsample, this association effectively disappears. Equations $(2R)$ and

TABLE 5—SPEARMAN RANK CORRELATION COEFFICIENT

Variable	Correlation Coefficient	*t*-Statistic
(a) World Sample		
G, R	−.39	2.71
G, E	−.49	3.60
(b) Industrialized Countries		
G, R	−.02	0.08
G, E	−.15	0.61
(c) Developing Countries		
G, R	.20	0.98
G, E	.12	0.58

$(2E)$ are the multiple-regression equations, where the control variables are basically the same as in the state-local equations. Within each of the samples, equation $(2R)$ is virtually identical with $(2E)$, suggesting that it makes little difference whether we use a revenue or expenditure measure of the extent of fiscal centralization. For the entire world sample, the multiple-regression equations have substantial explanatory power: they can "explain" nearly 80 percent of the variation in the size of the public sector. In particular, I find that other things equal, high-income countries typically have relatively large public sectors, populous nations tend to have comparatively small government sectors, and countries that rely heavily on intergovernmental grants have, on average, large public sectors. However, the measures of fiscal centralization, R and E, contribute virtually nothing to the explanatory power of the equations. The extent of centralization in the public sector appears to have little effect on the size of government.[10]

---

[10] Responding to the empirical findings for the international sample, Edwin Mills has offered the interesting suggestion that to measure Leviathan's monopoly power, the fiscal autonomy of decentralized governments is probably a better measure than their share of taxes or spending. Mills suggests a constitutional variable: the existence of a federal constitution. Following up on this, I find that if I divide the total sample into 8 federal and 35 nonfederal countries, the mean size of the public sector as a fraction of *GDP* (i.e., G in the earlier equations) is slightly larger for federal countries. Probably of more relevance, however, within the subsample of 18 industrialized countries, the mean value of G is somewhat less for the 6 federal countries than for the 12

TABLE 6—ESTIMATED REGRESSION EQUATIONS

(a) World Sample		
$(1R)$	$G' = \quad 0.8 \quad - 2.0R^*$ $\qquad (1.3) \quad (2.8)$	$R^2 = .16$
$(1E)$	$G' = \quad 0.6 \quad - 1.9E^*$ $\qquad (1.6) \quad (3.8)$	$R^2 = .26$
$(2R)$	$G' = -1.9 \quad + \quad .0003Y^* - .004P^* + .001U + 0.6I^* + 0.1R$ $\qquad (3.7) \qquad (5.0) \quad (2.8) \quad (0.4) \quad (2.5) \quad (0.2)$	$R^2 = .78$
$(2E)$	$G' = -1.9 \quad + \quad .0003Y^* - .004P^* + .001U + 0.6I^* + 0.1E$ $\qquad (4.6) \qquad (5.2) \quad (2.9) \quad (0.4) \quad (2.7) \quad (0.3)$	$R^2 = .78$
(b) Industrialized Countries		
$(1R)$	$G' = -0.3 \quad - \quad .07R$ $\qquad (0.5) \quad (0.1)$	$R^2 = .001$
$(1E)$	$G' = -\ .003 - 0.5E$ $\qquad (0.0) \quad (0.8)$	$R^2 = .04$
$(2R)$	$G' = -1.8 \quad + \quad .0004Y^* - .005P^* - .007U + 0.7I \quad + 0.4R$ $\qquad (2.3) \qquad (3.0) \quad (3.1) \quad (1.2) \quad (1.8) \quad (0.5)$	$R^2 = .57$
$(2E)$	$G' = -1.9 \quad + \quad .0004Y^* - .005P^* - .007U + 0.8I^* + 0.4E$ $\qquad (2.6) \qquad (3.2) \quad (3.2) \quad (1.3) \quad (2.3) \quad (0.7)$	$R^2 = .57$
(c) Developing Countries		
$(1R)$	$G' = -2.2 \quad + 0.9R$ $\qquad (1.8) \quad (0.7)$	$R^2 = .02$
$(1E)$	$G' = -1.5 \quad + 0.3E$ $\qquad (1.9) \quad (0.3)$	$R^2 = .004$
$(2R)$	$G' = -2.9 \quad + \quad .0004Y \quad + .0003P + .004U - 0.4I \quad + 1.0R$ $\qquad (2.2) \qquad (1.6) \quad (0.1) \quad (0.5) \quad (1.2) \quad (0.7)$	$R^2 = .59$
$(2E)$	$G' = -2.7 \quad + \quad .0004Y \quad + .0002P + .004U - 0.5I \quad + 0.7E$ $\qquad (2.9) \qquad (1.6) \quad (0.1) \quad (0.5) \quad (1.6) \quad (0.8)$	$R^2 = .59$

Note: The numbers in parentheses below the estimated coefficients are the absolute values of the associated t-statistic. An asterisk indicates that the estimated coefficient is statistically significant at the .05 level (using a two-tail test); Y = income per capita in U.S. dollars for 1977; P = population (in millions); U = percentage of population living in urban areas; I = intergovernmental grants as a percentage of total government general revenues.

nonfederal nations—a result that is presumably consistent with the Leviathan hypothesis. However, in neither case could a simple test for the difference between the means reject the null hypothesis that the observations come from the same population (at a .95 level of confidence). I also reestimated the regression equations in Table 6 substituting for the fiscal centralization ratios a dummy variable equal to one for those countries with a federal constitution and zero otherwise. In the multiple regression equations, the estimated coefficients on the dummy variable were of negative sign. Taking the point estimate for this coefficient from the equation for the industrialized countries, one finds that, *ceteris paribus,* the value of G for a federal country is about 5 percentage points less than for a nonfederal nation. However, in none of the equations was the t-statistic of sufficient size to reject the null hypothesis of no association. Related to this, Richard Bird (1984) using a sample of 13 countries from a study by Morris Beck (1981) finds that, over the period 1950–77, the rate of growth of real government expenditure in relation to GNP was actually slightly higher in federal than in nonfederal countries. It seems hard to find any really significant differences here.

The multiple-regression equations for the two subsamples tell pretty much the same story (except that the t-ratios for the subsample of developing countries tend to be somewhat smaller). The fiscal-centralization variables have positive coefficients, but the t-ratios remain quite small. Finally, like the results for the state-local analysis, the findings for the international sample seem quite robust. The use of a number of alternative specifications of the equations and variables did not alter the substance of the results.[11]

[11] As with the state-local sample, I reestimated the multiple-regression equations using $2SLS$ and treating intergovernmental grants (I) and the centralization ratios $(R$ and $E)$ as endogenous variables. The general pattern of the results remained similar to those reported in Table 6 although there was a substantial reduction in the t-statistic for the grant variable (I). The estimated coefficients for the centralization ratios remained statistically insignificant.

IV. Conclusion

Overall, the results of this study suggest that there does not exist a strong, systematic relationship between the size of government and the degree of centralization of the public sector. At the offset, I set forth as the null hypothesis the proposition that centralization and the size of government have little to do with one another. We certainly cannot reject this proposition from the findings in any of the samples or subsamples in this study.

What implications can we draw from all this? I would stress that the basic finding does not imply that there is no place in public economics for the revenue-maximization hypothesis. There is, in fact, considerable evidence to support budget-maximizing behavior by public agents in certain sorts of institutional settings (for example, the literature on bureaucracy). But it is another matter to try to characterize the entire public sector as a monolithic, monopolistic actor with the sole objective of making the government sector as large as possible. The results, it seems to me, cast considerable doubt on the usefulness of the Leviathan model. If, in fact, potentially pervasive revenue-maximizing forces are at work in the public sector, we should expect to see these forces manifest themselves in terms of larger budgets where given the opportunity to do so. As Brennan and Buchanan suggest, Leviathan will have much more scope for action in a relatively centralized public sector. But I seem to find no real difference in outcomes whether Leviathan is constrained by decentralization or not. Perhaps, after all, Leviathan is a mythical beast.

APPENDIX

Sample of countries:

Australia	Cyprus
Austria	Denmark
Bangladesh	Ecuador
Brazil	Ethiopia
Canada	Fiji
Chile	Finland
Costa Rica	France
Germany (West)	Norway
Greece	Pakistan
Honduras	Panama
Iceland	Paraguay
Iran	Philippines
Ireland	South Africa
Israel	Spain
Kenya	Sweden
Korea	Switzerland
Luxembourg	Thailand
Malawi	Tunisia
Mauritius	United Kingdom
Mexico	United States
Netherlands	Uruguay
New Zealand	

Sources of data for the state-local study:

Fiscal data: *1977 Census of Governments*, Vol. 4, No. 5, Tables 23, 24, 35, and 39. The same source was used for total population, urban population, number of local governments, and income per capita, but came from Table 46. The land area, population density, and date entered the union is from *The World Almanac...*, 1980.

Sources of data for the international study:

Fiscal data: IMF *Government Statistics Yearbook*, Vol. VI, 1982; the income per capita: Summers et al., pp. 19–66 (data used for 1977); *GDP*: United Nations *Yearbook of National Accounts Statistics, 1980*, Vol. 1, 1982; total population: *United Nations Demographic Yearbook 1981*, Table 6, 1983; urban population was from the same source but supplemented by *The World Almanac...*, 1983.

REFERENCES

Beck, Morris, *Government Spending, Trends and Issues,* New York: Praeger, 1981.

Bird, Richard M., "Federal Finance in Comparative Perspective," Working Paper No. 84–22, Department of Economics and Institute for Policy Analysis, University of Toronto, June 1984.

Brennan, Geoffrey, and Buchanan, James, *The Power to Tax: Analytical Foundations of a Fiscal Constitution,* Cambridge; New York: Cambridge University Press, 1980.

_____ and _____, "Tax Instruments as Constraints on the Disposition of Public Revenues." *Journal of Public Economics.* June 1978, *9*, 301–18.

_____ and _____, "Towards a Tax Constitution for Leviathan." *Journal of Public Economics*, December 1977, *8*, 255–73.

Epple, Dennis and Zelenitz, Allan, "The Implications of Competition Among Jurisdictions: Does Tiebout Need Politics?." *Journal of Political Economy*, December 1981, *89*, 1197–1217.

Musgrave, Richard, "Leviathan Cometh—or Does He?," in H. Ladd and T. N. Tideman, eds., *Tax and Expenditure Limitations*, COUPE Papers on Public Economics, *5*, Washington: The Urban Institute, 1981, 77–120.

Oates, Wallace, *Fiscal Federalism*. New York: Harcourt Brace Jovanovich, 1972.

Pindyck, Robert and Rubinfeld, Daniel, *Econometric Models and Economic Forecasts*, 2d ed., New York: McGraw-Hill, 1981.

Siegel, Sidney, *Nonparametric Statistics for the Behavioral Sciences*. New York: McGraw-Hill, 1956.

Summers, Robert, Kravis, Irving and Heston, Alan, "International Comparison of Real Product and its Composition: 1950–77." *Review of Income and Wealth*. March 1980, Series 26, No. 1, 19–66.

International Monetary Fund, *Government Finance Statistics Yearbook*, Vol. VI, Washington: International Monetary Fund, 1982.

United Nations, *Yearbook of National Accounts Statistics, 1980*. Vol. 1, New York: United Nations, 1982.

_____, *Demographic Yearbook, 1981*, New York: United Nations, 1983.

U.S. Bureau of the Census, *1977 Census of Governments*, Vol. 4, No. 5: *Compendium of Government Finances*. Washington: US-GPO, August 1979.

The World Almanac and Book of Facts, 1980; 1983.

[25]

Searching for Leviathan: A Reply and Some Further Reflections

By WALLACE E. OATES[*]

The dramatic growth of the public sector over the twentieth century has become a major source of concern. Not only academic economists, but policymakers around the globe have turned their attention to measures to contain the growth of government. One segment of work on this issue addresses the structure of the public sector and its implications for the size and growth of government. In particular, there is a widely held suspicion that the increasing centralization of the public sector is itself largely responsible for the rapid expansion of government. The issue, in short, is whether or not the public sector tends, *ceteris paribus*, to be larger the more centralized is its fiscal structure.

Some years ago, I (1972, pp. 209–213) explored this relationship in terms of a sample of 57 countries. My basic thought was that decentralization would constitute a disciplining force by providing a much closer link between revenues and spending; in a more centralized public sector, there would be wider opportunities for local residents to try to get local programs that would be financed from national revenue sources—more opportunities for logrolling of the sort described in Gordon Tullock's classic paper (1959). From this perspective, I looked for a positive relationship between the degree of fiscal centralization and the size of the public sector. Using cross-sectional data from the mid-1960s with tax revenues as a percentage of national income as the measure of government size, I found that the simple relationship between fiscal cen-

tralization and public-sector size was the exact reverse of what I had expected—I found an inverse and significant association. On closer inspection, however, it became clear that this finding resulted from the fact that the advanced, industrialized nations had both relatively large and relatively decentralized public sectors; the developing countries, in contrast, were characterized by small and centralized government. As a result, small government tended to be associated with a centralized fiscal system. If one controlled for the extent of economic development by including per capita income as an independent variable, the significance of the association between fiscal centralization and public-sector size disappeared. The results thus suggested that "The degree of fiscal centralization does not appear to have a systematic effect on the relative size of public spending" (pp. 210–211).

More recently, Geoffrey Brennan and James Buchanan (1980) have brought this relationship back under scrutiny in terms of their view of the public sector as "Leviathan"—a monolithic entity that seeks to maximize the revenues that it extracts from the economy. From this perspective, decentralization serves as a powerful constraint on Leviathan such that "Total government intrusion into the economy should be smaller, *ceteris paribus*, the greater the extent to which taxes and expenditures are decentralized..." (p. 185). With interest rekindled in this matter, I undertook a more extensive study with data from the 1980s (Oates, 1985) using both an international sample of 43 countries and a sample consisting of the 48 contiguous states in the United States. In neither set of regression equations did I have much success in finding evidence suggesting that fiscal centralization was positively associated with the size of the public sector. I thus came away from this later work with much the same

*Department of Economics and Bureau of Business and Economic Research, University of Maryland, and University Fellow, Resources for the Future. I am grateful to Robert Schwab and Jeffrey Zax for helpful comments on an earlier draft.

sense that I had earlier—namely, that the extent of centralization did not appear to have much to do with the size of the government sector.

However, several other economists have now undertaken investigations of this relationship with conflicting findings. The provocative papers, for example, by Jeffrey Zax and by Kevin Forbes and Ernest Zampelli in this issue both make use of counties in the United States as their units of observation. Zax finds evidence supporting Leviathan, while the Forbes-Zampelli results strongly reject the Leviathan view. This literature thus contains a number of puzzles. At the same time, it has helped to clarify the nature of the relationship under study. In particular, there are some subtle and tricky issues of interpretation that I believe would benefit from some explicit discussion here.

On a conceptual level, the recent work makes clear that there is more to this matter than simply examining the relationship between a fiscal centralization ratio (i.e., central government revenues or expenditures as a fraction of total government revenues or expenditures) and public-sector size. Brennan and Buchanan contend that competition among local governments in the context of the "interjurisdictional mobility of persons in pursuit of 'fiscal gains' can offer partial or possibly complete substitutes for explicit fiscal constraints on the taxing power" (1980, p. 184). The point here is that the share of the central government in the public sector represents only one dimension in the "degree of competition" within the public sector. Imagine, for example, two countries with the same relative role for the central government. Suppose, however, that in one country the lower tier of government consists of large regional governments with little mobility across their borders, while the other has a local sector with small jurisdictions that actively compete among one another for residents. Clearly, the second case would entail much more in the way of constraining forces on the public sector of the kind envisioned by Brennan and Buchanan.

The point then is that there is a second dimension to the measurement of competitiveness within the public sector. Zax

provides a nice, clear distinction between these two dimensions. He refers to the share of the top tier of government as "centralism" and to the extent of competition within the lower tiers as "fragmentation." Both dimensions clearly need to be integrated into the analysis.[1]

With this distinction in mind, let us turn to the recent empirical work. But, first, I should note that, prior to my second study, J. Fred Giertz (1981) published his findings on the effects of "centralism" on public-sector size. Using a cross-sectional sample of the fifty U.S. states with data for 1969, Giertz found a statistically significant positive association between his centralization ratio (state tax revenues as a percentage of total state and local tax revenues) and per capita state and local expenditure (after controlling for income and other relevant variables). In sharp contrast to my findings for the state and local sector using 1977 data, Giertz's results provide support for the centralism dimension of the competition hypothesis.

More recently, Michael Nelson (1987), in a follow-up study of the state and local sector, explored the relationship between the size of this sector and the size of local governments as measured by *average* population per local government unit. Although his results were not statistically significant for an equation involving all local governments, when he restricted the focus to general-purpose local governments, he found a significant relationship. Likewise, in a study of a single local function, he found a significant association between spending on fire protection and population per jurisdiction. Nelson's results suggest that increasing the number of general-purpose local governments serving a given population tends to reduce the size of the public sector. Note that (in contrast to Giertz) Nelson's study addresses only the second dimension of the centralization issue.

---

[1] In my more recent study (1985) involving the state and local sector in the United States, I used the number of local governments in the state as an alternative to the fiscal centralization ratio as a measure of decentralization. I would now regard these as complementary explanatory variables rather than as substitutes.

Nelson does not look at "centralism"; he examines only the size of local government units, the "fragmentation" dimension, where he finds that smaller general-purpose units (which presumably establish a more competitive environment within the local sector) are associated with a reduced size of government in the aggregate.[2]

However, there is some further evidence from another study of the state and local sector supporting the centralism relationship. Using a large panel data set with observations on the United States at decade intervals reaching back to the turn of the century, John Wallis and Oates (1988) find a positive and significant association between a fiscal centralization ratio and the size of the state and local sector measured as a fraction of state income. Employing an error-components estimation technique, the study finds that fiscal centralization and public-sector size are positively related for a range of specifications including centralization measures based both on the state's share of revenues and of expenditures. This finding runs directly counter to my earlier cross-sectional study of the states using 1977 fiscal data, but it is consistent with Giertz's results employing 1969 figures.

The two excellent studies in this issue turn to lower tier governments as their units of observation. Instead of examining the size of the state and local sector, both Zax and Forbes-Zampelli adopt the county sector as the subject of study on the grounds that population mobility is likely to be more important across county lines than across state boundaries. If, as Brennan and Buchanan contend, population mobility is an essential element in promoting intergovernmental competition, then we might expect to see the constraining force of competition manifest itself in its most compelling way at the local level.

On first inspection, the Zax and Forbes-Zampelli studies appear to reach strikingly

different results: Zax finds empirical support for Leviathan, while the Forbes and Zampelli findings clearly reject Leviathan. Closer examination, however, reveals that the two studies, although both look at counties, make use of quite different kinds of tests. Both have their strengths and weaknesses.

It is important to note at the outset that the dependent variables in the two studies are very different. In the Zax study, the size of government is measured in terms of the aggregate budget of *all* local government units within the county as a fraction of county income. Forbes and Zampelli, in contrast, use as a dependent variable the budget only of the county government as a fraction of income.

This difference in the choice of dependent variables reflects an important distinction in the focus of the two studies. Zax is examining the effect of *intra*-county competition on the size of the aggregate county fisc, while Forbes and Zampelli are looking at the effects of *inter*-county competition on the size of county government. With this difference in focus, the relevant explanatory variables for Zax are measures of centralism and of fragmentation *within* each county; for Forbes and Zampelli, the concern is with the number of *other* (potentially competitive) county governments within the same metropolitan area. The nature of these studies and their findings thus are not directly comparable.

Zax finds support for Leviathan on both dimensions of the centralization issue. Using a huge sample of over 3,000 U.S. counties and carefully controlling for the effects of other important variables, he finds that his measure of centralism, the county share of local revenues, is positively and significantly related to the size of the county-local fisc and that his measure of fragmentation, the number of governments per square mile, is negatively and significantly related to size. These results are thus consistent with the view that a more highly centralized county fisc tends to be larger and that smaller sub-county jurisdictions in terms of land area promote a smaller local public sector. It is of interest that, in contrast to Nelson, Zax does not find for general-purpose governments

---

[2] Nelson also finds that more state mandates to local governments (which indicate more central control in the state-local fisc) are associated with a larger state and local sector.

any tendency for jurisdictions that are smaller in terms of population to be associated with smaller government size. Nelson's finding for the state and local fisc does not manifest itself in Zax's results for the county-local fisc.

The Forbes-Zampelli study is less inclusive in that it examines the size of the county fisc in isolation from the other local governments within the county boundaries. There is, however, a control variable for county-local structure in the form of a measure of the county share in the county-local fisc. This precludes Forbes and Zampelli from examining the effect of centralism; however, it avoids certain complications in terms of the aggregation of what are, in some instances, overlapping and noncompeting jurisdictions. Instead, they focus on the potential competition from other county governments in the same SMSA. And they find that the more counties there are in the metropolitan area, other things equal, the larger is the county fisc—just the opposite of what a Leviathan view suggests! I have no ready explanation for this result, aside from the obvious possibility of some adminstrative economies of scale or Wallis' suggestion that residents may be willing to entrust a wider range of functions to smaller government units.[3]

In another recent (and ongoing) study of metropolitan and county finance, Randall Eberts and Timothy Gronberg (1988) have some interesting findings that confirm certain of the Nelson and Zax results. Eberts and Gronberg make use of a large U.S. data set for 1977 that includes over 2,900 counties and 280 SMSAs. The dependent variable in their study is local government expenditure on selected, key functions as a percentage of personal income. Like Nelson and Zax, they employ a number of different measures of

fragmentation, including the total number of local government units, the number of units normalized by population size, and the number of units normalized by land area. They also distinguish between general-purpose governments and single-purpose units. Experimenting with different levels of aggregation and measures of fragmentation, Eberts and Gronberg find that an increase in fragmentation of general-purpose local governments, measured by any one of their three measures, is significantly associated with a decrease in the local budget share of personal income. This result holds both for the cases where the dependent variable is defined in terms of counties or metropolitan areas. In contrast, the number of single-purpose units is positively and significantly related to budgetary share. Of further interest, they find that when this same type of equation is estimated using states as the unit of observation, the estimated coefficients are, in general, no longer statistically significant. The Eberts-Gronberg findings thus suggest that fragmentation of general-purpose local governments is a more effective constraining force within a metropolitan or county setting than at the state level.

There remains the issue of the effects of centralization at the national level. As I indicated, my own work has been unable to find any effects of "centralism"on public-sector size. However, I do have some concerns about comparability of data. My more recent study (1985) made use of IMF figures on government finances. These data are presented in a standard form that facilitates comparative study but, in discussions at a recent conference, some observers expressed reservations concerning their reliability for purposes of international comparisons. There is thus a need for further inter-country study making use of other data sources.

The alternative, of course, is time-series analysis at the national level. Michael Marlow (1988) has performed such a test using data on U.S. government from 1946 to 1985 in which he regresses total government expenditure as a share of GNP on the share of state and local expenditure in total public spending. Although the simple correlation is positive and significant (contrary to Levi-

---

[3] While one may quibble over certain matters of specification in these studies, it is hard to be very critical since there exists no basic theory from which to derive a fully specified standard model. The authors in both papers are careful to control for a wide range of other determinants of public-sector size and to use appropriate estimation procedures.

athan), Marlow finds in his expanded model corrected for autocorrelation that greater fiscal decentralization is significantly associated with a smaller public sector, thus providing support for the Leviathan view. All of this work at the national level, incidentally, looks solely at the centralism dimension of the centralization issue; it does not incorporate any measures of fragmentation of the subcentral public sector. While it would clearly be desirable to employ measures of both dimensions of centralization, it will be difficult to develop comparable measures of fragmentation for international cross-sectional studies because of the bewildering variety in jurisdictional structure among nations—a variety that would be hard to capture with conventional variables.

The empirical literature on fiscal centralization and government size thus contains a number of puzzles and inconsistent findings. Where does this leave us? Are things (as Zax asked me in a recent letter) in an "irresolvable muddle," or is it possible to construct a research agenda with the potential to clarify matters?

In attempting to answer this question, I would stress first that a review of the existing body of empirical work reveals some fairly well-grounded, and quite interesting, findings. For one, Nelson, Zax, and Eberts-Gronberg all find a basic and important difference between general-purpose and single-function local government. A proliferation of the former is associated in all these studies with a smaller local-government sector, while a larger number of single-purpose units seems to increase the size of the local government. This finding appears to make sense: a greater number of general-purpose governments (within the relevant area) should indicate a greater range of fiscal choice and potential competition in the local sector, while more single-function units reflect overlapping of governments that is unlikely to promote local competition. The findings in these studies in fact suggest that the additional costs of providing local services through numerous "special districts" may have come to exceed the savings from such specialized districts. Perhaps, as Zax argues, the potential scale efficiencies from

single-purpose units have been lost where these units serve relatively small populations.

More generally, most of the studies of the local sector seem to find some support for the centralization hypothesis, both on the centralism and fragmentation dimensions. The Forbes-Zampelli study is an exception, but (as discussed) this study is really looking at a somewhat different aspect of the issue. In addition, the Eberts-Gronberg work suggests that the effects of fragmentation are much more evident at the local level than at the state level—a finding that is consistent with the importance of household mobility as a constraining force on government size.

There are, I think, some useful directions for further work. First, I would like to see another international cross-sectional study with a new data base. In view of the forementioned reservations concerning the IMF data, I would have much more confidence in my finding of an absence of any relationship between fiscal centralization and public-sector size at the national level were it confirmed by another study using a new data set.

Second, as regards to the state and local sectors, I doubt that there is much new to be learned from simply another study like those described here. We now have several such studies, and I think that diminishing returns will set in quite rapidly from here on. However, there is a real need for a study that explicitly tries to unravel some of the inconsistencies in the existing literature. This will not be easy, but I think it is possible. What would be required is a large data base encompassing both state and local government finances. With these data, the researcher could explore systematically the effects of the various definitions that have been used of the key variables, the effects of different specifications of the equations, and the effects of using different levels of government. In short, what I envision is a study that will effectively "hold constant" other things and investigate one-by-one the differences in definition, specification, and aggregation that have been used in previous studies. The work by Zax and by Eberts and Gronberg goes some distance on this (for example, the

Eberts-Gronberg contrast of the results for the state-local sector with their findings for the local sector alone). But I think a further study that explicitly seeks to sort out the effects of each of these differences along both the centralism and fragmentation dimensions could help solve some of the remaining puzzles. At this juncture, it would be hard to disagree with Zax's conclusion that the effects of decentralization are "complex." But I think that this complexity is not impenetrable.

REFERENCES

Brennan, Geoffrey and Buchanan, James, *The Power to Tax: Analytical Foundations of a Fiscal Constitution*, Cambridge, New York: Cambridge University Press, 1980.

Eberts, Randal W. and Gronberg, Timothy J., "Can Competition Among Local Governments Constrain Government Spending?," *Economic Review* (Federal Reserve Bank of Cleveland), No. 1, 1988, *24*, 2–9.

Forbes, Kevin F. and Zampelli, Ernest M., "Is Leviathan a Mythical Beast?," *American Economic Review*, June 1989, *79*, 587–96.

Giertz, J. Fred, "Centralization and Government Budget Size," *Publius*, Winter 1981, *11*, 119–28.

Marlow, Michael L., "Fiscal Decentralization and Government Size," *Public Choice*, No. 3, 1988, *56*, 159–69.

Nelson, Michael A., "Searching for Leviathan: Comment and Extension," *American Economic Review*, March 1987, *77*, 198–204.

Oates, Wallace E., *Fiscal Federalism*, New York: Harcourt Brace Jovanovich, 1972.

———, "Searching for Leviathan: An Empirical Study," *American Economic Review*, September 1985, *75*, 748–57.

Tullock, Gordon, "Problems of Majority Voting," *Journal of Political Economy*, December 1959, *67*, 571–79.

Wallis, John Joseph and Oates, Wallace E., "Does Economic Sclerosis Set in with Age? An Empirical Study of the Olson Hypothesis," *Kyklos*, No. 3, 1988, *41*, 397–417.

Zax, Jeffrey S, "Is There a Leviathan in Your Neighborhood?," *American Economic Review*, June 1989, *79*, 560–67.

[26]

On the Nature and Measurement of Fiscal Illusion: A Survey

Wallace E. Oates

Wallace E. Oates lectures at the Department of Economics and Bureau of Business and Economic Research, University of Maryland. This chapter was written during sabbatical leave at Resources for the Future. I am grateful to RFF and to the Sloan Foundation for their support of this work. I am also indebted to Dennis Mueller, Paul Portney, and Robert Schwab for some most helpful comments on an earlier draft.

It is both a pleasure and an honour to contribute to this volume in recognition of the valuable and wide-ranging contributions of Russell Mathews to the study of fiscal structure and behaviour. Under Mathews's careful guidance, the Centre for Research on Federal Financial Relations at the Australian National University has provided a steady stream of published research on federal finance that occupies a central place in the field. Scholars throughout the world draw regularly on Mathews's and the Centre's work both for its substantive findings and for the rich bodies of comparative institutional information and data that they provide. All of us in the field are deeply in his debt.

For my contribution, I have chosen the very tantalising, but empirically elusive, phenomenon of 'fiscal illusion' — the notion that the systematic misperception of key fiscal parameters may significantly distort fiscal choices by the electorate.

Various elements of the tax structure, for example may be largely hidden so that voters do not perceive the entire cost of providing certain public services. There is now a small literature on this issue: its historic roots lie in Puviani (1903) and other Italian writers; and it has received impetus more recently from James Buchanan (1967).

The most recent work on fiscal illusion is largely empirical in character: it seeks to find particular manifestations of fiscal illusion in existing fiscal structure and choices. A central theme of my paper will be that this literature has been less successful than it might appear in establishing the presence and importance of various forms of fiscal illusion. For reasons that I will try to make clear, the detection and measurement of fiscal illusion is a difficult enterprise. In several instances where studies claim to find empirical support for a particular form of fiscal illusion, I believe that there are alternative, and more compelling explanations for the findings. In other cases, the evidence simply is not consistent with the illusion hypothesis. This is not to say that elements of fiscal illusion are not present in fiscal systems — I suspect they are — but rather that the existing empirical literature has not as yet made a persuasive case for their existence and importance.

The chapter begins with a general consideration of the nature of fiscal illusion and then turns to empirical efforts to substantiate various illusion hypotheses. Five forms (or sources) of fiscal illusion have received attention in the literature:

1. complexity of the tax structure;
2. renter illusion with respect to property taxation;
3. income elasticity of the tax structure;
4. debt illusion;
5. the flypaper effect.

I shall summarise and evaluate the work on each of them in turn.[1] But first we need a brief overview of fiscal illusion and of the general empirical approach to testing illusion hypotheses.

The Nature of Fiscal Illusion

Almost 30 years ago, Anthony Downs (1957) argued convincingly that the representative voter is likely to have highly imperfect information on which to base his decisions on public-sector activities. The costs of acquiring information imply, of course, less than perfect knowledge for private-sector choices as well. But as Downs pointed out, the incentives to obtain information on the benefits and costs of government programs are much less than for private activities. Since an individual ballot is unlikely to have a discernible effect on public-sector outcomes, there is little reason for the voter to invest substantial resources in learning about the relative costs and benefits of the various alternatives in the government sector. The individual determines his own pattern of purchases and consumption of private goods so that some investment in the acquisition of information is worthwhile. But for public-sector choices, his impotence with regard to outcomes implies that there will typically be little effort expended to learn about government progams. As Downs (1957) concludes: 'Ignorance of politics is not a result of unpatriotic apathy; rather it is a highly rational response to the facts of political life in a large democracy' (p. 147).

Imperfect information is not, however, synonymous with fiscal illusion. It is a necessary, but not a sufficient, condition for its existence. More specifically, fiscal illusion refers to a *systematic misperception* of fiscal parameters — a recurring propensity, for example, to underestimate one's tax liability associated with certain public programs. Imperfect information alone might well give rise to a random pattern of over- and underestimation of such tax liabilities. Fiscal illusion, in contrast, implies persistent and consistent behaviour. As such, it will give rise to recurring, and presumably predictable, biases in budgetary decisions.

It is by no means clear in which direction fiscal illusion will tend to bias public-sector outcomes. In the earlier literature on this matter, Downs (1960) and Galbraith (1958) argued that imperfect information would tend to make the public budget too small. It was Downs's contention that the benefits of most government programs tended to be 'remote' and largely unrecognised by the electorate, while the taxes to support these programs are more directly experienced and understood.[2] The more pronounced tendency towards a systematic underestimation of public-sector benefits than costs would lead the electorate to support an unduly small allocation of resources to the government sector.

However, in the more recent public choice literature, the view has shifted radically. The attention to special interest groups and associated lobbying efforts has called into question the presumed lack of support for public spending. At the same time, studies of revenue structure and 'tax consciousness' suggest that significant elements of the tax system are largely hidden and 'underperceived' by taxpayers. From this perspective, it is the costs of government programs, not their benefits, that are subject to significant and regular underestimation. This may stem, in part, from deliberate efforts by public agencies (of the sort Niskanen envisioned) to disguise the full costs of their programs and, where possible, to exaggerate the associated benefits. The tax system, in consequence, has come to include important elements like tax withholding and forms of taxation with obscure patterns of incidence that conceal the real cost of public programs (Brennan and Buchanan, 1980). Fiscal illusion, under this view, results in a public sector of excessive size.

Not surprisingly, the recent empirical literature on fiscal illusion has focused exclusively on the revenue side of the budget; it consists of studies of tax and debt illusion. These studies search for evidence linking relatively hidden elements in the revenue structure to higher levels of taxes or spending.

Before turning to this body of research, there is one general property of fiscal illusion that is worthy of note and that has some implications for empirical testing. Fiscal illusion (or at least tax illusion), by its very nature, can only operate over a limited range. Certain kinds of taxes may remain hidden while they absorb relatively modest fractions of personal income. But as they come to constitute larger and larger chunks of income, they become progressively harder to hide. To take a specific example, it has been argued that more income-elastic revenue systems are conducive to more rapid growth in the public sector, because they generate larger 'automatic' increases in public revenues as the economy grows (Oates, 1975). However, there are obviously limits to this — if the tax system were sufficiently income elastic, the argument would imply that the public sector could come to absorb virtually all of the taxpayer's income with little opposition. Fiscal illusion obviously cannot persist to such extremes; its potential is limited to some range of tax bills. Empirical work on tax illusion may, in consequence, need to make provision for various types of 'threshhold' effects or, more generally, for varying magnitudes of illusion over different values of the tax parameters.

Empirical Studies of Fiscal Illusion: The General Approach

The bulk of the empirical work on fiscal illusion consists of econometric studies based upon some kind of model of public spending. The models range from ad hoc expenditure equations to more rigorously founded demand functions for public goods (e.g., Bergstrom and Goodman, 1973). In both cases, these studies end up regressing a measure of budgetary size (either spending or revenues — or, in some instances, changes in spending or revenues) on a set of explanatory variables including income, often some kind of price term, and a series of 'taste' variables. In the Bergstrom and Goodman formulation, for example, this set of explanatory variables represents the determinants of the demand of the median voter for local public outputs. These are the variables that would determine public outputs in the absence of any fiscal illusion.

The next step is to add to the equation variables that will capture any illusion effects. As we shall see in the subsequent sections, these variables take a number of different forms in the attempt to test for the presence of tax or debt illusion. The typical model is thus of the form:

1. $E = \alpha X + \beta F + u,$

where E is a measure of budgetary size, X is a vector of explanatory variables in a world without fiscal illusion, F is a vector of variables designed to measure various types of fiscal illusion, and u is the usual disturbance term. The null hypothesis for each form of fiscal illusion is taken to be a zero coefficient on the relevant variable in the F-vector; since the illusion hypotheses usually imply particular signs for the variables, the alternative hypothesis is associated with either a positive or negative sign on β, and a one-tail test is employed to accept or reject the null hypothesis.

Case I: Complexity of the Revenue System

The first source of fiscal illusion that we shall examine is the complexity of the revenue system. Buchanan, incidentally, attributes the revenue-complexity hypothesis to Puviani (1903). As Buchanan puts it 'To the extent that the total tax load on an individual can be fragmented so that he confronts numerous small levies rather than a few significant ones, illusory effects may be created' (1967, p. 135). According to this hypothesis, the more complicated the revenue system, the more difficult it is for the taxpayer to determine the 'tax-price' of public outputs — and the more likely it is that he will underestimate the tax burden associated with public programs. In short, the hypothesis implies that, other things equal, the more complex the revenue system, the larger will be the public budget.

Richard Wagner (1976) undertook the first test of the revenue-complexity hypothesis. Wagner's approach, as discussed in the preceding section, was to regress total current expenditure for a sample of 50 large US cities on a set of socio-economic variables and a measure of the complexity of the revenue system. For the Wagner study, the vector F in equation (1) collapses into a single variable, f. Just how one measures the complexity of a revenue system is far from obvious. Wagner, interestingly, chose an index, the Herfindahl index, that is widely used in the industrial-organisation literature to measure the degree of concentration within an industry. More specifically, Wagner's measure of revenue-complexity is:

2. $$f = \sum_{i=1}^{4} r_i$$

where r_i is the fraction of total city revenue generated from tax source i. For the r_i, he adopted the Census Bureau classification of city-owned revenues into four categories: property taxes, general sales taxes, selective excise taxes, and charges and fees. The Herfindahl index will achieve its maximum value of unity if a city generates all of its own revenues from a single source; the minimum possible value would be one-fourth if revenues were divided equally amoung the four categories. A higher value of the index is thus associated with a less complex revenue system so that the revenue-complexity hypothesis posits a negative coefficient for the variable f.

Wagner's choice of the Herfindahl index has been an influential one, for, as we shall see shortly, *every* subsequent study of the revenue-complexity hypothesis has used this index as the measure of the illusion variable. In his estimated regression equation, Wagner found that the sign of the coefficient on the revenue-complexity variable was indeed negative and that he could reject the null hypothesis of non association at a .01 level of significance. Moreover, the point estimate of the coefficient suggested a very substantial magnitude for the effect: lower values of the Herfindahl index were associated with sizeable larger levels of public expenditure.

However, as Wagner acknowledged, the Herfindahl index has some serious deficiencies as a measure of tax illusion. In particular, the 'visibility' of the four classes of revenue is likely to vary greatly: a heavier reliance on charges and fees, for example, will surely provide a more direct sense of the cost of public outputs than a similar reliance on selective excise taxation. We might expect a city making extensive use of charges and fees to generate a lower level of spending than one which made relatively the same use of selective excise taxes. This absence of a measure of the visibility of various revenue sources suggests that Wagner's regression equation may be misspecified, raising the likelihood of biased estimators of the coefficients.[3]

Subsequent econometric work on the revenue-complexity hypothesis has yielded somewhat mixed results. Munley and Greene (1978), using a sample of cities much like that of Wagner, found that the results were quite sensitive to the specification of the equation. Making what appear to be some sensible alterations to the form of the regression equation, they found that the estimated coefficient of the revenue-complexity variable was no longer significantly different from zero, suggesting that Wagner's results may not be very robust. In another study exploring public spending for higher education, Clotfelter (1976) could find no evidence supporting a fiscal illusion. The estimated coefficient on the Herfindahl index was not statistically significant. Moreover, Clotfelter went a step further by trying to control for the visibility of different revenue sources. His results run counter to the illusion hypothesis; a heavier reliance on more visible revenue sources (direct taxation) was associated with more, not less, spending.

However, three other studies, drawing on samples from quite different sorts of jurisdictions, have found support for the hypothesis. Using data from 110 large Swiss municipalities, Pommerehne and Schneider (1978) estimated a series of multiple-regression equations in which the coefficients on the Herfindahl index had the hypothesised negative sign and were consistently significantly different from zero. Interestingly, they found that this result was much stronger in a subset of municipalities with representative democracy but no public referenda than where direct democracy or referenda were used. Baker (1983) regressed state and local tax revenues on the usual sorts of variables and obtained a negative and marginally significant estimated coefficient on his Herfindahl index. And, finally, Breeden and Hunter (1985), in a study of levels of tax revenues in 37 large US cities, found a negative and significant relationship between these revenues and the Herfindahl index.

While the results from the various studies of the revenue-complexity hypothesis are somewhat mixed, there appears to be considerable evidence, based on the Herfindahl-index variable, in support of this type of fiscal illusion. As we have seen, this evidence takes the form of a negative partial association between some measure of budgetary size and the value of the Herfindahl index. However, some further reflection suggests another, and I believe more compelling interpretation of this association. State and local officials tend to be painfully aware of tax rates in other jurisdictions and try to resist getting too far out of line with rates elsewhere. Levels of sales taxation in excess of those in neighbouring jurisdictions, for example, can induce shoppers to avoid local purchases of taxed goods. Likewise, relatively heavy taxation of business capital is often thought to deflect business investment and jobs away from the state or local economy. In consequence, as expenditures in a jurisdiction rise relative to those in nearby areas, officials are likely to seek out new sources of revenue to prevent tax rates on existing revenue bases from becoming excessively high relative to other jurisdictions. We thus tend to find that jurisdictions with relatively high levels of spending adopt more diversified revenue systems. The argument here is that the structure of the tax system is itself an endogenous variable, and, in particular, that the desired level of public expenditure influences the community's choice of a tax structure. If this is true, the existing econometric tests of the revenue-complexity hypothesis are subject to simultaneous-equation bias — and must be viewed with serious reservations.

We have two competing hypotheses here: the revenue-complexity hypothesis and what I will call the 'revenue-diversification hypothesis'. To discern between them is a difficult task, for they both imply a negative association between the level of the budget and the diversity (or complexity) of the revenue system. What we really need, of course, is a theory of the determination of the tax structure that would explain community choices among alternative sources of revenues. However, we are a long way from such a comprehensive theory.

Let me offer a couple of other suggestions. First, there are now some standard econometric tests for endogeneity (e.g., Wu, 1983). It would seem sensible to subject the revenue-complexity variable in the earlier studies to such testing to get some indication of whether or not this is a real issue. Second, and more fundamentally, it would be helpful to find some way to get at the revenue-diversification hypothesis empirically. One possibility suggests itself. Consider a period of rapid budgetary growth (like the decade of the 1960s for state and local governments in the United States). If we compare the revenue system at the beginning and at the end of such a period (especially for relatively high-spending jurisdictions), the revenue-diversity hypothesis would suggest that we should observe a shift from a more simplified revenue system initially to a more diversified system at the end of the period. The pressures of budgetary growth would, from this perspective, lead to the introduction of new sources of revenue. Such a test is admittedly not wholly free of some potential illusion effects, but it does seem to me that in a period of general growth (like that associated with the 'baby boom'), the presumption of a finding of increased revenue diversity would constitute support for the revenue-diversification hypothesis. As things stand now, I think that we must conclude that 'the jury is still out' as concerns the empirical verification of the revenue-complexity hypothesis.

Case II: Renter Illusion

In the course of estimating demand functions for local public goods, a variety of authors have consistently turned up a very striking result: other things equal, jurisdictions with a relatively large fraction of renters tend to spend more per capita on local public services (see, for example, Bergstrom and Goodman, 1973, and Peterson, 1975). This pervasive and intriguing finding has generally been attributed to a kind of 'renter illusion'. Property taxes, the primary source of local tax revenues, are levied on owners of rental dwellings — not on tenants. While such taxes may be passed forward in the form of higher rents to tenants, the renter-illusion hypothesis contends that renters do not perceive this to be the case. Illusion, in this instance, takes the form of a failure on the part of tenants to understand the link between the level of local spending and the level of rent that they pay. Renters thus misperceive their tax-price for local public outputs — they believe it to be zero, or at least less than the true tax-price — and, hence, support levels of local expenditure in excess of their counterparts who own homes and pay property taxes directly.

This empirical finding appears in multiple-regression studies of the general form discussed earlier. Referring back to equation (1), the F-vector in these studies consists of a single variable indicating the proportion of the residents in the jurisdiction who are renters. This variable has, in nearly all such studies, a positive and significant coefficient — and typically implies a substantial effect on levels of public spending.

Here again, however, the illusion interpretation of this finding is open to serious question. In one recent paper, Martinez-Vazquez (1983) suggests that there is no illusion here at all. Rather, he argues that renters do, in fact, have a lower tax-price than owner-occupants, because 'renters consume less housing than do homeowners of the same income level' (p. 244). Since one's property-tax liability is a function of the amount of housing consumed, it follows that the local tax share of a renter will be less than his home-owner counterpart.

There are additional reasons for scepticism concerning the illusion view. There is considerable uncertainty concerning the incidence of property taxes on rental housing. There are certainly circumstances under which one would expect forward shifting onto tenants; if the higher revenues are associated with improved local services, then the tax-expenditure increase should translate into a higher demand for rental housing in the jurisdiction that will drive up rents in a world of mobile consumers. Where tax differentials do not reflect service differentials, in contrast, the burden of the tax may remain on the owner. Moreover, even if forward shifting occurs ultimately, it may take a considerable period of time. The functioning of rental housing markets with leases for tenants may introduce substantial time lags into the process of tax shifting. In some ongoing research, Ellen Roche (1985) contends that these lags are, indeed, significant, and that their effect is to reduce the present discounted value of any increase in tax liability to tenants. The extreme case, of course, is that of rent control where, depending on the specific ordinances, owners may be limited in the extent to which they can pass along increases in property taxes into higher rents.

What all this suggests is that renter support for expanded budgets may not be based on fiscal illusion at all. Instead, it may well reflect quite rational behaviour: under local property taxation, renters may, in fact, have significantly lower tax-prices than do owner-occupants. If true, incidentally, this phenomenon has some troubling implications, for it suggests that renters may to some extent be getting a 'free ride' at the expense of home-owners. Perhaps voting on local budgetary measures (as suggested by Sonstelie and Portney [1978]) ought to be limited to those who own property?

Case III: Income Elasticity of the Revenue System

The third instance of fiscal illusion that has been examined empirically involves the income elasticity of the revenue system. The revenue-elasticity hypothesis has been stated succinctly by Buchanan (1967), who argues that: 'In a period of rapidly increasing national product, that tax institution characterized by the highest [income] elasticity will tend, other things equal, to generate the largest volume of public spending' (p. 65).

On first inspection, this proposition appears to imply some rather peculiar behaviour on the part of taxpayers. As I have put it earlier:

> We would expect that individual demands for public services would be based upon tastes, levels of income, and the cost of these services. With a given cost-sharing scheme (or set of tax shares), we could then determine the pattern of individual demands at some moment in time.
>
> But why should people care about the income elasticity of the tax structure? What the proposition under study seems to imply is that people will not object to increases in public expenditure if they can be funded with no increases in tax rates (that is, from increments to revenues resulting solely from growth in income), but they will not support an expanded public budget if it requires a rise in tax rates. This suggests what people care about is not their tax *bill*, but rather their tax *rate*. Viewed this way, the hypothesis simply is not consistent with our conventional description of rational behaviour; it implies that consumer-taxpayers are subject to a kind of 'fiscal illusion' [Oates, 1975, p. 141].

However, in the context of existing fiscal institutions, the hypothesis is surely plausible (Goetz 1977). As Richard Wagner has argued:

> There also exists a large body of casual evidence supporting the existence of faulty fiscal perception. Whenever a legislative assembly considers changes in tax rates, tortuous discussion takes place and considerable publicity is given to the deliberations. Yet no similar agonizing takes place over the continual, automatic increase in tax rates that is produced by progressivity in the national

tax structure. Everyone is aware of a consciously enacted tax surcharge; a similar surcharge is enacted each year when income grows under progressive taxation, but many taxpayers remain unconscious of this surcharge [p. 87].

The issue at this point becomes an empirical one: do revenue systems with a relatively high income elasticity tend, during periods of economic growth, to be associated with more rapid budgetary expansion? The initial empirical test of this issue (Oates, 1975) examined the growth in spending, first, by state governments in the US, and, second, by a sample of US city governments over the decade 1960 to 1970, a period of unusually rapid budgetary growth in the state and local sector. The study followed the general approach outlined earlier except that the dependent variables were changes in spending (over the decade) and the independent variables likewise took the form of changes instead of absolute levels. The multiple-regression equations thus seek to explain the growth in spending as a function of changes in the levels of the independent variables *and* of a measure of the income elasticity of the revenue system. In the cross-sectional equations both for state governments and for a sample of 33 large cities, I found a positive and statistically significant partial association of tax elasticity with expenditure growth, providing support for the revenue-elasticity hypothesis. However, the magnitude of the effect, as calculated from the point estimates, was, in my judgment, modest.

Subsequent empirical work has produced mixed results. In a study of US state government spending, Craig and Heins (1980) found a positive and significant relationship between tax elasticity and the *level* of expenditure. They claim, incidentally, that because of 'bounds' on spending, the appropriate dependent variable is the level of public spending, not the growth (or change) in expenditure. This is a tricky matter. As I suggested earlier, there are indeed limits to illusion effects. Fiscal illusion is likely to operate over certain ranges of budgetary variables, but all changes in these variables surely cannot go unnoticed. Thus, it is not entirely clear just how illusion relationships should be specified. My conjecture is that neither simple growth nor level measures are fully adequate; we probably need to think in terms of threshold effects, or, more generally, in terms of effects that vary in magnitude with budgetary levels. At any rate, Craig and Heins did find support for the revenue-elasticity hypothesis in terms of expenditure levels of state governments.

In contrast, DiLorenzo (1982) found a *negative* and significant relationship between his measures of tax elasticity and expenditure growth for a sample of 66 US county governments. DiLorenzo attributes this to Tiebout-like migration effects in response to fiscal differentials, which he contends could offset any illusion effects at the local level. However, it is hard to see how this could result in a negative effect! Other studies include Baker (1983), who finds only marginally significant effects of his tax-elasticity variables in explaining levels of tax revenues in the state-local sector, and Breeden and Hunter (1985), whose results on this issue I find a little hard to interpret.

Once again the evidence in support of the hypothesis is somewhat mixed. But there are certainly some results suggesting that tax elasticity matters. One problem that plagues all of these studies is measuring the income elasticity of the revenue system. This is not a simple matter where the system consists of a diverse set of tax bases with varying rates. In the United States, the Advisory Commission on Intergovernmental Relations (1968, Table 7; 1974, Table 173) has published some information on tax elasticity. But the ACIR estimates are seriously incomplete and typically apply only to a single year. Craig and Heins used the ACIR estimates, but Oates tried to develop some other proxy measures involving the extent of reliance on income taxation. There is a real need in this work for improved measures of revenue elasticity.

Ignoring these measurement problems, suppose that we accept the findings of Oates and Craig-Heins of a positive and significant association of expenditure growth (or level) with revenue elasticity. As mentioned earlier, there is still the troublesome issue of the endogeneity of the tax structure. Jurisdictions that prefer relatively high levels of spending may, for example, opt for more elastic revenue systems. The elasticity variable may itself be endogenous.

There is a further matter of interpretation that I find even more troublesome. Suppose that we were to conclude that the evidence supports the revenue-elasticity hypothesis. Can we infer from this the presence of fiscal illusion? I think not. There is another explanation for this phenomenon that I find at least as compelling as the illusion view: the *transactions costs* inherent in modifying budgetary parameters. Wagner (1971) argues that:

> As viewed by legislators, the cost of thus changing tax structures may exceed the benefits, in which case the required change in relative tax collections will not occur. Such legislative behavior may be interpreted as a form of habitual behavior, and may very well be rational. There is a cost incurred in failing to routinize many types of activity — the value of the resources consumed in examining the consequences of the alternative choices, in this case, choices among possible tax structures. If the costs incurred by continual reexamination exceed the benefits received from taking more timely actions, habitual behavior is efficient — it is the least inefficient of the attainable alternatives [pp. 85-86].

Note that the transactions-cost explanation does not rely on imperfect voter information or misperceptions. It simply recognises that there are costs associated with the legislative actions needed to raise tax rates. Such costs may impede desired rate increases, whereas with a more elastic revenue system the increase in 'effective' rates will be forthcoming automatically. The illusion and transactions-cost explanations for the revenue-elasticity phenomenon are certainly not mutually exclusive. But we cannot, I think, make an unequivocal leap from the verification of the revenue-elasticity hypothesis to the conclusion that we have discovered a form of illusion in the fiscal system.

Case IV: Debt Illusion

A further potential kind of fiscal illusion involves the choice between debt and tax finance. The argument here is that individuals are more likely to perceive the costs of public programs if they pay for them through current taxation than if tax liabilities are deferred through public-sector borrowing. Vickrey (1961), for example, has referred to '..."a public debt illusion" under which individuals pay no attention to their share in the liability represented by the public debt...' (p. 133). Reliance on debt, rather than tax finance should, from this perspective, tend to result in a larger public budget.

For rational and informed taxpayers, the choice between these two forms of finance (assuming a similar pattern of incidence) should make no difference. There is obviously an equivalence (Buchanan, 1964 calls it the 'Ricardian equivalence') between a current tax payment and the present discounted value of the future tax liabilities in the event of debt finance.[4] There is now a large literature on the nature of public debt and its effects on decisions (e.g., see Barro, 1974), which I shall not try to summarise. But the central proposition here is a straightforward one: there is a fiscal illusion present when taxpayers tend to underestimate the present discounted value of their future tax liabilities under bond finance. And with imperfect knowledge, the failure to recognise such future tax liabilities, at least to their full sum, seems a real possibility.[5]

The determination of the existence and the extent of such a debt illusion is an empirical issue. Once again, this is not an easy matter to get at empirically. There is, however, a straightforward approach in terms of local finance. As Daly (1969) and Oates (1972) have pointed out, the future tax liabilities associated with local public debt should be capitalised into local property values. Consider two otherwise identical communities that undertake identical capital projects. One community, call it A, finances the project out of current revenues, while community B chooses to employ bond finance so as to spread out the payments for the project over future years. At the end of the current year, the sole differences between a 'typical resident' of A and B will be that the latter will have a future tax liability whose present discounted value equals the recent differential tax payment by the resident of A. In a world of mobile consumers, this future tax liability associated with residing in community B will become capitalised into lower property values in B.[6]

This suggests an empirical test of the debt-illusion hypothesis. Other things equal, we should find, if there is a debt illusion, that the future tax liabilities associated with the debt are not fully capitalised into local property values. There has, in fact, been such a study by Epple and Schipper (1981) in which they examined the partial association between differentials in local property values across a sample of jurisdictions in the Pittsburgh metropolitan area and the extent of deferred funding for pensions for municipal-government employees. Epple and Schipper find no evidence of debt illusion. Their results suggest that unfunded pension obligations tend to be fully capitalised into local property values. We obviously cannot place great confidence in the findings from a single study, but, as yet, there is not to my knowledge any solid, systematic evidence supporting the debt-illusion hypothesis.

Case V: The Flypaper Effect

Our final example of fiscal illusion involves what is known in the public finance literature as the 'flypaper effect'. This is a phenomenon that has been regularly observed in econometric studies of inter-governmental grants-in-aid. More specifically, these studies have found that there is a significantly higher propensity for recipients to increase public expenditure in response to lump-sum inter-governmental grants than in response to equivalent increases in private income.

In principle, as Bradford and Oates (1971) have shown, there is no reason for rational and informed individuals in a particular jurisdiction to regard increases in income from grants any differently from increases in income from other sources. From this perspective, inter-governmental grants are simply a 'veil' (hence the 'veil hypothesis') for transfers of income directly to individuals.

However, existing econometric findings do not support the veil hypothesis. Instead, they indicate that communities direct much larger fractions (40 to 50 per cent) of revenue from lump-sum inter-governmental grants into state and local outlays than from private income (roughly 10 per cent).

How can we explain the flypaper effect? Courant, Gramlich, and Rubinfeld (1979) and Oates (1979) have proposed a form of fiscal illusion that can account for this phenomenon. In their models, budget-maximising public officials effectively conceal the lump-sum character of the grant revenues. What the electorate sees is a reduction in tax rates needed to finance local spending programs, and this reduction is erroneously viewed as a reduction *at the margin* in the 'tax-price' of these programs. The budgetary process thus transforms what is, in truth, a lump-sum inter-governmental grant into what is perceived by individuals as a reduction in the tax-price of local public goods. The result is a willingness on the part of the local electorate to support higher levels of spending than if they correctly perceived the relevant fiscal parameters.

Such an explanation for the existence of the flypaper effect is plausible.

But once again, there are competing explanations. It is by no means necessary to posit the existence of a fiscal illusion to rationalise such behaviour. Romer and Rosenthal (1979), for example, have shown that where public officials set the budgetary agenda, excessive public spending can result. In their model, the public agency takes advantage of a relatively unattractive alternative, the 'reversion level' of the budget which obtains if the electorate rejects the agency's proposed budget. The proposed budget is larger than that most preferred by the representative voter but still emerges victorious because it is preferred by the electorate to the alternative — relatively unappealing reversion level of public output. Note that this explanation does not presume any lack of information or 'illusion' on the part of taxpayer voters. Moreover, as Romer and Rosenthal (1980) show, their model generates a different budgetary response to an increase in income than to an equivalent increase in lump-sum grants. The model can give rise to a flypaper effect (although other outcomes are also possible).

The basic point is simply that it doesn't require any sort of fiscal illusion to generate a flypaper result. Plausible forms of local budgetary processes can do the trick. There is no real evidence that I know supporting the illusion explanation of the flypaper effect. It is one of the possibilities, but it needs empirical support.

Conclusion

In this chapter, we have examined five distinct forms that fiscal illusion might take, each of which has been explored in the public-finance literature.[7] Although forms of illusion are surely possible on the expenditure side of the budget, all five cases involve instances of revenue illusion. They are thought to be cases where individual taxpayers are likely to underestimate their true tax-prices and consequently to support excessively large levels of public outlays. It is my contention that although all five cases entail plausible illusion hypotheses, none of them has very compelling empirical support. In this regard, I wish to offer two concluding observations.

First, the general grounds on which I have expressed reservations about the existing econometric findings are two: endogeneity of the illusion variables and alternative explanations of the results. These are such commonplace objections to econometric studies that one might regard them as a 'cheap shot'. It is typically not hard to find some grounds for questioning the exogenous nature of an independent variable. Moreover, as we all know, statistical associations do not demonstrate causation — there is always room for another hypothesis. While this is true enough, the issue is really one of judgment and additional evidence. How compelling is the other explanation for the observed result? How likely and how serious is the potential endogeneity of the suspect variable? It is my sense, as I have tried to indicate in the paper, that these are probably serious matters in the fiscal-illusion literature. The likelihood of endogeneity in certain cases like the revenue-complexity hypothesis seems to me quite high. Further, the alternative explanations of a number of the findings strike me to be at least as persuasive as the illusion rationale. In short, I think that there really are sources of serious reservation that suggest the need for further, carefully designed empirical testing both to deal with the endogeneity issue and to distinguish among the various hypotheses.

My second observation concerns the theory of fiscal illusion. This survey has focused on empirical studies of illusion hypothesis for a good reason: there is very little underlying theory. The fiscal-illusion literature has identified a number of instances of potential illusion, but it has not explored with much care or rigour their conceptual underpinnings. To take a case in point, consider the revenue-complexity hypothesis. The assertion here is that as the revenue system becomes more 'complex' (meaning that it encompasses a more diverse set of revenue sources), individuals exhibit an increasing tendency to underestimate their true tax-prices. But how does this occur? One could imagine a very fragmented revenue system in which each revenue source was tied closely to a particular government activity. Such a system could provide quite accurate price signals to taxpayer voters on the costs of various public programs. There is also the important distinction between marginal tax-price and total tax liability (see Carter, 1982). What is presumably important is the individual's perception of his tax-price at the margin which may be fairly clear even though some illusion may be present as to total tax liability. Although the public sector employs numerous revenue sources, if it is clear where the *marginal* funds come from, tax-price may be readily evident (see Flowers, 1977). My point here is simply that the study of fiscal illusion requires a careful statement of the way in which tax-price is perceived and how this perception depends on revenue structure. The existing literature is suggestive and points to some important and tantalising hypotheses, but the supporting theoretical and empirical work remains, for the most part, to be done.

Notes

1. Since my concern in this paper is with *fiscal* illusion, I will not address a major source of potential illusion operating through the monetary sector: money creation and inflationary finance as an alternative to tax or bond finance.
2. Galbraith argued along somewhat different lines. It is his contention that extensive advertising activities in the private sector introduce a 'bias' in resource allocation away from publicly provided services toward private goods. On the potential for illusion on the benefit side, see also Musgrave (1981).
3. Robert Schwab has pointed out to me that there may well be a systematic relationship between the value of the Herfindahl index and the degree of revenue visibility. A high value of the index (indicating heavy reliance on a single revenue source) might well be correlated positively with the fraction of revenues from

property taxation. If the property tax is a relatively visible source of revenues, then the Herfindahl index might be serving as a proxy for visibility as well as a measure of revenue simplicity.

4. There are, of course, circumstances that will disturb this equivalence, as, for example, where public-sector borrowing can be undertaken at an interest rate other than that available to the individual tax-payer in the private market. But the basic point remains. For a careful examination of the Ricardian equivalence theorem, see Brennan and Buchanan (1980).

5. According to Buchanan (1967, pp. 132-3), Puviani (1903) had a somewhat more subtle view of debt illusion. While acknowledging the Ricardian equivalence of debt and tax finance, Puviani contended that taxpayers would still have a preference for debt finance, because they would retain 'control' over a captial value (even though it would be offset by a corresponding liability). The preference for bond finance based on this control consideration is called by Buchanan an 'asset illusion'.

6. This is a particularly straightforward case of debt finance: the issue of bonds to finance a capital project. Debt finance can, however, take other forms. One increasingly prevalent mode involves 'borrowing' from current public employees in the form of relatively low wages with compensation in the form of generous pensions to be paid upon retirement. Because of favourable tax treatment, this is an attractive way for local governments to compensate their employees; 'underfunding' of public pension programs may be a rational course of action for a community. On this, see Mumy (1978).

7. There are a few other cases of fiscal illusion that have received isolated study. DiLorenzo (1982), for example, has found that where municipal utilities use their profits to subsidise local spending, budgetary levels tend to be higher than in the absence of such subsidisation.

References

Advisory Commission on Inter-governmental Relations, *Federal-State-Local Finances: Significant Features of Fiscal Federalism* Washington, D.C.: ACIR, Feb., 1974.

Advisory Commission on Inter-governmental Relations, *Sources of Increased State Tax Collection: Economic Growth vs. Political Choice*, Report M-41 Washington, D.C.: ACIR, Oct., 1968.

Baker, Samuel H., 'The Determinants of Median Voter Tax Liability: An Empirical Test of the Fiscal Illusion Hypothesis', *Public Finance Quarterly 11* Jan., 1983, 95-108.

Barro, Robert J., 'Are Government Bonds Net Wealth?', *Journal of Political Economy 82* Nov.-Dec., 1974, 1095-1117.

Bergstrom, Theodore C., and Goodman, Robert P., 'Private Demands for Public Goods', *American Economic Review 63* June, 1973, 280-96.

Bradford, David, and Oates, Wallace, 'The Analysis of Revenue Sharing in a New Approach to Collective Fiscal Decisions', *Quarterly Journal of Economics 85* April, 1971 416-39.

Breeden. Charles H., and Hunter, William J., 'Tax Revenue and Tax Structure', *Public Finance Quarterly 13* April, 1985, 216-24.

Brennan, Geoffrey, and Buchanan, James M., 'The Logic of the Ricardian Equivalence Theorem', *Finanzarchiv 38* No. 1, 1980, 4-16.

Brennan, Geoffrey, and Buchanan, James M., *The Power to Tax: Analytical Foundations of a Fiscal Constitution* Cambridge: Cambridge University Press, 1980.

Buchanan, James M., *'Public Finance in Democratic Process'* Chapel Hill: University of North Carolina Press, 1967.

Carter, Richard, 'Beliefs and Errors in Voting Choices: A Restatement of the Theory of Fiscal Illusion'. *Public Choice 39* 1982, 343-60.

Clotfelter, Charles T., 'Public Spending for Higher Education: An Empirical Test of Two Hypotheses', *Public Finance 31* No. 2, 1976, 177-95.

Courant, Paul, Gramlich, Edward, and Rubinfeld, Daniel, 'The Stimulative Effects of Intergovernmental Grants: Or Why Money Sticks Where It Hits', in P. Mieszkowski and W. Oakland, eds., *Fiscal Federalism and Grants-in-Aid* Washington, D.C.: The Urban Institute, 1979, 5-21.

Craig, Eleanor D., and Heins, A. James, 'The effect of Tax Elasticity on Government Spending', *Public Choice 35* No. 3, 1980 267-75.

Daly, George G., 'The Burden of the Debt and Future Generations in Local Finance', *Southern Economic Journal 36* July, 1969, 44-51.

DiLorenzo, Thomas J., 'Tax Elasticity and the Growth of Local Public Expenditure', *Public Finance Quarterly 10* July, 1982, 385-92.

DiLorenzo, Thomas J., 'Utility Profits, Fiscal Illusion, and Local Public Expenditures', *Public Choice 38* No. 3, 1982, 243-52.

Downs, Anthony, *An Economic Theory of Democracy* New York: Harper and Row, 1957.

Downs, Anthony, 'An Economic Theory of Political Action in a Democracy', *Journal of Political Economy 65* April, 1957, 135-50.

Downs, Anthony, 'Why the Government Budget is Too Small in a Democracy', *World Politics* July, 1960.

Epple, Dennis, and Schipper, Katherine, 'Municipal Funding: A Theory and Some Evidence', *Public Choice 37* 1981, 141-78.

Flowers, Marilyn R., 'Multiple Tax Sources, Voting Equilibrium, and Budgetary Size', *Public Finance 32* No. 2, 1977, 210-24.

Galbraith, John K., *The Affluent Society* Boston: Houghton-Mifflin, 1958.

Goetz, Charles J., 'Fiscal Illusion in State and Local Finance', in T. Borcherding, ed., *Budgets and Bureaucrats: The Sources of Government Growth* Durham, North Carolina: Duke University Press, 1977, 176-87.

Martinez-Vazquez, Jorge, 'Renters' illusion or Savvy?', *Public Finance Quarterly 11* April, 1983, 237-47.

Mumy, Gene E., 'The Economics of Local Government Pensions and Pension Funding', *Journal of Political Economy 86* June, 1978, 517-28.

Munley, Vincent G., and Greene. Kenneth V., 'Fiscal Illusion, the Nature of Public Goods and Equation Specification', *Public Choice 33* No. 1, 1978, 95-100.

Musgrave, Richard A., 'Leviathan Cometh — Or Does He?', in H. Ladd and T.N. Tideman, eds., *Tax and Expenditure Limitations* Washington, DC: The Urban Institute, 1981, 77-120.

Oates, Wallace E., *Fiscal Federalism* New York: Harcourt Brace Jovanovich, 1972.

Oates, Wallace E., 'Automatic Increases in Tax Revenues — The Effect on the Size of the Public Budget', in W. Oates, ed., *Financing the New Federalism: Revenue Sharing, Conditional Grants, and Taxation* Baltimore: Johns Hopkins University Press, 1975, 129-60.

Oates, Wallace E., 'Lump-Sum Intergovernmental Grants Have Price Effects', in P. Mieszkowski and W. Oakland, eds., *Fiscal Federalism and Grants-in-Aid* Washington DC: The Urban Institute, 1979, 23-30.

Peterson, George E., 'Voter Demand for Public School Expenditures', in J. Jackson, ed., *Public Needs and Private Behavior in Metropolitan Areas* Cambridge, Mass.: Ballinger, 1975, 99-120.

Pommerehne, Werner W., and Schneider, Friedrich, 'Fiscal Illusion, Political Institutions, and Local Public Spending', *Kyklos 31* No. 3, 1978, 381-408.

Puviani, Amilcare, *Teoria della Illusione Finanziaria* Milan: Remo Sandon, 1903.

Roche, Ellen, 'The Incidence of Property Taxes on Renters', unpublished paper 1985.

Romer, Thomas, and Rosenthal, Howard, 'Bureaucrats vs. Voters: On the Political Economy of Resource Allocation by Direct Democracy', *Quarterly Journal of Economics 93* Nov., 1979, 562-87.

Romer, Thomas, and Rosenthal, Howard, 'An Institutional Theory of the Effect of Intergovernmental Grants', *National Tax Journal 33* December, 1980, 451-8.

Sonstelie, Jon C., and Portney, Paul R., 'Profit Maximizing Communities and The Theory of Local Public Expenditure', *Journal of Urban Economics 5* April, 1978, 263-77.

Vickrey, William, 'The Burden of the Public Debt: Comment', *American Economic Review 51* March, 1961, 132-37.

Wagner, Richard E., *The Fiscal Organization of American Federalism* Chicago: Markham, 1971.

Wagner, Richard E., 'Revenue Structure, Fiscal Illusion, and Budgetary Choice', *Public Choice 25* Spring, 1976, 45-61.

Wu, D.M., 'Alternative Tests of Independence between Stochastic Regressors and Disturbances', *Econometrica 41* July, 1973, 733-50.

Index